Exchange Rate Theory and Practice

Jan/98

A National Bureau
of Economic Research
Conference Report

Exchange Rate Theory and Practice

Edited by John F. O. Bilson
and
Richard C. Marston

The University of Chicago Press
Chicago and London

The University of Chicago Press, Chicago 60637
The University of Chicago Press, Ltd., London

Library of Congress Cataloging in Publication Data
   Main entry under title:

   Exchange rate theory and practice.

      (A Conference report / National Bureau of Economic
Research)
      Papers presented at a conference held in Jan. 1982
at the Rockefeller Foundation's Bellagio Conference
Center on Lake Como in northern Italy, and sponsored
by the National Bureau of Economic Research.
      Includes bibliographical references and index.
      1. Foreign exchange—Congresses.   I. Bilson, John
F. O.   II. Marston, Richard C.   III. National Bureau of
Economic Research.   IV. Series: Conference report
(National Bureau of Economic Research)

HG205 1984   332.4′5   84-2441
ISBN 0-226-05096-3 (cloth); 0-226-05097-1 (paper)

Contents

Introduction   1
John F. O. Bilson and Richard C. Marston

I. Recent Developments in Exchange Rate Theory
and Policy

1.   **The Theory of Exchange Rate Determination**   13
Michael Mussa
Comments: Jacob A. Frenkel, Rudiger Dornbusch,
Pentti J. K. Kouri

2.   **Exchange Rate Policy after a Decade of "Floating"**   79
William H. Branson
Comments: Willem H. Buiter, Peter B. Kenen

II. Short-Run Determinants of the Exchange Rate

3.   **International Interest Rate and Price Level
Linkages under Flexible Exchange Rates:
A Review of Recent Evidence**   121
Robert E. Cumby and Maurice Obstfeld

4.   **Properties of Innovations in Spot and Forward
Exchange Rates and the Role of Money
Supply Processes**   153
Hans Genberg

5.   **Exchange Rate Dynamics**   175
            John F. O. Bilson
            Comment on Chapters 4 and 5: Richard M. Levich

            III. Asset Demands and the Exchange Rate

6.   **International Portfolio Diversification:**
            Short-Term Financial Assets and Gold   199
            Jorge Braga de Macedo, Jeffrey A. Goldstein, and
            David M. Meerschwam
            Comments: Bernard Dumas, Jeffrey A. Frankel

7.   **Tests of Monetary and Portfolio Balance Models**
            of Exchange Rate Determination   239
            Jeffrey A. Frankel

8.   **The International Role of the Dollar: Theory**
            and Prospect   261
            Paul Krugman

            IV. Fundamental Determinants of the Real Exchange
            Rate

9.   **Real Exchange Rates in the 1970s**   281
            Louka T. Katseli
            Comment: Willem H. Buiter

10.   **The Real Exchange Rate, the Current Account,**
            and the Speed of Adjustment   335
            Francesco Giavazzi and Charles Wyplosz
            Comment: Paul Krugman

            V. Foreign Exchange Intervention

11.   **Exchange Market Intervention Operations:**
            Their Role in Financial Policy and Their Effects 357
            Dale W. Henderson
            Comment: Rudiger Dornbusch

12.   **Exchange Rate Unions as an Alternative to**
            Flexible Rates: The Effects of Real and
            Monetary Disturbances   407
            Richard C. Marston
            Comment: Peter B. Kenen

13.   **Multilateral Exchange Rate Determination: A**
             Model for the Analysis of the European
             Monetary System   443
             Giorgio Basevi and Michele Calzolari
             Comment: Francesco Papadia

             VI. Monetary Policy and Exchange Rates

14.   **Effects of United States Monetary Restraint on**
             the DM/$ Exchange Rate and the
             German Economy   469
             Jacques R. Artus
             Comment: William H. Branson

15.   **The Relationship between Exchange Rate Policy**
             and Monetary Policy in Ten Industrial Countries   499
             Stanley W. Black
             Comment: Paul de Grauwe

             List of Contributors   517
             Name Index   519
             Subject Index   521

Introduction

John F. O. Bilson and Richard C. Marston

In January 1982, the National Bureau of Economic Research held a conference on exchange rates at the Rockefeller Foundation's Bellagio Conference Center on Lake Como in northern Italy. This volume contains the fifteen papers presented at this conference on topics ranging from recent developments in exchange rate theory and policy to the empirical analysis of nominal and real exchange rates.

The theory of exchange rates has evolved quite rapidly in the last fifteen years. At the beginning of the 1970s, most economists had accepted Milton Friedman's conjecture that a system of flexible exchange rates would only be a system of unstable exchange rates if underlying economic conditions were unstable. According to this view, exchange rates would adjust to offset differences in national inflation rates, but these changes would be gradual and predictable. Even after accounting for the crisis leading to the breakdown of the Bretton Woods system and for the instability generated by higher oil prices, however, most economists by the mid-1970s agreed that exchange rates were more volatile than anticipated. Furthermore, it was clear that the existing theoretical and empirical models of the exchange rate were not capable of offering a believable description of the post–Bretton Woods experience. In the period from 1973 to 1975, economists set to work to build new theories of the exchange rate.

Some measure of the extent of this work, and of its remarkable productivity, became evident in the famous conference on flexible exchange rates and stabilization policy held in Sweden in the summer of 1975.[1] This conference witnessed the origins of not one but three new approaches to the economics of exchange rate determination: the overshooting model of Rudiger Dornbusch based on the differential speed of adjustment between the commodity and asset markets; the asset market variants of the monetary approach introduced by

---

1. The proceedings of the conference were published in the *Scandinavian Journal of Economics* 78, no. 2 (May 1976).

Jacob Frenkel and Michael Mussa; and the current account/portfolio approach developed by Pentti Kouri. Although each of these approaches was based on a distinct view of the way in which the exchange rate is determined, they shared an emphasis on the importance of the integration and efficiency of international asset markets for understanding exchange rate movements. Common to all three approaches was the idea that the anticipated return from holding a currency was an essential element in the determination of its value. This was an important first step in understanding the exchange rate volatility which has been such a striking characteristic of the recent period.

Since the Swedish conference, exchange rate analysis has continued to develop rapidly with interest focused increasingly on exchange rate dynamics, portfolio diversification, and current account adjustment. We asked Michael Mussa to begin the conference by surveying these developments. Three of the other contributors to the Swedish conference, Rudiger Dornbusch, Jacob Frenkel, and Pentti Kouri, served as discussants.

Mussa sets a standard for the rest of the volume with his masterful review of exchange rate theory. This review encompasses both monetary and balance of payments theories of exchange rate determination but extends both theories in interesting ways which highlight the central role played by expectations.

He begins his paper by citing five empirical regularities which have characterized recent exchange rate experience: (1) Monthly changes in exchange rates are large and almost entirely unpredictable. (2) Changes in spot rates correspond fairly closely to changes in expected future spot rates (with spot and forward rates changing together). (3) Monthly changes in nominal and real exchange rates are highly correlated. (4) There is no strong and systematic relationship between movements in nominal or real exchange rates and current account imbalances. (5) Movements in nominal and real exchange rates are not closely related to differential rates of monetary expansion. His study and those that follow in this volume help to explain many of these empirical regularities.

In order to explain both nominal and real exchange rates, Mussa specifies a full-scale model of a small open economy. If wages are flexible and real wealth effects are ignored, an economy can be dichotomized into real and monetary sectors with the monetary sector determining the nominal exchange rate and the real sector the real exchange rate (the inverse of the terms of trade). Mussa develops such a model in stages beginning with an asset market model of the nominal exchange rate. He uses this model to show how new information which alters expectations concerning future economic conditions can induce unexpected changes in exchange rates. Such unexpected changes can dominate actual exchange rate movements. Since new information often causes revision in future expected exchange rates as well as current rates, moreover, the asset market model can explain the high correlation between changes in spot and forward rates.

He organizes his discussion of the real sector around a balance of payments equation to emphasize a link to the more traditional flow model of the exchange rate. This section ties together a number of strands in the literature, from the elasticity and absorption approaches to analyzing the trade balance to the more recent analysis of foreign asset accumulation. The specification of demand behavior is general enough to encompass either the dependent economy model with traded and nontraded goods or the more traditional import-export model with specialization in each country. An important feature of the model is that both the level and the expected rate of change of the real exchange rate affect the current account (the latter through the real interest rate). Thus, as in the case of the nominal exchange rate, the real exchange rate is dependent on expected future conditions.

The combined model of nominal and real exchange rates provides a rich framework for analyzing the open economy. But because wages and prices are flexible it can explain deviations from purchasing power parity (PPP) only to the extent that disturbances originate in the real sector. Mussa therefore modifies his model by introducing price dynamics. With prices temporarily sticky, monetary disturbances can lead to temporary deviations from PPP and overshooting of the exchange rate can occur. The model is a long way from the flow models of the 1950s and the monetary models of the 1970s, but with the best of each being retained in a more general setting.

We asked the three discussants of this paper, Jacob Frenkel, Rudiger Dornbusch, and Pentti Kouri, to focus their comments on what they believed to be the main problem areas in exchange rate analysis. They responded to this challenge by describing three quite different areas in which further work needs to be done.

Frenkel discusses several difficult empirical problems which face any researcher trying to explain movements in exchange rates. The first is the "peso problem," where the forward discount on a currency reflects the expectation of some future change in the exchange rate but where in all but one period the spot exchange rate is unchanged. The forward rate may then appear to be a biased predictor of the spot rate. The second problem arises when changes in exchange rates are explained by the innovations in other variables. Since the innovations are unobservable, any empirical analysis depends on the way in which expectations, and hence the unexpected changes in variables, are modeled. Finally, Frenkel cites the difficulty in dealing with innovations when some variables are available at more frequent intervals than others.

Dornbusch cites another empirical problem, the sizable and persistent changes in real exchange rates involving the dollar. If the dollar were simply overshooting its long-run value, an appreciation should be followed by a steady depreciation. Since the dollar has instead stayed at a high level for many months, the overshooting model alone is insufficient to explain its movements. Dornbusch suggests several explanations which involve questioning the assumption of rational expectations as it is formulated in Mussa's paper and elsewhere. The first involves the possibility of speculative bubbles where the actual exchange rate can move even in a different direction than its "fundamental" value. The second involves the use of an incorrect exchange rate model for forming expectations of future exchange rates. The interesting point here is that it may be difficult for economic agents to discover the error in the model they are using because the autocorrelation in forecast errors may be too small to detect. In both cases, the exchange rate may deviate from its value based on "fundamentals," with all that that implies for trade and financial relationships.

Kouri argues that exchange rate theory has erred by focusing too much on monetary influences on the exchange rate and too little on the balance of payments flows which actually give rise to foreign exchange transactions. According to Kouri, international economists need to pay more attention to S. C. Tsiang's remarkable analysis of the forward exchange market (written in 1959) with its emphasis on how the flow transactions of traders, speculators, and arbitrageurs jointly determine the current exchange rate. This is not to deny that financial factors are dominant in determining the exchange rate. Indeed, Kouri argues that the formation of expectations and the wealth accumulation process are key elements in exchange rate determination. But the model which Kouri has in mind is quite different from the monetary models of the mid-1970s.

Following the paper on new developments in exchange rate theory, William Branson presented an analysis of exchange rate policy including an empirical section on the time series properties of exchange rates, prices, and the current account. Branson's theoretical model combines a balance of payments equation describing the accumulation of foreign assets with a model of short-run equilibrium in the asset market. The asset market is in continuous equilibrium but that equilibrium depends upon the stocks of assets and wealth in the economy; the equilibrium, therefore, changes through time as foreign assets are accumulated. The assumption of perfect foresight ties the current asset equilibrium to the future path of asset accumulation.

For the asset model Branson assumes imperfect substitutability between domestic and foreign bonds. As a result he can distinguish three types of financial operations: open market swaps of domestic bonds for money, exchange market intervention involving swaps of foreign bonds for domestic money, and sterilized intervention involving the swap of foreign bonds for domestic bonds. Branson suggests ways in which these operations can be used to modify the jump movements in exchange rates which follow unanticipated disturbances. In the case of a monetary disturbance, for example, the initial depreciation of the exchange rate could be limited by a discrete open market operation, with the specific form of the policy intervention depending upon whether the disturbance is permanent or not and upon the speed of price adjustment. In the case of a real disturbance, the policy action could involve the money supply or other asset supplies reacting to unanticipated changes in exchange rates, with the authorities leaning against the wind through their intervention.

Since policy actions can take a variety of forms, determining how policy has been pursued in practice is a difficult empirical problem. Branson tackles this problem by using vector autoregressions to obtain the innovations in exchange rates and other variables, then investigating the correlations among these innovations. (A typical vector autoregression relates the United States effective exchange rate to lagged values of that exchange rate, relative prices weighted the same way as the exchange rate, as well as the United States money supply, current account balance, interest rate, and foreign exchange reserves.) He draws inferences from these correlations about the extent of policy intervention in each of four industrial countries. The results are quite interesting. The theoretical model predicts, for example, two alternative relationships between unanticipated changes in exchange rates and money supplies: a positive correlation if changes in money supplies lead to changes in exchange rates (even if moderated by intervention) and a negative correlation if changes in exchange rates induce "leaning against the wind" monetary policy. The empirical results suggest a distinct pattern of policy reactions ranging from the domestic-oriented monetary policy of the United States (where changes in the money supply appear to drive changes in exchange rates) to the exchange-rate-oriented monetary policy of Germany and the United Kingdom.

Willem Buiter, in his comment on Branson's paper, describes several extensions of Branson's model which might alter behavior significantly. With lagged price adjustment, for example, the response to real disturbances could involve cyclical patterns rather than the monotonic pattern described in the paper. Similarly, with output endogenous, asset demands would respond directly to the level of transactions, thus altering the dynamic path toward equilibrium and possibly reversing the usual overshooting pattern.

Branson's empirical analysis comes under criticism both from Buiter and from Peter Kenen, the second discussant. Buiter questions Branson's choice of lag lengths based on univariate correlations, giving an example where such a procedure could lead to the omission of important variables. Moreover, he shows how difficult it is to draw inferences from correlations among variables without having strong priors on the signs of structural coefficients. Kenen focuses on the problem of explaining exchange rates in a multicountry world. Theoretical models, including Branson's, almost invariably describe small economies with but one exchange rate vis-à-vis the "foreign currency." Empirical models typically describe bilateral exchange rates of similar-sized countries or, in Branson's case, effective exchange rates for one large country relative to the rest of the world. Kenen gives several examples illustrating why the single country approach might be seriously misleading in empirical applications.

The second session of the conference provides further insight into the current state of empirical work on exchange rates. The paper by Robert Cumby and Maurice Obstfeld represents the best of one empirical tradition based on conventional econometric techniques, while the papers by Hans Genberg and John Bilson offer new approaches which explicitly reject traditional econometric methods in favor of time series analysis. Genberg analyzes the correlation between the innovations in exchange rates, while Bilson (like Branson in the second session) analyzes vector autocorrelations for exchange rates and other variables.

The Cumby-Obstfeld paper provides a series of sophisticated tests of three basic parity relationships, purchasing power parity and two versions of interest rate parity for nominal and real interest rates, respectively. The results are quite decisive in rejecting each of these parity relationships over the recent period. This evidence is important because most theoretical models of exchange rates rely on one or more of these parity relationships. Once the parity relationships are rejected, however, it is not at all clear how researchers should proceed. Some have sought to estimate alternative (structural) models of the exchange rate allowing for deviations from the parity relationships. Jeffrey Frankel's paper, which was presented in the next session, is in that tradition. Genberg and Bilson prefer instead to draw inferences on the basis of the time series properties of financial variables alone.

Genberg's paper makes imaginative use of data for the innovations in spot and forward rates. He posits a model of the process generating these rates, while remaining uncommitted about the variables in this process. He draws inferences from the term structure of innovations about the specific form of this process. He then specifies an autoregressive process generating the money supply and shows that there is a high correlation between the autoregressive parameter in this process and the pattern of exchange rate innovations. This interesting evidence is consistent with a simple monetary model of the exchange rate, although it is likely that more complex models of the exchange rate could equally well generate such patterns.

Overshooting of the exchange rate may occur in Genberg's model, but such overshooting can be attributed to the time series properties of the underlying variables driving the exchange rate rather than to any nominal rigidities in the economy. Bilson, in contrast, analyzes a simplified form of Dornbusch's celebrated overshooting model based on price rigidities. He does not attempt to estimate this model, but instead examines the time series properties of two financial variables, exchange rates and interest rates. The Dornbusch model offers two testable hypotheses regarding these variables: (1) negative contemporaneous correlation between the exchange rate and the domestic interest rate series and (2) negative autocorrelation within both series. Bilson examines both hypotheses using vector autoregressions. The results are mixed, but the specific form of the Dornbusch model is decisively rejected.

At the same time that the macroeconomic literature on exchange rates was developing, a quite distinct literature emerged on the microeconomics of portfolio choice under uncertainty. In the third session of the conference, the paper by Jorge de Macedo, Jeffrey Goldstein, and David Meerschwam showed how far this literature has progressed. Their paper derives an optimal portfolio for a "national investor." one who deflates returns by the consumer price index of a particular nation, and an "international investor" who uses a weighted average of many countries' CPIs as a deflator. The framework is quite general with asset prices as well as the CPIs treated as stochastic. They decompose the optimal portfolio into three elements, the first two of which constitute the minimum variance portfolio: a capital position, a (zero net worth) inflation hedge, and a (zero net worth) speculative portfolio. The empirical section then provides estimates of each of these portfolios. One particularly interesting result is the high percentage of the minimum risk portfolio invested in the national asset by investors from each country. This result indicates what an inhibiting influence exchange risk has on international portfolio diversification.

In the second paper of the session, Jeffrey Frankel estimates a variety of structural models of the exchange rate ranging from the flexible and sticky price versions of the monetary approach to portfolio models derived from microeconomic behavior. But he finds all of them wanting. The failure of monetary models has been attributed to many factors, including shifts in money demand and in the long-run terms of trade, as well as to changes in risk premiums. But, as Frankel observes, shifts in money demand and the terms of trade are more a manifestation than an explanation for the failure of the monetary models. As for risk premiums, Frankel shows that portfolio models fare as poorly as do the monetary models in explaining the exchange rate. The picture that emerges from his and other studies is a bleak one. Even though parity relationships are decisively rejected in studies like that of Cumby and Obstfeld, we have yet to replace them with structural models which fit recent exchange rate experience.

In the last paper of this session, Paul Krugman attempts to clarify many of the puzzling features of an international currency. According to Krugman, the importance of economies to scale explains why one currency may become the dominant international currency. Which currency assumes this role depends on a number of factors difficult to quantify, but once a currency becomes dominant its use may persist long after the factors responsible for its emergence have changed. Krugman shows how unstable a currency's position is in such a case. Some event may then precipitate the wholesale substitution of that currency for another with potentially disruptive effects on the financial system during the transition period.

Recent models of the exchange rate generally fall into two categories, those that focus on traded goods differentiated by country and those that have only one traded good but focus on the interaction between that good and a nontraded good specific to the country. Louka Katseli, in contrast, provides a general framework for analyzing both nontraded goods and differentiated traded goods. This framework is essential for the purpose at hand, which is to study competitiveness in the major industrial countries. But it is also very useful for showing how tenuous are many of the conclusions based on one or the other model alone. Katseli distinguishes between measures of the real exchange rate associated with the two models. When there are differentiated traded goods, the real exchange rate is naturally defined as the inverse of the terms of trade, while in models with nontraded goods, the real exchange rate is defined as the relative price of traded to nontraded goods. Katseli provides a comparative analysis of each of these series which shows just how much they vary relative to one another. This is followed by an extensive empirical analysis of the time series properties of prices and exchange rates from which inferences are drawn about the adjustment process.

In the second paper of this session, Francesco Giavazzi and Charles Wyplosz investigate the real exchange rate in a different type of model where the dynamic adjustment to a long-run steady state is explicitly analyzed. They actually specify two different models, both of which illustrate two important properties of dynamic models: the multiplicity of steady states and the dependence of the long-run equilibrium on the adjustment path. The second property is particularly interesting. In many models of the exchange rate, such as Dornbusch's overshooting model, the impact effects of disturbances depend on the speed of adjustment. The steady state properties typically are unaffected by the characteristics of the adjustment path. Giavazzi and Wyplosz, however, show in two different models, which illustrate the adjustment of capital and labor, respectively, how the parameters which set the speed of adjustment of the model have a permanent effect on the economy.

In the fifth session of the conference, on foreign exchange intervention, Dale Henderson offers a comprehensive and definitive assessment of intervention which incorporates recent insights into the role of policy under rational expectations. He uses a stochastic two-country model to analyze two types of foreign exchange intervention: (1) nonsterilized intervention where one country's money supply is increased and the other's is decreased and (2) sterilized intervention where relative bond supplies are varied. The second type of intervention is effective as long as the two countries' bonds are imperfect substitutes, and is the optimal form of intervention in the presence of portfolio shifts between these bonds. For other types of disturbances, Henderson compares two types of policies: an aggregates-constant policy where all asset supplies are held fixed and a rates-constant policy where interest rates and the exchange rate are held fixed. The results are reminiscent of those obtained by Poole for a closed economy. If disturbances in the market for the home good predominate, an aggregates-constant policy results in less variation in employment than a rates-constant policy. The opposite is the case in the presence of financial disturbances. Henderson goes on to expand this analysis to consider the effects of indexation and of contemporaneous feedback rules. The section on feedback rules is particularly interesting: If the authorities can base their intervention policy on whatever partial information about current disturbances they can glean from financial variables, then output variability can be reduced below that of either regime discussed above.

In the second paper of this session, Richard Marston examines intervention in a three-country setting where flexible rates are compared with an exchange rate union between two of the countries. As in Henderson's analysis, the desirability of a union depends upon the types of economic disturbances (monetary or real) typically encountered as well as the sources of the disturbances (domestic or foreign). But equally important are the degrees of wage indexation at home and abroad and the relative importance of trade between the potential partners in a union. These are factors which had figured in informal discussions of exchange rate unions but had never been formally analyzed before. The analysis of these factors yields several counterintuitive results which show how difficult it is to make an unambiguous case for a union. The case for a union is not necessarily stronger when the home country trades primarily with other countries in the union, nor is it necessarily stronger when disturbances originate primarily outside the union. In each case, the variability of output, for at least some disturbances, is greater in the union than under flexible rates.

The European Monetary System, which ties together the mark, franc, lira, and other European currencies, is the foremost example of an exchange rate union. Giorgio Basevi and Michele Calzolari estimate a multilateral model of exchange rates to analyze this union. The model is a multicountry version of Dornbusch's sticky price model with equations for the demand for money, aggregate demand, and a modified Phillips curve. The countries studied are Germany, France, and Italy (all members of the EMS), the United Kingdom, and the United States. This model is to be used in future work to analyze monetary policy within the EMS as well as the effects of shocks originating outside the EMS (for example, in the United States) on countries in the system.

One such shock which has dominated policy debates in the past few years is the shift toward monetary restraint in the United States beginning in 1980. The problems which this shift in policy caused for one major European country, the Federal Republic of Germany, are the subject of Jacques Artus's paper in the last session of the conference. Artus uses an econometric model of the German economy to trace the effects of United States policy on the DM/$ rate and macroeconomic conditions in Germany. Simulations of this model show that the impact of United States monetary policy depends crucially on whether or not other countries keep their real exchange rates constant vis-à-vis the dollar. Even more important, however, is the monetary policy response of the German authorities. If German money growth remains unchanged, the depreciation of the mark causes a significant increase in the German inflation rate. Alternatively, if the German authorities match United States monetary restraint with an equivalent policy, German output declines sharply, basically because in Artus's model nominal wages are slow to adjust. The simulations thus graphically describe a policy dilemma facing the German authorities: they can choose between higher prices or lower output through their choice of intervention policy.

The second paper in this session, by Stanley Black, investigates the link between methods of monetary control adopted in the leading industrial countries and exchange rate regimes. In general, countries choosing to control credit directly also prefer pegged exchange rates, while those relying on control of bank reserves typically adopt floating exchange rates. Black describes in detail why countries with credit controls often require extensive foreign exchange controls to prevent access to foreign loans from undermining credit measures. And if interest rates are also controlled, credit rationing is needed to limit the demand for loans to the available supply. In such a country, pegged exchange rates are a natural extension of this panoply of controls on financial transactions.

The view of exchange rates which emerges from this volume is markedly different from that of Milton Friedman and others prior to 1970. Many theoretical and empirical puzzles remain to be resolved, no doubt, but we believe this volume is an accurate reflection of the high quality and breadth of recent research on exchange rates.

The success of the conference owed much to the strong encouragement and support given by the director of the International Studies Program at the NBER, William Branson. We owe a deep debt of gratitude to the Ford Foundation for committing itself to the project at an early stage and to the Rockefeller Foundation for providing such an elegant setting, surrounded by the Italian and Swiss Alps, for contemplating exchange rates.

I   Recent Development in Exchange Rate Theory and Policy

1 The Theory of Exchange Rate Determination

Michael Mussa

1.1 Introduction

This essay develops an integrated model of exchange rate behavior that synthesizes many recent and older contributions to the theory of exchange rate determination. Since the task of exchange rate theory is to explain behavior observed in the real world, the essay begins (in sec. 1.2) with a summary of empirical regularities that have been characteristic of the behavior of exchange rates and other related variables during periods of floating exchange rates. This discussion continues (in sec. 1.3) with the presentation of a schematic model of the exchange rate as an "asset price" that depends on a discounted sum of economic factors that are expected to affect the foreign exchange market in present and future periods. This schematic asset price model implies a convenient decomposition of exchange rate changes into their expected and unexpected components; and it suggests a general explanation for the dominance of the random, unexpected component of exchange rate change in actual exchange rate movements.

Specific content for the schematic asset price model of the exchange rate is provided (in sec. 1.4) by considering a reduced-form expression for the condition of money market equilibrium in which both the level and the expected rate of change of the exchange rate affect the demand to hold domestic money. Under the assumption of rational expectations, this reduced-form equilibrium condition implies that (the logarithm of) the nominal exchange rate is an exponentially weighted average of expected future differences between (the logarithms of) the nominal money supply and the exogenous component of money demand. This result, which allows a key role for expectations concerning future money supply and money demand behavior in determining the current exchange rate, is contrasted with simple monetary models that focus on current money supplies and current money demands as the determinants of exchange rates.

An alternative asset price model of the exchange rate emerges (in sec. 1.5) from a reduced-form expression of the condition of balance of payments equilibrium that is derived from an extended version of the standard two-country model of international trade. This model, which focuses on the real exchange rate and other real variables, embodies the essential ideas of the elasticities and absorption approaches to the balance of payments and the traditional partial equilibrium model of the foreign exchange market. Under the assumption of rational expectations, the model yields an expression for the current real exchange rate as a discounted sum of the expected future values of the exogenous real factors that affect excess demands for foreign and domestic goods and the desired relationship between spending and income. From this result conclusions may be derived concerning the relationships among the real exchange rate, the current account balance, and the net stock of foreign assets.

Combination of the reduced-form models of monetary and balance of payments equilibrium yields (in sec. 1.6) an equilibrium model of the determination of the exchange rate. This model illustrates the coordinate importance of monetary factors affecting the supply and demand for money and real factors affecting excess demands for specific goods and of the desired relationship between spending and income in influencing the behavior of the exchange rate. Modification of this equilibrium model by the introduction of an appropriately specified adjustment rule for the domestic money price of domestic goods (in sec. 1.7) results in a disequilibrium model of the exchange rate in which monetary disturbances have real effects on levels of output, relative prices, and the real exchange rate. The model illustrates the phenomenon of exchange rate "overshooting" in response to monetary disturbances and the role of such disturbances in inducing temporary divergences from purchasing power parity. The essay concludes with a brief summary and a discussion of possible extensions.

1.2 Empirical Regularities and Their Theoretical Implications

A central objective of theoretical models of exchange rate determination ought to be a clearer understanding of the economic mechanisms governing the actual behavior of exchange rates in the real world and of the relationships between exchange rates and other important economic variables. In surveying theoretical models of exchange rate determination, therefore, it is appropriate to examine the empirical regularities that have been characteristic of the behavior of exchange rates and other related variables under floating exchange rate regimes. It is also relevant to discuss the minimum requirements for any theoretical model of exchange rate determination to be consistent with these empirical regularities.[1]

1. Empirical regularities in the behavior of exchange rates and their implications for exchange rate theory are discussed in Mussa (1979); see also Dooley and Isard (1978), Frenkel and Mussa (1980), Isard (1980), and Frenkel (1981).

1.2.1 The Stochastic Behavior of Exchange Rates and Related Variables

Experience with floating exchange rates between the United States dollar and other major currencies (the British pound, the German mark, the French franc, the Swiss franc, and the Japanese yen) during the 1970s has revealed five general characteristics of the behavior of exchange rates and related variables under a flexible exchange rate regime in which the authorities do not intervene too actively in the foreign exchange markets. These characteristics also apply, in general, to the experience with floating exchange rates between major currencies during 1920s and 1930s and, with some modifications, to the experience of floating exchange rates between the United States and Canadian dollars during the 1970s. They do not always apply, however, to situations in which exchange rates have been very actively managed, such as the exchange rate between the Mexican peso and the United States dollar or the exchange rates between currencies within the European Monetary System.

First, statistical examination of the behavior of (logarithms of) spot exchange rates reveals that they follow approximately random walks with little or no drift. The standard deviation of monthly changes in exchange rates between major currencies and the United States dollar (except the Canadian dollar) has been about 3% per month, with changes of more than 5% occurring with moderate frequency. (In comparison, changes in national price levels, measured by consumer price indices, have had a standard deviation of about 1% per month, and monthly changes have virtually never exceeded 5% in major industrial countries during the 1970s.) Moreover, there has been virtually no predictable pattern in monthly exchange rate changes, and, at most, only a small fraction of such changes has been anticipated by the market, as measured by the forward discount or premium. These facts may be summarized in a general characteristic: Monthly changes in exchange rates are frequently quite large and are almost entirely random and unpredictable.

Second, analysis of the correlation between contemporaneous movements in spot and forward exchange rates (for maturities extending out to 1 year) indicates that spot and forward rates tend to move in the same direction and by approximately the same amount, especially when changes are fairly large. Some evidence suggests that forward rates are marginally affected by risk premia and hence do not correspond exactly to the market's expectation of the spot exchange rate at the maturity date of the forward contract.[2] This evidence, however, is not sufficiently strong to overturn the assumption that forward rates are reasonable though approximate estimates of the market's expectation of corresponding future spot exchange rates. This assumption, together with the observed contemporaneous correlation of movements in spot and forward rates, implies a second general characteristic of exchange rate behavior: Changes in spot exchange rates which are largely unantici-

2. See, in particular, Hansen and Hodrick (1980).

pated correspond fairly closely to changes in the market's expectation of future spot exchange rates.

Third, contrary to the doctrine of purchasing power parity (PPP), there has not been a close correspondence between movements in exchange rates and movements in the ratio of national price levels, especially during the 1970s.[3] Monthly (or quarterly) changes in exchange rates have averaged about three times as great as monthly (or quarterly) changes in the ratio of consumer price indices, and the correlation between exchange rate changes and changes in the ratio of national price levels has been close to zero. Moreover, while there has usually been positive serial correlation of monthly changes in the ratio of consumer price indices, there has been no corresponding serial correlation of monthly exchange rate changes. Over longer time periods, such as a year, cumulative divergences from relative purchasing power parity between the major industrial countries have frequently been as large as 10%. Using the concept of the "real exchange rate" (defined as the price of a unit of foreign money in terms of domestic money, divided by the ratio of the home consumer price index to the foreign consumer price index), these facts may be summarized in the following characteristic: Monthly changes in nominal exchange rates are closely correlated with monthly changes in real exchange rates, and cumulative changes in real exchange rates over a period of a year have been quite large.

Fourth, during the recent period of floating exchange rates, there may have been a weak general tendency for countries that experienced sharp deteriorations in their current accounts subsequently to experience depreciation in the nominal and real foreign exchange value of their currencies. There also may have been a weak general tendency for countries that experienced sharp appreciations in nominal and real foreign exchange values of their currencies subsequently to experience deterioration in their current accounts. It has not been the case, however, that exchange rates have adjusted rapidly to eliminate current account imbalances, nor has there been strong correlation between exchange rate changes and either levels of changes in current account balances that has held up consistently over time and across countries.[4] These facts may be summarized in the following characteristic: There is no strong and systematic relationship between movements in nominal or real exchange rates and current account balances that allows for an explanation of a substantial fraction of actual exchange rate movements.

Fifth, countries that experience very rapid expansion of their domestic

3. See, for example, Kravis and Lipsey (1978) and Frenkel (1981a).
4. Some evidence has been presented that movements in current account balances are among the factors influencing movements in exchange rates; see Branson (1976), Branson, Haltunen, and Masson (1977), Dooley and Isard (1978), Dornbusch (1978, 1980a), Isard (1980), Artus (1981), and Driskill (1981). It has not been the case, however, that exchange rates have adjusted rapidly to eliminate current account imbalances or that a large fraction of monthly or quarterly movements in exchange rates is easily explained by movements in current account balances.

money supplies also experience rapid depreciation of the foreign exchange value of their money, relative to the monies of countries with much less rapid monetary expansion.[5] For countries with only modest differences in their rates of monetary expansion (such as has been true for the major industrial countries during the 1970s), however, there is only a tenuous, long-run relationship between high relative rates of monetary expansion and depreciation in the foreign exchange value of domestic money. In particular, there is little or no statistical correlation between monthly changes in exchange rates and monthly differences in rates of monetary expansion for the major industrial countries during the 1970s.[6] These facts may be summarized in the following characteristic: Movements in nominal and real exchange rates are not closely related to differential rates of monetary expansion, except possibly for some very highly inflationary economies.

1.2.2 Implications for Theories of Exchange Rate Behavior

One of the implications of these general facts is that no simple model of exchange rate determination provides an adequate explanation of most of the observed movement in nominal and real exchange rates under a floating exchange rate regime. The bulk of observed movements in exchange rates cannot be explained by a naive "payments flows" model, which suggests that exchange rates adjust either immediately or gradually to maintain balance of payments equilibrium. A naive monetary model that relates exchange rate movements to differential rates of monetary expansion (with or without some form of lagged adjustment) does not perform appreciably better in explaining the bulk of exchange rate movements, except possibly for highly inflationary economies. A naive PPP explanation (not really a theory) of exchange rate movements also performs rather poorly.

A second important implication of the observed characteristics of the behavior of exchange rates and related variables concerns the general conception of exchange rates as "asset prices." Exchange rates share many of the general behavioral characteristics of the prices of assets that are traded on organized exchanges, such as common stocks, long-term bonds, and various metals and agricultural commodities. Monthly changes in the prices of these assets, like monthly changes in exchange rates (but unlike monthly changes in consumer price indices) are largely random and unpredictable. For assets with quoted spot and future prices, there tends to be a strong correlation between changes in spot prices and contemporaneous changes in futures prices, indicating that changes in spot prices are largely unanticipated and correspond fairly closely to changes in the market's expectation of future spot prices. Monthly changes in the prices of assets traded in organized

5. See, in particular, Frenkel (1976).
6. For an assessment of the failures of simple monetary models to explain exchange rate movements in the 1970s, see Dornbusch (1978, 1980a), Frenkel (1979, 1982), Meese and Singleton (1980), and Meese and Rogoff (1982).

markets are not closely correlated with monthly changes in the general price level, as measured by the consumer price index, implying that most nominal price changes are also real price changes.

These common characteristics in the behavior of prices of assets traded in organized markets suggest that there should be important common elements in the theory of the behavior of such prices. In particular, for any asset that may be held in inventory at a relatively small storage cost and bought and sold with a relatively small transaction cost, we ought to expect that the price today would be reasonably closely linked to the price that is expected at some day in the near future, such as a month hence. The reason for this linkage is that if there were a substantial expected rise in the price of the asset over the course of a month, individuals would have a strong incentive to acquire and hold the asset, putting upward pressure on its current price and downward pressure on its expected future price, until the difference between these two prices was brought within the limits implied by storage and transactions costs.

This same argument implies that there should be a reasonably close linkage between the price of an easily storable and tradable asset that is expected 1 month from now and the price of that same asset that is expected 2 months from now, between the price of the asset expected 2 months from now and the price expected 3 months from now, and so on into the more distant future. Through this mechanism, the current price of an easily storable and tradable asset is linked to the economic conditions that are expected to affect the ultimate demand and supply of that asset in all future periods. Expected changes in the prices of such assets should reflect expected changes in the economic conditions that affect the ultimate demand and supply of the asset. In contrast, unexpected changes in the prices of such assets should reflect new information that changes expectations concerning the economic conditions that affect the ultimate demand for and supply of the asset. The observation that changes in many asset prices are largely random and unpredictable reflects the empirical preponderance of unexpected price changes due to new information over expected price changes in determining the actual behavior of most asset prices.[7]

1.3 The Asset Market View of Exchange Rate Determination

The gross similarities between the behavior of exchange rates and the behavior of the prices of other assets traded in highly organized markets suggests a common general approach to analyzing the behavior of such asset prices. The essential elements of this general approach, as applied to exchange rates, may be represented in a simple theoretical model that relates

---

7. It is not theoretically necessary that the unexpected component of price change should dominate actual movements in asset prices. Nevertheless, this appears to be true in all organized asset markets.

the current exchange rate to present and future conditions that are expected to affect the foreign exchange market.[8] This simple model assumes that the logarithm of the exchange rate at time t, $e(t)$; is determined by

$$(1) \qquad e(t) = X(t) + a \cdot E\{[e(t + 1) - e(t)]; t\},$$

where $E\{[e(t + 1) - e(t)]; t\}$ denotes the expected percentage rate of change of the exchange rate between t and $t + 1$, conditional on information available at t, and where $X(t)$ represents the basic conditions of supply and demand that affect the foreign exchange market at time t. The essential idea of equation (1) is that the exchange rate that yields equilibrium in the foreign exchange market at time t is affected not only by the basic factors of supply and demand summarized by $X(t)$, but also by the expected rate of change of the exchange rate which motivates domestic and foreign residents to move assets either into or out of foreign exchange depending on whether the price of foreign exchange is expected to rise or fall.

To close the model, it is necessary to specify how expectations of future exchange rates are determined. It is assumed that these expectations are "rational" in the sense that they are consistent with the validity of equation (1) in all future periods. By forward iteration of (1) and application of the appropriate boundary condition, we arrive at the conclusion that the exchange rate expected at any $t + j$, for $j \geq 0$, depends on a weighted average of expected future X's, starting at $t + j$ and extending farther into the future;[9] specifically,

$$(2) \qquad E(e(t + j); t) = (1/(1 + a)) \cdot \sum_{i=0}^{\infty} (a/(1 + a))^i$$
$$\cdot E(X(t + j + i); t).$$

Setting $j = 0$, we obtain the expression for the current exchange rate as a weighted average of present and expected future X's.

Using equation (2), we may obtain a convenient decomposition of the actual change in the exchange rate, $D[e(t)] = e(t + 1) - e(t)$, into its expected change component, $D^e[e(t)] = E\{D[e(t)]; t\} = E[e(t + 1); t] - e(t)$, and its unexpected change component, $D^u[e(t)] = e(t + 1) - E[e(t + 1); t]$. Specifically, applying the expected change operator $D^e(\ )$ to (2) with $j = 0$, we may conclude that

$$(3) \qquad D^e[e(t)] = [1/(1 + a)] \cdot \sum_{i=0}^{\infty} [a/(1 + a)]^i$$
$$\cdot E\{D[X(t + j); t]\}.$$

8. It is widely recognized that expectations are critically important in determining the behavior of exchange rates; see, for example, Dornbusch (1976, 1980b), Frenkel (1976), Kouri (1976a), Mussa (1976, 1982a), Ethier (1979), Rogoff (1979), and Wilson (1979). The present exposition of the asset price model is based on that given in Frenkel and Mussa (1980).

9. A boundary condition is imposed on the forward-looking solution of (1) to ensure an economically sensible, nonexplosive solution.

Thus, the expected change in the exchange rate is a weighted average of all expected future changes in the X's. This result may also be written in the alternative form,

(4) $$D^e[e(t)] = [1/(1 + a)] \cdot \{E[e(t + 1); t] - X(t)\},$$

which expresses the expected change in the exchange rate as proportional to the difference between the weighted average of all expected future X's that determines $E[e(t + 1); t]$ and the current $X(t)$, with a factor of proportionality of $[1/(1 + a)]$. The unexpected change in the exchange rate is determined by applying the unexpected change operator $D^u(\ )$ to (2) with $j = 0$;

(5)
$$D^u[e(t)] = [1/(1 + a)] \cdot \sum_{i=0}^{\infty} [a/(1 + a)]^i$$
$$\cdot \{E[X(t + j + 1); t + 1]$$
$$- E[X(t + j + 1); t]\}.$$

Thus, the unexpected component of the change in the exchange rate is a weighted average of the change in expectations about future X's, based on new information that is received between t and $t + 1$.

From these results, it is possible to argue that expected changes in exchange rates are unlikely to be very large. Specifically, consider the monthly expected change in the exchange rate between two countries with similar and modest inflation rates and nominal interest rates. It is reasonable to suppose that the parameter, a, that measures the sensitivity of the current exchange rate to the expected rate of change of the exchange rate is on the order of ten or twenty.[10] It follows that the factor $1/(1 + a)$ that appears on the right-hand side of (4) will be on the order of one-tenth or one-twentieth. This implies that it takes a difference of 10% or 20% between the current expected value of $X(t)$ and the weighted average of future expected X's summarized by $E[e(t + 1); t]$ to justify a 1% expected change in the exchange rate between t and $t + 1$.

No similar argument can be advanced for why the unexpected component of the change in the exchange rate should usually be small. This component of the change in the exchange rate is necessarily random and unpredictable because it depends on the effect of new information received between t and $t + 1$ on expectations of all future X's. A small unexpected change in X, for instance, might convey information that leads to a substantial revision of expectations of all future X's and hence to a substantial unexpected change in the exchange rate.

These results also explain why spot and forward exchange rates tend to move together, especially for when changes are fairly large. If expected exchange rate changes are usually small, then any large change in an ex-

---

10. A justification for this assumption is given in connection with the discussion of the monetary model of exchange rate determination in the next section; see specifically n. 18 below.

change rate is likely to be primarily attributable to a large unexpected component of the change in the exchange rate. Since the unexpected component of the change in the exchange rate depends on a weighted average of changes in expectations about all future X's, large unexpected changes in an exchange rate should generally be associated with substantial changes, in the same direction, in expectations about each of these future X's. From (2), it is apparent that substantial changes in the same direction in expectations about each future X should induce substantial movements in the same direction of both the current spot exchange rate and expectations of future spot exchange rates.

From this discussion, it should be apparent that the simple asset market model represented by equations (1) and (2) is capable at least of rationalizing some of the important empirical regularities that characterize the behavior of floating exchange rates. The critical result that allows for this rationalization is the pricing formula (2) which expresses the exchange rate as a discounted sum of the basic factors that are expected to affect the foreign exchange market in the present and in future periods. This formula is obviously similar to the standard formula for expected present discounted value that is relevant in determining the current value of an income-yielding asset. Any model of exchange rate determination that ultimately yields a pricing rule similar to (2), with a discount rate that is not too large, will possess the essential properties illustrated by the present simple model. Differences among such models reflect differences in the specification of the "basic factors affecting the foreign exchange market" or in the determinants of the sensitivity of the current exchange rate to the expected rate of change of the exchange rate. In this general conception of the exchange rate as an asset price, however, nothing has been said about the fundamental importance of asset market equilibrium conditions, as opposed to flow market equilibrium conditions, in determining the exchange rate. As subsequent analysis will show, it is perfectly possible to arrive at an asset price model of the exchange rate by focusing on the condition for equilibrium in balance of payments flows as the fundamental equilibrium condition that determines the exchange rate.[11]

1.4 Monetary Models of Exchange Rate Determination

Since an exchange rate is the relative price of one nation's money in terms of the money of another nation, it is natural to think of an exchange rate as

---

11. Many of the earlier papers that described the asset market approach to exchange rates, including some of my own papers, wrongly placed their emphasis on the conditions of asset market equilibrium as the critical determinants of exchange rates. It is clear to me that one can arrive at an asset price expression for the exchange rate from a model that focuses on flow market equilibrium conditions. More generally, one must recognize that in any sensible model of exchange rates both asset market and flow market equilibrium conditions are important, and it is a matter of expository convenience which of them one chooses to emphasize.

determined, at least proximately, by the outstanding stocks of these monies and by the demands to hold these stocks. This simple proposition is the starting-off point for two related but distinct classes of monetary models of exchange rate determination. The first class of monetary models, which have been widely applied in empirical studies of exchange rate behavior, expresses the current exchange rate as a function of the current stocks of domestic and foreign money and the current determinants of the demands for these monies, including domestic and foreign income and interest rates. The second class of monetary models, which has been more widely used in theoretical work, focuses on the influence on the current exchange rate of the expected future path of money supplies and of factors affecting money demands. The distinguishing features of these two classes of models requires that they should be given separate attention.

The essential content of the first class of monetary models may be summarized in an equation of the form

$$(6) \qquad e = m - m^* - (l[y, i, k] - l^*[y^*, i^*, k^*]),$$

where e is the logarithm of the price of foreign money in terms of domestic money, m is the logarithm of the domestic money supply, l is the logarithm of demand for domestic money (a function of domestic income, y, the domestic interest rate, i, and other factors k), and an asterisk (*) indicates variables for the foreign country.[12] In some presentations, equation (6) is derived from the following assumptions: (1) The logarithm of the domestic price level, P, is determined by domestic money market equilibrium to be $P = m - l(y, i, k)$. (2) The logarithm of the foreign price level, P^*, is determined by the foreign money market equilibrium condition to be $P^* = m^* - l^*(y^*, i^*, k^*)$. (3) The equilibrium exchange rate is determined by the requirement of purchasing power parity to be $e = P - P^* = m - m^* - (l[y, i, k] - l^*[y^*, i^*, k^*])$.

Monetary models of exchange rate determination have been criticized because of the inadequacy of the assumptions used to derive equation (6). In particular, the assumption of purchasing power parity has been criticized as not consistent with the facts, especially the facts of the 1970s.[13] The collapse of purchasing power parity in the 1970s, however, is not (in my judgment) adequate reason for rejecting equation (6) as a model (albeit an incomplete model) of exchange rate determination.[14] This equation can be derived without explicit reference to purchasing power parity; indeed, it can

---

12. Models of this type are examined in Bilson (1978, 1979), Hodrick (1978), Frenkel (1980), and Frenkel and Clements (1982).

13. For example, this is one of Dornbusch's (1980*a*) main criticisms of the monetary model of exchange rate determination.

14. In my own work on exchange rates, I have almost never assumed that purchasing power parity always holds, and have not regarded this assumption as essential to analyzing the role of monetary variables in influencing exchange rates; see Mussa (1976, 1977, 1979, 1981a, 1982*a*) and Frenkel and Mussa (1980).

be derived from a model that allows explicity for divergences from purchasing power parity. Moreover, some empirical studies employing equation (6) have noted that there are divergences from purchasing power parity and have argued that the conditions of money market equilibrium are more immediately relevant for determining the exchange rate (which is a freely adjusting asset price) than they are for determining national price levels.[15] This, of course, leaves open the important question of what determines the behavior of national price levels, which in turn is an important element in explaining the behavior of real exchange rates. Nevertheless, if equation (6) worked well in explaining the behavior of nominal exchange rates, this form of monetary model of exchange rate determination would clearly make a substantial contribution to our understanding of the economic forces influencing the behavior of exchange rates.

The principal empirical difficulty with this form of monetary model is that equation (6) does not work well in explaining actual movements in nominal exchange rates, unless we take into account shifts in the demands to hold different national monies that are difficult to explain in terms of traditional arguments appearing in money demand functions.[16] An example illustrates this difficulty as well as a set of regressions. Between October 1976 and October 1980, the British pound appreciated by 50% in terms of the United States dollar, from $1.60 to $2.40. During this same period, monetary aggregates in Britain grew more rapidly than corresponding monetary aggregates in the United States, while real income (a key variable affecting the demand for money) grew less rapidly in Britain than in the United States. Of course, the increase in dollar value of sterling might be explained by an increase in the demand to hold sterling combined with a decrease in the demand to hold dollars, resulting from increased confidence in the future value of sterling (due to North Sea oil and the policies of Prime Minister Thatcher) and from increased concern about the inflationary consequences of the policies of the Carter administration. However, it is difficult to take these effects into account in a rigorous and disciplined fashion in an empirical version of equation (6).

Another important deficiency of equation (6) as a model of exchange rate determination is that it does not explicitly reveal the critical role of expectations of future economic conditions in determining the current exchange rate. From equation (6), there is no immediately apparent reason why changes in exchange rates should be largely random and unpredictable, or why new information that alters expectations about future economic conditions (including supplies and demands for national monies) should induce such random and unpredictable changes in exchange rates.

15. Bilson (1979) advances this argument in his paper concerning the dollar-mark exchange rate.
16. The relatively poor empirical performance of monetary models in explaining exchange rate movements in the 1970s is documented in Meese and Rogoff (1982).

The second general class of monetary models of exchange rate determination does not suffer from this deficiency. These models usually treat a small or moderate size economy that takes conditions in the rest of the world as given.[17] The critical condition determining the exchange rate for this country is the requirement of money market equilibrium;

(7) $m = k + \zeta \cdot e - \eta \cdot D^e(e), \quad \zeta, \eta > 0,$

where m is the logarithm of the domestic money supply, e is the logarithm of the price of foreign money in terms of domestic money, k summarizes all exogenous factors affecting the logarithm of the demand for domestic money, and $D^e(e) = E(e(t + 1); t) - e(t)$ is the expected rate of change of the exchange rate. As will be made clear by the analysis in section 1.6, equation (7) should be thought of as a reduced-form equilibrium condition derived from a more basic model of goods and asset market equilibrium. In this reduced form, the parameter ζ captures all of the mechanisms through which an increase in the price of foreign money increases the demand for domestic money, and the parameter η captures all of the mechanisms through which an increase in the expected rate of change of the price of foreign money affects the demand for domestic money.

Since the reduced-form demand for domestic money depends on the expected rate of change of the exchange rate, it follows that the current equilibrium exchange rate depends not only on the current values of m and k, but also on the expectation of next period's exchange rate;

(8) $e(t) = [1/(\zeta + \eta)] \cdot [m(t) - k(t)] + [\eta/(\zeta + \eta)]$
$\cdot E(e(t + 1); t).$

Forward iteration of (8), justified by the assumption of rational expectations, leads to the conclusion that the exchange rate expected at any future date is an exponentially weighted sum of expected future differences between m and k;

(9) $E(e(s); t) = [\zeta/(\zeta + \eta)] \cdot \sum_{j=0}^{\infty} [\eta/(\zeta + \eta)]^j$
$\cdot E(w(s + j); t),$

where $w(u) = (1/\zeta) \cdot [m(u) - k(u)]$. The current exchange rate, $e(t) = E(e(t); t)$, is found by setting $s = t$ in (9). This result reveals the fundamental principle that the current exchange rate depends on the entire future expected path of differences between (the logarithms of) the money supply and the exogenous component of money demand.

Using the general procedure outlined in section 2.3, (9) may be used to decompose the change in the exchange rate into its expected and unexpected

17. Monetary models of the type examined here are considered in Mussa (1976, 1982c) and Barro (1978).

components. The expected change in the exchange rate is given by

(10) $$D^e[e(t)] = (\zeta/(\zeta + \eta)) \cdot [E(e(t + 1); t) - E(w(t); t)].$$

If, as is plausible to suppose, $\zeta/(\zeta + \eta)$ is on the order of one-tenth or one-twentieth, then large monthly expected changes in the exchange rate should be unlikely.[18] In contrast, the unexpected change in the exchange rate is given by

(11)
$$D^u[e(t)] = (\zeta/(\zeta + \eta)) \cdot \sum_{j=0}^{\infty} (\eta/(\zeta + \eta))^j$$
$$\cdot [E(w(t + j + 1); t + 1)$$
$$- E(w(t + j + 1); t)].$$

If the new information received between t and $t + 1$ leads to a substantial revision of expectations concerning all future w's (in the same direction), this random and unpredictable component of the change in the exchange rate could be quite large.

To proceed with the analysis of changes in the exchange rate, it is necessary to specify how expectations about m and k are formed and revised. One convenient *theoretical* assumption is that k is a known constant, $\bar{k}$, that the money supply is observed each period before the exchange rate is determined, and that the stochastic process generating the money supply is known to economic agents and used by them (together with data on the present and past money supplies) to project the future course of the money supply. To be specific, suppose that m is generated by a random walk plus noise but that economic agents observe only m and not its permanent (random walk) and transitory (noise) components. In this case, economic agents will form an estimate $\hat{m}(t)$, of the current level of the permanent component of m by taking a weighted average of present and past m's, and they will attribute the difference, $m(t) - \hat{m}(t)$, to the present transitory component of m. The expected level of m in any future period will equal $\hat{m}(t)$. The current exchange rate, $e(t) = (1/\zeta) \cdot [\hat{m}(t) - \bar{k}] + [1/(\zeta + \eta)] \cdot [m(t) - \hat{m}(t)]$, fully reflects the component of the money supply that is thought to be permanent, but is less strongly affected by the component of the money supply that is thought to be transitory. The expected change in the exchange rate, $D^e[e(t)] = -[1/(\zeta + \eta)] \cdot [m(t) - \hat{m}(t)]$, reflects the expected disappearance of the transitory component of m. The information received by economic agents between t and $t + 1$ is measured by difference between the actual level of $m(t + 1)$ and the level that was expected at time t, $E(m(t + 1); t) = \hat{m}(t)$. A fraction, α, of this difference is attributed to an increase in

---

18. In order to have an interest elasticity of money demand (given by $i \cdot \eta$) equal to 0.1, when the nominal interest rate is 1% per month, we must have $\eta = 10$. If $\zeta = 1$, as it would under strict purchasing power parity and no currency substitution, then $\zeta/(\zeta + \eta)$ would equal 1/11. If the interest elasticity of money demand were as large as 0.2 and ζ were as small as 0.5, then $\zeta/(\zeta + \eta)$ would be as small as 1/41.

the permanent component of m, and the remaining fraction, $1 - \alpha$, is attributed to the transitory component in $m(t + 1)$, where the fraction α is an increasing function of the ratio of the variance of disturbances to the permanent component of m to the variance of transitory disturbances to m.[19] The unexpected change in the exchange rate, $D^u[e(t)] = \{(\alpha/\zeta) + [(1 - \alpha)/(\zeta + \eta)]\} \cdot [m(t + 1) - \hat{m}(t)]$, reflects, as it should, the information received by economic agents between t and $t + 1$. Consistent with common sense, this unexpected change in the exchange rate is greater the greater is the deviation of the money supply from its expected level and the greater is the fraction of this deviation that is attributed to a change in the permanent component of the money supply.

This example illustrates the key point that the nature of the stochastic process governing the behavior of the exchange rate depends on the process generating the behavior of the money supply and on the information about this process that is available to economic agents. In particular, this example illustrates that the response of the exchange rate to a change in the money supply depends on the extent to which this change was unanticipated and on the extent to which any unanticipated change is thought to indicate a permanent change in the money supply.[20]

Aside from its theoretical usefulness, however, the assumption that economic agents use their knowledge of the (fixed) stochastic process generating the money supply as the primary ingredient in forming the expectations necessary for determining the exchange rate is not likely to provide a fully adequate empirical explanation of actual exchange rate movements. One likely reason for this inadequacy is that economic agents use many sources of information, other than the observed money supply series and other easily measured variables, in forming and revising their expectations concerning future money supply behavior. For example, the depreciation of the French franc on the day following the election of President Mitterand clearly was not due to any observed policy change (registered in the behavior of the money supply or other variables) since President Mitterand did not assume office until 3 weeks later. It must have been due to a change in expectations about future policy resulting from the fact of his election.

Another important barrier to monetary explanations of actual exchange rate movements arises from the lack of adequate measures of the exogenous factors affecting the demand for money and of expectations concerning the future behavior of these factors. Almost certainly, there have been shifts in the demands to hold national monies that are not accounted for either by changes in the traditional arguments appearing in money demand functions

19. See Muth (1960) for a description and derivation of this result.
20. For stochastic processes that allow for changes in the long-run growth rate of the money supply, as well as its long-run level, it is possible for unanticipated changes in the money supply to generate even stronger responses of the exchange rate. This possibility is examined in Mussa (1976).

(such as levels of national income) or by changes in expectations about future exchange rate movements induced by changes in expectations about money supply behavior. In theory, such demand shifts should play a role of coordinate importance with changes in money supplies (and changes in expectations about future money) supplies in determining movements in exchange rates. The inadequacy of measures of money demand shifts means, therefore, that a substantial fraction of actual exchange rate movements will not be adequately explained by monetary models.

One possible way around this difficulty is to adopt the view that changes in exchange rates which cannot be explained by changes in the actual or expected behavior of money supplies must be due to changes in the actual or expected behavior of money demands. The tautological view of the monetary model of exchange rate determination can be justified on the grounds that the money market equilibrium condition represented by equation (7) is a reduced form that incorporates all of the conditions of goods and asset market equilibrium. However, this tautological view of the monetary model still does not provide an explanation of many exchange rate movements, other than ascribing them to "shifts in money demands" arising from unknown sources. Moreover, while it is possible to view all economic forces affecting the exchange rate as operating through money demand or money supply, this may lead to a rather convoluted and unnatural view of the mechanisms through which some economic forces affect the exchange rate. In such circumstances, it is not sensible to insist on an exclusively monetary interpretation of the determination of exchange rates.

1.5 Balance of Payments Equilibrium and the Exchange Rate

The traditional approach to analyzing exchange rate behavior focuses on the condition of balance of payments equilibrium as the proximate determinant of the equilibrium exchange rate. A common feature of models that adopt this approach is the assumption that an increase in the price of foreign exchange implies an increase in the relative price of a country's imports in terms of its exports and (provided certain elasticity conditions are satisfied) an increase in the net inflow of foreign exchange arising from current account transactions.[21] The (momentary) equilibrium exchange rate in such a model is the exchange rate at which the net inflow of foreign exchange arising from current account transactions is balanced by the net outflow resulting from capital account transactions. In this section I consider a formulation of this traditional approach to the theory of exchange rate deter-

---

21. This assumption is made in the standard flow model of the foreign exchange market that is described in virtually every textbook on international economics. The elasticity condition that is required to ensure stability of the foreign exchange market is sometimes the Marshall-Lerner condition and sometimes the more complicated Robinson-Metzler-Bickerdike condition.

mination that results in an "asset price" model of the exchange rate which shares the general features of the schematic model examined in section 1.3.

1.5.1 Goods Market Equilibrium and the Trade Balance

To avoid the complexities of dealing with nominal prices and nominal exchange rates, it is convenient to phrase the present model of balance of payments equilibrium in terms of real variables. The model considers a moderate-size home country that trades two goods (domestic goods and foreign goods) and a single real asset (denominated in foreign goods) with the rest of the world (referred to as the foreign country). Real assets pay a fixed rate of return, r^*, in terms of foreign goods; and the net stock of such assets held by domestic residents, A, may be positive or negative.[22] Foreign residents are willing to exchange large flow amounts of foreign goods in exchange for foreign (real) assets at the prevailing rate of return r^*, but they are not willing to purchase large amounts of domestic goods (of the home country) in exchange for foreign goods at a fixed relative price of these two goods. Instead, the value of foreign demand for domestic goods (measured in units of foreign goods) is given by

$$(12) \qquad d^* = - \beta^* \cdot q + x^*,$$

where q is the logarithm of the relative price of domestic goods in terms of foreign goods, x^* is a shift parameter that takes account of all exogenous factors (including government commercial and expenditure policies) that affect foreign demand for domestic goods, and $\beta^* > 0$ reflects the relative price elasticity, equal to $- [1 + (\beta^*/d^*)]$, of foreign demand for domestic goods.

The desired trading position of the home country with respect to goods is described by that country's excess demand for foreign goods, f, and by the value (in terms of foreign goods) of its excess demand for domestic goods, d:

$$(13) \qquad f = (1 - \sigma) \cdot \psi + \beta \cdot q - x,$$

$$(14) \qquad d = \sigma \cdot \psi - \beta \cdot q + x,$$

where ψ is the excess of domestic spending over the value of domestic product (measured in terms of foreign goods), σ and $1 - \sigma$ are the (marginal) shares of domestic and foreign goods in domestic spending, x is a shift parameter that accounts for exogenous factors (including tariffs and government spending policies) that affect the distribution of home excess demand between foreign and domestic goods, and $\beta > 0$ reflects the relative

---

22. A nontradable domestic asset may be added to the model without altering its basic character or its analytical complexity. The equilibrium condition that the demand for this asset must equal the available supply can be used to determine the equilibrium rate of return on this asset and eliminate this variable from the model.

price elasticity, equal to $-(\beta/f)$, of home demand for imports of foreign goods.[23]

The system of excess demand functions (12), (13), and (14) can be interpreted as a modified and extended version of the standard two-country, two-commodity model of the real theory of international trade.[24] In this interpretation, equation (12) represents the offer curve of the foreign country and equations (13) and (14) represent the offer curve of the home country. The home offer curve is displaced from the origin of commodity trade by the excess of the domestic spending over the value of domestic product. There is no corresponding displacement of the foreign offer curve because, by assumption, the large foreign country absorbs the home country's excess spending through a flow of securities, without any effect on foreign demand for domestic goods of the home country. This interpretation of equations (12), (13), and (14) can also be applied in the special case of the standard two-country, two-commodity model that is widely used in discussions of macroeconomic issues in which it is assumed that each country produces a distinct output. To arrive at this form of model, all that is necessary is to assume, without any formal change in the equations, that the home country produces no foreign goods. Along a somewhat different line, equations (12), (13), and (14) can be interpreted as representing the standard model of a "dependent economy" which produces and consumes its own domestic non-traded good and also produces, consumes, and either exports or imports a traded good that is identical to traded goods sold on the world market. To arrive at this interpretation, all that is necessary is to regard the foreign good as the traded good (recognizing that domestic excess demand for this good could be positive or negative), to view d as domestic excess demand for the nontraded good (which must be zero in equilibrium), and to specify that foreign excess demand for this nontraded good, d^*, must be zero.

Consistent with all of these interpretations of the excess demand functions (12), (13), and (14), it is appropriate to express the requirement for equilibrium in the market for domestic goods (of the home country) by the requirement

(15) $d + d^* = 0.$

There is no similar condition for equilibrium in the market for foreign goods because, by assumption, the foreign country absorbs the home country's excess for these goods in exchange for a flow of securities. Thus, equation (15) represents the condition for goods market equilibrium.

23. It is noteworthy that the total value of home excess demand for foreign and domestic goods, $f + d$, is equal, as it should be, to the excess of domestic spending over the value of domestic product. Thus, given the value of ψ, there is really only one independent excess demand function specified by (13) and (14).

24. This is the model that is described, for instance, in Mundell (1960) and in most advanced texts in international economics.

From this goods market equilibrium condition and from the specification of the determinants of d and d^* given in (12) and (14), we may derive a critical relationship between the excess of domestic spending over the value of domestic product, ψ, the (logarithm of the) relative price of domestic goods in terms of foreign goods, q, and the shift parameters affecting domestic and foreign demand for domestic goods, x and x^*;

$$(16) \qquad -\psi = v \cdot (z - q),$$

where

$$(17a) \qquad v = (\beta + \beta^*)/\sigma$$

and

$$(17b) \qquad z = (x + x^*)/(\beta + \beta^*).$$

The significance of this relationship becomes apparent when we recognize that the trade balance of the home country (measured in units of foreign goods), T, must equal the excess of the value of foreign purchases of domestic goods, d^*, over domestic purchases of foreign goods, f; that is, $T = d^* - f$. Using this fact together with (12), (13), and (16), we arrive at the conclusion that

$$(18) \qquad T = -\psi = v \cdot (z - q).$$

This result expresses the fundamental equivalence between the ''absorption'' and the ''elasticities'' approaches to analyzing the behavior of the trade balance.[25] The absorption approach views that trade balance as the excess of the value of domestic output over domestic spending; that is, as $-\psi$. The elasticities approach views the trade balance as a function, $v \cdot (z - q)$, of the relative price of domestic goods in terms of imported goods and of the other (exogenous) factors affecting demands for imports in the two countries. From the perspective of the elasticities approach, it is noteworthy that the assumption that the parameters β and β^* are positive is sufficient to insure that the Marshall-Lerner condition is satisfied and hence that an increase in the relative price of domestic goods worsens the trade balance.

1.5.2 The Meaning and Implications of Balance of Payments Equilibrium

Ignoring unilateral transfers, and assuming that services such as transport, insurance, and tourism have been incorporated into the trade balance, the current account balance of the home country must equal its trade balance plus the interest income that home residents receive (or pay) on their net foreign asset holdings; that is,

$$(19) \qquad b = T + r^* \cdot A = v \cdot (z - q) + r^* \cdot A.$$

---

25. On the subjects of the elasticities and absorption approaches to the balance of payments, see Alexander (1959) and Johnson (1958).

In the absence of official intervention, the current account balance must correspond to the rate of accumulation of net foreign assets by home residents,

$$(20) \qquad D(A) = b = v \cdot (z - q) + r^* \cdot A,$$

where D is the forward difference operator.

As a matter of economic behavior, the rate of accumulation of net foreign assets must also correspond to the desired excess of domestic income (including net interest income) over domestic spending. The behavioral determinants of the desired excess of income over spending are indicated by the relationship

$$(21) \qquad r^* \cdot A - \psi = \alpha \cdot (R - \rho) + \mu \cdot (\hat{A} - A), \quad \alpha, \mu > 0,$$

where $r^* \cdot A - \psi$ represents the accounting value of the excess of income over spending, R is the domestic real interest rate, ρ is the natural level of the real interest rate at which domestic residents would want to spend exactly their income (provided that net foreign assets were at their target level), and $\hat{A}$ is the target level of net foreign assets that home residents would like to hold if R were equal to ρ. Since only the sum, $\alpha \cdot \rho + \mu \cdot \hat{A}$, matters in (21), and not either ρ or $\hat{A}$ independently, it can be assumed, without loss of generality, that $\rho = r^*$, and all exogenous changes in the desired excess of income over spending can be treated as arising from changes in the target level of net foreign assets.

The domestic real interest rate that influences the desired relationship between income and spending, R, depends on the foreign real interest rate, r^*, and the expected rate of change of the relative price of domestic goods, $D^e(q)$:

$$(22) \qquad R = r^* - \sigma \cdot D^e(q).$$

The idea underlying (22) is that spending behavior of home residents is affected by the rate of return they expect to earn on their assets measured in terms of a consumption basket that includes domestic and foreign goods with weights of σ and $1 - \sigma$. If the relative price of domestic goods in terms of foreign goods is expected to rise at a rate $D^e(q)$, the expected real rate of return on assets that have a fixed price in terms of foreign goods and pay a fixed rate of return of r^* in terms of such goods is less than r^* by an amount $\sigma \cdot D^e(q)$.

The desired rate of asset accumulation implied by the desired excess of domestic income over domestic spending, as determined by (21) and (22), must in equilibrium, be consistent with the net inflow of foreign assets resulting from the current account balance, as determined by (19) or (20). This consistency requirement is expressed by the condition

$$(23) \qquad v \cdot (z - q) + r^* \cdot A = -\alpha\sigma \cdot D^e(q) + \mu \cdot (\hat{A} - A).$$

This condition may be interpreted as the requirement for balance of payments equilibrium. It says that current account surplus, which is the sum of the trade balance surplus, $v \cdot (z - q)$, and the service account surplus, $r^* \cdot A$, must be equal to the capital account deficit, $-\alpha\sigma \cdot D^e(q) + \mu \cdot (\hat{A} - A)$, which is determined by desired asset accumulation by home residents.

A superior, but not necessarily conflicting, interpretation of (23) is that it represents two distinct sets of economic conditions that must simultaneously be satisfied in order for the economic system to be in (momentary) equilibrium. The left-hand side of (23) summarizes the implications of the excess demand functions (12), (13), and (14) and the requirement of goods market equilibrium (15). The left-hand side of (23) has real interpretation as a net flow of goods and services, and it has a financial interpetation as a corresponding flow of financial claims. The right-hand side of (23) summarizes the content of the behavioral equations and equilibrium conditions that underlie the determination of the desired excess of domestic income over domestic spending. It too has a real interpretation, as an excess of real income over real spending; and it has a financial interpretation, as a corresponding rate of accumulation of financial claims. Equation (23) simply requires that the real flows of goods and services and the corresponding flows of financial claims determined by the relationships that underlie the two sides of this equation be mutually consistent.

The determination of the momentary equilibrium "real exchange rate," which is identified with q, by the balance of payments equilibrium condition (23) is illustrated in figure 1.1. The negatively sloped line labeled $v \cdot (z - q) + r^* \cdot A$ shows the net flow demand for foreign exchange arising from current account transactions. The positively sloped line labeled $\alpha\sigma[q - E(q(t + 1); t)] + \mu(\hat{A} - A)$ shows the net flow supply of foreign exchange arising from desired asset accumulation by domestic residents.[26] The intersection of these two lines determines the current q that is consistent with balance of payments equilibrium, given the values of z, A, $\hat{A}$, and $E(q(t + 1); t)$. In many discussions, the positively sloped line in figure 1 (or its equivalent) is interpreted as representing the behavior of "foreign exchange speculators" who are distinguished from ordinary transactors in the foreign exchange market (whose behavior is represented by the negatively sloped line in fig. 1.1 or its equivalent). As the preceding analysis makes clear, however, this distinction between "speculators" and "ordinary transactors" is artificial and unnecessary. The two sides of equation (23) and the corresponding lines in figure 1.1 represent different behavioral equations and equilibrium conditions, but for the same set of economic agents.

26. The model of exchange rate determination that is represented in figure 2.1 is consistent with the rather naive descriptions of the foreign exchange market that appear in many textbooks and with more sophisticated "flow market" models of the exchange rate developed by Tsiang (1959), Stein (1965), Stein and Tower (1967), Black (1973), and Niehans (1977).

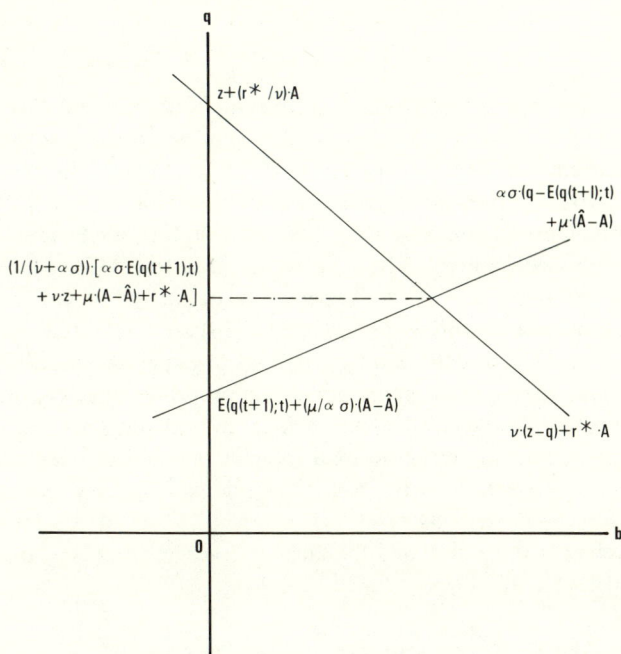

Fig. 1.1   Balance of payments equilibrium and the equilibrium real exchange rate.

Under the assumption of rational expectations, the difference equations (20) and (23) may be treated as a simultaneous, forward-looking system that jointly determines the expected future paths of A and q, conditional on the inherited level of net foreign assets, $A(t)$, and the expected future paths of the exogenous forcing variables z and $\hat{A}$. The solution of this system for the current value of q may be written in the form[27]

$$(24) \qquad q(t) = \overline{q}(t) + \gamma \cdot [A(t) - \overline{A}(t)],$$

where

$$(25) \qquad \overline{q}(t) = (r*/v) \cdot \overline{A}(t) + (1 - \theta) \cdot \sum_{j=0}^{\infty} \theta^j \cdot E(z(t + j); t),$$

$$(26) \qquad \overline{A}(t) = (1 - \theta) \cdot \sum_{j=0}^{\infty} \theta^j \cdot E(\hat{A}(t + j); t),$$

$$(27) \qquad \theta = [1/(1 + \lambda)], \quad \gamma = (\lambda/v) - (1/\alpha\sigma),$$

27. As in the case of the monetary model of the previous section, a boundary condition is imposed that ensures an economically sensible, nonexplosive solution for the difference equation system (20) and (23).

(28) $\lambda = (1/2) \cdot \{[r^* + (\nu/\alpha\sigma)]$
                    $+ \sqrt{[r^* + (\nu/\alpha\sigma)]^2 + 4 \cdot (\mu\nu/\alpha\sigma)}\}.$

These results may be interpreted in the following manner: $\overline{q}(t)$ represents the "long-run equilibrium exchange rate" that is expected to be consistent with the current account balance ($b = 0$) on average in the present and in future periods, with an appropriate rate of discount, λ, for future current account imbalances, and assuming that net foreign assets are currently at their long-run desired level. The long-run desired level of net foreign assets, $\overline{A}(t)$, is a discounted sum of the expected target levels of net foreign assets in the present and in future periods. The discount rate that is applied to expected future $\hat{A}$'s in determining $\overline{A}(t)$ and to expected future z's in determining $\overline{q}(t)$ depends, in an economically appropriate manner, on the sensitivity of the trade balance of changes in q and on the sensitivity of capital flows to changes in the domestic real interest rate and to changes in the net stock of foreign assets held by domestic residents. Finally, the current real exchange rate, $q(t)$, reflects both the current estimate of the long-run equilibrium exchange rate, $\overline{q}(t)$, and the current divergence of $A(t)$ from its long-run desired level, $\overline{A}(t)$.

1.5.3 The Real Exchange Rate as an Asset Price

The balance of payments equilibrium condition (23) that is the essential ingredient in deriving the results (24)–(28) is, on its face, a flow market equilibrium condition rather than an asset market equilibrium condition. Nevertheless, this equilibrium condition implies a solution for $q(t)$—which is identified with (the logarithm of) the real exchange rate—that may be thought of in two distinct ways as the expression for an asset price.

First, given $\overline{q}(t)$ and $\overline{A}(t)$, it is apparent from (24) that the current real exchange rate, $q(t)$, is related to the stock of net foreign assets, $A(t)$, in the manner that is suggested by a number of recent "asset market models" of the role of the current account in exchange rate dynamics.[28] The essential idea of these models is that the momentary equilibrium real exchange rate is determined by the price at which domestic residents are willing to hold their existing net position in foreign assets. The greater is the net stock of foreign assets, A, the lower is the price at which domestic residents will hold this stock; that is, the higher is the momentary equilibrium value of q (which is defined as the logarithm of the relative price of domestic goods in terms of foreign goods). Given the exogenous factors affecting trade balance, the higher is q the smaller is the trade balance surplus (or the greater is the trade balance deficit) and hence the slower is the rate of accumulation of foreign assets by domestic residents. These relationships imply a dynamic

---

28. Models of this type include those developed by Branson (1976), Kouri (1976a), Calvo and Rodriguez (1977), Dornbusch and Fischer (1978), and Rodriguez (1980).

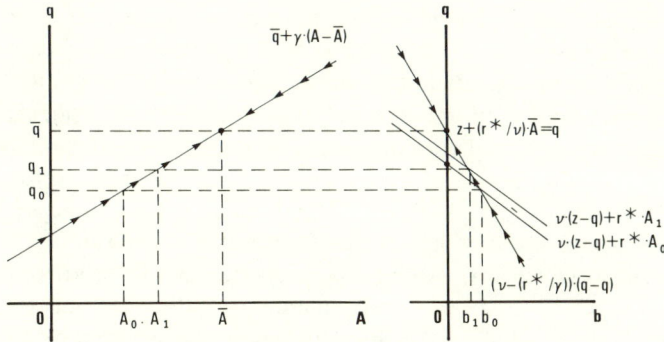

Fig. 1.2   Dynamic interaction among the exchange rate, asset stocks, and the current account.

process, which is illustrated in figure 1.2, in which an initial divergence of net foreign assets from their long-run equilibrium level, $\overline{A}$, implies a divergence of the momentary equilibrium level of q from the level that would yield a zero current account balance, and a subsequent sequence of current account imbalances and corresponding changes in net foreign assets that ultimately drive net foreign assets to their long-run equilibrium and q to the level that yields a zero current account balance. This is exactly the dynamic process that is implied by the results (24)–(28) when the exogenous forcing variables z and $\hat{A}$ are constant.

Second, the value of $q(t)$ determined by (24)–(28) is an "asset price" in the sense discussed in Section 1.3 because the long-run equilibrium exchange rate, $\overline{q}(t)$, and the long-run desired level of net foreign assets, $\overline{A}(t)$, which influence $q(t)$ are, respectively, forward-looking weighted averages of the present and expected future exogenous factors affecting the trade balance (the z's) and the present and expected future target levels of net foreign assets (the $\hat{A}$'s). The critical assumption that confers this "asset price" property on $q(t)$ is the assumption that the expected rate of change of q, $D^e(q)$, affects the desired excess of income over spending and hence the condition for balance of payments equilibrium. As previously explained, one justification for this assumption is in terms of the effect of $D^e(q)$ on the real interest rate that is relevant for domestic spending and saving decisions. Another, essentially equivalent justification is in terms of the effect of anticipated capital gains on net foreign asset holdings on the level of desired spending. When the relative price of domestic goods is expected to decline, domestic residents anticipate capital gains on their holdings of assets denominated in terms of imported goods. The expectation of such capital gains encourages domestic residents to save more than if such gains were not expected. Yet a third way of justifying an influence of $D^e(q)$ on the current q that is consistent with balance of payments equilibrium is in terms of the effect of an anticipated change in q on the temporal pattern of desired trading. If $D^e(q)$ is positive, then domestic residents have an incentive to expand purchases of domestic goods in the current period and to delay purchases of imported goods until they are relatively cheaper. Foreign residents have a similar incentive to expand current purchases of goods exported by the home country and delay purchases of their own goods. Together, these forces tend to improve the balance of payments of the home country and hence to raise the $q(t)$ that is consistent with balance of payments equilibrium.

The extent to which $q(t)$ exhibits the properties of an "asset price" that depends on expected future economic conditions, rather than only on current conditions, is determined by the discount rate λ that is given by (28). It is apparent that for λ to be small, ν and μ must be small relative to $\alpha\sigma$. This makes sense. Expected future economic conditions should have considerable weight, relative to current economic conditions, in determining $q(t)$ if divergences between $q(t)$ and $z(t)$ and between $A(t)$ and $\hat{A}(t)$ have relatively small effects on the balance of payments, in comparison with the effect of $D^e(q)$.

1.54 Dynamics of the Real Exchange Rate

Analysis of the causes of changes in the real exchange rate may be carried out by applying the general procedures of section 1.3 to the results (24)–(28). Specifically, the expected change in the real exchange rate is given by

$$(29) \qquad D^e[q(t)] = D^e[\overline{q}(t)] + \gamma \cdot D^e[A(t) - \overline{A}(t)].$$

In the special case where the long-run equilibrium exchange rate and the long-run desired level of net foreign assets are not expected to change, this result simplifies to

$$(30) \qquad D^e[q(t)] = \gamma \cdot D^e[A(t)] = \gamma \cdot E(b(t); t)$$

where $E(b(t); t)$ is the expected current account balance. In this special case, there is a positive relationship between $D^e[q(t)]$ and $E(b(t); t)$. More generally, however, there is no guarantee of such a relationship. The expectation of rising values of z implies a positive expected change in $\overline{q}$, but a negative contribution to the expected current account balance. The intuitive explanation of this relationship is as follows: The expectation of rising values of z means that the expected demand for domestic goods is less strong, and the expected demand for foreign goods is more strong, in the current period than it will be, on average, in future periods. The response to this situation is to allow the trade balance to go into deficit to absorb part of the strong demand for foreign goods and to reduce the relative price of domestic goods (increase the relative price of foreign goods) in order to reduce the excess demand for foreign goods in the current period relative to future periods. The result is a temporary expected deterioration in the current account combined with the expectation of a rise in the relative price of domestic goods. If this effect is sufficiently strong, it clearly could induce a negative, rather than a positive, relationship between the expected change in q and the expected current account balance.

The unexpected change in the real exchange rate, $D^u[q(t)]$, depends on the unexpected change in the long-run equilibrium real exchange rate, $D^u[\overline{q}(t)]$, and the unexpected change in the difference between A and $\overline{A}$;

$$(31) \qquad D^u[q(t)] = D^u[\overline{q}(t)] + \gamma \cdot D^u[A(t) - \overline{A}(t)].$$

If there are no unexpected changes in $\overline{q}$ or $\overline{A}$, then the unexpected change in q will depend exclusively on the unexpected change in net foreign assets which, in turn, must equal the "innovation" in the current account balance;

$$(32) \qquad D^u[q(t)] = \gamma \cdot D^u[A(t)] = \gamma \cdot [b(t) - E(b(t); t)].$$

More generally, however, the unexpected change in q will reflect changes in expectations about future z's and future $\hat{A}$'s which induce unexpected changes in $\overline{q}$ and $\overline{A}$. To the extent that unexpected movements in the trade balance are one of the sources of information that lead to revisions of expectations concerning future z's and A's, there is an additional channel for such innovations to affect the real exchange rate.[29]

1.6 Real and Monetary Factors in Exchange Rate Determination

Models of exchange rate behavior that focus on the condition of balance of payments equilibrium as the final determinant of the exchange rate are most directly relevant to understanding the real economic forces affecting the behavior of *real* exchange rates. In contrast, monetary models of exchange rate behavior are useful primarily in analyzing the influence of actual and anticipated movements in money supplies and money demands on *nominal* exchange rates. To arrive at a theoretical model that comprehends all of the factors that influence the actual behavior of exchange rates, it is necessary to combine the essential features of these two classes of models.

1.6 Monetization of the Real Model

To analyze the influence of the real sector of the economy on its monetary sector and arrive at a combined model of the determination of real and nominal exchange rates, it is convenient simply to expand the real model of the preceding section by introducing nominal prices and an appropriately specified money demand function. The logarithm of the domestic money price of domestic goods is denoted by p; the logarithm of the foreign money price of imported (or traded) goods is denoted by p^*; and the logarithm of the nominal exchange rate (defined as the domestic money price of a unit of foreign money) is denoted by e. These assumptions imply that the logarithm

29. The dynamic relationships between the current account and the exchange rate are explored more fully in Mussa (1981a).

of the relative price of domestic goods in terms of imported goods (previously identified with the real exchange rate) is given by

(33) $q = p - (e + p^*)$.

The logarithm of the general price level in the home country, denoted by P, is a weighted average of the domestic money prices of domestic and imported goods.

(34) $P = \sigma \cdot p + (1 - \sigma) \cdot (e + p^*) = e + p^* + \sigma \cdot q$,

where σ is the same as the σ of the preceding section and measures the weight of domestic goods in the expenditure of residents of the home country.

The logarithm of the demand for domestic money is given by

(35) $m^d = K + L \cdot P - N \cdot i - U \cdot D^e(e) + W \cdot A + V \cdot q$.

The parameter K represents all exogenous factors (such as real income) that affect money demand. The general price level affects money demand with a positive elasticity, L, which could equal unity. The exchange rate affects money demand (because of wealth valuation or currency substitution effects) with an elasticity J that is nonnegative. The domestic nominal interest rate, i, affects the demand for money with a negative semielasticity, $-N$. The expected rate of change of the nominal exchange rate, $D^e(e)$, affects the demand for domestic money through a "currency substitution effect" which is represented by a negative semielasticity, $-U$. Net holdings of foreign assets are assumed to affect the demand for domestic money with a positive semielasticity, W. Finally, the relative price of domestic goods in terms of imported goods affects the demand for domestic money with an elasticity, V, which may be either positive or negative.[30]

The money demand function specified in (35) may be converted into a reduced-form money demand function that is similar to that used in the simple monetary model of exchange rate behavior (see equation [7]). The general level of domestic prices can be eliminated as an explicit argument in the money demand function by substituting $e + p^* + \sigma q$ for P. The domestic nominal interest rate can be eliminated from the money demand function by utilizing the Fisher equation.

(36) $i = R - D^e(P)$,

where $D^e(P)$ is the expected rate of change of the domestic price level and

30. The relative price of domestic goods could affect money demand because of effects on the value of domestic product in terms of imported goods, on the distribution of income within the home country, on the value of domestic nontraded assets in terms of imported goods, or on the rate of return on such assets. In the next section, it will be assumed that whatever the signs of all of these effects, their cumulative impact is not very great.

R is the domestic real interest rate. Repeating equation (22), the domestic real interest rate is given by

(37) $$R = r^* - \sigma \cdot D^e(q),$$

where $D^e(q)$ is the expected rate of change of q and r^* is the exogenous foreign real interest rate. Further, assuming that expectations about domestic inflation take account of (34), it follows that

(38) $$D^e(P) = D^e(e) + \pi^* + \sigma D^e(q),$$

where $\pi^* = D^e(p^*)$ is the expected rate of change of the foreign money price of imported goods (i.e., the expected foreign inflation rate). Substituting the right-hand side of (38) for $D^e(P)$ in (36), and making all of the relevant substitutions in the money demand function (35), it follows that this money demand function can be rewritten in the form

(39) $$m^d = k + \zeta \cdot e \cdot \eta \cdot D^e(e),$$

where $\zeta = L + J > 0$ and $\eta = N + U > 0$, and

(40) $$k = \kappa + W \cdot A + (V + \sigma L) \cdot q$$

(41) $$\kappa = K + L \cdot p^* - N^*(r^* + \pi^*).$$

The distinction between k and κ is that k summarizes the influence on money demand of all factors that are exogenous to the monetary sector of the economy (including the endogenous real variables q and A), while κ summarizes the influence on money demand of all of the fully exogenous variables. It is noteworthy that the reduced-form money demand function (39) is consistent with the interest parity condition

(42) $$i = i^* + D^e(e) + \chi,$$

where $i^* = r^* + \pi^*$ is the foreign nominal interest rate and χ is a risk premium that may be specified as any linear function of e, $D^e(e)$, A, q, and $D^e(q)$.[31] The derivation of the reduced-form money demand function (39) establishes the point that the reduced-form money market equilibrium condition specified in equation (7) of section 1.3 is consistent with a very general specification of the structural factors influencing money demand.

1.6.2 Solution of the Combined Real and Monetary Model

The reduced-form money market equilibrium condition (7), together with equations (20) and (23) from the analysis of balance of payments equilib-

---

31. The implications of such a risk premium in the foreign exchange market are explored in papers by Kouri (1976b), Stockman (1978), and Fama and Farber (1980). Some evidence of such a premium is provided by Hansen and Hodrick (1982). The incorporation of such a risk premium in the present model alters only the structural interpretation of the parameters of the reduced-form money demand function.

rium, constitute a simultaneous system of difference equations that, under the assumption of rational expectations, determines the expected future paths of the real exchange rate, q, the net stock of foreign assets, A, and the nominal exchange rate, e, conditional on expectations concerning the future paths of the exogenous variables z, A, and $m - \kappa$. This system can be expressed in matrix form as

(43)
$$\begin{bmatrix} -\nu & r^* - D^e & 0 \\ \nu - \alpha\sigma \cdot D^e & \mu - r^* & 0 \\ V + \sigma L + \sigma N \cdot D^e & w & \zeta - \eta \cdot D^e \end{bmatrix} \cdot \begin{bmatrix} q \\ A \\ e \end{bmatrix} = \begin{bmatrix} -\nu \cdot z \\ \nu \cdot z - \theta \cdot A \\ m - \kappa \end{bmatrix}.$$

A key property of this dynamic system is determined by the two zeros that appear in the last column of the matrix on the left-hand side of (43). This property implies that dynamic system determining the expected future paths of the two real variables, q and A, is independent of the nominal exchange rate and of the exogenous monetary forcing variables, $m - \kappa$.[32] Indeed, the dynamic system determining the expected paths of q and A is identical to the dynamic system examined in section 1.5. This implies that the behavior of these variables is exactly as described by the analysis in that section. Moreover, given the behavior of q and A that is implied by the real subsystem of (43), we may treat the money demand parameter k (which is defined by [40] as a variable that is exogenous to the monetary sector of the economy); and we solve for the expected future path of the nominal exchange rate by using the reduced-form equilibrium condition given in (7). Thus, all that has been said in the preceding two sections concerning the behavior of the nominal and real exchange rates remains valid in the combined real and monetary model.

The fact that we determine the behavior of the nominal exchange rate by using a reduced-form model of monetary equilibrium, however, should not be allowed to obscure the important role that real variables play in determining the behavior of the nominal exchange rate. In the reduced-form monetary model, the influence of real variables on the nominal exchange rate is all subsumed into the influence of such variables on the money demand variable k. The influence of these real variables is brought into sharper focus by writing the solution for the expected path of the nominal exchange rate implied by the system (43) in the form

---

32. If desired expenditure were affected by the level of real money balances, then the real sector of the economy would not be independent of monetary influences. For some theoretical purposes, it is useful to assume that there is such a real balance effect. In the present context, however, the costs in terms of losing a convenient solution for the combined real and monetary model by introducing this effect outweigh its benefits.

(44) $$E(e(s); t) = E(F(s); t) - E(p^*(s); t) - \sigma \cdot E(q(s); t)$$

where

(45) $$F(s) = [1/(\zeta + \eta)]$$
$$\cdot \sum_{j=0}^{\infty} [\eta/(\zeta + \eta)]^j [m(s + j) - x(s + j)]$$

with

(46) $$x = K - N \cdot r^* + U \cdot [D^e(p^*) + \sigma \cdot D^e(q)]$$
$$+ W \cdot A + V \cdot q.$$

$F(s)$ is a weighted sum of differences between (the logarithm of) the nominal money supply, m, and the money demand shift variable, x, defined by (46). The economic significance of $F(s)$ is that its expected value is the common element influencing all nominal prices, as reflected in (44) and in the results

(47) $$E(p(s); t) = E(F(s); t) + (1 - \sigma) \cdot E(q(s); t)$$

(48) $$E((e(s) + p^*(s)); t) = E(F(s); t) - \sigma \cdot E(q(s); t)$$

(49) $$E(P(s); t) = E(F(s); t).$$

Comparing the results (44), (47), (48), and (49), it is apparent that movements in $E(F(s); t)$ are accommodated by equal movements in (the logarithms) of all nominal prices (measured in terms of domestic money). Movements in $E(p^*(s); t)$ are accommodated by offsetting movements in the nominal exchange rate which leave all domestic money prices unaltered. Movements in $E(q(s); t)$ are accommodated partly by movements in the nominal exchange rate (and corresponding movements in the domestic money price of imported goods) and partly by movements in the domestic money price of domestic goods, thereby allowing the general level of domestic prices, $E(P(s); t)$, to remain unaltered.

1.6.3 Exchange Rate Dynamics

Assuming that all current prices are observable, we obtain from (44) the following expression for the current nominal exchange rate:

(50) $$e(t) = E(F(t); t) - p^*(t) - \sigma \cdot q(t).$$

Applying the general procedures of section 1.3 to (50), it follows that the expected change in the exchange rate is given by

(51) $$D^e[e(t)] = D^e[F(t)] - D^e[p^*(t)] - \sigma D^e[q(t)],$$

where $D^e[p^*(t)] = \pi^*(t)$ is whatever people expect to be the rate of inflation in the foreign country, $D^e[q(t)]$ is determined by (29), and

(52) $$D^e[F(t)] = [\zeta/(\zeta + \eta)] \cdot \{E(F(t+1); t) - (1/\zeta) \cdot [m(t) - x(t)]\}.$$

The unexpected change in the exchange rate is given by

$$(53) \qquad D^u[e(t)] = D^u[F(t)] - D^u[p^*(t)] - \sigma \cdot D^u[q(t)],$$

where $D^u[p^*(t)]$ is the unexpected component of the foreign inflation rate, $D^u[q(t)]$ is determined by (31), and

$$(54) \qquad D^u[F(t)] = [1/(\zeta + \eta)] \cdot \sum_{j=0}^{\infty} [\eta/(\zeta + \eta)]^j$$
$$\cdot [E((m(t + j + 1) - x(t + j + 1)); t + 1)$$
$$- E((m(t + j + 1) - x(t + j + 1)); t)].$$

The general principle that is embodied in all of these results is that the change in the nominal exchange rate reflects expected and unexpected changes in the entire future time paths of the exogenous forcing variables that ultimately drive the behavior of the economy. One of these forcing variables is (the logarithm of) the nominal money supply, m. Its influence on (the logarithm of) the nominal exchange rate, $e(t)$, comes through the term $E(F(t); t)$ that involves an exponentially weighted sum of current and expected future m's. Since $E(F(t); t)$ is common to all nominal prices, it follows that expected and unexpected changes in $F(t)$ which are induced by expected and unexpected changes in m imply expected and unexpected changes in the exchange rate which are equal (proportionately) to the corresponding expected and unexpected changes in all domestic money prices and hence are consistent with purchasing power parity.

Another exogenous variable that affects the nominal exchange rate is the foreign money price of imported goods, p^*. It is apparent from (51) and (53) that expected and unexpected changes in p^* induce offsetting expected and unexpected changes in e which insulate domestic nominal prices from purely nominal disturbances in the foreign money price of imported goods. In addition, expected changes in p^* may influence e through a currency substitution effect on domestic money demand, as captured by the term $U \cdot D^e(p^*)$ appearing in the money demand parameter x defined in (46).

Real forcing variables affect the dynamic behavior of the exchange rate through two distinct channels. First, the real forcing variables z and $\hat{A}$ which enter into the determination of q (in the manner described in the preceding section) affect the expected and unexpected change in the exchange rate through the terms $-\sigma \cdot D^e[q(t)]$ and $-\sigma \cdot D^u[q(t)]$ that appear in (51) and (53). It is apparent that these contributions to the change in the nominal exchange rate, which are associated with changes in the relative price of domestic goods, give rise to deviations from purchasing power parity. Second, real forcing variables affect the change in the nominal exchange rate through their influence on expected and unexpected changes in the real demand for domestic money. In particular, the forcing variable K directly affects the demand for money, and the forcing variables z and $\hat{A}$ indirectly affect the demand for money through effects on the terms $W \cdot A$, and $(V + \sigma L) \cdot q$ that appear in the composite forcing variable x defined in (46). Since these effects come through the terms $D^e[F(t)]$ and $D''[F(t)]$ that are common to changes in all nominal prices, it is apparent that they induce exchange rate changes that are consistent with purchasing power parity.

1.7 Sticky Prices and Disequilibrium Dynamics

The combined real and monetary model of the preceding section assumes complete neutrality of money and allows no latitude for monetary disturbances to have real effects on output levels or relative prices. One way of modifying this result is by assuming that some nominal price is sticky and does not adjust immediately to its equilibrium value.[33] Usually, the nominal wage rate would be chosen as this sticky price; but, because the wage rate does not appear in our model, the domestic money price of domestic goods is selected to play this role. An adjustment rule that governs the behavior of this sticky price which may be derived from a microeconomic theory of price adjustment and shown to have desirable mathematical properties is given by

$$(55) \qquad D(p) = D^e(\bar{p}) + \delta \cdot (\bar{p} - p), \qquad \delta > 0,$$

where $\bar{p}$ is (the logarithm of) the "conditional equilibrium price" of domestic goods.[34] The "conditional equilibrium price" of domestic goods is defined as the price that would yield equilibrium in the market for domestic goods (and in all other markets) conditional on the actual expected path of net foreign assets.[35] The first term in the price adjustment rule, $D^e(\bar{p})$, causes the actual price of domestic goods to move in line with expected changes in its conditional equilibrium value. The second term in the price

33. This approach corresponds to "contracting approach" to introducing monetary nonneutralities into macroeconomic models that has been developed by Fisher (1977), Phelps and Taylor (1977), and Taylor (1980). An alternative approach is that developed by Lucas (1972, 1973, 1975), Sargent and Wallace (1975), and Barro (1976) which emphasizes incomplete information as the source of nonneutral effects of monetary disturbances. Differences between these approaches with respect to their implications for the usefulness of stabilization policy should carry over from closed to open economy models. For applications of these approaches to open economy macroeconomic models, see Flood (1979), Saidi (1980) and 1982), Stockman (1980), and Buiter and Miller (1981, 1982).

34. The economic justification for the assumption of this form of price adjustment rule is discussed in Mussa (1981b, 1982B).

35. The full equilibrium price of domestic goods is calculated on the assumption that domestic holdings of net foreign assets will follow their equilibrium path. When there is disequilibrium, the actual path of net foreign assets will not correspond to this full equilibrium path. For reasons of analytical convenience it is useful to specify that the conditional equilibrium price of domestic goods plays the role of the equilibrium price in the price adjustment rule. Designation of the full equilibrium price to play this role would not alter the basic conclusions of the analysis of this section, but it would make the analysis more complicated.

adjustment rule, $\delta \cdot (\bar{p} - p)$, causes any gap between the actual and the conditional equilibrium price of domestic goods to be eliminated at an exponential rate δ.

1.7.1 The Disequilibrium Situation

When the inherited value of $p(t)$ differs from $\bar{p}(t)$, there is disequilibrium in the market for domestic goods. Consistent with the assumption that producers of these goods are holding their prices temporarily fixed, it is assumed that this disequilibrium is absorbed by variations in the output of domestic goods. Formally, this assumption is represented by specifying that

$$(56) \qquad y = d + d^*,$$

where y denotes the *deviation* of the value of output of domestic goods from its equilibrium level, d^* is the value of foreign excess demand for domestic goods, and d is the excess of the value of domestic demand for domestic goods over the equilibrium level of output of such goods.

The value of foreign excess demand for domestic goods, d^*, is still determined by (12), namely,

$$(57) \qquad d^* = \beta^* \cdot q - x^*.$$

There must be some modification, however, in the specification of d and f to take account of the disequilibrium situation; specifically, (13) and (14) are replaced by

$$(58) \qquad f = (1-\sigma) \cdot \psi + \beta \cdot q - x + (1-\sigma) \cdot (1-\xi) \cdot y$$

$$(59) \qquad d = \sigma \cdot \psi - \beta \cdot q + x + \sigma \cdot (1-\xi) \cdot y,$$

where ψ is the excess of the equilibrium level of domestic spending over the equilibrium value of domestic output, and ζ is the marginal propensity to save out of a disequilibrium increase in the value of domestic output.

Since, by assumption, disequilibrium does not affect domestic output of foreign goods (if such goods are produced domestically), the excess of domestic demand for such goods over the equilibrium level of domestic output of such goods, which is measured by f, corresponds to the actual domestic excess demand for such goods even in the disequilibrium situation. It follows that the trade balance of the home country, T, is given by

$$(60) \qquad T = d^* - f = \sigma \cdot v \cdot (z - q) - (1 - \sigma) \\ \cdot \psi - (1 - \sigma) \cdot (1 - \xi) \cdot y$$

where, as before, $v = (\beta + \beta^*)/\sigma$ and $z = (x + x^*)/(\beta + \beta^*)$. Substituting (57) and (59) into the disequilibrium market-clearing condition (56), it is easily shown that

$$(61) \qquad \psi = v \cdot (q - z) + [(1 - \sigma + \xi\sigma)/\sigma] \cdot y.$$

Substitution of (61) into (60) yields the result that

(62) $$T = -(\psi - \xi \cdot y) = v \cdot (z - q) - [(1 - \sigma)/\sigma] \cdot y.$$

This result (which is the analogue of [18]) expresses the equivalence between the absorption and elasticities approaches to the trade balance when the economy is in disequilbrium.[36]

The budget constraints and accounting identities which must apply in disequilibrium as well as equilibrium situations imply that the rate of accumulation of net foreign assets by home residents must equal the current account balance of the home country; hence

(63) $$D(A) = b = v \cdot (z - q) + r^* \cdot A - ((1 - \sigma)/\sigma) \cdot y.$$

Further, adding disequilibrium savings, $\xi \cdot y$, to the equilibrium desired excess of domestic income over domestic spending, $r^*A - \psi = -\alpha\sigma D^e(q) + \mu(\hat{A} - A)$, it follows that the modified version of the balance of payments equilibrium condition that is relevant in disequilibrium is given by

(64) $$v \cdot (z - q) + r^* \cdot A - [(1 - \sigma)/\sigma] \cdot y = $$
$$-\alpha\sigma \cdot D^e(q) + \mu \cdot (\hat{A} - A) + \xi \cdot y.$$

The money market equilibrium condition must also be modified to take account of disequilibrium variations in the value of domestic output (and domestic income) on the demand for domestic money. Specifically, adding an amount $\omega \cdot y$ to the money demand function (35), it follows that the modified condition of money market equilibrium can be written as

(65) $$\zeta \cdot e - \eta \cdot D^e(e) + W \cdot A + (V + \sigma L) \cdot q$$
$$+ \omega \cdot y = m - \kappa,$$

where κ is the exogenous money demand parameter defined in (41).

1.7.2 Expected Convergence toward Conditional Equilibrium

Under the assumption of rational expectations, the difference equations (63), (64), and (65) are three of the four equations that are required for the system that determines the expected paths of the four endogenous variables, q, A, e, and y, conditional on the expected future paths of the exogenous forcing variables. To complete this system, we tentatively assume that

---

36. From the perspective of the absorption approach, the trade balance is given by $T = -(\psi - \xi \cdot y)$, and it appears that a disequilibrium increase in income improves the trade balance (since some of this income is saved). From the prospective of the elasticities approach, the trade balance is given by $T = v \cdot (z - q) - [(1 - \sigma)/\sigma] \cdot y$, and it appears that a disequilibrium increase in income worsens the trade balance (since it increases domestic demand for foreign goods). The two results are consistent, however, because for the absorption approach we are implicitly holding ψ constant, while for the elasticities approach we are implictly holding q constant.

(66) $y = \Lambda \cdot (\bar{p} - p)$,

where Λ is a constant whose value is yet to be determined. If (66) is valid, then it follows from the price adjustment rule (61) that

(67) $D^e(y) = \Lambda \cdot D^e[(\bar{p} - p)] = -\delta \cdot \Lambda \cdot (\bar{p} - p) = -\delta \cdot y$.

This difference equation completes the system required to determine the expected paths of q, A, e, and y.

The assumption of (66) is justified by showing that under this assumption all variables converge to their respective conditional equilibrium values (on an expected basis) in a consistent and correct manner. In the process of this demonstration, the appropriate value of the coefficient Λ is derived. The definition of the concept of conditional equilibrium implies that the current conditional equilibrium values of all endogenous variables (which are denoted by a tilde) must satisfy the equations of the combined real and monetary model developed in sections 1.4–1.6.[37] In particular, since q and e must be consistent with the balance of payments equilibrium condition and the money market equilibrium condition, it follows that the deviations $q - \tilde{q}$ and $e - \tilde{e}$ must satisfy the conditions[38]

(68) $v \cdot (q - \tilde{q}) - [(1 - \sigma)/\sigma] \cdot y =$
                    $-\alpha\sigma \cdot D^e(q - \tilde{q}) + \xi \cdot y,$

(69) $\zeta \cdot (e - \tilde{e}) - \eta \cdot D^e(e - \tilde{e}) + (V + \sigma L)$
                    $\cdot (q - \tilde{q}) + \omega \cdot y = 0.$

Further, consistent with (66) and (67), it may be assumed that q and e are expected to converge to their respective conditional equilibrium values, $\tilde{q}$ and $\tilde{e}$, at the same exponential rate δ that characterizes the expected speed of convergence of p to $\bar{p}$. This implies that the terms $D^e(q - \tilde{q})$ and $D^e(e - \tilde{e})$ appearing in (68) and (69) can be replaced by $-\delta \cdot (q - \tilde{q})$ and $-\delta \cdot (e - \tilde{e})$, respectively. In addition, the deviation $e - \tilde{e}$ can be replaced by $(p - \bar{p}) - (q - \tilde{q})$. The modified versions of (68) and (69) that result from these substitutions constitute a linear system in the three variables y, $q - \tilde{q}$, and $p - \bar{p}$, which may be solved to obtain the results

(70) $q - \tilde{q} = \Omega \cdot (p - \bar{p})$

(71) $y = -[\sigma/(1 - \sigma + \xi\sigma)] \cdot (v + \alpha\sigma\delta) \cdot \Omega \cdot (p - \bar{p})$,

---

37. The only difference between the conditional equilibrium and full equilibrium is that in conditional equilibrium we allow for the disequilibrium behavior of net foreign assets. This difference does not affect the applicability of the equilibrium conditions described in previous sections to the conditional equilibrium values of economic variables.

38. To derive these results, note (64) and (65) are satisfied when $q = \tilde{q}$, $e = \tilde{e}$, and $y = 0$.

where

(72)
$$\Omega = \cfrac{1}{1 - \left[\cfrac{V + \sigma L}{\zeta + \eta\delta}\right] + \left[\cfrac{\omega\sigma}{1 - \sigma + \xi\sigma}\right]\left[\cfrac{v + \alpha\sigma\delta}{\zeta + \eta\delta}\right]}.$$

It is apparent that (71) is equivalent to (66) under the stipulation that

(73) $\Lambda = [\sigma/(1 - \sigma + \xi\sigma)] \cdot (v + \alpha\sigma\delta) \cdot \Omega.$

Further, using the fact that $(e - \bar{e}) = (p - \bar{p}) - (q - \bar{q})$, it follows that

(74) $e - \bar{e} = \Phi \cdot (p - \bar{p}), \quad \Phi = (1 - \Omega).$

The results (70)–(74) justify the initial assumption of (66) and the future assumption that deviations of p, q, and e from their respective conditional equilibrium values are expected to be eliminated that the exponential rate δ. The results (72) and (73) give the appropriate value of the coefficient Λ.

These results permit a reasonably simple description of the state of disequilibrium of the economy at any moment and of how this state of disequilibrium is expected to evolve over time as the economy converges toward its equilibrium path. The state of disequilibrium is determined completely by the divergence between the inherited value of $p(t)$ and the conditional equilibrium value of this price, $\bar{p}(t)$. This divergence determines the deviation of the value of output of domestic goods from its equilibrium level, $y(t) = -\Lambda \cdot [p(t) - \bar{p}(t)]$, and also the deviations of the relative price of domestic goods and the exchange rate from their respective conditional equilibrium values, $q(t) - \bar{q}(t) = \Omega \cdot [p(t) - \bar{p}(t)]$ and $e(t) - \bar{e}(t) = \Phi \cdot [p(t) - \bar{p}(t)]$. Over time, it is expected that the price of domestic goods will converge toward its conditional equilibrium value at an exponential rate δ. Correspondingly, the deviation of the value of the value of domestic output from its equilibrium level, y, and the deviations of q and e from their respective conditional equilibrium values are also expected to disappear at the exponential rate δ.[39]

From all of these results, it is apparent that the coefficients Λ, Ω, and Φ are of critical importance in determining the magnitude of the effects disequilibrium created by divergences between p and $\bar{p}$ on other economic variables. Consider first the coefficient Ω which determines the response of $q - \bar{q}$ to $p - \bar{p}$. There is a strong presumption that $\Omega > 0$ and weaker

---

39. This same basic description of the state and expected evolution of disequilibrium applies to other endogenous variables of the economic system. In particular, if we assume that there is no risk premium in the foreign exchange market, then using the interest parity condition (42) we may show that the deviation of the domestic nominal interest rate from its conditional equilibrium value is given by $(i - \bar{i}) = -\delta\Phi \cdot (p - \bar{p})$. As disequilibrium is eliminated, the domestic nominal interest rate is expected to converge toward its conditional equilibrium value at the exponential rate δ.

presumption that $\Omega > 1$. The only thing that could make Ω negative is if $V + \sigma L$ were significantly greater than $\zeta + \eta\delta$. But, going back to (39), we find that $\zeta = L + J$ which is definitely greater than σL. Thus, the only thing that could make $\Omega < 0$ is if V were strongly positive, that is, if an increase in the relative price of domestic goods had a strong effect of increasing the nominal demand for domestic money. There is no reason to suppose that this relative price should have such a strong effect on nominal money demand. The weak presumption that $\Omega > 1$ comes from the notion that transitory changes in income associated with disequilibrium should have relatively weak effects on the demand for money. If this notion is correct, then the parameter ω which indicates the response of money demand to the deviation of the value of output from its equilibrium level should be small. If ω is small, then the third term in the denominator of Ω in (72) should be smaller (in absolute value) than the second term in this denominator, implying that $\Omega > 1$.

The conclusion that $\Omega > 1$ is of critical importance for the sign of the coefficient Φ and hence for the phenomenon of "exchange rate overshooting." If $\Omega > 1$, then $\Phi = 1 - \Omega < 0$, and from (74) it follows that $e - \bar{e}$ is inversely related to $p - \bar{p}$. In this case, we have Dornbusch's phenomenon of "exchange rate overshooting," in the sense that an increase in the conditional equilibrium price of domestic goods relative to the actual price of such goods (induced by an unexpected increase in the money supply) causes the actual exchange rate to increase by even more than the conditional equilibrium exchange rate. In the present model, however, overshooting of the exchange rate in response to monetary disturbances is not assured. If money demand responds strongly to deviations of the value of output from its equilibrium level (ω is large), or if increases in the relative price of domestic goods have a strong negative effect on money demand (V is large and negative), then Ω may be less than one and $\Phi = 1 - \Omega$ may be positive. In this case, the actual exchange rate will rise by less than the conditional equilibrium exchange rate in response to an unanticipated increase in the money supply that increases $\bar{p}$ relative to p.[40]

The coefficient Λ determines the response of the value of domestic output to divergences between p and $\bar{p}$. From (73) it follows that the strong presumption that Ω is positive translates into a strong presumption that Λ is positive. Since $y = -\Lambda \cdot (p - \bar{p})$, a positive Λ means that y is negatively related to $p - \bar{p}$. As one should expect, a high value of p implies a low demand for domestic goods, and the producers of these goods (who temporarily hold their price fixed) respond to this low demand by reducing the value of output of such goods below its equilibrium level.

---

40. In Dornbusch's (1976) original analysis of exchange rate overshooting, it is recognized that a strong response of income to an increase in the money supply may counteract the normal overshooting effect of a monetary disturbance.

1.7.3 Disequilibrium Dynamics

The preceding analysis indicates how current state of disequilibrium in the economy, at time t, is determined by the divergence between $p(t)$ and its conditional equilibrium value $\bar{p}(t)$, and how this disequilibrium is expected to disappear, at the exponential rate δ, as the economy converges toward its conditional equilibrium path. To obtain the complete picture of the dynamic behavior of the economy it is also necessary to describe how the conditional equilibrium price of domestic goods and the conditional equilibrium values of other endogenous variables are expected to change over time, how these expectations are altered by the receipt of new information, and how new disequilibrium is generated within the economic system.

To obtain the correct expressions for the expected conditional equilibrium paths of the endogenous variables of the economic system, it is only necessary to modify slightly the results which describe the expected equilibrium paths of these variables in the combined real and monetary model of section 1.6. Specifically, the solutions for the expected value of an endogenous variable as a weighted sum of expected future values of the exogenous forcing variables z, $\hat{A}$, and $w = (1/\zeta) \cdot (m - k)$ give the correct expressions for the expected conditional equilibrium value of that variable provided that

$$(75) \qquad z(t + j) \text{ is replaced by } z(t + j) - [(1 - \sigma)/\nu\sigma] \cdot (1 - \delta)^{j} \cdot y(t)$$
$$\hat{A}(t + j) \text{ is replaced by } \hat{A}(t + j) + (\xi/\mu) \cdot (1 - \delta)^{j} \cdot y(t)$$
$$w(t + j) \text{ is replaced by } w(t + j) + \omega \cdot (1 - \delta)^{j} \cdot y(t),$$

where $y(t)$ is determined by the divergence between $p(t)$ and $\bar{p}(t)$ in accord with $y(t) = \Lambda \cdot [\bar{p}(t) - p(t)]$.

From (75) it is apparent that if there is no disequilibrium at time t, then all of the forcing variables have the same values as in the equilibrium analysis, and hence the expected conditional equilibrium paths of all endogenous variables correspond exactly to the expected full equilibrium paths of these variables. Further, since the terms involving $y(t)$ in (75) (which are responsible for all differences between the expected full equilibrium and the expected conditional equilibrium values of endogenous variables) all decay with a factor $(1 - \delta)^{j}$, it follows that conditional equilibrium value of any endogenous variable is expected to converge toward its full equilibrium value at the exponential rate δ. For example, from (75) it follows that the difference between the current conditional equilibrium exchange rate and the current full equilibrium exchange rate—denoted by $\bar{\bar{e}}(t)$—can be written as

$$(76) \qquad \bar{e}(t) - \bar{\bar{e}}(t) = \theta \cdot y(t) = \theta\Lambda \cdot [\bar{p}(t) - p(t)],$$

where θ is a coefficient that is made up of weighted sums of the factors multiplying $y(t)$ in (75). Applying the expected forward difference operator to (76) and taking account of the price adjustment rule (55), we determine the expected rate of convergence of the conditional equilibrium exchange rate toward its full equilibrium value,

$$(77) \qquad D^e[\tilde{e}(t) - \overline{\overline{e}}(t)] = -\delta\Lambda \cdot [\tilde{p}(t) - p(t)]$$
$$= -\delta \cdot [\tilde{e}(t) - \overline{\overline{e}}(t)].$$

Similar results can be derived for the expected rate of convergence of the conditional equilibrium values of other variables, such as the real exchange rate, toward their full equilibrium values.

Expected changes in the actual values of endogenous variables can, in general, be decomposed into three parts: (i) the expected change in the full equilibrium value of the variable; as determined by the combined real and monetary model of section 1.6; (ii) the expected convergence of the actual value of a variable toward its conditional equilibrium value, which is equal to $-\delta$ times the existing divergence between the actual and the conditional equilibrium value of the variable; and (iii) the expected convergence of the conditional equilibrium value of the variable toward its full equilibrium value, which is equal to $-\delta$ times the existing divergence between the conditional and full equilibrium values of the variables. In particular, for the nominal exchange rate we have

$$(78) \qquad D^e[e(t)] = D^e[\overline{e}(t)] - \delta \cdot [e(t) - \tilde{e}(t)]$$
$$- \delta \cdot [\tilde{e}(t) - \overline{\overline{e}}(t)]$$
$$= D^e[\overline{\overline{e}}(t)] - \delta \cdot (\theta\Lambda - \Phi) \cdot [\tilde{p}(t) - p(t)],$$

where $D^e[\overline{\overline{e}}(t)]$ is given by the result (51). Similar results apply for the expected changes in the actual values of other endogenous variables.

The state of disequilibrium which influences expected changes in all endogenous variables is itself the consequence of past unexpected changes in the conditional equilibrium price of domestic goods. Specifically, since the price adjustment rule (55) specifies that the expected change in $\tilde{p}$ is incorporated into the actual change in p, it follows that the innovation in disequilibrium between t and $t + 1$ corresponds to the unexpected change in the conditional equilibrium price of domestic goods,

$$(79) \qquad D^u[\tilde{p}(t) - p(t)] = D^u[\tilde{p}(t)].$$

The total change in disequilibrium is the sum of this innovation and the expected change $D^e[\tilde{p}(t) - p(t)] = -\delta \cdot [\tilde{p}(t) - p(t)]$, that is,

$$(80) \qquad D[\tilde{p}(t) - p(t)] = D^u[\tilde{p}(t)] - \delta \cdot [\tilde{p}(t) - p(t)].$$

Taking the backward-looking solution of this difference equation, we find that the existing state of disequilibrium is a weighted average of past unexpected changes in the conditional equilibrium price of domestic goods;

$$(81) \qquad \bar{p}(t) - p(t) = \delta \cdot \sum_{j=0}^{\infty} (1 - \delta)^j \cdot D^u[\bar{p}(t - j - 1)].$$

Unexpected changes in the conditional equilibrium price of domestic goods that are the fundamental source of disequilibrium must themselves be the result of changes in expectations about the exogenous forcing variables, z, $\hat{A}$, and w, that ultimately determine $\bar{p}$. In particular, exploiting (47), it follows that

$$(82) \qquad \bar{p}(t) = E(F(t); t) + (1 - \sigma) \cdot E(\bar{\bar{q}}(t); t) + \Gamma \cdot y(t),$$

where $F(t)$ is the weighted sum of differences between money supply and money demand defined in (45), $\bar{\bar{q}}(t)$ represents the full equilibrium relative price of domestic goods as determined by the present stock of net foreign assets and the present and future values of the forcing variables z and $\hat{A}$, and Γ is the coefficient that indicates effect of $y(t)$ on $\bar{p}(t)$ implied by the modifications of the forcing variables listed in (75). Applying the unexpected difference operator to (83) and making use of (66) and (80), it follows that

$$(83) \qquad D^u[\bar{p}(t)] = [1/(1 + \lambda\Gamma)] \cdot \{D^u(E(F(t); t)) + (1 - \sigma) \cdot D^u[\bar{\bar{q}}(t)]\},$$

where the presumption is that $1 + \lambda\Gamma > 0$.

The price adjustment rule (55) prescribes that $D^u[p(t)]$ has no effect on the actual price of domestic goods in period $t + 1$, but is instead absorbed by the state of disequilibrium at $t + 1$. Because of its effect on the state of disequilibrium, however, $D^u[\bar{p}(t)]$ does influence the magnitudes of the unexpected changes in the values of all other endogenous variables between t and $t + 1$ by affecting both the divergence between the actual value of a variable and its conditional equilibrium value and the divergence between the conditional equilibrium value of the variable and its full equilibrium value. For example, from (74) and (76) it follows that the unexpected change in the nominal exchange rate is given by

$$(84) \qquad D^u[e(t)] = D^u[\bar{\bar{e}}(t)] + (\theta\lambda - \Phi) \cdot D^u[\bar{p}(t)].$$

The first factor affecting $D^u[e(t)]$ is the unexpected change in the full equilibrium exchange rate, $D^u[\bar{\bar{e}}(t)]$, as determined by (53). The second factor is the combined effect of the innovation in disequilibrium, $D^u[\bar{p}(t)]$, on the divergences between $\bar{e}$ and $\bar{\bar{e}}$ and between e and $\bar{e}$.

1.7.4 Disequilibrium Effects of Real and Monetary Disturbances

The principal advantage of disequilibrium model of the present section over the equilibrium model of the previous section is its capacity to deal with the disequilibrium effects of real and monetary disturbances, especially

52   Michael Mussa

their effects on real output and on the real exchange rate. Since unexpected changes in the conditional equilibrium price of domestic goods are the fundamental source of disequilibrium, it follows from (83) that "real disturbances" may conveniently be identified with unexpected changes in the full equilibrium relative price of domestic goods, $D^u[\bar{\bar{q}}(t)]$, and "monetary disturbances" may be identified with unexpected changes in the common element in the full equilibrium values of all nominal prices, $D^u(E(F(t); t))$. These disturbances would be "transitory" if the change in expectations due to new information received between t and $t + 1$ affected only expectations about the exogenous real and monetary factors (the z's, $\hat{A}$'s, and w's) in the near future and left expectations concerning their longer-run values unchanged. These disturbances would be "permanent" if the new information altered expectations concerning the exogenous real and monetary factors by approximately the same amount for all future periods.

With respect to their effects on the disequilibrium component of domestic output (and income), real and monetary disturbances have essentially the same effects in the sense that positive values of $D^u[\bar{\bar{q}}(t)]$ and $D^u(E(F(t); t))$ both induce positive innovations in y; formally,

$$(85) \qquad D^u[y(t)] = \lambda \cdot D^u[\bar{p}(t)] = [\lambda/(1 + \lambda\Gamma)]$$
$$\cdot \{D^u(E(F(t); t))$$
$$+ (1 - \sigma) \cdot D^u[\bar{\bar{q}}(t)]\}.$$

Moreover, for a given size disturbance, either real or monetary, it makes no difference for its effect on y whether the disturbance is transitory or permanent. As indicated by (66) and (81), however, the effect of any particular disturbance on y decays with the passage of time and the actual price of domestic goods gradually adjusts toward its conditional equilibrium value. Thus, a continuing sequence of real and monetary disturbances is necessary to sustain deviations of output from its equilibrium level.

With respect to their effects on the real exchange rate, there are important differences between real and monetary disturbances and between permanent and transitory disturbances. Formally, using the fact that $q - \bar{q} = p - \bar{p} - (e - \bar{e})$ and $\bar{q} - \bar{\bar{q}} = \bar{p} - \bar{\bar{p}} - (\bar{e} - \bar{\bar{e}})$, together with the results (74), (76), and (82), we may reach the conclusion that

$$(86) \qquad q(t) = \bar{\bar{q}}(t) = -\Delta \cdot [\bar{p}(t) - p(t)],$$

with $\Delta = 1 - \Phi + \theta\lambda - \Gamma\lambda$, where the presumption is that $\Delta > 0$.[41] The right-hand side of (86) measures the effect of disequilibrium on the real exchange rate (which is identified with the relative price of domestic goods).

41. Using (73) and (74) it may be shown that $\Delta = 1 + \Omega \cdot \{1 + (\theta - \Gamma) \cdot [\sigma/(1 - \sigma + \xi\sigma)] \cdot (\nu + \alpha\sigma\delta)\}$. As previously discussed, there is a strong presumption that $\Omega > 0$. The term multiplying Ω in the expression for Δ is also likely to be positive, except in the unlikely event that $(\theta - \Gamma)$ is both large and negative. Even if the term multiplying Ω is negative, it is still likely that Δ is positive.

Applying the expected and unexpected change operators to (86) yields the results

(87) $$D^e[q(t)] = D^e[\bar{\bar{q}}(t)] - \delta[q(t) - \bar{\bar{q}}(t)]$$

(88) $$D^u[q(t)] = D^u[\bar{\bar{q}}(t)] - \Delta D^u[\tilde{p}(t)].$$

Thus, the expected change in the real exchange rate reflects both the expected change in the full equilibrium real exchange rate and the expected convergence of the actual real exchange rate toward its full equilibrium value. The unexpected change in the real exchange rate reflects both the full equilibrium effect of the real disturbances measured by $D^u[\bar{\bar{q}}(t)]$ and the disequilibrium effect of the real and monetary disturbances summarized by $D^u[\tilde{p}(t)]$. It is noteworthy that full equilibrium effect of real disturbances on the real exchange rate will be permanent if the disturbances themselves are permanent, but that disequilibrium effect or real and monetary disturbances on the real exchange rate must be transitory, even if the disturbances are permanent, because the effect of any individual disturbance on the state of disequilibrium decays with the passage of time.

Further insight into the effects of real and monetary disturbances on the real exchange rate comes from substituting (83) into (88):

(89) $$D^u[q(t)] = [1 - (1 - \sigma) \cdot T] \cdot D^u[\bar{\bar{q}}(t)] - T \cdot D^u(E(F(t); t)),$$

where $T = \Delta/(1 - \Gamma\lambda)$. The second term on the right-hand side of (89) measures the effect of monetary disturbances. This effect is exclusively a disequilibrium effect which does not arise in the full equilibrium model of the preceding section. If the nominal exchange rate "overshoots" in response to monetary disturbances—in the sense that $D^u(E(F(t); t)$ has a more than one-for-one effect on $D^u[e(t)]$—then the coefficient T must be positive, and the real exchange rate must decline in response to a positive monetary disturbance. The first term on the right-hand side of (89) measures the combined equilibrium and disequilibrium effects of real disturbances on the real exchange rate. It is apparent that if the nominal exchange rate overshoots in response to monetary disturbances (for which the necessary and sufficient condition is $T > 0$), then the real exchange rate must undershoot in response to real disturbances or, in the extreme case where $(1 - \sigma) \cdot T > 1$, the real exchange rate may move in the opposite direction to the change in its full equilibrium value in response to real disturbances.

These results are directly relevant to the explanation of deviations from purchasing power parity, which are identified, one for one, with movements in the real exchange rate. In an economy where the prices of domestic goods are not immediately adjusted to unexpected changes in their equilibrium values, monetary disturbances will induce temporary divergences from purchasing power parity. Temporary real disturbances will also induce temporary deviations from purchasing power parity through both their equilibrium and disequilibrium effects. It is not necessary, however, that all deviations from purchasing power parity be temporary. Permanent real disturbances will require permanent adjustments in the relative price of domestic goods and hence permanent changes in the real exchange rate.

1.8 Summary and Extensions

It is desirable that theoretical models of exchange rate determination be consistent with the empirical regularities that have generally characterized the actual behavior of floating exchange rates. This requires that the exchange rate be treated as an asset price that is affected not only by current economic conditions but also, to an important extent, by expectations of future economic conditions. In such an asset price model, there is a general explanation of how new information that alters expectations concerning future economic conditions induces unexpected changes in exchange rates and of why such unexpected changes may dominate actual exchange rate movements. There is also an explanation of the empirically observed phenomenon that spot and forward exchange rates tend to move together, especially when there are fairly large changes. In such an asset price model of the exchange rate, it is desirable that the behavior of national money supplies and the demands to hold these monies play an important role in influencing the behavior of exchange rates, but, consistent with the observed facts, the model should not insist on too rigid a link between movements in money supplies and movements in exchange rates. It is also desirable that the model of exchange rate determination allow for variations in real exchange rates (and hence deviations from purchasing power parity) and that it permit real economic conditions relevant for determining relative prices to play a role in influencing the behavior of exchange rates. Consistent with the observed facts, however, the model should not insist that nominal or real exchange rates adjust rapidly to eliminate current account imbalances.

The theoretical model of exchange rate determination developed in this paper possesses these desirable properties. This model is a compendium of monetary and real models of exchange rate behavior, with equilibrium and disequilibrium features, that have been integrated into a unified theoretical framework in which the exchange rate is treated as an asset price. The model incorporates a simple, reduced-form condition of money market equilibrium that is consistent with a very general specification of the structural factors influencing money demand, including wealth and income effects, currency substitution effects, and the possibility of a risk premium in the foreign exchange market that affects the demand for money by influencing nominal interest rates. Under the assumption of rational expectations, the condition of money market equilibrium implies an asset price expression for (the logarithm of) the nominal exchange rate as a discounted sum of expected future differences between (the logarithms of) the domestic money supply and the exogenous (to the monetary sector of the economy) component of the demand for domestic money.

The model of exchange rate determination developed in this paper also incorporates a theory of the determination of the real exchange rate by means of a general equilibrium specification of the condition of balance of payments equilibrium. This specification is consistent with the standard two-country, two-commodity model of the real theory of international trade, with the dependent economy model in which the home country produces and consumes its own nontraded good as well as a traded good that is a perfect substitute for goods produced and consumed in the rest of the world, and with the usual "Keynesian" model in which the home country produces an output that is distinct from the output of the rest of the world. An important feature of this model of balance of payments equilibrium is that both the level and the expected rate of change of the real exchange rate affect the desired difference between domestic spending and domestic income and the current account balance. Under the assumption of rational expectations, it follows that (the logarithm of) the real exchange rate that is consistent with balance of payments equilibrium (but not necessarily with a zero current account balance) depends on the long-run equilibrium real exchange rate and on the divergence between the actual level of net foreign assets held by domestic residents and the long-run desired level of such asset holdings. The dependence of the real exchange rate on the level of net foreign assets is consistent with the relationship described in a number of recent models of the dynamic interaction between the current account and the exchange rate. The asset price property of the exchange rate is reflected in formulas expressing the long-run equilibrium real exchange rate and the long-run desired level of net foreign assets as discounted sums of expected future values of the exogenous factors affecting excess demands for domestic and foreign goods (and hence the trade balance) and the desired level of domestic spending.

In the equilibrium version of the model of exchange rate determination developed in this paper, money is strongly neutral and the real sector of the economic system functions independently of the monetary sector. For this reason, real economic conditions affecting the real exchange rate and the demand for real money balances can be taken as exogenous with respect to the monetary sector of the economic system, and the reduced-form condition for money market equilibrium may be treated as the proximate determinant of the nominal exchange rate, as is done in most simple monetary models of exchange rate behavior. An alternative (but analytically equivalent) solution for the equilibrium nominal exchange rate brings the influence of real economic conditions on the exchange rate into sharper focus. Real economic conditions influence the equilibrium nominal exchange rate because they affect the real demand for domestic money and thereby affect the common monetary element that influences the behavior of all domestic nominal prices. Real economic conditions also influence the equilibrium nominal exchange rate by affecting the equilibrium real exchange rate. Specifically, with the general level of domestic prices determined by the requirements of monetary equilibrium, an increase in the equilibrium relative price of domestic goods must be accomplished by an alteration of the nominal exchange rate which allows the domestic price of foreign goods to fall and the domestic price of domestic goods to rise. In the equilibrium model of exchange rate determination, such movements of the nominal exchange rate in response to movements in the equilibrium real exchange rate provide the only explanation for deviations from purchasing power parity.

In the disequilibrium version of the model of exchange rate determination developed in this paper, money is not neutral and monetary disturbances have temporary disequilibrium effects on real output, relative prices, the balance of payments, and real and nominal exchange rates. The source of monetary nonneutrality is the assumption that the domestic money price of domestic goods does not adjust immediately to its equilibrium value, but instead is governed by an adjustment rule that allows for expected changes in the equilibrium price of domestic goods and for gradual elimination of the existing divergence between the actual and equilibrium prices of these goods. The extent of this divergence determines the extent of disequilibrium in the economy, and the divergences of all endogenous variables from their respective equilibrium values are proportional to this measure of the extent of disequilibrium. Expected elimination of disequilibrium through expected convergence of the price of domestic goods toward its equilibrium value contributes an additional term to the expressions from the equilibrium model for expected changes in endogenous variables, including the nominal and real exchange rates. Unexpected changes in the equilibrium price of domestic goods constitute the innovations to disequilibrium in the economy, and the spillover effects of these innovations contribute an additional term to the expressions for unexpected changes in endogenous variables, including the nominal and real exchange rate. In particular, provided that the response of money demand to innovations in disequilibrium is not too strong, it is likely that a monetary disturbance that causes an unexpected increase in the equilibrium values of all domestic money prices will induce a more than proportionate response of the actual nominal exchange rate due to the spillover effect of the innovation to disequilibrium; that is, the nominal exchange rate will "overshoot" in response to monetary disturbances. Correspondingly, the real exchange rate will respond to the disequilibrium effect of a monetary disturbance, even though such a disturbance has no effect on the equilibrium real exchange rate. This effect of a monetary disturbance on the real exchange rate, however, will be temporary because the price of domestic goods will gradually adjust toward its equilibrium value and the disequilibrium created by the monetary disturbance will gradually be eliminated. In contrast, a real disturbance that permanently alters equilibrium relative prices will permanently affect the real exchange rate, and this long-run effect may be greater than the short-run effect of the real disturbance because the disequilibrium spillover effect of such disturbances is likely to work in the opposite direction of their long-run effect.

The results of this paper can be extended in a number of directions. One direction for such extensions is simply to apply the analytical results of the present paper to the examination of specific issues concerning the behavior of exchange rates and their relationships with other economic variables. For instance, we could investigate the effects of economic growth, of changes in desired spending patterns, of changes in government fiscal or commercial policy, and of a host of other economic changes on the behavior of real and nominal exchange rates and on the relationships among exchange rates, prices, interest rates, and the balance of payments, in both an equilibrium and a disequilibrium setting. The general procedure for conducting such investigations is to specify the nature of the initiating economic disturbance in terms of its effects on the paths of the exogenous forcing variables of the model, and then to examine the effects of these changes in the paths of the forcing variables on the paths of the endogenous variables of the model, including real and nominal exchange rates, prices, interest rates, and the balance of payments. Care must be taken in conducting these investigations because, in general, an initiating economic disturbance will affect the paths of all of the exogenous forcing variables. For example, economic growth in domestic goods sector of the home country will affect the demand shift parameter that is important for determining the relative price of domestic goods (the z's). It will also affect the exogenous monetary factor (the w's) by affecting the real demand for domestic money; and as domestic income grows there is also likely to be an effect of the target level of domestic net holdings of foreign assets (represented by an increasing level of $\hat{A}$).

Another direction for possible extensions of the analysis of this paper is by modifying some of the assumptions of the model without altering its basic character. One such modification would be to allow explicitly for a domestic, nontradable asset (other than domestic money) that is not regarded as a perfect substitute for either domestic money or foreign assets.[42] If the demand for this asset were a function only of variables that already appear in the model, its introduction would not require any alteration of the formal results of the present analysis. All that would happen is that the rate of return on this asset would be determined by the requirement that the demand to hold it should equal the supply available to be held. Explicit introduction of such a domestic asset, however, would allow explicit analysis of the effects of economic disturbances on its rate of return and of changes in the

---

42. Models that employ this type of specification of the structure of the asset markets have been investigated by Dornbusch (1975) and Branson (1976).

supply of this asset (resulting perhaps from open market operations) on the exchange rate and other variables. A more ambitious modification of the assumptions of the present model would be to allow for tradable domestic assets that are not regarded as perfect substitutes for foreign assets by either home or foreign residents. This modification would require alteration of some of the formal results of the present paper. It would permit explicit treatment of issues that arise in portfolio balance models of the exchange rate that assume a multiplicity of tradable securities. Yet another modification of the present model that is worthy of consideration is its extension to a two-country world in which events in the home country have a measurable effect events in the foreign country. This modification would also require alteration of some of the formal results of the present paper. It would permit analysis of issues relating to the dynamic interaction between large economies.[43]

A final direction for possible extension of the present paper is to examine the microeconomic foundations of the economic relationships that are employed in the present model. This direction has been taken in several recent papers that have explored the implications for exchange rate theory of different specification of the microeconomic foundations of the demand for money and of the demands for interest-bearing securities.[44] For these efforts to bear fruit, however, they must yield behavior functions whose implications for the behavior of exchange rates and other variables are at least broadly consistent with the observed empirical regularities.

Comment   Jacob A. Frenkel

Recent years have witnessed significant advances in theoretical and empirical research on exchange rate determination. One of the important characteristics of the modern approach is that the exchange rate is being viewed as a financial variable that is determined in general equilibrium within the macroeconomic setting and, like many other financial variables, its current value is strongly influenced by expectations concerning future policies and events. Characteristically, Mussa's paper on the theory of exchange rate determination is comprehensive and perceptive. He starts with a brief outline of empirical regularities which have characterized the regime of flexible rates and presents an outline of the asset market view of exchange rate determination which is consistent with the empirical regularities. He then presents and evaluates various monetary models of exchange rate determination

43. A limited amount of work has been done on genuine multicountry models of exchange rates determination in recent years; see, for instance, Bhandari (1982) and Saidi (1982).
44. See, for example, Krugman (1980), Helpman (1981), Kareken and Wallace (1981), Leviatan (1981), Obstfeld (1981), and Helpman and Razin (1982).

and proceeds to develop the relationship between balance of payments equilibrium and the exchange rate as well as the interaction between real and monetary factors in effecting the equilibrium exchange rate. The paper concludes with an analysis of sticky prices and disequilibrium dynamics.

My remarks will touch on several points in the paper and then will raise some unresolved issues. But in order to appreciate the extent of development in the theory of exchange rates, I should like to note questions that are not central to the paper and which probably would have been key questions in the early 1970s. For example, we do not expect any more flexible exchange rates to eliminate current account imbalances and we do not wonder why changes in exchange rates have not done so. Likewise, we no longer expect a unique relationship between exchange rates (nominal or real) and the current account since it is now obvious (as it should have been since the development of the absorption approach) that the effect of changes in relative prices on the current account depends on the effects of these changes on income as well as on spending, and that without additional assumptions and information on the source of the change in relative prices, on the composition of spending, on the perceived permanence of the change in prices, and the like, there can be no general presumption concerning the overall effect on the excess of income over spending.

The Monetary Models

Mussa discusses two classes of monetary models. The first, which was used in the early developments of the monetary approach to the exchange rate and has been applied to many empirical studies, expresses the exchange rate in terms of the supplies of domestic and foreign nominal balances and the demands for domestic and foreign real balances. Mussa notes correctly that the validity of the monetary approach does not depend on the assumption of purchasing power parity since the model can allow for divergences from parity. However, in empirical research allowances for divergences from parities and for a slow adjustment in the money market need to be introduced with great care. For example, one may not introduce these considerations into the final exchange rate equation by adding a lagged dependent variable. They need to be incorporated directly into the equations that summarize the more fundamental relationships (like the money markets, etc.). This procedure implies that the properties of the error term in the exchange rate equation may not be specified arbitrarily without reference to the properties of the error terms in the underlying relationships.

Mussa believes that the two major difficulties with the simple monetary models are (1) they have not performed well in explaining movements in nominal exchange rates and (2) they do not reveal explicitly the critical role of expectations. While I agree with both of these points, I believe they should be placed in the proper perspective. First, the poor performance in explaining short-term exchange rate movements is not specific to the monetary model of exchange rate determination. Rather, it has been a characteristic of virtually all simple structural models including the various varieties of the monetary models, the portfolio balance models, the current account models, and others. The key reason for the poor performance of the various models is the intrinsic characteristics of exchange rates as asset prices. As Mussa emphasizes, exchange rates are very sensitive to expectations concerning future events and policies. Periods that are dominated by rumors, announcements, and "news" which alter expectations are likely to induce a relatively large degree of exchange rate volatility. Since by definition "news" cannot be predicted on the basis of past information, it follows that by and large the resulting fluctuations of exchange rates are unpredictable. In a way, this asset market perspective suggests that we should not expect to be able to forecast exchange rate changes accurately with the aid of the simple structural models. The role of the simple structural models is to account for the systematic component of the evolution of exchange rates. Second, while there is no doubt that expectations should be central in modeling exchange rate behavior, it is relevant to note that the monetary models (as well as many other models) have incorporated forward-looking variables, like the rates of interest and/or the forward exchange rate, among the determinants of the spot exchange rate. As such, these models do provide for channels through which expectations about the future influence current values. Mussa is justified, however, in noting that the specific link between expectations concerning the future and the current value of the exchange rate should be consistent with the general principles which govern the pricing formulas for durable assets that are traded in organized markets.

Mussa concludes his insightful discussion of the monetary models by pointing out two conceptual difficulties in exchange rate modeling. First, the assumption that in forming expectations about the future money supply individuals use primarily their knowledge of the stochastic process generating the money supply may be inadequate. Rather, Mussa indicates that in forming expectations about the future money supply, it is likely that individuals use diverse sources of information other than the easily measured variables and, specifically, other than the observed money supply series. The second difficulty is the lack of adequate measures of the exogenous factors affecting the demand and the supply, and of expectations concerning the future behavior of these factors. It should be emphasized, however, that these difficulties do not pertain only to the monetary models of exchange rates. Rather, they are sufficiently general to be applicable to practically all available models of exchange rate determination.

The Balance of Payments

Mussa's analysis of the relation between the balance of payments and the exchange rates contains a novel exposition of the fundamental equivalence between the "absorption" and "elasticity" approaches to the analysis of the trade balance. Mussa demonstrates how the current account of the balance of payments may have a "real" interpretation as a net flow of real goods and services and a "financial" interpretation as a net flow of financial assets. But, most important, he shows that even though the model may be rather complex, its reduced-form exchange rate equation looks formally the same as the reduced-form equation of much simpler models. Analytically, the key difference between the various reduced-form equations lies in the determinants of D^e—the variable measuring expectations.

One of the significant implications of Mussa's analysis is that one may not validly criticize or praise a model just on the basis of its formal reduced-form equation. This implication follows from the fact that the various models can be solved so as to yield almost indistinguishable reduced-form equations. It is pertinent to note, however, that even though the exact expression of the reduced-form equation may be based on analytical and expository convenience, the interpretation of empirical reduced-form estimates must reflect the details of the underlying structural model.

Modeling Disequilibrium

Mussa concludes his paper with an analysis of sticky prices and disequilibrium dynamics. Disequilibrium arises whenever the predetermined value of the price of domestic goods differs from its conditional equilibrium value. However, for Mussa "disequilibrium" *is not* a situation in which anything can happen, the basic laws of economics cease to apply, and handwaving replaces economic theory as the tools of analysis. Mussa's concept of disequilibrium is much more attractive. It imposes structure and discipline on the art of modeling. Thus, when there is disequilibrium in the market for domestic goods, it "is necessary to specify how this disequilibrium is accommodated by the agents that participate in the market for domestic goods and also to examine how the disequilibrium in this market affects conditions in other markets." This modeling strategy is commendable in that it forces into the open the key microeconomic reasons which underlie the macroeconomic manifestation of apparent disequilibria. Further, in the context of exchange rate analysis the disequilibrium modeling provides for the mechanism which eliminates gradually divergences from purchasing power parities.

Additional Issues in Exchange Rate Modeling

To the fundamental issues discussed in Mussa's paper, I would like to add three more issues that are critical for empirical research in the area of exchange rate determination and which raise some difficulties that have not yet been resolved. The first issue may be referred to as the "peso problem." This phrase originally characterized the situation with the Mexican peso, which was devalued during the third quarter of 1976. Since this devaluation had been expected for several years, the peso was traded at a forward discount in the market for foreign exchange. Obviously, as long as the devaluation did not occur, the forward exchange rate proved (ex post) to have been a biased forecast of the realized future spot exchange rate. But once the devaluation took place, it exceeded the prediction that was implied by the forward discount on the peso.

Generally, the peso problem may be viewed as a situation in which there are many observations but only few events. In Mexico's case, there were many days (observations) during which the forward discount prevailed and yet only one event—the devaluation itself. These circumstances raise conceptual and practical difficulties for studies which attempt to examine the efficiency of foreign exchange markets and the bias of forecasts of future spot rates based on lagged forward rates. Likewise in such circumstances it is not clear whether a rise in the number of observations in any sample which is being brought about by a larger frequency of measurements should be treated as a corresponding increase in the number of effective degrees of freedom. In a way the peso problem could be cast in terms of a small-samples problem which has much wider application. However, because the foreign exchange market is strongly influenced by expectations of future events and of future policies, and because current expectations of future change in policies (like a devaluation or a specific change in intervention policies) are based on probabilistic evaluations, it seems that the peso problem is especially relevant in the foreign exchange market.

The second issue relates to the role of innovations. The anticipatory role of exchange rates suggests that empirical research of exchange rate determination should relate changes in exchange rates to the *innovations* in the relevant regressors. Because the innovations are intrinsically unobservable, any empirical analysis involves the *joint* examination of the model as well as the measurement of the innovation (i.e., the measurement of the expected values which are used in the construction of the innovations). Since there is no practical way to avoid the joint-hypotheses problem completely, it seems that inference from empirical estimates should be made with great care.

A third difficulty also relates to the anticipatory nature of exchange rates and the prompt response of asset prices to new information. It concerns the implications of different frequencies of data collection for various time series. For example, data on exchange and interest rates are available in a much greater frequency than data on national income or on the current account. These different frequencies of data availability are reflected in different patterns of revisions of expectations and may have a systematic effect on the time series characteristics of the innovations of the various data.

These issues and others—like the treatment and identification of risk premia, the proper definition of money, the specification of the demand for money in an open economy, the relative degree of substitution among various assets, and the role of portfolio balance in affecting exchange rates— remain at this point unresolved problems in exchange rate analysis.

Comment   Rudiger Dornbusch

Mussa's paper offers a definitive, comprehensive view of the asset market model of exchange rate determination. It is a restatement of the developments in exchange rate economics of the 1970s to which Mussa himself has been an important contributor. The task of his paper is to be integrative, not a border raid into the unknown or a broad questioning of received wisdom. As Mussa states the objective of his enquiry, "it assists in explaining why expected changes in exchange rates should generally be small and why actual exchange rate changes should be dominated by the random, unexpected component of exchange rate changes."

Mussa's paper gives us an excellent statement of established principles but unfortunately is not much help in explaining the large persistent real exchange rate movements that are at the center of policy debate. Nor does it offer any advice on exchange rate policy.

Real Interest Rates and the Real Exchange Rate

While the basic model that Mussa develops is familiar there are also new ideas well worth stressing. One of these is the definition of the real interest rate appropriate to an open economy macroeconomic model. Mussa notes that the relevant real interest rate, from consumers' point of view, is the nominal rate adjusted by the rate of inflation of the consumer price index. With $\dot{p}$ and $(\dot{e} + \dot{p}^*)$ the rates of inflation in home currency of domestic and imported goods, the real rate of interest then becomes

$$(1) \qquad r \equiv i - a\dot{p} - (1 - a)(\dot{e} + \dot{p}^*)$$
$$\equiv i - \dot{p} + (1 - a)(\dot{p} - \dot{e} - \dot{p}^*),$$

where a is the consumption share of domestic goods. But the equation can also be written in terms of the rate of producer price inflation, $\dot{p}$, and the rate of change of the terms of trade.

Thus there is a link between real interest rates and the rate of change of the real exchange rate. Mussa rightly notes that terms of trade effects on real interest rates are an important part of the trade balance adjustment process. This point emerges particularly when structural change over time affects both incomes and relative prices. Permanent income or life-cycle consumption patterns would lead us to predict that changes in full employment output would lead to increased *current* consumption, whatever the timing of the income growth. But the timing is important for the structure of relative prices over time and thus for real interest rates and consumption. A transitory increase in output today would tend to deteriorate today's terms of trade and thus increase real interest rates, other things equal. The same output change occurring tomorrow would imply a fall in the real interest rate. In bringing these real interest rate effects into an exchange rate and macro-economic setting, Mussa raises an important issue for further modeling of intertemporal exchange rate models. There is a parallel effort underway in barter models of trade that already offers interesting results.[1]

The Real Exchange Rate Problem

The accompanying figure 1.C.1 shows the real exchange rate for the United States dollar as measured by the value-added deflator in manufacturing. The extraordinary fact, of course, is that the fluctuations of the dollar in real terms have been so large. From 1979 to 1982 there has been a real appreciation in excess of 25% and in 1982 the real dollar was more than 10% above its average for the 1971–81 period. Now the striking fact is that these real exchange rate changes are presumably the by-product of asset market disturbances—tight money and expectations about the course of money and fiscal policy—not changes in full employment equilibrium real exchange rates. The magnitude of rate movements suggests that there may be a real exchange rate "problem" that calls for policy intervention. The trouble is that we would need models that identify the source of the real exchange rate change before we could confidently predict the cure. Asserting that exchange rates are too flexible—along with asset prices, and unlike goods prices and wages—is merely a guess, though probably a correct one.

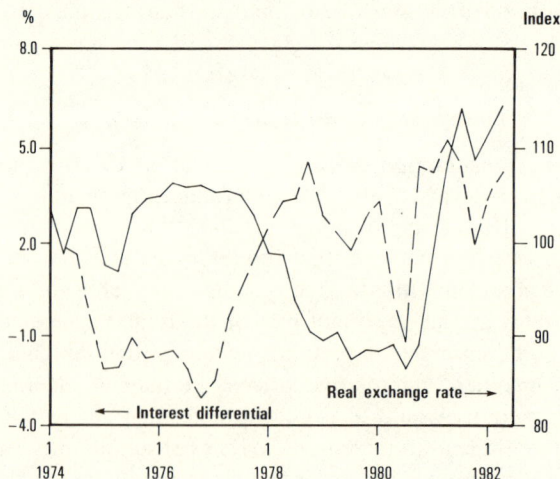

Fig. 1.C.1

1. See Svensson and Razin (1983) and Dornbusch (1983).

The discomfort goes further. As the figure shows, there has been over the last year an interest differential favoring the United States. Theory would predict that a tightening of money in the United States would raise United States interest rates (in the short run), lead to an appreciation of the spot exchange rate, with overshooting, but would then be followed by a rate of depreciation matching the interest differential. But the dollar has not been depreciating. On the contrary, there has been surprising stability in the face of what is broadly considered overvaluation. Mussa's paper is not at all inconsistent with such observations. After all it is spelled out in sufficient generality so that the right expectations can generate any path of nominal and real exchange rates. But the challenge of the evidence is to develop a more specific hypothesis about how markets are working and how overvaluation can be sustained.

Traps and Trips

One direction that I find particularly fruitful is suggested by Blanchard (1979) in his discussion of asset market bubbles. Blanchard notes that risk-averse speculators are willing to hold an asset known to be overvalued provided the expected losses associated with a collapse to fundamentals are offset by sufficient anticipated appreciation. Let e_t and $\bar{e}_t$ be the actual rate and the fundamental rate and x the probability of the fundamental rate prevailing in the next period. Then the arbitrage relation is

$$(2) \qquad e_{t+1} - e_t = \frac{i - i^*}{i - x} - \frac{x}{1 - x}(\bar{e}_{t+1} - \bar{e}_t)$$
$$+ \frac{x}{1 - x}(e_t - \bar{e}_t).$$

Suppose the fundamentals rate is constant and equal to $\bar{e}$. Then (2) shows that the home currency could be *appreciating* despite the fact that it is overvalued. In fact it is precisely because it is overvalued that it must, with a sufficient probability, be expected to appreciate further so that asset holders would be willing to carry the hot potato. This type of equilibrium is a very uncomfortable one because it implies that for some period real asset prices can be carried far away from the equilibrium levels appropriate in the goods markets. Speculation in asset markets prevails over fundamentals until some random event carries prices back to fundamentals. Note that (2) implies the possibility of a speculative trap. With an interest differential in favor of the home currency there is overvaluation that is larger the larger the interest differential and the smaller the risk of a collapse to fundamentals.

Models of exchange rate dynamics in the 1970s have stressed rational expectations and the perfect working of markets, mitigated by differential periods of adjustment of asset and goods prices. A new strand of ideas from finance theory now suggests that claims for asset market efficiency may be overrated. Shiller (1981), for example, argues that asset prices are more volatile than is warranted by the underlying fundamentals variability. In the same vein, it is shown that for particular structures of expectational errors it is in practice impossible to tell whether errors are persistent or white noise. Suppose, for example, a simple monetary model,

$$(3) \qquad m_t - e_t = -a(\bar{e}_{t+1} - e_t),$$

and a money supply process,

$$(4) \qquad m_{t+1} = \rho m_t + u_t,$$

where $\bar{e}_{t+1}$ is the current expectation of the exchange rate next period and u_t is a white noise process. Under rational expectations the solution for the exchange rate is given by

$$(5) \qquad e_t = xm_t; \ x \equiv 1/[1 + a(1 - \rho)].$$

But suppose instead that the public entertained the wrong exchange rate model, specifically,

$$(6) \qquad \bar{e}_{t+1} = xm_{t+1} + ve_t; \ v \geq 0.$$

Thus an irrelevant variable, e_t, is introduced into the forecasts. If (6) is the expectations model, the equilibrium exchange rate is

$$(5') \qquad e_t = \frac{(1 + a)x}{1 + a(1 - v)} m_t.$$

It is readily verified that forecast errors $e_{t+1} \equiv e_{t+1} - \bar{e}_{t+1}$ now are serially correlated:

$$(7) \qquad e_{t+1} = \rho e_t + \frac{(1 + a)x}{1 + a(1 - v)} u_t.$$

But note the capital point. If there is very little autocorrelation in money, so that ρ is close to zero, then autocorrelation in forecast errors will not be easy to detect. In fact with conventional samples the hypothesis of white noise cannot be rejected and thus economic agents will not uncover that they use the wrong model and make systematic errors. But these errors are of consequence. One of the implications, for instance, is excess variance in the actual exchange rate. The example here is simplistic, of course, but it suggests that modeling exchange rate models including plausible, irrelevant variables may well be an avenue toward explaining two facts: one, the large movements of exchange rates seemingly unrelated to fundamentals, and, two, the failure of any particular structural model to account for the experience of the 1970s.

Comment   Pentti J. K. Kouri

With hindsight I have come to feel that there was an unnecessary overshooting in exchange rate theory in the past ten years. This is particularly true of the extreme form of the monetary approach. As a partial equilibrium theory, the "old textbook model" of exchange rate determination, as formulated by Tsiang in particular, gave a basically correct description of the way the foreign exchange market works. It also identified most of the key variables that explain exchange rate fluctuations. Although the exchange rate is a relative price of the monies by definition, it is vacuous to say that "the exchange rate is determined by the relative supplies of and demands for the two monies."

Demand for foreign currency in the foreign exchange market is demand to *spend* foreign money on foreign goods and services, not to hold it over any extended period of time. As an empirical fact individuals and firms do not hold significant transactions balances in foreign currencies. Only commercial banks need to hold small working balances in their capacity as market makers. In advanced countries virtually no domestic transactions are paid for in foreign currency. What we have is a world of *national monies.* As McKinnon has emphasized, the key function of foreign exchange markets is to make each national money international money as well. If foreign exchange markets are efficiently organized, a system of convertible national monies can achieve many of the benefits of a truly global monetary system based on one world money, while still retaining national sovereignty over the creation of money. One may question whether an international rather than a global monetary system is desirable or even viable in the long run, but it certainly is a correct description of the past as well as of the present. For the future, one key factor in determining the viability of any system is bank regulation. If financial institutions were allowed to create a global means of payments, modern information and communications technology would certainly make it possible. We could have a world of global monies cutting across national boundaries.

But we do not have such a system yet. As we trade between different countries we have to go through the foreign exchange market, and therefore all payment flows between countries that belong to different currency areas are registered as supplies and demands in the foreign exchange market. Accordingly, it is both natural and correct to think of equilibrium in the foreign exchange market as a balance between such payment flows.

Now, if there are no capital movements because of government regulation, for example, and if we abstract from small changes in working balances, equilibrium in the foreign exchange market obtains when the trade balance is zero. This gives us the Bicherdicke-Robinson-Machlup supply-demand model. There is nothing wrong with it as far as it goes. However, the simple textbook model fails to explain the foreign exchange market because it does not incorporate speculation and capital movements. Once these features are brought in, the foreign exchange market begins to look like all speculative markets, responding immediately to all new information about the fundamentals. In his classic article, Milton Friedman argued that speculators would stabilize the exchange rate against reversible changes in supply and demand. This argument was simple and persuasive: speculators can make money and therefore survive only if they on average buy foreign exchange when the price is low and sell it when the price is high. Therefore, speculative activity must be stabilizing.

Friedman's paper prompted several authors, among them Baumol and Kemp, to come forward with counterexamples of destabilizing *and* profitable speculation. Baumol provided an example in which speculators sold after the exchange rate peaked and bought after it bottomed out. He was able to show, in the context of a simple dynamic model, that speculators who followed such a trading rule could still make money and, for certain parameter values, increase the amplitude of exchange rate fluctuations or even make the fluctuations explosive. Kemp provided another example in which there were multiple equilibria and demonstrated that speculators could push the market from one equilibrium to another and yet make money. The problem with these counterexamples is that they rely on ad hoc specifications of trading rules and do not allow for forward-looking behavior on the part of speculators. It was only later that Stanley Black (1973) introduced Muth's notion of rational expectations in the foreign exchange market and brought the analysis of speculation on a firmer analytical ground.

If the critics of Friedman were too eager to construct ad hoc counterexamples, the advocates of flexible exchange rates were too ready to conclude that the exchange rate would be quite stable under flexible exchange rates. The following quote from Machlup is typical of the views held by early advocates of flexible exchange rates: "Under a system of greater flexibility such serious disalignments of exchange rates would never, or hardly ever, arise, ... Profits from small changes can be only small, inviting only moderate speculation, which can be easily discouraged, if this is wanted, by relatively minor differentials in interest rates." Against these prior expectations, the volatility of exchange rates in recent years appeared to be a surprise. It has suggested to some that speculation may indeed be destabilizing. There is, however, an important point that was missed in the early discussion: the distinction between ex ante changes and ex post changes. Speculation can stabilize the exchange rate only in the ex ante sense that it eliminates all predictable future changes in the exchange rate in excess of differences in domestic and foreign interest rates. But it does not stabilize the exchange rate ex post when the market is subject to a steady flow of new information or surprises.

A parallel development in the literature of the 1950s and 1960s was the work on the theory of spot and forward markets. In a remarkable paper, S. C. Tsiang (1959) developed a "systematic reformulation of the theory of forward exchange." As Tsiang notes, previous work (e.g., by Keynes) on the forward market had been mostly concerned with covered interest arbitrage and the interest rate parity equation. Although the role of speculation and trade hedging had been recognized, no systematic theory existed which would explain "precisely how the interplay of all these different types of operation jointly determine the forward exchange rate and how the forward exchange market is linked to the spot exchange market." This is exactly what Tsiang's paper does exhaustively, leaving few relevant issues untouched. Stanley Black's important contribution in 1973 provided the finishing touches to a fully worked out model of the foreign exchange market, quite adequate to explain the behavior of exchange rates since then in terms of fundamentals and the intrinsic dynamics of the market. The partial equilibrium model did not imply PPP, nor did it rule out the possibility of exchange rate instability in an unstable environment. The literature of the past ten years largely neglected this earlier work on the foreign exchange market, in part because it followed the wave of the monetary approach in balance of payments theory.

The Chicago monetarist approach, represented by Jacob Frenkel and Michael Mussa, went furthest in throwing away the balance of payments framework. With the assumption of PPP, perfect capital mobility and instantaneous price flexibility import and export schedules or preferences between domestic and foreign assets no longer played a role in explaining exchange rate fluctuations. In effect, the monetarist model is not really a model of exchange rate determination. Rather it was a Cagan-Sargent-Wallace model of price level determination, in which exchange rates were determined simply as ratios of price levels. The monetarist model has failed so clearly as an empirically relevant theory that I need not discuss it further.

My own work on exchange rate theory in 1974 grew out of my work on capital movements with Michael Porter and Victor Argy at the International Monetary Fund. It occurred to me that the Kouri-Porter model would become a model of exchange rate determination if the stock of net foreign assets were exogenous and the exchange rate became endogenous with the domestic interest rate instead. Indeed the model could represent any exchange rate system—for example, Williamson's crawling peg—with appropriate specification of central bank behavior in the foreign exchange and domestic bond markets. Converting the KP model into a model of short-run exchange rate determination was straightforward, but it was not enough. It was necessary to explain the evolution of the exchange rate and asset stocks over time and also the dynamics of expectations formation.

To address these issues I started with an extremely simple model, far too simple if it is not confined to its narrow purpose. I assumed a small open economy producing only traded goods, so that the trade account could be explained simply as a difference between domestic output and absorption. Domestic price level would be determined by world prices and the exchange rate; domestic wage rate could be fixed or flexible. On the asset side, I stripped the KP model to its bare essentials, assuming that there are only two assets: domestic money and foreign money. The allocation of wealth between these two assets would depend on the expected rate of change of the exchange rate. This is the channel through which speculation entered exchange rate determination. I assumed that foreigners do not hold domestic money. With these elements, the short-run model was complete: given the stock of foreign assets and domestic money, the exchange rate would adjust in such a way that existing stocks would be willingly held. If domestic residents wanted to get out of domestic money into foreign money, they could not collectively do so—they would only drive up the price of foreign money. The only way for the stock of foreign assets to change in my model was through current account surpluses or deficits. Depreciation of the domestic currency would reduce domestic absorption and produce a current account surplus: this is the mechanism through which the desired capital transfer is effected over time.

This simple model suggested looking at exchange rate determination and balance of payments adjustment from the viewpoint of Tobin's q theory. The stock of foreign assets is like a stock of houses: it can change only slowly through investment (current account surplus) or disinvestment (deficit). But its valuation—exchange rate—can change immediately. In the same way that an increase in q stimulates capital formation, currency depreciation stimulates accumulation of foreign capital. Domestic currency is undervalued relative to its long-run equilibrium level when the stock of foreign asset is below its long-run equilibrium level and overvalued when the stock of foreign assets is above its equilibrium level.

In Kouri (1976), I developed this idea in a model that was too simple; other chapters of my dissertation introduce variations in the real exchange rate as well as in the real interest rate. The latter model is published in the Bigman-Taya volume (Kouri, 1980). I continue to think that the capital transfer perspective is a fruitful way to look at exchange rate behavior and balance of payments adjustment. It is rich enough to incorporate all relevant factors in a single unified framework. From the point of view of this model, the recent appreciation and continued strength of the dollar can be explained in terms of foreigners' desire to increase their holdings of United States assets, in part because of high real rates of return and in part for other reasons such as shifts in long-term confidence in the United States vis-à-vis Europe. Marketable world wealth can be counted in trillions of dollars; even a small shift in asset preferences can lead to a capital transfer that is very large relative to what can be effected through the current account. In the

1970s, for example, the United States current account deficit never exceeded $15 billion. Even the *flow* of savings in the world, at close to $2,000 billion for the OECD countries in 1982, is enormous relative to the feasible range of current account surpluses or deficits.

The capital transfer problem has been one of the themes in my work with Jorge de Macedo. In our joint paper (1978) we analyze the implications of differences in asset and consumption preferences. We also try to find microeconomic foundations for differences in asset preferences, linking them with differences in consumption preferences. Jorge has continued this work in his own subsequent research.

The second concern that I had in my early work was the modeling of expectations. In Kouri (1976) I considered alternative mechanisms of expectations formations, including perfect foresight or rational expectations. Introduction of perfect foresight in the portfolio balance model brought it closer and closer to the familiar capital models and their well-known problems of instability and indeterminacy. So much has been said and written about rational expectations that I need say no more.

In my early work I assumed price flexibility, not because I believed in it but in order to focus on the role of the exchange rate in balance of payments adjustment. I could just as well have assumed that the central bank pegs the domestic price level, leaving the exchange rate to be determined by supply and demand in the foreign exchange market (cf. Kouri 1983). In that paper I develop a dynamic partial equilibrium model of the foreign exchange market that does not restrict the macroeconomic framework. That paper focuses entirely on the process through which the foreign exchange market adjusts to new stationary equilibrium following disturbances in the trade account or in the capital account, assuming exogenously given interest rates, activity levels, and prices. In more recent work I have gone further in modeling the workings of the foreign exchange market with careful specifications of the behavior of various actors in the market, following the lead of Tsiang, 1959 (see my paper "Intertemporal Balance of Payments Equilibrium and Exchange Rate Determination," unpublished manuscript). I believe there is a great deal more to be done along these lines toward a more detailed understanding of the workings of the foreign exchange market.

This brings me to another point. In a world of instantaneous market clearing. there is very little difference between alternative exchange rate regimes—putting aside well-known monetary nonneutralities and asymmetries that may arise because of capital market imperfections. Behavior of relative prices, for example, would be identical in different exchange rate systems, as we know from the work of Lucas and Stockman. But clearly the system of flexible exchange rates is an entirely different system of collecting and disseminating information and coordinating economic activity. As an example, suppose that we have two economies producing differentiated consumer goods with monopolistically competitive market structures.

With a fixed exchange rate, the structure of relative prices would exhibit inertia, and prices would be preset on the basis of wage costs and conjectural demand schedules. If, in contrast, we had a flexible exchange rate between the two currencies, the exchange rate would be determined in a speculative auction market, while domestic currency prices would continue to be set in Hicksian "fix price" markets. Accordingly, relative prices would exhibit more variability under flexible than under fixed exchange rates, and the properties of the two systems in terms of resource allocation, information utilization, and risk sharing would be quite different.

Dornbusch's 1976 paper illuminates with a standard IS-LM model how differences in the mechanisms of market clearing can explain the overshooting of the exchange rate to monetary disturbances. Clearly, there is a great deal more to be done in this area. The optimum currency area literature is basically concerned with the same question from a normative point of view. I suspect that we have to abandon simple rational expectations concepts as we address these questions and recognize diversity of views, and imperfect information which does not permit knowledge of the model or of the expectations of others. We must analyze how alternative market arrangements utilize information, transmit it between individuals, and in the process help them to form a more coherent view of their environment. In saying this I am obviously indebted to my colleague Roman Frydman. Finally, I would also add that we have more or less exhausted the implications of the portfolio balance model. We need to move on from postulated asset demand and supply functions to a more careful consideration of the structure of financial assets, and of other arrangements that facilitate exchange and mediate between borrowers and lenders. My contribution to the Hawkins-Levich-Wihlborg volume is a first step in this direction. The work of Lucas, Helpman, Razin, Svensson, Stockman, and others should also be mentioned in this context. Toward this end, much more empirical work needs to be done on the nature of financial intermediation between different countries.

In summary, work on exchange rates is not finished. We need much less advocacy of simple-minded notions and much more painstaking, time-consuming work. I expect that such work will ultimately turn us against the current system of flexible exchange rates in favor of a more orderly monetary system.

References

Alexander, Sidney S. 1959. Effects of devaluation: A simplified synthesis of the elasticities and absorption approaches. *American Economic Review* 49 (March): 22–42.
Artus, Jacques R. 1981. Monetary stabilization with and without government credibility. *IMF Staff Papers* 28: 495–533.

Barro, Robert J. 1976. Rational expectations and the role of monetary policy. *Journal of Monetary Economics* 2 (January): 1–32.

———. 1978. A stochastic equilibrium model of an open economy under flexible exchange rates. *Quarterly Journal of Economics* 92 (February): 149–63.

Bhandari, Jagdeep. 1982. *Exchange rate determination and adjustment.* New York: Praeger.

Bilson, John F. O. 1978a. Rational expectations and the exchange rate. In *The economics of exchange rates: Selected studies,* ed. J. A. Frenkel and H. G. Johnson. Reading, Mass.: Addison-Wesley.

———. 1978b. The current experience with floating exchange rates: An appraisal of the monetary approach. *American Economic Review* 68 (May): 392–97.

———. 1979. The deutsche mark/dollar rate: A monetary analysis. In *Policies for employment, prices, and exchange rates,* ed. K. Brunner and A. H. Meltzer. Carnegie Rochester Conference Series, vol. 11. Amsterdam: North-Holland.

Black, Stanley. 1973. International money markets and flexible exchange rates. *Princeton Studies in International Finance,* no. 32. International Finance Section, Princeton University.

Blanchard, Olivier. 1979. Speculative bubbles, crashes, and rational expectations. *Economic Letters,* pp. 387–89.

Branson, William H. 1976. Portfolio equilibrium and monetary policy with foreign and non-traded assets. In *Recent issues in international monetary economics,* ed. E. Classen and P. Salin. Amsterdam: North-Holland.

Branson, William H.; Haltunen, Hannu; and Masson, Paul. 1977. Exchange rates in the short run: The dollar-deutschemark rate. *European Economic Review* 10: 303–24.

Buiter, Willem H., and Miller, Marcus. 1981. Monetary policy and international competitiveness: The problem of adjustment. *Oxford Economic Papers* 33 (suppl.; July): 143–75.

———. 1982. Real exchange rate overshooting and the output cost of bringing down inflation. In *Exchange rates and international macroeconomics,* ed. J. A. Frenkel. Chicago: University of Chicago Press.

Calvo, Guillermo, and Rodriguez, Carlos A. 1977. A model of exchange rate determination under currency substitution and rational expectations. *Journal of Political Economy* 85 (June): 617–25.

De Macedo, Jorge Barga. 1982. Portfolio diversification across currencies. In *The international monetary system under flexible exchange rates.* ed. R. N. Cooper, P. B. Kenen, J. de Macedo, and J. Von Ypersele. Cambridge, Mass.: Ballinger.

Dooley, Michael P., and Isard, Peter. 1978. A portfolio balance rational expectations model of the dollar-mark rate. Unpublished manuscript,

Board of Governors of the Federal Reserve System, Washington, D.C.

Dornbusch, Rudiger. 1975. A portfolio balance model of the open economy. *Journal of Monetary Economics* 1 (January): 3–20.

———. 1976. Expectations and exchange rate dynamics. *Journal of Political Economy* 84 (December): 1161–76.

———. 1978. Monetary policy under exchange rate flexibility. In *Managed exchange-rate flexibility: The recent experience*. Federal Reserve Bank of Boston Conference Series, no. 20. Boston: Federal Reserve Bank.

———. 1980a. Exchange rate economics: Where do we stand? *Brookings Papers on Economic Activity,* no. 1, pp. 143–85.

———. 1980b. *Open economy macroeconomics.* New York: Basic.

———. Equilibrium and disequilibrium exchange rates. *Zeitschrift für Wirtschaft- und Sozialwissenschaften* 102: 573–99.

Dornbusch, Rudiger, and Fischer, Stanley. 1978. Exchange rates and the current account. *American Economic Review* 70 (December): 960–71.

Driskell, Robert A. 1981. Exchange rate dynamics: An empirical investigation. *Journal of Political Economy* 89 (April): 357–71.

Ethier, Wilfred. 1979. Expectations and the asset approach to the exchange rate. *Journal of Monetary Economics* 5 (April): 259–82.

Fama, Eugene F., and Farber, Andre. 1979. Money, bonds and foreign exchange. *American Economic Review* 69 (September): 639–49.

Fischer, Stanley. 1977. Long-term contracts, rational expectations, and the optimal money supply rule. *Journal of Political Economy* 85 (February): 191–206.

Flood, Robert P. 1979. Capital mobility and the choice of exchange rate system. *International Economic Review* 20 (June): 405–17.

Frankel, Jeffrey A. 1979. On the mark: A theory of floating exchange rates based on real interest rate differentials. *American Economic Review* 69 (June): 610–22.

———. In this volume. On the mark, pound, franc, yen and Canadian dollar.

Frenkel, Jacob A. 1976. A monetary approach to the exchange rate: Doctrinal aspects and empirical evidence. *Scandinavian Journal of Economics* 78 (May): 200–24. Reprinted in *The economics of exchange rates: Selected studies,* ed. J. A. Frenkel and H. G. Jackson. Reading, Mass.: Addison-Wesley, 1978.

———. 1980. Exchange rates, prices and money: Lessons from the 1920's. *American Econmic Review* 70 (May): 235–42.

———. 1981a. The collapse of purchasing power parities during the 1970's. *European Economic Review* 7 (May): 145–65.

———. 1981b. Flexible exchange rates and the role of "news": Lessons from the 1970s. *Journal of Political Economy* 89 (August): 665–705.

Frenkel, Jacob A., and Clements, Kenneth. 1982. Exchange rates in the

1970's: A monetary approach. In *Development in an inflationary world,* ed. M. J. Flanders and Assaf Razin. New York: Academic Press.

Frenkel, Jacob A., and Mussa, Michael L. 1980. The efficiency of foreign exchange markets and measures of turbulence. *American Economic Review* 70 (May): 374–81.

Hansen, Lars P., and Hodrick, Robert J. 1980. Forward exchange rates as optimal predictors of future spot rates: An econometric analysis. *Journal of Political Economy* 88 (August): 829–53.

————. 1983. Risk averse speculation in the forward foreign exchange market: An econometric analysis of linear models. In *Exchange rates and international macroeconomics,* ed. J. A. Frenkel. Chicago: University of Chicago Press.

Helpman, Elhanan. 1981. An exploration in the theory of exchange rate regimes. *Journal of Political Economy* 89 (October): 865–90.

Helpman, Elhanan, and Razin, Assaf. 1982. Dyanamics of a floating exchange rate regime. *Journal of Political Economy* 90 (August): 728–54.

Hodrick, Robert J. 1978. An empirical analysis of the monetary approach to the determination of the exchange rate. In *The economics of exchange rates: Selected studies,* ed. J. A. Frenkel and H. G. Johnson. Reading, Mass.: Addison-Wesley.

Isard, Peter. 1980. Expected and unexpected changes in exchange rates: The role of relative price levels, balance of payments factors, interest rates, and risk. International Finance Discussion Paper no. 156, Board of Governors of the Federal Reserve System, April.

Johnson, Harry G. 1958. Towards a general theory of the balance of payment. In *International trade and economic growth,* ed. H. G. Johnson. London: Allen & Unwin.

Kareken, John, and Wallace, Neil. 1981. On the indeterminacy of equilibrium exchange rates. *Quarterly Journal of Economics* 96 (May): 207–27.

Kouri, Pentti J. K. 1976a. The exchange rate and the balance of payments in the short run and in the long run: A monetary approach. *Scandinavian Journal of Economics* 78 (May): 280–304.

————. 1976b. Determinants of the forward premium. Discussion Paper, Department of Economics, Stanford University.

————. 1980. Monetary policy, the balance of payments, and the exchange rate. In *The Functioning of floating exchange rates: Theory, evidence, and policy,* ed. D. Bigman and T. Taya. Cambridge, Mass.: Ballinger.

————. 1981. The effects of risk on interest rates: A synthesis of the macroeconomic and financial views. In *The Internationalization of financial markets,* ed. Robert G. Hawkins, Richard M. Levich, and Clas G. Wihlborg. Greenwich, Conn.: JAI Press.

————. 1983. Balance of payments and the foreign exchange market: A dynamic partial equilibrium model. In *International transmission under exchange rates,* ed. J. Bhandari and B. H. Putnam. Cambridge, Mass.: MIT Press.

———. Intertemporal balance of payments equilibrium and exchange rate determination. Manuscript.

Kouri, P., and de Macedo, Jorge. 1978. Exchange rates and the international adjustment process. *Brookings Papers on Economic Activity* 1: 11–50.

Kravis, Irving B., and Lipsey, Richard. 1978. Price behaviour in the light of balance of payments theories. *Journal of International Economics* 8 (May): 193–247.

Krugman, Paul. 1980. Consumption preferences, asset demands, and distribution effects in international financial markets. Unpublished manuscript, December 1980.

Leviatan, Nissah. 1981. Monetary expansion and real exchange rate dynamics. *Journal of Political Economy* 89 (December): 1218–27.

Lucas, Robert E. 1972. Expectations and the neutrality of money. *Journal of Economic Theory* 4 (April): 103–24.

———. 1973. Some international evidence on output inflation trade-offs. *American Economic Review* 63 (June): 326–34.

———. 1975. An equilibrium model of the business cycle. *Journal of Political Economy* 83 (December): 1113–44.

Meese, Richard, and Rogoff, Kenneth. 1983. The out of sample empirical failure of empirical exchange rate models: Sampling error or misspecification? In *Exchange rates and international macroeconomics,* ed. J. A. Frenkel. Chicago: University of Chicago Press.

Meese, Richard, and Singleton, Kenneth. 1980. Rational expectations and the volatility of floating exchange rates. Working Paper, Board of Governors of the Federal Reserve System, Washington, D.C.

Mundell, Robert A. 1960. The pure theory of international trade. *American Economic Review* 50 (March): 67–110.

Mussa, Michael L. 1976. The exchange rate, the balance of payments and monetary and fiscal policy under a regime of controlled floating. *Scandinavian Journal of Economics* 78 (May): 229–48. Reprinted in *The economies of exchange rates: Selected studies,* ed. J. A. Frenkel and H. G. Johnson. Reading, Mass.: Addison-Wesley.

———. 1977. A dynamic theory of foreign exchange. In *Studies in modern economic analysis: Proceedings of the Association of University Teachers of Economics,* ed. M. Artis and A. R. Nobay. Oxford: Basil Blackwell.

———. 1979. Empirical regularities in the behavior of exchange rates and theories of the foreign exchange market, In *Policies for employment, prices and exchanges rates,* ed. K. Brunner and A. H. Meltzer. Carnegie-Rochester Conference Series, vol. 11.

———. 1981a. The role of the current account in exchange rate dynamics. Unpublished manuscript, University of Chicago.

————. 1981b. Sticky prices and disequilibrium adjustment in a rational model of the inflationary process. *American Economic Review* 71 (December): 1020–27.

————. 1982a. A model of exchange rate dynamics. *Journal of Political Economy* 90 (February): 74–104.

————. 1982b. Sticky individual prices and the dynamics of the general price level. In *The cost and consequences of inflation,* ed. K. Brunner and A. H. Meltzer. Carnegie-Rochester Conference Series, vol. 15.

————. 1982c. Exchange rate and price level dynamics in a simple monetary model. In *Exchange rate determination and adjustment,* ed. J. Bhardari. New York: Praeger.

Muth, John F. 1960. Optimal properties of exponentially weighted forecasts. *Journal of the American Statistical Association* 55 (June): 299–306.

Niehans, Jurg. 1977. Exchange rate dynamics with stock/flow interaction. *Journal of Political Economy* 85 (December): 1245–57.

Obstfeld, Maurice. 1981. Macroeconomic policy, exchange-rate dynamics, and optimal asset accumulation. *Journal of Political Economy* 89 (December): 1142–61.

Phelps, Edmund S., and Taylor, John. 1977. Stabilizing powers of monetary policy under rational expectations. *Journal of Political Economy* 85 (February): 163–90.

Rodriguez, Carlos A. 1980. The role of trade flows in exchange rate determination: A rational expectations approach. *Journal of Political Economy* 88 (December): 1148–58.

Rogoff, Kenneth. 1979. Essays on expectations and exchange rate volatility. Ph.D. dissertation, Massachusetts Institute of Technology.

Saidi, Nasser H. 1980. Fluctuating exchange rates and the international transmission of economic disturbances. *Journal of Money, Credit and Banking* 12 (November): 575–91.

Saidi, Nasser H. 1983. *Essays on rational expectations and flexible exchange rates.* New York: Garland.

Sargent, Thomas J., and Wallace, Neil H. 1975. Rational expectations, the optimal monetary instrument, and the optimal money supply rule. *Journal of Political Economy* 85 (April): 241–54.

Shiller, R. 1981. The use of volatility measures in assessing market efficiency. *Journal of Finance* 36: 291–304.

Stein, Jerome. 1965. International short-term capital movements. *American Economy Review* 55 (March): 40–66.

Stein, Jerome. 1980. The dynamics of spot and forward prices in an efficient foreign exchange market with rational expectations. *American Economic Review* 70 (September): 565–83.

Stein, Jerome, and Tower, Edward. 1967. The short run stability of the foreign exchange market *Review of Economics and Statistics* 49 (May): 173–85.

Stockman, Alan. C. 1978. Risk, information, and forward exchange rates, In *The economics of exchange rates: Selected studies,* ed. J. A. Frenkel and H. G. Johnson. Reading, Mass.: Addison-Wesley.

————. 1980. A theory of exchange rate determination. *Journal of Political Economy* 88 (August): 673–98.

Svensson, L., and Razin A. 1983. The terms of trade, spending, and the current account. *Journal of Political Economy* 91: 97–125.

Taylor, John B. 1980. Aggregate dynamics and staggered contracts. *Journal of Political Economy* 88 (February): 1–23.

Tsiang, S. C. 1959. The theory of exchange rate and the effects of government intervention on the forward exchange market. *IMF Staff Papers* 7 (April): 75–109.

Wilson, Charles A. 1979. Anticipated shocks and exchange rate dynamics, *Journal of Political Economy* 87 (June): 639–47.

2 Exchange Rate Policy after a Decade of "Floating"

William H. Branson

2.1 Introduction and Summary

During the 1970s an extensive theoretical literature developed analyzing market determination of freely floating exchange rates. At the same time, there has been extensive and continuous intervention in the market by central banks. Exchange rates have not been floating freely; they have been managed, or manipulated, by central banks. However, most of the description of exchange rate policy, as actually practiced, has been informal, or "literary," not integrated with the formal theoretical literature. Examples are the surveys in Branson (1980) and Mussa (1981).

Rather than reproduce Mussa's excellent review (1981), in this paper I integrate exchange rate policy into a model of exchange rate behavior and examine the data econometrically to infer hypotheses about policy behavior in the 1970s. I focus on four major currencies, the United States dollar, the deutschemark, sterling, and the Japanese yen, and analyze movements in their effective (weighted) exchange rates as calculated by the International Monetary Fund for their relative cost and price data.

In section 2.2 a model of market determination of a floating exchange rate is laid out. It is a rational expectations version of the model in Branson (1977), and it draws on the model of Kouri (1978). The model shows how unanticipated movements in money, the current account, and relative price levels will cause first a jump in the exchange rate and then a movement along a saddle path to the new long-run equilibrium. Here the role of news in moving the exchange rate, as recently emphasized by Dornbusch (1980) and Frenkel (1981), is clear. The model emphasizes imperfect substitutability between domestic and foreign bonds, in order to prepare for the analysis of intervention policy in section 2.3.

Exchange rate policy is introduced in section 2.3. We analyze the options available to the central bank that wants to reduce the jump in the exchange rate following a real or monetary disturbance—news about the current account, relative prices, or money. This is the policy characterized as "leaning against the wind" in Branson (1976). The distinction is made between monetary policy and sterilized intervention. We also study a regime in which the domestic interest rate is used as the policy variable.

In sections 2.4 and 2.5 we turn to the data. These are described systematically in section 2.4, where we investigate the time series properties of the exchange rate, money, relative prices, and the current account, the short-term interest rate, and reserves for each of the four countries. It is difficult to summarize these data, but the time series behavior of exchange rates, money, relative prices, and current account balances are roughly consistent with the model of section 2.2.

In section 2.5 we estimate systems of vector autoregressions (VARs) for each of the countries and study the correlations among their residuals. These represent the innovations, or "news," in the time series. A clear pattern emerges in these correlations, in which policy in the United States and to a lesser extent Japan drives exchange rates, and policy in Germany and the United Kingdom reacts. It appears that United States monetary policy is essentially determined by domestic considerations, with the exchange rate moving as a consequence. In Japan, interest rates are varied in response to movement in the current account and relative price levels, and the effects on the exchange rate are partially neutralized by sterilized intervention. Germany and the United Kingdom react to movements in their exchange rates by moving interest rates and sterilized intervention.

2.2 An Asset Market Model with Rational Expectations

2.2.1 Introduction

The purpose of this section is to lay out a simple asset market model of exchange rate determination within which monetary policy reaction to movements in the exchange rate can be analyzed. The literature of the 1970s has identified three principal macroeconomic variables that influence movements in exchange rates. These are money supplies, relative price levels, and current account balances. Here I develop a representative model that explicitly includes all three elements. The model is an extension of the asset market model sketched in Branson (1975) and developed in full in Branson (1977). It is a close relative of Kouri (1978). In the early versions of this model the focus was on the roles of relative prices and asset markets, and static expectations were assumed. Here the model is extended to study the effects of underlying "real" disturbances influencing the current account and to include explicitly policy intervention in a rational expectations framework.

2.2.2 Asset Market Specification

To make the analysis manageable, let us consider one country in a many-country world. We can aggregate the assets available in this country into a domestic money stock M, which is a nonearning asset; holdings of domestically issued assets B, which are denominated in home currency; and net holdings of foreign-issued assets F, which are dominated in foreign exchange.[1] Bonds, B^p, is government debt held by the private sector, and B^c is government debt held by the central bank. Total government debt $B = B^p + B^c$. Foreign assets, F^p, is the net claims on foreigners held by the domestic private sector, and R is central bank foreign reserves. Total national net claims on foreigners $F = F^p + R$. The money stock M is equal to $R + B^c$, with a 100% reserve system. I assume the initial exchange rate is indexed to unity, and that the central bank does not permit capital gains or losses on R to influence M. Similarly, interest income on the central bank's holding of R is assumed to be turned over to the treasury so that it does not affect M. The current account in the balance of payments gives the rate of accumulation of F over time. The rate of accumulation of B is the government deficit. M is controlled by central bank purchases (or sales) of B or F from (or to) the domestic private sector.

The rate of return on F is given by $\bar{r}$, fixed in the world capital market, plus the expected rate of increase in the exchange rate, $\hat{e}$. The rate of return on B is the domestic interest rate r, to be determined in domestic financial markets. Total private sector wealth, at any point in time, is given by $W = M + B^p + eF^p$, so here the exchange rate e, in home currency per unit of foreign exchange (e.g., \$0.50 per DM), translates the foreign exchange value of F into home currency.

The total supplies of B and F to the national economy are given at each point in time. Each can be accumulated only over time through foreign or domestic investment.[2] Given the existing stocks of B and F at any point in time, the central bank can make discrete changes in M by swapping either

1. Since the analysis here applies to any single country in the international financial system, I use the terms "home" and "foreign" to denote the country being discussed and the rest of the system, respectively. At the level of generality of this discussion no damage would be done if the reader substituted United States for "home country," "dollar" for "home currency," and "Fed" for "central bank."

2. Since F is home claims on foreigners less home liabilities to foreigners, an asset swap which exchanges a claim and a liability with a foreign asset holder is a transaction within F, changing claims and liabilities by the same amount. This transaction would leave F and B unchanged. The reason for using this particular aggregation will become clear when we study dynamic adjustment below. Basically, we want to define net foreign assets consistently with the balance of payments and national income and product accounts, which record the capital account balance as the change in United States private holdings of net foreign assets. The assumptions outlined above make M and B nontraded assets. This implies that the total stocks of M, B, and F in domestic portfolios are given at any point in time.

B or F with the domestic private sector; these are open-market operations in government debt or foreign assets.

The demand for each asset by the private sector depends on wealth, $W = M + B^p + eF^p$, and both rates of return, r and $\bar{r} + \hat{e}$. As wealth rises, demands for all three assets increase. The demands for B and F depend positively on their own rates of return and negatively on those of the other assets. The demand for money depends negatively on both r and $\bar{r} + \hat{e}$; as either rises, asset holders attempt to shift from money into the asset whose return has increased.

These asset market equilibrium conditions are summarized in equations (1)–(6).

(1) $$M \equiv R + B^c = m(r, \bar{r} + \hat{e}) \cdot W.$$

(2) $$B^p = b(r, \bar{r} + \hat{e}) \cdot W.$$

(3) $$eF^p = f(r, \bar{r} + \hat{e}) \cdot W.$$

(4) $$W = M + B^p + eF^p.$$

(5) $$B^c + B^p = \bar{B}.$$

(6) $$F^p + R = F.$$

Equation (4) is the balance sheet constraint, which ensures that $m + b + f = 1$. The three demand functions give the desired distribution of the domestic wealth portfolio W into the three assets. Specifying the asset demand functions as homogeneous in wealth eliminates the price level from the asset market equilibrium conditions. Given the balance sheet constraint (4), and gross substitutability of the three assets, we have the constraints on partial derivatives of the distribution functions:

$$m_r + f_r = -b_r < 0 \quad m_{\bar{r}} + b_{\bar{r}} = -f_{\bar{r}} < 0.$$

Here a subscript denotes a partial derivative. The three market equilibrium conditions (1)–(3) contain two independent equations given the balance sheet constraint (4). In equation (5) the bar over B indicates that the total supply of government debt is fixed.

2.2.3 Asset Accumulation and the Current Account

Equations (1)–(6) provide the specification of asset markets in the model. The other main building block of the model is the current account equation. The balance of payments accounts provide the indentity.

$$\dot{F} \equiv \dot{F}^p + \dot{R} \equiv X + \bar{r}(F^p + R) \equiv X + \bar{r}F$$

where X is net exports of goods and noncapital services in terms of foreign exchange. Net exports depend on the real exchange rate e/P, private sector wealth W (given by equation [4] above), and an exogenous shift factor z

which represents real events such as changes in tastes in technology, oil discoveries, and so on, which increase net exports for given values of e/P and W. Thus we can write

$$X = X(e/P, W, z); X_e > 0, X_W < 0, X_z > 0.$$

The sign of X_e assumes the Marshall-Lerner condition holds; X_W reflects wealth effects on import demand.

Substitution of the function for net exports into the balance of payments identity gives us the equation for accumulation of national net foreign assets:

$$(7) \qquad \dot{F} = X(e/P, W, z) + \bar{r}F.$$

It is important to note that open-market swaps between the central bank and the domestic private sector have no direct effect on either W or F in (7). And the effect of accumulation of national net foreign assets through a current account surplus ($\dot{F} > 0$) on both W and F is the same regardless of the distribution of $\dot{F}$ between $\dot{F}^p$ and $\dot{R}$. Since an increase in R, ceteris paribus, increases the money stock, which is part of W, any increase in F will raise W by dF independently of the split between $\dot{F}^p$ and $\dot{R}$. Thus the central bank's intervention policy will have no effect on how a current account balance moves F and W in (7).

The effect of an increase in F on $\dot{F}$ in (7) is unclear; $\partial \dot{F}/\partial F = X_W + \bar{r}$, with $X_W < 0$ and $\bar{r} > 0$. Below we will conveniently assume that $\partial \dot{F}/\partial F = 0$; it will quickly become apparent why this is convenient. In Branson (1981), the case where $\partial \dot{F}/\partial F < 0$ is analyzed.

Equations (1)–(7) plus the assumption of rational expectations (or, more precisely, perfect foresight in this nonstochastic model) give us a complete dynamic model in $\dot{F}$ and $\hat{e}$. Price dynamics are suppressed, but we will discuss below exogenous price movements as delayed response to monetary shocks.

2.2.4 Solution of the Model

Solution of the model proceeds as follows. First, the rational expectations assumption is that $\hat{e}$ is the rate of change of e. Then two equations of (1)–(3), with wealth substituted from (4), can be used to solve for r and $\hat{e}$ as functions of M, W, eF^p. The $\hat{e}$ and $\dot{F}$ equations then are two dynamic equations in e and F that can be solved for the movement in these two variables.

Divide equations (1) and (3) by W and differentiate totally, holding $\bar{r}$ constant:

$$(8) \qquad d\left(\frac{M}{W}\right) = m_r dr + m_{\hat{e}} d\hat{e};$$

$$d\left(\frac{eF^p}{W}\right) = f_r dr + f_{\hat{e}} d\hat{e}.$$

These can be solved in matrix form as

(9)
$$\begin{pmatrix} dr \\ d\hat{e} \end{pmatrix} = \frac{1}{(m_r f_{\hat{e}} - f_r m_{\hat{e}})} \begin{bmatrix} f_{\hat{e}} & -m_{\hat{e}} \\ -f_r & m_r \end{bmatrix} \begin{bmatrix} d\left(\dfrac{dF^p}{W}\right) \\ d\left(\dfrac{M}{W}\right) \end{bmatrix}.$$

The solution for $d\hat{e}$ is then

(10)
$$d\hat{e} = \frac{1}{m_r f_{\hat{e}} - f_r m\hat{e}} \left[-f_r d\left(\frac{M}{W}\right) + m_r d\left(\frac{eF^p}{W}\right) \right].$$

The coefficients of eF^p/W and M/W are the partial derivatives of the $\hat{e}$ adjustment function,

(11)
$$\hat{e} = \phi\left(\frac{eF^p}{W}, \frac{M}{W}\right); \ \phi_1 > 0; \ \phi_2 < 0.$$

This is the dynamic equation to be solved along with (7) for $\dot{F}$ to obtain equilibrium e and F^p.

In the e, F^p space of figure 2.1, the $\hat{e} = 0$ locus is a rectangular hyperbola. This can be seen by observing that in ϕ, eF^p enters multiplicatively (in W as well as the numerator eF^p), so changes in e and F^p that hold the product eF^p constant will hold $\hat{e}$ constant. Combinations of e and F^p off the locus move e away from it, as the arrows show. For example, since $\phi_1 > 0$ an increase in e or F^p from a point on the locus makes $\hat{e} > 0$.

An increase in M/W, holding eF^p/W constant, would shift the $\hat{e} = 0$ locus in figure 2.1 upward. This would be the result of an expansionary open market operation in the government debt market with $dB^c = dM > 0$, and no change in R or F^p. An increase in eF^p/W, holding M/W constant, will shift $\hat{e} = 0$ downward; this could result from an open-market swap between

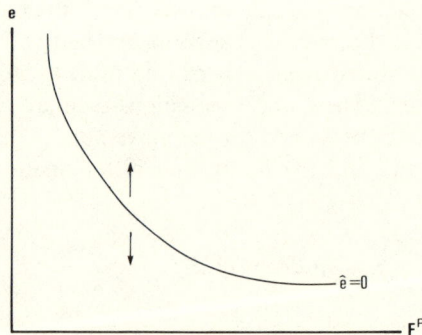

Fig. 2.1   Locus where $\hat{e} = 0$

F and B. An expansionary open-market operation in the foreign asset market, with the central bank altering reserves by exchanging M for F with the private sector, would shift $\hat{e} = 0$ up both by increasing M/W and reducing eF^p/W. This will provide the difference between intervention in the bond or foreign asset markets in the model.

For given values of z and P in the $\dot{F}$ equation (7), the $\dot{F} = 0$ locus in e, F^p space is a horizontal line at the e value where $X = -\bar{r}F$. This is shown in figure 2.2. If e is above this value, the current account is in surplus and $\dot{F} > 0$. In section 2.3 we will introduce a "leaning against the wind" exchange rate policy in which the authorities attempt to reduce the extent of jumps in the exchange rate but not to reverse them. Thus we rule out here the possibility that the monetary authority overintervenes and assume that the sign of $\dot{F}^p$ is the same as the sign of $\dot{F}$; this is the same as assuming $|\dot{R}| < |\dot{F}|$. This essentially assumes that the authorities permit the market to guide the system toward its long-run equilibrium, but perhaps slow the movement. The assumption gives the arrows showing movement in figure 2.2; above $\dot{F} = 0$, $\dot{F}^p > 0$, below it is negative.

An increase in z in (7) will shift the $\dot{F} = 0$ locus down. Given the assumption that $X_W + \bar{r} = 0$, the extent of the shift is simply given by the effect of a change in e on X:

$$\left.\frac{de}{dz}\right|_{\dot{F}=0} = -\frac{1}{X_e}.$$

If z rises, increasing X and giving a current account surplus, e must fall (currency appreciate) enough to restore the original value of X. An increase in P will shift $\dot{F} = 0$ upward, with

$$\left.\frac{de}{dP}\right|_{\dot{F}=0} = 1.$$

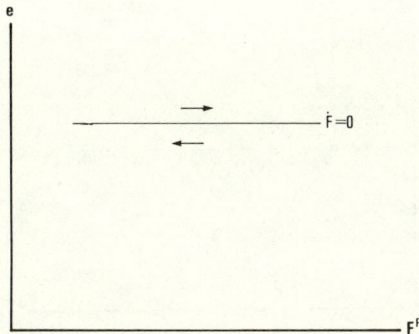

Fig. 2.2   Locus where $\dot{F} = 0$

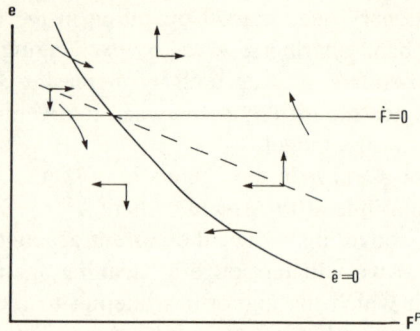

Fig. 2.3   Equilibrium path for e, F^p

Equilibrium of the system is shown in figure 2.3. There is one saddle path into the equilibrium shown by the dashed line. For a given value of F^p, it is assumed that following a disturbance, the market will pick the value for e that puts the system on the saddle path toward equilibrium. The system would have quite different properties under a policy regime of overintervention that reversed the pattern of movement in the horizontal direction.

2.2.5 Reaction to Exogenous Shocks

Monetary Disturbance

Consider an (unanticipated) expansionary open-market operation in government debt. This initially leaves W and F^p unchanged. There are two extreme assumptions on price adjustment to consider: no change in P, or $dP/P = dM/M$ immediately.

With no change in P as M increases, the $\dot{F} = 0$ locus in figure 2.4 does not shift, but $\hat{e} = 0$ shifts upward. With F^p initially given, the exchange rate jumps (currency depreciates) from initial equilibrium E_0 to E_1 on the

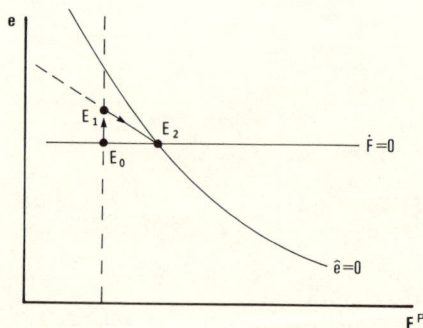

Fig. 2.4   Open-market operation in B, no change in F^p

new saddle path. This establishes $\hat{e} < 0$ as needed for asset holders to hold the existing stock of F^p given the lower interest rate. The rise in e/P generates a current account surplus, and F^p rises with e falling toward E_2. This is an extreme form of overshooting.

Suppose the domestic price level immediately reacts by rising by the same proportion as the money stock. Then $\dot{F} = 0$ also shifts upward by that same proportion. The extent of the upward shift in $\hat{e} = 0$ depends on initial portfolio distribution and the degree of substitutability among F, M, and B. One borderline case would be $M = eF^p$ and $m_r = f_r$. It can be seen in the expression for $d\hat{e}$ in equation (10) that in this case a proportional increase in e will maintain $\hat{e} = 0$. To the extent that $M > eF^p$ or $|f_r| > |m_r|$, the $\hat{e} = 0$ curve would shift upward more than $\dot{F} = 0$, requiring overshooting and $\hat{e} < 0$, $\dot{F}^p > 0$ moving to equilibrium. The reverse initial conditions would yield undershooting with $\hat{e} > 0$, $\dot{F}^p < 0$ in the movement to equilibrium.

Real Disturbance

The effect of an unanticipated fall in z (or an increase in P is shown in figure 2.5. The decrease in competitiveness shifts $\dot{F} = 0$ upward from its initial intersection with $\hat{e} = 0$ at E_0. The exchange rate jumps (currency depreciates) from E_0 to E_1 and then gradually rises to E_2 as F^p falls. The depreciation of the currency restores current account balance ($\dot{F} = 0$). The model undershoots in response to real disturbances.

Sluggish Price Adjustment

A limiting case of sluggish price adjustment could be modeled as a combination of figures 2.4 and 2.5. Expansionary monetary policy would begin this process illustrated in figure 2.4. The delayed price response would then resemble figure 2.5. To the extent that the price response is lagged and unanticipated, the e, F^p point would follow a path illustrated in figure 2.6.

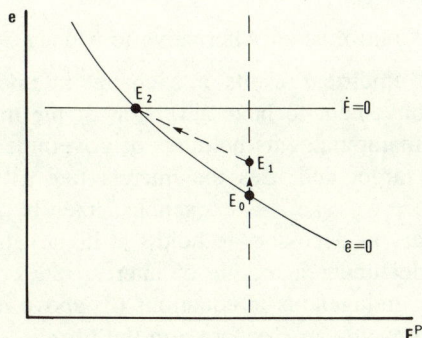

Fig. 2.5   Deterioration in competitiveness

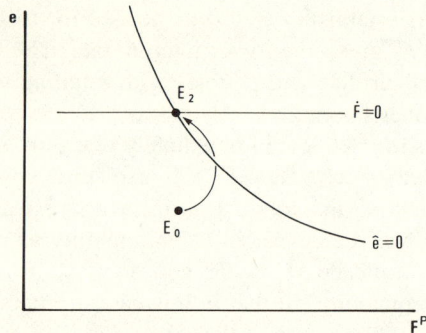

Fig. 2.6   Sluggish price adjustment

Quicker price response or anticipation would straighten the path to E_2, which may be to the right or left of E_0 depending on initial portfolio distribution and substitutability.

2.2.6 Conclusions and Empirical Implications

It is convenient to summarize here the basic conclusions from the analysis so far.

1. Unanticipated changes in money, the price level, or underlying real conditions should cause a jump in the exchange rate toward the new rational expectations saddle path.

2. Thus we should expect to see correlation between unanticipated movements in e and M, X, and P in the data. Some initial evidence was presented in Branson (1981); more is presented below.

3. Movement of the exchange rate following a real disturbance is likely to be monotonic, while monetary disturbances are likely to produce overshooting. Lagged price adjustment makes "multiple overshooting" possible. This can be seen in a combination of figures 2.4 and 2.6.

2.2.7 Interest Rate Control as an Alternative to Money Supply Control

In interpreting the empirical results on exchange rate policy in section 2.5 below, it will be convenient to have a version of the model in which the monetary authority manipulates its holdings of government debt in order to hit an interest rate target and uses the interest rate as the instrument of monetary policy. Here we take r as exogenous, fixed by policy, and permit B^p/W and M/W to vary as necessary to hold r at its target value.

To solve the model under a regime of interest rate control, we make r exogenous and M/W endogenous in equations (8) above, and then solve for $d\hat{e}$ and $d(M/W)$. This yields an $\hat{e}$ equation in the form

$$(12) \qquad \hat{e} = \psi\left(\frac{eF^p}{W}, r\right), \psi_1 > 0; \psi_2 > 0.$$

The interest rate simply replaces M/W here.

The $\hat{e} = 0$ locus is still a rectangular hyperbola in e, F^p space. A reduction in r, implying an increase in M/W and decrease in B^p/W, shifts the $\hat{e} = 0$ locus upward. Thus figure 2.4 provides a qualitative description of the effect of a reduction of the interest rate target in a regime of monetary control. The effects of movement in the interest rate on the path of the exchange rate are clearly the same as the effects of the corresponding change in M/W in the model with monetary control.

2.3 "Leaning against the Wind" as Exchange Rate Policy

2.3.1 Introduction

There is already ample evidence that monetary authorities have generally tried to slow the movement of exchange rates. This type of intervention has long been characteristic of United States domestic monetary policy; in Branson (1976) I labeled this "leaning against the wind" as exchange rate policy. Artus (1976) and Branson, Halttunen, and Masson (BHM) (1977) presented evidence that German monetary policy responded to movements in the exchange rate in this fashion. BHM (1977) estimated a reaction function of the form $\Delta M = \alpha \Delta e + \ldots$, with $\alpha < 0$ for Germany. As the exchange rate rose (DM depreciated), the money supply was reduced (relative to its trend). Amano (1979) describes Japanese monetary policy as attempting to stabilize the exchange rate similarly. United Kingdom exchange rate policy was discussed briefly in OECD (1977), where a regression of the form $\Delta r_m = \beta \Delta e + \ldots$, with r_m the minimum lending rate (MLR) and $\beta > 0$ is reported. This suggests that when sterling depreciated (e rose), the MLR was increased as a policy reaction. More recently, Mussa (1981) has presented a thorough review of exchange rate intervention which is consistent with a leaning-against-the-wind model.

In this section I shall characterize policy intervention in terms of the model of section 2.2., to prepare for interpretation of the empirical results in section 2.5 below. The objective is to describe policy, not evaluate it. The main difference from the previous models is the description of intervention as instantaneous and discrete changes in asset stocks via open-market operations to reduce the size of discontinuous jumps in exchange rates. This type of policy behavior is discernible in the "innovation" correlations in Section 2.5 below.

I shall begin with the description of monetary policy reaction to real disturbances via open-market operations in government debt or foreign assets. Then I will focus on sterilized intervention in the foreign asset market.

2.3.2 Monetary Policy

Consider a real disturbance to the current account that shifts $\dot{F} = 0$ up (rise in e), to restore equilibrium. This is illustrated in figure 2.7, where, in

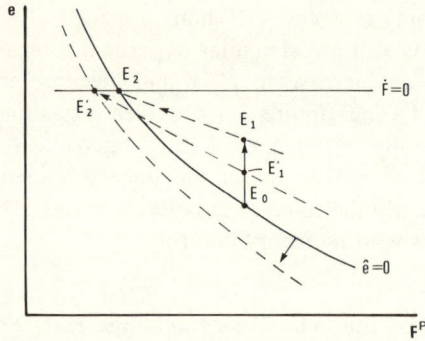

Fig. 2.7   Monetary policy reaction

the absence of policy intervention, the exchange rate would jump from the initial equilibrium E_0 to E_1 and then depreciate further to E_2. If the central bank tightened money by selling bonds to the public, holding F^p initially constant, the $\hat{e} = 0$ curve in figure 2.7 would shift downward as shown by the dashed $\hat{e} = 0$. This would shift the saddle path downward to the path running to E_2' and reduce the exchange rate jump to E_1'. Thus instantaneous intervention would reduce the initial jump in e. This would be an unexpected change in M, since the originating shift in z and X was unexpected. So this type of intervention could reduce the variability of e over time.

If the open-market operation were done in the foreign asset market, a smaller quantitative intervention would give the same shift in $\hat{e} = 0$ and in the saddle path in figure 2.7, because eF^p/W in equation (8) would rise. In addition, since F^p would rise, the initial jump would be to a point on the new saddle path below E_1'. Thus intervention on the foreign asset market would, in a sense, be more efficient than open-market operations in the bond market. This is essentially the same result that is obtained by Branson (1977) and Kenen (1982) under static expectations.

In a model with interest rate control, the same result as the bond market open market operation of figure 2.7 could be obtained by an appropriate increase in the interest rate target. The necessary increase in r could be reduced by performing the open-market operation in the foreign asset market.

2.3.3 Sterilized Intervention

There is ample evidence that central banks intervene in the foreign exchange markets but attempt to prevent the intervention from changing the path of M. The literature was cited in Whitman (1975); more recent results are discussed in Obstfeld (1980, 1982). In terms of the model of section 2.3, this is an open-market exchange of foreign assets for bonds by the central bank, with $\Delta B^p = -e\Delta F^p$ initially. The result is again a downward shift in $\hat{e} = 0$, as in figure 2.7, plus an outward shift in F^p. Thus the jump in the exchange rate is to a point below E_1', since F^p increases. This presents the possibility for intervention that does not move the path of the money supply.

2.3.4 Monetary Disturbances

Shifts in asset demand functions or the foreign interest rate would shift the $\hat{e} = 0$ locus, and the exchange rate would follow a path like that of figure 2.4, at least initially. Either monetary or sterilized intervention could reduce the extent of the shift in $\hat{e} = 0$, reducing the jump in e. The central bank would vary the supplies of the three assets to meet, at least partially, shifts in public demand for them. Again, this is a straightforward extension of leaning-against-the-wind policy reaction from the domestic to the international markets.

2.3.5 Empirical Implications

The principal empirical implication of the present model of policy intervention is that we should observe the intervention in the correlation of unexpected movements or "innovations" in exchange rates with innovations in money and/or reserves. Monetary intervention would give a negative correlation between exchange rate and money innovations. Intervention with interest rate control would give a positive correlation between exchange rate and interest rate innovations. If the monetary intervention is done in the foreign asset market, a positive correlation between exchange rate innovations and reserves would result. Sterilized intervention would give the reserve exchange rate correlation without a money exchange rate correlation. Thus we can study the correlation matrix of innovations in section 2.5. below to infer hypotheses about policy behavior.

2.4 The Data

2.4.1 Introduction

The asset market model of section 2.2 implies that unanticipated exogenous movements in the money stock, the current account balance, and relative price levels will cause unanticipated jumps in the exchange rate. The intervention model of section 2.3 implies that unanticipated jumps in exchange rates can cause unanticipated changes in the money stock, reserves, or interest rates. Thus innovations in money or interest rates may have a positive or negative correlation with innovations in exchange rates. If the correlation is negative, the inferred hypothesis would be that the underlying model is a monetary reaction function. A negative correlation between reserve and exchange rate innovations would indicate exchange market intervention. In this and the following section of the paper, we see that the quarterly data for the United States, Germany, Japan, and the United Kingdom can be interpreted within this framework. We are inferring testable hypotheses from the data in this exercise.

In this section and the next, we study relationships of movements in the exchange rate of each country, measured by the effective exchange rate as defined by the IMF, with movements in money stocks, current account balances, relative prices, reserves, and interest rates. The purpose is to see what policy stance is implied by the data. The data are described in detail in table 2.1.

Table 2.1   Variable Definitions and Data

I. Variable Name

e = effective nominal exchange rate, in units of foreign currency per unit of home currency as computed by the IMF. Note that this definition is the inverse of e in sections 2.2 and 2.3.

$P/\overline{P}$ = relative wholesale prices (ratio of home to competitors indices.

M1 = narrow money, as defined by the IMF in the *International Financial Statistics (IFS)*.

M3 = broad money, as defined by the IMF (M1 plus quasi-money) in the *IFS*.

CAB = current account balance.

IS = short-term interest rate, from *IFS*.

R = reserves, from *IFS*.

II. Countries

United States

United Kingdom

Federal Republic of Germany

Japan

III. Data

1. All data are quarterly, from IMF sources (in most causes from *IFS*) and cover 1973:IV–1980:IV.

2. *Exchange rates:* e_t is the log of the average effective exchange rate during quarter t. The units are foreign currency per unit of domestic currency. The index is based on a geometrically weighted average of bilateral rates between the home and 13 other industrial countries. The weights are the same as those used to calculate $P/\overline{P}$. Base: 1975 = 100. Source: IMF. Note that these are not the MERM rates published in *IFS*.

3. *Relative prices:* The index is a log of the ratio of home to foreign quarterly wholesale price indices. $\overline{P}$ is a composite and uses the same weights as does e (see above). Base = 1975. Source: IMF. This index is not the same as that published in the *IFS*. Our data is based on indices in local (not a common) currency.

4. *Money:* This is the log of the end of the quarter money stock. Source: *IFS*, line 34 ("money") for M1, lines 34 and 35 ("money" + "quasi-money") for M3.

5. *Current account:* This is the dollar value of the flow during the quarter (not measured in logs). Source: *IFS*, lines: 77aa (Merchandise: Exports, fob); 77ab (Merchandises: Imports, fob); 77ac (Other Goods, Services, and Income: Credits); 77ad (Other Goods, Services, and Income: Debits); 77ae (Private Unrequited Transfers); 77ag (Official Unrequited Transfers).

6. *Short-term interest rate:* Data are taken from *IFS* as indicated in the Table on "Money Market and Euro Dollar Rates." Source: *IFS* country pages: United States and United Kingdom, line 60c; Germany and Japan, line 60b.

7. *Reserves:* These are the dollar value of reserves measured at end of period. Source *IFS* line 1d.d. These series did not vary significantly from the series adjusted for valuation changes provided by the IMF.

The first step in analyzing the data is to investigate their time series properties. This provides a compact description of the "facts" and an initial indication of whether the facts are roughly consistent with the theory. The time series analysis of the data is done in this section. Then in section 2.5 we study systems of vector autoregressions, one for each country, to test the relations between unanticipated changes, or "innovations," in the variables.

2.4.2 Time Series Analysis

In this section the autoregressive structure of each time series is described by regression equations of the form

$$(12) \qquad X_t = \alpha_0 + \sum_{i=1}^{I} \alpha_i X_{t-i} + \sum_{j=1}^{3} \beta_j D_j + \gamma t + u_t,$$

where X_t is the log of the time series under consideration, X_{t-i} is its value lagged i quarters, D_i is a seasonal dummy, and t is time. Equation (12) is a univariate autoregression of the variable X on its own past values, and the estimated values of the α coefficients give the pattern of response of the time series to a disturbance u_t. The two cases that will appear prominently in our data are first-order autoregression, where only α_1 is significant, and second-order autoregression, where α_1 and α_2 are significant. One purpose of the analysis is simply to describe the data; the second is to see if the time series structure of the exchange rate data is consistent with that of the other data.

For each variable we began with a regression on four lags, seasonal dummies, and a time trend. We then shortened the lags by eliminating insignificant variables at the far end of the lag. The results are shown in tables 2.2–2.5, one for each country. Each column in the tables shows the results of a regression of the indicated variable on lagged values of itself. Coefficients of the time trend and seasonal dummies are not shown. The regressions are performed on quarterly data for the period 1973–IV to 1980–IV. The beginning date was chosen because it was after the major period of disequilibrium adjustment in 1971–73, including a major real devaluation of the United States dollar, and the last date was the most recent for which data were available when we began the study in June 1981. The regressions were run using the logs of exchange rates, relative prices, and money, and the levels of the current account balance, interest rates, and reserves. The current account and reserves are both time series that pass through zero in some cases.

2.4.3 Country Results

United States

The results for the United States are instructive and serve as an illustration of the technique. In the first two columns of table 2.2, we show the regressions for the log of the United States nominal effective exchange rate e,

Table 2.2 United States Univariate Autoregressions (Standard Errors in Parentheses)

Time Series

Lags:	e	e	P/P̄	P/P̄	M1	M1	M3	M3	CAB	CAB	IS	IS	IS	R	R
t-1	.86* (.21)	.78* (.10)	1.71* (.21)	1.36* (.17)	.33 (.24)	.55* (.18)	.70* (.24)	.78* (.14)	.92* (.21)	.80* (.14)	1.21* (.17)	.82* (.24)	.82* (.12)	1.31* (.26)	.87* (.15)
t-2	.24 (.29)	—	-1.41* (.38)	-.60* (.16)	.31 (.27)	—	.33 (.27)	—	-.19 (.30)	—	-1.19* (.26)	.00 (.24)	—	-.75 (.40)	—
t-3	.37 (.28)	—	.74 (.38)	—	-.16 (.29)	—	-.22 (.30)	—	.13 (.30)	—	1.49* (.30)	—	—	.28 (.40)	—
t-4	-.24 (.19)	—	-.20 (.21)	—	.22 (.24)	—	-.08 (.24)	—	-.20 (.22)	—	-.65* (.25)	—	—	.09 (.27)	—
Statistics:															
R^2	.86	.85	.92	.90	.99	.99	.99	.99	.76	.74	.92	.79	.79	.88	.84
D-W	1.89	1.82	2.16	1.51	1.57	1.96	1.98	2.15	1.86	1.66	2.24	1.68	1.68	1.78	1.28
SE	.027	.026	.008	.009	.012	.012	.009	.008	1.96	1.91	.82	1.28	1.26	36.7	38.8

Notes: (1) Sample period: 1973:IV–1980:IV for dependent variable.
(2) All regressions include constant, seasonal dummies, and time trend.
(3) An * indicates the coefficient is significant at the 5% level.
(4) Source for all data is IMF (but *e* is not merm, P/P̄ is WPI).

weighted by the IMF, in foreign currency per dollar. The first column shows the regression with four lags on the exchange rate; only the lag at $t - 1$ is significant with a coefficient of .86. When the lags at $t - 2$ through $t - 4$ are eliminated, the standard error of the estimated equation falls a bit, and the coefficient of e_{t-1} is .78. Thus the United States effective rate, measured as a quarterly average, can be described as a stable first-order autoregression (AR1). The coefficient of .78 on e_{t-1} indicates that a given disturbance u_t will eventually disappear from the time series as its effect is given by increasing powers of .78: $e_t = .78 \, u_t$; $e_{t+1} = .78^2 \, u_t$, and so on.

The third and fourth columns of table 2.2 show the results for the log of the United States relative price index $P/\overline{P}$. This is an index of the United States WPI relative to a weighted average of the WPIs of 13 other industrial countries. The variable $P/e\overline{P}$ is the IMF's measure of relative cost, published in the *International Financial Statistics*. It is the inverse of the real exchange rate of section 2.2.

The first regression for $P/\overline{P}$ in table 2.2 gives significant coefficients to the lags at $t - 1$ and $t - 2$. Elimination of the longer lags results in the second equation, with a standard error only slightly larger than the first. The result for $P/\overline{P}$ is a second-order autoregression (AR2), with a stable cyclical response to a distrubance.[3]

The next two pairs of columns in table 2.2 show the univariate autoregression results for the two United States money stocks. In both cases only the lag at $t - 1$ is significant. Both are stable first-order autocorrelations.

The next two columns in table 2.2 show the autoregressions for the current account balance. These are run on the level of CAB, rather than its log, since the time series passes through zero. The result is similar to that for the money stocks.

The next three columns in table 2.2 show the autoregressions for the United States short-term interest rate. All four lag coefficients are significant in the first column. In the second regression, with just lags at $t - 1$ and $t - 2$, the second is completely insignificant. Beyond $t - 1$, the important lags are at $t - 3$ and $t - 4$. The last of the three regressions includes only the lag at $t - 1$; the standard error is clearly higher than in the four-lag regression. Rather than include in the VAR system for the United States in section 2.5 four (or more) lags on the interest rate, which would greatly reduce degrees of freedom, I decided to include only the lag at $t - 1$. The last two columns of table 2.2 show the regressions for United States reserves. Only the lag at $t - 1$ is significant, giving a stable first-order autoregression.

In the case of the United States, then, money stocks, the balance on current account, reserves, and the nominal effective exchange rate all follow

3. The characteristic equation is given by
$$P/P_t - 1.36 \, P/P_{t-1} + 0.60 \, P/\overline{P}_{t-2} = 0.$$
The roots of this equation are $.68 + .37i$, with a modulus of $0.77 = 0.6^{1/2}$.

stable AR1 processes. This suggests that the behavior of money stocks, the current account balance, reserves, and the exchange rate are consistent, at this level, with the theoretical model of sections 2.2 and 2.3.

The relationships between interest rates and relative prices and the exchange rate is more complicated. With relative prices following an AR2, there is at best a loose relationship to the exchange rate. This is consistent with the evidence of high variability in purchasing power parity (PPP) in Frenkel (1981). The higher-order process for the interest rate suggests that it is being moved by all the exogenous variables simultaneously rather than reacting systematically to, or causing directly, the exchange rate.

West Germany

Table 2.3 shows the univariate autoregression results for Germany. The format is exactly the same as for the United States, so the discussion can be brief.

As in the United States case, the nominal effective rate, the money stocks, and the balance on current account all follow AR1 processes in Germany. All but M3 are stable. German M3 has a lag coefficient of unity, indicating that it is a "random walk": the change in M3 is (roughly) white noise. The German relative price series is AR2 with a stable cyclical response to disturbances.[4] The German interest rate is AR1 with a lag coefficient close to unity. Reserves have a barely significant lag at $t - 3$ but can be approximated by a stable AR1. Thus the impression from the German data is similar to the United States, except for the additional possibility that the interest rate is used as a policy instrument to control movements in the exchange rate.

United Kingdom

The United Kingdom results are summarized in table 2.4. Both the nominal effective rate and the M1 money stock in the United Kingdom have coefficients of unity on the $t - 1$ lag, indicating that they follow a random walk. The relative price series is AR2, as in the United States and Germany, but with a stable monotonic adjustment response to disturbances.

In the first regression for the current account balance, there are no significant lag terms. Thus the United Kingdom CAB is best described as random around the path described by the trend and seasonal dummy terms. This suggests that the innovations in the CAB in the United Kingdom should not be interpreted as conveying information about future movements in the exchange rate.[5]

[4]Note that the German price equation would not invert due to multicolinearity with more than two lags.
[5]A moving average specification of the equation for the United Kingdom CAB was also experimented with, with no improvement in results. The United Kingdom CAB does seem to be random about its trend.

Table 2.3   Germany Univariate Autoregressions

	e		P/P̄		M1		M3		CAB		IS		R	
Lags:														
t-1	.71*	.67*	—[a]	1.15*	.67*	.86*	1.08*	1.02*	.56*	.69*	.74*	.90*	.70*	.75*
	(.20)	(.18)		(.19)	(.21)	(.15)	(.20)	(.11)	(.22)	(.15)	(.21)	(.01)	(.19)	(.11)
t-2	-.15	—	—	-.58*	.23	—	-.10	—	.30	—	.27	—	-.19	—
	(.23)			(.19)	(.25)		(.30)		(.27)		(.26)		(.23)	
t-3	.37	—	—	—	.24	—	.24	—	-.15	—	-.04	—	.56*	—
	(.23)				(.24)		(.30)		(.28)		(.22)		(.23)	
t-4	-.29	—	—	—	-.32	—	-.50*	—	.05	—	-.15	—	-.33	—
	(.18)				(.19)		(.24)		(.24)		(.16)		(.17)	
Statistics:														
R^2	.96	.96		.99	.99	.99	.99	.99	.82	.81	.89	.88	.95	.93
D-W	1.11	1.43		2.50	2.11	2.20	2.06	1.73	1.64	1.95	1.90	2.25	1.80	2.01
SE	.024	.024		.003	.020	.020	.009	.009	1.33	1.28	1.02	1.01	74.5	79.8

[a]With more than two lags, the autoregression for P/P̄ would not invert due to collinearity.

Table 2.4   United Kingdom Univariate Autoregressions

	e		P/P̄		M1		M3		CAB		IS		R	
Lags:														
t-1	1.10*	1.04*	1.41*	1.53*	1.08*	.95*	.91*	.85*	.12	.12	1.21*	1.28*	1.14*	1.22*
	(.22)	(.07)	(.22)	(.17)	(.21)	(.12)	(.24)	(.16)	(.23)	(.21)	(.21)	(.18)	(.22)	(.19)
t-2	.01	—	-.48	-.57*	.21	—	-.04	—	-.02	—	-.29	-.52*	-.23	-.45*
	(.31)		(.36)	(.19)	(.25)		(.29)		(.26)		(.32)	(.18)	(.33)	(.18)
t-3	-.02	—	.19	—	-.62*	—	-.03	—	.02	—	-.23	—	-.20	—
	(.30)		(.35)		(.22)		(.29)		(.27)		(.31)		(.34)	
t-4	-.10	—	-.20	—	.08	—	-.14	—	.06	—	.04	—	.02	—
	(.23)		(.19)		(.20)		(.19)		(.24)		(.22)		(.23)	
Statistics:														
R^2	.94	.94	.99	.99	.99	.99	.99	.99	.50	.50	.83	.83	.95	.95
D-W	1.70	1.64	1.96	2.09	2.11	1.59	2.11	1.69	1.92	1.96	1.99	2.15	1.95	2.10
SE	.035	.033	.012	.012	.019	.024	.016	.016	912.71	853.07	1.33	1.30	56.8	55.1

Both the interest rate and reserves in the United Kingdom follow second-order autoregressions, with stable cyclical responses to disturbances. This would be consistent with interest rate policy being used to control reserves.

Japan

The results for Japan are summarized in table 2.5. There we see major differences from the other three countries. The nominal effective exchange rate, the relative price series, the current account balance, and the interest rate are all AR2 with stable cyclical response patterns. The two money stocks are AR1 with unitary lag coefficients. Reserves in Japan follow a complex autoregression of at least the fourth degree. Comparison of the first two reserve regressions in table 2.5 shows the importance of the lag at $t - 4$. To conserve degrees of freedom in the Japanese VAR system reported in section 2.5, I used the first-order approximation.[6] Thus in the Japanese case the time series behavior of the exchange rate is consistent with that of relative prices, the current account, and the interest rates, but the exchange rate does not follow the random walk pattern of money.

2.4.4 Summary on the Data

The univariate autoregressions of tables 2.2–2.5 provide a useful and compact description of the "facts." Comparing the country results, we see several common points.

1. All weighted relative price series are second-order autoregressions with stable responses to shocks. All but the United Kingdom series are cyclical.

2. All the money stocks are first-order autoregressions, many with unitary lag coefficients.

3. The United States and German exchange rate and current account series are first-order autoregressions and the Japanese are second-order. Thus these movements in exchange rate are consistent with movements in the current account balance, while the United Kingdom CAB contains no information about its future path.

4. The United States and German exchange rate and reserves follow AR1 processes that could reflect intervention. The United Kingdom and Japanese interest rates and exchange rates follow consistent processes, AR1 and AR2, respectively.

2.5 Empirical Results Using Vector Autoregression

2.5.1 Introduction

A useful technique for studying the relationships among the innovations in money, the current account balance, relative price levels, interest rates,

---

[6]The Japanese VAR results were reestimated using a 4-quarter lag on reserves, without much change.

Table 2.5   Japan Univariate Autoregressions

	e		P/P̄		M1		M3		CAB		IS		R		
Lags:															
t-1	1.18*	1.33*	1.24*	1.21*	.79*	1.03*	1.03*	1.10*	1.25*	1.50*	1.32*	1.56*	1.06*	1.07*	.80*
	(.22)	(.18)	(.20)	(.14)	(.22)	(.14)	(.22)	(.08)	(.22)	(.16)	(.23)	(.16)	(.16)	(.22)	(.12)
t-2	-.37	-.55*	-.85*	-.62*	-.56	—	.26	—	-.32	-.67*	-.39	-.72*	-.55*	-.30	—
	(.34)	(.18)	(.32)	(.12)	(.30)		(.32)		(.37)	(.16)	(.38)	(.17)	(.24)	(.31)	
t-3	.12	—	.45	—	-.04	—	-.21	—	.10	—	.05	—	.74*	-.05	—
	(.34)		(.32)		(.31)		(.32)		(.38)		(.56)		(.25)	(.21)	
t-4	-.26	—	-.27	—	-.24	—	-.01	—	-.34	—	-.23	—	-.072*	—	—
	(.22)		(.16)		(.28)		(.23)		(.25)		(.34)		(.17)		
Statistics:															
R^2	.91	.90	.99	.99	.99	.99	.99	.99	.91	.90	.93	.92	.92	.86	.84
D-W	1.74	2.06	1.82	1.81	1.77	2.42	1.79	1.96	1.85	2.17	2.00	2.34	1.47	2.01	1.40
SE	.044	.044	.014	.014	.023	.023	.008	.008	.97	1.00	1.00	1.00	58.8	78.5	80.4

reserves, and the exchange rate is vector autoregression (VAR). Here each variable of a system is regressed against the lagged values of all variables (including itself) in the system, to extract any information existing in the movements of these variables. The residuals from these "vector autoregressions" are the innovations—the unanticipated movements—in the variables. We can study the correlations of the residuals to see if they are consistent with the hypotheses implied by the theory of sections 2.2 and 2.3. The vector autoregression technique is introduced and justified by Sims (1980). A clear exposition is presented in Sargent (1979). Interesting and instructive applications are discussed in Taylor (1980), Ashenfelter and Card (1981), and Fischer (1981).

Here I estimate systems of VARs for each of the four countries, the United States, the United Kingdom, Germany, and Japan. Two systems were estimated for each country. Both include the effective exchange rate e, the current account balance CAB, and the effective relative price $P/\bar{P}$, the interest rate IS, and reserves R; the difference between the two is that one included M1 and the other M3. An obvious extension of the research would be to include cross-country effects, particularly of money stocks, but also the other variables. The difficulty in proceeding in this direction comes from the limited number of quarterly observations: 29 from 1973-IV to 1980-IV. Each VAR includes lagged values of four variables, a time trend, and three seasonal dummies. In order to expand the analysis, I am presently moving to a monthly data base.

Before estimating the VARs, one must consider the issue of the timing of the data. The effective exchange rate can be computed from public information on a daily basis. In fact, a United Kingdom effective rate is published daily in the Financial Times. Our data are averages during the quarter. The effective rate used here is the inverse of e as defined in sections 2.2 and 2.3. Money stock data are available on a weekly basis, so they are roughly contemporaneous with the exchange rate data. We use end-of-period money data. We would expect from Section II that the weekly changes in M would generate nearly simultaneous movements in e. Thus the innovation of the average e over a quarter would be most closely connected in our data with the innovation of the end-of-quarter money stock, which is the cumulation of the weekly innovations. Reserves are also end-of-period data, so that intervention to slow an unanticipated jump in e would appear as an innovation in reserves.

The relative price data are quarterly averages of monthly data, which become known soon after the month ends. Thus in our data set, the innovation in e_t would be most closely connected to the innovation in $P/\bar{P}_t$. Interest rates are also quarterly averages, so that if the interest rate were used to control the exchange rate we would see a correlation between the innovations in e_t and in IS_t.

On the other hand, the data on the quarterly balance on current account

Table 2.6   Variables Included in Vector Autoregression Systems

United States, Germany	United Kingdom	Japan
$\ln e_{t-1}$	$\ln e_{t-1}$	$\ln e_{t-1}$
$\ln M_{t-1}$	$\ln M_{t-1}$	$\ln e_{t-2}$
$\ln P/\overline{P}_{t-1}$	$\ln P/\overline{P}_{t-1}$	$\ln M_{t-1}$
$\ln P/\overline{P}_{t-2}$	$\ln P/\overline{P}_{t-2}$	$\ln P/\overline{P}_{t-1}$
CAB_{t-2}	CAB_{t-2}	$\ln P/\overline{P}_{t-2}$
IS_{t-1}	IS_{t-1}	CAB_{t-2}
R_{t-1}	IS_{t-2}	CAB_{t-3}
	R_{t-1}	IS_{t-1}
	R_{t-2}	IS_{t-2}
		R_{t-1}

Note: Two VAR systems were estimated for each country, one with M1, one with M3. The equations are estimated on data 1973 IV–1980 IV (described in table 2.1).

are not announced until well into the following quarter. Thus to the extent that the innovation in CAB signals a change in the equilibrium real exchange rate, it is the innovation in CAB_{t-1} that moves e_t.

The VAR residuals to be correlated, then, are those of e_t, M_t, $(P/\overline{P})_t$, CAB_{t-1}, IS_t, and R_t. We will use a tilde to designate residuals from the VARs. The variables in each VAR system are listed in table 2.6. The number of lags included in each variable was determined by the univariate autoregression of tables 2.2–2.5. This constraint provides a convenient way to limit the number of regressors and conserve degrees of freedom. A next step in research would be to reestimate the VAR systems with additional lags to see how much information is lost by application of this constraint.

After the VAR systems are estimated, we correlate their residuals to study the relationship among innovations. The correlations are given for the systems with M1 and M3 in tables 2.7–2.14 below, two for each country. Each table includes the correlation coefficients among the VAR innovations and in parentheses the probability of that correlation occurring under the null hypothesis that the true correlation is zero.

In discussing the correlations, we will focus on the correlations particularly relevant for analyzing exchange rate determination and policy. Detailed discussion of all the results would be far too tedious.

2.5.2 United States

The correlations of VAR innovations for the United States are shown in tables 2.7 and 2.8. Remember that here the effective nominal exchange rate is defined in units of foreign exchange per unit of home currency, the inverse of the theoretical definition of sections 2.2 and 2.3. So here an increase in e is an appreciation.

The first rows of table 2.7 and 2.8 give the correlations of exchange rate innovations. The negative signs for relative prices and money are consistent

Table 2.7   **Correlations of Innovations from United States Vector Autoregression System with M1**

	$\bar{e}$	$\bar{M}1$	$\bar{P}/\bar{P}$	$C\bar{A}B$	$I\bar{S}$	$\bar{R}$
$\bar{e}$	1.00	−.30	−.42	−.12	−.09	.14
		(.11)	(.03)	(.55)	(.65)	(.46)
$\bar{M}I$		1.00	−.35	−.41	−.03	−.56
			(.06)	(.03)	(.87)	(.00)^a
$\bar{P}/\bar{P}$			1.00	.44	.24	.26
				(.02)	(.20)	(.17)
$C\bar{A}B$				1.00	−.11	.55
					(.58)	(.00)^a
$I\bar{S}$					1.00	.35
						(.07)
$\bar{R}$						1.00

^{a}An entry of .00 indicates the number was less than .005.

with innovations in those variables driving e, as in the model of section 2.2. There is a weak correlation with reserves, consistent with intervention. Innovations in reserves, shown in the last columns of tables 2.7 and 2.8, are positively correlated with innovations in CAB, but not in money. It is useful here to recall that the CAB is lagged one period, so that the correlation is between the residual $C\bar{A}B_{t-1}$ and $\hat{R}_t$. Thus the indication in tables 2.7 and 2.8 is that intervention comes at the point where the CAB announcement would move the exchange rate, not during the period in which the actual CAB occurs.

The underlying vector autoregression for e (not shown here) also shows a strong Granger-causal role for lagged CAB. Thus the hypothesis I would infer from the United States data is as follows. The current account, money, and relative prices all move the exchange rate, the latter two through market

Table 2.8   **Correlation of Innovations from United States Vector Autoregression System with M3**

	$\bar{e}$	$\bar{M}3$	$\bar{P}/\bar{P}$	$C\bar{A}B$	$I\bar{S}$	$\bar{R}$
$\bar{e}$	1.00	−.48	−.37	−.08	−.02	.24
		(.01)	(.05)	(.68)	(.92)	(.22)
$\bar{M}3$		1.00	.23	.05	.50	.07
			(.24)	(.81)	(.01)	(.73)
$\bar{P}/\bar{P}$			1.00	.38	−.03	.03
				(.04)	(.89)	(.90)
$C\bar{A}B$				1.00	−.24	.47
					(.21)	(.01)
$I\bar{S}$					1.00	.30
						(.12)
$\bar{R}$						1.00

expectations and innovations. Monetary policy is essentially oriented toward domestic targets; movement in the exchange rate is a side effect. The United States monetary authorities intervene and sterilize, but do not follow a tight rule. This shows up in the strong correlation be $\bar{R}$ and $\widehat{CAB}$, and in the correlation between $\bar{R}$ and $\bar{e}$.

2.5.3 Germany

The innovation correlations for Germany are shown in tables 2.9 and 2.10. In the first row of both tables we see a very strong negative correlation between exchange rate and relative price innovations. This could come from exchange rates causing prices or vice versa, but through innovations and market expectations rather than a tight PPP relationship. The correlations of exchange rate innovations with short-term interest rates and reserves (in the

Table 2.9   Correlation of Innovations from German Vector Autoregression System with M1

	$\bar{e}$	$\bar{M}1$	$\bar{P}/\bar{P}$	$\widehat{CAB}$	$\widehat{IS}$	$\bar{R}$
$\bar{e}$	1.00	.17	−.44	.27	−.48	.40
		(.37)	(.02)	(.15)	(.01)	(.03)
$\bar{M}1$		1.00	.02	.25	−.47	.28
			(.94)	(.19)	(.01)	(.14)
$\bar{P}/\bar{P}$			1.00	.23	.07	.28
				(.22)	(.73)	(.14)
$\widehat{CAB}$				1.00	−.33	.43
					(.08)	(.02)
$\widehat{IS}$					1.00	−.13
						(.49)
$\bar{R}$						1.00

Table 2.10   Correlation of Innovations from German Vector Autoregression System with M3

	$\bar{e}$	$\bar{M}3$	$\bar{P}/\bar{P}$	$\widehat{CAB}$	$\widehat{IS}$	R
$\bar{e}$	1.00	−.09	−.59	.03	−.52	−.26
		(.63)	(.00)	(.90)	(.00)	(.17)
$\bar{M}3$		1.00	.18	.20	−.53	−.04
			(.34)	(.30)	(.00)	(.84)
$\bar{P}/\bar{P}$			1.00	.25	.05	.45
				(.20)	(.79)	(.01)
$\widehat{CAB}$				1.00	−.29	.25
					(.13)	(.19)
$\widehat{IS}$					1.00	−.01
						(.96)
$\bar{R}$						1.00

M1 system) must reflect leaning-against-the-wind policy in terms of both interest rates and intervention. The negative correlation of the interest rate and CAB innovations suggests that interest rate policy may respond to the state of the CAB as well as to the exchange rate. The lack of correlation between money and reserves or exchange rates indicates sterilized intervention. The correlation between $\tilde{CAB}$ and $\tilde{R}$ also supports the intervention hypothesis.

Thus the German data suggest fairly strongly a situation in which (1) price and exchange rate innovations go together, and (2) the authorities react to exchange rate and current account movements through changes in interest rates and sterilized intervention. This is consistent with the earlier results of BHM (1977) and of Herring and Marston (1977) for the fixed rate regime.

2.5.4 United Kingdom

The United Kingdom correlations are shown in tables 2.11 and 2.12. The exchange rate correlations with interest rates and reserves are a strong indication of leaning-against-the-wind intervention and interest rate policy. This effects M1 but not M3, as can be seen in the correlations of $\tilde{M}$ with $\tilde{e}$ and $\tilde{R}$. Innovations in the current account balance have the positive correlation with e that would come from the theory of section 2.2. Perhaps this suggests that while from the univariate autoregressions of section 2.4, CAB innovations have no predictive content, the market thinks they do.

In both tables there is a strong negative correlation between the CAB innovation and the interest rate. This would be consistent with interest rate policy determined by CAB as well as the exchange rate, similar to the German case. The United Kingdom data thus show influence of CAB on e, with interest rate and intervention policy reacting to innovations in e and CAB with M1 unsterilized.

Table 2.11   **Correlations of Innovations from United Kingdom Vector Autoregression System with M1**

	$\tilde{e}$	$\tilde{M}1$	$\tilde{P}/\bar{P}$	$\tilde{CAB}$	$\tilde{IS}$	$\tilde{R}$
$\tilde{e}$	1.00	.46	−.05	.29	−.59	.53
		(.01)	(.81)	(.12)	(.00)	(.00)
$\tilde{M}1$		1.00	.09	−.34	−.37	.52
			(.62)	(.07)	(.05)	(.00)
$\tilde{P}/\bar{P}$			1.00	−.02	.06	−.03
				(.91)	(.74)	(.89)
$\tilde{CAB}$				1.00	−.44	−.14
					(.02)	(.48)
$\tilde{IS}$					1.00	−.29
						(.12)
$\tilde{R}$						1.00

Table 2.12   **Correlations of Innovations from United Kingdom Vector Autoregression System with M3**

	$\tilde{e}$	$\tilde{M}3$	$\tilde{P}/\bar{P}$	$C\tilde{A}B$	$I\tilde{S}$	R
$\tilde{e}$	1.00	$-.04$	$-.04$	.47	$-.55$	.44
		(.82)	(.85)	(.01)	(.00)	(.02)
$\tilde{M}3$		1.00	.05	.46	$-.30$	$-.15$
			(.79)	(.01)	(.10)	(.43)
$\tilde{P}/\bar{P}$			1.00	.05	$-.05$	$-.04$
				(.80)	(.81)	(.85)
$C\tilde{A}B$				1.00	$-.61$	.08
					(.00)	(.67)
$I\tilde{S}$					1.00	$-.27$
						(.15)
$\tilde{R}$						1.00

2.5.5 Japan

The results for Japan are shown in tables 2.13 and 2.14. Let us focus on table 2.13 first. The correlation of innovations in the exchange and interest rates suggests a system of interest rate control with policy targets other than the exchange rate, rather than the reaction to exchange rates as found in the United Kingdom and Germany. The correlations of the interest rate with relative prices and the CAB suggest that these might be the targets.

The reserve correlations with the exchange rate and $C\tilde{A}B$ strongly suggest leaning-against-the-wind intervention, with the central bank absorbing part of the CAB innovations to reduce movement in the exchange rate. The lack of correlation of $\tilde{M}1$ with reserves or the exchange rate indicates sterilization.

An interesting picture emerges from the Japanese correlations. They sug-

Table 2.13   **Correlations of Innovations from Japan Vector Autoregression System with M1**

	$\tilde{e}$	$\tilde{M}1$	$\tilde{P}/\bar{P}$	$C\tilde{A}B$	$I\tilde{S}$	$\tilde{R}$
$\tilde{e}$	1.00	$-.06$	$-.08$	$-.03$	.55	.33
		(.77)	(.68)	(.89)	(.00)	(.08)
$\tilde{M}1$		1.00	$-.10$	$-.07$	$-.18$	.23
			(.59)	(.71)	(.36)	(.24)
$\tilde{P}/\bar{P}$			1.00	$-.32$	.42	$-.05$
				(.09)	(.02)	(.81)
$C\tilde{A}B$				1.00	$-.25$	.48
					(.19)	(.01)
$I\tilde{S}$					1.00	.31
						(.10)
$\tilde{R}$						1.00

Table 2.14   **Correlations of Innovations from Japan Vector Autoregression System with M3**

	$\bar{e}$	$\bar{M}3$	$\bar{P}/\bar{P}$	$C\bar{A}B$	$I\bar{S}$	$\bar{R}$
$\bar{e}$	1.00	.00	−.20	.05	.18	.12
		(.98)	(.30)	(.81)	(.35)	(.52)
$\bar{M}3$		1.00	.02	.12	−.28	.18
			(.93)	(.52)	(.14)	(.34)
$\bar{P}/\bar{P}$			1.00	−.36	.43	−.10
				(.05)	(.02)	(.61)
$C\bar{A}B$				1.00	−.60	.33
					(.00)	(.07)
IS					1.00	.14
						(.46)
$\bar{R}$						1.00

gest that policy sets interest rates with CAB and $P/\overline{P}$ among the objectives. The interest rate moves the exchange rate, as in section 2.2, and the authorities intervene to, in a sense, neutralize this effect. They also attempt to sterilize M1 from all of this. The VAR system with M3 is consistent with this picture in terms of signs of correlations, although significance levels vary from the M1 system (in both directions—see the correlation of IŜ and CÃB).

2.5.6 Summary of VAR Results on Policy

An interesting view of how the monetary system and interdependence have worked in the 1970s emerges from the VAR innovation correlations. My interpretation, or inferred set of hypotheses, is as follows. The United States sets monetary policy, largely by controlling quantities, with domestic objectives most in mind. The market looks to innovations in money and relative prices, and levels of the current account balance, to set the United States exchange rate. The monetary authority attempts sterilized intervention occasionally. In Japan, interest rates are set with relative prices (or rates of inflation) and the current account balance among the leading objectives. Interest rate innovations move the exchange rate, but an attempt is made to neutralize this effect through sterilized intervention.

Movement in the United States and Japanese effective rates, caused partly by fundamentals and partly by policy, are mirrored instantaneously in the United Kingdom and German effective rates, and their policy reacts. The reaction appears as "defensive" interest rate movements sensitive to exchange rate and CAB innovations, and largely sterilized intervention in the foreign exchange market. Thus a consistent story in which domestically oriented policy in the United States and Japan is transmitted in the United Kingdom and Germany is consistent with the VAR innovation results.

One final issue appears in the relations among exchange rate and interest rate innovations. The correlation in the United States is negligible, while in the United Kingdom and Germany it is strongly negative. An implication is that innovations in the dollar prices of the deutsche mark and sterling should be negatively correlated with innovations in the United States–German and United States–United Kingdom interest differentials, as noted by Frenkel (1981). The hypothesis advanced there was that nominal interest rates and exchange rates were both reacting to changes in inflation rates. The alternative hypothesis provided here is that United Kingdom and German interest rate innovations are policy reactions.

Comment   Willem H. Buiter

This interesting paper develops a theoretical open economy model that suggests certain associations between innovations in the exchange rate, the money stock, the current account, relative price levels, interest rates, and international reserves. The empirical part of the paper studies these correlations between innovations for the United States, the United Kingdom, the Federal Republic of Germany, and Japan. I shall discuss the theoretical and empirical sections in turn.

The Theoretical Model

The paper develops a model of a single open economy. The country is specialized in the production of its exportable and has some market power in the world market for the exportable. It consumes both its exportable good and an import whose world price in foreign currency is given. There are perfect international financial markets in the sense that instantaneous stock-shift portfolio reshuffles between domestic and foreign assets are possible. Domestic and foreign bonds are, however, imperfect substitutes. The interest rate on the foreign bond is exogenous. Exchange rate expectations are rational. Assumptions about price-level flexibility range from a fixed domestic currency price of the exportable to a freely flexible exportables price. External wealth adjustment through current account deficits and surpluses is allowed for. The model can be viewed as a flexible exchange rate version of Obstfeld (1980) or an imperfect asset substitutability version of Branson and Buiter (1983).

The decision to conduct the analysis conditional on the level of output and thus to avoid the need to consider the goods market or IS equilibrium condition certainly has expository advantages. However, the empirical observations have presumably been generated by a complete model in which output is endogenous. To infer what kinds of correlations between real world innovations are to be anticipated on the basis of the model, output would have to be endogenized. If output or income is an argument in the money demand function, some of the predictions of the complete model are likely to be different from those of the asset markets model, at any rate as regards the fixed and sluggish price adjustment versions.

The monotonic movement of the exchange rate following a real distur-bance holds true, even in the fixed price and perfectly flexible price versions of the model, only for unanticipated permanent disturbances. Anticipated future shocks are likely to give rise to nonmonotonic adjustment patterns. With lagged price adjustment the adjustment process is likely to be cyclical, even in response to unanticipated shocks. If, for example, sluggish price adjustment is modeled by $\frac{\dot{p}}{p} = \phi(y - \bar{y}) + \pi, \pi = \eta\left(\frac{\dot{p}}{p} - \pi\right)$ where y is real output, $\bar{y}$ is capacity output, and π is core inflation (ϕ, $\eta > 0$), a cyclical adjustment process is virtually guaranteed. Adding slug-gish price adjustment increases the dimensionality of the state vector by at least one. The example just given adds two state variables.

The implicit assumption is made throughout, that F^p and W are positive. From equation (11) we find that the $\dot{e} = 0$ locus can be given by either branch of the rectangular hyperbola in figure 2.C.1 depending on whether the stationary value of F is positive or negative. (It is assumed that while F^p can be negative as well as positive, W is positive throughout.)

Assuming with Branson that the $\dot{F}^p = 0$ locus is horizontal, the phase diagram is as figure 2.C.1. If there is a unique stationary solution for W and the domestic interest rate r, then there is a unique solution for F^p. If this

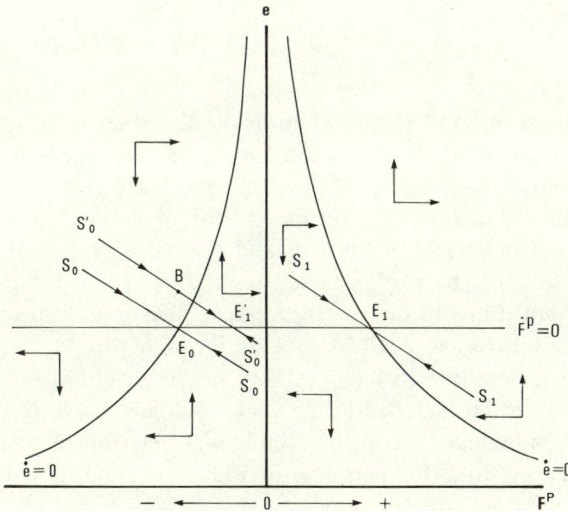

Fig. 2.C.1

solution is negative we are at E_0; if it is positive E_1 will be the stationary equilibrium.

The qualitative response of e and F^p to an unanticipated increase in M will be the same, whether the stationary equilibrium is at E_0 or E_1. From an initial position at E_0, the $\dot{e} = 0$ locus shifts down and to the right when M increases. There is a new long-run equilibrium at E_0', say, and a new convergent saddle path $s_0's_0'$ through E_0'. The exchange rate "jump-depreciates" to B and then gradually appreciates toward E_0' along $s_0's_0'$.

Most of the results in the theoretical part of the paper do not require the assumption of imperfect asset substitutability. The distinction between open market operations in domestic bonds and open market operations in foreign bonds would of course disappear if the two bonds were perfect substitutes.

The Empirical Work

The data analysis starts by estimating univariate autoregressions for money stocks, current account balances, effective exchange rates, relative prices, and interest rates. For the United States, the money supply, the current account balance, reserves, and the nominal exchange rate are found to follow stable AR1 processes. Branson argues that this suggests the behavior of these variables is "consistent, at this level, with the theoretical model of sections 2.2 and 2.3." However, the theoretical model only suggests that the innovations should be correlated. Consider, for illustrative purposes, the following structural model.

(1a) $$m_t = \alpha_1 m_{t-1} + \epsilon_t^m,$$

(1b) $$e_t = \beta_1 e_{t-1} + \beta_2 e_{t-2} + \beta e_{t-3} + \beta_4[m_t - E(m_t \mid I_{t-1})] + \epsilon^e t.$$

In this equation, ϵ_t^m and ϵ_t^e are white noise disturbances. Clearly the innovation in the univariate autogression for m_t, ϵ_t^m and the innovation in the univariate autogression for e_t, $\epsilon_t^e + \beta_4 \epsilon_t^m$, are correlated even if ϵ_t^m and ϵ_t^y are independently distributed. Yet m_t will follow an AR1 process and e_t an AR3 process. Conversely, even if m_t and e_t were each to follow "similar" AR1 processes, this by itself can tell us nothing about the correlation between the innovations in the two processes. That issue can only be settled by estimating a bivariate ARIMA process for m_t and e_t.

I am also unconvinced of the validity of the criterion for selecting the number of lags to be included in the vector autogressions. In the paper, the number of lags included for each variable was determined by the univariate autogressions. Assume for purposes of illustration that e_t and m_t follow a first-order vector autogressive process:

(2a) $$e_t = \alpha_1 e_{t-1} + \alpha_2 m_{t-1} + \epsilon_t^e,$$

(2b) $m_t = \beta_1 e_{t-1} + \beta_2 m_{t-1} + \epsilon_t^m.$

Repeated substitution in (2b) yields $m_t = \beta_1 \sum_{i=0}^{\infty} \beta_2^i e_{t-1-i} + \sum_{i=0}^{\infty} \beta_2^i \epsilon_{t-i}^m.$

That is,

(3a) $e_t = \alpha_1 e_{t-1} + \alpha_2 \beta_1 \sum_{i=0}^{\infty} \beta_2^i e_{t-2-i}$

$$+ \alpha_2 \sum_{i=0}^{\infty} \beta_2^i \epsilon_{t-1-i}^m + \epsilon_t^e.$$

Similarly,

(3b) $m_t = \beta_2 m_{t-1} + \beta_1 \alpha_2 \sum_{i=0}^{\infty} \alpha_1^i m_{t-2-i}$

$$+ \beta_1 \sum_{i=0}^{\infty} \alpha_1^i \epsilon_{t-1-i}^e + \epsilon_t^m.$$

If in (2a)–(2b) α_1, α_2, β_1, and β_2 are all nonzero, then the univariate autoregressions would be characterized by an infinite lag distribution. If ϵ_t^e and ϵ_t^m are white noise, the disturbances in the univariate autogressions would be infinite-order MA processes. Clearly, (2a) and (2b) are only consistent with univariate autoregressive representations for e_t and m_t if $\alpha_2 = \beta_1 = 0$.

Finally, a remark about the interpretation of any observed contemporaneous correlation between the innovations in a vector autoregression. Branson argues, for example, that a positive correlation between innovations in the money supply and the exchange rate reflects the response of the exchange rate to unanticipated open market operations, while a negative correlation suggests monetary ("leaning against the wind") intervention aimed at stabilizing the exchange rate in response, say, to current account disturbances.

While I have no quarrel with Branson's interpretation of the correlations contained in the paper, it is important to realize that the stochastic properties of the data themselves cannot establish whether m responds to innovations in e, e responds to innovations in m, or both respond to each other's innovations. The effect of unanticipated e on m is observationally equivalent with the effect of unanticipated m on e (Buiter 1983). Consider the following example:

(4a) $e_t = a_1 + b_1[m_t - E(m_t \mid I_{t-1})] + \epsilon_t^e,$

(4b) $m_t = a_2 + b_2[e_t - E(e_t \mid I_{t-1})] + \epsilon_t^m.$

The reduced form of this model is given by

(5a) $e_t = a_1 + (1 - b_1 b_2)^{-1}(\epsilon_t^e + b_1 \epsilon_t^m) = a_1 + u_t^e,$

(5b) $m_t = a_2 + (1 - b_1 b_2)^{-1}(\epsilon_t^m + b_2 \epsilon_t^e) = a_2 + u_t^m.$

Let ϵ_t^e and ϵ_t^m be white noise disturbances that are also contemporaneously uncorrelated.

The covariance between the reduced-form disturbances u^e and u^m in (5a) and (5b) is given by

$$(6) \qquad E(u^e u^m) = (1 - b_1 b_2)^{-2}(b_1 \sigma_\epsilon^2 m + b_2 \sigma_\epsilon^2 e)$$

If we know on a priori grounds that money does not respond to exchange rate surprises ($b_2 = 0$), then $E(u^e u^m) = b_1 \sigma_\epsilon^2 m$ and b_1 can be identified and estimated using the estimated variance-covariance matrix of the reduced-form disturbances since $b_1 = E(u^e u^m)/E(u^m)^2$. If instead the exchange rate does not respond to money surprises ($b_1 = 0$), then $E(u^e u^m) = b_2 \sigma_\epsilon^2 e$, $E(u^e u^m)/E(u^m)^2 = b_2 \sigma_\epsilon^2 e/(\sigma_\epsilon^2 m + b_2^2 \sigma_\epsilon^2 e)$ and $b_2 = E(u^e u^m)/E(u^e)^2$. The data themselves cannot tell us whether $b_1 = 0$, $b_2 = 0$, or both b_1 and b_2 are nonzero.

Prior information must be used to overcome this identification problem. If it can be assumed, for example, that $b_1 \geq 0$ and $b_2 \leq 0$, then a negative value for $E(u^e u^m)$ is (from [6]) only consistent with a (negative) policy response of m to e. Even if we accept the constraint $b_1 \geq 0$, one may well be able to imagine policy scenarios under which $b_2 > 0$. "Leaning with the wind" in the foreign exchange market can be shown to be optimal under certain conditions (Buiter and Eaton 1981). In that case the positive correlation between u^e and u^m reflects both any positive structural effect of m on $e(b_1 \geq 0)$ and the positive policy response of m to $e(b_2 > 0)$. Only detailed prior knowledge of the actual form of the policy response rules will enable us to extract useful information from correlations between the innovations in vector autoregressions.

Comment   Peter B. Kenen

If I had read only the summary of findings at the start of Branson's paper, I would have had no quarrel with him. His descriptions of national policies seem eminently sensible. Having read his whole paper carefully, I find myself in difficulty. I agree with most of his conclusions but have many doubts about the way that he obtains them.

I do not have much trouble with the model that Branson uses to define the questions he wants to investigate. It is a standard asset market model of exchange rate determination that is made forward looking by introducing rational expectations. (If I understand the model, most of the comparative static results could be obtained with stationary expectations. The rational expectations form serves mainly to draw the distinction between anticipated and unanticipated shocks—a distinction Branson needs later to treat his regression residuals as proxies for unanticipated shocks.)

I do have one small complaint and one unanswered question. It would have been easier for me to follow his presentation if Branson had told us from the start that "reserves" held by the central bank do not differ in character from the foreign assets held by the public (that R is part of F); this is why reserve use for official intervention is the same as an open market sale of foreign assets to domestic asset holders. My question has to do with the assumption that $(\delta \dot{F}/\delta F) = 0$. In most asset market models, this term or one like it must be negative for the model to be stable; an increase in F is an increase in wealth, and it must reduce $\dot{F}$, the capital outflow or current account surplus, if the economy is to reach a stationary state. I wonder, then, whether Branson's assumption could impair the stability of his model.

I have somewhat more serious questions about the use of this standard model for the main purpose of the paper—empirical work on exchange rate determination and official intervention. The model describes a small country facing a homogeneous world. There is one exchange rate and one foreign asset. The countries with which Branson deals in his empirical work are large in every sense, and the outside world is not homogeneous. Branson does not face this problem squarely, and when the numbers force him to do something about it, whether he wants to or not, he tries to make the countries fit his model rather than making his model fit the countries.

Let me add right away that it would be very difficult to make the model fit the countries. It would be necessary to deal simultaneously with a number of interdependent economies, each one holding assets in the others' currencies and affecting by its policies all of the bilateral exchange rates for its currency. One could, of course, determine the effects of policies, domestic and foreign, on the behavior of the effective exchange rate. But one would have to begin with the effects on the relevant bilateral exchange rates and to take account of the foreign repercussions relevant to each such rate. One could thus measure the influence of United States monetary policy on the effective exchange rate for the dollar by determining its impact on the mark-dollar rate, the yen-dollar rate, and so on, allowing fully for the German and Japanese responses, including both endogenous and policy responses.

What has Branson done? He has tried to fit four large countries into his small-country model by working directly with effective exchange rates and making no allowance for foreign repercussions or for the effects of other countries' policies. His vector autoregressions for the United States include the effective exchange rate for the dollar, the ratio of domestic to foreign prices corresponding conceptually to the effective rate, and the current account balance. They also include United States reserves, the United States money supply, and the United States short-term interest rate. The price ratio and current account balance may take some account implicitly of events in other countries, including endogenous responses to events in the United States, but they are far from adequate for this purpose.

When I made these observations at Bellagio, during the discussion of Branson's paper, several participants came to his defense. It would be impossible, they said, to execute the strategy implied by my criticism. To capture the impact of official intervention on the effective exchange rate for the dollar, one would have to estimate vector autoregressions for all of the relevant bilateral exchange rates and include a larger number of variables in *every* vector autoregression. Each equation would have to include all of the bilateral exchange rates, all of the current account balances, and all of the other variables for the foreign countries. Branson does not have enough degrees of freedom. I was at first inclined to accept this defense, but I am increasingly dissatisfied with it. If one cannot do things right, one should perhaps refrain from doing them at all.

What are the practical consequences of following Branson's procedure? Two examples lead me to believe that it must misrepresent the influence of official intervention. My first example illustrates the need to disaggregate—to work separately with the bilateral exchange rates for each currency. For most of the period covered by this study, exchange rate arrangements in Western Europe pegged bilateral rates between the mark and certain other European currencies. The German authorities had to intervene whenever the relevant bilateral rates reached the limits of the bands set first by the "snake" and then by the EMS. I have not worked carefully through the implications, but I venture a conjecture. When the effective exchange rate for the mark is used to "explain" the behavior of German reserves, the vector autoregression will be unsatisfactory. The coefficients of the German reaction function implicit in its coefficients will not be unbiased, and the residuals will not represent the "innovations" needed later on. To measure the effects of intervention accurately, one has to disaggregate—to separate the two types of intervention residing in the German data and link each type of intervention to the relevant bilateral exchange rates.[1]

My second example illustrates the need to include foreign variables in each country's vector autoregressions. During most of the period covered by this study, the United States authorities did not intervene regularly on foreign exchange markets. When they did intervene, moreover, they concentrated on two or three bilateral exchange rates. But foreign central banks intervened extensively. To capture the effects of intervention on the effective exchange rate for the dollar, one should thus try to estimate the effects of United States intervention on the two or three bilateral exchange rates and, simultaneously, the effects of foreign intervention on those and the other bilateral rates that make up the effective rate.

For reasons given earlier, it would be difficult to do this correctly. If

1. One would expect both types of intervention to affect both types of rates—those that are pegged by intra-European arrangements and those that are not—and the "cross effects" may be quite strong. (Some of the intervention undertaken to defend the pegged rates is done in dollars rather than in European currencies, and therefore it should affect the bilateral exchange rate between the mark and dollar directly.) But the correlations between the two types of intervention and two types of rates are apt to be different, and they should be identified instead of being "averaged" into a single correlation between "innovations" in total intervention and in the effective exchange rate.

intervention is not exogenous but can and should be described by a reaction function, we should include in the vector autoregressions for the United States all variables for all foreign countries, and this is not possible. But there may be rough and ready ways to take account of foreign intervention:

1. Using the small-country approach adopted by Branson (i.e., using only United States variables) but working with bilateral exchange rates for the dollar, not with the effective rate, we could obtain new sets of exchange rate residuals. We could then calculate the simple correlations between German reserves and the mark-dollar residuals, between Japanese reserves and the yen-dollar rate, and so on.

2. If we were to look at Branson's vector autoregressions for reserves, we would probably find that very few of the right-hand-side variables are significant. In this event, it would be possible to run three new equations— one for the mark-dollar exchange rate containing all of the United States and German variables, one for German reserves containing the mark-dollar rate (or the effective exchange rate for the mark) and one or two other variables, and an equation for United States reserves containing the mark-dollar rate (or the effective exchange rate for the dollar) and one or two other variables. We could then run simple correlations between the residuals from the exchange rate equation and the residuals from the reserve equations.

These methods are imperfect. The second, for example, runs afoul of my earlier objection—that some German intervention is mandated by intra-European monetary arrangements. But they may take us farther than Branson's approach.

As I have concentrated heavily on intervention, let me continue in that vein. I have two more problems. In Branson's paper, intervention is identified with quarter-to-quarter changes in official foreign exchange holdings (in the series on line 1.d.d of *International Financial Statistics*). If these are the figures he has used, he is wrong to say that they can turn negative. Furthermore, Branson mentions the valuation problem but says that it is small. He does not mention a much larger problem: changes in the figures are not necessarily due to intervention. During the fourth quarter of 1978, when the United States began to intervene heavily to keep the dollar from depreciating, it sold large quantities of foreign exchange. Nevertheless, its official foreign exchange holdings rose by $4.34 billion. Why? Because the United States drew on its reserve position in the IMF and issued the Carter bonds. It borrowed more foreign exchange than it used. There are other instances of this sort, and one must make careful corrections for them before using changes in foreign exchange holdings to represent official intervention. We cannot correct them completely, but we should do what we can. There is no excuse for running data from a tape into a regression program without inspecting, let alone correcting them.

My last point has to do with the reliability of the results reported in Branson's paper. For example, the results in table 2.13, which deals with Japan, come from vector autoregressions that use M1 to represent the Japanese money supply. The correlation between innovations in reserves and in the exchange rate is .33 and is significant. The results in table 2.14, also dealing with Japan, come from vector autoregressions that use M3 to represent the money supply. The correlation between the same sets of "innovations" is .12 and is not signficant. What conclusion should we draw about the effectiveness of intervention? It may be best to render the old Scottish verdict—not proven—until we can discriminate decisively between the reduced forms implicit in alternative specifications. I have grave doubts about the validity of the rational expectations hypothesis. Even those who think that it is valid, however, should entertain doubts about using residuals from reduced-form regressions to represent the unexpected.

References

Amano, A. 1979. Flexible exchange rates and macroeconomic management: A study of the Japanese experience in 1973–1978. Mimeographed. Kobe University.

Artus, J. 1976. Exchange rate stability and managed floating: The experience of the Federal Republic of Germany. *International Monetary Fund Staff Papers* 23 (July): 312–33.

Ashenfelter, O., and Card, D. 1981. Time-series representations of economic variables and alternative models of the labor market. Working Paper. University of Bristol.

Branson, William H. 1975. Comment on M.v.N. Whitman: Global monetarism and the monetary approach to the balance of payments. *Brookings Papers on Economic Activity* 6:537–42.

————. 1976. Leaning against the wind as exchange rate policy. Paper presented at Graduate Institute of International Studies, Geneva, revised 1981 for book publication by the Institute.

————. 1977. Asset markets and relative prices in exchange rate determination. *Sozialwissenschaftliche Annalen* 1:69–89.

————. 1980. Monetary and fiscal policy with adjustable exchange rates. In *The international economy: U.S. role in a world market*. U.S. Congress, Joint Economic Committee. Washington, D.C.: Government Printing Office.

————. 1981. Macroeconomic determinants of real exchange rates. NBER Working Paper no. 801, November.

Branson, William H., and Buiter, Willem H. 1983. Monetary and fiscal policy with flexible exchange rate. In *Economic interdependence and flexible exchange rates*, ed. J. Bhandari and B. Putnam. Cambridge, Mass.: MIT Press.

Branson, William H.; Halttunen, H.; and Masson, P. 1977. Exchange rates in the short run: The dollar-deutschemark rate. *European Economic Review* 10 (December): 303–24.

Buiter, Willem H. 1983. Real effect of anticipated and unanticipated money: Some problems of estimation and hypothesis testing. *Journal of Monetary Economics* 11 (March):207–24.

Buiter, Willem H., and Eaton, J. 1981. Policy decentralization and exchange rate management in interdependent economics. Mimeographed. University of Bristol.

Dornbusch, R. 1980. Exchange rate economics: Where do we stand? *Brookings Papers on Economic Activity* 2:143–86.

Fischer, Stanley. 1981. Reiative shocks, relative price variability, and inflation. *Brookings Papers on Economic Activity* 2:381–431.

Frenkel, Jacob. 1981. Flexible exchange rates, prices and the role of "news": Lessons from the 1970s. *Journal of Political Economy* 89 (August): 665–705.

Herring, R. J. and Marston, R. C. 1977. *National monetary policies and international financial markets,* Amsterdam: North-Holland.

Kenen, P. B. 1981. Effects of intervention and sterilization in the short run and the long run. In *The international monetary system under flexible exchange rates: Essays in honor of Robert Triffin,* ed. R. N. Cooper et al. Cambridge, Mass.: Ballinger.

Kouri, Pentti J. K. 1978. Balance of payments and the foreign exchange market: A dynamic partial equilibrium model. Yale University, Cowles Foundation Discussion Paper no. 510.

Mussa, Michael. 1981. The role of official intervention. Occasional Paper 6. New York: Group of 30.

Obstfeld, Maurice. 1980. Portfolio balance, monetary policy, and the Dollar-Deutschemark exchange rate. Columbia University Economics Department, Discussion Paper No. 62, March 1982.

———. 1980. Imperfect asset substitutability and monetary policy under fixed exchange rates. *Journal of International Economics,* 10:177–200.

———. 1982. Can we sterilize? Theory and evidence. *American Economic Review* (May).

OECD Interfutures. 1977. Long-term aspects of the monetary system. Mimeographed. Paris: OECD, September 30.

Sargent, Thomas. 1979. Estimating vector autoregressions using methods not based on explicit economic theories. *Federal Reserve Bank of Minneapolis Quarterly Review* (Summer), pp. 8–15.

Sims, C. 1980. Macroeconomics and reality. *Econometrica* 48 (January): 1–48.

Taylor, J. 1980. Output and price stability: An international comparison. *Journal of Economic Dynamics and Control* 2 (February): 109–132.

Whitman, M. v. N. 1975. Global monetarism and the monetary approach to the balance of payments. *Brookings Papers on Economic Activity* 3:471–536.

II   Short-Run Determinants of the Exchange Rate

3 International Interest Rate and Price Level Linkages under Flexible Exchange Rates: A Review of Recent Evidence

Robert E. Cumby and Maurice Obstfeld

3.1 Introduction

International linkages between goods and asset markets are the key factors in exchange rate determination. The scope for activist stabilization policy depends on both the nature of the equilibrium implied by these linkages and the speed with which equilibrium is attained. Two important relationships—purchasing power parity, which links the exchange rate to relative national price levels, and uncovered interest rate parity, which links the expected future path of the exchange rate to relative nominal interest rates—have received extensive empirical attention in recent years and are main building blocks of several empirical exchange rate models.[1] The purpose of this paper is to review and extend recent empirical evidence on these classical parity relationships within a rational expectations framework.

When an economy is small and both classical parity relations hold even in the short run, monetary policy cannot influence the ex ante real rate of interest. Insofar as the ex ante real rate is an important determinant of saving and investment decisions, an important channel for stabilization policy disappears.[2] In theoretical models of Dornbusch (1976) and Mussa (1982),

We thank J. Frenkel, R. Hodrick, B. Loopesko, R. Meese, and F. Mishkin for helpful comments and discussions. Assistance from N. Killefer and J. Withers is acknowledged with thanks. Obstfeld's research was supported in part by a grant from the National Science Foundation.

1. Examples include Frenkel (1976), Bilson (1979), Frankel (1979a), Hodrick (1978), and Hooper and Morton (1982).

2. In these circumstances, monetary policy also loses its power to exert a systematic influence on the terms of trade or real exchange rate, and a second avenue of demand management is thus closed. Even so, monetary policy can be effective if nominal wages are sticky (see Obstfeld 1982a). But this possibility disappears as well when wages are fully and instantaneously indexed to the aggregate price level. While monetary policy may be ineffective, tax policy can always succeed in driving a wedge between home and foreign ex ante real rates. The discussion below abstracts from taxes. Also ignored is the possibility that changes in monetary growth rates might influence the terms of trade through real effects of the Tobin-Sidrauski sort.

temporary price level stickiness allows money to influence the real interest rate in the short run even though uncovered parity holds exactly. Portfolio balance models of exchange rate determination (such as those of Girton and Henderson [1977] and Branson [1979]) stress imperfect substitution between bonds of different currency denomination. In these models, central banks can influence real interest rates if they can alter relative outside debt supplies.

As emphasized by Roll and Solnik (1979), among others, the classical parity relations need not hold in a setting of uncertainty and risk aversion, even when prices are fully flexible and agents efficiently exploit all welfare-augmenting arbitrage opportunities.[3] Unless at least one parity relationship fails, monetary policy cannot affect the expected real rate of interest; but the invalidity of a parity condition does not, in itself, imply that monetary policy has this power (see Henderson [in this volume] and Obstfeld [1982b]). Thus, the series of tests performed below is at best a single component of a more extensive inquiry into the role of monetary policy in the open economy.

A central theme in our review of empirical work is the conditional heteroscedasticity of inflation and exchange rate forecast errors, and the bias this econometric problem may impart to tests of international parity relationships. Below, we propose and implement a test for conditional heteroscedasticity which in many cases produces strong evidence that the problem is indeed important.

The paper is organized as follows. Section 3.2 reviews the classical parity conditions and examines the recent behavior of bilateral ex post real interest rate differentials between the United States and the United Kingdom, Germany, Switzerland, Canada, and Japan. Section 3.3 carries out bilateral tests of ex ante real interest rate equality between the United States and these countries. Section 3.4 is devoted to empirical tests of uncovered interest rate parity. Finally, section 3.5 tests the hypothesis that relative purchasing power parity has held ex ante during the recent era of exchange rate flexibility.

3.2 Classical Parity Relationships and Real Interest Rates

To facilitate formal discussion of the classical parity relations, we introduce the following notation:

P_t = price level in the "home" country at the end of period t;

P_t^* = price level in the "foreign" country at the end of period t;

3. If there are no default risks, covered interest arbitrage is riskless (in home currency terms), and so *covered* interest parity must always hold exactly in the absence of transaction costs. In contrast, uncovered arbitrage involves home currency risk in an essential way. The relation between covered and uncovered interest parity is discussed in Section III, below.

S_t = the exchange rate at the end of period t, defined as the home currency price of foreign currency;

$R_{k,t}$ = $\ln(1 + I_{k,t})$, where $I_{k,t}$ is the home country k-period nominal interest rate at the end of period t;

$R^*_{k,t}$ = $\ln(1 + I^*_{k,t})$, where $I^*_{k,t}$ is the foreign country k-period nominal interest rate at the end of period t;

$E_t(\cdot)$ = Conditional expectation operator, based on information available at the end of period t.

Purchasing power parity (PPP), in its relative form, states that the rate at which the relative price of two currencies changes over time must equal the difference between the national inflation rates. The doctrine of PPP has a long intellectual history, which is surveyed by Frenkel (1976, 1978). Using the foregoing notation, the PPP relation may be written as

$$(1) \qquad \ln(S_t/S_{t-1}) = \ln(P_t/P_{t-1}) - \ln(P^*_t/P^*_{t-1}).$$

An implication of (1) is that relative PPP must be expected to hold ex ante, that is, for any k,

$$(2) \qquad E_t[\ln(S_{t+k}/S_t)] = E_t[\ln(P_{t+k}/P_t) - \ln(P^*_{t+k}/P^*_t)].$$

The ex ante relative PPP condition (2) is weaker than (1), of course. Magee (1978) and Roll (1979) have suggested an "efficient markets" interpretation of ex ante PPP for a world with low transport costs.

Uncovered interest rate parity (UIP) states that the nominal interest differential between similar bonds denominated in different currencies must equal the expected change in the logarithm of the exchange rate over the holding period. This explanation of international differences in nominal interest rates is associated with Fisher (1930). UIP implies that, for any k,

$$(3) \qquad R_{k,t} - R^*_{k,t} = E_t[\ln(S_{t+k}/S_t)].$$

Condition (3) must hold when bonds differing only in their currencies of denomination are perfect substitutes in investors' portfolios.

Define the expected or ex ante k-period real interest rates for the home and foreign countries by

$$(4a) \qquad r_{k,t} \equiv R_{k,t} - E_t[\ln(P_{t+k}/P_t)],$$

$$(4b) \qquad r^*_{k,t} \equiv R^*_{k,t} - E_t[\ln(P^*_{t+k}/P^*_t)].$$

By combining (2) and (3) with (4a) and (4b), we find that

$$(5) \qquad r_{k,t} = r^*_{k,t}.$$

Thus, under ex ante relative PPP and uncovered interest rate parity, ex ante real rates of interest must be equalized internationally. The classical parity relationships imply that policymakers in a small open economy cannot affect domestic economic activity through financial policy measures aimed at influencing the expected real interest rate.

Figures 3.1 through 3.5 plot monthly series of ex post 1-month real interest rate differentials between the United States and the United Kingdom, Germany, Switzerland, Canada, and Japan. (The data are expressed on an annualized basis.) The series begin in January 1976 and are based on wholesale price index inflation rates and 1-month Eurocurrency deposit rates.

Because the figures use nonoverlapping monthly data involving 1-month-ahead forecasts, the deviations from ex post real rate equality should be serially uncorrelated and trendless if agents' expectations are rational and real rates are equal across countries ex ante. All five figures suggest some degree of both serial dependence and trend, however. Ex post real rates in both the United Kingdom and Germany, for example, appear to have been on the whole above those in the United States over the period lasting from roughly July 1977 to December 1979. Between early 1976 and mid-1978, Swiss and Japanese ex post real rates were persistently above those in the United States. The figures show a pronounced rise in United States ex post real rates relative to those in the five other countries beginning around the end of 1980.

While the figures suggest the existence of ex ante real interest rate differ-

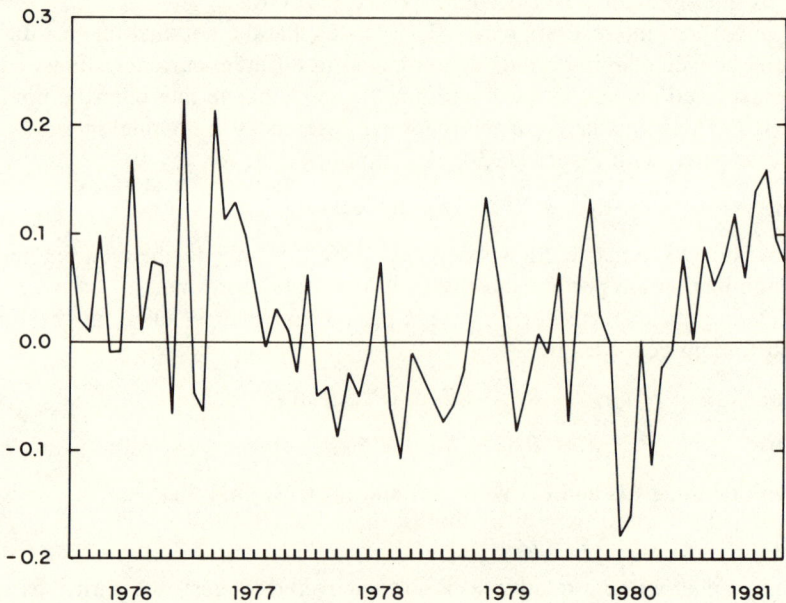

Fig. 3.1   Ex post U.S.–U.K. 1-month real interest differential

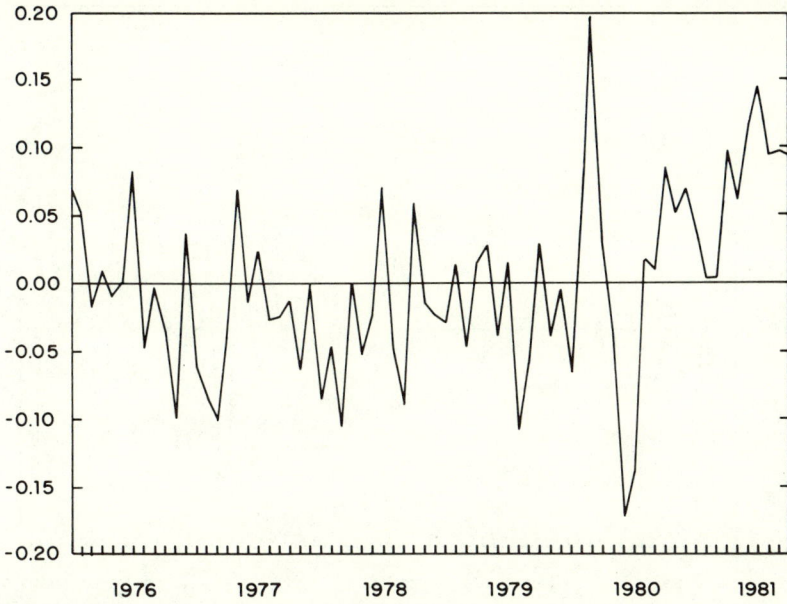

Fig. 3.2   Ex post U.S.–Germany 1-month real interest differential

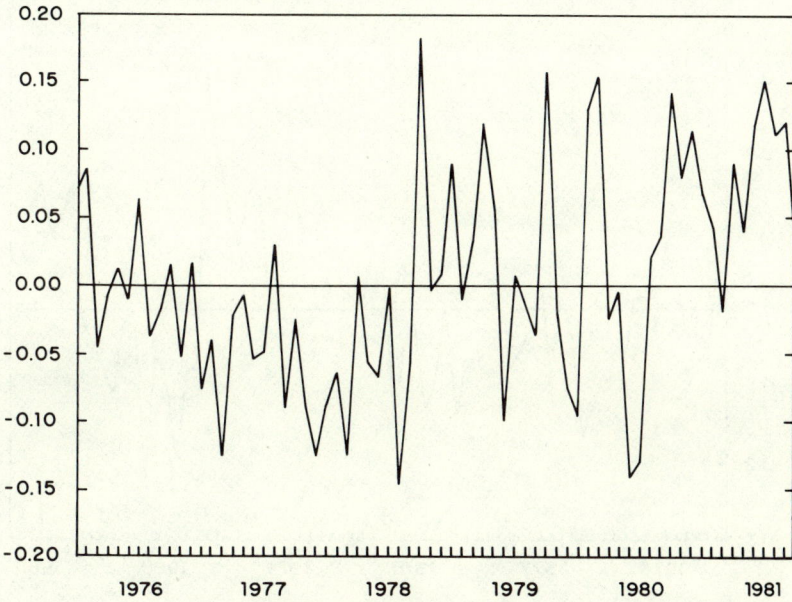

Fig. 3.3   Ex post U.S.–Switzerland 1-month real interest differential

125

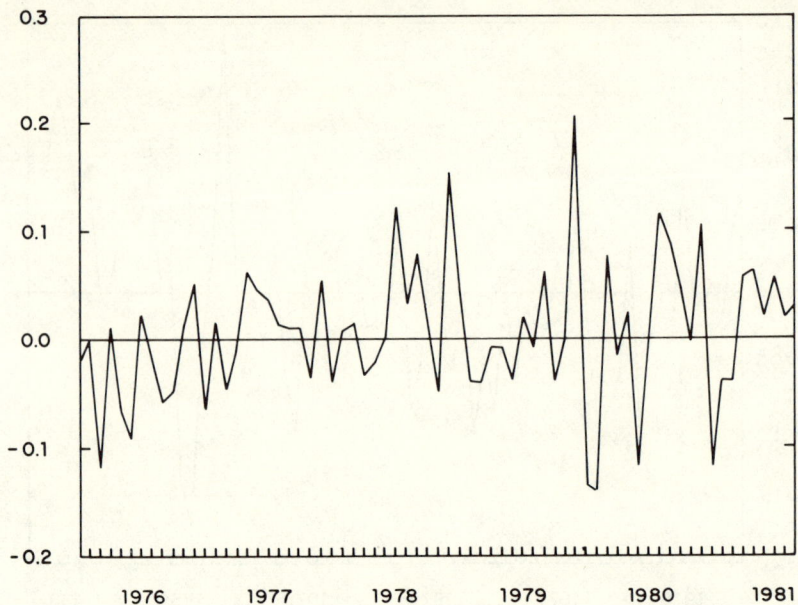

Fig. 3.4   Ex post U.S.–Canada 1-month real interest differential

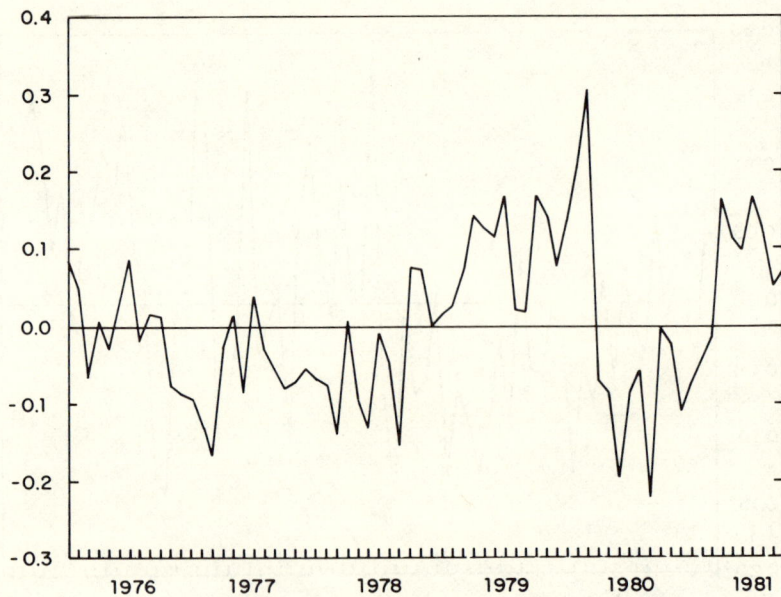

Fig. 3.5   Ex post U.S.–Japan 1-month real interest differential

entials over the period since January 1976, conclusive evidence can be provided only by econometric tests. We now turn to these.

3.3 The Equality of Ex Ante Real Interest Rates

The equality of ex ante real interest rates across countries has been tested in papers by Hodrick (1979) and Mishkin (1982). Hodrick (1979), using monthly data on 3-month rates, performs bilateral tests to compare ex ante real rates in the United States and four other OECD countries over the period of generalized floating. He concludes that the empirical record, though mixed, is not inconsistent with the validity of condition (5). Mishkin (1982) carries out multilateral tests of equality using quarterly data for the United States and six other OECD countries. Over both the 1967:II–1979:II and 1973:II–1979:II sample periods, he obtains strong rejections of the hypothesis that ex ante real interest rates in the seven countries were equal.

In this section we test equation (5), taking into account the possible dependence of the conditional covariances of relative inflation forecast errors on nominal interest differentials. Such dependence induces a heteroscedasticity problem which invalidates hypothesis tests unless standard errors are estimated in an appropriate manner. Below, we establish the presence of a conditional heteroscedasticity problem and then use appropriate estimators to conduct a test similar to one of Hodrick's (1979). The results, based on monthly data, are on the whole unfavorable to the hypothesis that expected real interest rates have been equalized internationally in recent years.

3.3.1 A Test of the Hypothesis

The assumption of rational expectations yields a simple bilateral test of the hypothesis that ex ante real rates are equal across countries. Let π_{t+k} and π^*_{t+k} denote the realized inflation rates in the home and foreign countries between the end of period t and the end of period $t + k$. Then

(6a) $$\pi_{t+k} = E_t[\ln (P_{t+k}/P_t)] + u_{t+k},$$

(6b) $$\pi^*_{t+k} = E_t[\ln (P^*_{t+k}/P^*_t)] + u^*_{t+k},$$

where u_{t+k} and u^*_{t+k} are mean-zero inflation forecast errors uncorrelated with any variables observed by the market by the end of period t. Because subsequent forecast errors are not part of that information set, $E(u_{t+k}u_{t+k-j})$, $E(u^*_{t+k}u^*_{t+k-j}) \neq 0$ for $j < k$ even though $E(u_{t+k}u_{t+k-j}) = E(u^*_{t-k}u^*_{t+k-j}) = 0$ for $j \geq k$. Combining (4a), (4b), and (5) with (6a) and (6b), we obtain the relation

(7) $$\pi_{t+k} - \pi^*_{t+k} = R_{k,t} - R^*_{k,t} + u_{t+k} - u^*_{t+k}.$$

Because the composite forecast error $e_{t+k} \equiv u_{t+k} - u^*_{t+k}$ is uncorrelated with $R_{k,t}$ and $R^*_{k,t}$ (both of which are known to agents at the end of period t), the parameters a and b in the regression equation

(8) $$\pi_{t+k} - \pi^*_{t+k} = a + b(R_{k,t} - R^*_{k,t}) + e_{t+k}$$

may be estimated consistently by ordinary least squares (OLS). A test of the hypothesis $[a \; b]' = [0 \; 1]'$ is a test of the hypothesis that expected real interest rates are equal in the home and foreign country.[4]

While OLS is consistent when applied to equation (8), it is generally inefficient relative to an instrumental variables estimator of the type discussed by Cumby, Huizinga, and Obstfeld (1983) and by Hansen (1982).[5] Because e_{t+k} is orthogonal to *any* variables in agents' information set at time t, many instrumental variables are available. Below, we use third-country interest rates as additional instruments to estimate the parameters of (8) by the two-step two-stage least squares (2S2SLS) technique described by Cumby, Huizinga, and Obstfeld (1983).[6]

Let Q_t denote the row vector $[1(R_{k,t} - R^*_{k,t})]$ and stack the T observations on (8) to obtain the regression model $\pi - \pi^* = Qd + e$, where $d \equiv [a \; b]'$. Let X_t be a row vector of instrumental variables (including Q_t), all of which are uncorrelated with e_{t+k}. Then the 2S2SLS estimate of d can be written as

(9) $$\hat{d} = (Q'X\hat{\Omega}^{-1}X'Q)^{-1}Q'X\hat{\Omega}^{-1}X'(\pi - \pi^*),$$

---

4. This test is suggested by Hodrick (1979). However, he uses the k-period forward premium rather than the k-period nominal interest differential on the right-hand side of (8). The two procedures should yield very similar results when Eurocurrency interest rates are being compared (see section 3.4).

5. The reason is that the latter uses more information. As noted in the next paragraph of the text, OLS is a special "just identified" case of this type of instrumental variables estimator.

6. When the forecast horizon k exceeds 1 period, e_{t+k} is serially correlated and, under the null hypothesis, has the covariance matrix of a moving average (MA) process. As Hansen and Hodrick (1980) note, two-step serial correlation corrections of the generalized least squares type are inconsistent, even though QLS is consistent. The inconsistency is due to the fact that the nominal interest differential is not a strictly exogenous variable. To see this, suppose that $k = 3$, so that the hypothesis involves 3-month interest rates observed monthly. Assume that the vector stochastic process $[(\pi_t - \pi^*_t)(R_{3,t} - R^*_{3,t})]'$ is covariance stationary and has the indeterministic bivariate Wold representation

$$\pi_t - \pi^*_t = \sum_{i=1}^{\infty} \psi_i v_{t-i} + \sum_{i=1}^{\infty} \theta_i \omega_{t-i} + v_t,$$

$$R_{3,t} - R^*_{3,t} = \sum_{i=1}^{\infty} \rho_i v_{t-1} + \sum_{i=1}^{\infty} \delta_i \omega_{t-i} + \omega_t,$$

where $E_t(v_{t+j}) = E_t(\omega_{t+j}) = 0$ for $j > 0$ (see Sargent 1979, p. 257). Under the null hypothesis,

$$E_t(\pi_{t+3} - \pi^*_{t+3}) = \sum_{i=0}^{\infty} \psi_{i+3} v_{t-i} + \sum_{i=0}^{\infty} \theta_{i+3} \omega_{t-i} = R_{3,t} - R^*_{3,t} = \sum_{i=1}^{\infty} \rho_i v_{t-i} + \sum_{i=1}^{\infty} \delta_i \omega_{t-i} +$$

ω_t. Thus, if ex ante real interest rates are equal, $\psi_3 = 0$, $\theta_3 = 1$, $\rho_i = \psi_{i+3}$, and $\delta_i = \theta_{i+3}$. This implies that $\pi_{t+3} - \pi^*_{t+3} - R_{3,t} + R^*_{3,t} = v_{t+3} + \psi_1 v_{t+2} + \psi_2 v_{t+1} + \theta_1 \omega_{t+2} + \theta_2 \omega_{t+1} = e_{t+3}$. Now e_{t+3} has the covariance matrix of an MA process and, by Granger's lemma (see Ansley, Spivey, and Wrobleski 1977), can be written as an invertible second-order MA process, $e_{t+3} = \zeta_{t+3} + \lambda_1 \zeta_{t+2} + \lambda_2 \zeta_{t+1}$. But even though e_{t+3} is uncorrelated with the regressors in (8), ζ_{t+3} need not be; and therefore application of a generalized least squares transformation to (8) will generally induce a nonzero correlation between the filtered disturbance ζ_{t+3} and the filtered regressors. For a more detailed argument, see Cumby, Huizinga, and Obstfeld (1983). Hansen and Hodrick (1980) use the Wold theorem to provide a similar characterization of the form of the forward exchange rate forecast error when contract periods overlap in the data.

where $\hat{\Omega}$ is a consistent estimate of $\Omega = \lim_{T \to \infty} ((1/T)E(X'ee'X)$. Under standard regularity conditions (which include covariance stationarity of all series), $\sqrt{T}(\hat{d} - d)$ converges to a normal random vector with mean zero and asymptotic covariance matrix plim $T^2(Q'X\Omega^{-1}X'Q)^{-1}$. When $X = Q$, $\hat{d}$ reduces to the QLS estimator $(Q'Q)^{-1}Q'(\pi - \pi^*)$.

Computation of $\hat{d}$ and its asymptotic covariance matrix requires a consistent estimate of Ω. If we assume that for all j, the conditional covariance

(10) $$E(e_{t+k}e_{t+k-j} \mid X_t, \ldots, X_{t-j}) = \sigma_j,$$

a constant, then $\hat{d}$ may be written as

(11) $$\hat{d} = [Q'X(X'\hat{\Sigma}X)^{-1}X'Q]^{-1}Q'X(X'\hat{\Sigma}X)^{-1}X'(\pi - \pi^*)$$

where $\hat{\Sigma}$ is an estimate of the variance-covariance matrix $E(ee')$, formed using the residuals from a first-step, consistent estimation of (8) (by OLS, say). The matrix

(12) $$T[Q'X(X'\hat{\Sigma}X)^{-1}X'Q]^{-1}$$

provides a consistent estimate of the asymptotic covariance matrix of $\sqrt{T}(\hat{d} - d)$ in this special case. (The usual textbook formula for the asymptotic covariance matrix of the two-stage least squares estimator [see Dhrymes 1974] is based on assumption [10] and the assumption that $\sigma_j = 0$ for $j > 0$.)

Formula (12) is used by Hodrick (1979) to calculate the asymptotic confidence ellipse for OLS estimates of (8). But (12) is not justified, even in the OLS case, unless the conditional covariances of forecast errors with respect to lagged interest differentials are constants.[7] Condition (10) would be valid if the variables included in X_t were all strictly exogenous; but that is certainly not the case here.[8] The validity of (10) is thus an issue of considerable importance in constructing hypothesis tests concerning the coefficients of (8). Below, we describe and implement a test of (10).

When (10) fails, estimation of the matrix Ω is more involved. Hansen (1982) suggests the following procedure. As before, generate estimates $\hat{e}_t$ of the residuals of (8) using some consistent (but not necessarily efficient) estimation procedure, for example, OLS. Then, calculate a consistent estimate $\hat{s}(\xi)$ of the spectral density matrix of the vector stochastic process $[X_t'\hat{e}_t]$,

(13) $$s(\xi) = \frac{1}{2\pi} \sum_{l=-\infty}^{\infty} \exp(-i\xi l)(X_t'\hat{e}_t\hat{e}_{t-l}'X_{t-l}).$$

---

7. See Dhrymes (1974), pp. 183–84. A more recent discussion of the failure of assumption (10) in regression models with i.n.i.d. residuals appears in White (1980). For time series models, see Engle (1982) and Hansen (1982). It is important to note that even if (10) does not hold, the estimator given in (11) still yields consistent (but relatively inefficient) estimates of parameters.

8. The condition would also be valid if the instruments and disturbances were jointly normally distributed. Without the joint normality assumption, however, lack of correlation need not imply statistical independence.

A consistent estimate of Ω is provided by $2\pi\hat{s}(0)$. This heteroscedasticity-consistent covariance matrix estimator is convenient, as it does not require detailed specification of either the nature of the heteroscedasticity or the nature of the serial correlation in the residuals of (8).[9]

3.3.2 A Test of Conditional Homoscedasticity

To determine the appropriate estimator for the matrix Ω in (9), the empirical validity of assumption (10) must be examined. Here, we test (10) for the case $j = 1$. In that case, (10) asserts that

$$(14) \qquad E(e_{t+k}^2 \mid X_t) = \sigma^2,$$

a constant, so that the forecast error e_{t+k} is *conditionally homoscedastic* with respect to time t values of the instrumental variables. Rejection of (14) is clearly a sufficient indication that formula (12) is inappropriate and may lead to faulty inferences.

Since our ultimate goal is to test whether $a = 0$ and $b = 1$ in (8), it is reasonable to test for conditional heteroscedasticity under the tentative assumption that the null hypothesis of ex ante real interest rate equality is valid. That assumption implies that e_{t+k} is simply the composite forecast error $\pi_t - \pi_t^* - R_{k,t} + R_{k,t}^*$, which is observable. By the properties of conditional means, the random variable $\eta_{t+k} \equiv e_{t+k}^2 - E(e_{t+k}^2 \mid X_t)$ has unconditional mean zero and is uncorrelated with any variable in the information set generated by X_t. If (14) is valid, $\eta_{t+k} = e_{t+k}^2 - \sigma^2$, and so (14) can be tested by estimating an equation of the form

$$(15) \qquad e_{t+k}^2 = \alpha + \beta(R_{k,t} - R_{k,t}^*) + \gamma(R_{k,t} - R_{k,t}^*)^2 + \eta_{t+k}.$$

A test of the hypothesis $\beta = \gamma = 0$ is a test of conditional homoscedasticity. Because η_{t+k} is uncorrelated with the regressors in (15) (all of which are included in the information set generated by instrumental variables dated t or earlier), OLS yields consistent parameter estimates. But 2S2SLS again yields an efficiency gain in general. Any variables in the information set generated by X_t may be used as instrumental variables.[10]

The foregoing test is similar in spirit to one proposed by White (1980) for cross-sectional estimation environments. White suggests regressing *estimated* equation residuals on cross-products of regressors. His procedure thus

---

9. One can of course obtain covariance matrix estimates by imposing such information if it is known. Cumby, Huizinga, and Obstfeld (1983) describe one way of doing this. Their method is implemented in obtaining the empirical results reported in this paper. White (1980 has proposed a heteroscedasticity-consistent covariance matrix estimator in a cross-sectional context, along with a test of homoscedasticity. White's test is discussed further below.

10. Any product of instrumental variables is a legitimate regressor in (15), but we have excluded all but two in the a priori belief that the others are less likely to be significant in explaining e_{t+k}^2. It is worth emphasizing that the possibility of conditional heteroscedasticity does not contradict the assumption that e_{t+k} follows a covariance stationary process. The latter assumption requires only that the *unconditional* variance of e_{t+k} be constant over time.

imposes no a priori coefficient constraints. The present setting, however, is one in which a *simple* null hypothesis is to be tested. Absence of conditional heteroscedasticity when the null is imposed is clearly necessary if formula (12) is to lead to valid inferences.

Table 3.1 contains the homoscedasticity test results based on monthly data. Five countries—the United Kingdom, Germany, Switzerland, Canada, and Japan—are compared with the United States in the tests of ex ante real interest rate equality carried out below. Choosing an appropriate price index and interest rate is in itself an issue of considerable importance. Thus, the

Table 3.1   **Conditional Homoscedasticity of Inflation Forecast Errors**

Countries	Interest Rate	Price Index	Test Statistic
U.S./U.K.	1-month Euro	CPI	3.42
U.S./U.K.	1-month Euro	WPI	2.58
U.S./U.K.	3-month Euro	CPI	7.21*
U.S./U.K.	3-month Euro	WPI	7.53*
U.S./U.K.	3-month money market	CPI	8.24*
U.S./U.K.	3-month money market	WPI	9.40**
U.S./Germany	1-month Euro	CPI	6.20*
U.S./Germany	1-month Euro	WPI	4.23
U.S./Germany	3-month Euro	CPI	16.54**
U.S./Germany	3-month Euro	WPI	11.00**
U.S./Germany	3-month money market	CPI	32.35**
U.S./Germany	3-month money market	WPI	72.07**
U.S./Switzerland	1-month Euro	CPI	4.45
U.S./Switzerland	1-month Euro	WPI	11.97**
U.S./Switzerland	3-month Euro	CPI	74.08**
U.S./Switzerland	3-month Euro	WPI	42.38**
U.S./Switzerland	3-month money market	CPI	58.22**
U.S./Switzerland	3-month money market	WPI	11.64**
U.S./Canada	1-month Euro	CPI	2.56
U.S./Canada	1-month Euro	WPI	4.22
U.S./Canada	3-month Euro	CPI	21.49**
U.S./Canada	3-month Euro	WPI	9.93**
U.S./Canada	3-month money market	CPI	2.19
U.S./Canada	3-month money market	WPI	5.95
U.S./Japan	1-month Euro	CPI	2.14
U.S./Japan	1-month Euro	WPI	2.55
U.S./Japan	3-month Euro	CPI	127.83**
U.S./Japan	3-month Euro	WPI	6.23*
U.S./Japan	3-month money market	CPI	9.58**
U.S./Japan	3-month money market	WPI	35.85**

Note: Data for tests using 1-month interest rates run from January 1976 to September 1981. Data for tests using 3-month interest rates run from January 1976 to July 1981. The test statistic is distributed asymptotically as $\chi^2(2)$. An * = rejection at the 5% level; ** = rejection at the 1% level.

tests are performed for both consumer price index (CPI) and wholesale price index (WPI) inflation rates and for three nominal interest rates, the 1-month and 3-month Eurocurrency rates and a domestic 3-month money market rate.[11] All the resulting possibilities are represented in table 3.1.[12]

The results illustrate the empirical relevance of the conditional heteroscedasticity problem in tests of real interest rate equality. In 20 of the 30 tests, the hypothesis of conditional homoscedasticity can be rejected at the 5% level. In five of the remaining cases, the hypothesis can be rejected at the 20% level. Taken together, these results contradict the simplifying assumptions under which formula (12) is a consistent estimator of the asymptotic covariance matrix. Accordingly, a heteroscedasticity-consistent covariance matrix estimator is used to obtain the test results analyzed below.

3.3.3 Empirical Results

Tables 3.2A, 3.2B, and 3.2C report the results of bilateral tests of equality between the United States real interest rate and those of the United Kingdom, Germany, Switzerland, Canada, and Japan.[13] Except in the United Kingdom and Japanese cases, equality is strongly rejected for all combinations of price index and interest rate. The rejections in tests using onshore money market interest rates (table 3.2c) may in some cases be plausibly ascribed to the existence or prospect of capital controls. However, the rejections are almost equally strong when Eurocurrency interest rates are used in place of money market rates; and arbitrage between differently denominated Eurocurrency deposits has not been restricted.[14] On the whole, it seems difficult to explain the rejections of real interest rate equality by appealing to institutional factors that hinder international movements of capital.

11. In order to distinguish empirically between inflation risk and default risk, studies of United States real interest rates focus on United States treasury bills, which yield a riskless *nominal* return (Fama 1975; Shiller 1980; Mishkin 1981). As Mishkin (1982) observes, cross-country comparisons of real interest rates are most informative when the bonds being compared have the same default and political risk characteristics. This is true of Eurocurrency deposits denominated in different currencies, but not of onshore bonds traded in different countries' financial centers. Thus, tests of real rate equality using domestic money market interest rates should be interpreted with caution. Another cause for caution is the fact that the prices entering CPIs and WPIs are not all sampled every month in revising the previous month's index; indeed some prices are observed only once a year (see Fama 1977; Nelson and Schwert 1977; Shiller 1980). This means that over short periods, changes in the price indices correspond only imperfectly to actual price level movements. Because the implied measurement errors are serially correlated, our tests of real interest rate equality are, to some extent, biased. It would be of considerable interest to perform these tests on 12-month interest and inflation rates.

12. The instrumental variables in these regressions were the time t nominal interest differentials for all countries in the sample and the time t nominal interest differentials squared. All data are described in the Appendix.

13. The instrumental variables in the regressions were the time t nominal interest differentials for all countries in the sample.

14. Further, any political risks attaching to Eurocurrency deposits are not denomination-specific, and thus should not influence ex ante real interest differentials in the Eurocurrency market (see n. 11, above).

Table 3.2   Equality of Ex Ante Real Interest Rates

A. One-Month Eurocurrency Rates (January 1976–September 1981)

Countries	Price Index	$\hat{a}$	$\hat{b}$	Test Statistic
U.S./U.K.	CPI	−.0119 (.0086)	.7362 (.2351)	2.22
U.S./U.K.	WPI	−.0216 (.0093)	.8197 (.2713)	5.34
U.S./Germany	CPI	.0278 (.0095)	.5031 (.2264)	9.13*
U.S./Germany	WPI	.0484 (.0148)	−.1371 (.3529)	11.21**
U.S./Switzerland	CPI	.0350 (.0125)	.3708 (.1970)	10.25**
U.S./Switzerland	WPI	.0844 (.0178)	−.3187 (.2655)	25.16**
U.S./Canada	CPI	.0010 (.0054)	.4043 (.1915)	12.61**
U.S./Canada	WPI	−.0111 (.0070)	.0317 (.3429)	8.01*
U.S./Japan	CPI	−.0028 (.0177)	.9623 (.2902)	.24
U.S./Japan	WPI	.0379 (.0125)	.0467 (.2350)	16.81**

B. Three-Month Eurocurrency Rates (January 1976–July 1981)

Countries	Price Index	$\hat{a}$	$\hat{b}$	Test Statistic
U.S./U.K.	CPI	−.0156 (.0084)	.7464 (.2135)	3.47
U.S./U.K.	WPI	−.0165 (.0093)	1.0665 (.1544)	4.15
U.S./Germany	CPI	.0380 (.0075)	.2997 (.1520)	26.02**
U.S./Germany	WPI	.0488 (.0122)	−.0972 (.2690)	17.68**
U.S./Switzerland	CPI	.0335 (.0085)	.2945 (.1436)	25.32**
U.S./Switzerland	WPI	.0815 (.0137)	−.2740 (.1883)	46.04**
U.S./Canada	CPI	.0076 (.0040)	.3302 (.1238)	62.72**
U.S./Canada	WPI	−.0091 (.0039)	.2541 (.1816)	17.35**
U.S./Japan	CPI	.0060 (.0107)	.8323 (.1806)	1.40
U.S./Japan	WPI	.0446 (.0114)	−.1133 (.2223)	26.06**

Table 3.2 (continued)

C. Domestic Money Market Rates (January 1976–July 1981)

Countries	Price Index	$\hat{a}$	$\hat{b}$	Test Statistic
U.S./U.K.	CPI	−.0134 (.0074)	.7554 (.2400)	3.34
U.S./U.K.	WPI	−.0153 (.0102)	1.1464 (.1974)	6.34*
U.S./Germany	CPI	.0379 (.0043)	.3137 (.1276)	78.85**
U.S./Germany	WPI	.0355 (.0088)	.1643 (.2569)	16.44**
U.S./Switzerland	CPI	.0352 (.0074)	.3451 (.1438)	23.11**
U.S./Switzerland	WPI	.0707 (.0108)	−.1144 (.1461)	58.37**
U.S./Canada	CPI	.0018 (.0049)	.2721 (.1015)	73.85**
U.S./Canada	WPI	−.0056 (.0046)	.2942 (.2032)	14.60**
U.S./Japan	CPI	.0180 (.0077)	.7229 (.1822)	5.47
U.S./Japan	WPI	.0385 (.0097)	−.5492 (.2290)	48.06**

Note: Standard errors appear in parentheses. The test statistic is distributed asymptotically as $\chi^2(2)$. * = rejection at the 5% level; ** = rejection at the 1% level.

In the case of the United Kingdom, the evidence is on the whole very favorable to the hypothesis that ex ante real rates in the United States and United Kingdom have been equal during the recent years of floating exchange rates. While the United States/United Kingdom test statistic lies in the 5% critical region in one case and is quite high in the others, the large size of the estimated constant term ($\hat{a}$) relative to its estimated standard error is often the cause. In contrast, the estimated slope coefficient ($\hat{b}$) is, in half the cases, within a standard deviation of unity. This evidence is consistent with the existence of a constant ex ante real interest differential between the United States and the United Kingdom. The evidence therefore suggests that real interest rates in the two countries, though possibly different, are closely linked.

Tests for Japan using CPI inflation rates and Eurocurrency interest rates support the hypothesis of real interest rate equality. When WPI inflation rates are used in defining real interest rates, however, the hypothesis is easily rejected. Use of the CPI inflation rate together with the domestic money market nominal interest rate yields a χ^2 statistic that is quite close to the critical value of 5.99.

An interesting feature of the results is that nominal interest differentials have significant explanatory power in equations with the CPI inflation differential as the dependent variable, but do not usually help in forecasting relative WPI inflation rates. The United Kingdom is again an exception in this respect: nominal United States–United Kingdom interest differentials are significant (and relatively unbiased) predictors of CPI *and* WPI inflation rates. The greater importance of the interest differential in CPI regressions is not surprising, for the expected future CPI is probably a better measure of the anticipated future "real" value of money to consumers than is the expected WPI.[15]

The tests demonstrate that ex ante real interest rate equality is often rejected decisively over the recent floating exchange rate period. In an attempt to shed light on the reasons for rejection, we now examine the two components of the hypothesis, uncovered interest parity and ex ante purchasing power parity.

3.4 Expectations and Nominal Interest Differentials

The hypothesis that expected exchange rate movements offset nominal interest differentials so as to equalize expected nominal yields internationally has been tested extensively. Work in this area by Frenkel (1981) generally supports the view that uncovered interest rate parity (UIP) has held quite closely over the period of generalized floating. However, a number of other studies reject the same hypothesis quite strongly (see Geweke and Feige 1979; Tyron 1979; Hansen and Hodrick 1980, 1983; Bilson 1981; Cumby and Obstfeld 1981; Hakkio 1981; Longworth 1981; Hsieh 1982; among others).

We discuss below some econometric issues that arise in tests of UIP. Among these, once again, is the problem of conditional heteroscedasticity, which is found to be important in the recent data. Tests of UIP which take this problem into account are performed, and these provide strong evidence against that hypothesis.

3.4.1 A Test of the Hypothesis

In the absence of default risk or transaction costs, covered interest arbitrage equates the forward premium on foreign exchange to the nominal interest differential between home and foreign currency bonds. Keynes (1923) provides the classic exposition. Denoting by $F_{k,t}$ the k-period forward price of foreign exchange, the covered interest parity condition may be written as

$$(16) \qquad R_{k,t} - R_{k,t}^* = \ln (F_{k,t}) - \ln (S_t).$$

Empirical studies such as Frenkel and Levich (1975, 1977, 1981), Marston

---

15. Fama (1975) uses the CPI inflation rate in his study of the predictive power of United States short-term interest rates.

(1976), and McCormick (1979), show that (16) holds quite closely in the Eurocurrency market, where the interest-bearing assets being compared have identical default and political risk characteristics.

If UIP holds, then (3) and (16) imply that

(17) $$E_t[ln\ (S_{t+k})] = \ln\ (F_{k,t})$$

or, equivalently, that

(18) $$\ln\ (S_{t+k}) = \ln\ (F_{k,t}) + v_{t+k},$$

where v_{t+k}, the k-period forecast error $\ln\ (S_{t+k}) - E_t[\ln\ (S_{t+k})]$, has mean zero and is uncorrelated with information available at the end of period t. According to (18), the logarithm of the forward rate is an unbiased predictor of the future spot rate, and 1-period-ahead forecast errors ($k = 1$) are serially uncorrelated. When UIP fails, (17) becomes

(19) $$E_t[\ln\ (S_{t+k})] = \ln\ (F_{k,t}) + \phi_t$$

where ϕ_t is a risk premium which may fluctuate through time and may be serially correlated. Recent theoretical work shows that when asset holders are risk averse, market efficiency is consistent with the existence of a non-zero, possibly time-varying, risk premium (see, e.g., Grauer, Litzenberger, and Stehle 1976; Kouri 1977; Stockman 1978; Frankel 1979b; Hodrick 1981; Stulz 1981). When a nonzero risk premium exists, bonds denominated in different currencies are imperfect substitutes in portfolios. The empirical implications of imperfect asset substitutability are that $\ln\ (F_{k,t})$ is not in general an unbiased predictor of $\ln\ (S_{t+k})$ and that the forward forecast error $\ln\ (S_{t+k}) - \ln\ (F_{k,t})$ need not be uncorrelated with information available to the market at time t.

Frenkel (1981) tests UIP by estimating the parameters of the equation

(20) $$\ln\ (S_{t+1}) = a + b\ \ln\ (F_{1,t}) + v_{t+1}$$

using monthly data (sampled from June 1973 to July 1979) on the spot and 1-month-forward dollar prices of the pound sterling, the French franc, and the deutsche mark.[16] A test of the hypothesis $[a\ b]' = [0\ 1]'$ is a test of the UIP condition. Frenkel finds that the results of estimation are "broadly consistent" with the hypothesis that nominal interest differentials can be explained entirely by expected exchange rate movements.

A problem with the foregoing test, pointed out by Hansen and Hodrick (1980) and by Meese and Singleton (1982), is that the stochastic processes generating the logarithms of spot and forward exchange rates may be nonstationary. Even though least squares estimates of a and b in (20) will often

16. Similar tests have been conducted by Frenkel (1976) (for the German experience of the 1920s), Stockman (1978), and Frankel (1980). Levich (1978, 1979) surveys the early literature in this area.

be consistent in a nonstationary estimation environment, the usual asymptotic theory invoked to construct hypothesis tests becomes inapplicable. Mussa's (1979) observation that the logarithms of exchange rates seem to follow approximately a random walk is supported by statistical tests implemented by Meese and Singleton (1982). These tests, which involve the United States dollar's exchange rate against the Canadian dollar, the Swiss franc, and the deutsche mark, cannot reject the hypothesis that unit roots are present in the univariate autoregressive representations of the logarithms of spot and forward rates. The Meese-Singleton findings suggest that the possibility of nonstationarity needs to be taken seriously in designing and evaluating hypothesis tests involving exchange rates.

A procedure that often avoids the unit-root problem is to test whether $a = 0$ and $b = 1$ in the equation

$$(21) \qquad \ln (S_{t+k}/S_t) = a + b \ln (F_{k,t}/S_t) + v_{t+k}.$$

Under the hypothesis of UIP, (21) is equivalent to (20), and states that the k-period forward premium is the market's expectation of the change in the logarithm of the spot rate over the next k periods. Like the tests cited above as rejecting UIP, the test just described works in terms of first differences rather than levels. Thus, the asymptotic theory used in testing is more likely to be justifiable.

Equation (21) is estimated below, and the hypothesis that $a = 0$ and $b = 1$ is tested. The tests are bilateral (unlike Bilson's [1981]), but expand Frenkel's (1981) information set by using third-currency forward premia observed at time t (which are uncorrelated with the disturbance v_{t+k}) as instrumental variables in forming 2S2SLS estimates of $[a\ b]'$. This yields parameter estimates more efficient than those produced by OLS, and so a more stringent test of the null hypothesis. Like Hansen and Hodrick (1980), we use weekly data on 3-month forecasts.

3.4.2 A Test of Conditional Homoscedasticity

Tests of UIP have almost universally assumed that the conditional covariances of forecast errors do not depend on lagged forward premia.[17] Because the forward premium is not a strictly exogenous variable, this assumption may be false, in which case the customary standard error estimators have no asymptotic justification. As in the previous section, it is therefore of interest to test the conditional homoscedasticity assumption formally under the null hypothesis that UIP holds.

This can once again be done by estimating the equation

$$(22) \qquad v_{t+k}^2 = \alpha + \beta \ln (F_{k,t}/S_t) + \gamma \ln (F_{k,t}/S_t)^2 + \epsilon_{t+k}.$$

17. Hansen and Hodrick (1980) make this assumption explicitly. In a later paper, Hansen and Hodrick (1983) allow for conditional heteroscedasticity in testing a forward foreign exchange pricing model. Hsieh (1982) accounts for conditional heteroscedasticity in his tests and obtains results similar to those reported in table 3.5 below.

Table 3.3   **Conditional Homoscedasticity of Forward-Rate Forecast Errors (Weekly Data January 1976–June 1981)**

Exchange Rate	Test Statistic
U.S./U.K.	308.13**
U.S./Germany	26.38**
U.S./Switzerland	13.20**
U.S./Canada	2.57
U.S./Japan	141.05**

Note: The test statistic is distributed asymptotically as $\chi^2(2)$. * = rejection at the 5% level; ** = rejection at the 1% level.

Under conditional homoscedasticity, the expected value of v_{t+k}^2 conditional on forward premia observed at time t is a constant. Thus, we should find that $\beta = \gamma = 0$ in (22). As before, any variable in the conditioning set may be used as an instrumental variable in forming 2S2SLS estimates of (22).

Table 3.3 reports the results of testing the conditional homoscedasticity of 3-month forward rate forecast errors.[18] The tests involve the United States dollar's exchange rate against the pound sterling, the deutsche mark, the Swiss franc, the Canadian dollar, and the Japanese yen. Weekly data running from January 7, 1976 to June 24, 1981 are employed. The data are aligned to account for timing problems caused by bank holidays and weekends.[19]

In four of five cases, the null hypothesis of conditional homoscedasticity is strongly rejected. For the Canadian dollar, there is weak evidence against conditional homoscedasticity. The results suggest that a heteroscedasticity-consistent covariance matrix estimator should be used in conducting hypothesis tests on the coefficients of equation (21).

3.4.3 Empirical Results

Results of estimating (21) and testing UIP appear in table 3.4.[20] In all cases save that of the dollar–deutsche mark exchange rate, the null hypothesis of UIP can be rejected at the 5% level. In the case of Canada, however, rejection is entirely due to the large size of $\hat{a}$ relative to its estimated standard error. As the estimated slope coefficient $\hat{b}$ is quite close to unity, the rejection in the Canadian case cannot be considered very strong.

In four of five cases, the 3-month-forward premium has on average mispredicted the direction of movement of the subsequently observed spot rate.

18. The instrumental variables were the time t forward premia and squared forward premia for all countries in the sample.

19. See Riehl and Rodriguez (1977) and Meese and Singleton (1982).

20. The instrumental variables were the time t forward premia for all countries in the sample.

Table 3.4   **Tests of Uncovered Interest Parity (Weekly Data, January 1976– June 1981)**

Exchange Rate	$\hat{a}$	$\hat{b}$	Test Statistic
U.S./U.K.	.0086	−.2881	16.16**
	(.0156)	(.9741)	
U.S./Germany	.0214	−.7815	3.59
	(.0113)	(1.1579)	
U.S./Switzerland	.0481	−2.2145	9.11*
	(.0214)	(1.1177)	
U.S./Canada	−.0076	.8285	12.44**
	(.0023)	(.7922)	
U.S./Japan	.0311	−2.8316	41.58**
	(.0097)	(.6740)	

Note: Standard errors appear in parentheses. The test statistic is distributed asymptotically as $\chi^2(2)$. * = rejection at the 5% level; ** = rejection at the 1% level.

In the remaining case (that of Canada), the slope coefficient, while of the correct sign, is insignificantly different from zero. The test results are on the whole inconsistent with UIP, and they also suggest that forward premia contain little information regarding subsequent exchange rate fluctuations. As emphasized by Dornbusch (1978, 1980), Mussa (1979), and Frenkel (1981), exchange rate changes over the recent period of floating seem to have been largely unanticipated.

3.4.4 An Additional Test

As a check on the validity of the conclusions reached above, an additional test, suggested by Geweke and Feige (1979) and by Hansen and Hodrick (1980), was performed. If UIP holds, then with weekly data and 3-month forward rates, the forward forecast error v_{t+13} must be uncorrelated with any information dated t or earlier. In particular, if v_{t+13} is regressed on a constant, on v_t, and on the time t forward forecast errors for the other four currencies, one should not be able to reject the hypothesis that all coefficients equal zero. The results of this test are reported in table 3.5. The equations were estimated by OLS, but the standard errors were calculated using a heteroscedasticity-consistent technique.

Rejection at the 5% level again occurs in all cases except that of Germany. Thus, the results of the present test are quite similar to those of table 3.4. In addition, most of the estimated constant terms (Canada is the exception) are quite insignificant. None of the rejections in table 3.5 appears to be caused exclusively by the large size of an estimated constant term relative to its standard error. Note that while the present tests are unable to reject UIP for dollar and deutsche mark deposits, tests by Hansen and Hodrick (1980) using a different data sample do reject that hypothesis.

While the two tests performed above cast considerable doubt on the hy-

Table 3.5   Tests of Uncovered Interest Parity (Weekly Data, April 1976–June 1981)

Exchange Rate	$\hat{a}$	$\hat{b}_1$	$\hat{b}_2$	$\hat{b}_3$	$\hat{b}_4$	$\hat{b}_5$	Test Statistic
U.S./U.K.	.0088	.1147	.5759	−.1979	.3059	.0054	22.91**
	(.0112)	(.2102)	(.3178)	(.2050)	(.3963)	(.1809)	
U.S./Germany	−.0049	−.0176	.0925	.2396	.2117	.0187	7.61
	(.0098)	(.1509)	(.2750)	(.1695)	(.4463)	(.1785)	
U.S./Switzerland	−.0071	−.1493	−.0304	.1529	.4762	.2333	13.00*
	(.0137)	(.2137)	(.3820)	(.3087)	(.6477)	(.2621)	
U.S./Canada	−.0093	−.0464	−.0231	.0089	−.2190	−.1060	50.97**
	(.0030)	(.0462)	(.1037)	(.0598)	(.1479)	(.0430)	
U.S./Japan	.0042	−.1462	.0066	−.0121	.5836	.4679	21.69**
	(.0115)	(.2070)	(.3304)	(.2530)	(.4316)	(.1439)	

Note: Standard errors appear in parentheses. The coefficient a represents a constant. The b_i ($i = 1, \ldots , 5$) are the coefficients of the lagged forecast errors for the five currencies. b_1 = U.K., b_2 = Germany, b_3 = Switzerland, b_4 = Canada, and b_5 = Japan. The test statistic is distributed asymptotically as $\chi^2(6)$.
* = rejection at the 5% level; ** = rejection at the 1% level.

pothesis of perfect asset substitutability, their results should be interpreted with caution. First, political uncertainties or fears of bank failures may have introduced an element of default risk into forward transactions during the sample period. A second issue is the "peso problem" (Rogoff 1979 and Krasker 1980), which is essentially a problem of finite sample inference. If agents, over some significant time period, expect a major central bank intervention which does not materialize, nonoverlapping forward forecast errors will be correlated in the sample even if the expectation of intervention is rational in the light of past central bank behavior. While agents would be correct on average given an infinite sample containing infinitely many such episodes, econometricians have only a finite history at their disposal. The dramatic central bank interventions in the fourth quarters of 1978 and 1979 are examples of the type of event which, if incorrectly anticipated ex post, may give rise to a spurious correlation in nonoverlapping forecast errors.

3.5 Exchange Rates and National Price Levels

The absolute version of the purchasing power parity (PPP) doctrine has not fared well in econometric tests on recent data, at least not in tests involving the United States (see, e.g., Krugman 1978; Frenkel 1981). Figures 3.6–3.10 display the time series of monthly first differences of the logarithm of the real exchange rates of the United Kingdom, Germany, Switzerland, Canada, and Japan against the United States. The real exchange rate is defined as the dollar "value" of the foreign WPI divided by the United States WPI. The figures reveal that for all countries, the floating rate period has been a period of much higher real exchange rate variability vis-à-vis the United States than was the Bretton Woods era.[21] The increase in the amplitude of deviations from PPP begins abruptly with the adoption of flexible rates.[22]

Here, we test whether relative PPP holds ex ante, that is, whether expected exchange rate depreciation reflects the expected inflation differential between the home and foreign countries. If ex ante PPP does not hold, ex ante real interest rates will generally differ internationally. As Magee (1978) and Roll (1979) observe, under certain assumptions ex ante PPP is a consequence of the efficiency of international commodity markets. Both Roll (1979) and Frenkel (1981) present evidence that changes in real exchange rates are serially uncorrelated, and thus possess a key property of forecast error series.

21. There are two sharp jumps in the German series over the Bretton Woods period. These correspond to the deutsche mark revaluations of 1961 and 1969. The spike in the United Kingdom series corresponds to the sterling devaluation of 1967.
22. Genberg (1978) also notes this phenomenon.

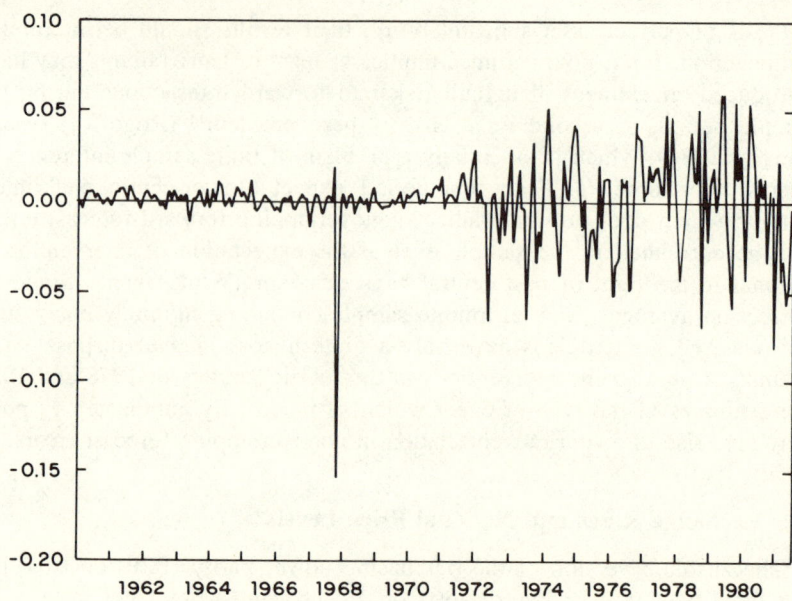

Fig. 3.6   Change in the real exchange rate between the United States and
the United Kingdom (monthly data).

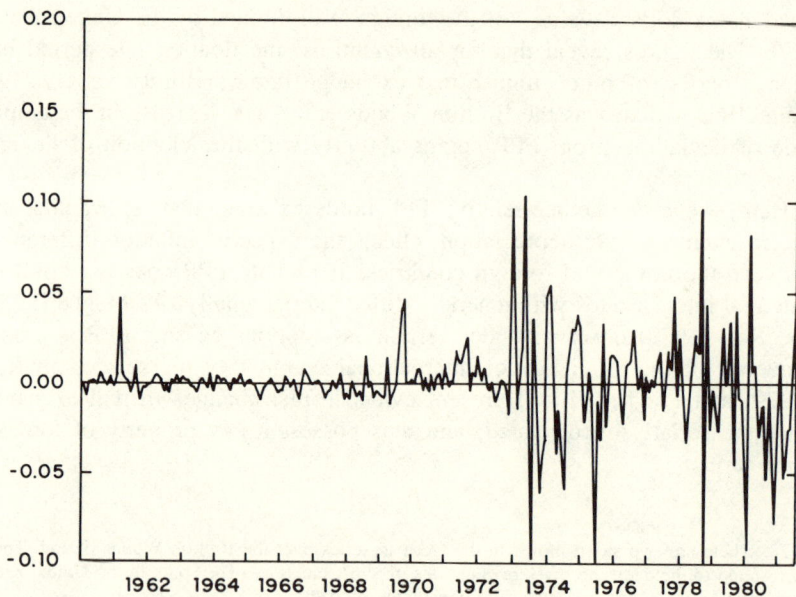

Fig. 3.7   Change in the real exchange rate between the United States and
Germany (monthly data).

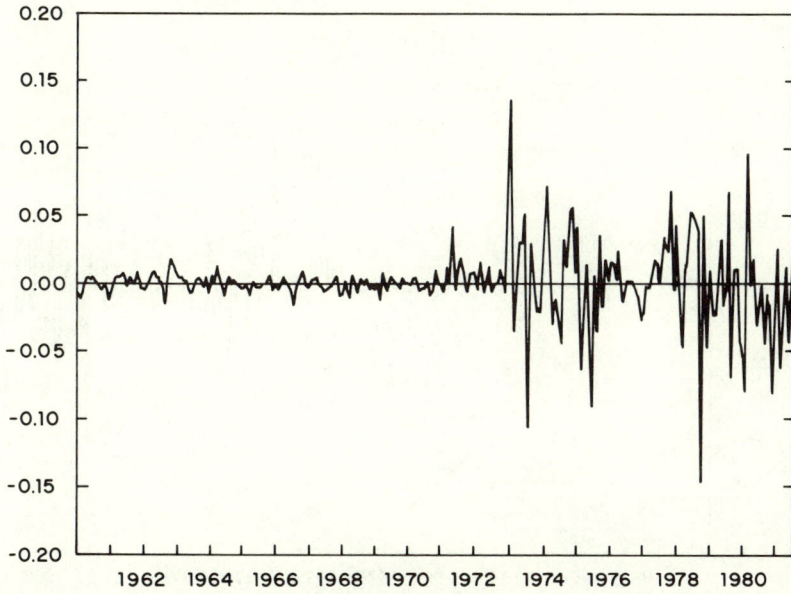

Fig. 3.8   Change in the real exchange rate between the United States and Switzerland (monthly data).

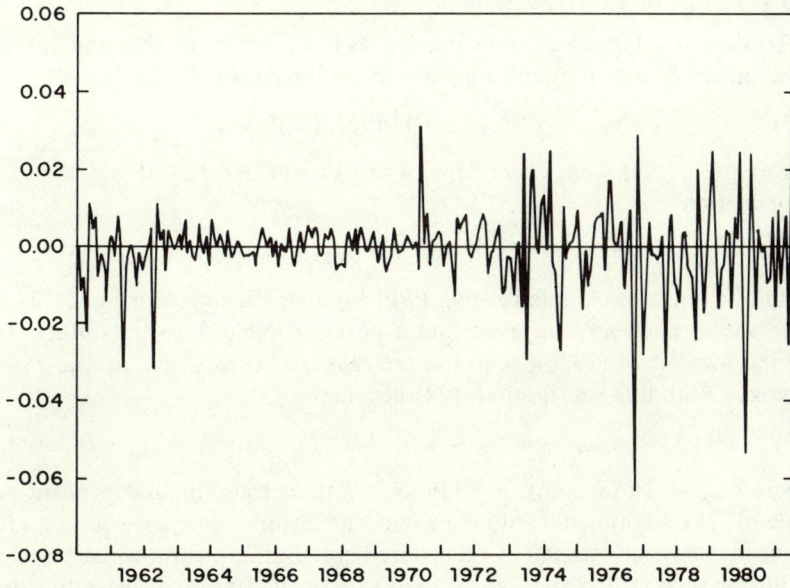

Fig. 3.9   Change in the real exchange rate between the United States and Canada (monthly data).

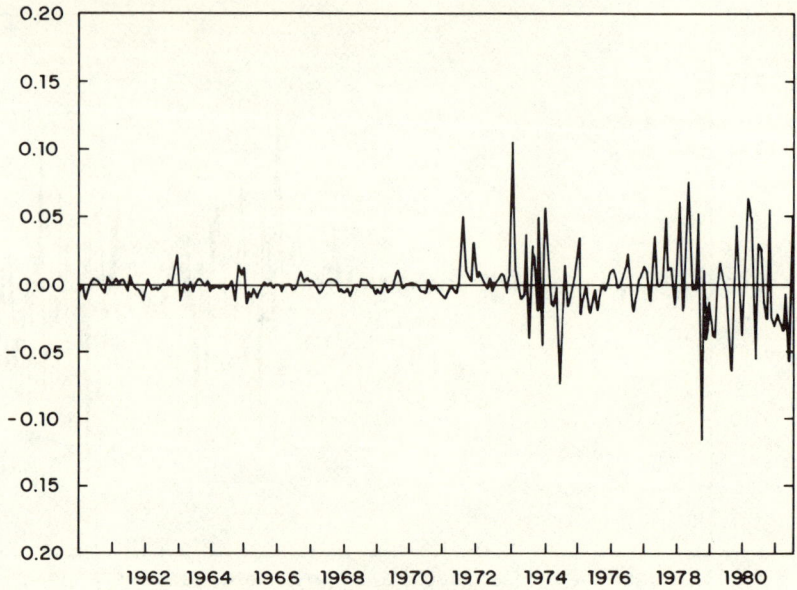

Fig. 3.10   Change in the real exchange rate between the United States and Japan (monthly data).

3.5.1 A Test of the Hypothesis

To design a test of ex ante relative PPP we return to equation (2). By combining (2) with (6a) and (6b) we obtain the equation

$$(23) \qquad \pi_{t+k} - \pi^*_{t+k} = E_t[\ln (S_{t+k}/S_t)] + u_{t+k} - u^*_{t+k}.$$

If $E_t[\ln (S_{t+k}/S_t)]$ were observable, a test of whether $a = 0$ and $b = 1$ in the equation

$$(24) \qquad \pi_{t+k} - \pi^*_{t+k} = a + b\, E_t[\ln (S_{t+k}/S_t)] + e_{t+k}$$

would be a test of ex ante relative PPP. Because the regressor in (24) is not observable, however, we must find a proxy variable. One possibility, following McCallum (1976), is to use the *realized* depreciation $\ln (S_{t+k}/S_t)$ as a proxy. With this substitution, (24) becomes

$$(25) \qquad \pi_{t+k} - \pi^*_{t+k} = a + b \ln (S_{t+k}/S_t) + e_{t+k} - bv_{t+k},$$

where $v_{t+k} = \ln (S_{t+k}/S_t) - E_t[\ln (S_{t+k}/S_t)]$. Because the independent variable in (25) is correlated with the composite disturbance $e_{t+k} - bv_{t+k}$, OLS is an inconsistent estimation procedure here. But an instrumental variables estimator such as 2S2SLS can be used to estimate $[a\ b]'$ consistently. Since e_{t+k} and v_{t+k} are rational forecast errors, any relevant variables in the time t information set may be used as instrumental variables.

Table 3.6   **Tests of Ex Ante PPP (September 1975–May 1981)**

Countries	Price Index	$\hat{a}$	$\hat{b}$	Test Statistic
U.S./U.K.	CPI	−.0033	.1660	48.32**
		(.0010)	(.1205)	
U.S./U.K.	WPI	−.0048	−.1763	17.07**
		(.0012)	(.3415)	
U.S./Germany	CPI	.0033	.1902	166.21**
		(.0006)	(.0789)	
U.S./Germany	WPI	.0034	−.1707	94.25**
		(.0009)	(.1218)	
U.S./Switzerland	CPI	.0037	.1174	63.98**
		(.0007)	(.1111)	
U.S./Switzerland	WPI	.0073	−.2333	29.94**
		(.0018)	(.2255)	
U.S./Canada	CPI	−.0003	.0822	65.13**
		(.0005)	(.1395)	
U.S./Canada	WPI	−.0002	.1984	26.87**
		(.0007)	(.1786)	
U.S./Japan	CPI	.0007	.1523	21.46**
		(.0012)	(.1848)	
U.S./Japan	WPI	.0037	.0330	180.79**
		(.0008)	(.0725)	

Note: Standard errors appear in parentheses. The test statistic is distributed asymptotically as $\chi^2(2)$. * = rejection at the 5% level; ** = rejection at the 1% level.

3.5.2 Empirical Results

Results of estimating (25) over a 1-month forecasting horizon with monthly data are reported in table 3.6.[23] As in the previous tests, a heteroscedasticity consistent covariance matrix estimator was employed. Tests of the null hypothesis for a 3-month forecasting horizon were also performed, but these are not reported as they only reinforce the message of table 3.6.

That message is that expected exchange rate changes have been poor and biased predictors of relative inflation rates over the years of generalized floating. The hypothesis $a = 0$ and $b = 1$ is decisively rejected for all countries, regardless of the price index used. Further, the estimated slope coefficients are almost always insignificant and frequently of the wrong sign. The one exception to this occurs in the case of the dollar–deutsche mark rate, where we find that the expected depreciation rate does help forecast the United States–German CPI inflation differential.

Table 3.7 uses the adjusted Q-statistic of Ljung and Box (1978) to test whether real exchange rate changes have been serially uncorrelated in recent

23. Instruments were lagged inflation differentials vis-à-vis the United States for all countries in the sample.

Table 3.7   Tests for Serial Correlation of Real Exchange Rate Changes (September 1975–May 1981)

Countries	Price Index	Test Statistic	Marginal Significance Level
U.S./U.K.	CPI	7.79	.80
U.S./U.K.	WPI	10.63	.56
U.S./Germany	CPI	7.09	.85
U.S./Germany	WPI	7.73	.81
U.S./Switzerland	CPI	4.30	.98
U.S./Switzerland	WPI	5.00	.96
U.S./Canada	CPI	17.62	.13
U.S./Canada	WPI	16.11	.19
U.S./Japan	CPI	11.88	.46
U.S./Japan	WPI	8.08	.78

Note: The test statistic is distributed asymptotically as $\chi^2(12)$.

years. The test statistics, which are computed for 12 lags using monthly data, confirm the Roll-Frenkel finding that real exchange rate changes are not serially correlated. Only in the Canadian case can the null hypothesis of no serial correlation be rejected at better than the 20% significance level. While the foregoing evidence supports ex ante relative PPP, the results of table 3.6 are strongly at variance with that hypothesis. On balance, it seems reasonable to conclude that the "efficient markets" version of relative PPP has not characterized the recent experience with floating rates.

3.6 Conclusion

This paper has studied the interplay among price levels, interest rates, and exchange rates over the recent period of managed exchange rate flexibility. Attention was focused on the two classical parity conditions that link prices and nominal interest rates internationally and on their corollary, the international equality of ex ante real rates of interest. Econometric tests of these propositions within a rational expectations framework provided significant evidence against them. As a by-product of the investigation, we found that inflation and exchange rate forecast errors appear to be conditionally heteroscedastic.

When monetary disturbances are dominant, the classical parity relationships may be a reliable guide to the comovements of nominal macro variables. But the past decade has been characterized by moderate inflation coupled with substantial real disturbances. In such circumstances, the classical conditions appear to be too simple and aggregative to provide an adequate explanation of macroeconomic events in a world of differentiated commodities and assets.

Whether the failure of the parity relations has conferred monetary autonomy on small open economies is an entirely distinct question. Further theoretical and empirical research is needed before a confident answer can be ventured.

Appendix: The Data

Section 3.3

Prices: WPIs are taken from *International Financial Statistics* (IFS), line 63. CPIs come from IFS, line 64.
Interest Rates: The 1- and 3-month Eurocurrency deposit rates come from Data Resources, Inc. (for the United Kingdom, Germany, and Switzerland) and from the Harris Bank of Chicago *Weekly Review* (for Canada and Japan). The 3-month domestic money market rates come from Morgan Guaranty's *World Financial Markets,* and are quoted at or near the end of the month. For the United States, the rate on prime industrial paper is used. Interbank deposit rates are used for the United Kingdom, Germany, and Switzerland. For Canada, the rate used is that on prime finance company paper. The interest rate on 3-month repurchase agreements is used as the Japanese money market rate.

Section 3.4

Spot and 3-month-forward exchange rates are noon rates collected by the Federal Reserve System. Spot rates are matched to the maturity of the corresponding forward contract, as described by Riehl and Rodriguez (1977). Morgan Guaranty's *World Calendar of Holidays* is used to account for bank holidays, weekends, etc.

Section 3.5

Prices: Same as Section 3.3.
Exchange Rates: End-of-month rates taken from *IFS,* line ag.

References

Ansley, C. F.; Spivey, W. A.; and Wrobleski, W. J. 1977. On the structure of moving average processes. *Journal of Econometrics* 6 121–34.
Bilson, J. F. O. 1979. Recent developments in monetary models of ex-

change rate determination. International Monetary Fund *Staff Papers* 26 (June): 201–23.

————. 1981. The 'speculative efficiency' hypothesis. *Journal of Business* 54 (July): 435–52.

Branson, W. H. 1979. Exchange rate dynamics and monetary policy. In *Inflation and Employment in Open Economies,* ed. A. Lindbeck. Amsterdam: North-Holland.

Cumby, R. E., and Obstfeld, M. 1981. A note on exchange-rate expectations and nominal interest differentials: A test of the Fisher hypothesis. *Journal of Finance* 36 (June): 697–704.

Cumby, R. E.; Huizinga, J.; and Obstfeld, M. 1983. Two-step two-stage least squares estimation in models with rational expectations. *Journal of Econometrics* 21 (April): 333–55.

Dhrymes, P. J. 1974. *Econometrics: Statistical foundations and applications.* New York: Springer-Verlag.

Dornbusch, R. 1976. Expectations and exchange rate dynamics. *Journal of Political Economy* 84 (December): 1161–76.

————. 1978. Monetary policy under exchange rate flexibility. In *Managed exchange-rate flexibility: The recent experience.* Federal Reserve Bank of Boston Conference Series no. 20. Boston: Federal Reserve Bank of Boston.

————. 1980. Exchange rate economics: Where do we stand? *Brookings Papers on Economic Activity* 11:143–85.

Engle, R. F. 1982. Autoregressive conditional heteroscedasticity with estimates of the variance of United Kingdom inflation. *Econometrica* 50 (July): 987–1007.

Fama, E. F. 1975. Short-term interest rates as predictors of inflation. *American Economic Review* 65 (June): 269–82.

————. 1977. Interest rates and inflation: The message in the entrails. *American Economic Review* 67 (June): 487–96.

Fisher, I. 1930. *The theory of interest.* New York: Macmillan.

Frankel, J. A. 1979a. On the mark: A theory of floating exchange rates based on real interest differentials. *American Economic Review* 69 (September): 610–22.

————. 1979b. The diversifiability of exchange risk. *Journal of International Economics* 9 (August): 379–94.

————. 1980. Tests of rational expectations in the forward exchange market. *Southern Economic Journal* 46 (April): 1083–1101.

Frenkel, J. A. 1976. A monetary approach to the exchange rate: Doctrinal aspects and empirical evidence. *Scandinavian Journal of Economics* 78 (May): 200–224.

————. 1978. Purchasing power parity: Doctrinal perspectives and evidence from the 1920's. *Journal of International Economics* 8 (May): 169–91.

————. 1981. Flexible exchange rates, prices, and the role of 'news': Lessons from the 1970s. *Journal of Political Economy* 89 (August): 665–705.

Frenkel, J. A., and Levich, R. M. 1975. Covered interest arbitrage: Unexploited profits? *Journal of Political Economy* 83 (April): 325–38.

―――. 1977. Transaction costs and interest arbitrage: Tranquil versus turbulent periods. *Journal of Political Economy* 85 (December): 1209–26.

―――. 1981. Covered interest arbitrage in the 1970's. *Economics Letters* 8: 267–74.

Genberg, H. 1978. Purchasing power parity under fixed and flexible exchange rates. *Journal of International Economics* 8 (May): 247–76.

Geweke, J. F., and Feige, E. L. 1979. Some joint tests of the efficiency of markets for forward foreign exchange. *Review of Economics and Statistics* 61 (August): 334–41.

Girton, L., and Henderson, D. W. 1977. Central bank operations in foreign and domestic assets under fixed and flexible exchange rates. In *The Effects of exchange rate adjustments,* ed. P. B. Clark, D. Logue, and R. Sweeney. Washington, D.C.: U.S. Government Printing Office.

Grauer, F.; Litzenberger, R.; and Stehle, R. 1976. Sharing rules and equilibrium in an international capital market under uncertainty. *Journal of Financial Economics* 3 (June): 233–56.

Hakkio, C. S. 1981. The term structure of the forward premium. *Journal of Monetary Economics* 8 (July): 41–58.

Hansen, L. P. 1982. Large sample properties of generalized method of moments estimators. *Econometrica* 50 (July): 1029–54.

Hansen, L. P., and Hodrick, R. J. 1980. Forward exchange rates as optimal predictors of future spot rates: An econometric analysis. *Journal of Political Economy* 88 (October): 829–53.

―――. 1983. Risk averse speculation in the forward foreign exchange market: An econometric analysis of linear models. In *Exchange rates and international macroeconomics,* ed. J. A. Frenkel. Chicago: University of Chicago Press (for the National Bureau of Economic Research).

Henderson, D. W. Exchange market intervention operations: Their effects and their role in financial policy. This volume.

Hodrick, R. J. 1978. An empirical analysis of the monetary approach to the determination of the exchange rate. In *The economics of exchange rates,* ed. J. A. Frenkel and H. G. Johnson. Reading: Addison-Wesley.

―――. 1979. Some evidence on the equality of expected real interest rates across countries. Working Paper, Graduate School of Industrial Administration, Carnegie-Mellon University.

―――. 1981. International asset pricing with time-varying risk premia. *Journal of International Economics* 11 (November): 573–87.

Hooper, P., and Morton, J. 1982. Fluctuations in the dollar: A model of nominal and real exchange rate determination. *Journal of International Money and Finance* 1 (1982): in press.

Hsieh, D. A. 1982. Tests of rational expectations and no risk premium in forward exchange markets. Working Paper no. 843, National Bureau of Economic Research, Cambridge, Mass.

Keynes, J. M. 1923. *A tract on monetary reform.* London: Macmillan.

Kouri, P. J. K. 1977. International investment and interest rate linkages under flexible exchange rates. In *The political economy of monetary reform,* ed. R. Z. Aliber. London: Macmillan.

Krasker, W. S. 1980. The 'peso problem' in testing the efficiency of forward exchange markets. *Journal of Monetary Economics* 6 (April): 269–76.

Krugman, P. R. 1978. Purchasing power parity and exchange rates: Another look at the evidence. *Journal of International Economics* 8 (August): 397–407.

Levich, R. M. 1978. Further results on the efficiency of markets for foreign exchange. In *Managed exchange-rate flexibility: The recent experience.* Federal Reserve Bank of Boston Conference Series no. 20. Boston: Federal Researve Bank of Boston.

———. 1979. On the efficiency of markets for foreign exchange. In *International economic policy: Theory and evidence,* ed. R. Dornbusch and J. A. Frenkel. Baltimore: Johns Hopkins University Press.

Ljung, C. M., and Box, G. E. P. 1978. On a measure of lack of fit in time series models. *Biometrika* 65: 297–303.

Longworth, D. 1981. Testing the efficiency of the Canadian–U.S. exchange market under the assumption of no risk premium. *Journal of Finance* 36 (March): 43–9.

McCallum, B. T. 1976. Rational expectations and the natural rate hypothesis: Some consistent estimates. *Econometrica* 44 (January): 43–52.

McCormick, F. 1979. Covered interest arbitrage: Unexploited profits? Comment. *Journal of Political Economy* 87 (April): 411–17.

Magee, S. P. 1978. Contracting and spurious deviations from purchasing power parity. In *The economics of exchange rates,* ed. J. A. Frenkel and H. G. Johnson. Reading: Addison-Wesley.

Marston, R. C. 1976. Interest arbitrage in the Eurocurrency markets. *European Economic Review* 7 (January): 1–13.

Meese, R. A., and Singleton, K. J. 1982. A note on unit roots and the empirical modeling of exchange rates. *Journal of Finance* 37 (Sept.): 1029–36.

Mishkin, F. S. 1981. The real interest rate: An empirical investigation. In *The costs and consequences of inflation,* ed. K. Brunner and A. H. Meltzer. Carnegie-Rochester Conference Series on Public Policy vol. 15 (supplementary series to the *Journal of Monetary Economics,* 1981).

———. 1982. The real interest rate: A multi-country empirical study. Parts I and II. Working Paper, Department of Economics, University of Chicago.

Mussa, M. 1979. Empirical regularities in the behavior of exchange rates and theories of the foreign exchange market. In *Policies for employment, prices, and exchange rates,* ed. K. Brunner and A. H. Meltzer. Carnegie-Rochester Conference Series on Public Policy vol. 11 (supplementary series to the *Journal of Monetary Economics,* 1979).

————. 1982. A model of exchange rate dynamics. *Journal of Political Economy* 90 (February): 74–104.

Nelson, C. R., and Schwert, G. W. 1977. Short-term interest rates as predictors of inflation: On testing the hypothesis that the real rate of interest is constant. *American Economic Review* 67 (June): 478–86.

Obstfeld, M. 1982a. Relative prices, employment, and the exchange rate in an economy with foresight. *Econometrica* 50 (Sept.): 1219–42.

————. 1982b. Can we sterilize? Theory and evidence. *American Economic Review, Papers and Proceedings* 72 (May): 45–50.

Riehl, H., and Rodriguez, R. M. 1977. *Foreign exchange markets.* New York: McGraw-Hill.

Rogoff, K. S. 1979. Essays on expectations and exchange rate volatility. Unpublished Doctoral Dissertation, Massachusetts Institute of Technology.

Roll, R. 1979. Violations of purchasing power parity and their implications for efficient international commodity markets. In *International Finance and Trade,* ed. M. Sarnat and G. P. Szego. Vol. 1. Cambridge: Ballinger.

Roll, R., and Solnik, B. 1979. On some parity conditions frequently encountered in international economics. *Journal of Macroeconomics* 1: 267–83.

Sargent, T. J. 1979. *Macroeconomic theory.* New York: Academic Press.

Shiller, R. J. 1980. Can the Fed control real interest rates? in *Rational expectations and economic policy,* ed. S. Fischer. Chicago: University of Chicago Press (for the National Bureau of Economic Research), 1980.

Stockman, A. C. 1978. Risk, information, and forward exchange rates. In *The economics of exchange rates,* ed. J. A. Frenkel and H. G. Johnson. Reading, Mass.: Addison-Wesley.

Stulz, R. M. 1981. A model of international asset pricing. *Journal of Financial Economics* 9 (December): 383–406.

Tryon, R. 1979. Testing for rational expectations in foreign exchange markets. International Finance Discussion Papers no. 139, Board of Governors of The Federal Reserve System, Washington, D.C.

White, H. 1980. A heteroskedasticity-consistent covariance matrix estimator and a direct test for heteroskedasticity. *Econometrica* 48 (May): 817–38.

4   Properties of Innovations in Spot and Forward Exchange Rates and the Role of Money Supply Processes

Hans Genberg

4.1 Introduction and Summary

This paper aims to provide some new evidence concerning the determination of exchange rates by investigating relationships between innovations in spot and forward exchange rates.[1] In section 4.2 it is shown that under fairly general conditions this relationship depends on the properties of the stochastic processes generating the underlying determinants of exchange rates such as relative money supplies. In section 4.3 weekly data on spot and forward rates for eight countries and for five maturities are used to calculate innovations in these series which then are shown to conform to simplified versions of the model set out in section 4.2. It appears that only first-order processes generating the exogenous variables in exchange rate equations are necessary to explain the expected exchange rate dynamics contained in the data. But it is also shown that the parameters describing this first-order process tend to vary over time.

In section 4.4 the estimates, obtained from data in the foreign exchange markets, of these time-varying parameters are related to estimates of the same parameters obtained from first-order autoregressions of relative money supplies. The expected relationship between these two estimates is found

I would like to thank George Jung and Marc Vanheukelen for very efficient research assistance. This research was partially financed by a grant from the Fonds National Suisse de la Récherche Scientifique (grant no. 4.367-0.79.09).

1. In a previous paper written with Mario Blejer (Blejer and Genberg 1981), I investigated this relationship, hoping to distinguish between permanent and transitory shocks to exchange rates and to use this distinction in an explanation of deviations from purchasing power parity.

and taken as evidence that foreign exchange markets conform to at least some implications of the rational expectations hypothesis.

Section 4.5 of the paper discusses some implications of the empirical results for formulating and estimating exchange rate models, for interpreting the instability observed in estimated exchange rate equations, for explanations of the overshooting hypothesis, and for the influence of innovations in interest rate differentials on exchange rates. The last section of the paper contains some suggestions for extensions of the analysis.

4.2 A Model of Exchange Rate Determination

Suppose that the exchange rate is determined according to equation (1),[2] where z represents a vector of exogenous variables,[3] and u is a serially uncorrelated random variable

$$(1) \qquad S_t = \alpha Z_t + \beta E_t S_{t+1} + u_t, \qquad \beta > 0.$$

With rational expectations and $\beta < 1$ this equation can be rewritten in the familiar form (2):

$$(2) \qquad S_t = \alpha \sum_{i=0}^{\infty} \beta^i E_t Z_{t+i} + u_t.$$

Suppose furthermore that Z_t is determined by (3),

$$(3) \qquad Z_t = a_0 + \sum_{i=1}^{k} a_i Z_{t-i} + v_t,$$

where v_t is another serially uncorrelated random variable. Then (2) can be transformed into

$$(4) \qquad S_t = \pi_0 + \sum_{i=1}^{k} \pi_i Z_{t-i} + \pi_{k+1} v_t + u_t,$$

where the $k + 2$ $\pi:s$ are functions of α, β and the $k+1$ $a:s$. A joint test of rationality and the models of S and Z can be achieved by estimating (3) and (4) simultaneously while taking into account the restrictions on the $\pi:s$ mentioned above. Under the joint null hypothesis the estimates of the structural parameters will be more efficient than if the overidentifying restrictions were not taken into account. Extending this argument further by hypothesizing that the forward exchange rate is equal to the expected future spot rate plus a random error as in (5),[4]

$$(5) \qquad F_t^{t+1} = E_t S_{t+i} + \epsilon_t^i,$$

---

2. Frenkel and Mussa (1980) argue that a reduced-form equation of this type for the exchange rate can be derived from a wide variety of structural models of exchange rate determination.

3. In the algebra which follows, for simplicity Z is assumed to contain only one element.

4. I denote by F_t^{t+i} the i-period forward exchange rate observed in period t.

one can see the efficiency is improved still further by estimating jointly equations (3), (4), and (6) where the latter is derived from (2) and (3)

$$(6) \qquad F_t^{t+1} = \pi_0^i + \sum_{j=1}^{k} \pi_j^i Z_{t-k} + \pi_{k+1}^i v_t + \epsilon_t^i,$$

$$i = 1, \ldots, M.$$

As in (4), the $\pi^i{:}s$ in (6) are functions of α, β and the $a{:}s$ Hence, by including the reduced-form equations for forward rates of various maturities in an estimation system containing equations for the spot rate and the Z-process, information is added, yet the number of parameters to be estimated is not increased. A strong case can thus be made for following such a procedure if the purpose of the estimation is to test the model as specified above. However, I shall argue in the next two sections that the processes determining some of the Z variables, especially the money supplies, are not stable over time, implying that estimation of (3), (4), and (6) would lead to coefficients which vary with the sample period used. In order to investigate the empirical content of this assertion, I shall therefore proceed in a different manner by first isolating certain empirical regularities which exist in data on spot and forward rates and in particular in their innovations. I shall then relate these regularities to corresponding features of the process described in equation (3) and show that the data are consistent with the basic implication of the above analysis. That is, exchange rate movements are consistent with the rational expectations hypothesis in the sense that properties of the stochastic process generating the underlying determinants of exchange rates are appropriately reflected in spot and forward exchange rates.

From (2) and (5) I can write the current innovation in the spot rate as

$$(7) \qquad IS_t = S_t - F_{t-1}^t + \epsilon_{t-1}^1 = \alpha \sum_{i=0}^{\infty} \beta^i [E_t Z_{t+1} - E_{t-1} Z_{t+1}]$$

$$+ \epsilon_{t-1}^1 + u_t.$$

Similarly, the innovation in the i-period forward rate is

$$(8) \qquad IF_t^i = F_t^{t+i} - F_{t-1}^{t+i} = \alpha \sum_{j=0}^{\infty} \beta^j [E_t Z_{t+i+j} - E_{t-1} Z_{t+i+j}]$$

$$+ \epsilon_t^i - \epsilon_{t-1}^{i+1}.$$

Using (3) these innovations can be written as functions of α, β, the $a{:}s$, and v_t, the current forecast error of Z_t. In general these functions will be fairly complicated and will allow for many types of relationships between IS and IF^i for various maturities i. Substantial simplication is obtained if one restricts the Z-process to be of order one in either the level or the first difference.[5] Thus if

$$(9) \qquad Z_t = a_1 Z_{t-1} + v_t,$$

5. These two cases were analyzed in Mussa (1976).

it follows that

$$E_t Z_{t+i} - E_{t-1} Z_{t+i} = a_1^i v_t, \qquad i = 0, 1, \ldots ,$$

and that

(10) $$IS_t = \frac{\alpha}{1 - \beta a_1} v_t + \epsilon_{t-1}^1 + u_t$$

(11) $$IF_t^i = \frac{\alpha}{1 - \beta a_1} a_1^i v_t + \epsilon_t^i - \epsilon_{t-1}^{i+1}.$$

Combining (10) and (11), we get

(12) $$IF_t^i = a_1^i \, IS_t + \eta_t$$

where $\eta_t = \epsilon_t^i - \epsilon_{t-1}^{i+1} - a^i(\epsilon_{t-1}^1 + u_t)$.

Similarly, if

(13) $$Z_t - Z_{t-1} = b_1(Z_{t-1} - Z_{t-2}) + v_t,$$

then

(14) $$IS_t = \frac{\alpha}{(1-\beta)(1-\beta b_1)} v_t + \epsilon_{t-1}^1 + u_t,$$

(15) $$IF_t = [\beta + (1 - \beta)(1 + b_1 + b_1^2 + \ldots + b_1^i)]$$

$$\frac{\alpha}{(1-\beta)(1-\beta b_1)} v_t + \epsilon_t^i - \epsilon_{t-1}^{i+1},$$

and

(16) $$IF_t^i = [\beta + (1 - \beta)(1 + b_1 + \ldots + b_1^i)] \, IS_t + \eta_t',$$

where

$$\eta_t = \epsilon_t^i - \epsilon_{t-1}^{i+1} + [\beta + (1 - \beta)(1 + b_1 + \ldots + b_1^i)](\epsilon_{t-1}^1 + u_t).$$

From (12) and (16) one sees that if Z follows a first-order Markov process in the levels, the innovations in forward rates tend to be smaller than the innovations in the spot rates, whereas if the *first difference* of Z follows the same process the opposite would be the case. These relationships would furthermore be more pronounced the longer is the maturity of the forward rate considered.

Rather than pursuing the theoretical analysis further, I would now like to turn to the data in order to establish that regularities exist in the relationship between IS and IF across countries, over time for a single country, and along the term structure of forward rates which are consistent with the simplified Z-processes (9) and (13) if the a_1 parameter in these processes is allowed to vary over time.

4.3 Empirical Regularities in the Relationship Between *IS* and *IF*

Weekly data on spot rates and forward rates were used to calculate innovations in spot rates and forward rates as follows:[6]

$$IS_t = S_t - F_{t-4}^1$$

$$IF_t^i = F_t^i - F_{t-4}^{i+1}, \ i = 1, 3, 6, 9, 12,$$

where the time subscript spans weeks and the superscript spans months.[7] The sample period was April 27, 1973–August 7, 1981, and the countries included were Canada, the United Kingdom, France, Germany, Italy, the Netherlands, Switzerland, and Japan.

The analysis in the previous section suggested that innovations in forward rates are proportional to innovations in spot rates if the exogenous variable in the exchange rate equation is generated by a first-order autoregressive process in either the level or rate of change of that variable. Furthermore, the factor of proportionality should be larger than unity and increase with the length of the forecast horizon if the rate of change follows a first-order Markov process, and it should be less than one and decrease with the forecast horizon if the level is generated by this process. If the factor of proportionality did not change monotonically with the horizon the stochastic process generating the Z variable could not be of first order.

Tables 4.1–4.8 were compiled to determine whether the data contain any of the regularities suggested in the paragraph above. In the tables each row contains the mean value of IF^i/IS for the observations for which IF^1/IS was contained in the interval given in column 1 of that row. Column 2 gives the number of such observations. Inspection of these tables reveals that almost uniformly the data are consistent with the relationship predicted by first-order processes.[8] In particular, there are only two cases out of 64 in which the factor of proportionality changes from being less than unity to being greater than unity as the forecast horizon is lengthened. An implication of this finding for the formulation of models of exchange rate determination will be discussed in section 4.5.

A second regularity apparent in these tables is that between 50% and 90% of all observations of IF^1/IS lie in the interval 0.9–1.1, suggesting that shocks to exchange rates (either to the level or to the rate of change) have a high degree of persistence.[9] If one instead looked at the distribution of observations on IF^{12}/IS among the same intervals as in tables 4.1–4.8, one would notice a bimodality with peaks in the (0.5, 0.9) and (1.1, 1.5) intervals reflecting the monotonicity noted above.

---

6. See Appendix 1 for a description of data sources and of the calculations involved.

7. In addition, the spot and forward rates (all expressed as US$/domestic currency units) were transformed into natural logarithms before the innovations were calculated.

8. The main exceptions are row 4 for Italy and the Netherlands.

9. This is of course nothing but the familiar statement that exchange rates follow (approximately) random walks.

Table 4.1   **United Kingdom**

IF^1/IS	No. Obser- vations	IF^1/IS	IF^3/IS	IF^6/IS	IF^9/IS	IF^{12}/IS
< 0	9	−.31	−1.61	−3.50	−4.28	−4.62
		(−4.15)	(−5.88)	(−5.20)	(−4.67)	(−4.83)
0–.5	11	.33	−.36	−.64	−.93	−1.04
		(7.53)	(−2.19)	(−1.68)	(−.67)	(−1.34)
.5–.9	47	.80	.41	−.06	−.46	−.80
		(64.15)	(2.21)	(−.13)	(−.65)	(−.79)
.9–1.0	117	.96	.91	.86	.83	.83
		(370.28)	(84.75)	(41.30)	(27.63)	(21.51)
1.0–1.1	145	1.03	1.09	1.12	1.17	1.23
		(445.41)	(101.17)	(43.68)	(31.18)	(18.91)
1.1–1.5	76	1.21	1.54	1.87	2.17	2.44
		(107.58)	(38.57)	(20.87)	(17.12)	(15.26)
1.5–3.0	9	1.85	2.56	3.36	4.04	4.06
		(15.67)	(7.84)	(4.19)	(3.73)	(3.03)
3.0–10.0	1	4.25	6.33	7.98	9.50	9.60

Note: As an aid in interpreting tables 4.1–4.8, consider the following example: row 3 of table 4.1 refers to observations for which IF^1/IS was in the range .5–.9 (col. 1). There were 47 such observations in the entire sample (col. 2). The mean value of IF^1/IS for these 47 observations was .80 with a *t*-value of 65.15 (col. 3). The mean value of IF^3/IS for the same 47 dates in the sample was .41 with a *t*-value of 2.21 (col. 4). The interpretation of cols. 5–7 is the same as that of col. 4.

Table 4.2   **Canada**

IF^1/IS	No. Obser- vations	IF^1/IS	IF^3/IS	IF^6/IS	IF^9/IS	IF^{12}/IS
< 0	1	−.006	−.42	−.39	−.14	−.97
0–.5	7	.33	−.63	−.98	−1.86	−2.14
		(9.05)	(−1.59)	(−.99)	(−2.07)	(−2.00)
.5–.9	71	.78	.55	.33	.33	.24
		(69.90)	(17.55)	(5.27)	(4.00)	(2.66)
.9–1.0	129	.97	.94	.88	.84	.85
		(406.25)	(93.62)	(45.04)	(29.88)	(23.27)
1.0–1.1	118	1.04	1.08	1.13	1.16	1.17
		(401.06)	(98.61)	(46.23)	(34.37)	(25.44)
1.1–1.5	53	1.20	1.49	1.78	1.98	2.00
		(106.86)	(29.27)	(19.12)	(12.56)	(13.36)
1.5–3.0	9	1.97	3.58	4.83	5.56	5.76
		(14.44)	(9.81)	(7.57)	(7.31)	(5.66)
3.0–10.0	0					

Table 4.3   France

IF^1/IS	No. Observations	IF^1/IS	IF^3/IS	IF^6/IS	IF^9/IS	IF^{12}/IS
< 0	3	−.65	−2.14	−3.58	−3.90	−5.55
		(−1.17)	(−4.26)	(−6.99)	(−10.29)	(−10.07)
0–.5	7	.23	−.39	−1.27	−1.14	−1.80
		(3.83)	(−1.29)	(−1.77)	(−1.26)	(−1.43)
.5–.9	81	.78	.57	.37	.30	.08
		(69.03)	(10.13)	(4.20)	(2.79)	(.53)
.9–1.0	135	.96	.93	.89	.88	.85
		(450.85)	(81.81)	(47.59)	(33.70)	(24.34)
1.0–1.1	113	1.04	1.10	1.16	1.14	1.20
		(428.78)	(82.55)	(52.43)	(40.92)	(31.36)
1.1–1.5	68	1.21	1.38	1.57	1.58	1.77
		(90.75)	(41.08)	(21.92)	(18.32)	(15.30)
1.5–3.0	7	1.81	2.20	3.52	3.05	3.62
		(9.69)	(3.95)	(3.64)	(4.49)	(3.81)
3.0–10.0	3	3.24	3.17	5.45	3.98	4.40
		(26.65)	(1.42)	(2.49)	(4.57)	(5.68)

Table 4.4   Germany

IF^1/IS	No. Observations	IF^1/IS	IF^3/IS	IF^6/IS	IF^9/IS	IF^{12}/IS
< 0	2	−.58	.77	−3.10	−3.79	−4.98
		(−2.30)	(1.42)	(−28.88)	(−3.37)	(−4.15)
0–.5	7	.24	−.08	−.94	−1.24	−1.78
		(3.31)	(−.21)	(−1.02)	(−1.23)	(−1.32)
.5–.9	67	.80	.74	.62	.65	.57
		(63.23)	(17.85)	(8.09)	(6.52)	(4.23)
.9–1.0	185	.96	.95	.94	.95	.94
		(473.30)	(101.08)	(29.70)	(22.73)	(17.04)
1.0–1.1	117	1.03	1.05	1.09	1.13	1.21
		(53.97)	(42.37)	(40.64)	(30.35)	(65.23)
1.1–1.5	33	1.21	1.30	1.51	1.65	1.83
		(65.23)	(25.55)	(12.62)	(9.67)	(8.33)
1.5–3.0	4	1.94	2.43	2.77	2.54	2.97
		(19.89)	(2.76)	(2.18)	(2.85)	(2.30)
3.0–10.0	0					

Table 4.5   **Italy**

IF^1/IS	No. Observations	IF^1/IS	IF^3/IS	IF^6/IS	IF^9/IS	IF^{12}/IS
< 0	25	−.79 (−7.61)	−2.37 (−7.35)	−3.86 (−5.91)	−4.32 (−5.88)	−6.17 (−6.11)
0–.5	37	.27 (10.86)	−.23 (−2.09)	−.85 (−4.71)	−.88 (−2.96)	−1.46 (−3.64)
.5–.9	83	.73 (51.09)	.64 (14.12)	.37 (4.02)	.37 (2.80)	.21 (1.18)
.9–1.0	70	.96 (357.22)	1.10 (28.44)	1.15 (14.71)	1.18 (13.40)	1.29 (10.72)
1.0–1.1	71	1.04 (303.77)	1.22 (40.41)	1.38 (19.86)	1.55 (15.16)	1.78 (12.71)
1.1–1.5	76	1.25 (109.31)	1.71 (35.63)	2.10 (23.55)	2.05 (16.34)	2.48 (14.76)
1.5–3.0	26	1.92 (26.70)	2.82 (19.28)	3.84 (10.01)	4.00 (11.53)	4.94 (10.90)
3.0–10.0	3	4.24 (5.50)	6.32 (5.86)	9.85 (29.60)	8.24 (6.36)	10.36 (5.88)

Table 4.6   **Netherlands**

IF^1/IS	No. Observations	IF^1/IS	IF^3/IS	IF^6/IS	IF^9/IS	IF^{12}/IS
< 0	5	−.43 (−1.57)	−1.63 (−1.79)	−3.45 (−2.09)	−3.28 (−2.37)	−4.43 (−2.38)
0–.5	3	.15 (2.70)	−.47 (−1.31)	−1.61 (−3.33)	−1.74 (−2.45)	−2.55 (−2.69)
.5–.9	76	.79 (68.09)	.65 (20.46)	.41 (6.10)	.38 (4.96)	.20 (2.02)
.9–1.0	168	.96 (445.19)	.94 (84.33)	.89 (40.61)	1.08 (5.74)	1.11 (4.59)
1.0–1.1	115	1.04 (384.70)	1.09 (84.52)	1.14 (44.38)	1.16 (31.58)	1.21 (24.83)
1.1–1.5	37	1.23 (68.38)	1.57 (11.30)	1.93 (8.87)	1.96 (7.61)	2.27 (6.41)
1.5–3.0	11	1.92 (17.25)	2.74 (6.77)	4.07 (4.85)	4.04 (4.27)	5.00 (3.90)
3.0–10.0	0					

Table 4.7   **Switzerland**

IF^2/IS	No. Obser- vations	IF^1/IS	IF^3/IS	IF^6/IS	IF^9/IS	$IF^{12}IS$
< 0	2	−.29	−1.32	−2.81	−3.12	−4.32
		(−3.07)	(−1.66)	(−1.26)	(−1.06)	(−1.16)
0–.5	5	.36	.35	−.24	−.30	−.60
		(6.12)	(2.85)	(−1.18)	(−.72)	(−1.11)
.5–.9	45	.79	.76	.68	.59	.52
		(49.46)	(15.80)	(8.89)	(5.45)	(3.61)
.9–1.0	159	.96	.95	.92	.89	.87
		(426.18)	(92.63)	(34.27)	(26.24)	(19.56)
1.0–1.1	156	1.03	1.07	1.10	1.12	1.16
		(555.76)	(153.96)	(86.31)	(58.57)	(45.63)
1.1–1.5	41	1.20	1.40	1.61	1.73	1.95
		(88.87)	(18.08)	(9.06)	(7.26)	(6.00)
1.5–3.0	6	1.64	1.48	2.00	2.51	2.78
		(29.56)	(2.52)	(1.98)	(2.71)	(2.12)
3.0–10.0	0					

Table 4.8   **Japan**

IF^1/IS	No. Obser- vations	IF^1/IS	IF^3/IS	IF^6/IS	IF^9/IS	IF^{12}/IS
< 0	5	−1.36	−1.40	−1.89	−1.98	−2.68
		(−5.27)	(−1.73)	(−1.27)	(−1.83)	(−1.83)
0–.5	12	.27	.20	−.03	−.29	−.53
		(6.33)	(1.41)	(−.15)	(−.83)	(−1.13)
.5–.9	46	.75	.86	.74	.49	.45
		(45.61)	(13.86)	(8.60)	(6.02)	(3.96)
.9–1.0	96	.97	.97	.93	.91	.90
		(385.82)	(68.82)	(43.83)	(38.30)	(27.12)
1.0–1.1	94	1.03	1.13	1.16	1.12	1.17
		(423.83)	(62.60)	(47.96)	(40.81)	(31.92)
1.1–1.5	31	1.26	1.65	1.78	1.63	1.88
		(62.56)	(18.72)	(15.95)	(12.28)	(10.41)
1.5–3.0	8	1.91	2.84	3.68	3.29	4.19
		(16.90)	(10.46)	(10.15)	(10.50)	(9.76)
3.0–10.0	0					

In order to investigate the relationship between *IS* and *IF* over time, I next estimated equations of the form

$$(17) \qquad IF_t^i = \alpha IS_t + u_t$$

and

$$(18) \qquad IS_t = \beta IF_t^i + v_t.$$

As is clear from equations (10)–(16), the error terms in (17) and (18) are correlated with the independent variable in each equation. OLS estimates of α and β will hence be biased and inconsistent. Under certain conditions (see, e.g., Koutsoyiannis 1977, pp. 268–69), a consistent estimate of α, α^*, can be obtained from the OLS estimates, $\hat{\alpha}$ and $\hat{\beta}$, by computing

$$(19) \qquad \alpha^* = \left(\frac{\hat{\alpha}}{\hat{\beta}}\right)^{1/2}.$$

The value of α^* was calculated from OLS estimates of α and β for moving samples of length 53 weeks, the overlap between each sample being 40 weeks. The resulting time series for α^* are plotted in figures 4.1–4.8, the general features of which evoke three observations.

First, there appears to be a substantial amount of variation over time in the relationship between innovations in spot and forward rates even if on average they change by approximately the same amount. In particular, there is generally a marked reduction in α^* toward the end of the sample and a peak occurring around 1977–78 for a number of countries. Second, there are differences between countries both in the level of α^* and in its fluctuations over time. The latter are substantially larger for France, Italy, and the

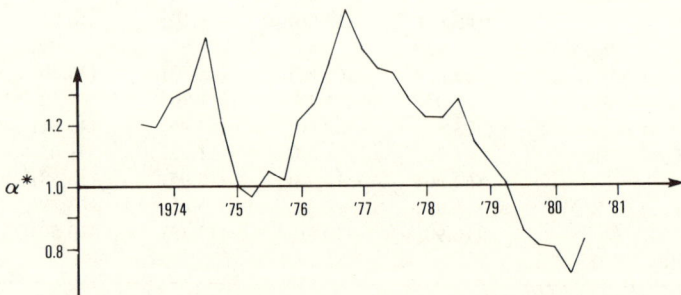

Fig. 4.1   United Kingdom
Note: Figs. 4.1–4.8 contain point estimates of α^* as defined in the text. The 1980-I observation for Italy is excluded because the estimate of β in the denominator of (19) was not significantly different from zero. The 1973 and 1974 observations for Japan are excluded due to unavailability of data.

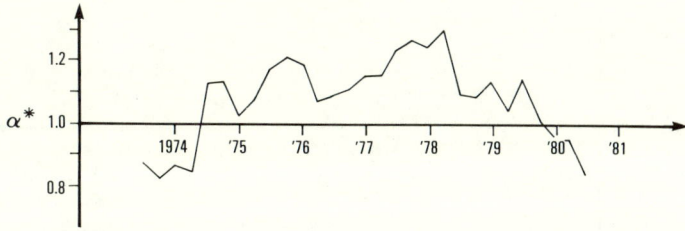

Fig. 4.2   Canada

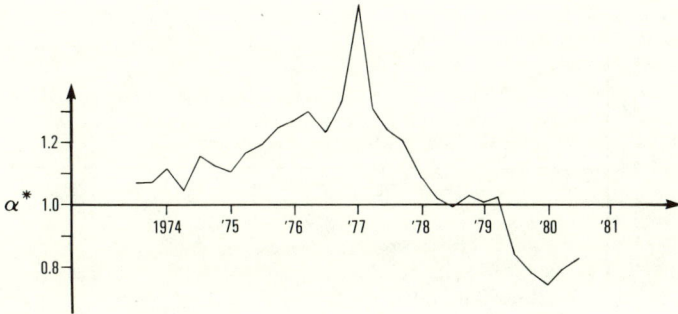

Fig. 4.3   France

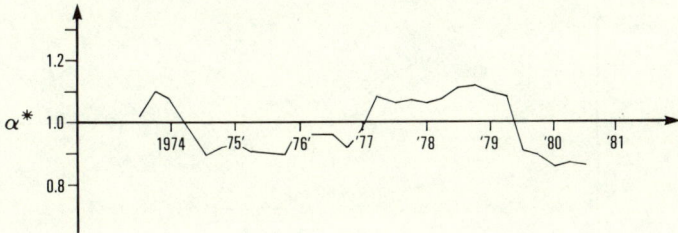

Fig. 4.4   Germany

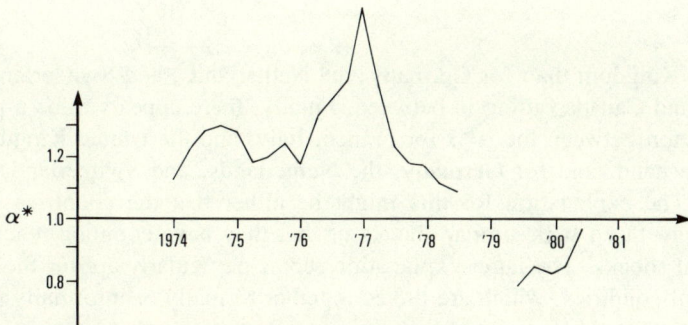

Fig. 4.5   Italy

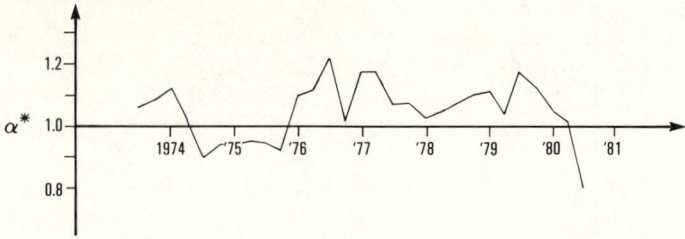

Fig. 4.6   Netherlands

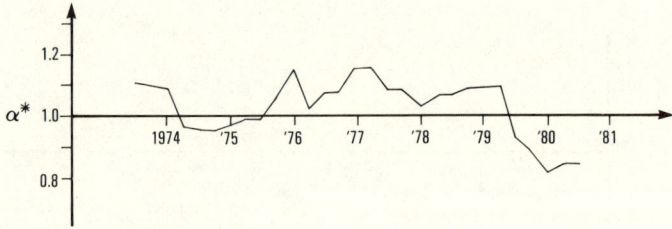

Fig. 4.7   Switzerland

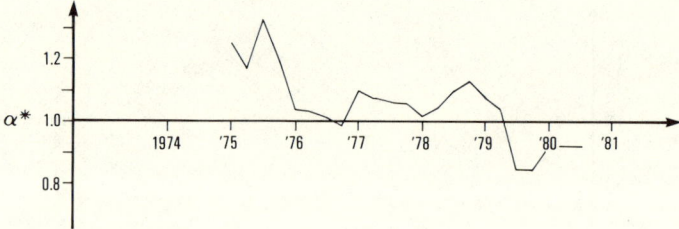

Fig. 4.8   Japan

United Kingdom than for Germany, the Netherlands, and Switzerland, with Japan and Canada falling in between. Finally, there appears to be a positive correlation between the α^*:s for France, Italy, and the United Kingdom, on the one hand, and for Germany, the Netherlands, and Switzerland, on the other. The explanation for this might be either that the countries in each group are faced with similar shocks or that they have common reactions to external shocks. The latter explanation seems particularly apt for the second group of countries, which are linked together formally or informally through a desire to avoid large intragroup exchange rate movements.

In the next section the variability over time and across countries noted in these figures will be related to variations in monetary policy. Some implications of the other empirical regularities in the relationship between IF and IS noted above will be taken up in the next section of the paper.

4.4 The Role of Differences in Monetary Policy

Two views may be taken of the differences over time in the responses of the spot and forward exchange rates to common shocks. One is that the differences are due to changes over time in the stochastic processes governing the underlying determinants of the exchange rate. Such changes might occur because of changes in monetary policy regimes from, say, a strategy of preannounced growth rates to a feedback rule for the money supply. Changes in the money supply process might also result from changes over time in the degree of intervention in the foreign exchange market.[10] Another view is that the differences over time and across countries we observe in figures 4.1–4.8 are due to changes over time in the *sources* of the shocks (monetary versus real shocks, for example), and that the stochastic properties governing each type of shock are invariant with respect to time.

In what follows I shall investigate the implications of the first of these views, concentrating exclusively on monetary policy by assuming that the money supply of each country relative to the money supply in the United States is an important determinant of that country's exchange rate. I shall then hypothesize that (the natural logarithm of) the ratio of money supplies, $m_{i,t}$, follows a first-order autoregressive process with an autoregressive parameter which varies over time.[11] Hence,

$$(20) \qquad m_{i,t} = a_{i,0} + a_{i,1,t}\, m_{i,t-1} + u_{i,t}.$$

According to equation (12) of section 4.2, the autoregressive parameter a_1 obtained from (20) should be related to the factor of proportionality between innovations in forward and spot exchange rates under the joint hypothesis described by (1), $Z_t = m_t$, (5), (20), and rational expectations. In order to investigate this hypothesis, I first estimated (20) for each of the countries in the sample, using monthly money supply data from January 1972 to May 1981. The a_1 parameter was estimated for 36-month-long moving samples with the overlap between adjacent samples being 24 months. The resulting point estimates were then correlated with the estimate of α obtained from (19), both over time and across countries.[12] Under the null hypothesis these

10. These examples were chosen because I believe that they have been important in a number of countries in recent years.

11. In fact $m_{i,t} = \ln (M_t^{us}/M_t^i)$ where M^{us} is the money supply for the United States and M^i is the money supply for country i. See Appendix 1 for data sources.

12. For point estimates, see table 4.A.1. For the resulting coefficients, see table 4.A.2. In this part of the paper, I worked only with estimates of α obtained with innovations in 12-month forward rates.

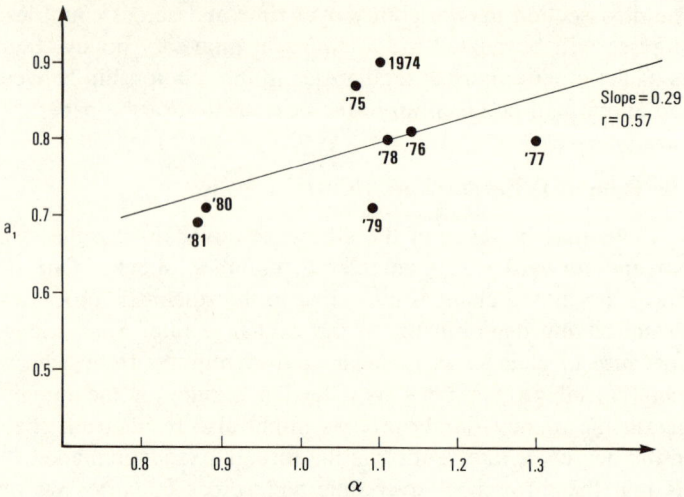

Fig. 4.9   Averages of eight countries

correlations should be positive. Figures 4.9 and 4.10 contain scatter diagrams of the estimates of the autoregressive parameter obtained from (19) and (20) for cross-country and time series sample averages. The correlation coefficient between the two variables (denoted *r* in the figures) is in both cases significantly larger than zero at the 90% level. On this criterion, there-

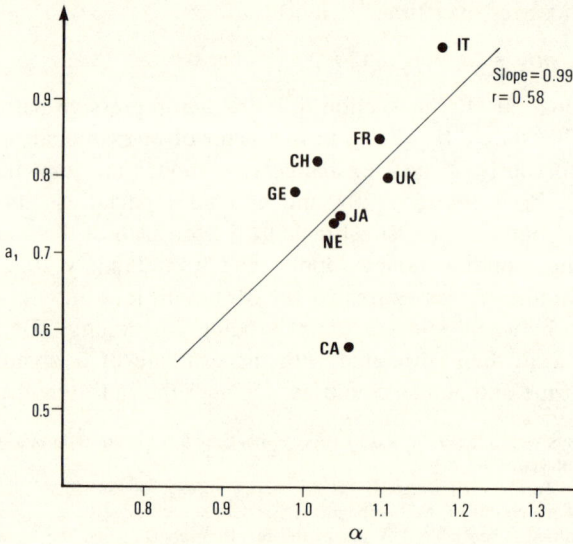

Fig. 4.10   Averages of 8 years

fore, the null hypothesis is not rejected by the data and one may conclude that when agents form expectations about future spot rates the properties of the stochastic process generating the money supply are indeed taken into account in a manner consistent with the rational expectations hypothesis.

Confirmation of this assertion is obtained if first-order autoregressive parameters are estimated for the logarithms of the own-country money supplies (i.e., not relative to the United States) and the resulting point estimates are correlated (across countries) with the coefficient obtained from (19). The correlation coefficient here is .68, significantly larger than zero at the 95% level. If individual countries are examined one finds that the data from the United Kingdom, France, Italy, and Japan corroborate the null hypothesis; that the evidence from Canada is mixed; and that Germany, the Netherlands, and Switzerland fail to corroborate the hypothesis. Similar ambiguities appear when cross-country correlations are calculated for each of the 8 years. Given the exclusion of all variables which affect exchange rates except money supplies, and especially given the problems of dating exactly changes in the autoregressive parameter in the two ways suggested here, it is probably too much to hope that each country and each year should conform to the predictions of the theory. Hence I view the average data as more appropriate for examining the null hypothesis as posed here, and I retain the conclusion that changes in monetary policy strategies which manifest themselves as changes in the money supply processes are taken into account by agents in forming expectations. I now turn to some implications of this conclusion, and of those of the previous section, for the appropriate conduct of empirical estimation of exchange rate equations, for interpretation of existing empirical work, and for judging the empirical validity of alternative theoretical models of exchange rate determination.

4.5 Implications

The theoretical framework for exchange rate determination set out in section 4.2 incorporating the rational expectations hypothesis implied that the relationship between innovations in spot rates, IS, and innovations in forward rates, IF, should depend, inter alia, on the stochastic process generating the underlying determinants of exchange rates. In the previous section it was shown that part of the differences in the ratio of IF to IS observed in data over time and between countries can indeed be explained by differences over time and between countries in the processes generating relative money supplies as suggested by the theory. In section 4.3 it was also shown that the size of the ratio of innovations in forward rates to innovations in spot rates depends on the maturity of the forward rate involved. This dependence was shown to be monotonic in the sense that the ratio increased (decreased) steadily with the maturity of the forward rate if the ratio for the 1-month forward rate was greater (less) than unity. Oscillations around unity were extremely rare. Some implications of these and other empirical findings will now be taken up.

4.5.1 Formulating and Estimating Exchange Rate Equations

In section 4.2, it was shown that if agents form expectations partly on the basis of their estimate of the process generating the exogenous variables, increased efficiency can be obtained in estimation of exchange rate equations if the latter are estimated jointly with the process for the exogenous variable and if the appropriate cross-equation restrictions are taken into account. The evidence presented here implies that this gain in efficiency will be achieved in practice since agents do seem to rely on information contained in the money supply processes. The results also imply that further gains in efficiency will be obtained if equations for forward exchange rates of different maturities are included in the joint estimation because these forward rates will be determined as spot rates are, and the processes generating the exogenous variables will have an identifiable impact on them as well.

The results of the previous section suggest, however, that in implementing the joint estimation mentioned above it is necessary to allow for changes over time in the process generating the exogenous variables, at least as far as the money supply is concerned. This increases the complexity of the procedure, but it is essential if problems of parameter instability are to be avoided.

4.5.2 Instability of Coefficients in Empirical Exchange Rate Equations

It has been argued that explanations of exchange rate movements based on movements in money supplies are inadequate because, among other reasons, estimated exchange rate equations which restrict themselves to using current and lagged money supplies as regressors appear to be unstable in the sense that the coefficients on the money supply terms vary with the sample period (see, e.g., Hodrick 1979; Dornbusch, 1980). An implication of the results presented here is that such instability is not necessarily a result of an inadequacy of the monetary model, but rather a consequence of inappropriate implementation of that model. If the processes generating money supplies change over time, then the model presented in section 4.2 implies that the coefficients relating the current spot rate to current and lagged money supplies should change. Hence observed instability may simply be a reflection of instability of monetary policy rather than inadequacy of any particular theoretical framework.[13]

---

13. This is of course not to suggest that only money supply processes matter. Coefficient instability will appear whenever the process generating the exogenous variable, whatever it may be, changes.

4.5.3 Overshooting

The concept of overshooting has become a popular one in the discussion of exchange rate movements and exchange rate policy. The most common reasons given for the emergence of overshooting are some forms of stickiness somewhere in the economic system which prevent prices and quantities from adjusting rapidly. In the framework presented here overshooting may be related to the relative size of *IS* or *IF*. If *IS* is larger than *IF* then we might say that the spot rate is overshooting in the sense that the current spot rate moves by more than does the expected future spot rate. Concerning the reason for such movements, the present paper has emphasized an alternative to the stickiness explanation which is the role of the processes generating underlying determinants of exchange rates in general and money supplies in particular. As noted above, if the *levels* of money supplies follow first-order autoregressive processes, one should expect to observe overshooting as defined here. On the other hand, if the *rates of change* of money supplies follow first-order autoregressive processes, then one should expect to observe undershooting. In tables 4.1–4.8 it appears that, far from being a dominant feature of the recent period of flexible rates, overshooting is no more common than undershooting for the countries examined here.

4.5.4 The Role of "News"

Frenkel (1981) implemented the idea that *unexpected* movements in exchange rates should be related only to *unexpected* movements in their determinants by using as a regressor in an exchange rate equation the innovation in the interest rate differential between the countries in question. Letting i_t stand for this interest differential and assuming that uncovered interest parity holds, we have $i_t = E_t S_{t+1} - S_t$, which can be rewritten as

$$(21) \qquad i_t = (E_t S_{t+1} - E_{t-1} S_{t+1}) - (S_t - E_{t-1} S_t) + E_{t-1} S_{t+1} - E_{t-1} S_t$$

or

$$(22) \qquad i_t = IF_t - IS_t - E_{t-1} i_t.$$

Equation (22) shows that the innovation in the interest differential is equal to the difference between the innovations in the forward rate and the spot rate. Letting $IF/IS = \alpha$, it then follows that if one runs a regression of innovations in the spot exchange rate on innovations in the interest differential, then one should expect to find a positive, negative, or zero slope coefficient according to whether α is larger, smaller, or equal to one. Frenkel's sample included France, Germany, and the United Kingdom for the period June 1973–July 1979. Looking at figures 4.1, 4.3, and 4.4, it appears that α was systematically greater than unity for France and the United Kingdom but was both smaller and greater than unity for Germany during this sample period. On the argument presented here, the two former countries should yield significantly positive coefficients in Frenkel's regressions, whereas for Germany one would expect a coefficient not significantly different from zero. An examination of Frenkel's results shows this to be the case, thus providing an additional bit of evidence in favor of the interpretation of the relationship between *IS* and *IF* suggested in this paper.

4.5.5 Structure of Theoretical Models of Exchange Rate Determination

The relationship between *IS* and *IF* depends in theory on both the structure of the economy and the processes generating the exogenous variables in the exchange rate equations. Under some simplifying assumptions noted in section 4.2, it was shown that this relationship varies monotonically with the maturity of the forward rate. In section 4.3 it was found that the data contain almost exclusively such monotonic relationships. This finding implies that, whatever economic model one chooses to work with, it need not result in more complicated exchange rate dynamics than those generated by a first-order difference equation in order to be compatible with the data. Models which generate more complicated adjustment patterns, such as overshooting followed by undershooting (as defined in the previous subsection), may be theoretically interesting, but they do not appear to warrant serious empirical consideration because the data simply do not contain such adjustment patterns.

In the same vein, in order to construct models to allow for the possibility of overshooting, it is not necessary to rely on slow adjustment and various degrees of sticky prices. Overshooting may simply be a result of the properties of the money supply process responsible for movements in the exchange rate. This explanation ought to be given more attention, especially in discussions of the policy implications of the overshooting hypothesis.

4.6 Extensions

The present paper has presented a bit of new evidence consistent with the rational expectations hypothesis as applied to exchange rate behavior. As already noted, further tests of this hypothesis and more efficient estimations of exchange rate equations can be obtained by following the methods suggested in sections 4.2 and 4.5.1. The main difficulty of implementation would seem to stem from the hypothesized time dependence of the coefficients in the money supply equations. The procedure followed in this paper represents a first rough attempt to deal with this problem. More detailed treatment would seem to be an area of potentially significant payoff. Two different paths may be followed. One is to attempt to model the time dependence directly in terms of the presumably shifting objectives of the monetary policy authorities. This would involve attempts to model changes in the strategy of the central bank and would be subject to all the usual difficulties encountered in trying to estimate policy reaction functions.

Another possible path to follow would be to assume that agents view the money supply (and other variables) as being generated by a combination of temporary and permanent shocks and then to use results from signal extraction analysis to describe the nature of the current shocks. Kalman filtering techniques offer a possible tool for this line of inquiry.

Appendix 1: Data

The data on exchange rates were those published by the Harris Bank. Weekly spot rates and 30-, 60-, 90-, 180-, and 360-day forward rates were available for all eight countries. In addition, 270-day forward rates were available for the United Kingdom and Canada. To calculate innovations in forward rates for 90, 180, 270, and 360 days, forward rates of 120, 210, 300, and 390 days were necessary. These were obtained by interpolation using the forward rate with the closest matching maturity. Money supply data were taken from the International Monetary Fund's *International Financial Statistics* data tape. The M_1 (line 34 of *International Financial Statistics*) definition of money was used. For the United States it was necessary to supplement the data from the tape with data from the *Federal Reserve Bulletin* starting in 1979. The money supply data were seasonally adjusted prior to the estimation of the autoregressive processes.

Appendix 2: Calculation of Estimates of α and a_1 over Time

Given the overlapping sample periods used to estimate the first-order autoregressive process for the ratio of the money supplies, it is possible to justify calculating the a_1 coefficient appropriate for any given year in a number of ways. Only one method was explored here. This took the following form:

Let $a_{1,t}$ be the estimated first-order autoregressive parameter in equation (20) for the sample period ending with December of year t. Then the parameter for year t, $\hat{a}_{1,t}$, used in the correlation analysis was calculated according to

$$\hat{a}_{1,t} = (\hat{a}_{1,t} + 2a_{1,t+1} + a_{1,t+2})/4, \qquad t = 1974, \ldots, 1979;$$

$$\hat{a}_{1,t} = (\hat{a}_{1,t} + 2a_{1,t+1})/3, \qquad t = 1980;$$

$$\hat{a}_{1,t} = \hat{a}_{1,t}, \qquad t = 1981.$$

The resulting parameters are contained in table 4.A.1.

Table 4.A.1   Estimates of First-Order Autoregressive Parameter in Relative Money Supply Series

	United Kingdom	Canada	France	Germany	Italy	Netherlands	Switzerland	Japan
1974	.87	.86	.94	.94	.94	.90	.83	—
1975	.98	.77	.91	.89	.96	.93	.63	.89
1976	.97	.56	.85	.79	.99	.84	.65	.83
1977	.97	.47	.83	.79	1.01	.79	.78	.76
1978	.92	.53	.88	.74	1.01	.74	.84	.71
1979	.74	.54	.85	.65	.98	.64	.90	.68
1980	.55	.49	.78	.69	.94	.57	.96	.67
1981	.43	.45	.74	.77	.92	.54	.99	.69

Table 4.A.2   **Estimates of the Parameter α (cf. Equation [19])**

	United Kingdom	Canada	France	Germany	Italy	Netherlands	Switzerland	Japan
1974	1.29	.87	1.12	1.08	1.13	1.12	1.09	—
1975	1.00	1.03	1.11	.93	1.28	.95	.97	1.26
1976	1.21	1.20	1.27	.98	1.19	1.10	1.15	1.04
1977	1.45	1.16	1.66	.99	1.68	1.18	1.16	1.10
1978	1.22	1.25	1.09	1.06	1.18	1.02	1.04	1.03
1979	1.08	1.14	1.01	1.10	1.32	1.11	1.10	1.06
1980	.80	.96	.75	.87	.84	1.06	.82	.93
1981	.83	.85	.83	.87	.97	.80	.85	.93

For the calculation of the parameter α (cf. eq. [19] in section 4.3) corresponding to a given year t, the estimate α_t^* (as defined in the equation following [19] in the main text) corresponding to the sample ending with the last week of year t was used. The resulting parameters are contained in table 4.A.2.

References

Blejer, Mario, and Genberg, Hans. 1981. Permanent and transitory shocks to exchange rates: Measurement and implications for purchasing power parity. Manuscript.

Dornbusch, Rudiger. 1980. Exchange rate economics: Where do we stand? *Brookings Papers on Economic Activity,* no. 2, pp. 143–85.

Frenkel, Jacob. 1981. Flexible exchange rates, prices and the role of "news": Lessons from the 1970s. *Journal of Political Economy* 89:665–705.

Frenkel, Jacob, and Mussa, Michael. 1980. The efficiency of foreign exchange markets and measures of turbulence. *American Economic Review* 70:374–81.

Hodrick, Robert. 1979. On the monetary analysis of exchange rates, a comment. In *Policies for employment, prices, and exchange rates,* ed. Karl Brunner and Allan H. Meltzer. Carnegie-Rochester Conference Series on Public Policy no. 11. Amsterdam: North-Holland.

Koutsoyiannis, A. 1977. *Theory of econometrics.* London: Macmillan.

Mussa, Michael. 1976. The exchange rate, the balance of payments, and monetary and fiscal policy under a regime of controlled floating. *Scandinavian Journal of Economics* 78:229–48.

5 Exchange Rate Dynamics

John F. O. Bilson

Exchange rates adjust until the existing stocks of currencies are willingly held. While this statement may be considered a tautology, economists have not reached a consensus on the mechanism by which an increase in the price of a currency reduces the demand for it. Seen in the light of the recent experience, the early versions of the elasticities and monetary approaches to exchange rate determination failed because of two considerations. First, these approaches specified that the exchange rate influenced the relative demand for money through its influence on a transmitting economic variable— the trade balance in the first instance and the price level in the second. Second, empirical observation suggested that the speed of transmission was not rapid enough to maintain equilibrium in the foreign exchange market on a day-to-day basis. Either viable models of the foreign exchange market must specify the mechanism by which the exchange rate directly influences the demand for money, or they must rely on a transmission variable which is as free to move as the exchange rate itself.

During the past decade, the most popular model of the second type has been Rudiger Dornbusch's (1976) model of exchange rate dynamics. In the Dornbusch model, the exchange rate "works" through its influence on interest rate differentials. An appreciation of sterling against the dollar in the spot market creates an anticipated depreciation in the future. In order to maintain interest rate parity, nominal interest rates must increase in the United Kingdom relative to the United States, and it is the increase in nominal interest rates which directly reduces the demand for sterling relative to dollars. This description of the Dornbusch mechanism may be reversed in order to directly assign a market-clearing role to the local interest rate. Suppose that the demand for sterling should increase for some reason. Those who attempt to build up their currency holdings will do so by attempting to

This research was financed in part by a grant from the National Science Foundation.

sell assets. Since the quantity of currency is fixed, the result of this attempt will be lower bond prices and higher interest rates. However, at the existing exchange rate, the higher local interest rates will create an incipient capital inflow into the United Kingdom. Since the current account is fixed in the short run, the exchange rate must appreciate in order to clear the foreign exchange market. It will continue to appreciate until the anticipated depreciation of sterling offsets the international interest rate differential.

Although this description of the adjustment mechanism has gained wide acceptance in both academia and the financial markets, attempts to apply it empirically have not been notably successful.[1] In a recent survey of empirical models of exchange rate determination, Meese and Rogoff (1981) demonstrate that none of the simple econometric models of the exchange rate outperform a random walk specification in which the best forecast of the future spot rate is the current spot rate. In addition, Rogoff and Meese cast doubt on the efficient market underpinnings of the Dornbusch model by demonstrating that the spot rate forecast is also superior to the forecast embodied in the forward rate.

In part, the lack of success in the empirical implementation of theoretical models of the exchange rate may be due to the instability experienced during the 1970s. The oil crisis, the freezing of Iranian assets, the debt problems of the LDCs and the Eastern European countries, and the changing institutional arrangements in the international monetary system are all factors that are difficult to account for within the confines of traditional econometric analysis. It may also be the case that the foreign exchange market, as an asset market, is not amenable to standard econometric techniques. In the domestic financial literature, attempts to forecast asset prices typically are left to commercial forecasters, and the finding that the exchange rate was generated by a random walk during the first decade of floating would not be a source of dismay but an affirmation of market efficiency.

There is, however, no theoretical ground for rejecting econometric models of asset prices. The theory simply states that the most important source of a change in the price of an asset is a revision in the market's expectations of its future value. The empirical problem arises because it is extremely difficult to quantify the revisions in market expectations. Since it is to be expected that standard empirical proxies are inexact, it is also to be expected that the power of tests based upon these proxies is low.

In this paper, an attempt is made to avoid the problem of directly modeling market expectations. It is based upon the idea that the innovations in market "fundamentals," whatever they may be, can be observed from the innovations in the financial asset prices themselves. Suppose, for example,

---

1. See Bilson (1978), Frankel (1979), and Driskill (1981). The discussion in the December 1981 *American Economic Review* of Frankel's paper is directed toward estimation problems with this type of model.

that an economist was left in a room with a computer terminal, a copy of Dornbusch's paper, and the past history of exchange rates and interest rate differentials for two unknown currencies. Would that economist be able to infer that the data were generated by the theoretical model?

The object, then, is to make inferences about the adjustment mechanism in international financial markets through an analysis of the dynamics of international asset prices. As it stands, the paper is more an exercise in methodology and exploratory data analysis than an attempt to present definitive tests of alternative hypotheses. There are, of course, a number of other models of exchange rate dynamics which are broadly consistent with observed empirical regularities.[2] In more sophisticated applications of the approach, it should be possible to present dynamic models which distinguish between these alternatives. For the moment, however, a simple variant of the Dornbusch model will be considered as a case study to be applied to the recent history of the £/$ and DM/$ exchange rates.

5.1 A Theoretical Model of Exchange Rate Dynamics

In this section, vector autoregressions for exchange rates and interest rate differentials are derived from a discrete time, two-country version of the Dornbusch model of exchange rate dynamics. The model is described in the following five equations:

(1) $$m - p = -\alpha x$$

(2) $$x = \theta(\bar{e} - e)$$

(3) $$p = \phi Le + (1 - \phi) Lp$$

(4) $$m = Lm + u$$

(5) $$\bar{e} = L\bar{e} + u + v,$$

where m = log (net supply of sterling/net supply of dollars);
$\quad x$ = forward premium on the dollar;
$\quad$ = sterling interest rate − dollar interest rate;
$\quad e$ = log (exchange rate, i.e., £/$);
$\quad \bar{e}$ = log (expected exchange rate);
$\quad \alpha$ = interest rate semielasticity of the demand for money;
$\quad \phi$ = velocity of price adjustment parameter;
$\quad \theta$ = expectations parameter;
$\quad u$ = innovation in net relative supply of sterling;
$\quad v$ = innovation in expected exchange rate that is independent of the innovation in the net supply of sterling;
$\quad L$ = the lag operator, i.e., $Lz_t = z_{t-1}$.

2. Frenkel (1981) discusses the role of "news" in models of exchange rate determination.

Equation (1) represents the equilibrium condition in the foreign exchange market: the demand for sterling, relative to dollars, is assumed to depend positively on relative prices and negatively on the interest rate differential. All other influences on the relative demand for the two currencies are subsumed into the net relative supply term. Equation (2) is the Dornbusch version of the interest rate parity condition: the forward premium, which is assumed to be equal to the expected increase in the price of sterling, is assumed to be proportional to the difference between the expected long-run exchange rate, $\bar{e}$, and the spot rate, e. Equation (3) is a simple relative price adjustment equation in which the current level of relative prices is assumed to be a weighted average of the exchange rate and the level of relative prices in the previous period. This specification does not allow for any immediate pass-through of the exchange rate into relative prices. Apart from certain simplifications and notational changes, the first three equations are standard components of the Dornbusch model.

In equation (4), the relative supply of money is assumed to be generated by a random walk process. This assumption is implicit in the original model, and Driskill (1981) presents some evidence in favor of its empirical relevance. In equation (5), however, an important modification is introduced. In the Dornbusch model, and in the majority of other models of exchange rate dynamics, expectations of future money growth are often tied to current changes in the money supply. As Wilson (1979) and others have demonstrated, the dynamic response to an anticipated future change in the money supply within this framework is quite different from the response to a current realized innovation. In equation (5), the fact is recognized by the introduction of an additional source of disturbance to the system: an innovation in the expected future exchange rate which is unrelated to current changes in the relative net supply of money.

These v innovations may be justified on a number of grounds. Within the framework of monetary models, v innovations may represent changes in the expected future path of monetary policy which are unrelated to changes in the current money supply. Alternatively, the v innovations could represent temporary real disturbances, speculative factors, or pure noise.

One could obviously extend this approach to allow for additional sources of disturbances in the system. One obvious extension to the present model would be to introduce innovations into the real exchange rate in equation (3). Another approach would be to allow for separate disturbances in the two countries. For the moment, however, we are primarily interested in the relationship between exchange rates and interest rate differentials and, for this purpose, the simple model specified above provides a convenient starting point.

There are a number of approaches that could be taken to the estimation of the model specified in equations (1) through (5). Frankel (1979) estimates a quasi-reduced form which allows for the nominal interest rate differential to enter as an independent variable. Bilson (1978) estimated a three-equation version with exchange rates, interest rates, and prices as dependent variables, and Driskill (1981) has estimated a two-equation system explaining prices and exchange rates. More recently, Driskill and Shefferin (1981) have estimated a three-equation system accounting for prices, exchange rates, and interest rates using full-information maximum likelihood techniques. As the discussion of Frankel's paper in the December 1981 issue of the *American Economic Review* indicates, this brief survey only touches the top of an econometric iceberg. In general, history has not been kind to these econometric models. Equations which appeared to fit the data well within the sample period did not retain their forecasting ability in postsample experiments. The results reported by Meese and Rogoff (1981) suggest, in fact, that the simple random walk hypothesis, in which the best forecast of the future spot rate is its current value, outperforms most standard econometric models.

For this reason, it may be worthwhile to approach the estimation of the model from a different perspective. One of the problems with standard econometric procedures is that the models of expectations formation are very simple and unrealistic. Although it may be useful for some purposes to assume that market participants base their expectations of future money supplies on a simple autoregression of past money, any reader of the *Wall Street Journal* must realize that this type of approach is unlikely to capture accurately the expectational influences on the exchange rate. In addition, the flexible exchange rate period has probably been subject to as many important shifts in the demand for currencies as in the supply, and these demand shocks are unobservable. While the introduction of dummy variables may help to explain the past, they are of limited value for predicting the future.

In the present paper, these problems are addressed through the assumption that both the forcing series, m_t, and the gradually adjusting series, p_t, are unobservable variables. This assumption is based on the idea that current market participants are making their decisions on the basis of expectations of the future values of these fundamental series. Published estimates, or ad hoc forecasting rules, thus are likely to be very poor approximations to the true expectations. This issue, which is quite separate from that of the accuracy of the money supply series, may explain which equations relating the innovation in the exchange rate to innovations in relative money supplies have been unsuccessful.

The task, then, is to demonstrate that the exchange rate and interest rate differentials observed during the floating rate period are consistent with the model described in equations (1) through (5). Furthermore, this consistency must be demonstrated using only the past history of the two financial asset prices. For an informal view of the solution procedure, consider the simple Dornbusch model in which there are only money supply shocks. This model predicts a number of well-defined characteristics of the exchange rate and interest rate differential series: *(a)* the innovations in the two series should be negatively correlated, since an increase (depreciation) of the price of the local currency works by lowering local interest rates relative to world rates; *(b)* the anticipated changes in the two series should also be negatively correlated, since this is required by the overshooting scenario; and *(c)* the change in the anticipated change in both series should be negatively related to the current innovations. In other words, if we observe a depreciation of the exchange rate today, the anticipated appreciation for the future should increase. If the actual data demonstrated these characteristics, then it would be possible to conclude that the dynamics of the exchange rate and the interest rate differentials are consistent with the model.

The main advantage of this approach, in contrast with traditional econometric procedures, is that we are able to obtain good estimates of the innovations in relative money supply and demand from the innovations in the asset prices themselves. A second advantage of the approach is that it allows the use of higher frequency data. Although exchange rate and interest rate data are available almost continuously, most of the presumed determinants of these prices are only available on a monthly or quarterly basis. Restricting the econometric research to the two financial prices allows the use of weekly, or even daily, data.

At the present time, economists have fairly diffuse priors over the economic determinants of exchange rates. In addition to the variables stressed by monetary models, more recent theories have assigned a role to the current account, the stock of wealth, and the supply of currency-denominated debt. Given that these controversies are unlikely to be resolved soon, the model-free approach based on time series analysis may be a useful nonjudgmental tool for studying the adjustment dynamics of international financial markets.

5.2 Theoretical Autoregressions for Exchange Rates and Forward Premia

In this section, the "unobservable" variables, relative prices and the net relative supply of money, will be eliminated from the model in order to arrive at the joint process generating the exchange rate and the forward premium. This process will then be estimated using weekly data on the two time series. As a first step, solve the money market equilibrium condition for the relative price and substitute this equation into the price adjustment equation. Since the forward premium is the price that maintains the equilibrium condition in the foreign exchange market in the short run, the resulting expression is solved for this variable.

$$(6) \qquad x = -\frac{1}{\alpha} m + \frac{\phi}{\alpha} Le + \frac{1 - \phi}{\alpha} Lm + (1 - \phi) Lx.$$

Since the money supply is assumed to follow a random walk, equation (6) is differenced and the relative money supply variable is replaced by its innovation.

$$(7) \qquad \Delta x = \frac{\phi}{\alpha} L\Delta e + (1 - \phi) Lx + w - (1 - \phi) Lw.$$

In equation (7), the relative money supply innovation, u, has been replaced by the innovation in the forward premium, w. The two innovations are related in equation (8).

$$(8) \qquad w = -\frac{1}{\alpha} u.$$

By making use of the fact that the autoregressive and the moving average structure in (7) are the same, equation (7) can be restated in the following form.

$$(9) \qquad \Delta x = \frac{(\phi/\alpha) L}{[1 - (1 - \phi)L]} \Delta e + w.$$

Equation (9) imposes a number of testable restrictions on the process generating the forward premium. First, the predictable part of the change in the premium is an exponentially declining distributed lag of the past changes in the exchange rate. Second, given the past history of the exchange rate, lagged changes in the forward premium should not have any significant predictive power over current changes. Third, only the relative money supply innovations induce changes in the current value of the premium; changes in expected future relative money supplies have no influence.

The economics behind these results is straightforward. In the Dornbusch model, the role of the forward premium is to maintain equilibrium in the foreign exchange market. The exchange rate only influences the current demand for the two currencies through its influence on the forward premium. Consequently, all of the burden of adjusting to future shocks is placed directly on the exchange rate. As far as the predictable part of the change in the premium is concerned, the results follow from the fact that there is only one variable in the system which adjusts over time. Hence the past history of the system can be represented by the past history of either of the endogenous variables.

The solution for the exchange rate begins by differencing equation (2) and introducing the process generating $\Delta \bar{e}$. This yields

$$(10) \qquad \Delta e = -\frac{1}{\theta} \Delta x + w + v.$$

If equation (9) is used to eliminate the relative money supply innovation from (10), the following final form for the exchange rate may be obtained.

$$(11) \qquad \Delta e = - \frac{1 + \alpha\theta}{\theta} \Delta x + \frac{\phi}{[1 - (1 - \phi)L]} L\Delta e + v.$$

As an alternative, it would be possible to use (9) to eliminate the contemporaneous change in the forward premium from (10). Equation (11), however, has the important advantage that the θ parameter can be identified from the coefficient relating the change in the exchange rate to the change in the forward premium. Since the change in the premium is uncorrelated with the *v* innovation by construction, the estimates of the parameters will be unbiased.

Before proceeding to the empirical analysis, it may be useful to check the validity of the model through a simulation experiment. For the structural parameters, it is assumed that prices adjust to the real exchange rate at a rate of 1% per week, hence φ equals .01, and that the interest elasticity of the demand for money is −.1. If monthly interest rates are approximately 1% per month, the semielasticity would then be 10. Given these assumed values, the value of the expectations coefficient, θ, is defined by the rational expectations condition:

$$(12) \qquad \theta_1, \theta_2 = \frac{-\phi\alpha \pm \sqrt{(\phi\alpha)^2 + 4\phi\alpha}}{-2\alpha}.$$

Choosing the positive root, and introducing the assumed values of the other parameters, we arrive at an estimate of θ of .037. These values will serve as a useful standard of comparison with the actual estimates.

The estimates of the constrained system are provided in table 5.1. The first notable fact from these results is that the parameters are generally estimated imprecisely. The exception to this rule is the price adjustment parameter, which is significantly different from zero in both cases. The results for

Table 5.1   **Estimates of the Constrained Model**

Parameter	Control	£/$	DM/$
φ	.01	.066	.054
		(.029)	(.027)
α	10	15.24	180.59
		(26.07)	(1488.26)
θ	.037	.140	.076
		(.536)	(3.324)
σ_v		.012	.013
σ_w		.003	.006
D-W (v)		2.150	2.011
D-W (w)		2.920	2.730

Notes: The parameters were estimated from a weekly sample of 393 observations using the spot rate and the 1-month forward premium from the Harris Bank *Weekly Review* data tape. The sample runs from January 1974 to September 1981.

the £/$ rate are, however, reasonably consistent with prior expectations. The two adjustment parameters are larger than one might expect, but the interest semielasticity of the demand for money is very close to prior expectations. The main surprise in the DM/$ results is the very large estimate of the interest rate semielasticity. Even with interest rates as low as 5% on an annual basis, this estimate suggests an interest elasticity of about .75 in the DM/$ rate.

The large estimated interest elasticity in the German case results in a pattern of exchange rate dynamics which is familiar from the discussion of near perfect currency substitution. In the currency substitution literature, a high degree of currency substitution results in greater variability in the exchange rate because the expected change in the exchange rate must be kept small. Consider, as an example, a 1% increase in the demand for either sterling or deutsche marks relative to dollars. The adjustment pattern predicted by the models is given in table 5.2.

The control solution is surely familiar to students of the Dornbusch model. In response to a 1% increase in the relative demand for money, the exchange rate appreciates immediately by 3.7% on an annual basis and the interest rate differential increases by 1.2% per annum. As prices adjust, the exchange rate depreciates and the interest rate differential declines. The results for the £/$ rate mirror this pattern: the initial overshooting is smaller, and the adjustment is more rapid, but the dynamics are certainly consistent with the underlying model.

Table 5.2   **Dynamic Response to an Increase in the Relative Demand for Money**

	Control		£/$		DM/$	
t	$e - e_0$	$x - x_0$	$e - e_0$	$x - x_0$	$e - e_0$	$x - x_0$
-1	0	0	0	0	0	0
0	-3.7	1.2	-1.56	.84	-1.16	.07
5	-3.2	.99	-1.36	.50	-1.14	.05
10	-2.8	.82	-1.25	.30	-1.13	.04
15	-2.5	.68	-1.17	.18	-1.12	.03
20	-2.3	.56	-1.13	.11	-1.11	.02
25	-2.1	.46	-1.11	.07	-1.10	.02
30	-1.9	.38	-1.09	.04	-1.10	.01
35	-1.8	.32	-1.08	.02	-1.09	.00
40	-1.6	.27	-1.08	.01	-1.09	.00
45	-1.5	.22	-1.07	.01	-1.09	.00

Note: The $e - e_0$ column represents the % deviation of the exchange rate from the rate that would have existed in the absence of the 1% increase in the demand for money in period 0. The $x - x_0$ column represents the deviation of the interest rate differential—expressed in annual percentage terms—from the interest rate differential that would have occurred in the absence of the 1% increase in the demand for money in period 0.

In the DM/$ rate, the characteristics of closely substitutable currencies are evident. The extent of the overshooting is small relative to the other results, and the increase in the interest rate differential is also small. Clearly these factors are interrelated. The overshooting must be small in order for the expected rate of change in the exchange rate to be small, given that the adjustment velocities are about the same as in the £/$ case.

In this section, it has been demonstrated that simple dynamic models of exchange rate determination can be formulated and estimated as vector autoregressive processes. Estimates of the Dornbusch model were not particularly precise, but the dynamic response of the exchange rate and the interest rate differential to an increase in the demand for money was broadly consistent with the predictions of the model. This fact, however, does not represent a test of the model. In the next section, the constrained model will be tested against a less constrained alternative.

5.3 Unconstrained Vector Autoregressions

A more general specification of the joint process generating the exchange rate and the forward premium is presented in equations (13) and (14):

(13) $[1 - A11(L)] \Delta e + A22(L) \Delta x = Cw + v$

(14) $A21(L) \Delta e + [1 - A22(L)] \Delta x = w.$

In these equations, the $A(L)$ functions are polynomials in the lag operator and C is a parameter relating the innovation in the forward premium to the exchange rate. This general model differs from the constrained model in two important respects: the distributed lags are unconstrained across equations and the lagged values of the change in the premium are introduced into both equations. In the estimation, fourth degree polynomials are used to test the alternative hypothesis.

Estimates of equations (13) and (14) are presented in table 5.3. It is obvious that the constrained model will be rejected by the sample data. In fact, the lagged values of the forward premium are important predictors of both the change in the exchange rate and the change in the forward premium. This impression is confirmed by a likelihood ratio test of the alternative models. Twice the difference between the log likelihood ratios of the constrained and unconstrained models is 182.42 in the £/$ case and 86.28 in the DM/$ case. Under the hypothesis that the constrained model is correct, this variable is distributed X^2 with 17 degrees of freedom. The probability that a X^2 variable with 17 degrees of freedom is greater than 33.4 is 1%. The estimates consequently reject the hypothesis that the constrained model is correct.

Given the simplicity of the model, the fact that it is rejected by the data should not be a cause for undue dismay. What is required is a more general

Table 5.3   **Estimates of the Unconstrained Model**

Parameter	£/$	DM/$
A11–1	− .011	.056
	(.049)	(.050)
A11–2	.128**	.135**
	(.049)	(.049)
A11–3	.062	− .064
	(.049)	(.050)
A11–4	.103**	.048
	(.050)	(.050)
A12–1	.698**	.555
	(.225)	(.552)
A12–2	.685**	− .736
	(.265)	(.595)
A12–3	.102	− 2.344**
	(.266)	(.595)
A12–4	− .496**	− .346
	(.229)	(.559)
A21–1	.008	− .007
	(.011)	(.004)
A21–2	.001	.002
	(.011)	(.004)
A21–3	− .014	.002
	(.011)	(.005)
A21–4	.004	.001
	(.011)	(.005)
A22–1	− .669**	− .408**
	(.051)	(.051)
A22–2	− .451**	− .094
	(.059)	(.054)
A22–3	− .291**	.016
	(.060)	(.054)
A22–4	.012	− .006
	(.051)	(.051)
C	− .418	− .023
	(.224)	(.548)
v	.011	.012
w	.003	.001

Note: Constants were estimated but not reported.

specification of the dynamic interaction between exchange rates and interest rates that will allow for tests of dynamics which are not model specific. In the following, such tests will be developed and tested for two important concepts in the literature on exchange rate dynamics: magnification and overshooting.

Before proceeding to the tests, it may be worthwhile to describe these theories in general terms. The overshooting hypothesis, which was a theoretical feature of the Dornbusch model, refers to a situation in which the short-run change in an endogenous variable in response to an innovation is greater than the long-run change. This implies that an innovation that causes the endogenous variable to increase on impact must also create an anticipated decline in the endogenous variable during the adjustment period. Hence the anticipated change is negatively correlated to the innovation. The magnification effect, on the other hand, is generally based upon the idea that the exogenous variables which generate exchange rates are positively correlated. Hence an innovation, for example, in the money supply affects the exchange rate both directly and by increasing the future money supply. Since the expected future increase creates an anticipated depreciation of the currency, which reduces the demand for it, the depreciation of the exchange rate will be more than proportional to the increase in the money supply. During the adjustment period, the exchange rate will continue to depreciate in the absence of new disturbances. Hence, in contrast to the overshooting hypothesis, the magnification effect posits a positive correlation between the current innovation and the expected future change in the endogenous variable.

These concepts may be formally specified and tested within the framework of the model specified in equations (13) and (14). The first step in the development of the tests is to derive the univariate representations of the vector autoregressive processes. The univariate processes are defined in equations (15) and (16):

(15)
$$[(1 - A\,11)\,(1 - A22) - A12A21]\,\Delta e =$$
$$[C(1 - A22) - A12[\,u + (1 - A22)\,v$$

(16)
$$[(1 - A11)\,(1 - A22) - A12A21]\,\Delta x =$$
$$[(1 - A11) - C*A21]\,u - A21\,v.$$

The gain in a time series is defined as the change in the expected terminal value, conditional upon the new information at time t. If

$$A11 = a_{11-1}\,L + a_{11-2}\,L^2 + a_{11-3}\,L^3 + \ldots + a_{11-n}\,L^n,$$

then define

$$B11 = a_{11-1} + a_{11-2} + a_{11-3} + \ldots + a_{11-n}.$$

Using this definition, we have that

$$\underset{t}{E}\,e_{t+i} - \underset{t-1}{E}\,e_{t+i} = \frac{[C(1 - B22) - B12]}{[(1 - B11)\,(1 - B22) - B12B21]}\,u$$
$$+ \frac{(1 - B22)}{[(1 - B11)\,(1 - B22) - B12B21]}\,v$$

and

$$E_t x_{t+i} - E_{t-1} x_{t+i} = \frac{[(1 - B11) - C*B21]}{[(1 - B11)(1 - B22) - B12B21]} u$$
$$- \frac{B21}{[(1 - B11)(1 - B22) - B12B21]} v$$

as i tends to infinity. It is reasonable to define these expressions as the change in the expected permanent exchange rate in response to the innovations at time t. Based upon the information at time t, the model predicts a dynamic path for the exchange rate with some stable terminal value, at $t + 1$, new innovations are observed and new terminal values are calculated. The change in the expected terminal values is the change in the permanent exchange rate.

With these concepts in hand, definitions of magnification and overshooting effects are straightforward. A magnification effect, which we might also call an undershooting effect, refers to a situation in which the change in the actual exchange rate in response to the innovation at time t is less than the change in the permanent exchange rate. This implies that the actual rate must continue to move in the same direction in order to reach the terminal value.

On the other hand, a magnification effect occurs when the actual change in the exchange rate in response to the innovation exceeds the change in the permanent exchange rate. This pattern implies that the future changes in the rate must, to some extent, reverse the current change in order to reach the terminal point. These definitions are fairly general in that they do not require a specific pattern of adjustment toward the terminal value. For example, the exchange rate might increase in response to an innovation, continue to increase in the following weeks, and then decline as prices adjusted. As long as the terminal point fell below the initial change, this would be characterized as an overshooting situation.

There are two innovations in the version of the Dornbusch model described above, and they imply different patterns of exchange rate dynamics. A current money supply shock, a u innovation, implies overshooting: the exchange rate must initially increase by more than its long-run value in order to induce a market-clearing interest rate differential. On the other hand, a future shock, a v innovation, leads to undershooting. To see this, consider an anticipated future tightening of the money supply. Since the interest rate must remain fixed, all of the burden of adjustment is placed upon the exchange rate in the short run, and it must appreciate in proportion to the anticipated fall in the money supply. During the subsequent adjustment, prices will tend to fall, and interest rates will have to increase in order to maintain equilibrium in the money market. Through the forward parity condition, the increase in interest rates will lead to a further appreciation of the exchange rate.

A simple test of magnification and/or overshooting involves an examination of the long-run response to an innovation with the impact response. Table 5.4 presents a comparison of these values for the two cases under study.

The results reported in table 5.4 for the £/$ rate are broadly consistent with the theoretical model. For contemporaneous money shocks, overshooting is evident in both the exchange rate and the forward premium, and the degree of overshooting in the forward premium is certainly statistically significant. In addition, a magnification effect is evident in the response of the exchange rate to a future innovation in relative money supply: a 1% increase in per one leads to an eventual increase of 1.4%.

In the DM/$ case, the results are more mixed. While there is strong evidence of overshooting in the forward premium in response to a contemporaneous money shock, the exchange rate appears to be independent of these shocks in both the short run and the long run. While the random walk nature of the exchange rate may be due to currency substitution, this explanation is difficult to reconcile with the evidence of reasonably strong negative correlation in the forward premium. However, the results are more supportive of the model in the case of future shocks. As in the £/$ case, future shocks are associated with undershooting in the exchange rate and in the forward premium.

Table 5.4   Magnification and Overshooting Effects

Relation	£/$	DM/$
$\Delta e : u$		
Impact	−.4183	−.0225
	(.224)	(.548)
Permanent	−.0004	−.0215
	(.011)	(.006)
$\Delta e : v$		
Impact	1.000	1.000
Permanent	1.3919	1.220
	(.176)	(.138)
$\Delta x : u$		
Impact	1.0000	1.0000
Permanent	.4166	.6746
	(.039)	(.062)
$\Delta x : v$		
Impact	.0000	.0000
Permanent	−.0077	−2.3675
	(.543)	(1.416)

5.5 Conclusions

The purpose of this paper has been to outline an approach to the testing of dynamic models of exchange rate determination. This approach is based upon the idea that it is difficult to measure directly the process by which market participants revise their expectations about current and future money supplies. On the other hand, it is possible to make indirect inferences about these expectations through a time series analysis of related financial prices. In an application of the process to the Dornbusch model of exchange rate dynamics, it was shown that all of the key parameters of the model could be identified from a vector autoregression of the weekly time series of the exchange rate and the forward premium.

The restrictions placed upon the parameters of the vector autoregression by the Dornbusch model were firmly rejected by the data. Given the simplicity of the model, this rejection was probably to be expected. In the final section of the paper, a more general characterization of exchange rate overshooting and magnification effects was developed and tested against the data. In the £/$ case, the more general specification did appear to match the broad empirical regularities present in the time series process generating the two prices. In the DM/$ case, the results were more problematic.

Given the exploratory nature of the paper, it is worthwhile to close the paper with some suggestions for extending the method. In the empirical research, the parameters of the time series models were found to be quite unstable over time. Hence an important future step would be to take account of the drift in the parameters through varying parameter regression techniques. In addition, the relative variance of the two innovations was also not constant over time, and it could be the case that the parameter drift is related to this variation. Finally, there is a need to develop similar autoregressive models for other popular models of exchange rate dynamics. This step would allow for multimodel tests of exchange rate dynamics.

Comment   Richard M. Levich

The papers by Hans Genberg and John Bilson are both engaged in exploratory research to understand the short-run dynamic behavior of exchange rates. The explicit motivation for both studies is the view that previous research has not adequately explained the recent trends and volatility in major exchange rates. The erratic relationship between the theory and the reality of exchange rate behavior leads Bilson to observe that "economists currently have fairly diffuse priors on the economic determinants of exchange rates." As a consequence, both Bilson and Genberg propose a new line of research—one that looks at the "tracks" of recent exchange rate behavior and asks what type of exchange rate theory (i.e., exogenous variables, their interrelationships and stochastic processes) would be consistent with this behavior.

As I suggested above, this new line of research stems from Genberg's and Bilson's frustration with the explanatory (i.e., in sample) and predictive (i.e., postsample) performance of popular exchange rate models. In capsule form, what do these two authors propose?

Genberg proposes to remain agnostic about the fundamental variables, the Z_t driving exchange rates. He also decides not to entertain complicated time series processes for his Z_t. Instead, he considers only AR(1) processes in the levels and percentage changes. With these assumptions, Genberg derives relationships between forward rate innovations *(IF)* and spot rate innovations *(IS)*. Empirical analysis of the *IF* and *IS* series can therefore be used to infer the nature of the Z_t process. Genberg concludes that: AR(1) processes on the Z_t seem sufficient to explain the time series behavior of spot and forward rate innovations; there is little evidence for exchange rate overshooting; and the foreign exchange market appears to anticipate and reflect changes in expected monetary behavior.

Bilson, on the other hand, begins with the basic Dornbusch exchange rate dynamics model. This model fosters two testable hypotheses: (1) negative contemporaneous correlation between the exchange rate and domestic interest rate series, and (2) negative autocorrelation *within* both the exchange rate and domestic interest rate series. Bilson adapts the basic model by assuming that in the current period both the money supply and domestic prices are unobservable. This leads him to adopt a vector autoregression (VAR) technique for testing his hypothesis. Bilson's empirical results offer only mixed evidence on the hypothesis.

Both Genberg and Bilson appear to be pursuing a nontraditional style of empirical analysis. Rather than specify the exchange rate as a function of certain independent variables in a tightly specified model, the authors seem to ask a more limited question: Are certain broad empirical findings (e.g., autocorrelation or cross-correlation patterns among series) consistent with the predictions of a general class of exchange rate models? If so, Genberg and Bilson will interpret these empirical regularities as evidence supporting a general model of exchange rate behavior.

I will argue that while new studies of exchange rate behavior are always welcome, we should not be surprised by the poor ability of earlier studies to explain short-run exchange rate behavior. Part of my argument is general, applicable to any asset pricing situation, and part is specific to the foreign exchange market.

In my view, the most important finding to come from the last decade of research is the realization that foreign exchange is a financial asset. Therefore, foreign exchange rates will exhibit behavior closely identified with stock and bond prices—that is, prices will adjust quickly and sometimes by a large amount in response to new information about current variables, the future values of these variables or simply the confidence with which these expectations are held. The implication of this is that over the long run, asset prices should be set in accordance with well-known asset pricing formulas, but over the short run there is considerable scope for prices to be a noisy series and at variance with observable fundamentals. (I am not suggesting here that asset markets are inefficient in the short run or that profit opportunities exist. Costly information whose implications and accuracy are highly uncertain and the psychological state of market agents are real factors in the short run.)

Existing economic theories seem to be quite capable of explaining cross-sectional variation—why there are 10,000 Argentinian pesos per dollar, 1,300 Italian lire per dollar, and only 0.5 British pounds per dollar. Existing theory is also capable of explaining the bulk of currency movements over a long time period—why the mark rose from $0.35 in 1973 to $0.50 in 1980. Existing theories fail to adequately explain short-run currency fluctuations— why the mark rose from $0.50 on Monday to $0.52 on Tuesday or Friday. Some of these currency movements can be attributed to unexpected changes in fundamental variables (i.e., "news"). But the remainder are attributable to "purely technical" factors (e.g., large corporations meeting contractual obligations on prearranged dates, large financial institutions taking short-term positions in markets with little net speculative capital), central bank intervention, and other factors that contribute to what we often label "noise" from the standpoint of a highly stylized macro model. My point here is that economists know a good deal about exchange rate determination, as evidenced by the cross-section and long-run comparisons. The analysis of short-run currency movements puts the foreign exchange market very much "under the microscope," where most of our existing theories do not have a comparative advantage for explaining observed behavior.

While the above discussion on valuation problems describes both the equity market and the foreign exchange market, I believe the problems are fundamentally more difficult in the foreign exchange market. Consider the example of a large consumer products company such as Kraft Foods, General Mills, or Proctor and Gamble. Many of the directors and officers of these firms may have been employed for 5 years, 10 years, or more. They may make and publicize 5-year plans. Both the demand side and supply side of these industries may be fairly stable, or at least predictable, in response to known demographics and spending habits. In short, it is conceivable that market analysts might come to know these firms so that their share prices and returns were fairly stable or predictable.

In contrast, the fundamental variables which effect foreign exchange rates—namely, monetary and real events—are heavily influenced by government action. The nature of governmental planning (monetary or fiscal policy) is that it is short term (generally no longer than one year), somewhat uncertain to the extent that legislative approval is required, and totally uncertain given that a new administration with completely different policies may be voted in at the next election. This setting suggests to me that the foreign exchange market is starved for information relative to the stock market. My point here is that currency analysts are not likely to know very much about the fundamental determinants of exchange rates at horizons past one or two years. Consequently, expectations concerning fundamental variables are likely to be weakly held and uncertainty acts to deter a large pool of risk capital. Both factors contribute toward short-run exchange rate volatility.

A final point that inhibits easy empirical tests in the foreign exchange market is that most models hypothesize shocks of known size and duration that occur one at a time. In practice, however, these conditions are never satisfied. An initial disturbance may occur on Monday. A disturbance with an opposite effect occurs on Wednesday. And news arrives on Friday that causes us to revise our assessment of Monday's shock. In a multiple factor, lagged adjustment model, it may be nearly impossible to isolate individual disturbances and follow their effects through to the exchange rate.

*   *   *

Hans Genberg's paper begins by setting up the Z_t processes and deriving the relationship between spot and forward innovations *(IS* and *IF)* that appear in expressions (12) and (16). The thrust of the empirical work, then, is to determine whether the data on *IS* and *IF* are consistent with rational expectations on the Z_t. This procedure raises two issues. First, no alternative hypothesis for the Z_t is specified. A common interpretation of many early empirical studies of floating exchange rates was that the data were so volatile that few hypotheses could be rejected. Testing one hypothesis on the Z_t versus an alternative would be the preferred procedure. Second, the procedure assumes for simplicity that there is only one Z_t. As we argued earlier, it is more likely that Z_t is a vector and that disturbances occur in one variable while the market is still adjusting to an earlier disturbance in another variable. Thus the exchange rate series probably reflects a complicated overlay of disturbances and adjustments that is both difficult to model theoretically and test for empirically.

Another assumption that might be questioned is Genberg's definition of *IS* and *IF*. Note that the definition of an innovation does not allow any role for transaction costs, risk premia, or the technical (but real) factors I discussed earlier. What concerns me here is that the empirical values for these innovations, which will be subjected to close scrutiny, are likely to be very small numbers. I suggest that it is an exaggeration to define *IS* and *IF* as reflecting only innovations in the Z_t rather than transaction costs, risk premia, or other variables.

Genberg's analysis relies on the so-called news model, wherein today's exchange rate depends on deviations between expected and realized values for the Z_t. It seems to me that this formulation is not compatible with a model that incorporates risk premia for risk-averse investors. The news model suggests that if analysts expect 10% money supply growth and 10% growth is realized, then no exchange rate change is required. But surely if analysts were worried that actual money growth might reach 20% (there must also have been some probability of money growth less than 10%), this announcement, which confirms expectations, must make risk-averse investors feel relieved. The value of domestic currency should rise on this news that removes uncertainty.

Also on the topic of news, I would argue that in an efficient market the source of news is necessarily shifting. Suppose the market sees that inflation is volatile and unpredictable. More resources should be spent to understand and forecast inflation with more precision. Once this is accomplished, inflation ceases to be a newsworthy variable. But now relative ignorance about some other variable causes it to be an important source of news driving exchange rates.

On the positive side, Genberg's paper marks an important step by analyzing the term structure of forward rate innovations. Both the magnitude and duration of disturbances are important factors for analyzing exchange rate behavior. Genberg's approach here is innovative, and it seems to be a promising avenue for gauging the persistence if not the magnitude of exchange market disturbances.

John Bilson's approach also is to analyze correlation and time series properties of exchange rates and interest rates to see if they are consistent with the Dornbusch exchange rate dynamics model. Bilson does not offer an alternative hypothesis. The null hypothesis—negative contemporaneous correlation between exchange rates and domestic interest rates, and negative autocorrelation within the exchange rate and interest rate series—are supported in only half the cases. The second hypothesis is poorly stated since the dynamics model predicts a positive shock in period 1 to be followed by a negative shock in period 2 (i.e., negative autocorrelation), but then the negative shocks continue in periods 3 on (i.e., positive autocorrelation). This null hypothesis seems especially susceptible to the problem of multiple and overlapping disturbances upsetting the autocorrelation pattern.

Bilson's analysis includes only 1-month forward contracts, so these tests are more limited than for Genberg. Bilson's regressions of correlations against volatility measures for spot and forward rates are provocative but very likely confuse short-term noise in the independent variables with real disturbances. My preference would be toward analyzing the large disturbances in the driving variables and testing for announcement effects, perhaps by a variance criterion. M. F. Melhem (NYU, Ph.D. in progress) is currently analyzing the data in this way. Melhem finds that during the period 1973–78, the $/DM and $/$C rates were roughly twice as volatile over the 1-day interval Thursday (9:00 A.M.) to Friday (9:00 A.M.) than over any other similar interval. Over this sample period, the weekly United States money supply figures were announced during the Thursday/Friday interval. Melhem also finds that these daily exchange rate changes respond significantly to the unexpected money supply component, and insignificantly to the expected money supply component. For the $/$C rates, the pattern of response is stronger for spot rates and short-term forward rates, consistent with an overshooting model.

The papers by Genberg and Bilson have embarked on exploratory research to compare short-run exchange behavior to the predictions of a general class of exchange rate model. In this comment, I have argued that current economic models are very useful to explain cross-sectional exchange rate differences and major currency swings over long time periods. Existing economic models, applied in an environment with major monetary and structural uncertainties, cannot be expected to gauge exchange rate values with a 5% or 10% tolerance limit. Since these figures are within the range of current month-to-month exchange rate changes, we cannot expect that existing exchange rate models will be useful for pinpointing exchange rate values, although they should get the rough direction of movement correct.

The general problem with both papers is that they may put the foreign exchange market "too much under the microscope" relative to the sophistication of current models. Genberg's paper, however, which looks at the term structure of innovations, seems to offer some promise for gauging the magnitude and duration of economic disturbances.

References

Bilson, John F. O. 1978. The current experience with floating exchange rates: An appraisal of the monetary approach. *American Economic Review, Papers and Proceedings* 68 (May): 392–97.

Calvo, Guillermo A., and Rodriguez, Carlos A. 1977. A model of exchange rate determination with currency substitution and rational expectations. *Journal of Political Economy* 85 (June): 55–65.

Driskill, Robert A. 1981. Exchange rate dynamics: An empirical investigation. *Journal of Political Economy* 89 (April): 357–71.

Driskill, Robert A., and Sheffrin, Steven M. 1981. On the mark: Comment." *American Economic Review* 71 (December): 1068–74.

Dornbusch, Rudiger. 1976. Expectations and exchange rate dynamics. *Journal of Political Economy* 84 (December): 1161–76.

Frankel, Jeffrey. 1979. On the mark: A theory of floating exchange rates based on real interest rate differentials, *American Economic Review* 69 (September): 610–22.

————. 1981. On the mark: Reply. *American Economic Review* 71 (December): 1075–82.

Frenkel, Jacob A. 1981. Flexible exchange rates, prices, and the role of "news": Lessons from the 1970s. *Journal of Political Economy* 89 (August): 665–705.

Johnson, Harry G. 1976. The monetary approach to balance of payments theory. In *The monetary approach to the balance of payments,* ed. Jacob A. Frenkel and Harry G. Johnson. London: Allen & Unwin.

Kouri, Pentti J. K. 1976. The exchange rate and the balance of payments in the short run and the long run. *Scandinavian Journal of Economics* 78: 280–304.

Meese, R. A., and Rogoff, K. 1981. Empirical exchange rate models of the seventies: Are any fit to survive?" International Finance Discussion Paper no. 184, Board of Governors of the Federal Reserve System, Washington, D.C.

Niehans, Jurg. 1977. Exchange rate dynamics with stock/flow interaction. *Journal of Political Economy* 85 (December): 1245–57.

Wilson, Charles A. 1979. The impact of anticipated shocks in Professor Dornbusch's model of "Expectations and exchange rate dynamics. *Journal of Political Economy* 87 (June): 639–97.

III   Asset Demands and the Exchange Rate

6 International Portfolio Diversification: Short-Term Financial Assets and Gold

Jorge Braga de Macedo, Jeffrey A. Goldstein, and
David M. Meerschwam

6.1 Introduction

During the last decade, there has been a relaxation of international capital controls, a dramatic expansion in the volume of trading in international financial markets, and, more generally, an increase in international financial integration. The period of generalized floating has also been associated with a significant increase in uncertainty about exchange rates, interest rates, and prices. In this context, our paper discusses international portfolio selection by individuals, firms, and government agencies. Specifically, we present a model of optimal portfolio diversification by risk-averse agents who consume goods produced in various countries. They are able to continuously reshuffle the composition of their wealth, which is held in assets with known nominal interest rates denominated in different currencies. Given risk and consumption preferences and uncertainty about the prices of goods, prices of assets, and exchange rates, this model indicates the optimal combination of assets chosen by an agent who wishes to maximize returns and minimize fluctuations in the purchasing power of his portfolio. The theory of international portfolio diversification thus explains how risk-averse investors may reduce uncertainty about real rates of return and provides a way of understanding the portfolio behavior of a given agent with an international horizon.

This analysis is an extension of the classic mean-variance framework of Tobin (1965). When continuous trading is possible, Merton (1971) spelled out the conditions under which intertemporal maximization of expected util-

The research described in this paper was partly financed by a NSF grant to the International Finance Section, Princeton University (NSF PRA-8116473).

199

ity would allow the separation of the portfolio rule from the consumption rule. In particular, he showed that, if asset prices are generated by stationary and lognormally distributed continuous-time stochastic processes (geometric Brownian motion) and if the instantaneous utility function of the agent is homothetic with constant relative risk aversion, a time-invariant portfolio rule could be derived. Furthermore, this rule would be the same as the one obtained if the agent was maximizing period by period a linear function of mean real return and the variance of return.

There have been several applications of the Tobin-Merton framework to international finance. Most have been surveyed out by Branson and Henderson (1984). In section 6.2, we present a version of the model developed in Meerschwam (1983) which allows the international investor to hold assets with uncertain prices, such as gold. This generalizes the currency diversification rules derived by Kouri and Macedo (1978) and Macedo (1979, 1983). Section 6.3 adds gold to the optimal portfolios of short-term financial assets analyzed by Goldstein (1983). Using monthly data and quarterly holding periods from April 1973 to March 1981, the evolution of optimal portfolios is discussed. The conclusion summarizes the main results.

6.2 Optimal Portfolio Rules

In this section, we present the optimal diversification rule for an agent who consumes fixed proportions of N composite goods produced in N countries and who holds a portfolio (that can be continuously reshuffled) of M assets with known nominal returns in domestic currency. The prices of the N goods, the prices of the M assets, and the $N - 1$ exchange rates are uncertain and are specified as continuous stochastic processes. As a result, real wealth accumulation, equal to the difference between the real rate of return on the portfolio and the rate of real consumption, is described by a stochastic differential equation. Given this flow budget constraint, the agent chooses at each moment in time a portfolio of assets and a consumption bundle. The optimal portfolio rule is thus one of the outcomes of the intertemporal constrained maximization of the expected utility of consumption from time 0 to time T.[1] Since we are interested in the problem of an individual agent rather than in the determination of goods and assets prices and exchange rates in general equilibrium, we assume that prices are exogenous.[2] We specify prices in terms of the numeraire (arbitrarily defined as

1. A constant discount rate could easily be introduced. For a variable discount rate and infinite time horizon, see Nairay (1981).
2. For an endogenous determination of these processes, see Nairay (1981). Simplified applications to international finance are in Bortz (1982) and Stulz (1982).

the currency of country N) as stationary and lognormally distributed stochastic processes.[3] Then, for $M = N$ and $i = 1, \ldots, N$, we have

$$(1) \qquad \frac{dG_i}{G_i} = \pi_i dt + \sigma_i dz_i$$

$$\frac{dP_i}{P_i} = \mu_i dt + \delta_i du_i,$$

where G_i is the price of the asset i expressed in terms of the numeraire, so that $G_i = G_i^d/S_i$ and $G_N = G_N^d$, G_i^d being the domestic currency price of asset i and S_i the price of currency i in terms of the numeraire; P_i is the price of the good produced in country i expressed in terms of the numeraire, so that $P_i = P_i^d/S_i$ and $P_N = P_N^d$, P_i^d being the domestic currency price of the good; $\pi_i(\mu_i)$ is the instantaneous conditional mean proportional change per unit of time of $G_i(P_i)$; $\sigma_i^2(\delta_i^2)$ is the instantaneous conditional variance per unit of time of $G_i(P_i)$, σ_{ij}, δ_{ij}, θ_{ij} being the instantaneous conditional covariances per unit of time between G_i and G_j, P_i and P_j, and G_i and P_j, respectively; and dz_i and du_i are Wiener processes with zero mean and unit variance, and instantaneous correlation coefficients ρ_{ij} (between dz_i and dz_j) and $\bar{\rho}_{ii}$ (between dz_i and du_i).

It is convenient to measure (positive or negative) asset holdings as a proportion of real wealth, W. The share of wealth held in asset i is defined as

$$(2) \qquad x_i = \frac{N_i Q_i}{W}, \quad i = 1, \ldots, N;$$

where N_i are the holdings of asset i and $Q_i = G_i/\Pi_j^N P_j^{\alpha_j}$ is the purchasing power of asset i over the N goods,[4] α_j being the share of good j in total expenditure.

Utility is a strictly concave function of the instantaneous rate of consumption X_j of the N goods, constant expenditure share α_j, and constant relative risk aversion $1 - \gamma$. Given the state of the system, described by real wealth, we use the method of dynamic stochastic programming in order to find the optimal paths of the control variables x_i and X_j. Hence, we define the value function,

$$(3) \qquad J(W) = \max E_t \int_t^T \frac{1}{\gamma} \Pi_j^N X_j(\tau)^{\alpha_j \gamma} \, d\tau,$$

---

3. More general exogenous processes are used in Macedo (1983), Macedo, Golstein, and Meerschwam (1982), henceforth MGM, and Meerschwam (1983).

4. The purchasing power of a currency is the optimal price index when the indirect utility functions are separable. See more on the concept in Kouri and Macedo (1978) and Macedo (1982). Work with more general utility functions has been done by Stulz (1980).

where E_t denotes the expectation conditional upon information available at time t. From intertemporal utility maximization subject to the wealth accumulation constraint and the unity constraint on asset shares, we obtain first-order conditions from which the consumption and portfolio rules can be derived.[5] Stacking the M first-order conditions on portfolio shares, we obtain

(4) $$r + (1 - \gamma)\Theta\alpha - (1 - \gamma)Gx - (\lambda/J_W)e = \underline{0},$$

where r is the vector of real returns; $1 - \gamma = -(\delta^2 J/\delta W^2)(W\delta J/\delta W)$; α is the vector of expenditure shares; x is the vector of portfolio shares; λ is the Lagrange multiplier; $J_W = W\delta J/\delta W$; e is an N column vector of ones; $\underline{0}$ is an N column vector of zeros; $G = \{\sigma_{ij}\}$ is the N-by-N variance-covariance matrix of changes in asset prices expressed in terms of the numeraire; and $\Theta = \{\theta_{ij}\}$ is the N-by-N covariance matrix of changes in asset prices and changes in goods prices both expressed in terms of the numeraire. Note that the expected real return on each asset is obtained by adding the expected proportional change in the purchasing power of the asset to its known nominal return in domestic currency: $r_i = R_i + dQ_i/Q_i$, $i = 1, \ldots, N$.

Using the unity constraint on the portfolio shares (multiplied by $\gamma - 1$), we augment (4) by another row, to get

(5) $$\left[\frac{x}{\lambda/J_W(1 - \gamma)}\right] = \left[\begin{array}{c|c} G & e \\ \hline e' & 0 \end{array}\right]^{-1} \left\{\left[\begin{array}{c|c} \Theta & 0 \\ \hline \underline{0}' & 0 \end{array}\right]\left[\begin{array}{c} \alpha \\ \hline 0 \end{array}\right] \right.$$
$$\left. + \frac{1}{1 - \gamma}\left[\begin{array}{c} r \\ 1 - \gamma \end{array}\right]\right\}.$$

Now we invert the augmented G matrix in (5):

(5') $$\left[\begin{array}{c|c} G & e \\ \hline e' & 0 \end{array}\right]^{-1} = \left[\begin{array}{c|c} G^{-1}K & y \\ \hline y' & -1/e'G^{-1}e \end{array}\right],$$

where $y = G^{-1}e/e'G^{-1}e$ and $K = I - ey'$, I being the identity matrix of order N. Omitting the $N + 1$ row (which is the definition of λ) and substituting (5') into (5), we obtain an expression for the vector of N optimal portfolio shares:

(6) $$x = y + G^{-1}K\Theta\alpha + \frac{1}{1 - \gamma} G^{-1}Kr.$$

The optimal portfolio decomposes into a capital position y, such that $e'y = 1$, and two zero-net-worth portfolios. The latter are constructed by comparing the mean and variance of the real return on the particular asset

---

5. The derivations are in MGM.

(respectively involving r and $\Theta\alpha$) with the mean and variance of the real return on the capital position. This is done through the "comparison matrix" K, such that $e'G^{-1}K = \underline{0}'$. We refer to $y + G^{-1}K\Theta\alpha$ as the minimum variance portfolio, x^m, and to $G^{-1}Kr/1 - \gamma$ as the speculative portfolio, x^s.[6]

To interpret (6) further, it is convenient to decompose the N-by-N variance-covariance matrix of changes in numeraire prices of assets (G) and the N-by-N covariance matrix of changes in numeraire prices of assets and goods (Θ), namely,

$$
(7) \qquad\qquad G = G^d + \hat{S} - \hat{E} - \hat{E}'
$$
$$
\underline{\Theta} = H + \hat{S} - \hat{E} - \hat{\Psi},
$$

where $G^d = \{g_{ij}\}$ is the N-by-N variance covariance matrix of changes in the domestic currency price of assets; $\hat{S}$ is $S = \{\bar{\sigma}_{ij}\}$, the N-1-by-N-1 variance-covariance matrix of exchange rate changes, bordered by zeros; $\hat{E}$ is $E = \{\epsilon_{ij}\}$, the N-by-$N - 1$ covariance matrix between changes in domestic currency prices of assets and bilateral exchange rates, augmented by a column vector of zeros; $H = \{\eta_{ij}\}$ is the N-by-N covariance matrix of changes in domestic currency prices of assets and goods, and $\hat{\Psi}$ is $\psi = \{\psi_{ij}\}$ the N-1-by-N covariance matrix between changes in bilateral exchange rates and domestic goods prices, augmented by a row vector of zeros.

Next consider the case where the Nth asset has a known domestic currency price, so that it is essentially a short bond or deposit denominated in the numeraire currency. The G and $\underline{\Theta}$ matrix can then be rewritten as

$$
(8) \qquad\qquad G = \left[\begin{array}{c|c} G & \underline{0} \\ \hline \underline{0}' & 0 \end{array}\right], \quad \underline{\Theta} = \left[\begin{array}{c} \Theta \\ \hline \underline{0}' \end{array}\right],
$$

where $\underline{0}$ is a $N - 1$ column vector of zeros.

Substituting (8) into (4), the last row becomes

$$
(9) \qquad\qquad r_N + \lambda/J_W = 0.
$$

Using (9) to eliminate λ/J_W from (5), we now solve for $\underline{x}$, the $N - 1$ column vector of portfolio shares:

---

6. Kouri (1975) referred to the "hedging demand for forward exchange which is proportional to the value of imported goods consumed" and to the "speculative demand" in a two-country model where national investors have different preferences. The decomposition between minimum variance and speculative portfolios for the international investor holding N currencies when prices and exchange rates are lognormally distributed is in Kouri and Macedo (1978). Equation (6) is written out in full in the Appendix.

(10) $$x = G^{-1}\Theta\alpha + \frac{1}{1-\gamma}G^{-1}(r - er_N),$$

where $r = (r_1 \quad r_{N-1})'$ and e is a $N - 1$ column vector of ones. To obtain x_N, we use the unity constraint:

(10') $$x_N = 1 - e'x.$$

Denoting the identity matrix of order $N - 1$ by I, the rule for the N assets is then written as

(11) $$x = \Gamma\alpha + \frac{1}{1-\gamma}\Sigma r,$$

where $\Gamma = \begin{bmatrix} G^{-1}\Theta \\ \hline e'(I - G^{-1}\Theta) \end{bmatrix}$

is such that $e'\Gamma = e'$, and

$$\Sigma = \begin{bmatrix} G^{-1} & -G^{-1}e \\ \hline -e'G^{-1} & e'G^{-1}e \end{bmatrix}$$

is such that $e'\Sigma = 0'$ and $\Sigma e = 0$.

Comparing (6) to (11), it is clear that when one asset has a known price in terms of the numeraire the structure of the minimum variance portfolio changes. In this case, $\Gamma\alpha$ cannot be decomposed into a capital position depending on asset price uncertainty and a zero-net-worth hedge portfolio determined by the covariance of changes in assets and goods prices in terms of the numeraire, weighted by preferences $(G^{-1}K\Theta\alpha)$. Also, the zero-net-worth speculative portfolio is computed in terms of real returns relative to the Nth asset $(\Sigma r/1 - \gamma)$ rather than relative to the capital position $(G^{-1}Kr/1 - \gamma)$.[7]

When all asset prices are known, G^d, E, and H in (7) vanish and the G and Θ matrices can be written as

(7') $$G = S$$
$$\Theta = \tilde{S} - \Psi$$

where

$$\tilde{S} = [S \mid 0].$$

---

7. Note that, by Itô's lemma, mean real return differentials depend on the variance of the exchange rate as well as on the covariance of prices and exchange rates, weighted by α. This implies that $\partial x_i/\partial\alpha_i > 0$ if $\gamma < 0$, that is to say the individual is more risk averse than the Bernouilli investor. See references in Macedo (1982).

The Σ matrix used to weight real returns in (11) now becomes the augmented inverse of the variance-covariance matrix of exchange rate changes. The Γ matrix used to weight consumption preferences in (11) decomposes further, so that the minimum variance portfolio for the $N - 1$ assets can be written as

$$(12) \qquad \underset{\sim}{x}^m = (\hat{I} - S^{-1}\Psi)\alpha,$$

where $\hat{I} = S^{-1}\hat{S}$ is the $(N - 1$ by $N)$ matrix obtained by augmenting $\underline{I}$ by an $N - 1$ column vector of zeros.

Using the unity constraint to obtain x_N we can express the total portfolio and its components as

$$(13) \qquad x = (I - \Phi)\alpha + \frac{1}{1 - \gamma}\Sigma r$$

$$(13a) \qquad x^m = (I - \Phi)\alpha$$

where $\Phi = \begin{bmatrix} S^{-1}\Psi \\ \hline -\underline{e}'S^{-1}\Psi \end{bmatrix}$

is such that $e'\Phi = \underline{0}'$;

$$(13b) \qquad x^s = \frac{1}{1 - \gamma}\Sigma r.$$

It is clear from (13a) that the capital position is given by the expenditure shares so that the minimum variance portfolio reduces to α when goods prices are known.[8] Also, we again have the two zero-net-worth portfolios of (6), one hedging against changes in domestic currency prices of goods and in exchange rates $(-\Phi\alpha)$, the other, x^s, based on real returns relative to the Nth currency.

Consider now the special case of purchasing power parity. In that case there are no relative price changes, so that there is only one random domestic currency good price, say in the Nth currency, and $P_i = P_N$ for all i in (1) above. Then the Θ matrix in (7') can be expressed as

$$(7'') \qquad \Theta = -\Psi_N e',$$

where Ψ_N is the Nth column of Ψ. Using (7'') in the minimum variance portfolio, we see that preferences drop out and that the capital position is all in the Nth asset:[9]

$$(14) \qquad x^m = \underline{1}_N - \Phi_N$$

---

8. This result is emphasized by Adler and Dumas (1982).

9. In Kouri (1977), the assumption of purchasing power parity and no inflation in the Nth country eliminates hedging so that the minimum variance portfolio is all in the Nth currency, $x^m = \underline{1}_N$. A similar result holds in the model of Solnik (1973).

where $\underline{1}_N$ is an N column vector with zeros in the first $N - 1$ rows and one in the Nth row, and $\Phi_N = \begin{bmatrix} S^{-1} \\ \hline -\underline{e}'S^{-1} \end{bmatrix} \Psi_N.$

The rule in (14) is applicable to the case where $P_j^d = P_i S_j$ is the only random price and $\Theta = -\Psi_j e'$ and also to an investor who only consumes the jth good because then $I - \Phi$ reduces to $\underline{1}_j - \Phi_j.$[10]

Finally, consider the problem of the investor who holds currencies and one asset with an uncertain price in terms of the numeraire. In this case, a rule in the form of (13) still applies. This is shown in the Appendix. The reason for this equivalence is that the asset with an uncertain price has the same effect on the portfolio rule as the currency of a country whose good is not consumed by the investor. Henceforth, we will interpret the portfolio rule in (13) as an $N + 1$ rule, where the first element in x is the gold share and α has a zero in the first row.

6.3 Optimal Portfolios of Short-Term Financial Assets and Gold Computed

6.3.1 Overview

In this section, we apply the $N + 1$ time-invariant portfolio rule derived in section 6.2 to investors holding gold and short-term financial assets (with 3-month maturities) denominated in eight major currencies; the United States dollar ($), used as the numeraire currency, the Canadian dollar (C$), the French franc (FF), the German mark (DM), the Italian lira (IL), the Japanese yen (¥), the Swiss franc (SF), and the pound sterling (£). Interest rates and the domestic currency prices of these short-term financial assets are assumed known. Gold (GO), in turn, is a non-interest-bearing asset with an uncertain domestic price, G_0, which is expressed in terms of the numeraire. The $N - 1$ bilateral exchange rates, S_i, are defined in (1) as units of domestic currency per dollar. It is convenient to express the price of gold in ounces per dollar or as $1/G_0$. As defined above, real returns are equal to the known interest rate plus the proportional rate of change of the purchasing power of the currency (or of gold) over the previous 3 months. Investors are assumed to have static expectations about the rate of change of exchange rates, the price of gold, and numeraire prices of the goods in their consumption basket.

In section 6.2, we assumed that the investor consumes a basket composed

---

10. If exchange rate changes are typically not passed on to prices, (14) is the relevant rule, making $\phi_N = \phi_{CPI}\beta$ where ϕ_{CPI} captures the covariance between exchange rates and the components of the Nth country's CPI and β are the CPI weights as in Macedo (1982). See Branson and Henderson (1984).

of goods produced in the various countries with weights given by constant expenditure shares α_j. We refer to these goods by the country name: Canada (CA), France (FR), Germany (GE), Italy (IT), Japan (JA), Switzerland (SZ), the United Kingdom (UK), and the United States (US). For empirical purposes, however, we identify each one of these national goods with the consumer price index of the country in question. As a consequence of this simplification, we refer to an investor consuming only the goods included in the consumer price index of, say, Germany as the "German investor" even though the German CPI includes imported goods. In terms of the utility function in (5) above, the "national investor" of country j is defined as having $\alpha_j = 1$ and $\alpha_i = 0$ for $i \neq j$. This contrasts with the "international consumer-investor" who weights national consumer price indexes by the share of each country in total trade and can thus be thought of as a weighted average of national investors.[11] The role of preferences in optimal portfolios is shown by comparing different national investors to the international investor.

In section 6.3.2, we focus on optimal portfolios and their determinants for the 3-month holding period, April 1–June 30, 1981. We refer to these as March 1981 portfolios given that, with the exception of known interest rates, real returns and their distribution are computed on the basis of data available prior to the holding period, that is, April 1973–March 1981. The use of all available data since April 1973 in the computation of the matrix of covariances between exchange rates and price changes and the variance-covariance matrix of exchange rate changes is motivated in part by the results of tests for the stationarity of these variance-covariance structures.[12]

The analysis of the joint distribution of the uncertain component of real returns which determines the composition of optimal portfolios is interesting because it offers a convenient summary of assets' risk and return characteristics and indicates the scope for risk-reducing diversification. In addition, these determinants serve to depict explicitly the substitutability and complementarity relationships between assets. We emphasize the total portfolios of United States and international investors, but the total portfolios of other

11. These weights are given as the simple average of the dollar value of imports and exports of the eight countries. The United States dollar share is 25%, which makes the comparison of the United States investor (with a share of 100% in the United States consumer price index) to the international investor particularly instructive in attempts at bracketing the dollar share in optimal portfolios. See a discussion of weighting schemes in Macedo (1982).

12. Results in Goldstein (1983, chap. 3) show that the structure of the $S^{-1}\Psi$ matrix has remained significantly the same since the widespread introduction of floating exchange rates. This implies that the best forecast of the determinants of the inflation hedge portfolio is based on all available data since April 1973 to the period immediately prior to the chosen holding period. Tests for the stationarity of the variance-covariance matrix of exchange rate changes used in the calculation of the speculative portfolio are less conclusive. This may imply that shorter sample periods should be used in the estimation of the joint distribution of returns in order to avoid the bias which would result if there has been structural change in the parameters of the stochastic processes generating exchange rate changes. These results exclude consideration of gold.

national investors can easily be calculated. This is done by adding the computed speculative portfolio which does not depend on consumption preferences to the national investor's minimum variance portfolio. Section 6.3.3 investigates the evolution of these portfolios since September 1974 as investors revise their estimates of variances and covariances at the end of every quarter by including the new observations on the risk and return characteristics of each asset.

6.3.2 Optimal Portfolios and Their Determinants, March 1981

In table 6.1, we present the pattern of correlations and covariances between exchange rate (and gold price) changes which underlies the computation of the speculative portfolio as well as the computation of the minimum variance portfolios of different investors. The upper triangular matrix reports estimates of the S matrix (including the price of gold). Since mean changes in exchange rates are expressed in number per quarter, we multiply their variances and covariances by 100 and refer to the units as percentages. Since variances and covariances are not directly comparable (because the variables have different means), correlation coefficients are reported in the lower triangle. It is clear from the table that the correlation coefficients between "Ecu area" currencies—including the Swiss franc but excluding the pound sterling—are uniformly higher than all other correlation coefficients. The lowest of the Ecu area correlations, between the lira and the Swiss franc, is 0.5. The table also shows that the correlation coefficients between the Canadian dollar and the other currencies are the lowest (and negative). Between these two extremes, we find the correlation coefficients of gold, the yen, and the pound with the other currencies. The highest variance is the variance of the price of gold. On the other hand, the Canadian dollar ranks lowest in variance of dollar exchange rate changes. The two "hard currencies" of Europe (DM and SF) exhibit a somewhat higher variance than the other currencies.

As was mentioned in section 6.2, the speculative portfolio is based on the inverse of S, each element of which shows the effect of change in the return differential relative to the United States dollar on the speculative demand of all investors for a particular currency or gold. Therefore, the elements of S^{-1} provide estimates on the degree of substitutability (negative entries) and complementarity (positive entries) between assets. For an investor with unitary risk aversion ($\gamma = 0$), the own and cross effects of an increase in the real return of a given asset on speculative shares are obtained by augmenting S^{-1} by a row (column) equal to minus the sum of the elements of all other columns (rows). The resulting matrix, which we denoted above by Σ, is reported in table 6.2 using an ordering of the assets which emphasizes the strength of the substitutability ($-$) and complementarity ($+$) relationships between assets.

It is clear from table 6.2 that, in addition to the strong substitutability

Table 6.1   Exchange Rates and Gold: Covariances and Correlations (April 1973–March 1981)

	GO (ounces/$)	C$ (Canadian dollars/$)	FF (French francs/$)	DM (DM/$)	IL (Lira/$)	¥ (Yen/$)	SF (Swiss francs/$)	£ (pounds/$)
GO	2.281	.032	.326	.461	.245	.042	.411	.308
C$	.1	.044	−.016	*	.025	.020	*	−.001
FF	.4	−.1	.287	.268	.205	.190	.267	.140
DM	.5	*	.8	.377	.190	.123	.346	.149
IL	.3	−.2	.7	.6	.287	.084	.188	.143
¥	*	−.2	.4	.4	.3	.300	.184	.107
SF	.4	*	.7	.8	.5	.5	.461	.156
£	.4	−.1	.5	.5	.5	.4	.5	.257

Note: Upper-triangular matrix is $G_o = \{\sigma_i \sigma_j \rho_{ij}\}$, defined in equation (A.8) of the Appendix (in number per quarter squared times 100). Lower-triangular matrix reports ρ_{ij}.
*Less than .05 in absolute value.

Table 6.2   Own and Cross Effects (%, April 1973–March 1981)

	SF	DM	FF	IL	C$	$	¥	£	GO
SF	2.0	−1.5	−.4	*	−.3	.6	−.7	.2	−.1
DM	−1.5	3.2	−1.6	*	−.5	.3	.2	−.1	−.1
FF	−.4	−1.6	3.7	−1.2	.7	−1.0	*	−.2	*
IL	*	*	−1.2	2.0	.7	−1.1	.1	−.5	*
C$	−.3	−.5	.7	.7	6.7	−7.4	.5	−.2	−.1
$	.6	.3	−1.0	−1.1	−7.4	9.7	−1.1	−.3	.1
¥	−.7	.2	*	.1	.5	−1.1	1.4	−.5	.2
£	.2	−.1	−.2	−.5	−.2	−.3	−.5	1.8	−.2
GO	−.1	−.1	*	*	−.1	.1	.2	−.2	.2

Notes: Σ_0 matrix defined by equation (A12) in the Appendix. Columns and rows may not add to zero due to rounding.
*Less than .05%.

between the United States and the Canadian dollar and, to a lesser degree, between the Deutschemark and the Swiss franc, there are two partly overlapping currency blocs: the Ecu bloc and the dollar bloc. The criterion for a bloc is a cross effect of at least 1%. While the French franc and the lira belong to both blocs, the pound does not belong to either one, as all its cross effects are less than or equal to 0.5% in absolute value. Table 6.2 also shows that gold's own and cross effects are quite small.[13]

The Canadian and United States dollars' own effects far exceed those of other currencies. In the Canadian dollar's case, this is partly the result of the fact that, as noted, it exhibits the lowest variance of exchange rate changes. The high value of the United States own effect is observed here because it equals the sum of all elements of the S^{-1} matrix. In general, the own effects are much greater than the absolute value of the cross effects. One notable exception is the cross effect between United States and Canadian dollar assets which exhibits, by far, the highest degree of substitutability. A 1% increase in the real rate of return on one asset decreases the other's share in the speculative portfolio by 7.4% of the initial share (when $\gamma = 0$). Contrary to the presumption in two-country models, we find that the United States dollar and German mark as well as United States dollar and Swiss franc are complements in the speculative portfolio.[14] Also, with the exception of the observed complementarity between the pound and the Swiss franc, the cross effects between all other European currencies are negative.

For given consumption preferences, the inflation hedge portfolio is determined by the estimates of the degree of substitutability and complementarity between assets shown in the Σ matrix (table 6.2), together with the covariances between changes in exchange rates and domestic currency prices of national goods. In table 6.3, we report the correlation coefficients between changes in dollar exchange rates (and in the price of gold) and national inflation rates, which we denoted in (1) above by $\bar{\rho}_{ij}$. It is evident that these correlations are generally small. Note that the negative correlations in the Canadian row imply that the Canadian dollar appreciates relative to the United States dollar not only when foreign consumer prices rise but also when Canadian prices increase. Similarly, a rise in United States prices is associated with a depreciation of the French franc, the German mark, the yen, and the Swiss franc vis-à-vis the dollar. While the low values of the elements of table 6.3 (particularly the underlined ones) indicate little correlation between domestic price and exchange rate movements, they do not, by themselves, imply the rejection of the relative purchasing power parity hypothesis. We can derive the correlation coefficients which would obtain if

13. As can be seen in equation (A8) in the Appendix, if the price of gold is uncorrelated with exchange rate changes, G_0^{-1} becomes block diagonal. Further details on this case can be found in MGM.

14. See, e.g., Dornbusch (1980).

Table 6.3   **The Correlation Matrix of Exchange Rates and National Consumer Price Indices (1973:4–1981:3)**

Asset	Good							
	CA	FR	GE	IT	JA	SZ	UK	US
GO	.1	−.1	−.1	−.4	−.3	*	*	−.2
C$	−.1	−.3	−.3	−.1	−.3	−.2	*	−.2
FF	.1	.1	.2	.1	.1	.2	−.1	.1
DM	.3	.2	.2	*	*	.3	*	.2
IL	*	.1	.3	.3	.2	.2	−.1	−.1
¥	*	.2	.3	.3	.2	.4	.1	.2
SF	.2	.1	.3	.1	*	.3	.1	.2
£	*	*	*	.1	.2	.1	.1	−.2

Note: ψ_0 matrix defined in equation (A7′) of the Appendix.
*Less than .05 in absolute value.

purchasing power parity (PPP) prevailed. In all cases, they are vastly different from those reported in table 6.3.

Note further that each vector $-S^{-1}\Psi_i$ has a simple interpretation: it gives the shares of the $N - 1$ currencies in the inflation hedge portfolio of the national investor of country i.[15] The dollar share of the inflation hedge portfolio is then obtained residually. Adding this portfolio to the expenditure share of the national investor of country i (given by a vector with one in row i and zeros elsewhere) we obtain the minimum variance portfolio of the national investor of country i. These portfolios are reported in table 6.4. Together they form what we denoted in section 6.2 as the $I - \Phi$ matrix (expressed in percent). For example, the minimum variance portfolio of the German investor (table 6.4, col. 3) would include long positions in marks (98%), Canadian dollars (8%), French francs (5%), pounds (2%), and gold (1%), and short positions in lire (5%), United States dollars (5%), Swiss francs (3%), and yen (1%). We find that inflation risk is minimized for most national investors by holding gold, pound, French franc, and Canadian dollar assets, while borrowing in United States dollars, Swiss francs, yen, and marks.

15. Notice that each element ij of the $S^{-1}\Psi$ matrix involves the ratio of the standard deviation of the change in the price of good j to the standard deviation of the change in the dollar exchange rate of currency i. These ratios are in the 20%–40% range for Italy, Japan, and the United Kingdom, countries with a relatively high variance of inflation, and in the 10%–20% range for the other countries. Thus, for example, when $N = 3$ the 1, 2 element of $S^{-1}\Psi$ would be $\Phi_{12} = (\zeta_2/\sigma_1)R_{12}$ where $R_{12} = \bar{\rho}_{12} - \rho_{12}\rho_{22}/1 - \rho_{12}^2$. When gold is included, we have instead

$$R_{12} = \frac{(1 - \rho_1^2)(\bar{\rho}_{12} - \rho_1\bar{\rho}_2) - (\rho_{12} - \rho_1\rho_2)(\bar{\rho}_{22} - \rho_2\bar{\rho}_2)}{1 - \rho_1^2 - \rho_2^2 - \rho_{12}^2 + 2\rho_{12}\rho_1\rho_2},$$

where $\rho_i(\bar{\rho}_j)$ refers to the correlation of the price of gold with exchange rate i (price of good j).

The underlined element in each column of table 6.4 may also be interpreted as the extent to which a long position in the domestic currency of a given national investor is chosen in the construction of the inflation hedge portfolio. This is consistent with the domestic currency being a "preferred monetary habitat" and is thus only supported for those currencies whose "diagonal" element in table 6.4 is greater than 100, that is, Canada, France, and Switzerland.[16] Hence, a "preferred local currency habitat" may be observed as a result of the inflation-hedging portfolio provided by one's domestic money, even in the absence of transaction or information costs.

The last column of table 6.4 is of particular interest because, as noted at the end of section 6.2, if relative prices between national goods do not change, the minimum variance portfolio is invariant to consumption preferences. In this context, relative purchasing power parity would imply that uncertainty with respect to the N national goods prices collapses into uncertainty about the price of a single national good, for example, the good pro-

Table 6.4   **The Minimum Variance Portfolio of National Investors (%, April 1973–March 1981)**

Currency of Holding	Home Country of Investor							
	CA	FR	GE	IT	JA	SZ	UK	US
GO	−.1	.7	.8	4.4	4.8	.1	.5	1.2
C$	105.1	7.6	8.1	−4.9 (−2.5)	21.0	6.7	8.4	8.5
FF	3.6	100.6	4.6	4.0	−5.8	3.3	19.7	1.6
DM	−6.5	−3.3	98.4	1.6 (2.9)	−4.0 (−2.5)	−10.4	−6.6	−6.0
IL	2.2	.3	−5.3	86.8	−3.3	−.5	−.3	5.0
¥	.9	−.8	−1.3	−4.3 (−8.4)	98.5 (94.0)	−7.2	−2.9	−.9 (−2.1)
SF	−.1	.3	−3.0	−1.3	8.3 (11.8)	96.6	−5.8	−3.0
£	.4	.8 (1.6)	2.3	−.8 (4.2)	−9.6 (−4.1)	3.6	95.7	3.9 (5.3)
$	−5.5	−6.2	−4.5	14.6 (11.6)	−9.8 (−13.1)	1.1	−8.7	89.7

Notes: Numbers in parentheses refer to the corresponding element in the $I - \Phi$ matrix without gold (noted only when significantly different). Columns may not add to 100 due to rounding. Φ_0 matrix defined by equation (A11) in the Appendix subtracted from the identity matrix times 100.

16. This correspond to a negative "diagonal" element in the $S^{-1}\Psi$ matrix. Using the expression in the previous footnote, we see that the "own" inflation hedge in table 6.4 of −3.4% for Switzerland corresponds to $(\zeta/\sigma)_{SZ} = 14\%$ and $R_{SZ} = -0.24$ (while the underlined element in table 6.3 was $\bar{\rho}_{SZ} = 0.3$) and that the value of 13.2% for Italy corresponds to $(\zeta/\sigma)_{IT} = 28\%$ and $R_{IT} = 0.47(\bar{\rho}_{IT} = 0.3)$.

duced in the country of the numeraire currency.[17] With the United States dollar chosen as the numeraire, the minimum variance portfolio of the United States investor would also be the "universal" minimum variance portfolio under purchasing power parity. The portfolio is dominated by a long position in United States dollars (90%). The United States (cum universal PPP) investor holds less than his consumption share in dollars in order to maintain an 8.5% long position in Candian dollar assets, while mark, yen, and Swiss franc–denominated liabilities finance short-term investments in gold, French franc, lira, and pound assets.

Contrasting the last column of table 6.4 with the other columns reveals that relative price changes were important, particularly in the cases of Italy and Japan. Specifically, we find that the Japanese investor's minimum variance portfolio differs significantly from the universal PPP portfolio. Of particular note are the sign and magnitude of positions in Canadian dollar, French franc, lira, Swiss franc, and pound sterling assets. The last row of table 6.4, which reports the residually determined shares of the United States dollar, also reflects the significance of relative price changes. Note that the 89.7% dollar share in the "universal" minimum variance portfolio stems from − 10.3% dollar share in the "universal" inflation-hedge portfolio. It is thus smaller than the dollar share in the minimum variance/inflation-hedge portfolios of all national investors, especially those of the Italian and Swiss investors. In sum, this analysis shows that, since national inflation rates are not fully anticipated and relative prices change, not even investors who consume only domestic goods (and are infinitely risk averse) will hold a portfolio consisting only of home-currency-denominated claims. Rather, national investors exploit inflation risk-minimizing gains to diversification as provided by the variance-covariance structure of exchange rate changes relative to the covariance of exchange rate and domestic price changes.

Having presented and interpreted the Σ and $I - \Phi$ matrices, we are now in a position to report the components of the total portfolio computed under alternative assumptions about consumption preferences and risk aversion. This is done in table 6.5 for the United States investor (left panel) and an international investor (right panel). The speculative portfolio of the Bernouilli investor ($\gamma = 0$) is reported in the center column. It is common to both investors because there is no significant difference in the speculative portfolio when computed with real rates of return relevant to the international investor compared with real returns relevant to national investors. This is a consequence of the fact that own and cross effects in the Σ matrix

---

17. If price indices in different countries were constructed using identical goods and weights, the composition of the universal PPP minimum variance portfolio would be independent of the choice of the numeraire. However, when goods and weights and hence price indexes vary by country, the universal minimum variance portfolio is determined according to the choice of the numeraire. See 10 above.

Table 6.5   Optimal Portfolio Shares and Their Components (%, April 1973–March 1981)

| | U.S. Investor | | | | International Investor | | |
| | | Minimum Variance Portfolio | | | Minimum Variance Portfolio | | |
Asset	Total Portfolio (1)	Capital Position (2a)	Inflation Hedge (2b)	Speculative Portfolio (R.A. = 1) (3)	Capital Position (4a)	Inflation Hedge (4b)	Total Portfolio (5)
GO	4	0	1	3	0	2	5
C$	0(3)	0	8	−8(−6)	8	8	8(11)
FF	1(1)	0	2	−1(−1)	12	4	15(15)
DM	−5(−4)	0	−6	1(2)	19	−4	16(17)
IL	0(−1)	0	5	−5(−6)	8	−1	2(2)
¥	4(0)	0	−1	5(2)	14	−2	17(12)
SF	−3(−1)	0	−3	0(2)	3	−1	2(6)
£	3(9)	0	4	−1(3)	11	0	10(15)
$	96(94)	100	−10	6(4)	25	−6	25(22)
Total	100(100)	100	0	0(0)	100	0	100(100)

Notes: Col. 1 = col. 2a + col. 2b + col. 3. Col 5 = col. 4a + col. 4b + col. 3. Numbers in parentheses in cols. 1, 3, and 5 refer to the optimal shares when gold is excluded. Risk-aversion (R.A.) is unity (Bernouilli investor).

are far greater in magnitude than differences in national versus international investor's real rates of return. In fact, the composition of the speculative portfolio is invariant to the choice of real returns versus nominal interest rates adjusted for exchange rates changes.

As expected, the United States and international investor's minimum variance portfolios are significantly different (col. 2a + 2b vs. col. 4a + 4b). With the exception of the lira, however, we find that the sign of the difference between expenditure shares and minimum variance portfolio shares is independent of consumption preferences. For example, both United States and international investors have greater holdings of gold, Canadian dollars, and French francs than is implied by their respective capital position (i.e., inflation hedge portfolio shares greater than zero). On the other hand, the zero-net-worth inflation hedge portfolio decreases the share of mark, yen, Swiss franc, and United States dollar assets in the minimum variance portfolio.

The relationship between the minimum variance portfolio and consumption preferences can be illustrated by multiplying each element ij of the $I - \Phi$ matrix by the ratio of the expenditure share j (column) to the minimum variance portfolio share i (row). We then obtain a matrix of elasticities of the shares of the international investor's minimum variance portfolio with respect to shares in expenditure. For example, the own elasticity for the United States dollar is 1.16. A 10% increase in the international investor's share of expenditure on United States goods would increase the dollar component of the minimum variance portfolio from 19% to 22% ($= 19 \times 1.16$). Other countries with own elasticities greater than one are Germany, Italy, Japan, Switzerland, and the United Kingdom. Sizable cross elasticities with respect to an increase in the United States expenditure share are on holdings of Canadian dollars and lire.

The speculative portfolio, dependent on own and cross effects between assets and real return differentials with the United States dollar, includes long positions in United States dollars (6%), yen (5%), and gold (3%) and short positions in Canadian dollars (-8%) and lire (-5%). The relatively large positive share of the United States dollar is attributable less to its mean real return (-1.9%) than to its substitutability with Canadian dollar, French franc, and lira assets and to its complementarity with the Swiss franc. Return differentials with the dollar largely explain the attractiveness of yen assets (4% return differential) and gold (20% differential) and the short position in lire (-1.5% differential). While the return differential for the Swiss franc was the same as for the yen, its share is zero rather than 5%. The primary reason is the interaction between these assets' risk and return characteristics and gold. If gold is excluded from the portfolio the shares are the same. The high degree of substitutability between the Canadian and United States dollars is reflected by the fact that a relatively small difference in mean real returns results in a long position in United States dollar assets financed by Canadian dollar liabilities.

The total portfolios of the international and United States investors are computed under the assumption of unitary risk aversion. Of course, the higher the degree of risk aversion, the smaller the contribution of the speculative to the total portfolio. At the limit, when risk aversion is infinite, the speculative portfolio disappears so that the minimum variance and total portfolios are the same and optimal shares are independent of returns. It is clear from table 6.5, column 5, that the total portfolio of the international investor is dominated by the minimum variance portfolio. The long positions of gold, marks, yen, and United States dollars in the latter are reinforced by the speculative portfolio.

We now analyze the effect of excluding gold from the available menu of assets, reported in parentheses in tables 6.4 and 6.5. The elements of the Σ matrix are not sensitive to the exclusion of gold, as expected from the low own effect in table 6.2. We note from table 6.3 that the price of gold has the largest correlation with the Italian and Japanese consumer price indexes (respectively, -0.4 and -0.3). Accordingly, the exclusion of gold results in significant changes in the minimum variance portfolio of the Italian and Japanese investors (col. 4 and 5 of table 6.4). These differences do not affect the international investor, however, as can be seen in column 4b of table 6.5, while the last column of table 6.4 suggested little change in the United States (cum universal PPP) investor minimum variance portfolio.

In fact, larger effects can be seen in the speculative portfolio. Excluding gold, the asset with the highest mean return, leads to an increase in the share of the mark, the Swiss franc, the pound, the Canadian dollar, and the French franc totaling 13% (to 49%) and a decline of the share of the yen and the dollar totaling 8% (to 39%), the difference being the (5%) share in gold. These shifts illustrate the interaction of the change in the variance-covariance structure and of the change in return differentials on the speculative portfolio, a topic to which we return at the end of the next subsection.

6.3.3 The Evolution of Optimal Portfolios over Time

Table 6.5 reported March 1981 minimum variance speculative and total optimal portfolios calculated with data from the full sample period. It must be emphasized that these portfolios are period specific, that is, optimal for a single holding period. If, as we have assumed, the variance-covariance structure generating Σ and Φ were stationary and, in addition, investors had perfect knowledge of these true underlying structures, the inflation hedge portfolio would not change over time and speculative portfolios would change only as a consequence of changes in real returns. In the absence of such knowledge, investors must compute sample moments from observed exchange rate and price data and utilize these statistics to infer their true values. That is, investors' expectations regarding the determinants of optimal portfolios change over time as their information set is enlarged by the availability of new data. Thus, optimal inflation hedge and speculative portfolios may be reshuffled as investors improve their estimates of both variance-covariance structures and real returns.

In the preceding subsection, optimal portfolios and their determinants were calculated with data from April 1973 to March 1981 for the April 1–June 30, 1981 holding period. In this subsection, we study the evolution of these optimal portfolios for interim periods and assess whether changes in these portfolios were attributable to changes in expected real returns differentials or to changes in observed variance-covariance structures. It should be emphasized that in computing these portfolios we avoid the use of ex post data as if the information were known ex ante.[18] In other words, the information set available to an investor choosing an internationally diversified portfolio is limited to data available prior to the holding period in which optimal shares are calculated.

In table 6.6, we report the United States dollar share in the inflation hedge portfolios of the different investors as well as of the international investor. The inflation hedge portfolio share of the dollar is the minimum variance portfolio share for all but the United States and international investors. In the case of the United States investor (international investor), the minimum variance portfolio share of the dollar is obtained by adding the capital position of 100 (25) to the inflation hedge portfolio share. Movements in the United States dollar shares are implied by changes in the sum of all other inflation hedge portfolio shares since dollar shares are determined residually. It is clear from table 6.6 that the dollar shares of all investors change substantially from year to year. Some patterns, however, do emerge. Since 1978, the short positions in United States dollars of both the international (col. 9) and the German investor decline. The reduction in the Japanese investor's short position in dollars begins in 1976. The decline in the long position in dollars held by the Italian investor begins in 1977 but is reversed in 1981. This strengthening in the inflation hedge demand for the dollar (smaller short positions and larger long positions) in 1981 is evidenced in all minimum variance portfolios except those of the Swiss and the United States investors. Over the entire period, we observe like movements in the minimum variance dollar shares of the United States and international investors. Although it is only roughly reflected in table 6.6, we also found that the change over time in the share of many of the assets in the minimum variance portfolio is similar regardless of the choice of expenditure weights.

Next, we turn to table 6.7, which summarizes the evolution of the own and cross effects of changes in the rate of return on the United States dollar.

18. This procedure, developed in Goldstein (1983), is motivated by critiques of earlier finance-theoretic work on international portfolio selection along the lines of Tobin (1982).

Table 6.6   The U.S. Dollar Share in the Inflation Hedge Portfolio of Different National Investors (%)

From April 1973 to March of:	Investor Consuming Only the Good of								International Investor[a]
	Canada	France	Germany	Italy	Japan	Switzerland	U.K.	U.S.	
1975	-2	-33	-4	-28	-43	20	-70	-7	-22
1976	21	-6	-2	-6	-50	29	-33	6	-8
1977	-2	-7	-11	30	-47	-2	-9	-13	-11
1978	-1	-6	-13	23	-45	2	-20	-15	-13
1979	-9	-11	-10	15	-33	-4	-8	-17	-12
1980	-7	-8	-6	10	-13	3	-7	-14	-8
1981	-6	-6	-5	15	-10	1	-9	-10	-6

[a]Weighted sum of national investor's inflation hedge portfolio where weights are given by the capital position in table 6.3, col. 4a.

Table 6.7   Cross and Own Effects with the U.S. Dollar (%) and the U.S. Dollar Share in the Speculative Portfolio

1973: April to March of	GO	CA	FR	GE	IT	JA	SZ	UK	US	Speculative Share of the U.S. Dollar
1975	.6	-33.5	-8.2	4.2	-2.5	2.7	-.9	4.5	33.0	33.0
1976	-.3	-27.8	-7.0	4.4	-4.3	.8	.9	4.0	29.4	-14.6
1977	-.4	-10.5	-2.6	1.3	-1.7	-1.5	1.9	.5	13.1	7.1
1978	-.5	-10.8	-2.5	2.2	-2.0	-2.7	1.1	.3	14.8	7.6
1979	-.2	-9.1	-1.4	.7	-1.8	-1.0	.9	-.3	12.2	10.0
1980	.0	-8.0	-1.3	.5	-1.4	-1.3	.7	.1	10.9	3.8
1981	.1	-7.4	-1.0	.3	-1.1	-1.1	.6	-.3	9.7	6.4

Specifically, this table reports the last row of Σ. It is determined residually so that each element of this row is minus the sum of the column elements of the inverse of the variance-covariance matrix of exchange rate (and gold price) changes. The sum of all the elements of this matrix is equal to the element in the United States column (own effect) of table 6.7. In the last column of this table we report the United States dollar share in the speculative portfolio.

Except for a slight increase in 1978, there has been a steady and substantial decline in the own effect of an increase in the real return on the United States dollar–denominated asset on its speculative share. Similarly, the magnitude of the cross effects of changes in dollar asset returns on the speculative shares of other assets has generally declined over the sample period. This pattern is most apparent in the Canadian and French columns. The reduction in the size of own and cross effects of changes in United States real returns on speculative portfolios shares is associated with the observed pattern of increased variances and covariances of exchange rate and gold price changes. Between December 1975 and March 1981, the observed variance of exchange rate changes increased for all currencies except the German mark and French franc. We also found that the own and cross effects of changes in other assets' real returns have generally declined over the sample period. The cross effects between the European currencies have exhibited the greatest stability over time, with respect to both sign and magnitude.

As noted in the preceding subsection, the elements of Σ indicate the degree of substitutability and complementarity between assets. We thus interpret the first eight columns of table 6.7 as reporting the evolution of the substitutability/complementarity relationships of all assets with the United States dollar. The consistently strong substitution effects between the Canadian and United States dollars, noted above, are evident in their negative signs and high absolute values. For example, in the late 1970s, they were close to 10%, showing that a 10% increase in the return on United States dollar assets decreases the speculative demand for Canadian dollars by 1%. For the pound sterling, the strong complementarity before the dramatic mid-1976 depreciation is followed by a very weak and erratic relationship. The degree of dollar-mark complementarity has significantly diminished over time. The increasing weakness in this relationship became particularly pronounced following the decline in the value of the United States dollar in late 1978.

In figure 6.1, we show the evolution of the optimal United States dollar share in the total portfolio for the Bernouilli ($\gamma = 0$) United States and international investors. These shares correspond to the sum of the appropriate column of table 6.6 plus the last column of table 6.7, to which we add the capital position (100 for the United States investor and 25 for the international investor). The similarity of the evolution in these shares is apparent.

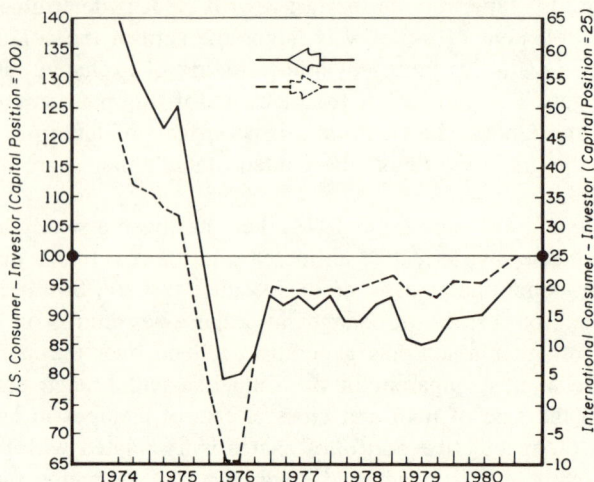

Fig. 6.1   Total optimal U.S. dollar shares (%) April 1974–March 1981

We noted above that the choice of expenditure weights did not greatly affect the sign of inflation hedge portfolio shares. This is also evident when comparing movements in the United States and international investors' minimum variance portfolios. Further, the speculative portfolio is, for empirical purposes, common to all investors regardless of their expenditure patterns.

Figure 6.1 reveals that the sharp decline in the attractiveness of the dollar between 1974 and mid-1976 was partly reversed in 1976, and that since 1977 rather stable shares obtained. Over the late 1975 to early 1977 period, both the precipitous decline and the subsequent increase in the total optimal share of the United States dollar were the result of similar movements in the speculative portfolios. In the period prior to September 1975, we found that the United States dollar held the dominant share in the speculative portfolio. After that time, no asset clearly dominated this portfolio. Finally, it should be noted that the increase in the total dollar share for both the United States and the international investor in the 1980–81 period was caused by like movements of the dollar share in both the inflation hedge portfolio (becoming less negative) and the speculative portfolio.

Table 6.8 reports expected mean real returns on both United States dollar assets and optimal portfolios computed with different degrees of relative risk aversion. It is evident that the expected mean real return on the United States dollar is consistently negative and less than the expected return on the minimum variance portfolio (and a fortiori less than the expected return on

Table 6.8   **Expected Mean Real Return on the U.S. Dollar and on the Optimal Portfolios[a] (% p.a.)**

From April 1973 to March of:	Return on U.S. Dollar (1)	Minimum Variance Portfolio (2)	Speculative Portfolio (3)	Total Portfolio		
				$\gamma = 0$ (4a)	$\gamma = -1$ (4b)	$\gamma = 1/2$ (4c)
1975	−6.4	−2.1	3.2	1.1	−.5	4.3
1976	−2.9	−1.9	3.1	1.2	−.2	4.3
1977	−2.5	−1.4	1.3	−.1	−.7	1.2
1978	−3.7	−1.5	2.1	.6	.2	2.7
1979	−3.8	−1.0	1.3	.3	−.3	1.6
1980	−3.1	−.5	1.1	.6	.1	1.6
1981	−1.9	−.3	.9	.6	.3	1.5

Notes: Col. 4a = col. 2 + col. 3. Col. 4b = col. 2 + (1/2 × col. 3). Col. 4c = col. 2 + (2 × col. 3).

[a]These returns are computed for the international investor.

the speculation and total portfolios). We also found that the return on the speculative portfolio is always lower than the mean real return on gold (the lowest return on gold ranged from 7.3% to 2.3% over this period). The yield on the speculative portfolio was also less than the return on the German mark asset in all reported periods except March 1976 and March 1981. As a result, the expected return on the total portfolio for the Bernouilli investor is relatively low. The expected return on the total portfolio is even lower when we increase the degree of relative risk aversion (e.g., $\gamma = -1$).

Changes in speculative shares were, in many periods, the dominant factor in the determination of movements in the total optimal portfolio. Clearly, observed changes in the speculative portfolio were a consequence of changes both in real returns and in the inverse of the augmented variance-covariance matrix of gold price and exchange rate changes, Σ. In table 6.9, we report

Table 6.9   **Real Return Differentials with the U.S. Dollar (% p.a.)**

From April 1973 to March of:	GO	C$	FF	DM	IL	¥	SF	£
1975	40.7	−.7	8.9	13.9	−.2	−.9	13.7	2.1
1976	15.3	.8	4.1	5.4	−5.5	.7	8.1	−3.3
1977	12.8	.3	2.0	5.6	−3.9	2.7	6.4	−4.3
1978	14.1	−.8	3.4	7.1	−1.1	5.8	10.5	−1.1
1979	15.6	−1.3	4.2	6.8	.0	6.5	10.1	.4
1980	26.4	−.7	3.6	5.6	.2	2.5	7.4	4.1
1981	20.2	−.7	1.3	2.8	−1.4	4.2	4.2	2.4

Note: Mean real return on assest in column minus mean real return on U.S. dollar (see table 6.8).

expected real return differentials with United States dollar assets observed in March of each year from 1975 to 1981. The importance of capital gains on gold, which bears no interest, is evident. The consistently positive expected yield differentials in favor of French franc-, mark-, yen-, and Swiss franc–denominated assets are also apparent. It is interesting to note that while the expected real return differential between Canadian and United States dollar assets is low, we have observed large movements in the speculative shares of these assets in response to small changes in their return differential. This is a consequence of the high degree of substitutability between these currencies.

In table 6.10, we record the percentage of the year-over-year change in speculative portfolio shares attributable to changes in real return differentials. That is, we decompose the relative effects of changes in expected real returns and in the observed variance-covariance matrix of exchange rate (and gold price) changes on movements over time in the speculative portfolio shares of all assets. It should be emphasized that under the assumption that the variance-covariance structure of exchange rate (and gold price) changes is stationary and known with certainty by the investor, movements in speculative portfolio shares would be entirely due to changes in real returns. This would imply that investors' estimates of the true stationary Σ matrix are not subject to sampling error. In this case, all of the elements in table 6.10 would be 100%, indicating that changes in speculative portfolios are fully attributable to real returns. In those cases where the reported percentage is 0%–100%, changes in the observed variance-covariance structure were found to reinforce the effect of changes in the real return differentials on (positive or negative) movements in speculative shares. Alternatively, elements greater than 100% imply that changes in the observed variance-covariance structure were a countervailing influence. A negative element in the table indicates that the movement in the speculative share was dominated by changes in the observed Σ matrix while the countervailing influence became the change in the real return vector.

Only in 1976 and 1978 were year-over-year changes in the speculative share of the United States dollar dominated by changes in real return differentials. For example, between March 1977 and March 1978 the optimal dollar share increased by 0.5%. If the observed Σ matrix had remained constant over this period, however, the share of United States assets in the speculative portfolio would have increased by 2.1%. Alternatively, the March 1979 dollar share increased by 2.4% over the previous year. If the Σ matrix observed in March 1978 had prevailed, the dollar speculative share would have fallen by 0.5% as a consequence of increased gold, French franc, yen, and pound assets' return differentials (see table 6.9). Thus, the increase in the share of the dollar over the year was entirely the consequence of favorable changes in its substitutability-complementarity relationships with other assets. Similarly, between March 1980 and March 1981, we ob-

Table 6.10   Percentage Change in Speculative Portfolio Shares Due to Changes in Real Returns

12-Month Change in Portfolio in March of:	GO	CA	FR	GE	IT	JA	SZ	UK	US
1976	67.3	79.2	76.3	99.6	−84.8	107.5	61.8	72.4	86.4
1977	−5.1	16.1	40.0	51.9	431.5	73.4	24.6	−8.0	16.6
1978	324.9	179.0	186.3	144.0	330.4	141.3	114.9	−304.1	445.8
1979	96.0	−90.3	131.4	−23.0	−20.0	−16.2	17.5	44.3	−22.4
1980	73.9	50.1	87.7	53.5	88.4	86.4	79.4	49.1	39.8
1981	70.8	−39.2	52.0	23.9	28.1	75.8	91.7	68.0	−39.0

Note: $\sum (r - r_{-12})$ as a percentage of $\left(\sum r - \sum_{-12} r_{-12}\right)$, the change in Bernoulli investor speculative portfolio changes in the previous 12-month period.

serve a 2.7% increase in the optimal dollar share. Changes in return differentials alone would have resulted in a 1% decline in the optimal share. This effect, however, was overwhelmed by a 3.7% increase in the dollar share attributable to changes in the observed variance-covariance structure (i.e., the optimal dollar share would have increased by 3.7% if real return differentials had remained constant at their March 1980 level).

In contrast to the case of the United States, changes in German mark speculative portfolio shares were, in most periods, principally due to changes in differentials. In 1976, for example, the 14.1% drop in the optimal German mark share was entirely the consequence of changes in real return differentials (e.g., between March 1975 and March 1976, the return differential in favor of German mark assets declined from 13.9% to 5.4%). In March 1978, the 304% decline in the optimal German mark share was fully attributable to changes in the vector of real returns. In this instance, however, changes in the observed variance-covariance structure served to reduce the magnitude of this effect.

In table 6.10, we also observe a similarity in the relative contribution of changes in real return differentials across assets in a given year. That is, in 1977 and 1978, changes in the observed Σ matrix played a significant role in the determination of changes in most speculative shares. In comparison, in March of 1976, 1980, and 1981, movements in real return differentials were of relatively greater importance in the reshuffling of the observed speculative portfolios.

6.4 Conclusion

Using a continuous-time finance-theoretic framework, section 6.2 of this paper presented the optimal portfolio rule of an international investor who consumes N national composite goods and who holds M domestic-currency-denominated assets with known nominal interest rates in an environment where prices of goods, assets, and exchange rate follow geometric Brownian motion. It is shown that the optimal portfolio decomposes into a capital position and two zero-net-worth portfolios. The derivation presents a capital position which depends only on the relative variances and covariances of changes in asset prices in terms of the numeraire. The first zero-net-worth portfolio, scaled by risk aversion, depends on a comparison of mean real return to the return on the capital position.

When the portfolio is restricted to N short-term financial assets with known prices and one asset with a random price in terms of the numeraire (e.g., gold), both the general rule of Meerschwam (1983) and the currency rule derived in Macedo (1983) are applicable, as shown in the Appendix. In this case, the capital position depends only on expenditure shares. The zero-net-worth inflation hedge portfolio is determined by the covariances between exchange rate and gold price changes and by their interactions with goods price changes. The zero-net-worth speculative portfolio depends on the risk preferences of the consumer-investor, the returns on the assets, and exchange rate and gold price changes.

Optimal portfolios are presented in section 6.3. These portfolios are based on the inflation-hedging potential provided by short-term financial assets denominated in different currencies and gold as well as on the substitutability/complementarity relationships among these assets.

In general, optimal diversification involves departures from both the "preferred monetary habitat" hypothesis, according to which portfolio shares would match expenditure shares, and the "purchasing power parity" hypothesis, according to which preferences would not affect the minimum variance portfolio. Specifically we found that the optimal portfolio of an investor who consumed goods from all major industrialized countries (according to their weight in total trade) would be dominated in March 1981 by long positions in United States dollars (25%) yen (17%), German marks (16%), French francs (15%), and pounds sterling (10%). An investor who consumed only United States goods, by contrast, would hold 96% of his optimal portfolio in United States dollars. The inflation hedge portion of this portfolio reveals that inflation risk is minimized, for both the international and United States investor would hold lire and pounds, while the international investor would borrow lire.

In March 1981, the optimal speculative portfolio, maximizing mean real returns, would include long positions in United States, German, and Japanese assets and in gold and short positions in Canandian dollars, French francs, lire, and pounds. The exclusion of gold generates substantial reshuffling in the speculative portfolio. With the exception of the pound, however, there is no change in the sign of optimal positions. The analysis of the speculative portfolio also reveals strong substitutability between United States and Canadian dollars and, to a lesser extent, between United States dollars and French francs and Italian lire. Weak complementarity relationships are observed between United States dollar and German mark and Swiss franc assets.

The analysis of the evolution of portfolios over time showed that even if the optimal portfolio rule is time invariant, optimal portfolios are not. Shares changed as expectations about the joint distribution of returns were revised. Share movements were most dramatic at the beginning of the period, and optimal positions did not begin to approach their March 1981 levels until the end of 1976.[19] In the case of the yen and the pound there were oscillations throughout the period. With respect to the dollar share in the optimal portfolio of the United States and international investor, we found that, in the period between late 1974 and mid-1976, a period in which the dollar is

---

19. Optimal portfolio shares computed with constant (two-year) sample length but different base periods exhibit even greater variability. See Goldstein (1983, chap. 5).

considered to have been strong, a large decline in its optimal share took place. This shows the importance of the variability (and the associated uncertainty) of the changes in the value of the United States dollar, even when the currency itself is strong. After the lows reached in mid-1976, the share increased again and stabilized in mid-1977 at levels well below those of before the end of 1974.

In sum, the finance-theoretic framework presented in this paper is motivated by the need to analyze the microeconomic foundations of international portfolio demands. The theory of optimal international portfolio selection highlights both the importance of risk and return considerations in the determination of the composition of a multicurrency portfolio and the potential for risk-reducing gains from diversification. Together with consumption and risk preferences, the demand for a given asset by a utility-maximizing investor is determined by its relative return as well as by its inflation-hedging potential and substitutability and complementarity relationships with assets and liabilities denominated in other currencies.

Ultimately, the analysis of market portfolio behavior will be facilitated by the relaxation of assumptions regarding the stochastic processes generating goods prices, asset prices, and exchange rates in a general rather than partial equilibrium model. The analysis of macroeconomic policy in interdependent economies also requires knowledge about the portfolio behavior of major participants in international financial markets. The theoretical and empirical framework developed in this paper provides a useful foundation for studying actual portfolio diversification across currencies by individual investors. For example, regression results in Goldstein (1984) cast doubt on the correspondence between observed United States banks' portfolio behavior and optimal international diversification. This may be explained by the estimation of cross-spectral densities between rates of return and asset positions: his results suggest that there are significant differences in portfolio demands across currencies and maturities, as well as in the portfolio behavior of smaller versus larger banks. Pursuing the line of research of Healy (1981), reserve diversification by central banks can also be studied using the model presented here.

By understanding agents' sensitivity to changes in real and nominal rates of return and to uncertainty deriving from exchange rate and price variability, one is better able to explore questions relating to the effects of monetary policy on portfolio shifts across currencies, the effectiveness of interventions policy, and the determination of exchange rates.

Appendix

Equation (6) in the proper can be written in full as:

(A1)
$$x = \frac{G^{-1}e}{e'G^{-1}e} + G^{-1}\left[I - e\frac{e'G^{-1}}{e'G^{-1}e}\right]\underset{\sim}{\Theta}\alpha$$
$$+ \frac{1}{1-\gamma}G^{-1}\left[I - e\frac{e'G^{-1}}{e'G^{-1}e}\right]r.$$

Rearranging terms, we see that

(A2)
$$x = G^{-1}\underset{\sim}{\Theta}\alpha + \frac{1}{1-\gamma}G^{-1}r$$
$$+ \frac{G^{-1}e}{e'G^{-1}e}\left[1 - e'G^{-1}\underset{\sim}{\Theta}\alpha - \frac{1}{1-\gamma}e'G^{-1}r\right].$$

Since $e'x = 1$, a consistent solution for x is that

(A3)
$$e'G^{-1}\underset{\sim}{\Theta}\alpha + \frac{1}{1-\gamma}e'G^{-1}r = 1.$$

Using (A3) in (A2) we get the portfolio rule for the $N - 1$ assets as

(A4)
$$x = G^{-1}\underset{\sim}{\Theta}\alpha + \frac{1}{1-\gamma}G^{-1}\, r.$$

Equation (28) in Meerschwam (1983) shows a similar result for the case where there is one asset with an uncertain price and one asset with a certain price in each country, so that the vector of portfolio shares (excluding the numeraire currency) is $2N - 1$. Here we only have one asset with an uncertain price in the numeraire country, gold (subscript 0), and $N - 1$ exchange rates (subscript 1 to N), so that the vector of portfolio shares excluding the numeraire has dimension N and

(A5)
$$x_0 = G_0^{-1}\, \Theta_0\alpha + \frac{1}{1-\gamma}\, G_0^{-1}\, r_0$$

where $X_0(r_0)$ is an $n \times 1$ column vector of portfolio shares (return differentials) obtained by adding row zero to the previous vector $x(r)$; G_0 is an $N \times N$ variance-covariance matrix of exchange rates and gold price changes; Θ_0 is an $N \times N$ covariance matrix of numeraire currency goods price changes with exchange rates and gold price changes.

Using the decomposition described in equation (7) in the text and preserving the notation introduced there, we get

(A6)
$$G_0 = \left[\begin{array}{c|c} g^2 & \underset{\sim}{0}' \\ \hline \underset{\sim}{0} & 0 \end{array}\right] + \left[\begin{array}{c|c} 0 & \underset{\sim}{0}' \\ \hline \underset{\sim}{0} & S \end{array}\right] - \left[\begin{array}{c|c} 0 & \epsilon' \\ \hline \underset{\equiv}{0} & 0 \end{array}\right] - \left[\begin{array}{c|c} 0 & \underset{\sim}{0}' \\ \hline \epsilon & 0 \end{array}\right]$$

$$= \left[\begin{array}{c|c} g^2 & -\epsilon' \\ \hline -\epsilon & S \end{array}\right]$$

(A7)
$$\Theta_0 = \left[\begin{array}{c|c} \eta' & \\ \hline \underline{0} & \underline{0} \end{array}\right] + \left[\begin{array}{c|c} \underset{\sim}{0}' & 0 \\ \hline S & \underline{0} \end{array}\right] - \left[\begin{array}{c|c} 0 & \epsilon' \\ \hline \underline{0} & 0 \end{array}\right] - \left[\begin{array}{c|c} \underset{\sim}{0}' & 0 \\ \hline & \psi \end{array}\right]$$

$$= \left[\begin{array}{c|c} -\epsilon' & 0 \\ \hline S & 0 \end{array}\right] - \left[\begin{array}{c} -\eta' \\ \hline \psi \end{array}\right] = \tilde{S}_0 - \psi_0,$$

where 0 is an $N - 1$-by-$N - 1$ matrix of zeros, g is the variance of gold price changes, ϵ is an $N - 1$ column vector of the covariance of gold price with exchange rate changes, and η is an N column vector of the covariance of gold price with goods price changes. Since gold is priced in the numeraire currency it is useful to decompose the ψ_0 matrix using the notation of (7'') in the text and the covariance η_N between the price of gold and the good of the numeraire currency:

(A7')
$$\psi_0 = \left[\begin{array}{c|c} -\tilde{\eta}' & -\eta_N \\ \hline \tilde{\psi} & \psi_N \end{array}\right].$$

We now invert G_0 and operate

(A8)
$$G_0^{-1} = \left[\begin{array}{c|c} \sigma_0 & \sigma_0 \epsilon' S^{-1} \\ \hline S^{-1} \epsilon \sigma_0 & S^{-1} + \sigma_0 S^{-1} \epsilon \epsilon' S^{-1} \end{array}\right],$$

where $\sigma_0 = (g^2 - \epsilon' S^{-1} \epsilon)^{-1}$.

(A9)
$$G_0^{-1} \tilde{S}_0 = \left[\begin{array}{c|c} \underset{\sim}{0}' & 0 \\ \hline \underline{I} & \underset{\sim}{0} \end{array}\right] \alpha = \left[\begin{array}{c} \underset{\sim}{0}' \\ \hline \underline{I} \end{array}\right] \alpha$$

(A10)
$$G_0^{-1} \psi_0 =$$

$$\left[\begin{array}{c|c} \sigma_0 \tilde{\eta}' - \sigma_0 \epsilon' S^{-1} \tilde{\psi} & \sigma_0 \eta_N - \sigma_0 \epsilon' S^{-1} \psi_N \\ \hline \sigma_0 \tilde{\eta}' S^{-1} \epsilon - S^{-1}[\underline{I} + \sigma_0 \epsilon \epsilon' S^{-1}] \tilde{\psi} & \sigma_0 \eta_N S^{-1} \epsilon - S^{-1}[\underline{I} + \sigma_0 \epsilon \epsilon' S^{-1}] \psi_N \end{array}\right].$$

It is clear from (A9) and (A10) that these matrixes are the ones given in (12) in the text, with the first row referring to gold. The $N + 1$ rule is therefore obtained by constructing the ϕ_0 and Σ_0 matrixes which are the exact counterparts of the ϕ and Σ matrixes defined in equations (13) and (11) of the text, respectively:

(A11)
$$\phi_0 = \left[\begin{array}{c} G_0^{-1}\psi_0 \\ \hline -e'G_0^{-1}\,\psi_0 \end{array}\right]$$

(A12)
$$\Sigma_0 = \left[\begin{array}{c|c} G_0^{-1} & -G_0^{-1}e \\ \hline -e'G_0^{-1} & e'G_0^{-1}e \end{array}\right].$$

An alternative procedure, described in detail in MGM and alluded to in the text, interprets gold as the currency of a country whose good is not concerned by the international consumer inventory and hence has $\alpha_0 = 0$ not generalize when there are several assets with uncertain prices in each country. In order to provide further insight, however, we do illustrate it for the case of gold and two currencies, modifying a similar presentation of the three-currency portfolio in Goldstein (1983, pp. 37–38). We chose currency 2 as the numeraire and denote the correlation coefficient between gold price and exchange rate changes by ρ and write

(A13)
$$\begin{pmatrix} x_0 \\ x_1 \end{pmatrix} = \begin{pmatrix} 0 \\ \alpha_1 \end{pmatrix} - \begin{bmatrix} (\delta_1/g)l_{01} & (\delta_2/g)l_{02} \\ (\delta_1/\sigma)l_{11} & (\delta_2/\sigma)l_{12} \end{bmatrix}\begin{pmatrix} \alpha_1 \\ \alpha_2 \end{pmatrix}$$
$$+ \frac{1}{1-\gamma}\frac{1}{g^2\sigma^2(1-\rho^2)}\begin{bmatrix} \sigma^2 & -\rho g \\ -\rho g\sigma & g^2 \end{bmatrix}\begin{pmatrix} r_0 - r_2 \\ r_1 - r_2 \end{pmatrix},$$

where $l_{0i} = \tilde{\rho}_{0i} - \rho\tilde{\rho}_{1i}/(1-\rho^2)$

and

$l_{1i} = \tilde{\rho}_{1i} - \rho\tilde{\rho}_{1i}/(1-\rho^2)$,

for $i = 1, 2$. Using the unity constraint $x_2 = 1 - x_0 - x_1$, we get

(A14)
$$\begin{pmatrix} x_0 \\ x_1 \\ x_2 \end{pmatrix} = \begin{pmatrix} 0 \\ \alpha_1 \\ \alpha_2 \end{pmatrix} - \begin{bmatrix} (\delta_1 l_{01}) & (\delta_2/g)l_{02} \\ (\delta_1/\sigma)l_{11} & (\delta_2/\sigma)l_{12} \\ (\delta_1/g\, l_{01} + \delta_1/\sigma\, l_{11}) & -(\delta_2/g\, l_{02} + \delta_2/\sigma\, l_{12}) \end{bmatrix}\begin{pmatrix} \alpha_1 \\ \alpha_2 \end{pmatrix}$$

$$
+ \frac{1}{(1 - \gamma)(1 - \rho^2)}
$$

$$
+ \begin{bmatrix} 1/g^2 & -\rho/g\sigma & (\rho/\sigma - 1)g \\ -\rho/g\sigma & 1/\sigma^2 & (\rho/g - 1)\sigma \\ (\rho/\sigma - 1)g & (\rho/g - 1)\sigma & 1/g^2 + 1/\sigma^2 - 2\rho/g\sigma \end{bmatrix} \begin{pmatrix} r_0 \\ r_1 \\ r_2 \end{pmatrix}.
$$

Comment   Bernard Dumas

The recent work of Kouri, de Macedo, and others represents a welcome attempt by macroeconomists to use Markowitz portfolio theory as a way to determine asset demands. This attempt is long overdue; for years, macroeconomic analysis has postulated asset demand schedules without microeconomic foundations. However, it comes at a time when the Finance profession itself begins to seriously question the virtues of this approach. This reappraisal is motivated by theoretical and statistical considerations which I will review after some comments and clarifications pertaining to the specific contribution of Macedo, Goldstein, and Meerschwam.

The basic separation result of mean-variance portfolio theory, formulated in a way which makes it relevant for international finance, can be stated as follows: "Every investor in the world holds a combination (with weights based on his risk tolerance) of two portfolios: the portfolio of minimum variance in real terms (weight = one minus the risk tolerance); and the portfolio which would be held by a logarithmic investor (weight = risk tolerance). Under purchasing power parity the minimum variance portfolio is the same for all investors; otherwise it is specific to each one of them,[1] and it depends on the commodities price index used by the investor. The logarithmic portfolio, however, is universal and is independent of the price index used."[2]

Against this background, I would make two observations on the paper of de Macedo et al. that appear to call their results into question. One is mostly a matter of presentation, but the other is more fundamental. First, recall that Macedo et al. present the optimal portfolio composition in terms of *three* component portfolios: the capital position, the (zero net worth) inflation

---

1. Solnik (1974) and Sercu (1980) examine the case where each investor takes his anticipated home inflation to be zero. In that case, the minimum variance portfolio is entirely made up of the home currency short-term asset.

2. This observation appeared first in Hakansson (1969).

hedge, and the (zero net worth) speculative portfolio. As a means of describing the optimal choices, this approach seems inferior to the separation theorem I stated above: it uses three components when only two are required by the mean-variance framework, and two of these components (the inflation hedge and the speculative portfolio) are specific to the particular national investor being considered. As a consequence of this added complexity, the picture which emerges from the numerical results being presented is not as clear as it might have been.[3]

The second, more fundamental observation pertains to the authors' choice of the commodities price indexes. The results are quite sensitive to this choice. De Macedo et al. compute their own brand of price index based on home and foreign consumer price indexes and the shares of the imports from the various countries, in home consumption. An alternative procedure would be simply to use the home consumer price index of the investors. Quite obviously the two types of indexes behave very differently; the computed index reflects immediately the strong impact of exchange rates on foreign goods whereas the CPI does so very little. The consequences of the choice of the index on portfolio choice are momentous. In de Macedo et al. the minimum variance portfolio composition reflects mostly the geographic origin of the goods consumed by the investor, whereas using the CPI would let practically 100% of this portfolio fall on the home short-term nominal asset,[4] which appears minimally risky even in real terms (for countries of residence with ''reasonable'' inflationary processes). A strong ''home currency preference'' pattern comes out of the second specification.

At least two interpretations may be offered for the de Macedo et al. procedure. The first one is the one they themselves apparently advocate: they intend to refer to an international ''average'' investor. This reference to the aggregate seems to be the reason for computing a weighted average of national CPIs. This seems questionable, as aggregation of national portfolio compositions should not be performed by means of trade weights, but by using weights related to national wealths. (Which could perhaps be proxied by GNPs?)

A second (and to my mind more satisfactory) interpretation would consider the de Macedo price index as a proxy for home and foreign *output prices* weighted by the shares of import in the home consumption of one particular nation. In that case, the choice between the de Macedo index and the straight CPI is not simple to make. In principle, investors are confronted with consumption prices and not with import prices directly so that the CPI

---

3. Numerical results in the two-fund format are given in Adler and Dumas (1982), table 5.
4. See Adler and Dumas (1982), table 5.

should be used. Yet the impact of exchange rates on import prices must somehow have an impact on asset selection.[5]

In short, de Macedo et al. do not provide sufficient justification for the particular price index which they use in portfolio choice as against using the straight CPI and the results of the empirical analysis are markedly affected by this choice of an index. One cannot therefore consider them as definitive.

I now come to some general remarks on the validity and testability of portfolio theory, in its specific version used here. First, let us examine the validity of the analytical derivations as they are presented in the paper. Some Ito stochastic processes are postulated for prices and exchange rates, but for empirical purposes these processes are restricted to being stationary Brownian motions, and portfolio optimization based on some time-additive von Neuman–Morgenstern objective function is then performed.[6] If the equilibrium resulting from these asset demands were computed, some restriction (called the capital asset pricing model) on the parameters of the various Brownian motions would typically be reached. To be rigorous, however, one should then verify that prices do follow the postulated processes. That is rarely done. But we can be more negative: we know from Lucas (1978) that the processes governing asset prices cannot be stationary Brownian motions, as risk aversion implies that rates of return must be serially correlated. Hence the specific formulation presented here is contradictory as it is not compatible with general equilibrium. What we need, therefore, is a complete theory of asset prices based on more general processes for prices, and we must await this theory before optimal portfolios are presented.[7] This is apparently forthcoming, since the conclusion of the paper announces that one of the authors (Meerschwam) is working on such a theory and another (Goldstein) is attempting empirically to measure the nonstationarity of the postulated processes.

I now come to some remarks on the testability of portfolio theory. They will throw some light on the validity of the numerical calculations produced by de Macedo et al. At the root of most of the statistical problems is the fact that *the sample distribution of optimal portfolio compositions is not*

5. But, contra de Macedo et al., the proper vehicle for this influence is not the minimum variance fund. If exchange rate changes are not immediately reflected in the CPI, it must be because firms engaged in import trading keep a stable sales price which they do not adjust very quickly to the import price. In the ideal case, where the shares of these firms would be traded on a stock exchange and included as separate investment lines into an optimal portfolio based, as it should be, on the CPI, investors would hold these shares in their logarithmic fund and would tend to hedge them by holding some foreign currency deposits. But note that this portfolio modification takes place via the logarithmic fund which is universal and not via the inflation hedge.

6. There may be an additional assumption that the invested wealth (a variable combination of asset prices) of each investor also follows an Ito process.

7. This is not being unduly cautious. There is considerable evidence of instability in the drift and standard deviation parameters of the postulated Brownian motions. Investors would therefore hold a number of hedge funds designed to anticipate on the shifts of the various state variables. The portfolio choice picture is likely to be *qualitatively* modified by these considerations.

known. Consider, for instance, the logarithmic portfolio. Its optimal composition is given by the inverse of the covariance matrix of returns premultiplying the vector of expected returns in excess of the reference currency interest rate. There is no difficulty in obtaining efficient unbiased (in the expected value sense) estimates of the covariance matrix and the excess returns, but we have no reason to think that these estimates would yield efficient (or even unbiased) estimates of portfolio compositions. If returns are normally distributed, the inverted covariance matrix estimate is distributed according to the inverse Wishart distribution and the expected return estimates are normal, but we know nothing of their product, especially because all these estimates are generally not independent. Casual reasoning suggests that the estimated optimal portfolio compositions have a very high variance:[8] the optimization procedure presumably rushes headlong on the securities whose sample risk happens to be low and whose sample return happens to be large, assigning very large positive weights to them and very large negative weights to other securities, while another sample might do just the reverse. And, indeed, every study based on actual rates-of-return data which I have seen produces such "unreasonable" optimal portfolio choices (in the absence of constraints such as short-selling limitations).

Simulation studies can clarify this issue to some extent. Consider the choice between two assets: one riskless with an interest rate of 10% and one risky with an average return of 11% and a standard deviation of return of 10% so that the true optimal weight (for a logarithmic investor) to be placed on the risky asset is equal to one. Drawing six times a sample of thirty-two observations,[9] the average estimated optimal weight has been found to be 0.8576 *with a standard deviation of this estimate equal to 1.2988*. Hence for any given sample one may easily obtain an optimal weight of $+2$ or -1 when the true optimal weight is $+1$. Estimates of optimal portfolio composition are not reliable.

Perhaps even more crucial is the restricted menu of assets considered here: only gold and short-term nominal assets. The diversification motive is central to portfolio choice; as a result, adding just one asset to a prior list of eight assets is quite easily capable of drastically changing the relative weights assigned to the eight assets themselves. For so long as we do not look at a reasonably complete list of individual assets available across the world, sample calculations of optimal portfolios yield almost arbitrary results. On the other hand, of course, a reasonably complete list would entail impossible data and computation requirements.

Assuming the above two problems solved, there would remain the actual task of testing the theory (an issue which de Macedo et al. do not touch upon) before we venture to provide advice to decision makers. One way to proceed would be to aggregate the optimal portfolios of all the economic

8. This is quite apart from nonstationarity questions.
9. This is the same sample size *relative* to the number of assets as in de Macedo et al. (128 observations for eight assets).

entities and compare the result with the observed world market capitalizations of the various assets (the so-called world market portfolio). As Roll (1977) has pointed out, identifying this portfolio with sufficient precision is quite difficult. Another way to proceed, which, to my knowledge, has not been attempted, would be to confront optimal portfolio revisions computed as above with balance of payments data on international capital flows. This is a possible, if hazardous, avenue for future research.

Comment   Jeffrey A. Frankel

I would like to follow up on Bernard Dumas's call for going beyond econometric estimation of optimal portfolios, to econometric testing of the hypothesis that they in fact correspond to the actual portfolios held by investors. That this hypothesis is in doubt should be clear from the fact that the optimal portfolios estimated by Macedo, Goldstein, and Meerschwam, as in the earlier study by Kouri and Macedo, prescribe negative holdings of some countries' assets. These assets could be "shorted" by individual investors, but it is not possible that all investors hold negative amounts, as the net supplies of these assets to the market, that is, the net liabilities of governments, are known to be positive.

The hypothesis of portfolio optimization can be tested by nesting it within framework in which asset demand functions are of the portfolio balance variety but are not necessarily optimizing. Let x_t be a vector of demands for various assets as proportions of wealth, let r_t^e be the vector of expected returns, and let β be the matrix of coefficients in the demand function:

$$(1) \qquad x_t = \alpha + \beta r_t^e.$$

If we invert the portfolio balance function and assume rational expectations, then we can use equation-by-equation OLS to estimate the system because the regression error ϵ_{t+1} is the expectational error $r_{t+1} - r_t^e$ that is independent of all variables known at time t:

$$(2) \qquad r_{t+1} = -\beta^{-1}\alpha + \beta^{-1}x_t + \epsilon_{t+1}.$$

Under assumptions like those made by Macedo et al., it can be seen that if investors optimize with respect to the mean and variance of end-of-period wealth, the coefficient matrix will be given by

$$(3) \qquad \beta^{-1} = \rho\Sigma,$$

where ρ is defined as the coefficient of relative risk aversion and Σ is defined as the return variance-covariance matrix: $\Sigma \equiv E\epsilon_{t+1}\epsilon_{t+1}'$. It is an unusual problem in econometrics to estimate an equation like (2) subject to a constraint like (3), a constraint not within the coefficient matrix but rather between the coefficient matrix and the variance-covariance matrix of the error term. But it can be done by maximum likelihood estimation. Then the like-

lihood from estimating equation (2) unconstrained can be compared to the
likelihood from estimating it constrained. If the fit does not worsen significantly, as decided by the likelihood ratio test, then we have failed to reject
the null hypothesis.

If one accepts the optimizing hypothesis, either on the grounds of such a
test or a priori, then the constrained estimates can be taken as efficient estimates of the parameters. The Macedo et al. paper is an important step forward over most previous work in the respect that it allows expected returns
to vary over time, as they surely do both in the standard macroeconomic
models and in the recent history of the world economy. However, it is still
limited by the assumption that investors form expectations solely on the
basis of past history. One might wish for coefficients in the portfolio balance
function estimated under the assumption that investors form expectations
rationally given all contemporaneous data. This can be done by using data
on actual portfolios to infer expectations, as in the estimation framework
suggested here; the expected returns are simply the fitted values of equation (2).

References

Adler, Michael, and Dumas, Bernard. 1982. International portfolio choice
    and corporate finance: A survey. *Journal of Finance* 38:925–84.
Bortz, Gary. 1982. The determination of asset yields in a stochastic two-
    country model. Ph.D. diss., Princeton University.
Branson, William, and Henderson, Dale. 1984. The specification and influ-
    ence of asset markets. In *Handbook of international economics,* ed. R.
    Jones and P. Kenen. North-Holland.
Dornbusch, Rudiger. 1980. Exchange rate economics: Where do we stand?
    Brookings Papers on Economic Activity 1:143–85.
Frankel, Jeffrey. 1982. In search of the exchange risk premium: A six-cur-
    rency test assuming mean-variance optimization. *Journal of International
    Money and Finance* 1 (December): 225–74.
Goldstein, Jeffrey. 1983. Essays in international portfolio selection. Ph.D.
    diss., Yale University.
———. 1984. International portfolio diversification: The case of U.S. com-
    mercial banks. In *The modeling and control of national economies,* ed.
    Tamer Basar and Louis Pau. Washington, D.C.: Pergamon Press.
Hakansson, N. H. 1969. On the relevance of price-level accounting. *Journal
    of Accounting Research* 7 (Spring): 22–31.
Healy, James. 1981. A simple regression technique for the optimal diversi-
    fication of foreign exchange reserves. IMF Departmental Memorandum
    (August), Washington, D.C.
Kouri, Pentti. 1975. Essays on the theory of flexible exchange rate. Ph.D.
    diss., MIT.

————. 1977. International investment and interest rate linkages under flexible exchange rates. In *The political economy of monetary reform,* ed. Robert Z. Aliber. New York: Macmillan.

Kouri, Pentti, and de Macedo, Jorge. 1978. Exchange rates and the international adjustment process. *Brookings Papers in Economic Activity* 1:397–407.

De Macedo, J. 1979. Portfolio diversification and currency inconvertibility: Three essays in international economics. Ph.D. diss., Yale University. Also rev.; Lisbon: New University of Lisbon Press, 1982.

————. 1982. Portfolio diversification across currencies. In *The International monetary system under flexible exchange rates,* ed. R. Cooper et al. Cambridge, Mass.: Ballinger.

————. 1983. Optimal currency diversification for a class of risk-averse international investors. *Journal of Economic Dynamics and Control* 5:173–85.

De Macedo, J.; Goldstein, J.; and Meerschwam, D. 1982. International portfolio diversification: Short-term financial assets and gold. International Finance Section, Princeton University, Working Paper in International Economics 6-28-01.

Meerschwam, David. 1983. On causes and effects of exchange rate volatility. Ph.D. diss. Princeton University. Also available as Financial Research Memorandum no. 44.

Merton, Robert. 1971. Optimal consumption and portfolio rules in a continuous-time model. *Journal of Economic Theory* 3:373–413.

Nairay, Alain. 1981. Consumption-investment decisions under uncertainty and variable time preference. Ph.D. diss., Yale University.

Roll, R. 1977. A critique of the asset pricing theory's tests, part 1: On past and potential testability of the theory. *Journal of Financial Economics* 4 (March): 129–76.

Sercu, P. 1980. A generalization of the international asset pricing model. *Revue de l'Association française de finance* 1 (June): 91–135.

Solnik, Bruno. 1973. *European capital markets.* Lexington, Mass.: Lexington Books.

————. 1974. An equilibrium model of the international capital market. *Journal of Economic Theory* 8 (August): 500–524.

Stulz, Rene. 1980. Essays in international asset pricing. Ph.D. diss., MIT.

————. 1982. Currency preferences, purchasing power risks, and the determination of exchange rates in an optimizing model. University of Rochester Working Paper GPB 82-2.

Tobin, James. 1965. The theory of portfolio selection. In *The theory of interest rates,* ed. F. Hahn and J. Brechlings. New York: Macmillan.

————. 1982. The state of exchange rate theory: Some skeptical remarks. In *The international monetary system under flexible exchange rates,* ed. R. Cooper et al. Cambridge, Mass.: Ballinger.

7   Tests of Monetary and Portfolio Balance Models of Exchange Rate Determination

Jeffrey A. Frankel

Such titles of recent papers as "Exchange Rate Economics: Where Do We Stand?" and "Exchange Rate Models of the 1970's: Are Any Fit to Survive?" indicate that the field has entered an introspective and skeptical phase, after the initial enthusiastic burst of model building and estimation that followed the beginning of floating exchange rates. In the same spirit of "taking stock," I was asked in the present paper to present some econometric tests of competing monetary and portfolio balance models of exchange rate determination.[1]

7.1 The Monetary Model

The first part of the paper deals with the monetary approach to the exchange rate, as it was developed in the first five years after 1973. Because the theory is by now well known, we go through it as quickly as possible—the version that assumes perfectly flexible goods prices as well as the version that assumes sticky goods prices—and pass on to the econometric estimation. The estimation, for five currencies from 1974 up to mid-1981, turns out to favor the sticky price monetary equation over the flexible price equation, if one must choose between them. However, the results must be pronounced poor for both versions. Thus we are led to consider possible ways of "patching up" the monetary model.

7.1.1 The Flexible Price Monetary Equation

We begin with the version of the monetary approach attributed to Frenkel (1976), Mussa (1976), and Bilson (1978). This version assumes that goods

I would like to thank Charles Engel for very capable research assistance and the National Science Foundation for research support (grant no. SES-8007162).
1. The two classes of models are surveyed by Dornbusch (1980) and Frankel (1980).

prices are perfectly flexible and thus that purchasing power parity holds instantaneously:

(1) $s = p - p^*,$

where s is the log of the spot exchange rate, defined as the price of foreign currency in terms of domestic and p and p^* are the logs of the domestic and foreign price levels, respectively. We assume conventional money demand functions at home and abroad,

(2) $m = p + \phi y - \lambda i$
$$m^* = p^* + \phi y^* - \lambda i^*,$$

where m and m^* are the logs of the domestic and foreign money supplies, respectively; y and y^* are the logs of domestic and foreign real income; and i and i^* the domestic and foreign interest rate. For simplicity, we assume that the elasticity with respect to income, ϕ, and the semielasticity with respect to the interest rate, λ, are equal across countries. Combining equations (1) and (2) we have one representation of the flexible price monetary equation:

(3) $s = (m - m^*) - \phi(y - y^*) + \lambda(i - i^*).$

The monetary approach, if it is to maintain that bond supplies do not affect interest or exchange rates as money supplies do, must assume that domestic and foreign bonds are perfect substitutes and thus that uncovered interest parity holds,

(4) $i - i^* = \Delta s^e,$

where Δs^e is the expected depreciation of domestic currency. The market will be aware of the purchasing power parity condition (1), and so we will have

(1') $\Delta s^e = \pi - \pi^*,$

where π and π^* are the expected inflation rates, at home and abroad, respectively. Substituting (4) and (1') into (3), we get an alternative representation of the flexible price monetary equation:

(3') $s = (m - m^*) - \phi(y - y^*) + \lambda(\pi - \pi^*).$

Equation (3') says that the exchange rate, as the relative price of moneys, is determined by the supply and demand for money. An increase in the supply of domestic money causes a proportionate depreciation. An increase in the demand for domestic money, such as results from an increase in domestic income or a decrease in expected inflation, causes an appreciation. The equation has been widely estimated econometrically.

7.1.2 The Sticky Price Monetary Equation

Dornbusch (1976) took exception with the assumption that prices are perfectly flexible even in the short run, as unrealistic. Instead, purchasing power parity is assumed to hold only in the long run:

$$(5) \qquad \bar{s} = \bar{p} - \bar{p}^*,$$

where a "bar" over a variable denotes long-run equilibrium.[2] Thus the Frenkel-Mussa-Bilson equation (3') holds only in long-run equilibrium:

$$(6) \qquad \bar{s} = (\bar{m} - \bar{m}^*) - \phi(\bar{y} - \bar{y}^*) + \lambda(\bar{\pi} - \bar{\pi}^*).$$

In the short run, the spot rate can deviate from its equilibrium value, but the market expects the spot rate to regress toward equilibrium at a rate proportional to the gap:

$$(7) \qquad \Delta s^e = -\theta(s - \bar{s}) + \bar{\pi} - \bar{\pi}^*.$$

This form of expectations turns out to be rational in a model in which prices adjust gradually over time in response to excess goods demand but also move in line with the underlying inflation rate $\bar{\pi}$.[3] Combining (7) with the monetary approach's assumption of uncovered interest parity (4), which is retained in the Dornbusch model, we have an expression for the gap between the current spot rate and its equilibrium level:

$$(8) \qquad s - \bar{s} = -\frac{1}{\theta}[(i - \bar{\pi}) - (i^* - \bar{\pi}^*)].$$

A tight monetary policy raises the real interest differential, attracts a capital inflow, and appreciates the currency above its equilibrium value.

We combine equations (6) and (8) to obtain the sticky price monetary equation of exchange rate determination:

$$(9) \qquad s = (\bar{m} - \bar{m}^*) - \phi(\bar{y} - \bar{y}^*) + \left(\lambda + \frac{1}{\theta}\right)(\bar{\pi} - \bar{\pi}^*)$$
$$- \frac{1}{\theta}(i - i^*).$$

2. Evidence that purchasing power parity holds in the long-run despite large short-run deviations is offered by Genberg (1978) and Krugman (1978). One survey of the PPP literature is Katseli-Papaefstratiou (1979).

3. This is the Dornbusch model as extended to the case of secular inflation in Frankel (1979). The inflation rate $\bar{\pi}$ and $\bar{\pi}^*$ can be thought of as the countries' expected money growth rates. An implication of this formulation is that a sudden decline $\Delta\bar{\pi}$ in the expected money growth rate, in addition to its appreciation of the currency in equilibrium by $\lambda\Delta\bar{\pi}$, will cause the currency to overshoot its equilibrium by $\frac{1}{\theta}\Delta\bar{\pi}$. Buiter and Miller (1981) offer an alternative way of extending the Dornbusch model to the case of secular inflation; the money growth rate is assumed to have less than the full impact on $\bar{\pi}$ and therefore on s in the short run. Both formulations are very suggestive of the recent experience of the United Kingdom and United States vis-à-vis other countries.

The flexible price version can be viewed as the special case in which adjustment to long-run equilibrium is instantaneous, so $\theta = \infty$ and the coefficient on the interest differential is not less than zero. In the following section we estimate this equation econometrically.

7.1.3 Estimation for Five Currencies

Prior empirical studies of the monetary model have produced different results depending on the currency used. For example, Bilson (1978) claimed support for the flexible price version from the pound/dollar data, while I found evidence for the sticky price version in the mark/dollar data in Frankel (1979). In this section we test equation (9) for five exchange rates at the same time: the mark, pound, franc, yen, and Canadian dollar, each against the United States dollar.

The sample begins in January 1974 and ends in mid-1981, with the exact limits for each currency depending on data availability. The "equilibrium" money supplies are represented by their current values, though we must recognize that much of the monthly fluctuation in the monetary aggregates is in fact transitory. The equilibrium income levels are represented by industrial production. The equilibrium expected inflation rates are measured by actual CPI inflation over the preceding 12 months. Finally, the nominal interest rates are represented by annualized short-term money market rates.

Table 7.1 presents estimates for the five exchange rates using the iterative Cochrane-Orcutt technique to correct for high serial correlation. Only in the case of France are all four coefficients of the hypothesized sign. The coefficient on the interest differential is always of the negative sign hypothesized by the sticky price model. In the case of England, this represents a reversal in sign over earlier studies. The reversal is attributable to the unprecedented variation in interest rates of 1980–81, and confirms a finding of Hacche and Townend (1981). But overall, the presence of wrong signs on the other coefficients and the predominance of low significance levels render the results discouraging for the monetary equation.

There are several ways that one can bring more information to bear in order to get more efficient estimates. First, one can impose the constraint of a unit coefficient on the relative money supply.[4] The results in table 7.1 indicate no improvement, except for the case of Japan. Second, we can impose the constraint that the coefficients are the same across all five equations. This technique is achieved by "stacking" the regressions. The results, reported in table 7.2, show some improvement. The negative coefficient on the interest differential is now highly significant. But the other three coefficients, though of the correct sign, are still not significantly different from

---

4. Imposition of this constraint has the added benefit that if the money stocks are endogenous, as they surely are, then it allows consistent estimation of the other coefficients.

Table 7.1   Monetary Equation (Dependent Variable: Log of Exchange Rate per United States Dollar)

Country	Constant	$m1 - m1_{US}$	$y - y_{US}$	$INFL - INFL_{US}$	$i - i_{US}$	Sample	ρ	s.e.r.
Germany:	.80	-.05	.07	1.34	-.61[a]	90	.95	.033
	(.21)	(.33)	(.22)	(.82)	(.27)			
	1.37	1.00	.12	1.59	-.62[a]		.96	.034
	(.12)	(Constrained)	(.23)	(.86)	(.28)			
France:	1.34	.17	-.23	2.41[a]	-.24	87	.81	.029
	(.07)	(.17)	(.13)	(.69)	(.24)			
	1.07	1.00	-.16	1.53	-.28		.90	.032
	(.06)	(Constrained)	(.14)	(.83)	(.27)			
United Kingdom:	-.20	.12	-.13	-.06	-.28	89	.97	.029
	(.61)	(.22)	(.17)	(.05)	(.21)			
	2.10	1.00	-.09	-.07	-.24		.98	.032
	(.23)	(Constrained)	(.18)	(.05)	(.22)			
Japan:	4.39	.21	.27	.53	-.40	89	.98	.031
	(1.00)	(.20)	(.23)	(.33)	(.27)			
	.44	1.00	.60[b]	.73[a]	-.61[a]		.98	.034
	(.17)	(Constrained)	(.23)	(.36)	(.29)			
Canada:	.44	.08	.18	-.48	-.27	89	.98	.014
	(.32)	(.12)	(.12)	(.32)	(.17)			
	2.85	1.00	.18	-.31	-.29		.99	.018
	(.15)	(Constrained)	(.15)	(.41)	(.22)			

[a]Significant at the 95% level and of the correct sign.

[b]Significant at the 95% level and of the incorrect sign. (Standard errors in parentheses.)

Technique: Cochrane-Orcutt.

Samples: $90 = 2/74–7/81$, $87 = 2/74–4/81$, $89 = 2/74–6/81$.

Table 7.2   Five Monetary Equations "Stacked" (Dependent Variable: Log of Exchange Rate per United States Dollar)

Constant Terms					Coefficients					
Germany	France	U.K.	Japan	Canada	$m1 - m1_{US}$	$y - y_{US}$	$INFL - INFL_{US}$	$i - i_{US}$	ρ	s.e.r.
.77	1.46	−1.08	4.98	.35	.09	−.05	.24	−.36[a]	.97	.028
(.10)	(.09)	(.40)	(.49)	(.25)	(.09)	(.08)	(.19)	(.11)		
1.28	1.10	−4.93	.31	2.66	1.00	−.03	.31	−.39[a]	.96	.031
(.09)	(.09)	(.09)	(.09)	(.09)	(Constrained)	(.08)	(.21)	(.12)		

[a]Significant at the 95% level. (Standard errors in parentheses.)

Technique: Cochrane-Orcutt.

Sample: same as table 7.1; 444 observations.

zero. It appears that we must consider theoretical modifications of the monetary model.[5]

7.1.4 Drift in Velocity and the Real Exchange Rate

Some recent literature on exchange rate determination has proposed modifications in the monetary models, partly in response to poor results like those reported in section 7.1.3. As a matter of logic, one or more of the assumptions, or building blocks, in sections 7.1.1 and 7.1.2 would have to be modified.

First, one could question assumption (5), that purchasing power parity holds, even in the long run.[6] The most commonly cited sources of recent shifts in the long-run terms of trade are the oil price rises of the 1970s,[7] though these shifts do not automatically imply changes in the long-run real exchange rate between pairs of industrialized countries, as pointed out by Krugman (1980). Other possible sources include nontraded goods prices that rise more rapidly in countries with more rapid income growth, as argued years ago by Balassa (1964). Whatever the source of shifts in the long-run real exchange rate, they are easily integrated into the monetary equation of exchange rate determination, as in Hooper and Morton (1982). If (5) is replaced by

$$(5') \qquad r \equiv \bar{s} - \bar{p} + \bar{p}^*,$$

then the long-run real exchange rate r simply appears as an additional term in (9).

A second building block that has been called into question is the money demand equation (2). A downward shift in United States money demand in the 1970s has been widely noted. In Frankel (1982) I argue that there has also been an upward shift in German money demand, and that the two shifts

---

5. A third way to obtain still more efficient estimates is to take advantage of the joint distribution that the error terms must have in a world of multilateral floating, through Zellner's technique of seemingly unrelated regressions. The membership of Germany and France in the European Monetary System, for example, provides particularly strong grounds for expecting their exchange rates against the dollar to be highly correlated. However, the results obtained from using Zellner's technique suggest that the cost exceeds the benefit of the slight gain in efficiency. Of course, the theory may be correct and yet the economic estimation plagued by more serious problems than high standard errors, that is, by inconsistency resulting from misspecification or simultaneity. Haynes and Stone (1981) argue against imposing the constraint that the money demand parameters in eq. (2) are equal across countries. But the results in table 7.1 are little affected by relaxing the constraints. Driskill and Sheffrin (1981) and others argue that the interest differential is endogenous, requiring simultaneous-equation estimation. In Frankel (1981) I use the ratio of the monetary base to government debt as an instrumental variable to estimate the coefficient of the interest differential.

6. The turnabout on purchasing power parity is strikingly symbolized by the title of Frenkel (1981), in contrast to the title of Katseli-Papaefstratiou (1979).

7. The role of an oil shock in determining the real exchange rate is examined by Obstfeld (1980) and Giavazzi and Wyplosz (in this volume).

explain the fall in the mark/dollar rate of the late 1970s. If we add a shift term to each money demand function,

(2')
$$\overline{m} = \overline{p} + \phi\overline{y} + \lambda\overline{i} + v$$
$$\overline{m}^* = \overline{p}^* + \phi\overline{y}^* + \lambda\overline{i}^* + v^*,$$

they show up as two more terms in the exchange rate equation:

(9')
$$s = (\overline{m} - \overline{m}^*) - \phi(\overline{y} - \overline{y}^*) + \left(\lambda + \frac{1}{\theta}\right)(\overline{\pi} - \overline{\pi}^*)$$
$$- \frac{1}{\theta}(i - i^*) + r - (v - v^*).$$

The third building block that has been called into question is the uncovered interest parity condition (4). If domestic and foreign bonds are imperfect substitutes, then the interest differential will differ from the expected rate of depreciation by a term that is most naturally thought of as a risk premium. The risk premium can be integrated into the monetary equation as yet another additional term in (9).

The question remains how to represent for empirical work our additional terms arising from shifts in purchasing power parity, money demand, and the risk premium. In each case, authors who have proposed the additional terms have constructed fairly ad hoc measures based largely on the current account. The current account is argued, alternatively, to give signals regarding long-run competitiveness, to constitute an important component of wealth which in turn belongs in the money demand function, and to be a determinant of the risk premium. Indeed, a major motivation for these modifications has been to "get the current account back into the monetary model." One obvious disadvantage with using these ad hoc measures is that it would be difficult to discriminate among the three alternative rationales.

The aim of this section is the very limited one of identifying which of the possible shifts is responsible for the apparent breakdown in the monetary model, without attempting to model the particular shift in question. This is possible by making use of the one structural variable in the monetary model that does not appear in the "reduced form" (9): the price level. In equation (9') we represent r by a 1-year polynomial distributed lag of the real exchange rate ($e - p + p^*$), and we represent $v - v^*$ by a 1-year polynomial distributed lag of relative velocity, $(p + y - m) - (p^* + y^* - m^*)$, both in log form. If one variable or the other gets the equation running smoothly again, then at least the source of the malfunction will have been localized.

In table 7.3 the lags on velocity and the real exchange rate are in every case but one highly significant and of the correct sign. Far more interestingly, the coefficients on each of the original four variables are now usually significant and of the correct sign. These results suggest that shifts in the money demand function and the long-run real exchange rate may equally be responsible for the problems of the monetary equation. The results tell us

Table 7.3   Monetary Equation with Drift in Velocity and the Real Exchange Rate (Dependent Variable: Log of Exchange Rate per United States Dollar)

Country	Constant	$m1 - m1b_{US}$	$y - y_{US}$	$INFL - INFL_{US}$	$i - i_{US}$	Sum of Lag Coefficients — Velocity	Sum of Lag Coefficients — Real Exchange Rate	Sample	ρ	s.e.r.
Germany	-.19	.46[a]	-.26	.81[b]	-.59[a]	.65[a]	1.00[a]	78	.24	.018
	(.15)	(.17)	(.18)	(.45)	(.17)	(.09)	(.11)		(.11)	
France	-.49	.64[a]	-.50[a]	.54	-.54[a]	.38[a]	1.05[a]	86	.51	.019
	(.20)	(.18)	(.12)	(.51)	(.17)	(.17)	(.12)		(.09)	
United Kingdom	.75	.88[a]	-.54[a]	.04[b]	-.14	.52[a]	1.06[a]	88	.49	.021
	(.27)	(.09)	(.13)	(.02)	(.15)	(.12)	(.07)		(.09)	
Japan	1.84	.61[a]	-.81[a]	.51[a]	.06	.77[a]	81[a]	89	.46	.020
	(.50)	(.13)	(.10)	(.24)	(.14)	(.09)	(.07)		(.09)	
Canada	.27	-.02	.30[c]	.40[b]	-.43[a]	-.38[c]	.98[a]	89	.85	.010
	(.24)	(.10)	(.10)	(.22)	(.13)	(.08)	(.11)		(.06)	

[a]Significant at the 95% level and of the correct sign.

[b]Significant at the 90% level and of the correct sign.

[c]Significant at the 95% level and of the incorrect sign. (Standard errors reported in parentheses.)

Technique: Cochrane-Orcutt.

Samples: 78 = 2/75–7/81, 86 = 3/74–4/81, 88 = 3/74–6/81, 89 = 2/74–6/81.

nothing about what is causing these shifts, but they do indicate that these are two promising areas for future research.

It is clearer how to go about modeling the third factor, shifts in the risk premium, than the first two. This leads us to the portfolio-balance approach, the subject of the remainder of the paper.

7.2 The Portfolio Balance Model and Synthesis

7.2.1 The Portfolio Balance Equation

The portfolio balance approach to flexible exchange rates was pioneered in a small country framework by Black (1973), Kouri (1976a), Branson (1977), and Girton and Henderson (1977). In this paper we will consider a simple model in which only two assets are held in the portfolio: those denominated in domestic currency, and those denominated in foreign currency (dollars). We assume that domestic investors allocate a proportion β_d of their total financial wealth W_d to domestic assets B_d and the remainder to dollars F_d:

$$(10) \qquad B_d = \beta_d W_d,$$

where $W_d \equiv B_d + SF_d$. If we could assume that domestic assets were not held by foreign residents, so that all current account imbalances were necessarily financed in dollars, then we could compute F_d as the accumulation of past current account surpluses. With B_d computed as the accumulation of past government budget deficits, and both variables corrected for any foreign exchange intervention, it would be a simple matter to solve (10) for the exchange rate S and estimate the parameter β_d. This is how Porter (1979), for example, proceeds.

However, the "small country" assumption that foreigners hold no domestic bonds is unrealistic for most countries, at least most with floating exchange rates. We must, at a minimum, specify another portfolio balance equation for United States investors:

$$(11) \qquad B_{us} = \beta_{us} W_{us},$$

where $W_{us} \equiv B_{us} + SF_{us}$, and a third equation for residents of the rest of the world:

$$(12) \qquad B_r = \beta_r W_r,$$

where $W_r \equiv B_r + SF_r$. Data on B_d, B_{us}, and B_r, or on F_d, F_{us}, and F_r, are not normally available. We can compute only the totals $B \equiv B_d + B_{us} + B_r$ and $F \equiv F_d + F_{us} + F_r$, as the cumulation in each country of the government deficit plus foreign exchange intervention. It is not clear how to express S as a function of B, F, W_d, and W_{us}. But it is clear that the signs in such a relationship would be, respectively, positive, negative, negative, and positive. An increase in the supply of dollar assets F lowers their price S; an increase in B has the opposite effect. An increase in United States wealth W_{us} through a current account surplus, raises the net demand for dollar assets, assuming United States residents choose to allocate a greater share of their portfolio to dollar assets than do residents in the rest of the world, and thus raises their price S; an increase in W_d has the opposite effect. Branson, Haltunnen and Masson (1977, 1979) and Frankel (1980) regress the exchange rate against four variables similar to these, for the mark/dollar rate.

Table 7.4 presents estimates of the portfolio balance model.[8] Though the own asset and wealth variables are significant for some of the countries, the results in general are as poor as those for the monetary equation in table 7.1. Particularly dismal is the equation for Germany: the coefficients on mark and dollar assets have the wrong signs. The supply of mark bonds, like the German money supply, has increased during precisely those periods in which the mark has *appreciated* rather than depreciated, due largely to the Bundesbank's habit of resisting such appreciation through foreign exchange intervention.

7.2.2 The Risk Premium and Synthesis with the Monetary Equation

The portfolio balance model has always specified that the shares β_d and β_f depend on rates of return: the domestic and foreign interest rates i and i^*, and the expected rate of depreciation Δs^e. But recent applications of finance theory by Kouri (1976b), Kouri and de Macedo (1978), Macedo (1980), Krugman (1981) and Dornbusch (1983), have shown the precise nature of this dependence, on the assumption that investors determine the parameters in their asset demand functions by mean-variance optimization rather than arbitrarily. The asset demand functions are

$$(10') \qquad B_d = [a_d + b(i - i^* - \Delta s^e)]W_d,$$

$$(11') \qquad B_{us} = [a_{us} + b(i - i^* - \Delta s^e)]W_{us},$$

$$(12') \qquad B_r = [a_r + b(i - i^* - \Delta s^e)]W_r.$$

The coefficient b is related inversely to the coefficient of relative risk aversion, assumed to be the same in both countries, and to the variance of the exchange rate; it multiplies the risk premium to give the "speculative portfolio." The constant terms a_d, a_{us}, and a_r are related positively to the shares of consumption that residents of the three countries allocate to domestic goods; they constitute the "minimum variance" portfolio.

To use aggregate world data, we must add the three equations,

$$B = a_d W_d + a_{us} W_{us} + a_r W_r + b(i - i^* - \Delta s^e)W,$$

---

8. The data are described in an Appendix.

Table 7.4   Portfolio Balance Equation (Dependent Variable: Exchange Rate per United States Dollar)

Country	Constant	Asset	Asset$_5$	W_d	W_{US}	Sample	ρ	s.e.r.
Germany	3.36	$-.009^b$	$.006^b$	.002	$-.004^c$	83	.77	.056
	(.16)	(.002)	(.002)	(.002)	(.002)			
France	10.66	$.002^a$	.005	$-.019^a$	$-.009^b$	83	.90	.100
	(1.40)	(.004)	(.005)	(.004)	(.003)			
United Kingdom	1.07	$-.014^b$	.000	$.010^b$	$-.000$	83	.97	.013
	(.27)	(.005)	(.001)	(.004)	(.001)			
Japan	782.16	$.015^a$	$-.069$	$-.014^a$	$-.099$	79	.90	6.067
	(71.67)	(.002)	(.307)	(.002)	(.275)			
Canada	.94	$.007^a$	$-.000$	$-.005$	.000	86	.86	.016
	(.08)	(.002)	(.000)	(.004)	(.000)			

[a]Significant at the 95% level and of the correct sign.
[b]Significant at the 95% level and of the incorrect sign.
[c]Significant at the 90% level and of the incorrect sign.
(Standard errors reported in parentheses.)
Technique: Cochrane-Orcutt.

where we have defined world wealth $W \equiv W_d + W_{us} + W_r$. We solve for the risk premium:

$$(13) \qquad i - i^* - \Delta s^e = \frac{1}{b}\left(\frac{B}{W}\right) - \frac{a_d - a_r}{b}\frac{W_d}{W} + \frac{a_r - a_{us}}{b}\frac{W_{us}}{W}$$
$$- \frac{a_r}{b}.$$

Notice first that an increase in the relative supply of domestic assets that must be held in investor portfolios requires a higher relative return on domestic assets. Now assume that domestic residents have the greatest preference for domestic asset and United States residents for dollar assets. (Krugman [1981] has shown that this requires not only that residents of each country consume relatively more of their own goods but also that the constant of relative risk aversion be greater than one.) Then equation (13) implies also that a redistribution of wealth from the rest of the world toward domestic residents will raise the net world demand for domestic assets, and thus lower the relative returns that must be paid on them. A redistribution of wealth toward United States residents will have the opposite effect.

One might wish to make the risk premium equation (13) into a complete model of exchange rate determination like that estimated in the last section. It would be necessary to specify the determination of the interest rates (e.g., by the proportions of money and bonds within the asset variables) and of expected depreciation (e.g., by a rationally expected future path of the asset supplies and a saddle-point stability assumption).

Here, instead, we integrate the portfolio balance model with the monetary model of the first part of the paper. We simply allow for deviations from the uncovered interest parity condition (4), substituting instead our new risk premium equation (13), much as we earlier allowed for deviations from the long-run purchasing power parity condition and the money demand equations. The risk premium is added to the monetary equation of exchange rate determination (9), in the form of the relative asset supply and the distribution of wealth variables:

$$(14) \qquad s = (\overline{m} - \overline{m}_{us}) - \phi(\overline{y} - \overline{y}_{us}) + \left(\lambda + \frac{1}{\theta}\right)(\overline{\pi} - \overline{\pi}_{us})$$
$$- \frac{1}{\theta}(i - i_{us})$$
$$+ \frac{1}{\theta b}\left(\frac{B}{W}\right) - \frac{a_d - a_r}{\theta b}\left(\frac{W_d}{W}\right)$$
$$+ \frac{a_r - a_{us}}{\theta b}\left(\frac{W_{us}}{W}\right) - \frac{a_r}{\theta b}.$$

We have special cases (a) uniform asset demand preferences ($a_d - a_r = a_r - a_{us} = 0$) and (b) perfect substitutability ($b = \infty$) in addition to the

Table 7.5   Monetary and Risk-Premium Synthesis Equation (Dependent Variable: Log of Exchange Rate per United States Dollar)

Country	Monetary Model					Risk Premium			Sample	ρ	s.e.r.
	Constant	$m1 - m1_{US}$	$y - y_{US}$	$INFL - INFL_{US}$	$i - i_{US}$	$\frac{B}{W}$	$\frac{W_D}{W}$	$\frac{W_{US}}{W}$			
Germany	−.05 (.22)	.15 (.10)	.06 (.05)	−.24 (.24)	.05 (.08)	−.06 (.44)	−2.21[a] (.32)	1.13[a] (.16)	83	.98	.008
France	.16 (.29)	.01 (.08)	−.00 (.05)	.02 (.32)	−.06 (.10)	7.40[a] (.73)	−6.92[a] (.39)	1.16[a] (.19)	83	.98	.001
United Kingdom	−2.07 (.24)	−.03 (.05)	.03 (.04)	.00 (.01)	.03 (.05)	−3.44[c] (.32)	2.26[c] (.44)	1.67[a] (.14)	83	1.00	.007
Japan	4.57 (.39)	−.03[c] (.06)	−.05 (.07)	−.10 (.10)	−.10 (.10)	3.64[a] (.30)	−2.99[a] (.12)	1.47[a] (.15)	79	.96	.009
Canada	.37 (.33)	.07 (.13)	.16 (.12)	−.55 (.34)	−.38[a] (.19)	3.25[a] (.88)	−4.08[a] (1.12)	.003[b] (.002)	86	.91	.014

[a]Significant at the 95% level and of the correct sign.
[b]Significant at the 90% level and of the correct sign.
[c]Significant at the 95% level and of the incorrect sign.
(Standard errors in parentheses.)

usual special case within the monetary model of *(c)* perfect price flexibility $(\theta = \infty)$.

The synthesis equation is estimated in table 7.5. The results are surprising. Contrary to what one might expect from the earlier poor portfolio balance results, each of the three risk premium variables has a coefficient that appears significant and of the correct sign for most of the countries. But one cannot claim that the synthesis works better than the sum of the parts, because the coefficients on the variables from the monetary model are almost invariably insignificant.

To sum up the empirical findings of this paper, only those in table 7.3 could be described as favorable.[9] The implication is that further research into shifts in money demand and in the long-run real exchange rate, within the framework of the monetary model, appears justified.

Appendix
Data

Monetary Models

For each of the countries, the exchange rate against the United States dollar was obtained from the IMF's *International Financial Statistics,* and the money market interest rates from Morgan Guaranty Trust's *World Financial Markets.* The source for M1, industrial production, and the Consumer Price Index for the United States was the *Federal Reserve Bulletin* (tables 1.21, 2.10, and 2.10, respectively). The source for Germany was the *Statistical Supplement to the Monthly Report* of the Deutsche Bundesbank, series IV (tables 33, 7, and 11, respectively). The source for France, the United Kingdom, Japan, and Canada was *International Financial Statistics* (lines 34b, 66c, and 64, respectively).

Portfolio Balance Models

The supply of each country's asset is calculated as the cumulation of its government debt corrected for (1) issuance of debt denominated in foreign currency, if any; (2) foreign exchange market intervention by the country's central bank; and (3) foreign exchange market intervention by *other* countries' central banks in the domestic currency. The corrections are necessary

---

9. Adding the three risk premium variables to the regressions in table 7.3—the monetary model with drift in velocity and the real exchange rate—turns out only to vitiate the relatively positive results. And attempts to relate the risk premium variables directly to the excess return on countries' assets as in equation (13) have not been successful (Dooley and Isard 1983).

under the assumption that what matters for asset demand functions is currency of denomination and exchange risk, rather than location of issuance and political risk. These calculations give the net supply of assets denominated in a country's currency, including both money and bonds. It is easy enough to use the monetary base in regressions like those in table 7.4, if one believes that only the net supply of money should matter (as in "currency substitution" models), or to subtract off the monetary base from total assets if one believes that only the net supply of bonds should matter (as in Dooley and Isard 1979). However, such regressions yield results similar to those in table 7.4. (See Frankel 1980.)

United States Dollar Assets

DOASST = world supply of dollar assets. Calculated as DODEBT + FEDINT − NDOLCB.

DODEBT = gross public debt of the United States Treasury and other United States government agencies, excluding that held by United States government agencies and trust funds—i.e., debt held by the Federal Reserve, private domestic investors, and foreigners, at end of month (source: *Treasury Bulletin,* table FD-1, as reported by DRI); minus two issues of "Carter notes," which are denominated in foreign currency: $1,595.2 million dating from December 1978 and another $1,351.5 million from March 1979 (source: Federal Reserve press release, June 1979).

FEDINT = dollars supplied by the Fed in cumulative foreign exchange intervention. Computed by $FEDINT_t = FEDINT_{t-1} + \Delta FEDINT_t$, on a benchmark of the dollar value of all United States international reserve assets (gold, foreign exchange, SDRs, and IMF position) in January 1974 (source: Federal Reserve *Annual Statistical Digest 1973–1977,* table 51, or *F. R. Bulletin,* table 3, p. A59, e.g., June 1975).

$\Delta FEDINT$ = intervention, equal to increases in reserves, corrected for valuation changes. Computed as change in gold holdings (there have been no valuation changes since 1973), plus change in foreign exchange holdings in dollars minus valuation change (last period's foreign exchange holdings times the change in the dollar/mark rate; most of the holdings have been in marks during the only period in which they have been significant, i.e., since November 1978), plus change in SDRs and IMF position in dollars minus valuation change (last period's SDRs and IMF position times the change in the dollar/SDR rate; relevant since July 1974), minus new SDR allocations (nonzero only for January 1979, 1980, and 1981). Source for reserve holdings through 1977: F. R. *Annual Statistical Digest 1973–1977,* table 51; source for reserve holdings 1978–81: *F. R. Bulletin,* table 3.12. Source for dollar/SDR rate: IMF *International Financial Statistics,* line 78bd.

NDOLCB = holdings of dollar assets (regardless whether government securities) by foreign central banks as foreign exchange reserves. Source for 1973II–1979: IMF; 1979IV: IMF *Annual Report,* 1980, tables 15 and 16. Monthly numbers obtained by interpolation.

Deutsche Mark Assets

DMASST = world supply of mark assets. Calculated as DMDEBT + BBINT − NDMCB.

DMDEBT = debt of the German federal government, end of month. Source: Deutsche Bundesbank, *Monthly Report,* table VIII-10.

BBINT = cumulative Bundesbank sales of mark assets for international reserves in exchange market intervention, calculated as GRES − GADJ.

GRES = net external position of the Bundesbank, valued in marks, at end of month. Source: Bundesbank, *Statistical Supplements to the Monthly Report,* Series 3, table 9a.

GADJ = "balancing item to the Bundesbank's external position," an adjustment by the Bundesbank every December to reflect capital gains on foreign exchange and other reserves (these numbers are also available from table IX-6 [1], col. 12) and every January (except when zero: 1975–78) to reflect new SDR allocations. These items must be taken back out of GRES so that only changes in reserves due to purchases or sales of mark assets are counted. Cumulated with a benchmark of zero in 70:1. Source: Bundesbank, *Monthly Report,* table IX-1, col. 7.

NDMCB = holdings of mark assets (regardless whether government securities) by foreign central banks as foreign exchange reserves. Source for 1973II–1979I: IMF; for 1979IV: IMF *Annual Report* 1980, tables 15 and 16. Monthly numbers obtained by interpolation.

Pound Sterling Assets

PSASST = world supply of pound assets. Calculated as PSDEBT + BEINT − NPSCB.

$PSDEBT_t$ = pound sterling debt of the British government. Computed by $PSDEBT_t = PSDEBT_{t-1} - UKDFCT$ (source: IMF *IFS,* line 80) on a March 1973 benchmark of £37,156 million (source: *UN Statistical Yearbook 1977,* Public Finance table #201). The government deficit was used for UKDFCT rather than the better-known Public Sector Borrowing Requirement because the deficit "corresponds to a negative figure of net acquisition of financial assets" while the PSBR (according to *Central Statistical Office Financial Statistics,* 2.3, col. 1) exceeds the deficit by "net government lending to private sector and overseas" and "other financial transactions."

BEINT = cumulative Bank of England sales of pound assets for international reserves in exchange market intervention. Computed by $BEINT_t = BEINT_{t-1} + \Delta BEINT_t$ (U.K. Balance for Official Financing; source: *CSO Financial Statistics,* HI), on a 1973:1 benchmark of total international reserves in dollars (source: IMF *IFS,* line 1 d..d) times the pound/dollar exchange rate.

NPSCB = holdings of pound assets (regardless whether government securities) by foreign central banks as foreign exchange reserves. Source for 1973 II–1979I: IMF; for 1979IV: IMF *Annual Report* 1980, tables 15 and 16. Monthly numbers obtained by interpolation.

Japanese Yen Assets

JYASST = world supply of yen assets. Calculated as JYDEBT + BJINT − NJYCB.

JYDEBT = yen-denominated debt of Japanese government. Computed as JADEBT − JYCURD.

JADEBT = total Japanese debt, computed by $JADEBT_t$ = $JADEBT_{t-1}$ + JSURP (government surplus; source: *IFS*, line 80), on a benchmark of yen debt in January 1970 (source: *IFS*, line 88b).

JYCURD = Japanese debt denominated in foreign currency. Source: *IFS*, line 89b.

BJINT = cumulative Bank of Japan sales of yen assets for international reserves in exchange market intervention. Computed as yen/dollar exchange rate × BJINTD, which is cumulative intervention expressed in dollars and is in turn computed by $BJINTD_t$ = $BJINTD_{t-1}$ + $\Delta BJINTD_t$, on a benchmark of the dollar value of all Japanese international reserve assets in November 1973 (source: *IFS*, line 1).

ΔBJINTD = intervention in dollars. Computed as increases in reserves (source: *IFS*, minus of line 79 k.d) minus new SDR allocations (source: *IFS*, line 78 bd; nonzero only for January 1978, 1980, 1981), minus capital gains (source: *IFS*, line 78 dd).

NJYCB = holdings of yen assets (regardless whether government securities) by foreign central banks as foreign exchange reserves. Source: IMF *Annual Report* 1980, tables 15 and 16. Monthly numbers obtained by interpolation.

French Franc Assets

FFASST = world supply of franc assets, calculated as FFDEBT + BFINT − NFFCB.

FFDEBT = franc-denominated debt of French government. Computed as FRDEBT − FYCURD.

FRDEBT = total French debt, computed by $FRDEBT_t$ = $FRDEBT_{t-1}$ + FSURP (government surplus; source: *IFS*, line 80), on a June 1974 benchmark of F137.345 billion of franc debt (source: *IFS*, line 88b).

FYCURD = French debt denominated in foreign currency. Source: *IFS*, line 89b.

BFINT = cumulative Banque de France sales of franc assets for international reserves in exchange market intervention. Computed as franc/dollar exchange rate times BFINTD, which is cumulative intervention expressed in dollars and is in turn computed by $BFINTD_t$ = $BFINTD_{t-1}$ + $\Delta BFINTD_t$, on a benchmark of the dollar value of all French international reserve assets in January 1973 (source: *IFS*, line 1).

ΔBFINTD = intervention expressed in dollars. Computed as increases in reserves (source: *IFS*, minus line 79 k.d), minus new SDR allocations (source: *IFS,* line 79 bd; nonzero only for January 1979, 1980, 1981), minus capital gains (source: *IFS,* line 78 dd).

NFFCB = holdings of franc assets (regardless whether government securities) by foreign central banks as foreign exchange reserves. Source: IMF *Annual Report,* 1980, tables 15 and 16. Monthly numbers obtained by interpolation.

Canadian Dollar Assets

CDASST = world supply of Canadian dollar assets. Calculated as CDDEBT + BCINT. (Canadian dollars are not held as reserves by other central banks.)

CDDEBT = net debt of the Canadian federal government. Computed by CADEBT − CINTRA (intragovernmental debt; source: *IFS,* line 88s).

CADEBT = gross debt of the Canadian federal government. Source for 1970:1 to 1976:4: *IFS,* line 80. For 1976:5 to 1981:4, *CADEBT* computed by $CADEBT_t = CADEBT_{t-1} + CSURP$ (government surplus; source: *IFS,* line 80).

BCINT = cumulative Bank of Canada sales of Canadian dollar assets for international reserves in exchange market intervention. Computed as Canadian dollar/United States dollar exchange rate times BCINTD, which is cumulative intervention expressed in United States dollars and is in turn computed as $BCINTD_t = BCINTD_{t-1} + \Delta BCINTD_t$, on a benchmark of the dollar value of all Canadian international reserve assets in January 1972 (source: *IFS,* line 1).

ΔBCINTD = intervention expressed in dollars. Computed as increases in reserves (source: *IFS,* minus line 79 k.d), minus new SDR allocations (source: *IFS,* line 78 bd; nonzero only for January 1979, 1980, 1981), minus capital gains (source: *IFS,* line 78 dd).

Wealth Variables

Wealth in each country is computed as the cumulation of the current account surplus and government debt. Sources for the current account were as follows. Germany: *Monthly Report* of the Deutsche Bundesbank, table IX, 1. United States: *Survey of Current Business,* using the monthly balance of trade to interpolate between the quarterly current account figures. France, United Kingdom, Japan, and Canada: *IFS* lines 77 aad, abd, acd, add, aed, and agd summed and divided by 3 to get monthly figures.

The benchmarks for wealth were computed in a very ad hoc manner, since accurate data on the *level* of wealth are difficult to get, and since they are only constant terms in the regressions anyway. For the United States and Germany the benchmarks were taken from Dooley and Isard's (1983) figures for wealth "estimated from end-of-1972 stocks in Federal debt, monetary bases, and net claims on foreigners" (p. 699). For the other four countries end-of-1973 benchmarks were constructed by assuming that their wealths (expressed in own currency) at that time were proportional to United States wealth, with the proportionality constants taken to be GNP (nominal, 1977, as reported in *IFS*). The wealth series, observed at the end of 1973, translate into billions of dollars as follows: United States 415.041, Germany 80.779, France 86.95, United Kingdom 58.452, Japan 169.427, and Canada 42.136.

References

Balassa, Bela. 1964. The purchasing-power parity doctrine: A reappraisal. *Journal of Political Economy* 72:584–96.

Bilson, John. 1978. The monetary approach to the exchange rate—some empirical evidence. *IMF Staff Papers* 25 (March): 48–75.

Black, Stanley, 1973. International money markets and flexible exchange rates. *Studies in International Finance,* no. 25. Princeton University.

Branson, William. 1977 Asset markets and relative prices in exchange rate determination. *Sozialwissenschaftliche Annalen* 1:69–89.

Branson, William; Halttunen, Hannu; and Masson, Paul. 1977. Exchange rates in the short run: The dollar-deutschemark rate. *European Economic Review* 10:303–24.

Branson William; Halttunen, Hannu; and Masson, Paul. 1979. Exchange rates in the short run: Some further results. *European Economic Review* 12 (October): 395–402.

Buiter, Willem, and Miller, Marcus. 1981. Monetary policy and international competitiveness: The problems of adjustment. *Oxford Economic Papers* 33 (July): 143–75.

Dooley, Michael, and Isard, Peter. 1983. The portfolio-balance model of exchange rates and some structural estimates of the risk premium. *IMF Staff Papers* 30 (December): 683–702.

Dornbusch, Rudiger. 1976. Expectations and exchange rate dynamics. *Journal of Political Economy* 84:1161–76.

———. 1980. Exchange rate economics: Where do we stand? *Brookings Papers on Economic Activity,* 1:143–94

———. 1983. Exchange risk and the macroeconomics of exchange rate determination. In *The Internationalization of Financial Markers and National Economic Policy,* ed. R. Hawkins, R. Levich, and C. Wihlborg. Greenwich, Conn.: JAI Press.

Driskill, Robert, and Sheffrin, Steven. 1981. On the mark: Comment. *American Economic Review* 71 (December): 1068–74.

Frankel, Jeffrey. 1979. On the mark: A theory of floating exchange rates based on real interest differentials. *American Economic Review* 69 (September): 610–22.

———. 1980. Monetary and portfolio-balance models of exchange rate determination. NBER Summer Institute Paper 80–7. In *Economic Interde-*

pendence and Flexible Exchange Rates, ed. J. Bhandari. Cambridge, Mass.: MIT Press, 1983.

———. 1981. On the mark: Reply. *American Economic Review AER* 71 (December): 1075–82.

———. 1982. The mystery of the multiplying marks: A modification of the monetary model. *Review of Economics and Statistics* 64 (August): 515–19.

Frenkel, Jacob. 1976. A monetary approach to the exchange rate: Doctrinal aspects and empirical evidence. *Scandinavian Journal of Economics* 76 (May): 200–224.

———. 1981. The collapse of purchasing power parities during the 1970s. *European Economic Review,* 16:145–65.

Genberg, Hans. 1978. Purchasing power parity under fixed and flexible exchange rates. *Journal of International Economics* 8 (May): 247–76.

Girton, Lance, and Henderson, Dale. 1977. Central bank operations in foreign and domestic assets under fixed and flexible exchange rates. In *The effects of exchange rate adjustment,* ed. P. Clark, D. Logue, and R. Sweeney. Washington: United States Treasury.

Hacche, Graham, and Townend, John. 1981. Exchange rates and monetary policy: Modelling Sterling's effective exchange rate, 1972–1980. In *The Money Supply and the Exchange Rate,* ed. W. A. Eltis and P. J. N. Sinclair. Oxford: Clarendon Press.

Haynes, Steven, and Stone, Joe. 1981. On the mark: Comment. *American Economic Review* 71 (December): 1060–67.

Hooper, Peter and Morton, John. 1982. Fluctuations in the dollar: A model of nominal and real exchange rate determination. Journal of International Money and Finance 1, no. 1:39–56.

Katseli-Papaefstratiou, Louka. 1979. The reemergence of the purchasing power parity doctrine in the 1970s. Special Papers in International Economics no. 13. Princeton: Princeton University, December.

Kouri, Pentti. 1976a. The exchange rate and the balance of payments in the short run and in the long run: A monetary approach. *Scandinavian Journal of Economics* 78 (May): 280–308.

———. 1976b. The determinants of the forward premium. Institute for International Economic Studies Seminar Paper 62. Stockholm: University of Stockholm, August.

Kouri, Pentti, and Macedo, Jorge de. 1978. Exchange rates and the international adjustment process. *Brookings Papers on Economic Activity* 1:111–57.

Krugman, Paul. 1978. Purchasing power parity and exchange rates: Another look at the evidence. *Journal of International Economics* 8 (August): 397–407.

———. 1980. Oil and the dollar. NBER Working Paper no. 554. In *Economic Interdependence and Flexible Exchange Rates,* ed. J. Bhandari. Cambridge, Mass.: Press, 1983.

————. 1981. Consumption preferences, asset demands, and distribution effects in international financial markets. NBER Working Paper no. 651 (March).

Macedo, Jorge de. 1980. Portfolio diversification across countries. Princeton International Finance Section. Working Paper (November).

Meese, Richard, and Rogoff, Kenneth. 1981. Empirical exchange rate models of the seventies: Are any fit to survive? International Finance Discussion Paper no. 184. Washington, D.C.: Federal Reserve Board, June. *Journal of International Economics,* March 1983.

Mussa, Michael. 1976. The exchange rate, the balance of payments, and monetary and fiscal policy under a regime of controlled floating. *Scandinavian Journal of Economics* 78 (May): 229–48.

Obstfeld, Maurice. 1980. Intermediate imports, the terms of trade, and the dynamics of the exchange rate and current account. *Journal of International Economics* (November). 10:461–80.

Porter, Michael. 1979. Exchange rates, current accounts, and economic activity. Federal Reserve Board, June.

8 The International Role of the Dollar: Theory and Prospect

Paul Krugman

8.1 Introduction

What do people use as money? In studying national economies we usually do not worry about this question very much, assuming that governments are able to create fiat monies and enforce their acceptance. There are some problems, such as the role of inside monies and near monies, and the cases of "dollarization" (as in Israel) where the national currency is partly supplanted by some other currency. But these problems are the exception rather than the rule, and theorists are generally comfortable with the idea of assuming a demand for M/P without having to explain why it is these pieces of paper, rather than something else, which appear in the numerator.

When we study the international economy, however, we can no longer avoid the question. International economic activity, like domestic activity, requires the use of money, and the same forces which lead to convergence on a single domestic money lead the world to converge on a limited number of international monies. Before World War I, the pound sterling was the international currency; in the interwar period the dollar and the pound shared the role; in the Bretton Woods era the dollar was dominant. But there is no world government to enforce the role of international monies. The preeminence of sterling and its displacement by the dollar were largely the result of "invisible hand" processes, ratified more than guided by international agreements. The future of the United States monetary system is largely a political question; the future international role of the dollar is largely an economic one.

Yet it is a question which, though central to international monetary discussion in the 1960s and still a major policy issue, has virtually disappeared from the research agenda. The reason for this neglect lies in the change in the field of international monetary economics. Traditionally dominated by a

I would like to thank Peter Kenen for helpful suggestions.

historical and institutional approach, international monetary economics in the 1970s essentially became a branch of macroeconomics. This meant a drastic change in style. Formal models replaced well-written essays; brief journal articles replaced books. Adjustment, Confidence, Liquidity became $\dot{p}/p = \lambda(y - \bar{y})$, $i = i^* + \pi$, $\Delta R = \Delta M - \Delta D$. And the change in style meant a change in substance. What we know how to model formally are frictionless markets, where transactions are costless and agents make full use of the information available. The microeconomics of money, however, whether domestic or international, is fundamentally about frictions. Thus the explosion of theory in international economics in the 1970s was concerned with macroeconomic issues and ignored the traditional issues regarding the role of the dollar.

The problem is that the fact that an issue is hard to model rigorously is no guarantee that the issue is unimportant. Fortunately, even a less than fully worked out model can be useful, if one does not demand too much of it. Over the years, a number of economists, especially Swoboda (1969), Cohen (1971), McKinnon (1979), and Kindleberger (1981), have developed what amounts to a theory of international money. This theory is not embedded in formal models in the way that, say, the monetary approach to the balance of payments is; but it is tight enough to be informative. The purpose of this paper is to provide a unified exposition of this theory and to apply it to the history and the future of the role of the dollar.

The basic concepts of this theory are drawn from the (equally informal) theory of money in a closed economy. Frictions—costs of transacting, costs of calculation—cause agents to use national monies as international media of exchange, units of account, stores of value; economies of scale lead them to concentrate on only a few—often only one—currency for these purposes. The differences between the theory of international money and the ordinary theory of money arise from two facts. First, we are not dealing with a choice among commodities but with a choice among monies, demanded not for their intrinsic usefulness but because of their privileged role in domestic transactions. Second, part of the international role of the dollar reflects choices made by official bodies, the central banks, rather than private agents. A crucial question is, How closely linked are the official and private roles? Would replacing the dollar with some other reserve asset reduce its role in private transactions? Conversely, can central banks be induced to hold a reserve asset which is not a "live" international money?

This paper is in five sections. Section 8.2 reviews the basic roles of international money and provides an overview of the argument. Section 8.3 examines the role of the dollar as a medium of exchange; it presents a simple model of convergence on a limited number of international media of exchange and discusses the ways in which transitions from one vehicle currency to another might happen. Section 8.4 turns to the unit-of-account role. It tries to combine arguments by several authors to provide a stylized account of the choice of invoice currency in private transactions. Section 8.5 then reviews the store-of-value role, presenting evidence on and an interpretation of recent trends toward diversification in the currency denominations of reserve holdings, Euro-currency holdings, and international lending.

The final section of the paper takes a tentative look forward. It reviews the forces leading to a reduction in the dominance of the dollar; a comparison is made between the position of the dollar today and the position of sterling in the 1910s and 1920s. I argue that a "collapse" of the dollar's role is possible, though it is by no means necessary, and I discuss briefly what such a collapse might involve.

8.2 The Six Roles of the Dollar

Money, the classical economists argued, serves three functions: it is a medium of exchange, a unit of account, and a store of value. International money does the same: it is used to settle international payments, it is used to fix prices, it is held as a liquid asset for international transactions. An added dimension is provided by the distinction between private behavior and the decisions of central banks (although the central banks of small countries may behave more like private agents than like Group of Ten monetary authorities). Thus there are six roles of the dollar, presented schematically in table 8.1 (closely based on Cohen 1971). The dollar is used as a medium of exchange in private transactions, or "vehicle," and is also bought and sold by central banks, thus making it an "intervention" currency. Trade contracts are sometimes denominated in dollars, making it an "invoice" currency, and the par values for exchange rates are sometimes stated in terms of the dollar, which makes it serve as a "peg." Finally, private agents hold liquid dollar-denominated assets—the "banking" role—and central banks hold the dollar as a reserve.[1]

In principle and to some extent in practice these roles are separable. The separation of roles can be either horizontal or vertical. Thus under the gold standard the official roles were filled by gold, yet sterling played the private roles. In the European snake in the mid-1970s the currencies were pegged

Table 8.1   **Roles of an International Currency**

	Private	Official
Medium of exchange	Vehicle	Intervention
Unit of account	Invoice	Peg
Store of value	Banking	Reserve

1. Kindleberger (1981) treats the denomination of loans in dollars as a seventh role, that of "standard of deferred repayment." I prefer to regard this as a particular case of the "invoice" role.

to one another, yet the dollar was used as a reserve and intervention currency. One can even separate medium of exchange and unit of account—the famous example is those small Persian Gulf nations which until 1974 set their oil prices in dollars but required payment in sterling. But the roles are not independent. In ways which I hope will become clearer, the more the dollar is used in one role, the more incentive there is to use it in the others.

Let us briefly review the actual extent to which the dollar plays the different roles:

1. *Vehicle*. It is important to distinguish three types of transaction here. First is settlement between nonbank firms, which is closely tied to invoicing; as discussed below, the dollar plays a special but not exclusive role here. Second is the "retail" foreign exchange market in which firms deal with banks; here the dollar plays no special role; a Swedish bank will sell, say, kronor for pesetas and vice versa. Finally there is the interbank market: here the dollar is *the* medium of exchange. "Virtually all interbank transactions, by market participants here and abroad, involve a purchase or sale of dollars for a foreign currency. This is true even if a bank's aim is to buy German marks for sterling" (Kubarych 1978, p. 18).

2. *Intervention*. Central banks usually intervene in the existing private interbank market; thus the dollar is the intervention currency. This is true even for some of the interventions which maintain parities within the European Monetary System.

3. *Invoice*. Data on this are not as good as we might like, but a few generalizations seem possible. In manufactured goods trade between any two countries, there is a preference for invoicing in exporter's currency, but also a preference for invoicing in the currency of the larger country. This in itself gives the United States, as the world's largest economy, a disproportionate share of the invoicing. In addition, much raw materials trade, even if it does not involve the United States, is also invoiced in dollars. In financial transactions, the dollar is the dominant currency for international borrowing and lending, though this dominance is not complete.

4. *Peg*. This is the best-known aspect of the story. In 1970 most of the world was pegged to the dollar; now only a limited number of smaller countries still are. This does not, however, represent the rise of a rival currency, but the abandonment of fixed rates altogether.

5. *Banking*. Dollars in New York and Eurodollars in London constitute the main liquid international asset, although there has been some diversification into other currencies, especially Deutsche marks.

6. *Reserve*. The dollar accounts for the bulk of nongold reserves, with some accounting complications introduced recently by the EMS. As will be discussed further below, there is again some trend toward diversification.

It is clear from this brief description that the dollar *is* an international money, though its moneyness is less than it might be, less than it was eleven years ago, and less than that of sterling in 1913. The natural questions are how this position is likely to change and what difference it makes. To answer these—as best we can, for the answers will be based on loose theory and casual empirics—we need to examine the forces which make the dollar an international money.

8.3 The Dollar as an International Medium of Exchange

8.3.1 Economies of Scale and Indirect Exchange

The role of the dollar as a vehicle currency can be attributed to economies of scale in foreign exchange markets, which in turn arise from the lumpiness of transactions. "Since the dollar is the main currency for international trade and investment the dollar market for each currency is much more active than between any pair of foreign currencies. By going through the dollar, large amounts can be traded more easily" (Kubarych 1978, p. 18).

The nature of the economies of scale can be illustrated if we ignore the distinction between retail and interbank markets and simply think of firms offering to buy and sell foreign exchange. Suppose that at the going exchange rate the total demand and supply for foreign exchange in some market are equal over the course of a year, but that offers to exchange currencies in either direction are of finite size and arrive at random times. Then a firm offering to exchange currencies may find a complementary offer waiting for it in the marketplace, but it may have to wait for one to arrive, and may have to wait until earlier offers are consummated. Thus there will on average be some delay before a transaction can be completed. Now suppose the flow through the market were to double. It is obvious that the average waiting time would fall. It is easier to find a match in a thick market than a thin one.[2]

Adding market-making banks, who hold currency stocks, will not much alter this picture. Firms may no longer have to wait, but the law of large numbers will imply that the trade-off between the size of currency stocks and the probability of a stockout will improve as the market gets larger. So bid-ask spreads will be lower in larger markets.

To go from economies of scale in the exchange markets to the emergence of a vehicle currency, it is useful to make a distinction between what I have called (Krugman 1980) the *structure of payments* and the *structure of exchange*. By the structure of payments we will mean the matrix of final demands for foreign exchange for the purposes of trade and investment. By the structure of exchange we will mean the matrix of actual foreign exchange transactions. The distinction between these may be illustrated by considering, say, trade and investment flows between Ecuador and the Neth-

---

2. An ingenious and suggestive model along these lines of the emergence of a domestic medium of exchange is Jones (1976).

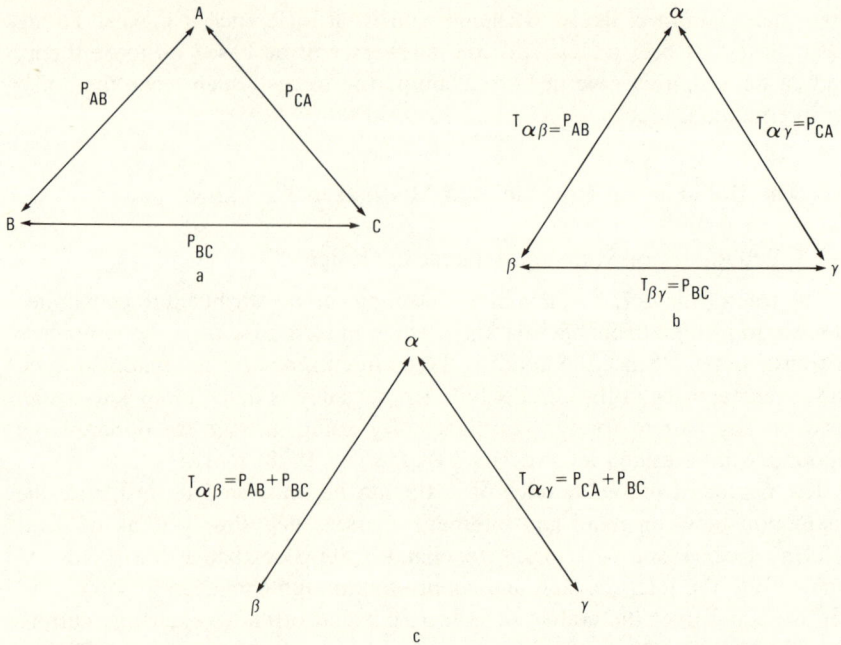

Fig. 8.1   The structure of payments *(a);* the structure of exchange: direct exchange *(b);* the structure of exchange: indirect exchange *(c).*

erlands. These will appear as positive entries in the Ecuador-Netherlands and Netherland-Ecuador boxes of the structure of payments; but there will be a zero in the guilder-sucre box of the structure of exchange, because the actual transactions will take place in the dollar-guilder and dollar-sucre markets. To a first approximation, we can regard the structure of payments as independent of the choice of medium of exchange, determined by "fundamental" trade and investment motives. The question then becomes one of determining the structure of exchange given these fundamentals.

Consider first a world of three countries, A, B, and C. They have national currencies, the α, the β, and the γ. In figure 8.1a is illustrated the structure of payments in this world: P_{AB}, P_{BC}, P_{CA} are the final demands for foreign exchange flows, measured in the same (arbitrary) units; they are assumed to be bilaterally balanced.[3]

How will these payments be carried out? One possibility, illustrated in figure 8.1*b,* is that payments will take place directly, with all three pairs of

3. If the structure of payments is not bilaterally balanced, the model becomes much more complicated. It becomes possible that some but not all payments are made indirectly through the vehicle currency; this "partial indirect exchange" will be associated with a systematic difference between the direct exchange rate and the cross rate. For an unfortunately unreadable analysis, see Krugman (1980).

currencies actively traded. If so, the volume of exchange transactions in each market will equal the final payments. But suppose that A is much more important a trading and investment partner of B and C than either is of the other; that is, P_{AB}, P_{CA} $>>$ P_{BC}. Then it will be cheaper to trade β's and γ's indirectly, through the vehicle of the α, and the structure of exchange will collapse to that illustrated in figure 8.1c, where there is no active βγ market. An important point to note is that this channeling of transactions between B and C through A's currency itself swells the markets in that currency, reinforcing its advantage.[4]

8.3.2 N-Country Complications

When we go beyond three countries, the picture becomes somewhat more complicated, though the principles don't change. Two new possibilities emerge: First, that the currency of a country which is not very dominant in world payments will emerge as vehicle through a process of "snowballing"; second, that there may emerge a multipolar world with several vehicle currencies.

Snowballing may be illustrated by the following example. Suppose that the world consists of several large countries, one only slightly larger than the others, and a number of small countries. Simple trilateral comparisons would lead us to expect payments between large countries to take place through direct exchange; yet the presence of the smaller countries can lead to a complete "super-monetization" of world payments. The process would work as follows: payments between small countries will take place indirectly, through the medium of the largest country's currency; this will swell these markets, creating an incentive for other large countries to carry out their exchanges with the small countries via the same medium; this will swell all of the markets in the largest country's currency, perhaps enough to eliminate all direct bilateral markets. It may not be too far-fetched to suggest that this process explains the rise of sterling to an extraordinary position of dominance at a time when Britain, though the economic leader, was far from having the sort of preeminence that, say, the United States had in 1950.

On the other hand, a many-country world can support several vehicle currencies. Figure 8.2 illustrates a possible structure of exchange among five countries—A, B, C, D, E—whose currencies are the α, β, γ, δ, ε, respectively. Payments between the countries are P_{AB}, P_{BC}, etc.; transactions on the markets are $T_{\alpha\beta}$, $T_{\beta\gamma}$, etc. The illustrated pattern is one in which A and B are both vehicle currency countries. There is an "alpha area" (A and C)

---

4. Cohen (1971 p. 60) quotes A. C. L. Day: "In general the more connexions a country has and the stronger they are, the more connexions she is likely to attract. This meant that because Britain had very extensive trading . . . connexions, sterling would be all the more useful to a country which chose to use it; and as more people came to use it, sterling would be all the more attractive as a means of international payment to everyone."

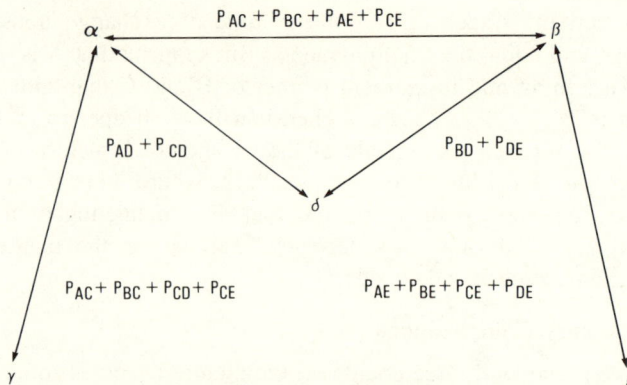

Fig. 8.2   A bipolar structure of exchange

in which all payments go through α's, and a "beta area" (B and E) in which payments go through the β. One country, D, is a part of neither area, so that there is both an active $\alpha\delta$ and an active $\beta\delta$ market. A bipolar structure of exchange of this type existed in the dollar-sterling system of the interwar period, and is a possible future.

8.3.3 Multiple Equilibria and Changes in the Vehicle

The model of vehicle currencies we have sketched out contains an obvious possibility for multiple equilibria. If the choice of a currency as a vehicle is a response to the relative size of the markets in it, and if a currency's becoming a vehicle itself swells those markets, then the choice of vehicle may be self-justifying. This in turn suggests that once a country's currency gets established as the international medium of exchange it will continue in that role, even if the country loses the position in the structure of payments which originally gave it that position. Thus sterling remained a vehicle currency long after Britain had ceased to be number 1.

It might be objected that a structure of exchange which does not minimize worldwide transaction costs offers a profit opportunity. A bank could act as market maker and reap the gains. I would offer a guess here: market making probably involves a one-time fixed cost in getting market participants informed and inducing them to change their behavior. In existing markets this is a sunk cost, which need not be expended again; to change the structure of exchange requires a new expenditure. The result is that the structure of exchange will change only if it is very far from what the structure of payments would suggest, so that the choice of a medium of exchange exhibits a good deal of inertia. On the other hand, a temporary disruption of the foreign exchange markets can shift the structure of exchange from one equilibrium to another and thus have lasting effects. The choice of a vehicle currency reflects both history and hysteresis.

The actual decline of sterling as a medium of exchange, and its replacement by the dollar, appears to have taken place in a sharp slump, a long slow slide, and a final crash. World War I exchange restrictions disrupted the sterling system and led to the emergence of the dollar, and also the French franc, as rivals; and the dollar slowly gained ground for fifty years. (Remarkably, sterling remained the more important medium of exchange during the interwar period, and may even still have been more important than the dollar in the late 1940s). Finally, sterling vanished from the map in the late 1960s and the early 1970s. The impressive fact here is surely the inertia; sterling remained the first-ranked currency for half a century after Britain had ceased to be the first-ranked economic power.[5]

8.3.4 Relationships to Other Roles of Money

The discussion in this section has concentrated on the medium-of-exchange role of international money in isolation. In fact, there is some interdependence among roles. The links which seem clear are these: if the dollar is a good store of value, the costs of making markets against the dollar are lower, thus encouraging the vehicle role. Conversely, the medium-of-exchange role encourages both invoicing in dollars and holding dollars, we will discuss below.

8.4 The Dollar as an International Unit of Account

Most of the analytical work on the use of currencies as international units of account has focused on the official role: on the decision on whether to peg to another currency, and on the choice of peg. I will not attempt to add to this extensive literature; in any case, hardly anyone still pegs to the dollar. Instead, this section will focus on the private use of currencies as units of account. A good place to start, because there are relatively abundant data, is the invoicing decision.

Even in the 1960s, trade contracts were by no means exclusively written in dollars. In influential work, Grassman (1973) showed that most Swedish trade was invoiced in exporting country currency. It seems to be generally true that trade between industrial countries is invoiced in either the exporter's or the importer's currency, with no major role for the dollar in trade between third parties.

Table 8.2 presents some comparative numbers on the share of exports and imports invoiced in a country's currency and on the share of exports to the United States invoiced in dollars. The countries are ranked in order of the value of their 1978 exports. An impressionistic look at this table suggests that much of the variation can be explained by three rules. First, other things equal the exporter's currency is preferred. For every country for which data

5. This account is drawn from Yeager (1976) and Cohen (1971).

Table 8.2   Invoicing of Merchandise Trade

	Share of Domestic Currency Used to Invoice:		Share of Exports to United States Invoiced in Dollars
	Exports	Imports	
Germany	86.9	42.0	36
Japan	—	—	94
France	68.3	31.5	52
United Kingdom	73.0	—	44
Italy	—	—	68
The Netherlands	50.2	31.4	81
Canada	—	—	87
Belgium	47.7	25.4	78
Sweden	66.1	25.8	27
Austria	54.7	24.7	—
Denmark	54.0	24.0	—
Finland	15.5	—	—

Source: Page (1977), Rao and Magee (1980).

on both are available, a higher share of exports than imports is invoiced in domestic currency. Second, other things equal the currencies of large are used more than those of small countries. Thus Germany has the highest proportion of exports in domestic currency and a sizable fraction of imports in marks as well; the fraction of exports to the United States invoiced in dollars is noticeably high, even for countries which mostly invoice in home currency.

The third rule is that the yen is hardly used. As shown in the table, virtually all Japanese exports are invoiced in dollars; it is also true where data are available that the yen is much less used as an invoice currency in exports to Japan than Japan's size would lead one to expect. This may in part reflect a political decision on the part of Japan not to allow the yen to become an international currency.

In additional to these generalizations, we have one more observation: raw materials trade, and with it most of LDC exports, is generally invoiced in dollars. McKinnon has proposed the terms "tradables I" and "tradables II" to describe the relevant distinction. Tradables I are differentiated manufactured products, typically produced by oligopolists, and normally invoiced in exporting country currency—except, we might add, when the importer is large relative to the exporter, in which case the importer's currency is used. Tradables II are primary products, sold in a world market, and normally invoiced in dollars.

Figure 8.3 shows a stylized version of the facts about choice of invoice currency. Four types of countries are distinguished: the United States, large advanced countries, small advanced countries, and LDCs. An arrow indi-

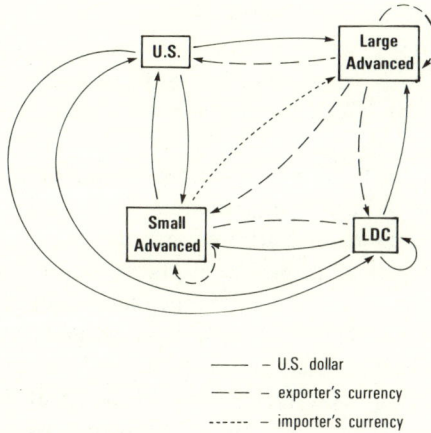

— – U.S. dollar
— — – exporter's currency
------ – importer's currency

Fig. 8.3   Choice of currency in world trade

cates the direction of exports.[6]

These, then, are our stylized facts about invoicing. What explains them? I would argue that they reflect essentially the cost of calculation.

Note that risk sharing by itself cannot explain the pattern of invoicing. The reason is that firms can always avoid exchange risk by entering the forward market, and that the choice between invoicing in exporter and importer currency is simply a question of deciding who does the forward contract. (Even if no forward market exists, firms can "roll their own" forward contracts by international borrowing and lending.) Admittedly, forward contracting does involve some costs, but then it is on the "frictions" rather than on risk per se that we should focus.

The simplest explanation seems to be this. To deal with contracts denominated in foreign currency, one must be sophisticated about foreign exchange—and acquiring this sophistication has a real if hard-to-measure fixed cost. In the case of tradables I, the exporter is typically a firm selling a differentiated product; its costs are mostly fixed in domestic currency, so its normal pricing strategy will be to keep the domestic currency price fixed. This being the case, it is natural that the firm should leave worrying about the exchange rate to the importer, who has to deal with exchange markets as a matter of course in any case. The special case where a small country exports to a large country then falls into place—in small countries, everyone is obliged to be sophisticated about foreign exchange; in large countries nobody wants to worry about it.

Exporters of tradables II, by contrast, sell products whose prices depend

6. This scheme is essentially that offered by Magee and Rao (1980).

very little on domestic factors. For them the easiest procedure—in the sense that each contract does not involve a simultaneous speculation on future exchange rates—is to have all contracts anywhere in the world written in the same currency, for which the international medium of exchange is the most natural.

Kindleberger has used the analogy between money and language to explain the role of the dollar; in this situation it fits very well. If I want to communicate with someone of a different nationality, one or both of us must invest in learning a second language. If she is from a large country and I from a small one, we will probably use her language; if we are both from small countries, we will both use some international language. If a Dutch businessman and a German businessman make an agreement, they will probably converse in German and quote prices in marks; if the Dutch businessman then deals with a Brazilian, the conversation will more likely be in English and the price in dollars.

This is a very loose argument, and we would not want to lean too hard on it. Nevertheless, we will push it just a bit further, to suggest that international capital markets—especially under fixed rates—resemble tradables II in that bond prices are very much internationalized. LIBOR and the Chicago wheat price both are watched around the world, and in both cases this makes it convenient to denominate international contracts in dollars.

Is there anything in the unit-of-account role of the dollar which corresponds to the possibility of multiple equilibria in its medium of exchange role? In trade among the advanced countries, the choice of a unit of amount seems to be determined by fundamentals; the use of the dollar is comparable to the use of the mark, that is, the dollar plays no more of a role than the size of the United States entitles it to. Where there is an arbitrariness in the use of the dollar is in LDC/tradables II trade and, perhaps, in international lending. Here there is again a situation where the dollar is used because it is used, and its place could be taken by the mark or the yen.

8.5 The Dollar as an International Store of Value

8.5.1 Sterling and the Dollar as Banking Currencies

In 1913 working balances in sterling were held by banks and firms all around the world, reflecting in part the demand for sterling created by its other monetary roles, in part the economies of scale which made London the most efficient financial center. Thus settlement of trade contracts in sterling, servicing of sterling-denominated debt, and interbank transactions in sterling all required holding of sterling balances; the vehicle role of sterling made it more liquid than other currencies; and the scale of the London market made Lombard Street sterling balances an attractive proposition.

The dollar today holds a similar, but less striking, position. As we have seen, the dollar is dominant in interbank markets, still acounts for most international lending, and plays a disproportionate though not dominant role in trade invoicing. Economies of scale also play a role—but in a more confusing way. Dollar balances can be held not only in New York but also in London, so that the advantages of the dollar are not so much tied to the scale of activities in a particular geographical center as they are to the scale of activities in that currency. Nonetheless, these economies are real—imagine asking a London bank to offer a Euro-drachma account or a Euro-escudo account, and the importance of having at least some minimum scale becomes apparent.

As a store of value, however, the dollar has one disadvantage prewar sterling did not have. This is the uncertainty caused by floating exchange rates. Uncertain exchange rates push wealth holders toward diversification, opposing the forces encouraging convergence on a single currency. The result has apparently been a gradual diversification away from the dollar since 1973. The first line of table 8.3 presents some evidence from the Eurocurrency markets, where a slow drift away from the dollar seems to have occurred.

8.5.2 The Dollar as a Reserve Currency

Probably the most important reason for holding reserves in dollars is that the dollar is an intervention currency. This means that reserves initially accrue to central banks in dollars and must be converted to other currencies if the central banks want to diversify. It also means that reserves must be converted back to dollars to be used for intervention. For large countries such operations carry more than a transaction cost: movements into and out of nondollar currencies amount to intervention in other countries' foreign exchange markets which are likely to be resented (the United States is used to it). Because of this political aspect, jointly floating European countries (in the snake and later in the EMS) have continued to hold reserves in dol-

Table 8.3 **The Dollar as a Store of Value**

	1970	1973	1980
Share of dollars in "offshore" holdings of European banks[a]	77.1	70.4	69.0
Share of dollars in world foreign exchange reserves[b]	75.6	84.5	73.1
Share of pounds in world foreign exchange reserves[b]	12.6	5.9	3.0
"International currency" share in foreign exchange reserves[c]	88.2	84.5	73.1

[a]BIS *Annual Report*.
[b]This number includes dollars exchanged by members of the EMS for ECUs. See IMF, *Annual Report* 1981, p. 69.
[c]See text for explanation.

lars, not in each others' currencies; and they have often maintained cross-parities by simultaneous buying and selling of dollars, not by direct swaps of European currencies.

Opposing these advantages of the dollar is the desire of central banks to diversify agains exchange risk. As table 8.3 shows, the dollar's share of world foreign exchange reserves actually rose in the early 1970s, then declined. But in a sense this is misleading as a measure of "demonetization" of reserves, because sterling was still a partial international money in 1970. The last line of the table adds the dollar and pound shares in 1970, but not afterward, to give a rough measure of the share of international money in reserves. It suggests a continual and substantial shift on the part of central banks toward less liquid but less risky portfolios.

8.6 Prospects for the Dollar's Role

8.6.1 Determinants of the Dollar's Role

The theory of international money sketched out in the preceding section emphasized two kinds of influence on the choice of currency as international money and on the importance of its role. First, the currency of a country which is important in world markets will be a better candidate for an international money than that of a smaller country. Second, the use of a currency as an international money itself reinforces that currency's usefulness, so that there is an element of circular causation. This circularity was clearest in the case of choice of a medium of exchange, where a given structure of payments—a type of market fundamentals—might be consistent with several different structures of exchange, because of the self-justifying effect of making a currency serve as vehicle.

It is this circularity which raises the most worries about the future prospects of the dollar. The troublesome possibilities are either that the dollar's fundamental advantages will drop to some critical point, leading to an abrupt unraveling of its international role, or that a temporary disruption of world financial markets will permanently impair the dollar's usefulness. These are not purely academic speculations, since they have precedent in the history of sterling's decline. The disruption of World War I led to a permanent reduction in sterling's role, while the gradual relative decline of Britain's importance in the world was reflected not in a smooth decline in sterling's role but in surprising persistence followed by abrupt collapse.

These possibilities are illustrated in figure 8.4. We assume that it is possible to define some index of the use of the dollar as international money (though we have emphasized that the different roles are at least partly separable). The *desired* use of the dollar as international money will then be an increasing function of the actual use, as illustrated by the curve *UU*. The position of this schedule depends on fundamentals, such as the relative size

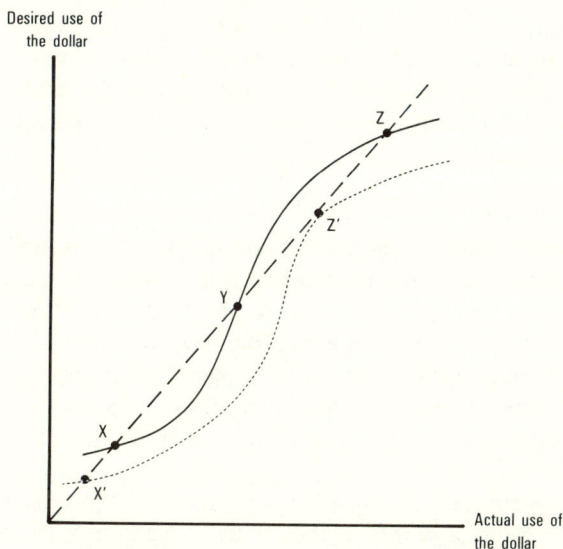

Fig. 8.4   Possibilities for a collapse of the dollar's role

of the United States economy and the openness and efficiency of its capital markets, as well as the stability of exchange rates and thus the strength of the incentives for diversification. Given these fundamentals, however, there may be several equilibria, as illustrated. Even without a formal specification of dynamics, it seems clear that X and Z will be the locally stable equilibria here; Z might correspond to the current state of dollar standard with diversification, X to a multipolar world where the mark and yen serve as regional international currencies.

Suppose that the fundamental strength of the dollar were gradually to weaken (as it surely has). Then UU would shift downward. Initially the role of the dollar would also gradually decline, from Z to Z'. At that point, however, a critical level would have been reached; a small further decline in the fundamentals would produce an unraveling of the dollar's role. As it was used less, the desired use would fall, and the role of the dollar would decline to X' even without any further weakening in the fundamentals.

Alternatively, a temporary disruption of the system could shift the world from one equilibrium to another. It is depressingly easy to imagine scenarios; for example, a war scare in Europe. This could lead to capital flight and the imposition of exchange controls. If the controls lasted long enough they could break the habit of doing business in dollars, so that when they were lifted the world would end up at X instead of Z.

This may seem to be an extremely casual and oversimplified way to think about the future of the dollar. Oversimplified it certainly is; we would very much like to be able to treat the subject rigorously. But this analysis seems to be if anything more formal and less casual than most discussion of the international monetary system and monetary reform. And this analysis points to a useful way of framing the question of the future role of the dollar: namely, is the fundamental position of the dollar strong enough to sustain its world role?

8.6.2 Is America Big Enough?

The question of whether the role of the dollar in sustainable should, in principle, be answered with a quantitative model. Unfortunately, this is not feasible. What we *can* do is to compare the position of the United States with that of the United Kingdom before the First World War, when sterling was the international currency to a much greater extent than the dollar has ever been. To the extent that the United States position is as strong or stronger, the continuation of a dollar-based international monetary system looks possible.

Table 8.4 presents some comparisons between the position of the United States in recent years and that of the United Kingdom at the peak of sterling's preeminence. The United Kingdom was the largest trading nation in 1913, by a small margin which was however bigger than the United States margin in the late 1970s. The United Kingdom domestic economy was, however, proportionately far smaller. Also, the relatively large share of Germany in trade reflects its geographical position in Europe; outside Europe the United States still has a pronounced lead.

On the basis of these comparisons, then, there does not seem to be any reason why the dollar cannot continue to be the basic international money; indeed, why it could not expand its role to something like that of sterling at its peak. There are, however, two features of the world which have changed—a less important one and a crucial one.

The less important aspect of the world which has changed is the increased

Table 8.4   Pax Brittanica vs. Pax Americana

	United Kingdom 1913	United States Late 1970s
(a) Share of world trade	16^a	12.1^c
(b) Share of world output	14^b	24.3^d
(c) Trade share of largest rival	12^a	11.5^c
	(Germany)	(Germany)
(d) Output share of largest rival	36^b	10.1^d
	(US)	(Japan)

[a]Exports plus imports, from Rostow (1978).
[b]Industrial production, from Rostow (1978).
[c]1979 export figures, from *Report of the President on US Competitiveness*, 1980.
[d]1978 GNP figures, from *World Bank Atlas*.

relative importance of trade in manufactures as opposed to primary products. In McKinnon's terms, world trade has shifted from tradables II to tradables I. This in itself reduces the role of the center country's currency, since that currency is more likely to be used for the denomination and settlement of trade contracts in tradables II than tradables I.

The crucial difference is, of course, the advent of generalized floating with no end in sight. This creates incentives for diversification which reduce the usefulness of the dollar as a store of value. Perhaps this will be enough to tip the balance. If so, the dollar's role will unravel, not because of the relative decline of the United States, but essentially because of the general problem of controlling inflation.

8.6.3 After the Fall

What would happen if the dollar's role were to decline sharply? There are really two questions here. The first is one of the transition; would a decline in the dollar's role as a store of value, in particular, amount to a devastating run on the bank? Second, once the transition is accomplished, how much harm would the dethroning of the dollar do the world economy?

The important point to notice in discussing the transition is that the problem is *not* one of the United States having given the world paper in exchange for real goods and services. Very little of the "dollar" holding of the world is backed up by high-powered money; essentially it consists of short-term securities and bank deposits, many of the latter outside the United States. In principle, then, a change in the desired currency composition of liquid assets could be accommodated without any redistribution of wealth. Banks could convert their depositors' Eurodollar deposits into Euromark or European deposits at the current exchange rate; the Federal Reserve could buy up Treasury bills while selling mark-denominated securities. The currency transformation need not involve capital gains and losses to anyone.

Where the problem would arise is in the increased exposure of financial intermediaries to exchange risk. International banks borrow short and lend long, both at present mostly in dollars. A shift away from dollars would force a transition period during which the short borrowing and long lending are not in the same currency, posing obvious risks to the stability of the financial system. The example of Britain shows that the transition can be made—indeed, the unraveling of the pound as an international money went along with continuing growth of London as a financial center. But it would not be a good idea to be too complacent.

What about the long-run costs? Replacing the dollar in all its roles, with, say, the mark would not seem to make much difference. A more likely outcome, however, is a multipolar system with the dollar, mark, and yen all playing some role as international money. The cost would be a loss of economies of scale. Transactions costs in the interbank market would be higher, as would the operating costs of international banks—but these costs are so low at present than even a huge proportionate increase would still be a small number. More important, perhaps, would be the increased difficulty of calculation in a world without a single international unit of account. But surely the use of three currencies to quote raw materials prices would be a far less important cost than what we have already experienced from inflation and floating exchange rates.

The moral, then, seems to be that it is not a collapsed but a collapsing role of the dollar that we should worry about.

References

Cohen, B. J. 1971. *The future of sterling as an international currency.* London: Macmillan.

Grassman, A. 1973. A fundamental symmetry in international payment patterns. *Journal of International Economics* 3:105–16.

Jones, R. 1976. The origin and development of media of exchange. *Journal of Political Economy* 84:757–76.

Kindleberger, C. 1981. *International money.* London: George Allen & Unwin.

Krugman, P. 1980. Vehicle currencies and the structure of international exchange. *Journal of Money, Credit, and Banking* 12:513–26.

Kubarych, R. 1978. *Foreign exchange markets in the United States.* New York: Federal Reserve Bank.

Magee, S., and Rao, R. 1980. Vehicle and non-vehicle currencies in international trade. *American Economic Review Papers and Proceedings* 70:368–73.

McKinnon, R. 1979. *Money in international exchange.* New York: Oxford University Press

Page, S. A. B. 1977. The currency of invoicing in merchandise trade. *National Institute Economic Review* 81:77–81.

Rostow, W. W. 1978. *The world economy: History and prospect.* Austin: University of Texas Press.

Swoboda, A. 1969. Vehicle currencies in the foreign exchange market: the case of the dollar. In *The international market for foreign exchange,* ed. Robert Z. Aliber. New York: Praeger.

Yeager, L. 1976. International monetary relations: Theory, history, and policy. New York: Harper & Row.

IV   Fundamental Determinants of the Real Exchange Rate

9   Real Exchange Rates in the 1970s

Louka T. Katseli

9.1 Introduction

There is by now a substantive literature and a growing consensus on the failure of the purchasing power parity (PPP) doctrine to explain exchange rate movements in the 1970s. With the advent of floating exchange rates, PPP was rediscovered and presented as a simple and potentially powerful theory of exchange rate determination. Then it was reburied under a strong wave of criticism. The main objections were equivalent to those which had been raised in the 1920s,[1] and included the tenuous empirical validity of perfect commodity arbitrage and the noncomparability of general price indices due to weighting and/or productivity differences. Critics pointed to the predominance of nonmonetary disturbances that can substantially alter the equilibrium terms of trade among countries; they finally highlighted the role of expectations, and potentially asymmetric behavior of governments and/or private market participants in asset and good markets whose actions can produce "overshooting" phenomena.[2]

This latest round of debate on the theoretical and empirical validity of PPP has raised a number of interesting and still unresolved questions that focus explicitly on the role of the real exchange rate in macroeconomic adjustment.

Real exchange rates have moved differently across countries as a consequence of both structural differences and policy responses. The origin of the shocks has also varied. In some cases the predominant shocks originated in

I would like to thank Steven Marks and Paul McGuire for research assistance and my colleagues T. N. Srinivasan, Jonathan Eaton, and Zvi Eckstein for their helpful comments. Financial support by the German Marshall Fund is gratefully acknowledged.

1. For a review of the most recent round of debates on PPP, see Katseli-Papaefstratiou (1979a) and Frenkel (1981).
2. This point was first raised and elaborated by Dornbusch (1976).

the home country: increases in domestic costs of production due to growing government budget deficits adversely affected international competitiveness through real appreciation of the exchange rate. Careful management of the nominal exchange rate through a policy of minidevaluations has in some instances mitigated these effects. Alternatively, in countries with open financial markets, the real appreciation of the currency has occasionally been dampened due to actions of private market participants who diversified internationally in light of expected nominal depreciation of the currency.[3]

In other cases the origin of the disturbance was external to the particular economy: confronted with rising foreign prices, some central banks appreciated their effective nominal exchange rates in an attempt to insulate the domestic economy from external inflationary pressures. Nominal appreciation of the exchange rate in the face of external price increases could also be consistent with private market behavior where agents perceive the deterioration of the terms of trade as a permanent improvement in international competitiveness. More often, however, at least among smaller European countries, increases in foreign prices have been transmitted to domestic prices through substitution and income effects in consumption or production. This process could even be accompanied by exchange rate depreciation if the rise of internal prices exceeds that of traded goods.[4] Finally, changes in nominal exchange rates among hard currencies have led to changes in effective exchange rates which have in turn been transmitted to domestic prices and, in the case of countries with market power, to the foreign currency price of exports.[5]

Thus real exchange rate movements reflect different economic processes which result from the interaction of private market participants and policy authorities. Even in those cases where real exchange rates have remained roughly constant, it is interesting to analyze the economic forces behind the process of real exchange rate determination. Such analysis can highlight the effectiveness of exchange rate policy and can illuminate the fundamental reasons for alternative targets in the exercise of exchange rate policy. Thus in a country where nominal exchange rate devaluation quickly raises domestic prices by the full extent of the devaluation, an active exchange rate policy can only become an instrument of anti-inflation policy rather than balance of payments adjustment. Alternatively, if the speed of adjustment is low, nominal exchange rate policy can potentially become a useful instrument of external balance.

3. Increases in domestic cost conditions could also be associated with a drop in foreign prices due to labor market behavior in the foreign country (Branson and Rotemberg 1980) or the presence of intermediate goods (Katseli and Marion 1982).

4. For a discussion of overshooting of internal prices of home goods, see Corden and Jones (1976) and Katseli-Papaefstratiou (1979b).

5. If the demand elasticity for exports is not infinite, devaluation by the home country reduces the foreign price of exports.

In countries where nominal exchange rates are market determined, the transmission from nominal exchange rate movements to relative prices and from prices to exchange rates can highlight the role of the current account in the process of exchange rate determination. In a rational expectations framework, the instantaneous adjustment of the nominal exchange rate following a given disturbance will critically depend on expectations about the movement of relative prices. Similarly, the dynamic path of the nominal exchange rate to its new equilibrium level will depend on the actual and expected movement of the real exchange rate which determines the current account and hence the rate of accumulation of foreign assets.[6]

In light of these considerations, this paper presents a comparative analysis of the implied linkages between nominal exchange rates and relative prices for 13 industrialized countries during the 1974–80 period of floating rates. Section 9.2 highlights the theoretical differences between two commonly used indices of real exchange rate movements, namely, the terms of trade and the relative price of traded to nontraded goods. This is done in a pure two-country, four-good trade model following the work by Bruno (1976), Jones (1979), Katseli (1980), and more recently Srinivasan (1982). The model is solved for the equilibrium terms of trade and relative price of nontraded goods in response to a number of disturbances in the home or foreign country. Even in the context of this stark framework, it can be readily seen that the movement of the two indices is not analytically equivalent so that the choice of index becomes crucially important for empirical work.

Section 9.3 provides a comparative study of the two relative price indices for thirteen OECD countries during the period of floating rates and analyzes their time series properties for that same period. The lack of any systematic correspondence in the movement of the two indices, which is suggested in the theoretical analysis of section 9.2, is also evident in the empirical findings of this section.

In section 9.4, movements in the real exchange rate, defined now as the relative price of nontraded to traded goods, are decomposed into movements of the nominal exchange rate, a foreign price, and a domestic price component. The analysis of their time series properties supports the view that in the floating rate period there has not been a one-to-one correspondence between movements in exchange rates and prices, as a simple PPP view would maintain. Instead exchange rates have generally followed an AR1 process while prices all followed cyclical AR2 processes. This provides partial support to the theoretical argument that the process of exchange rate determination is qualitatively different from the process of relative price determination, and does not contradict the conventional hypothesis that exchange

---

6. Whether or not news about the current account affects nominal exchange rate movements will depend on the market's expectations about real exchange rate movements (Branson 1977, 1981).

rates are determined in assets markets which clear faster than goods markets. Statistical exogeneity, however, is harder to ascertain.

Section 9.5 investigates different patterns of statistical exogeneity among nominal exchange rates, domestic, and foreign prices and simulates the implied adjustment to unexpected shocks in each of these variables for the OECD countries in the sample. The analysis highlights some of the observed differences of behavior and the appearance of vicious circles.

The last section of the paper summarizes the results.

9.2 The Equilibrium Real Exchange Rate: Alternative Interpretations

In static trade theory long-run equilibrium is usually identified with balance on current account.[7] The equilibrium real exchange rate is thus identified with the vector of relative prices that balances the current account (Katseli 1979a).

Depending on the object of the analysis most models of real exchange rate determination have focused either on the terms of trade or the relative price of traded to nontraded goods. In traditional two-country, two-good models, the equilibrium real exchange rate has almost always been identified with the terms of trade.[8] Alternatively in models where nontraded goods play an important role in balance of payments adjustment, the terms of trade are usually assumed to be determined exogenously and traded goods are assumed to be perfect substitutes and thus aggregated into a composite good (Dornbusch 1973; Bruno 1976). Given the importance of nontraded goods and trade in differentiated products in most OECD countries (Krugman 1980), such restrictive assumptions are not necessarily warranted except for analytical purposes. It is important to realize that in the process of adjustment both relative prices are involved, that is, the terms of trade and the relative price of traded to nontraded goods. This fundamental insight goes back to Pearce (1961) if not still earlier to Keynes (1930) and Ohlin (1929a, 1929b). Introduction of nontraded goods into a simple two-country model where each country is completely specialized in the production of a traded commodity allows the relationship between the two relative price indices in both flow and stock equilibrium to be demonstrated clearly.[9] The effects of different shifts such as technological change in either sector on both equilibrium relative prices can then be easily derived.

This is the structure of the theoretical model that is presented in this section. It is a static trade model where all goods are final and where there is

7. Most analyses at least in the finance literature abstract from long-run structural imbalances that may be planned especially in the context of developing economies with substantial foreign borrowings. Most notable exceptions are the works by Bardhan (1970) and Bruno (1976).

8. Besides most trade theory models one should include in that tradition the work by Branson (1981), Krugman (1981), and Sachs (1981).

9. In the flow equilibrium solutions, the stock of money is held fixed while in stock equilibrium it becomes endogenous as the current account is assumed to be balanced.

only one tradeable private asset, money, that can be accumulated through the trade balance. All these assumptions could in turn be relaxed along the lines of recent papers (Giavazzi 1980; Obstfeld 1981a; Katseli and Marion 1982). The objective here is not to present a complete list of factors that could affect the real exchange rate but rather to highlight the differences between the equilibrium properties of the two relative indices in the simplest general equilibrium model.

Each country is assumed to produce a nontraded good (H and H^*, where a "*" indicates the foreign country) using a fixed amount of sector-specific capital ($\overline{K}_h$ and $\overline{K}_h^*$) and labor (N) which is free to move between the nontraded and traded good sector in each country but not internationally. The two trading countries are assumed to be completely specialized with the home country producing an exportable commodity (X) and importing the foreign country's traded good (M). The assumption of complete specialization can be justified on grounds that each of the major OECD countries produces a different bundle of products. It also makes the model solvable, as it reduces the number of relative prices that need to be endogenously determined to three. Using the home country's exportable price as the numeraire,[10] the relevant relative prices are the home and foreign country's relative prices of nontraded goods (P_h and P_h^*) and the terms of trade (P_m) between the two countries.

The exogenous shifts that are analyzed in the comparative-static exercises are increases in the stock of capital used by different sectors, representing capital-augmenting technical progress; increases in the desired real wage that could be attributed to rising degrees of unionization; changes in the marginal propensity to save which could result either from shifts in intertemporal preferences or from policy; and a money transfer from one country to the other. Money is assumed to be the only asset that constitutes private wealth.[11] Thus saving, which is equal to the trade balance, is also equal to the flow excess demand for money by the private sector. The effects of all disturbances on relative prices will be presented both on impact when the stock of money is given, but there is positive saving or dissaving in each country through the balance of payments, and in the long run where the actual money holdings equal their desired level and hence saving and the trade balance are zero.

The full model is set out and described below and a more detailed explanation of the workings of the labor and goods markets follows.[12] A complete list of symbols is presented in table 9.1.

10. The choice of the numeraire turns out to be important and linked to the homogeneity postulates of the demand functions.

11. The capital stock is assumed to be held by the public sector and profits earned by the government are returned to the public in a lump-sum transfer.

12. The exchange rate is assumed to be held constant or at least to be determined separately in asset markets (Katseli and Marion 1982). This will be shown to be consistent with the empirical findings later on. The model could be significantly enriched if financial markets are introduced and expectations explicitly modeled.

Table 9.1   Notation

H = nontraded (home) good.
X = home country's exportable good.
M = foreign country's exportable (home country's importable).
P_h = price of home country's nontraded good relative to exportable.
P_m = terms of trade (an increase in P_m is equivalent to a deterioration in the terms of trade of the home country).
K_i, $i = x, m, h, h^*$ = sector-specific capital used in each sector i.
A = shift parameter of labor supply function in each country.
W = real wage in terms of the exportable commodity.
N_i, $i = x, m, h, h^*$ = employment in each sector.
C = desired real consumption expenditures in terms of the home country's exportable.
λ = speed of adjustment of actual to desired money holdings.
k = inverse of velocity of circulation.
$\lambda k = s$ = marginal propensity to save.
Y = real income in terms of the home country's exportable.
M = real money supply in terms of the home country's exportable.

Note: Asterisks refer to foreign variables denominated in foreign exchange. Subscripts s and d attached to quantities refer to supplies or demands of goods, while subscript $i = x, m, h, h^*$ refers to sector-specific variables.

The Model

(1) $$H_s(P_h, P_m, K_h, A) - H_d(P_h, P_m, C) = 0.$$

(2) $$H_s^*(P_h^*, P_m, K_h^*, A^*) - H_d^*(P_h^*, P_m, C^*) = 0.$$

(3) $$X_s(P_h, P_m, K_x, A) - X_d(P_h, P_m, C) - X_d^*(P_h^*, P_m, C^*) = 0.$$

(4) $$M_s^*(P_h^*, P_m, K_m^*, A^*) - M_d^*(P_h^*, P_m, C^*) - M_d(P_h, P_m, C) = 0.$$

(5) $$C = Y - S.$$

(6) $$C^* = Y^* - S^*.$$

(7) $$Y = P_h H_s + X_s.$$

(8) $$Y^* = P_h^* H_s^* + P_m M_s^*.$$

(9) $$S = \lambda[kY - M].$$

(10) $$S^* = \lambda^*[k^* Y^* - M^*].$$

(11) $$X_s(P_h, P_m, K_x, A) - X_d(P_h, P_m, C) - P_m M_d(P_h, P_m, C) = 0.$$

As in Katseli (1980), equations (1) and (2) specify the equilibrium condition in the nontraded good markets of both countries, while equations (3) and (4) impose the overall equilibrium clearing conditions in the international market for the traded commodities X and M. Equations (3) and (4) together imply that in flow equilibrium one country's deficit should be the other country's surplus.

The specification of the labor markets follows the work by Argy and Salop (1979) and Katseli and Marion (1982), where firms determine the demand for labor by equating the nominal wage to the value of the own marginal product of labor while the supply of labor in each sector is assumed to depend on the nominal wage divided by the expected price level (W/P^e); the expected price level (P^e) is assumed to be a function of the consumer price index. It is due to this assumption that the terms of trade enter the supply function of the nontraded goods. The shift parameter A represents exogenous movements in the supply of labor schedule. Appendix 1 gives a derivation of the functional forms for the supply curves presented in equations (1) and (2) and by extension (3) and (4).

Demand for home goods depends on the own relative price, the terms of trade, and real consumption expenditures, the latter defined by equations (5) and (6). All goods are assumed to be gross substitutes and indifference curves homothetic.

Finally, real output, or income in terms of commodity X, is defined in equations (7) and (8), and real saving in equations (9) and (10). Desired saving is equal to the flow excess demand for money. In the absence of government debt or domestic money creation, the private sector accumulates money through the balance of payments.

The condition for stock equilibrium, characterized by a zero rate of asset accumulation, is equation (11).

By appropriate substitution of equations (5)–(10) in equations (1)–(4), and by invoking Walras's law, the model can be reduced to a system of three equations in three unknowns, namely, the two relative prices of nontraded goods, P_h and P_h^*, and the relative price of imports, P_m. Table 9.1 reports the comparative static effects of percentage changes in each of the exogenous variables, K_h, K_x, K_h^*, K_m^*, A, A^*, on P_h and P_m, holding the stock of money fixed. Table 9.2 also reports the effects on relative prices of a money transfer from the foreign country to the home country (i.e., when $\hat{M}^* = -\hat{M}$) and the effects of a change in the marginal propensities to save in both countries.

Table 9.2   **Effects of Various Disturbances on Relative Prices Holding the Real Money Stock, M, Fixed**

Disturbance	$\hat{K}_h$	$\hat{K}_x$	$\hat{K}_h^*$	$\hat{K}_m^*$	$\hat{A}$	$\hat{A}^*$	$\hat{M}^* (= -\hat{M})$	ds	ds^*
$\hat{P}_h$	−	+	?	−	?	?	?	?	+
$\hat{P}_m$	?	?	?	−	?	?	?	+	+

In Appendix 2 it is shown that a sufficient condition for local stability of the system is that the reduction in the labor supply due to an increase in the expected consumer price relative to the price of the exportable is adequately low.

It can be seen from table 9.2 that with few exceptions the movement of the two relative prices is hard to sign unambiguously. The results depend on the relative size of the structural parameters in the two countries such as the relative own-price and cross-price elasticities of demand and supply for each good and the relative marginal propensities to consume. For the convenience of the reader, Appendix 3 gives a complete listing of the solutions, so that the existing ambiguities can be interpreted more easily.

A few general conclusions can be drawn which can be related to known results:

1. An increase in the capital stock used by the home country's nontraded good sector unambiguously lowers the relative price of nontraded goods. This result is well known from the growth and trade literature and is also derived in Bruno (1976). The opposite can be said for expansion of the capital stock in the home country's traded good sector. The effects of these disturbances on the equilibrium terms of trade are ambiguous, however, depending on the relative size of the income and substitution effects in the demand for the three available goods.

2. Increases in the capital stock of the trading partner's nontraded good have ambiguous effects on P_h and P_m. The reason for this is that the ensuing decrease in the foreign country's relative price of nontraded goods causes substitution away from the traded goods at the same time that foreign income probably increases. It is not clear therefore if overall demand by foreigners for the two traded goods increases or not.

3. Contrary to the previous case, growth of the capital stock in the foreign country's traded good reduces the home country's relative price of nontraded goods and the relative price of importables. Expansion of supply of importables unambiguously reduces their price, causing substitution away from the home country's nontraded and traded goods. Thus, if we define the real exchange rate as the relative price of traded goods and the terms of trade as the relative price of exportables (that is, the inverse of $\hat{P}_h$ and $\hat{P}_m$, respectively), it follows that trade-biased growth in the foreign country causes the home country's real exchange to depreciate and its terms of trade to improve.

4. A push for higher real wages in either country has, as one would expect, ambiguous effects on the relative price of goods. The outcome will depend once again on the relative size of the supply and demand elasticities.

5. The results from the transfer experiment are interesting in light of the Ohlin-Keynes insights and can be studied in conjunction with the *ds* experiment. If the home country's money supply is increased by the same amount as the reduction in the money supply of the trading partner, home saving

falls. As in the case of a reduction in the marginal propensity to save, the ensuing change in P_h depends on the marginal propensities to consume the home and exportable commodities. If m_h is sufficiently larger than m_x, then P_h unambiguously increases. The effects on P_m are harder to ascertain. A reduction in saving unambiguously reduces P_m as consumption of both the nontraded good and the exportable rises in the home country. However, the effects of a transfer which increases M in the home country depend not only on the home country's reaction but also on the foreign country. Hence, as is shown in Appendix 3, the relative size of both the home and foreign marginal propensities to consume is important.

The ambiguities that characterize the flow equilibrium solutions reappear in the stock equilibrium version, which is characterized by a balanced current account and an endogenous money supply. In stock equilibrium the system consists of four equations in four unknowns and can be solved recursively, as is shown in Appendix 4.

From the above, it is evident that both the origin of any given disturbance and the choice of the relative index will determine the effects of any given real shock on what is called the "equilibrium real exchange rate." In the empirical section that follows, the two indices will be approximated first by the relative price of foreign to domestic wholesale prices, a proxy for the relative price of traded goods between countries and hence the terms of trade, and second by the price of traded goods relative to the value-added deflator, a proxy for the relative price of traded to nontraded goods.[13]

9.2 Indices of Real Exchange Rates

An index usually used to describe the real exchange rate in empirical studies is the ratio of foreign to domestic wholesale prices expressed in a common currency (Branson 1981). As wholesale prices exclude services, a major component of nontraded goods, they can be considered proxies for relative traded good prices and thus the terms of trade. Data for the construction of this index (R^w) come from the International Monetary Fund and are based on quarterly observations.[14]

The R^{tn} index, that is, the relative price of traded to nontraded goods, is constructed by deflating the home currency price of traded goods by the value-added deflator which is used as a proxy for the price of nontraded goods. The home currency price of traded goods is calculated by taking a weighted average of export and import unit value indices for each country as these are given by the IMF's *International Financial Statistics*.

13. The relevant wholesale price index was also used in subsequent tests as a proxy for traded good prices. The results are not reported here but are available upon request.

14. The weights used in these calculations are based on trade in manufacturing commodities among 14 countries, 13 of which are included in our sample. (The sole exception is Switzerland.) They can be readily obtained from the author.

Figures 9.1–9.5 plot the two relevant indices for five major industrialized countries, namely, the United States (A), Japan (J), Germany (G), United Kingdom (E), and France (F).

The United States is the only country which has experienced a continuous depreciation of its real exchange rate almost for the whole period, regardless of which index is used. The other countries' experience can be roughly subdivided into three subperiods. During the first period, which ends around the second quarter of 1974, the relative price of traded to nontraded goods increased while domestic wholesale prices rose rapidly. This trend is especially characteristic of Japan and Germany. The second period, roughly extending from 1974 to 1978, is quite dissimilar across countries. The two real price indices stayed roughly constant in the case of the United States and Japan, while they exhibited substantial fluctuations in the other countries. After 1978, France and England experienced real appreciations and the United States and Germany real depreciations. The evidence on Japan is mixed.

Table 9.3 provides some information on the stochastic properties of the two real exchange rate indices for the whole period of the 1970s by comparing the variability of each index around trend and the correlation coefficient between the two for each country. The correlation coefficient between each index and the current account balance is also included, even though

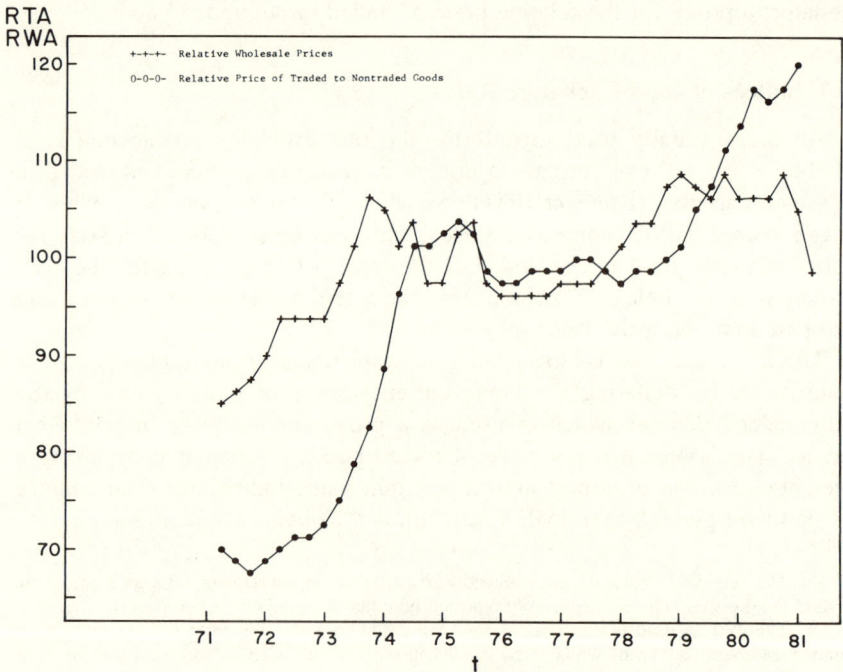

Fig. 9.1   Alternative measures of real exchange rates—United States

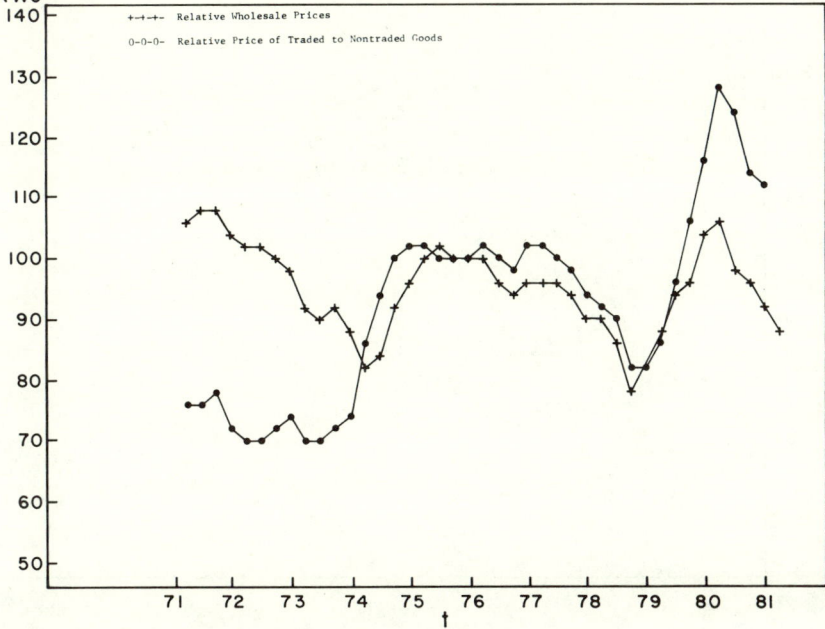

Fig. 9.2   Alternative measures of real exchange rates—Japan

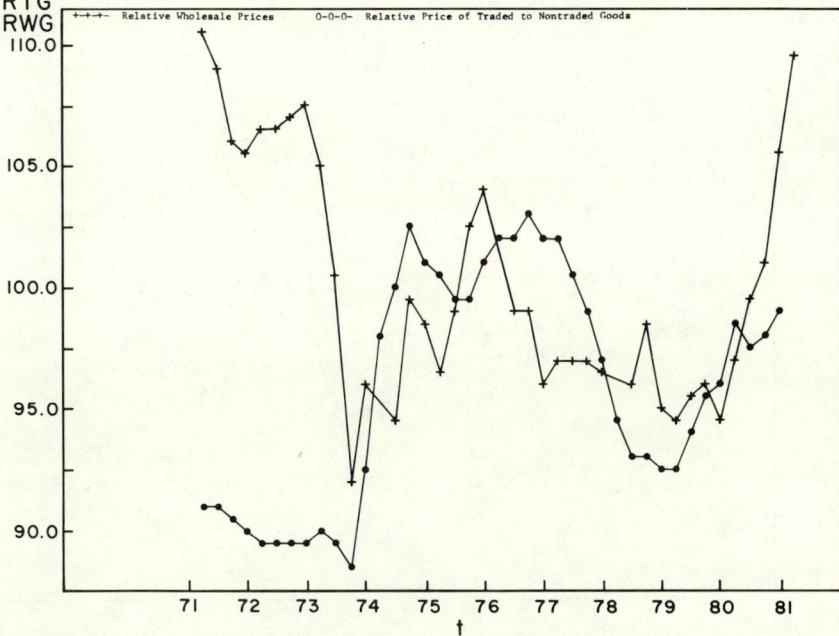

Fig. 9.3   Alternative measures of real exchange rates—Germany

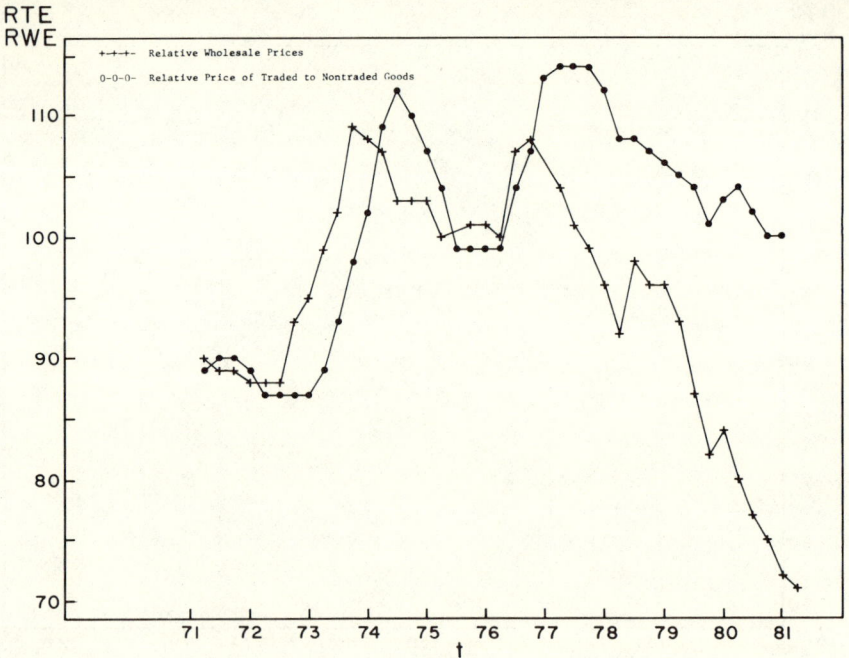

Fig. 9.4 Alternative measures of real exchange rates—United Kingdom

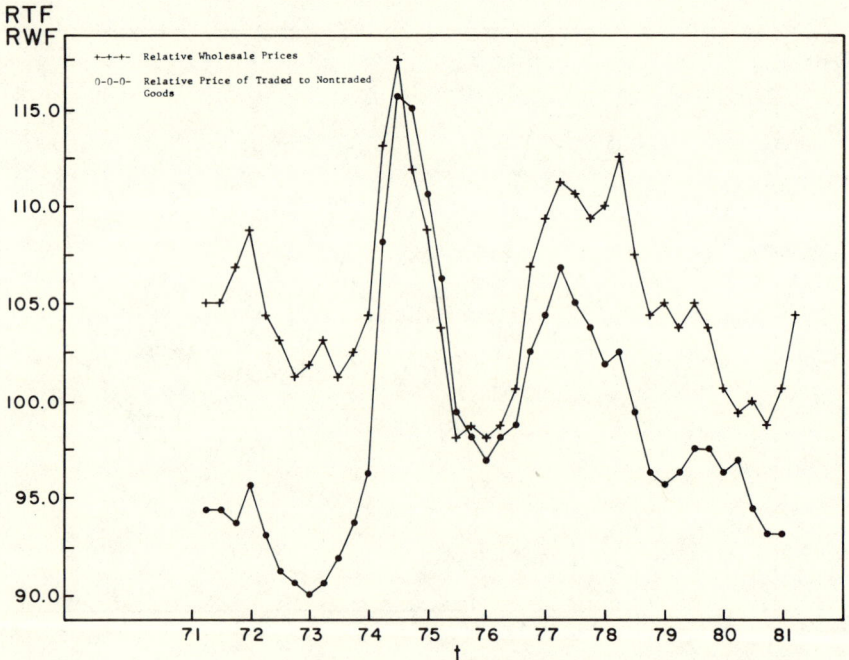

Fig. 9.5 Alternative measures of real exchange rates—France

Table 9.3   **Comparison of Real Exchange Rate Variability and Correlations (1971.1–1980.4)**

Countries	Real Exchange Rates (R)		Correlations		
	$\sigma_R tn$	$\sigma_R w$	$\rho(R_t^{tn}, R_t^{w})$	$\rho(CA_t, R_t^{tn})$	$\rho(CA_t, R_t^{w})$
United States	7.7	4.3	.307	.559	.258
Canada	3.2	3.6	.141	−.043	.140
Japan	11.1	7.2	.561	−.443	−.239
United Kingdom	6.7	10.3	.784	−.491	−.537
West Germany	4.4	6.4	−.116	.287	−.642
Austria	2.0	3.1	.259	−.069	−.015
Netherlands	5.5	3.3	.420	.103	−.301
Denmark	5.4	5.8	.194	−.177	−.079
Belgium	4.7	4.4	.112	−.330	−.653
France	6.3	4.4	.738	−.417	−.204
Italy	7.7	3.8	.334	−.542	.041
Norway	5.6	5.8	−.124	.351	.639
Sweden	2.4	5.1	−.334	−.518	.383

1. Data are detrended and deseasonalized.
2. Source of all data is the IMF.
3. Both indices are defined as relative prices of foreign to domestic variables; $R^{tn} = \dfrac{E\,(w_1 P^x + w_2 P^m)}{P^y}$ and $R^{w} = \dfrac{E\,(FP^w)}{P^w}$.

this study will stop short of investigating the properties of current account adjustment. It is interesting to note, however, that ρ is in most cases negative, probably reflecting strong J curve effects.

Comparing the standard deviations of the two indices which are used as measures of variability around trend, it is interesting to note that experiences differ across countries even though the underlying reasons for these differences are not apparent in such aggregate analysis. In terms of variability of the R^{tn} index during the floating rate period, Japan has clearly the lead, followed by the United States, Italy, and England. In terms of R^{w}, the United Kingdom and Japan are the two leading countries. Germany and countries in the deutsche mark currency area have experienced considerably less real exchange rate variability, regardless of the index. In all cases, these developments could be attributed either to private market behavior, to policy, or even to differences in structural characteristics which account for different transmission processes. It is evident, however, that whatever the reason, the real exchange rates of most countries moved sufficiently to contradict a PPP view of exchange rate determination. This is consistent with most available empirical findings (Frenkel, 1981). Section 9.4 below will pursue this line of inquiry further.

The correlation coefficient between the two relative price indices (detrended and deseasonalized) is highest in the case of the United Kingdom (.784) but low and sometimes negative in most other cases. Thus, the choice of the real exchange rate index becomes crucial.

This becomes clearer if the time series properties of the two indices are compared more closely. Given the instability of the international system during the first 3 years of the 1970s, which is evident in figures 9.1–9.5, 1974.2 was chosen as the base period of the empirical investigation.

Table 9.4 presents the autoregressive structure of the two quarterly time series where each variable is regressed on its own past lags. In each regression and in all subsequent tables, a constant and seasonal dummy variables are included while a log-linear trend has been removed. All variables in this and subsequent tables are stated as natural logarithms. Significance at the 5% and 10% levels is indicated by one or two asterisks, respectively.

For each of the thirteen countries in the sample, the fourth-order univariate autoregression (AR4) obtained by least squares fit over the 1974.2–1980.4 period is presented. The lags are subsequently shortened and the results of the appropriate second-order or first-order autoregressive structures are also reported. In all cases the standard errors increase only slightly.

As was expected, the two time series have quite different properties. In all countries except Austria, Norway, and Sweden, R^{tn} exhibits AR2 properties with convergent cyclical responses to disturbances,[15] while R^w is in most cases an AR1 stable process. Exceptions are Canada, Japan, France, and Sweden, where R^w is a stable AR2 process, and the United Kingdom, where the system could be considered explosive. These differences in the properties of the two time series can be attributed to the relative sluggishness of domestic nontraded good prices which causes a lengthier adjustment process. It should also be noted that the coefficient of R^w_{t-1} is in some cases over .90 and in the United Kingdom, Denmark, Norway, and Italy not significantly different from unity. This would make the R^w close to a random walk process in which a given disturbance to the system is sustained indefinitely. It is thus evident both from the theoretical analysis of section 9.2 and the empirical evidence provided so far that the two indices do not exhibit similar time series properties.

The analysis of the remaining two sections will be cast in terms of R^{tn}. The choice of the index is influenced by the fact that the properties of R^w have received relatively more attention in the recent literature (Branson 1981) and that in the presence of nontraded goods, R^{tn} is a better proxy of overall competitiveness.

Given the choice of R^{tn} as the relevant real exchange rate index, sections 9.4 and 9.5 below investigate further the movements of nominal effective exchange rates, foreign prices of traded goods, and domestic prices, and their interactions.

---

15. In a second-order difference equation with complex roots convergence requires that the modulus $R(= \sqrt{a_2})$ be smaller than unity.

Table 9.4   Cross-Country Univariate Regressions of the Real Exchange Rate (1974:2–1980:4)

	R^m_{t-i}							R^w_{t-i}						
	$t-1$	$t-2$	$t-3$	$t-4$	R^2	SSE	D-W	$t-1$	$t-2$	$t-3$	$t-4$	R^2	SSE	D-W
United States	1.49*	−.39	−.26	.10	.98	.002	2.0	.66*	−.12	.35	−.21	.76	.012	1.9
	1.56*	−.64*			.98	.002	2.3	.61*	.08			.74	.014	1.8
Canada	1.18*	.03	−.50		.96	.002	1.8	1.20*	−.60**	.47	−.35	.96	.005	1.5
	1.49*	−.67*		.05	.94	.003	2.3	1.23*	−.43*			.95	.006	1.9
Japan	1.41*	−.56**	−.03	−.04	.92	.025	1.8	1.07*	−.37	.17	−.35	.85	.020	2.1
	1.49*	−.69			.91	.026	1.9	1.24*	−.54*			.81	.026	2.2
United Kingdom	1.34*	−.51	−.04	−.02	.87	.007	1.9	1.00*	−.04	−.03	−.01	.93	.025	1.9
	1.39*	−.59*			.87	.007	1.9	1.01*	−.08			.93	.025	1.9
West Germany	1.35*	−.41	−.04	−.04	.92	.002	1.8	.96*	−.14	.30	−.48	.67	.008	1.6
	1.45*	−.56*			.92	.002	2.0	.80*	.05			.52	.011	1.6
Austria	.77*	−.03	.13	−.17	.89	.003	2.5	.89*	−.27	.22	−.18	.72	.006	1.5
	.77*	.02			.88	.003	2.4	.79*	−.10			.71	.006	1.6
Netherlands	1.14*	−.24	.07	−.16	.88	.006	2.0	.84*	.20	.31	−.43*	.84	.005	2.0
	1.27*	−.38*			.86	.006	2.2	.79*	.22			.80	.006	2.1
Denmark	1.34*	−.62	.28	−.17	.93	.007	1.7	.97*	−.18	.31	−.23	.85	.007	2.0
	1.31*	−.44*			.93	.007	1.8	.92*	−.00			.85	.008	2.1
Belgium	1.11*	−.28	.32	−.45	.92	.007	1.6	1.05*	−.35	.39	−.51*	.95	−.004	1.9
	1.36*	−.47*			.90	.008	2.1	1.18*	−.37			.93	.005	2.1
France	1.18*	−.60*	.05	−.11	.96	.004	2.2	1.14*	−.54**	.32	−.36	.85	.010	2.1
	1.32*	−.69*			.96	.004	2.5	1.24*	−.52*			.82	.012	2.4
Italy	.49*	.05	−.01	−.32*	.74	.013	1.8	.93*	−.35	.23	−.28	.65	.013	1.9
	.91*	−.30**			.61	.020	2.4	.92*	−.26			.63	.014	2.0
Norway	.74*	.31	−.12	−.28	.85	.014	1.9	.89*	−.15	.02	−.15	.89	.009	2.0
	.99*	−.10			.81	.018	2.3	.97*	−.30			.89	.010	2.1
Sweden	.57*	−.09	−.34	−.03	.79	.002	1.9	1.13*	−.25	−.16	−.06	.89	.008	1.8
	.76*	−.25						1.26*	−.53*			.88	.009	2.1

Notes: All regressions include a time trend and seasonal dummies.

One asterisk implies that the coefficient is significant at the 5% confidence level. Two asterisks imply that the coefficient is significant at the 10% confidence level.

9.4 Decomposition of R^{tn} and Analysis of Time Series Properties of Its Components

Variability of the real exchange rate, R^{tn}, around trend can be decomposed further. Determination of the principal source of variability, if at all possible, can illuminate the importance and effects of "news" relative to the long-run movement of R^{tn}, which is determined by expected changes in competitiveness due to technological innovations, decreasing money illusion or other factors.

Table 9.5 shows that for most countries much of the R^{tn} variability can be attributed to the detrended foreign price of tradeables index. Its standard deviation is considerably higher than that of either the nominal effective exchange rate or the value added deflator with the exception of the United Kingdom where nominal exchange rate variability is dominant. This is not surprising given the fact that the time period under consideration in table 9.5 includes 1973 and hence the dramatic increase in the prices of all imported intermediate goods, most notably oil. The second point to be noted is that for most countries the standard deviation of the value added deflator is the lowest. Austria, the Netherlands, and Belgium, whose exchange rates have been tied to the deutsche mark, are the only exceptions. Low variability of P^v probably reflects countercyclical policies that have been pursued during the period. Finally, contrasting the results of tables 9.3 and 9.5, real exchange rate variability is consistently higher than nominal exchange rate variability in all countries except Canada, the United Kingdom, Austria, and Sweden. The result runs counter to existing perceptions about real exchange rates which in a PPP world are assumed to stay roughly constant, and at least not to exhibit greater variability than nominal exchange rates.

The correlation analysis presented in table 9.5 sheds some light on the process underlying the variability in the real exchange rate index. Once again, experience is quite varied across countries. Foreign and domestic prices have moved closely together in all countries, especially in Japan ($\rho = .909$), but in most cases the nominal exchange rate has moved in the opposite direction from foreign and domestic prices. A notable exception is Japan. The Scandinavian countries (Denmark, Norway, Sweden) and Austria exhibit the highest negative correlations between exchange rates and each of the two price indices.

With the exception of Japan and the United Kingdom, where the correlation coefficient between nominal and real exchange rates is relatively high, in most countries it is relatively small. This could be the outcome of a PPP market view of nominal exchange rate determination which is probably unlikely given the high variability of the real exchange rates in most countries, or policy-enforced correlations (positive and negative respectively) among the nominal exchange rate and domestic and foreign prices. As was argued in section 9.1, causality can run either way. With respect to domestic prices,

Table 9.5   **Comparison of Price and Nominal Exchange Rate Variability and Correlation Analysis (1971:1–1980:4)**

	Effective Exchange Rate (E) σ_E ($\times 100$)	Prices (P)		Correlation Analysis				
		σ_{PV}	σ_{FPt}	$\rho(E, R^m)$	$\rho(P^v, R^m)$	$\rho(P^v, FP^f)$	$\rho(E, FP^f)$	$\rho(E, P^v)$
United States	4.6	2.7	9.0	.255	.040	.566	−.425	−.487
Canada	4.5	3.2	7.4	.131	.456	.791	.667	−.247
Japan	8.2	5.0	8.6	.938	.581	.909	.538	.469
United Kingdom	10.6	4.7	7.0	.680	.001	.296	−.571	.307
West Germany	4.0	1.5	6.7	−.088	.693	.698	−.564	.017
Austria	2.9	3.2	5.8	−.111	.333	.901	−.771	−.505
Netherlands	2.5	2.8	8.1	−.283	.333	.708	−.618	−.366
Denmark	4.7	2.9	7.8	.200	−.138	.674	−.670	−.731
Belgium	2.2	3.4	6.1	.474	.286	.774	.053	−.140
France	4.1	3.4	7.3	.116	−.223	.297	−.486	.024
Italy	4.8	3.7	9.4	.268	.412	.562	−.152	.347
Norway	5.1	3.0	9.1	−.001	−.130	.629	−.789	−.701
Sweden	5.0	3.3	8.9	−.214	.765	.847	−.814	−.428

$R_t^m = E(w_1 P^x + w_2 P^m)/P^v$

Notes: Data are detrended and deseasonalized. Source of all data is the IMF; P^x and P^m series come from the IMF's *International Financial Statistics*. Exchange rates are effective rates, defined as home currency per foreign exchange.

a nominal devaluation could be passed on rapidly to domestic prices or alternatively domestic inflationary pressures could influence authorities or the market to depreciate the nominal exchange rate. This process will be consistent with the evidence on Japan, United Kingdom, and Italy, where the correlation coefficient between E and P^v is positive.

A nominal devaluation can induce a decline in the foreign currency price of traded goods if countries possess market power in traded good markets. Alternatively, an increase in foreign prices might lead monetary authorities to appreciate the nominal exchange rate in order to insulate the economy from external inflationary pressures. This would be consistent with the evidence on most other industrialized countries, especially the Scandinavian countries. Given the observed high variability of the real exchange rate and foreign prices and the relatively low variability of the domestic price index, intervention by the monetary authorities is suspected. Section 9.5 investigates more thoroughly the evidence on causality and the adjustment process of individual countries.

Before proceeding with the analysis, however, a few more points should be raised. Table 9.6 describes the dynamic time series properties of the three indices, the nominal effective exchange rate, the value-added deflator, and the foreign price of traded goods for the period 1974.2–1980.4 after the 1973 major realignment of nominal parities. As with the real exchange rate indices, each variable is regressed against past values of itself in a regression which includes a constant, a time trend and seasonal dummies. Lags are subsequently eliminated successively and the final choice is based on the significance level of the estimated coefficient and the standard error of the restricted equation. The F-test of the joint elimination of the third- and fourth-period lags shows that the three indices generally demonstrate properties of an AR1 or AR2 autoregressive process with the exception of West Germany and the United Kingdom.

With the exception of Canada, Japan, France, and Sweden, the exchange rate can be described as an AR1 process. The process is generally stable except in the cases of the United Kingdom and Italy, where the estimated coefficients of E_{t-1} exceed unity while the second lag coefficient is not significantly different from zero. Also for Norway, one of the smaller European countries, the respective estimates in the restricted equation are 1.12 and $-.32$. The coefficients for some of the other small European countries, especially the Scandinavian countries, are close enough to unity that the nominal exchange rate can be effectively characterized as a random walk. This probably explains why the nominal exchange rate in most of these countries has not been allowed to vary much (see table 9.5).

The two prices can be described effectively on the other hand as AR2 processes. According to the reported F-tests, P^v, in the United Kingdom and Germany exhibit even higher-order autoregressive properties. This underlines the sluggishness of the domestic price index which is probably the

Table 9.6   **Cross Country Univariate Regressions of Exchange Rates and Prices (1974.2–1980.4)**

		E						
	-1	-2	-3	-4	R^2	SEE	D-W	$F(3,4)$
United States	.88*	−.06	.33	−.34	.88	.012	1.6	1.5(.24)
	.82	.03			.86	.014	1.5	
Canada	1.39*	−.75**	.41	−.25	.98	.005	1.6	0.7(.49)
	1.36*	−.52*			.98	.006	1.8	
Japan	1.16*	−.19	−.12	−.21	.95	.002	2.1	2.0(.17)
	1.45*	−.69			.94	.027	2.4	
United Kingdom	1.13*	−.04	−.02	−.09	.93	.023	1.9	0.2(.85)
	1.16*	−.15			.93	.023	2.0	
West Germany	.94*	−.11	.24	−.48*	.97	.009	1.5	3.3(.06)
	.80*	.01			.96	.012	1.5	
Austria	.84*	−.37	.18	−.42*	.97	.004	1.4	2.7(.09)
	.76*	−.27			.96	.005	1.6	
Netherlands	.69*	−.13	.24	−.44	.93	.004	1.5	2.0(.16)
	.67*	−.09			.91	.005	1.7	
Denmark	.94*	−.18	.32	−.24	.83	.007	1.8	0.6(.56)
	.88*	−.00			.82	.007	1.9	
Belgium	.75*	−.05	.25	−.35	.90	.005	1.6	1.0(.39)
	.78*	−.01			.89	.006	1.7	
France	1.05*	−.44	.29	−.37**	.86	.009	2.3	2.0(.16)
	1.13*	−.44*			.82	.010	2.4	
Italy	1.13*	−.43	.24	−.22	.98	.017	1.9	0.4(.65)
	1.11	−.33			.98	.018	2.0	
Norway	.99*	.00	−.13	−.10	.88	.005	2.0	0.9(.44)
	1.12*	−.32			.87	.006	2.2	
Sweden	1.25*	−.44	.01	−.09	.94	.008	1.8	0.3(.78)
	1.32*	−.55*			.94	.008	2.0	

1. All regressions include a constant, seasonal dummies, and a time trend.

2. A "*" indicates the coefficient is significant at the 5% level. A "**" indicates the coefficient is significant at the 10% level.

3. The source of data is the IMF. FP' was computed by division of the P' index by the effective exchange rate.

4. The F-test is conducted under the null hypothesis that the third and fourth-lag coefficients are equal to zero; the number in parenthesis is the significance level at which the null hypothesis can be accepted. Germany and Austria are the only countries for which the F-test on the E and P autoregressions point to an AR3 or AR4 structure.

5. The behavior of the stochastic equations is stable in all cases.

6. For Sweden the FP' autoregression was estimated for the period 1974:2–1979:4.

outcome of pricing or stabilization policies. FP' is generally an AR2 process, except possibly in West Germany and Norway.

The observed differences between the properties of nominal exchange rate time series data and those of relative prices, which have also been noted elsewhere (Branson 1981; Frenkel 1981), would be consistent with the

Table 9.6   (Continued)

			P^v					
	-1	-2	-3	-4	R^2	SEE	D-W	$F(3,4)$
United States	1.30*	$-.62$	.00	.00	.99	.001	2.0	0.0(.99)
	1.30	$-.61$			.99	.001	1.9	
Canada	1.49*	$-.61**$	.16	$-.21$	1.00	.001	2.2	0.7(.49)
	1.67*	$-.78*$			1.00	.001	2.3	
Japan	1.19*	$-.52**$	.49**	$-.26$	.94	.002	1.4	1.6(.23)
	1.03*	$-.16$			.93	.002	1.4	
United Kingdom	.90*	$-.00$	.24	.40*	1.00	.001	1.9	5.7(.01)
	1.37*	$-.54*$			1.00	.002	2.4	
West Germany	.96*	.08	$-.05$	$-.29**$	1.00	.000	1.8	6.4(.01)
	1.45*	$-.55$			1.00	.000	2.2	
Austria	1.12*	$-.73*$	.66**	$-.39**$	.99	.001	1.9	2.1(.15)
	1.03*	$-.37*$			.99	.001	2.0	
Netherlands	1.00*	$-.26$	$-.02$	$-.12$	.99	.002	2.0	0.4(.65)
	1.11*	$-.43*$			.99	.002	2.2	
Denmark	1.16*	$-.18$	$-.25$	.08	1.00	.001	2.4	0.3(.73)
	1.26*	$-.44*$			1.00	.001	2.4	
Belgium	1.01*	$-.20$	$-.16$	.14	1.00	.001	2.6	0.8(.47)
	1.02	$-.23**$			1.00	.001	2.2	
France	1.32*	$-.14$	$-.32$	$-.06$	1.00	.002	2.1	1.6(.23)
	1.59*	$-.70*$			1.00	.002	2.5	
Italy	1.42*	$-.97*$	.32	$-.08$	1.00	.002	2.0	0.5(.61)
	1.23*	$-.58*$			1.00	.002	1.7	
Norway	1.17*	$-.45$	.17	$-.16$	1.00	.001	2.3	0.4(.65)
	1.23*	$-.47*$			1.00	.001	2.4	
Sweden	.94*	$-.12$	$-.23$	$-.01$	1.00	.002	2.0	0.9(.44)
	1.12*	$-.47*$			1.00	.003	2.3	

hypothesis that exchange rates are determined in assets markets, which clear markedly faster than goods markets. Since price adjustments generally are more sluggish than exchange rate adjustments, nominal exchange rates tend to overshoot their equilibrium value as private market participants respond to new information. This would also be consistent with the observed high real exchange rate variability and would apply particularly well to the United States, the United Kingdom, and Germany among the major hard currency countries. The interaction of exchange rates and prices in the other floating countries—Japan, Canada, and France—is harder to ascertain at least from the evidence presented in table 9.6. Section 9.5 provides some further insights into these cases and into the underlying process of real exchange rate determination in the smaller European countries.

9.5 Statistical Exogeneity and Responses to Unexpected Shocks

Following the work of Sargent (1979), Sims (1980a), and Taylor (1980), and more recently of Ashenfelter and Card (1981), the stochastic dynamics

Table 9.6 (Continued)

	-1	-2	-3	-4	R^2	SEE	D-W	$F(3,4)$
United States	1.00*	$-.18$	.27	$-.32*$	.98	.013	1.5	2.8(.08)
	1.18*	$-.30**$			.97	.017	1.8	
Canada	1.38*	$-.45$	$-.05$	$-.04$	.98	.006	2.1	0.2(.81)
	1.49*	$-.63*$			.98	.007	2.3	
Japan	.89*	$-.24$	.23	$-.27**$	.98	.015	2.1	1.9(.18)
	1.04*	$-.23**$			.97	.018	2.4	
United Kingdom	1.15*	$-.19$	.05	$-.24$	.98	.017	2.0	1.1(.35)
	1.34*	$-.43*$			.98	.019	2.3	
West Germany	.85*	$-.30$	.13	$-.28*$	.99	.005	1.5	3.1(.07)
	1.09*	$-.54*$			.99	.007	2.1	
Austria	.90*	$-.19$	$-.12$	$-.10$	.99	.005	1.8	1.0(.38)
	1.18*	$-.54*$			.99	.005	2.0	
Netherlands	1.26*	$-.51**$	.05	$-.09$	.99	.005	1.9	0.3(.78)
	1.37*	$-.53*$			.99	.005	2.2	
Denmark	1.02*	$-.09$	$-.14$	$-.05$	.99	.003	1.9	0.8(.46)
	1.20*	$-.42*$			.99	.004	2.3	
Belgium	1.01*	$-.39$	.02	$-.17$	.99	.006	1.8	1.0(.39)
	1.26*	$-.64*$			.99	.007	2.4	
France	1.06*	$-.13$	$-.06$	$-.16$	.99	.006	1.9	1.4(.26)
	1.32	$-.53*$			.98	.007	2.4	
Italy	.95*	.04	$-.08$	$-.17$	.97	.017	2.0	2.0(.17)
	1.23*	$-.36$			.96	.021	2.4	
Norway	.83*	.26	$-.22$	$-.22$	.98	.015	1.7	4.3(.03)
	1.27*	$-.45*$			.97	.022	2.5	
Sweden	1.52*	$-.86*$	.30	$-.15$	.98	.006	1.7	0.3(.76)
	1.47*	$-.66*$			.98	.006	1.8	

of the nominal exchange rate and relative price series are investigated further in this section. The objective here is twofold: to estimate the observed adjustment of current nominal exchange rates (and prices) to lagged known values of relative prices (and exchange rates) and, more important, to investigate the response of each time series to unanticipated disturbances. The failure of most well-known models of exchange rate determination to explain the variability of nominal exchange rates in the 1970s suggests that "news" is the main explanatory variable of the observed large swings in exchange rates. News is captured by the error term in vector autoregression systems, which include as independent variables lagged values of all the relevant dependent variables.

In the context of real exchange rate determination, news about the current account position, money supply, or output will affect both nominal exchange rates and prices. Thus, residuals in vector autoregressions which include as independent variables only lagged values of nominal exchange rates and prices will capture unanticipated movements in these two variables due to such news. A high negative correlation coefficient among residuals therefore could imply either that agents move nominal exchange rates and prices in opposite directions as a response to a particular source of news or that nominal exchange rates and prices respond to different sets of news which are themselves negatively correlated.

In light of these considerations, a second-order vector autoregression system is estimated for each country in the sample. The two variables are the nominal effective exchange rate and relative prices defined as the ratio of the value-added deflator to the foreign price of traded goods. Each of the two variables is regressed against lagged values of both variables. All regressions are run on quarterly observations and include a constant, a linear trend, and seasonal dummies. Given the analysis of section 9.4, two lags are used for each variable. The only exception is Germany, for which the vector autoregression is also run with three lags on exchange rates and relative prices.

Each of the estimated equations can be interpreted as a forecasting equation. To determine whether or not inclusion of the other variable improves its explanatory power, F-tests are conducted under the null hypothesis that *(a)* the two lagged relative price terms in the exchange rate equation are zero or *(b)* the two lagged exchange rate terms in the relative price equation are zero. The results are reported in table 9.7 with significance levels in parentheses. Table 9.7 also reports the correlation between the residuals of the two estimated equations, which can be interpreted as the correlation between "innovations." Subject to our previous interpretation, a strong positive correlation between the two residuals would imply that the two series respond similarly to a given source of news (e.g., money supply news) or to different sets of news (e.g., money supply and current account) that are positively correlated.

The results of table 9.7 support the intuitive arguments so far. At a 10% significance level, it is shown that the exchange rate can be considered statistically exogenous or predetermined vis-à-vis relative prices in all cases except the United Kingdom and possibly Denmark, Austria, and Belgium. Past movements of the exchange rate are important expected determinants of the relative price ratio in Japan, Belgium, and Norway. This supports the previous findings of differential speed of adjustment in assets and goods markets and the stronger *expected* transmission linkages in the smaller and more open economies.

The correlation among residuals is positive in all cases but it is around .8 to .9 in the cases of the United States, the United Kingdom, West Germany, and France. This finding is consistent with the hypothesis that, despite relatively low expected transmission from exchange rates to prices and from prices to exchange rates in the hard-currency industrialized countries as compared to smaller and more open economies (tables 9.5 and 9.7), innovations have a similar effect on both nominal exchange rates and domestic prices. In the other smaller countries, relative price and exchange rate movements seem to respond independently to innovations.

Table 9.7 **Correlation of Residuals and Granger Exogeneity Tests in Vector Autoregression System of Exchange Rates and Relative Prices^a (1974:2–1980:4)**

Countries	$\rho(\hat{V}_E, \hat{V}_{P^v/FP}t)$	$F(P^v/FP')^b$	$F(E)^b$
United States	.92	1.09 (.36)	1.82 (.19)
Canada	.73	1.63 (.22)	.95 (.41)
Japan	.62	.25 (.78)	4.80 (.02)*
United Kingdom	.83	3.59 (.05)*	6.99 (.57)
West Germany	.92	.66 (.53)	1.96 (.17)
	.93	.45 (.72)	.81 (.51)
Austria	.72	3.21 (.06)**	.04 (.96)
Netherlands	.16	1.66 (.22)	1.44 (.26)
Denmark	.36	2.75 (.09)**	.70 (.51)
Belgium	.31	2.69 (.09)**	3.95 (.04)*
France	.79	1.23 (.32)	1.77 (.20)
Italy	.45	.66 (.53)	.44 (.65)
Norway	.33	.52 (.60)	2.68 (.09)**
Sweden^c	.77	.31 (.74)	.46 (.64)

^{a}For all countries the vector autoregressions include two lags on all relevant variables, with the sole exception of Germany where the results of the vector autoregression with three lags on E, P^v, and hence P^v/FP' are also reported.

$^b F(P^v/FP')$ is the F-test under the null hypothesis that $(P^v/FP')_{t-1}$ and $(P^v/FP')_{t-2}$ are zero in the E equation. Similarly, $F(E)$ is the F-test under the null hypothesis that E_{t-1} and E_{t-2} are zero in the relative price equation. Significance levels are given in parentheses. An asterisk indicates that the null hypothesis can be rejected within a 10% confidence interval.

^{c}Sample period: 1974.2–1979.4.

Based on the underlying estimation of the vector autoregression system (VAR), figures 9.6 and 9.7 plot the response of each of the two independent variables to one standard deviation shock in the residual of the cross-equation for France, Germany, Japan, and the United States.[16] Note that the impulse reaction functions presented in these figures reveal substantial cross-country differences in the dynamic path of adjustment to an unexpected disturbance.

16. The impulse reaction functions are run under the assumption that the variance-covariance matrix of the disturbances is in fact diagonal. This assumption is hard to justify in the case of the large industrialized countries where the correlation coefficient of residuals is high. Three factors prompted this choice, however: *(a)* there is no unique way of orthogonalizing the disturbances and thus the only acceptable alternative would have been to investigate all possible orthogonalizations; *(b)* the impulse reactions could be interpreted as a shock to the distinct part of each residual in the VAR system; and *(c)* since there is no a priori reason why the appropriate orthogonalization is different across the chosen subset of countries, cross-country comparisons of impulse reactions are still informative.

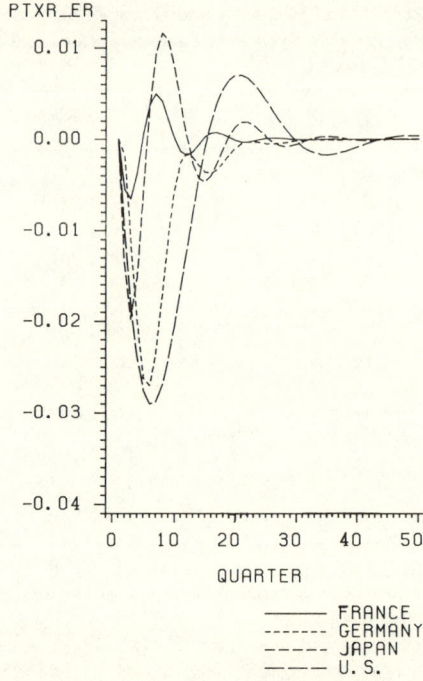

Fig. 9.6   Responses of relative prices, nontraded to traded goods, to shock in exchange rate (period of estimation 1974:2–1980:4).

In all four countries, news that causes an unexpected nominal depreciation induces a decrease in the relative price of nontraded to traded goods. The drop is largest and the adjustment slowest in the case of the United States, which is the least open country in the sample and which possesses a high degree of market power. The system in all cases converges roughly after 50 quarters.

Oscillations of nominal exchange rates in response to an unexpected shock in relative prices are once again larger and more prolonged in the case of the United States. The nominal exchange rate depreciates in value after a short period of small appreciation (two quarters). After 50 quarters it did not converge to its equilibrium value. The dynamic path of adjustment is quite different in the other countries, with adjustment almost monotonic in the case of Germany. The exchange rate converges approximately after 35 quarters. The pronounced nominal and real appreciations probably reflect anti-inflationary policies and possibly, in the case of the European countries, the sluggishness in nominal exchange rate adjustment imposed by monetary arrangements.

In conclusion, the evidence in table 9.7 and figures 9.6–9.7 suggests that even though innovations affect nominal exchange rates and relative prices

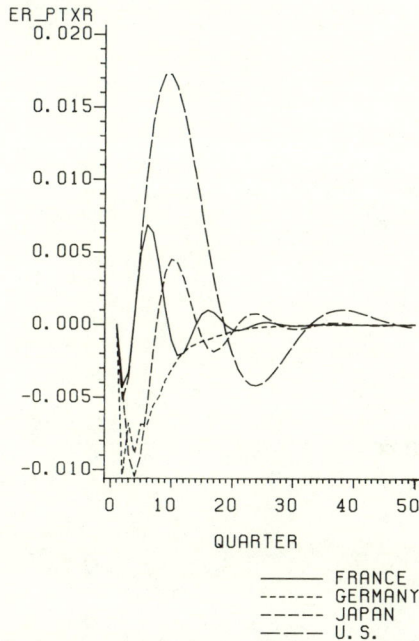

Fig. 9.7   Response of exchange rate to shock in relative prices, nontraded to traded goods (period of estimation 1974:2–1980:4).

symmetrically in the large countries as opposed to the smaller countries, the impulse reaction functions even for these countries are not identical due to differences in structure and policy behavior.

Movements in the relative price index can now be decomposed further into movements of the domestic and foreign price components, and the properties of the system can be analyzed further. Here again each variable in the trivariate autoregression system is regressed against lagged values of all three variables. As with the bivariate VAR, two lags are used in the autoregressive structure. Tables 9.8, 9.9, and 9.10 present estimates of each of the forecasting equations as well as the results of F-tests on the successive elimination of cross variables. The numbers in parentheses under the estimated coefficients report the t-statistics.

Table 9.8 confirms the hypothesis of exogeneity of the nominal exchange rate that was postulated in table 9.7, except in the case of Germany. While in table 9.7 it was reported that current values of the exchange rate do not seem to depend on lagged values of relative prices, the results here indicate that lagged values of P^v independently affect the nominal exchange rate. Furthermore, in the case of Belgium, joint elimination of the two lags on P^v is hard to justify. This gives partial justification for the preoccupation with vicious circles by Belgian economists.

Table 9.8   **Responsiveness of E to Lagged E, P^y and FP^i (1974.2–1980.4)**

	E_{t-1}	E_{t-2}	E_{t-3}	P^y_{t-1}	P^y_{t-2}	P^y_{t-3}	FP^i_{t-1}	FP^i_{t-2}	FP^i_{t-3}	R^2	D-W	$F(P^y)$	$F(FP^i)$
United States	.97	−.50		1.76	−.73		.12	−.58		.92	2.3	2.5	2.2
	$(2.3)^a$	(.9)		(2.2)	(2.2)		(.3)	(1.0)				(.11)	(.15)
Canada	1.24	−.35		−.49	−.25		.30	.30		.99	2.1	3.0	2.1
	(4.3)	(1.2)		(.09)	(.4)		(1.2)	(.1)				(0.08)	(.15)
Japan	1.42	−.68		−.41	.59		.29	−.17		.94	2.4	.2	.3
	(7.0)	(3.4)		(0.5)	(.5)		(.8)	(.5)				(.84)	(.70)
United Kingdom	.68	.27		.86	−.38		−.27	.15		.96	1.9	3.0	.2
	(1.6)	(.8)		(1.2)	(.6)		(.7)	(.5)			(0.7)	(.08)	(.80)
West Germany	.71	−.36		−.50	2.11	−2.89	.41	−.32		.98	1.6	6.4	.7
	(2.1)	(.8)		(.5)	(1.9)	(2.3)	(1.2)	(1.1)				$(.01)^{*c}$	(.50)
	1.43	−1.03	.21	−2.81	6.17		.82	−1.01	.44	.99	2.4	7.2	1.1
	(3.3)	(1.5)	(.4)	(2.0)	(3.4)		(1.7)	(1.3)	(1.0)			(.00)*	(.30)
Austria	.91	.25		−.39	−.05		−.14	.56		.98	1.8	.9	3.6
	(3.0)	(.9)		(.8)	(.1)		(.6)	(2.6)				(.42)	(.52)
Netherlands	.44	.08		.16	−.62		−.21	.30		.93	1.9	1.9	2.8
	(1.6)	(.3)		(.4)	(1.5)		(1.2)	(2.0)				(.18)	(.09)
Denmark	.74	.05		−.45	.12		.17	.11		.86	2.1	.6	1.8
	(2.7)	(.2)		(.7)	(.2)		(.5)	(.3)				(.55)	(.19)
Belgium	.49	.35		−.93	.17		−.21	.29		.94	2.4	4.4	1.6
	(1.8)	(1.3)		(1.6)	(.3)		(1.3)	(1.7)				(.03)*	(.23)
France	1.03	−.41		−.80	.84		.38	−.44		.85	2.4	.08	1.2
	(4.6)	(1.9)		(1.2)	(1.1)		(1.1)	(1.5)				(.47)	(.34)
Italy	1.05	−.30		−.43	.30		−.16	.15		.98	2.0	.2	.3
	(4.1)	(1.2)		(.7)	(.6)		(.7)	(.7)				(.74)	(.74)
Norway	.91	−.28		.21	−.41		−.17	.11		.89	2.4	1.2	1.0
	(3.4)	(1.1)		(.6)	(1.2)		(1.4)	(.9)				(.32)	(.38)
Sweden^b	1.10	−.36		.12	−.12		−.28	.23		.94	1.9	.0	.2
	(2.5)	(.8)		(.2)	(.2)		(.6)	(.6)				(.98)	(.78)

^{a} t-statistics in parentheses. ^{b} Sample period = 1974:2–1979:4.

^{c} Significance level for F-test under null hypothesis that the coefficients of relevant variable are zero. An asterisk indicates that the null hypothesis can be rejected within a 5% confidence interval.

Table 9.9 Responsiveness of P^y to Lagged P^y, E and FP^t (1974:2–1980:4)

	E_{t-1}	E_{t-2}	E_{t-3}	P^y_{t-1}	P^y_{t-2}	P^y_{t-3}	FP^t_{t-1}	FP^t_{t-2}	FP^t_{t-3}	R^2	D-W	$F(E)$	$F(FP^t)$
United States	−.70 (.7)[a]	.25 (2.0)		.73 (4.0)	−.70 (3.8)		−.10 (1.0)	.32 (2.5)		1.00	2.1	8.6 (.00)*	9.1 (.00)*
Canada	.09 (.6)	−.01 (.1)		1.45 (5.1)	−.57 (1.8)		.05 (.4)	−.03 (.2)		1.00	2.1	.8 (.48)	.1 (.91)
Japan	.03 (.6)	.01 (.2)		.66 (3.7)	−.22 (1.0)		.16 (2.1)	.04 (.6)		.97	1.8	1.4 (.27)	5.0 (.02)*
United Kingdom	−.11 (.8)	.04 (.3)		1.18 (5.3)	−.35 (1.6)		−.13 (1.0)	−.07 (.7)		1.00	2.2	.8 (.47)	.5 (.60)
West Germany	.05 (.9)	−.15 (1.9)		1.07 (5.2)	−.10 (.5)		.17 (2.7)	−.13 (.7)		1.00	1.9	2.1 (.15)	3.6 (.05)*
	.19 (2.2)	−.30 (2.3)	.12 (1.2)	.86 (3.1)	.52 (1.6)	−.61 (2.5)	.22 (2.4)	−.28 (1.8)	.10 (1.2)	.99	2.3	1.9 (.18)	2.1 (.15)
Austria	−.01 (.0)	.19 (1.1)		.79 (3.0)	−.30 (1.4)		.10 (.8)	.07 (.6)		.99	2.1	.7 (.51)	1.0 (.41)
Netherlands	.39 (1.9)	−.21 (1.1)		.85 (3.3)	−.12 (.4)		.20 (1.5)	−.09 (.8)		.99	1.9	1.8 (.20)	1.7 (.21)
Denmark	−.11 (1.3)	.41 (1.6)		.65 (3.2)	−.07 (.4)		−.25 (2.5)	.37 (3.7)		1.00	2.3	1.4 (.28)	8.7 (.00)*
Belgium	.03 (.3)	.09 (.9)		.81 (3.5)	−.02 (.1)		−.00 (.1)	.05 (.7)		1.00	2.4	1.7 (.21)	1.4 (.27)
France	.06 (.6)	−.02 (.2)		1.16 (4.6)	−.20 (.7)		.29 (2.1)	−.25 (2.2)		1.00	2.6	.2 (.79)	2.7 (.10)
Italy	.17 (2.1)	−.12 (1.5)		.99 (4.8)	−.49 (3.2)		.05 (.6)	.06 (.9)		1.00	1.8	2.2 (.14)	1.2 (.32)
Norway	−.10 (.8)	.20 (1.6)		1.12 (6.4)	−.36 (2.2)		−.06 (1.0)	.09 (1.5)		.99	2.3	1.5 (.25)	1.3 (.30)
Sweden[b]	.25 (1.4)	.12 (.6)		.32 (1.0)	−.21 (.9)		.44 (2.1)	−.12 (.8)		1.00	2.1	2.0 (.18)	2.3 (.14)

[a] t-statistics in parentheses.

[b] Sample period = 1974.2–1979.4.

Table 9.10   Responsiveness of FP^i to Lagged FP^i, E, and P^v (1974:2–1980:4)

	E_{t-1}	E_{t-2}	E_{t-3}	P^v_{t-1}	P^v_{t-2}	P^v_{t-3}	FP^i_{t-1}	FP^i_{t-2}	FP^i_{t-3}	R^2	D-W	$F(E)$	$F(P^v)$
United States	.43	.15		-2.17	.63		1.34	.12		.98	1.7	5.8	3.4
	(.9)	(.2)		(2.5)	(.7)		(2.7)	(.2)				(.01)*	(.06)
Canada	.06	-.07		.77	-.07		1.11	-.62		.98	2.9	.0	2.7
	(.2)	(.2)		(1.3)	(.1)		(4.0)	(2.0)				(.98)	(.10)
Japan	.42	-.34		.50	.02		.90	-.32		.99	2.2	5.6	.6
	(3.3)	(2.6)		(.9)	(.0)		(4.0)	(1.5)				(.01)*	(.55)
United Kingdom	.33	-.61		-1.24	.95		1.29	-.55		.99	1.7	5.5	3.5
	(1.0)	(2.3)		(2.3)	(1.8)		(4.2)	(2.2)				(.02)*	(.06)
West Germany	.74	-.32		-.24	-.81		1.32	-.55		.99	1.8	5.2	3.7
	(2.7)	(.9)		(.3)	(.9)		(4.8)	(2.3)				(.02)*	(.05)*
	.06	.54	-.45	1.30	-4.03	2.55	.79	.44	-.62	.99	2.3	1.3	5.0
	(.2)	(1.0)	(1.0)	(1.1)	(2.9)	(2.5)	(2.03)	(.7)	(1.7)			(.32)	(.02)*
Austria	-.29	.12		.83	-.60		.90	-.47		.99	2.2	.3	1.4
	(.8)	(.4)		(1.6)	(1.5)		(3.6)	(1.9)				(.71)	(.28)
Netherlands	.53	-.08		-.61	.37		1.53	-.63		.99	2.1	2.3	1.9
	(1.9)	(.3)		(1.8)	(.9)		(9.1)	(4.5)				(.13)	(.18)
Denmark	.22	-.24		.05	-.01		1.29	-.51		.99	2.1	.7	0
	(1.0)	(1.1)		(.1)	(.0)		(5.1)	(2.0)				(.53)	(.98)
Belgium	.39	-.17		.86	-.83		1.14	-.44		.99	2.2	.9	1.0
	(1.2)	(.5)		(1.2)	(1.4)		(5.8)	(2.2)				(.40)	(.38)
France	.30	-.27		.31	-.13		1.30	-.53		.99	2.3	1.5	.2
	(1.6)	(1.5)		(.6)	(.2)		(4.4)	(2.2)				(.26)	(.79)
Italy	.10	-.28		.47	-.70		.99	-.19		.96	2.1	.7	1.3
	(.4)	(1.1)		(.7)	(1.5)		(4.4)	(.8)				(.51)	(.31)
Norway	-.94	1.21		-.28	.23		.95	-.07		.98	2.4	3.5	.1
	(1.9)	(2.6)		(.4)	(.4)		(4.3)	(.3)				(.06)	(.90)
Sweden[b]	-.0	.08		-.38	.21		1.57	-.69		.98	2.0	.0	.2
	(.0)	(.2)		(.5)	(.3)		(3.4)	(2.0)				(.97)	(.86)

[a] t = statistics in parentheses.   [b] Sample period–1974:2–1979:4.

Table 9.9 presents the forecasting equation for P^y. Based on the F-test, the domestic price index is clearly responsive to past exchange rate movements only in the case of the United States with an insignificant first-period lag and a significantly positive second-period lag. Based on the estimated equation, the first-period lag (E_{t-1}) has a significantly positive sign in Germany and Italy. The second-period lag is significantly negative in Germany alone.

Past values of the foreign price index for the post-1973–74 oil price increase period are significant determinants of the domestic price index only in the United States, Japan, Germany, and Denmark. The first-period lag is significantly positive also in France and Sweden and surprisingly negative in the case of Denmark. The second-period lag is significantly negative in Germany and France and positive in Denmark and the United States. In general, it can be concluded that current values for P^y do not seem to be as affected by lagged values of E and FP^t as one would expect. This limited backward-looking linkage could be the outcome of domestic price stabilization policies during the 1970s.

Finally, table 9.10 presents the forecasting equation for the price of traded goods in units of foreign exchange. There are two reasons why one could expect past exchange rate and domestic price movements to affect the foreign currency price of traded goods: the possession of market power and a dominant position in international trade. Thus it is not surprising that in the case of the leading countries—the United States, Japan, England, and Germany—lagged values of exchange rates if not domestic prices are important determinants of the foreign price index. This kind of international linkage can work in many directions. An effective nominal devaluation of the dollar, for example, would raise United States domestic prices of home and exported goods (cf. table 9.9). Inflation in the United States will be transmitted to its trading partners and induce an increase in their domestic price despite the initial nominal appreciation of their currency. Eventually it could raise the United States' effective foreign price of traded goods (FP^t). On the other hand, possession of market power on the export and import markets could lower the foreign price of traded goods, at least in the short run.

Finally, an increase in the domestic price of any of the leading countries might induce other nations to establish restrictive policies in an attempt to insulate their economies from the negative transmission effects. The results in table 9.10 are difficult to interpret further without reference to other macroeconomic variables. However, they support the view that there exist sufficiently important negative transmission links between the most developed of the industrialized countries and the rest of the world to require a more careful analysis.

The major findings so far are quite supportive of established theories. *(a)* In most cases (with the possible exception of the United States and

Belgium), the exchange rate can be considered a predetermined variable in domestic price determination. *(b)* Prices of nontraded relative to traded goods are affected by lagged values of exchange rates only in the cases of Japan among "large" countries and Belgium and Norway among "small" countries. In the other large countries, news seems to affect exchange rates and prices in similar patterns even though there are cross-country differences in the speed of adjustment to innovations. *(c)* Again in the case of "large" countries (United States, Japan, United Kingdom, and Germany), the foreign price of traded goods cannot be considered exogenous as it is affected by past exchange rates and domestic prices. *(d)* The domestic price index, P^v, does not seem to depend on lagged exchange rates and/or foreign prices in almost all countries, probably due to stabilization policies.

The correlations of residuals among all pairs in the autoregressive system are presented in table 9.11. For all countries, an innovation in the exchange rate, the predominantly exogenous variable, is associated with a negative innovation in the foreign price index. Once again for the large countries (United States, United Kingdom, and Germany) the correlation coefficient is highly significant (greater than $-.70$). This high negative ρ in the countries with open and developed financial markets would be consistent with a rational expectations asset market view of exchange rate determination where an unexpected increase in foreign prices induces expectations of a

Table 9.11   **Correlation of Residuals in Vector Autoregression System of Exchange Rates, Value Added Deflator and Foreign Price of Traded Goods (1974:2–1980:4)**

Countries	$\rho(\hat{V}_E, \hat{V}_{Pv})$	$\rho(\hat{V}_E, \hat{V}_{FPt})$	$\rho(\hat{V}_{Pv}, \hat{V}_{FPt})$
United States	$-.52$	$-.91$	.55
Canada	$-.04$	$-.58$	.53
Japan	$-.36$	$-.73$	.39
United Kingdom	$-.33$	$-.87$	.47
West Germany	.47	$-.83$	$-.28$
	$.23^a$	$-.75$	.07
Austria	.15	$-.59$	.28
Netherlands	$-.20$	$-.39$	.51
Denmark	$-.54$	$-.56$	.22
Belgium	.44	$-.25$	.17
France	$-.52$	$-.88$	.62
Italy	.13	$-.36$	.34
Norway	$-.49$	$-.45$	.25
Sweden	$-.16$	$-.79$	.40

[a]Correlation of residuals in system of equations estimated with three lags on each independent variable.

current account surplus and thus an immediate appreciation of the exchange rate. In the case of the other countries, the negative correlation probably reflects intervention by authorities in the exchange market.

The correlation coefficient between innovations in the domestic and foreign price indices is positive, as expected, but relatively low. Given all the empirical findings so far, and the low overall variability of the P^v index, it should be concluded that during the 1970s stabilization policies focused on domestic inflation. This finding is also consistent with the mixed evidence on the correlation coefficient between the exchange rate and domestic price residuals. It is positive only in the cases of Germany, Austria, Belgium, and Italy, and negative for all other countries. The results for Belgium and Italy once again give some empirical support to the vicious circle theorizing in connection with these two countries (Basevi and de Grauwe 1977) and sharply contrasts their experience with that of the Scandinavian small and open economies.

In general, it can be concluded that innovations in the two price indices move generally together with causality running from foreign to domestic prices in the smaller countries and usually in both directions in the larger countries. Innovations in exchange rates and foreign prices are negatively correlated. In the case of small countries with managed nominal exchange rates, the negative correlation would be consistent with contemporaneous intervention in the exchange market as a result of innovations in the foreign price level. In the large countries, where both the nominal exchange rate and foreign price level are market determined, the high negative correlation would be consistent with opposite impact responses of the two indices to the same set of news or responses to different sets of news which are negatively correlated. Finally, the evidence on the correlation in innovations between the exchange rate and the domestic price vector is mixed, with positive correlations in the most open economies (Germany, Austria, Belgium, and Italy) and negative correlations elsewhere, probably because of stabilization policies.

These results are only indicative of the complicated nature of the adjustment process and differences across countries which can have their origin in the nature of the unexpected shock, the structural responses to the disturbance, or the policy reaction of the authorities. What is striking is that some systematic patterns emerge.

It could be said that the process of adjustment in the smaller European countries is perhaps the most varied and complicated despite the "smallness" of the economy. As an example of differences in behavior, figures 9.8 and 9.9 plot the response of the value-added deflator to unexpected shocks in foreign prices and the exchange rate for three small European countries which follow the deutsche mark closely: Belgium, the Netherlands, and Norway. Here again, substantial differences emerge in the dynamic path of adjustment of the domestic price index. Differences occur,

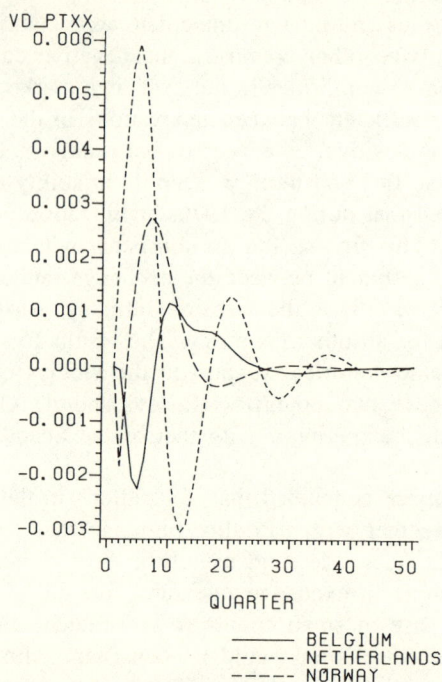

Fig. 9.8   Response of value added deflator to shock in foreign prices of
traded goods.

not only in the magnitude of oscillations, the oscillatory path itself, and the
speed of convergence, but also in the direction of the short-run impulse
response to disturbances.

The response of domestic prices to unexpected shocks in foreign prices
for the three countries is presented in figure 9.8. Adjustment is quite varied
with an initial decrease in P^v in Belgium and Norway and a sharp increase
in the Netherlands, and subsequent oscillations which are damped relatively
quickly in the first two countries (in less than 30 quarters) but more slowly
in the case of the Netherlands. Figure 9.9 demonstrates the cross-country
differences in the response of P^v to innovations in E. The Norwegian response, where the value-added deflator decreases following an unexpected
depreciation, could have its origin in the importance of intermediate goods
(Katseli 1980) or in the role of policy. Any hypothesis, however, would be
only that unless one possesses knowledge of the specific institutional and
economic characteristics of the country.

The negative response of domestic prices following an unexpected nominal depreciation induces a larger depreciation of the real exchange rate rel-

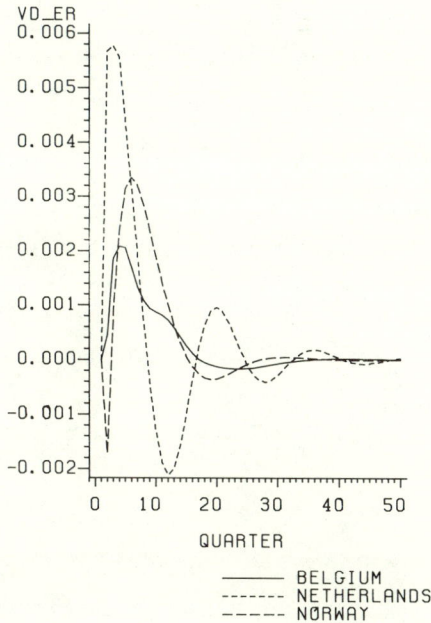

Fig. 9.9   Response of value added deflator to shock in exchange rate

ative to the nominal exchange rate. Interestingly enough, the same pattern is observed in Denmark and Austria. This pattern of response to innovations in exchange rates is quite different in the case of the other small European countries, as can be seen in table 9.12. The induced movement in domestic prices following an unexpected depreciation probably makes real exchange rate adjustment easier in the Scandinavian countries and Austria than in the other small countries of Europe. Given that current account adjustment is dependent on movements in the real rather than the nominal exchange rate, this tentative conclusion suggests that the attainment of external balance requires a greater nominal devaluation in the case of the smaller countries of central Europe than in the case of their northern neighbors.

9.6 Conclusions

The objective of this paper was to study the movements of real exchange rates in the 1970s and to explore some of the inherent complications in the process of real exchange rate determination. Real factors such as technological change, decreasing money illusion, and changes in intertemporal preferences were shown to affect the equilibrium terms of trade and the relative

Table 9.12 **Impulse Reaction Functions: Responses of P^y to One Standard Deviation Shock in E (20 quarters)**

Quarter	Denmark	Sweden[b]	Norway	Austria	Netherlands	Belgium	Italy
				Country			
1	.0	.0	.0	.0	.0	.0	.0
2	-.20 D-02[a]	.59 D-02	-.17 D-02	-.13 D-03	.56 D-02	.45 D-03	.53 D-02
3	-.13	.11 D-01	.84 D-03	.21 D-02	.57	.19 D-02	.71
4	.43 D-03	.11	.24 D-02	.31	.56	.21	.45
5	.17 D-02	.66 D-02	.31	.39	.43	.21	.33 D-04
6	.23	.33 D-02	.33	.44	.32	.17	-.35 D-02
7	.23	.17	.32	.46	.19	.13	-.51
8	.20	.11	.28	.46	.70 D-03	.11	-.51
9	.14	.76 D-03	.24	.44	-.40	.94 D-03	-.43
10	.70 D-03	.43	.19	.41	-.13 D-02	.88	-.34
11	.94 D-04	.12	.14	.38	-.19	.82	-.26
12	-.38 D-03	-.11	.10	.35	-.21	.73	-.20
13	-.70	-.24	.64 D-03	.33	-.20	.58	-.15
14	-.85	-.29	.32	.32	-.16	.42	-.10
15	-.86	-.28	.62 D-04	.30	-.10	.26	-.60 D-03
16	-.77	-.23	-.13 D-03	.29	-.38 D-03	.12	-.27
17	-.62	-.15	-.26	.28	.19	.16 D-04	-.32 D-04
18	-.44	-.71 D-04	-.33	.26	.62	-.52	.13 D-03
19	-.25	-.11 D-05	-.36	.25	.88	-.95	.21
20	-.96 D-04	.47 D-04	-.35	.24	.95	-.12 D-03	.25

[a]Divided by 100; D-02 applies to all numbers below it. Same for D-01, D-03, D-04.
[b]Sample period of estimation 1974:2–1979:4.

price of traded to nontraded goods differently. Given the latter definition of the real exchange rate, deviations around trend were shown to be quite varied across countries. So were the economic processes that dictated them. Three rough country groupings emerged: the large industrialized countries (with the possible exception of Japan), the Scandinavian countries, and the smaller European countries.

In the major industrialized countries, exchange rates can be considered predetermined with respect to relative prices. Past movements of nominal exchange rates, however, influence foreign prices in a way that is consistent with these countries' possession of market power. There is a strong positive correlation among residuals of nominal exchange rates and relative prices. This would be consistent with economic theorizing where unexpected increases in the money supply or other news cause a depreciation of the nominal exchange rate and an increase in the price of nontraded goods relative to the foreign currency price of traded goods. However, the strong positive correlation between innovations in E and P^v/FP^t cannot be accounted for by a strong positive correlation between innovations in E and P^v. The evidence is rather mixed (table 9.11), but it seems to suggest that this correlation is the outcome of strong negative correlations between innovations in E and FP^t, negative correlations between innovations in E and P^v, and strong positive correlations between innovations in P^v and FP^t. This suggests that one should look more closely at patterns of interdependence among major industrialized countries.

The evidence also suggests that a nondiscriminatory application of the "small country" model to European experiences will be problematic unless one understands internal targets of policy and differences in structural characteristics.

In all small countries, with the exception of Belgium, the nominal exchange rate does not seem to be affected by lagged values of domestic or foreign prices. The foreign price level of traded goods can be considered similarly predetermined. The domestic value-added deflator, however, is strongly influenced by lagged values of foreign prices (tables 9.8–9.10).

Differences across countries come with respect to their adjustment to innovations. "News" that affects nominal exchange rates and domestic prices are positively correlated in Austria, Belgium, and Italy and negatively correlated in the Netherlands and the Scandinavian countries. There is similarly a strong negative correlation of the E and FP^t residuals in the Scandinavian countries as opposed to the other smaller European countries. This could be the outcome of more independent nominal exchange rate policies in the northern countries as opposed to the countries in the European Monetary System. There are also substantial differences in the path of adjustment as a response to innovations. The fundamental economic processes behind these systematic differences are not well understood. They merit closer attention and more careful analysis.

Appendix 1

In each country each sector uses a fixed stock of capital $\overline{K}_i$ and labor N_i which is free to move between sectors. The overall stock of labor is given and there is full employment. In each sector profit maximizing behavior would imply that the nominal wage is equated to the value of the own marginal product of labor. Thus, taking the nontraded goods sector as an example, and using again the exportable as a numeraire,

(A1) $\qquad W = P_h \cdot f(\overline{K}_h, N_h); f_N < 0, f_K > 0,$

where W = the real wage in terms of the exportable commodity. The supply of labor is assumed to depend on the expected real wage (W/P^e), where the expected price level is itself a function of the consumer price index, and a shift parameter A. Thus,

(A2) $\qquad W = P^e \cdot g(\overline{N}, A); g_N > 0; g_A > 0,$

where

(A3) $\qquad P^e = h(P); 1 \geq h' \geq 0$

and

(A4) $\qquad P = \alpha_1 P_h + \alpha_2 + \alpha_3 P_m.$

Substituting (3′) and (4′) in (2′) and equating the demand and supply of labor in each sector, it follows that

(A5) $\qquad W = P_h \cdot f(\overline{K}_h, N_h) = h(\alpha_1 P_h + \alpha_2 + \alpha_3 P_m)$
$\qquad\qquad \cdot g(\overline{N}, A).$

Assuming that all initial prices and hence $g(\overline{N}, A)$, $h(P)$, and $f(\overline{K}_h, N_h)$ are set equal to unity, equation (A5) can be differentiated totally and solved for dN_h. Then,

(A6) $\qquad f_N dN_h = (h'\alpha_1 - 1)dP_h + h'\alpha_3 dP_m + g_A dA - f_K dK_h.$

From (A6) it follows that employment, and hence output in the nontraded good sector, is a positive function of P_h and K_h and a negative function of A and P_m. These are the assumed signs of the partial derivatives in the supply functions of the model. This is the most general specification of the labor markets that allows explicit consideration of different types of wage rigidities or degrees of money illusion.

Appendix 2

Local stability of a three-by-three system requires that the trace is negative and the determinant is negative. In the present case, sign ambiguities arise in elements a_{32}, a_{13}, and a_{33}, which are defined below. If a_{13} is positive and a_{32} and a_{33} are negative, then stability is guaranteed. This is equivalent to assuming that the cross elasticities of supply, E_{mh}^*, E_{hm}, and E_{xm}, are sufficiently low. In other words, the determinant of the system can be described as follows:

$$|D| = \begin{bmatrix} a_{11} & 0 & a_{13} \\ 0 & a_{22} & a_{23} \\ a_{31} & a_{32} & a_{33} \end{bmatrix},$$

where

$$a_{11} = -(B_h - 1) - (1 + E_{hh})[1 - m_h(1 - s)]$$
$$- (1 - s)m_h \frac{X_s}{P_h H_d} E_{xh} < 0$$

$$a_{21} = 0$$

$$a_{31} = -E_{xh}X_s[1 - m_x \frac{1}{P_x}(1 - s)] - B_{xh}X_d - m_x \frac{1}{P_x}P_h H_s(1 + E_{hh}) < 0$$

$$a_{22} = -(B_h^* - 1) - (1 + E_{hh}^*)[1 - m_h^*(1 - s^*)]$$
$$- m_h^*(1 - s^*)\frac{P_m M_s^*}{P_h H_d^*} E_{mh}^* < 0$$

$$a_{32} = -B_{xh}^* X_d^* - m_h^* \frac{1}{P_x}(1 - s^*)[P_h^* H_s^*(1 + E_{hh}^*) - P_m M_s^* E_{mh}^*]?$$

$$a_{13} = E_{hm} + B_{hm} - m_h(1 - s)\left[E_{hm} + \frac{X_s}{P_h H_d}E_{xm}\right]?$$

$$a_{23} = E_{hm}^*[1 - m_h^*(1 - s^*)] + B_{hm}^* + m_h^*(1 - s^*)\frac{P_m M_s^*}{P_h^* H_d^*}(1 + E_{mm}) > 0$$

$$a_{33} = -E_{xm}X_s - B_{xm}X_d - B_{xm}^* X_d^* + m_x \frac{1}{P_x}(1 - s)(P_h H_s E_{hm} + X_s E_{xm})$$
$$+ m_x^* \frac{1}{xP_x}(1 - s^*)[P_h^* H_s^* E_{hm}^* - P_m M_s^*(1 + E_{mm}^*)]?$$

The elasticities used in the solutions, all converted to be positive numbers, are defined below:

B_h = own-price elasticity of demand for home goods;
B_{ij} = cross-price elasticities of demand where i is the relevant sector and j the relevant price vector;

E_{ii} = own-price elasticity of supply;
E_{ij} = cross-price elasticities of supply;
m_i = marginal propensity to consume goods of sector i.

Appendix 3

Two sets of solutions are presented below. Holding M constant, P_h and P_m can be expressed as functions of all the exogenous variables. The first term in parenthesis is the numerator, and its sign is given above it. Elements from the determinant matrix are presented as elements a_{ij} and their sign is specified in Appendix 2. The determinant, D, is assumed to be negative as required for stability. A complete listing of the elasticity terms is presented in Appendix 2.

$$\hat{P}_h = \left\{ \overset{+}{[1 - m_h(1 - s)]E_{h,K_h}(a_{22}a_{33} - a_{32}a_{23})} \right.$$
$$\left. + m_x \frac{1}{P_x}(1 - s)P_h H_s E_{h,K_h}(-a_{22}a_{13}) \right\} D^{-1}\hat{K}_h < 0$$

$$\overset{?}{=} \left\{ -[1 - m_h^*(1 - s^*)]E_{h,K_h}^*(-a_{32}a_{13}) \right.$$
$$\left. + m_x^* \frac{1}{P_x}(1 - s^*)P_h^* H_s^* E_{h,K_h}^*(-a_{22}a_{13}) \right\} D^{-1}\hat{K}_h^*$$

$$\overset{-}{=} \left\{ -\frac{X_s}{P_h H_d}m_h(1 - s)E_{x,K_x}(a_{22}a_{33} - a_{32}a_{23}) \right.$$
$$\left. - E_{x,K_x}X_s\left[1 - m_x\frac{1}{P_x}(1 - s)\right](-a_{22}a_{13}) \right\} D^{-1}\hat{K}_x > 0$$

$$\overset{+}{=} \left\{ -\frac{P_m M_s^*}{P_h^* H_d^*}m_h^*(1 - s^*)E_{m,K_m}^*(-a_{32}a_{13}) \right.$$
$$\left. + m_x^* \frac{1}{P_x}(1 - s^*)P_m M_s^* E_{m,K_m}^*(-a_{22}a_{13}) \right\} D^{-1}\hat{K}_m^* < 0$$

?

$$= \left(\left\{ -[1 - m_h(1 - s)]E_{h,A} + m_h\frac{(1 - s)}{P_h H_d}X^s E_{x,A} \right\}(a_{22}a_{33} - a_{32}a_{23}) \right.$$

$$+ \left\{ E_{x,A}X_s\left[1 - m_x\frac{1}{P_x}(1 - s) \right] \right.$$

$$\left. \left. - P_h H_s E_{h,A}m_x\frac{1}{P_x}(1 - s) \right\} \cdot (-a_{22}a_{13}) \right)D^{-1}\hat{A}$$

?

$$= \left(\left\{ [1 - m_h^*(1 - s^*)]E_{h,A}^* - m_h^*(1 - s^*)\frac{P_m M_s^*}{P_h^* H_d^*}E_{m,A}^* \right\}(-a_{32}a_{13}) \right.$$

$$- m_x^*\frac{1}{P_x}(1 - s^*)(P_h^* H_s^* E_{h,A}^* + P_m M_s^* E_{m,A}^*)$$

$$\left. (-a_{22}a_{13}) \right)D^{-1}\hat{A}*$$

?

$$= \left[m_h\frac{Y}{P_h H_d}(a_{22}a_{33} - a_{32}a_{23}) - m_x\frac{Y}{P_x}(-a_{22}a_{13}) \right]D^{-1}ds$$

$$-$$

$$= \left[-m_h^*\frac{Y*}{P_h^* H_d^*}(-a_{32}a_{13}) - m_x^*\frac{Y*}{P_x}(-a_{22}a_{13}) \right]D^{-1}ds* > 0$$

$$= \left[-m_h\frac{1}{P_h H_d}\lambda M(a_{22}a_{33} - a_{32}a_{23}) - m_h^*\frac{1}{P_h^* H_d^*}\lambda M*(-a_{32}a_{13}) \right.$$

$$+ \left(m_x\frac{1}{P_x}\lambda M - m_x^*\frac{1}{P_x}\lambda*M* \right)$$

$$\left. (-a_{22}a_{13}) \right]D^{-1}\hat{M}.$$

?

$$\hat{P}_m = \left\{ [1 - m_h(1 - s)]E_{h,K_h}(-a_{31}a_{22}) + \right.$$

$$\left. m_x\frac{1}{P_x}(1 - s)P_h H_s E_{h,K_h}(a_{11}a_{22}) \right\}D^{-1}\hat{K}_h$$

$$= \left\{ -[1 - m_h^*(1 - s^*)]E_{h,K_h}^*(a_{11}a_{32}) \right.$$

$$\left. + m_x^* \frac{1}{P_x}(1 - s^*)P_h^*H_s^*E_{h,K_h}^*(a_{11}a_{22}) \right\}D^{-1}\hat{K}_h^*$$

$$?$$

$$= \left\{ -\frac{X_s}{P_hH_d}m_h(1 - s)E_{x,K_x}(-a_{31}a_{22}) - \right.$$

$$\left. E_{x,K_x}X_s\left[1 - m_x\frac{1}{P_x}(1 - s) \right](a_{11}a_{22}) \right\}D^{-1}\hat{K}_x$$

$$+$$

$$= \left[\frac{P_mM_s^*}{P_h^*H_d^*}m_h^*(1 - s^*)E_{m,K_m}^*(a_{11}a_{32}) + \right.$$

$$\left. m_x^*\frac{1}{P_x}(1 - s^*)P_mM_s^*E_{m,K_m}^*(a_{11}a_{22}) \right]D^{-1}\hat{K}_m^* < 0$$

$$?$$

$$= \left(\left\{ -[1 - m_h(1 - s)]E_{h,A} + m_h\frac{(1 - s)}{P_hH_d}X^sE_{x,A} \right\}(-a_{31}a_{22}) \right.$$

$$+ \left[E_{x,A}X_s\left(1 - m_x\frac{1}{P_x}(1 - s) \right) \right]$$

$$\left. - m_x\frac{1}{P_x}(1 - s)P_hH_sE_{h,A}(a_{11}a_{22}) \right)D^{-1}\hat{A}$$

$$?$$

$$= \left\{ [1 - m_h^*(1 - s^*)]E_{h,A}^* - m_h^*(1 - s^*)\frac{P_mM_s^*}{P_h^*H_d^*}E_{m,A}^* \right\}\left[(a_{11}a_{32}) \right.$$

$$\left. - m_x^*\frac{1}{P_x}(1 - s^*)(P_h^*H_s^*E_{h,A}^* + P_mM_s^*E_{m,A}^*)(a_{11}a_{22}) \right]D^{-1}\hat{A}^*$$

$$-$$

$$= \left[m_h\frac{Y}{P_hH_d}(-a_{31}a_{22}) - m_x\frac{Y}{P_x}(a_{11}a_{22}) \right]D^{-1}ds > 0$$

$$-$$

$$= \left[-m_h^*\frac{Y^*}{P_h^*H_d^*}(a_{11}a_{32}) - m_x^*\frac{Y^*}{P_x}(a_{11}a_{22}) \right]D^{-1}ds^* > 0$$

$$= \left[-m_h \frac{1}{P_h H_d} \lambda M (-a_{31} a_{22}) - m_h^* \frac{1}{P_h^* H_d^*} \lambda M^* (a_{11} a_{32}) \right.$$

$$\left. + \left(m_x \frac{1}{P_x} \lambda M - m_x^* \frac{1}{P_x} \lambda^* M^* \right) (a_{11} a_{22}) \right] D^{-1} \hat{M}$$

Appendix 4

Total differentiation of equation (11) yields the following expression:

$$(1'') \qquad \gamma_1 \hat{P}_h + \gamma_2 \hat{P}_m - \gamma_3 \hat{M} = \delta_1 \hat{K}_x + \delta_2 \hat{K}_h + \delta_3 \hat{A} + \delta_4 ds,$$

where

$$\gamma_1 = -E_{xh} X_s - B_{xh} X_d - B_{mh} P_m M_d$$

$$- (m_x + m_m)(1 - s)[P_h H_s (1 + E_{hh}) - X_s E_{xh}], \quad <0;$$

$$\gamma_2 = -E_{xm} X_s - B_{xm} X_d - P_m M_d (1 - B_{mm})$$

$$+ (m_x + m_m)(1 - s)(P_h H_s E_{hm} + X_s E_{xm})?$$

$$\gamma_3 = -(m_x + m_m)\lambda M, \quad <0$$

$$\delta_1 = -E_{x,K_x} X_s [1 - (m_x + m_m) X_s (1 - s)], \quad <0$$

$$\delta_2 = (m_x + m_m)(1 - s) P_h H_s E_{h,K_h}, \quad >0$$

$$\delta_3 = E_{x,A} X_s - (m_x + m_m)(1 - \lambda k)(P_h H_s E_{h,A} + X_s E_{x,A}), \quad ?$$

$$\delta_4 = -(m_x + m_m)Y, \quad <0.$$

Substituting the flow equilibrium solutions for $\hat{P}_h$ and $\hat{P}_m$ with respect to each of the disturbances (see App. 3), equation $(1'')$ can be solved for $\hat{M}$ as a function of each of the exogenous variables. The effects on the relative prices can then be inferred from the $\hat{P}_h/\hat{M}$ and $\hat{P}_m/\hat{M}$ flow equilibrium solutions. Given the ambiguity of γ_2 and the noted ambiguities in Appendix 3, the relative movements of the two prices are hard to ascertain.

Comment   Willem H. Buiter

Introduction

I found this an interesting paper. The first half, containing the theoretical analysis, develops a specification of the real side of an open economy that should become part of the "standard" open macroeconomic model. The empirical second half contains some interesting data description and analysis.

In this paper, as in her earlier work, Louka Katseli emphasizes the importance of differences in economic structure for the way in which external and internal shocks are transmitted through the economy. This attention to the details of economic structure, on both the demand side and the supply side, can also be found in the work of Bruno and Sachs.

Following the paradigm developed by Koopmans and Montias (1971), outcomes are the result of the interaction of the external environment, economic structure and economic policies. Macroeconomists have had quite a bit to say about policy and the external environment while paying scant attention to economic structure. Homogeneous output and inputs and a minimal role for relative prices were the norm until recently. The oil shocks of the seventies have ended this complacency. Those who, like Louka Katseli, combine knowledge of the industrialized capitalist world with an understanding of the semi-industrialized world have been well ahead of the rest of us in appreciating the importance of differences in economic structure.

This does not mean that I agree with all or even most of what is said in the paper. But my comments, even if occasionally critical, should always be footnoted with my appreciation for the general thrust of this research. I certainly learned something by studying this paper.

One general criticism I have is that the paper really is two papers. The theoretical model of the first half does not contribute significantly to our understanding of the empirical analysis contained in the second half. I therefore shall discuss the two parts separately.

The Theoretical Model

The theoretical model is a two-country, four-good model. Each country produces a (possibly distinct) nontraded good and specializes in the production of a single distinct exportable. Both the terms of trade and the relative price of traded and nontraded goods are endogenous. I consider this to be a useful production structure for the analysis of contemporary macroeconomic adjustment problems. For a number of important policy issues, (imported) intermediate inputs will of course have to be incorporated in the model.

The model analyzes a short-run flow equilibrium with static expectations and a stationary, long-run stock equilibrium. If the role of intertemporal prices were brought out explicitly, and if forward-looking, rational expectations were included, the current momentary equilibrium could of course no longer be determined with reference only to current conditions. To be integrated successfully into the open-economy macroeconomics tradition, the roles of intertemporal allocation and of model-consistent expectations formation should be further developed.

As it stands, the model is entirely "real"; it belongs to the pure theory of international trade. Only relative prices are determined. M is identified with "money" but in fact stands for home country nonhuman wealth in terms of the home country's exportable. This misleading identification with money has led to the omission of interest-bearing internationally traded assets and to the loss of the distinction between the trade balance and the current account. Another problem is that while the saving function $S = \lambda(kY - M)$ clearly identifies M with (nonhuman) private wealth, there are other assets in the model: the sector-specific capital stocks. Even if physical capital goods are neither internationally tradable nor shiftable between sectors within a country, the financial ownership claims on these physical capital goods certainly are part of private wealth. In a model with an explicit intertemporal dimension their market values would be endogenous. Along the lines of Tobin's q, sectoral capital formation could then be endogenized.

The current model does not have any international mobility of financial capital in a stock-shift sense. In the absence of public sector deficits and domestic credit creation, the given world stock of M is redistributed between countries through the "flow" trade balance deficit or surplus. Of course, this is a long way removed from the asset market approach to exchange rate determination. In a suitably modified form, however, it may provide a theory of the long-run determinants of the real exchange rate—one of the anchors that helps pin down the behavior of the short- and medium-term adjustment processes that have been the traditional concern of open macroeconomics.

A rather minor comment is that the ambiguities in the comparative statics are probably even worse than reported. Two of the unambiguous results were, first, that an increase in the capital stock used by the home country's nontraded good sector lowers the relative price of the nontraded good and, second, that an expansion of the capital stock in the home country's traded good sector raises the relative price of the nontraded goods. Both these results can be reversed once it is recognized that such additions to the sector-specific capital stocks represent increases in wealth that will affect demand directly.

Finally on the theoretical side, since the model is entirely real, it should be feasible to root it more firmly in optimizing behavior. This would also be the most satisfactory way of introducing expectations explicitly. Analytically, the simplest way to proceed would be to model an infinite-lived consumer (see, e.g., Obstfeld 1981b). In view of the rather tenuous empirical status of that hypothesis, an overlapping generations approach may be preferred (see, e.g., Buiter 1981a).[1]

---

1. For a discussion of some of the problems involved in modeling infinite-lived agents, see Matt. 19:16–30.

The Empirical Analysis

As someone interested in the "real exchange rate overshooting" (Dornbusch 1976) phenomenon, I was struck by the dissimilarities in the behavior of the various different real exchange rate and competitiveness indices. Clearly, empirical work aimed at testing the Dornbusch proposition will have to proceed very carefully in selecting an empirical counterpart to the theoretical construct of "competitiveness."

The rest of my comments, on Katseli's empirical work, amount to quite general reflections on modern time series analysis, that is, the vector autoregressions, impulse response functions, and Granger-causality tests that are the bread and butter of so much recent macroeconometric work, including this paper.

Diagnostic Tests of Residuals from Vector Autoregression

Valid use of vector autoregressive models requires that the estimated residuals be not too different from white noise. Even when no lagged dependent variables are present in time series models, the standard Durbin-Watson statistic is strictly only a test against a first-order autoregressive process in the disturbances of a single equation, although its usefulness as a general test of misspecification in linear regression models has been argued by some (e.g., Harvey 1981). It is not an appropriate test for first-order autocorrelation even in univariate autoregressions, because the presence of a lagged dependent variable biases the Durbin-Watson statistic toward 2. Furthermore, in the paper, the Durbin-Watson test is applied equation by equation, and does not therefore provide a test against noncontemporaneous correlations between the disturbances in different equations. What is required is a test that considers the entire autocorrelation and cross-correlation function of the estimated residuals. For a univariate autoregression, the Box-Pierce Q-statistic provides a useful diagnostic, as do tests based on the Lagrange multiplier principle or indeed simple visual inspection of the autocorrelation function. For multivariate autoregressions, the Lagrange multiplier principle may be used to derive an asymptotically valid test for serial correlation when the system of equations is estimated under the null hypothesis that the disturbances are white noise. In principle the alternative hypothesis could be that the disturbances follow any higher-order AR or MA process. Without asking for the moon, it is clearly desirable that the single-equation Durbin-Watson tests be supplemented by more appropriate diagnostics.

Innovation Accounting and Impulse Response Functions

The impulse response function or transfer function analysis performed in the paper and advocated, for example, by Sims (1980a, 1980b) is often less informative than it seems. The estimation of an unrestricted vector-auto-regressive process will ideally yield a representation of the data-generating process as in (1).[2]

(1) $A(L) x(t) = \epsilon_t$

x_t is an n-vector, $A(L)$ is a matrix polynomical in the lag operator L with $A(0) = I$ and ϵ_t is an n-vector of random disturbances with $\epsilon_t \sim NID(0, \Omega)$. The variance-covariance matrix of the disturbances Ω will not in general be diagonal: the disturbances will tend to be contemporaneously correlated. To be able to answer the question, ''What is the dynamic response of the system to a unit impulse in the ith equation?'' Sims proposes to transform the residuals ϵ_t in such a way that the transformed residuals have a diagonal variance covariance matrix. To see what this means, consider the moving average representation of (1) given by

(2) $x_t = [A(L)]^{-1}\epsilon_t = B(L)\epsilon_t = \displaystyle\sum_{i=0}^{\infty} B_i\epsilon_{t-i}, B_0 = I.$

Sims (1980*b*) proceeds by premultiplying ϵ_t by a lower-triangular matrix D which has ones along its main diagonal and which transforms ϵ_t into a vector of contemporaneously independent disturbances. That is, let

(3a) $C_i = B_i D^{-1},$

(3b) $r_t = D\epsilon_t,$

and

(4b) $E[r_t r_t'] = [\sigma_{r_i r_j}]; \sigma_{r_i r_j} = 0, i \neq j.$

This permits us to write (2) as

(2') $x_t = C(L)r_t = \displaystyle\sum_{i=0}^{\infty} C_i r_{t-i}.$

With this representation of the disturbances, we can identify clearly the jth element of r_t, r_{jt}, as the innovation specific to the jth equation. We now can perturb just the jth equation in period t with a unit impulse. While in period t this affects only the jth element of x, in subsequent periods the effects of r_{jt} will spread through the entire system, propagated by the C_i matrices. In the bivariate examples considered in Louka Katseli's paper,

$$\epsilon_t = \begin{bmatrix} \epsilon_{1t} \\ \epsilon_{2t} \end{bmatrix}, D = \begin{bmatrix} 1 & 0 \\ d_{21} & 1 \end{bmatrix},$$

2. For empirical purposes the order of the autoregression will generally have to be finite. All processes are assumed to be covariance stationary.

and

$$r_t = D\epsilon_t = \begin{bmatrix} \epsilon_{1t} \\ d_{21}\epsilon_{1t} + \epsilon_{2t} \end{bmatrix}.$$

The contemporaneous variance-covariance matrix of r_t is

$$E[r_t r_t'] = \begin{bmatrix} \sigma_{\epsilon_1}^2 & d_{21}\sigma_{\epsilon_1}^2 + \sigma_{\epsilon_1 \epsilon_2} \\ d_{21}\sigma_{\epsilon_1}^2 + \sigma_{\epsilon_1 \epsilon_2} & d_{21}^2\sigma_{\epsilon_1}^2 + \sigma_{\epsilon_2}^2 + 2d_{21}\sigma_{\epsilon_1 \epsilon_2} \end{bmatrix}.$$

This will be a diagonal matrix if and only if $d_{21} = -\sigma_{\epsilon_1 \epsilon_2}/\sigma_{\epsilon_1}^2$ in which case

$$D = \begin{bmatrix} 1 & 0 \\ -\dfrac{\sigma_{\epsilon_1 \epsilon_2}}{\sigma_{\epsilon_1}^2} & 1 \end{bmatrix}$$

and

$$E[r_t r_t'] = \begin{bmatrix} \sigma_{\epsilon_1}^2 & 0 \\ 0 & \sigma_{\epsilon_2}^2 - \dfrac{(\sigma_{\epsilon_1 \epsilon_2})^2}{\sigma_{\epsilon_1}^2} \end{bmatrix}.$$

The problem with this procedure is that there is no unique way of diagonalizing the variance-covariance matrix of the disturbances. In an n-variable system there are $n!$ linearly independent ways of orthogonalizing the disturbances. The impulse response function will be different for different orthogonalizations.

In the bivariate example, we could instead orthogonalize the disturbances by using the upper-triangular matrix $\overline{D} = \begin{bmatrix} 1 & d_{12} \\ 0 & 1 \end{bmatrix}$. In this case we require

$$d_{12} = -\frac{\sigma_{\epsilon_1 \epsilon_2}}{\sigma_{\epsilon_2}^2}, \text{ in which case}$$

$$\overline{D} = \begin{bmatrix} 1 & -\dfrac{\sigma_{\epsilon_1 \epsilon_2}}{\sigma_{\epsilon_2}^2} \\ 0 & 1 \end{bmatrix}$$

and

$$E[r_t r_t'] = \begin{bmatrix} \sigma_{\epsilon_1}^2 - \dfrac{(\sigma_{\epsilon_1 \epsilon_2})^2}{(\sigma_{\epsilon_2})^2} & 0 \\ 0 & \sigma_{\epsilon_2}^2 \end{bmatrix}.$$

The C_i matrices that propagate the unit impulses will, unless the disturbances are orthogonal to begin with ($\sigma_{\epsilon_1\epsilon_2} = 0$), differ under D and $\overline{D}$ transformations. Unless one performed the full range of orthogonalizations and established that the impulse response functions are similar for all of them, it is difficult to see what interest attaches to a particular orthogonalization.

Testing for Stability

Vector autoregressions are not immune to the Lucas critique. More generally, changes in the stochastic process generating the data may have occurred over the sample period. Stability tests such as the Chow test can be performed if one has prior reason to suspect a break in the data generating process at a given data. Graphical techniques such as the CUSUM and CUSUM SQUARED tests are helpful as are tests of out-of-sample predictive ability.

Granger Causality Tests

My comments under this heading are not so much a specific criticism of Louka Katseli's use of Granger causality or econometric exogeneity tests as a general warning against the widespread misinterpretation of these tests. I do this with little hope that it will have any significant effects as the tide of lemmings rushing toward the sea appears to be almost unstoppable.

For simplicity, my examples will be bivariate. Let $E(\mid .)$ be the conditional expectation operation. For any variable x_t let $X^t \equiv \{x_s, s < t\}$.

Definition 1: x_t is said to Granger cause y_t *in mean* if

(5a) $$E(y_t \mid Y^t, X^t) \not\equiv E(y_t \mid Y^t).$$

x_t fails to Granger cause y_t *in mean* if

(5b) $$E(y_t \mid Y^t, X^t) \equiv E(y_t \mid Y^t).$$

Instead of referring to Granger causality *in mean,* I shall follow common usage and refer to definition 1 as the definition of Granger causality. A stronger form of Granger causality does, however, relate to the entire conditional distribution of random variables instead of merely to their conditional means. For any variable x, let $F(x_t \mid .)$ denote the conditional distribution function of x_t. Then (Granger 1980):

Definition 2: x_t is said to Granger cause y_t *in distribution* if

(6a) $$F(y_t \mid Y^t, X^t) \not\equiv F(y_t \mid Y^t).$$

x_t fails to Granger cause y_t *in distribution* if

(6b) $$F(y_t \mid Y^t, X^t) \equiv F(y_t \mid Y^t).$$

For policy design and evaluation, the following property is essential.

Definition 3: y_t is said to be *invariant in mean* with respect to x_t if changes in the deterministic components of the structural stochastic process governing x_t do not have any effect on the mean of y_t.

A stronger invariance property is

Definition 4: y_t is said to be *invariant in distribution* with respect to x_t if changes in the deterministic components of the structural stochastic process governing x_t do not have any effect on the distribution function of y_t.

Tests of Granger causality are tests of *incremental predictive content* (Schwert 1979, p. 82), they are not tests of invariance. In fact, there is two-way nonimplication between the two properties, "absence of Granger causality" and "invariance." Yet applied economists almost without fail make invariance propositions on the basis of Granger causality tests. The "two-way nonimplication" can be established using two examples.

Example 1: x Granger causes y does not imply y is not invariant with respect to x.

The example is due to Sargent (1976).

$$(7) \qquad y_t = \lambda y_{t-1} + \beta_0[x_t - E(x_t \mid I_{t-1})]$$
$$+ \beta_1[x_{t-1} - E(x_{t-1} \mid I_{t-2})] + u_t,$$

$$(8) \qquad x_t = \sum_{i=1}^{n} \delta_i x_{t-i} + \epsilon_t.$$

u_t and ϵ_t are white noise disturbances. I_t is the information set in period t conditioning expectations formed in period t. It is easily seen that x_t Granger causes y_t, since

$$E(y_t \mid Y^t, X^t) = \lambda y_{t-1} + \beta_1(x_t - \sum_{i=1}^{n} \delta_1 x_{t-1-i}) \neq E(y_t|Y^t) = \lambda y_{t-1}.$$

However, changes in the deterministic components of the stochastic process governing x, that is, changes in δ_i, $i = 1, \ldots , n$, do not affect the density function of y_t which, for (7) and (8), is given by

$$(9) \qquad y_t = \lambda y_{t-1} + \beta_0 \epsilon_t + \beta_1 \epsilon_{t-1} + u_t.$$

Note, however, that if it is possible to have an instantaneous feedback rule for x_t which makes it a function of some element(s) of I_t, then changes in the deterministic components of the instantaneous feedback rule will in general alter the density function of y.

Example 2: x fails to Granger cause y does not imply that y is invariant with respect to x.

The failure of Granger causality tests always to flag the presence or absence of invariance is due to their inability to detect effects of x on y operating currently (x_t on y_t) and through anticipations of the future

$[E(x_{t-i} \mid I_{t-j})$ on y_t, $i \geq 1$, $j \geq 0]$. Granger causality tests are "backward looking." According to Granger (1980, p. 330), "The past and present may cause the future but the future cannot cause the past." While this is, by definition, correct for Granger causality, it is misleading for causality in the sense of noninvariance, which is the one relevant for policy design and evaluation. The following example shows how current "policy actions" and current and past anticipations of future policy actions can have effects that are not detected by Granger causality tests. This means that Granger causality tests fail to signal the presence or absence of instantaneous feedback rules or automatic stabilizers. Ironically, they also fail to reveal the presence or absence of anticipated future policy actions. Thus the rational expectations revolution is the final nail in the coffin of the idea that Granger causality tests can settle the issue of policy effectiveness or neutrality. Sargent's assertion that "failure of monetary and fiscal policy variables to cause unemployment and other real variables is sufficient to deliver classical policy implications" (Sargent 1976, p.222) is false. (See also Buiter 1981*b*.)

Consider the following:

$$(10) \qquad y_t = \alpha_1 y_{t-1} + \alpha_2 E(x_{t+1} \mid I_t) + \alpha_3 x_t + \alpha_4 x_{t-1} + \epsilon_t^y;$$

$$(11) \qquad x_t = \beta y_{t-1} + \epsilon_t^x,$$

where ϵ_t^y and ϵ_t^x are mutually serially independently distributed random disturbances. Eliminating $E(x_{t+1} \mid I_t)$, x_t, and x_{t-1} in (10) using (11) we get

$$(12) \qquad y_t = (1 - \alpha_2\beta)^{-1}(\alpha_1 + \alpha_3\beta)y_{t-1}$$
$$+ (1 - \alpha_2\beta)^{-1}\alpha_4\beta y_{t-2} + (1 - \alpha_2\beta)^{-1}\alpha_3\epsilon_t^x$$
$$+ (1 - \alpha_2\beta)^{-1}\alpha_4\epsilon_{t-1}^x + (1 - \alpha_2\beta)^{-1}\epsilon_t^y.$$

Now,

$$E(y_t \mid Y^t) = (1 - \alpha_2\beta)^{-1}(\alpha_1 + \alpha_3\beta)y_{t-1} + (1 - \alpha_2\beta)^{-1}\alpha_4\beta y_{t-2}$$
$$+ (1 - \alpha_2\beta)^{-1}\alpha_4 E(\epsilon_{t-1}^x \mid Y^t).$$

Therefore (assuming ϵ^y and ϵ^x to be contemporaneously independent),

$$(13a) \qquad E(y_t \mid Y^t) = (1 - \alpha_2\beta)^{-1}(\alpha_1 + \alpha_3\beta)y_{t-1}$$
$$+ (1 - \alpha_2\beta)^{-1}\alpha_4\beta y_{t-2}$$
$$+ \frac{\alpha_4\alpha_3\sigma_x^2}{(\alpha_3^2 + \alpha_4^2)\sigma_x^2 + \sigma_y^2}(1 - \alpha_2\beta)^{-1}(\alpha_3\epsilon_{t-1}^x$$
$$+ \alpha_4\epsilon_{t-2}^x + \epsilon_{t-1}^y).$$

Also,

$$(13b) \qquad E(y_t \mid Y^t, X^t) = (1 - \alpha_2\beta)^{-1}(\alpha_1 + \alpha_3\beta)y_{t-1}$$
$$+ (1 - \alpha_2\beta)^{-1}\alpha_4\beta y_{t-2}$$
$$+ (1 - \alpha_2\beta)^{-1}\alpha_4\epsilon_{t-1}^x.$$

Comparing (13a) and (13b), we see that x Granger causes y. (It should be obvious that y also Granger causes x.) Since y is obviously not invariant with respect to x (changes in β alter the mean and the higher moments of y_t), the presence of Granger causality from x to y appears to be a good indicator of the presence of noninvariance of y with respect to x. All the Granger test does, however, is pick up the effect of x_{t-1} in (10). If we set $\alpha_4 = 0$ in (10), x affects y_t only through x_t and through $E(x_{t+1} \mid I_t)$. With $\alpha_4 = 0$, inspection of (12) reveals that y again is not invariant with respect to x: changes in β affect all moments of y. Inspection of (13a) and (13b) reveals, however, that with $\alpha_4 = 0$, x fails to Granger cause y: the Granger test cannot reveal current and anticipated future effects. Even if $\alpha_4 \neq 0$ and lagged effects are present, x will not Granger cause y if the function (11) is nonstochastic, that is, if $\sigma_x = 0$. If x is a policy instrument whose value is determined by some nonstochastic feedback rule, $x_t = \beta y_{t-1}$ might well apply. If x is chosen optimally, this will always be the case.

Of course, Granger causality tests do have their uses in time series analysis. The three most important ones are the following.

First, together with the entire modern time series apparatus of vector autoregressive–moving average processes, "innovation accounting," and the analysis of the contemporaneous correlations between the innovations in the various equations, they are an important tool for *data description*. They represent compact and parsimonious ways of representing the dominant time series properties of a data sample. Data-coherent structural models should be consistent with these representations.

Second, in empirical rational expectations models that fall short of being complete general equilibrium models, there frequently is a problem about what to include in the information set conditioning the expectations. The answer would seem to be that anything that Granger causes the variable to be predicted and can reasonably be assumed to be widely available at low cost should be part of the information set.

Third, in structural model estimation heroic assumptions are often made about statistical exogeneity. Systematic use of Granger causality tests will establish whether these exogeneity assumptions are consistent with the data.

What Granger causality tests cannot do is shed light on such issues as whether the authorities can use the money supply to influence the behavior of real output or prices. Granger causality tests may be sophisticated post hoc, ergo propter hoc; using them as the basis for invariance propositions represents a "sophisticated" fallacy.

These critical general observations do not affect my opinion that the data description contained in the empirical part of this paper is informative. Any theory that cannot generate the kinds of stochastic behavior documented in the paper is not worth having.

References

Argy, V., and Salop, J. 1979. Price and output effects of monetary and fiscal expansion in a two-country world under flexible exchange rates. Mimeographed. Geneva: International Monetary Fund.

Ashenfelter, O., and Card, D. 1981. Time-series representations of economic variables and alternative models of the labor market. Discussion Paper no. 81/109. Princeton University.

Bardhan, P. K. 1970. Economic growth, development, and foreign trade: A study in pure theory. New York: Wiley-Interscience.

Basevi, G., and de Grauwe, P. 1977. Vicious and virtuous circles: A theoretical analysis and a policy proposal for managing exchange rates. *European Economic Review* 10:277–301.

Branson, W. 1977. Asset, markets, and relative prices in exchange rate determination. *Sozialwissenschaftliche Annalen* 1:69–89.

———. 1981. Macroeconomic determinants of real exchange rates. NBER Working Paper no. 801.

Branson, W., and Rotemberg, J. 1980. International adjustment with wage rigidity. *European Economic Review* 13:309–32.

Bruno, M. 1976. The two-sector open economy and the real exchange rate. *American Economic Review* 66:566–77.

Buiter, W. H. 1981a. Time preference and international lending and borrowing in an overlapping generations model. *Journal of Political Economy* 89:769–97.

———. 1981b. Granger causality and stabilization policy. NBER Technical Paper no. 10. To appear in *Economica,* 1984.

Corden, M., and Jones, R. M. 1976. Devaluation, non-flexible prices, and the trade balance for a small country. *Canadian Journal of Economics* 9 (February): 150–61.

Dornbusch, R. 1973. Devaluation, money, and non-traded goods. *American Economic Review* (December).

———. 1976. Expectations and exchange rate dynamics. *Journal of Political Economy* 84:1161–76.

Findlay, R., and Rodriquez, C. 1977. Intermediate imports and macroeconomic policy under flexible exchange rates. *Canadian Journal of Economics* 10 (May): 208–17.

Frenkel, J. 1981. Flexible exchange rates, prices, and the role of "news": Lessons from the 1970s. *Journal of Political Economy* 89 (August): 665–705.

Giavazzi, F. 1980. Exchange rate and current account dynamics following real disturbances. Mimeographed.

Granger, C. W. J. 1980. Testing for causality: A personal viewpoint. *Journal of Economic Dynamics and Control* 2:329–52.

Harvey, A. C. 1981. *The econometric analysis of time series*. Oxford: Philip Allan.

Jones, R. 1979. Technical progress and real incomes in a Ricardian trade model. In *International trade: Essays in theory*. Amsterdam: North-Holland.

Katseli, L., and Marion, N. P. 1982. Adjustment to variations in imported input prices: The role of economic structure. *Weltwirtschaftliches Archiv* 118:131–47.

Katseli-Papaefstratiou, L. 1979*a*. The reemergence of the purchasing power parity doctrine in the 1970s. Special Paper in International Economics, no. 13. Princeton N.J.: International Finance Section, Princeton University.

————. 1979*b*. *Transmission of external price disturbances in small, open economies*. New York: Garland.

————. 1980. Transmission of external price disturbances and the composition of trade. *Journal of International Economics* 10 (August): 357–75.

Keynes, J. M. 1930. *A treatise on money*. Vol. 1. London: Macmillan.

Koopmans, T. C., and Montias, J. 1971. On the description and comparison of economic systems. In *Comparisons of economics studies,* ed. A. Eckstein. Berkeley: University of California Press.

Krugman, P. 1980. Scale economies, product differentiation, and the pattern of trade. *American Economic Review* 70 (December): 950–59.

————. 1981. Real and financial determinants of the real exchange rate. NBER Working Paper no. 584.

Obstfeld, M. 1981*a*. Aggregate spending and the terms of trade: Is there a Laursen Metzler effect? NBER Working Paper no. 686.

————. 1981*b*. Capital mobility and devaluation in an optimizing model with rational expectations. *American Economic Review* 71:217–21.

Ohlin, B. 1929*a*. The reparation problem: A discussion. I. Transfer difficulties, real and imagined. *Economic Journal* 39 (June): 172–78.

————. 1929*b*. A rejoinder. *Economic Journal* 39 (September): 400–404.

Pearce, I. F. 1961. The problem of the balance of payments. *International Economic Review* 2 (January): 1–28.

Sachs, J. 1981. The current account in the macroeconomic adjustment process. NBER Working Paper no. 796.

Sargent, T. J. 1976. A classical macroeconometric model for the United States. *Journal of Political Economy* 84:207–37.

————. 1979. Estimating vector autoregressions using methods not based on explicit economic theories. *Federal Reserve Bank of Minneapolis Quarterly Review* (Summer), pp. 8–15.

Schwert, G. W. 1979. Tests of causality: The message in the innovations. In *Three aspects of policy and policy making: Knowledge, data, and institutions,* ed. K. Brunner and A. H. Meltzer. Amsterdam: North-Holland.

Sims, C. A. 1980*a*. Macroeconomics and reality. *Econometrica* 48 (January): 1–47.

———. 1980*b*. Comparison of interwar and postwar business cycles: Monetarism reconsidered. *American Economic Review* 70:250–57.

Srinivasan, T. N. 1982. International factor movements, commodity trade, and commercial policy. Economic Growth Center Discussion Paper no. 399. New Haven, Conn.: Yale University.

Taylor, J. B. 1980. Output and price stability: An international comparison. *Journal of Economic Dynamics and Control* 2 (February): 109–32.

10 The Real Exchange Rate, the Current Account, and the Speed of Adjustment

Francesco Giavazzi and Charles Wyplosz

10.1 Introduction

A stylized recent model of exchange rate determination would include the following features: high capital mobility, rational expectations, and continuous clearing of asset markets. Such a model would exhibit saddle-path stability and, in order to solve it, one would typically first determine its long-run (steady state) equilibrium following a disturbance and then identify the unique path along which convergence would be obtained.[1] In this paper we present and discuss a class of models for which the steady state equilibrium seems to admit a priori an infinity of solutions so that there would appear to exist an infinity of convergence paths.[2] It will be shown that this indeterminacy is only apparent: the long-run equilibrium, and the path that leads to it, are uniquely determined by the dynamic characteristics of the model. In other words, the parameters which set the speed of adjustment of the model have a permanent effect on the evolution of the economy.

This interesting property is obtained in two-country models with infinite intertemporal optimization where agents typically consume their permanent income, which, in the stationary state, coincides with their actual income. Consequently, under assumptions to be specified later, the requirement that the current account be in equilibrium vanishes, opening up the possibility of

We gratefully acknowledge the benefit of remarks by Jeff Sachs and Joshua Aizenman. This work has been partially supported by a grant from the Délégation Générale à la Recherche Scientifique at Technique.
1. For a representative sample of these studies, see Dornbusch (1976), Wilson (1979), Dornbusch and Fischer (1980), Mussa (1980), and Kouri (1981).
2. This indeterminacy should not be confused with the well-known problem associated with saddle-path stability, according to which one needs additional conditions, such as ruling out explosive solutions, to identify a unique convergence path. On this problem, see for example Blanchard (1979).

an indeterminacy of the real exchange rate. Models of real exchange rate determination with intertemporal optimization have received considerable attention recently, especially in Dornbusch (1981), Obstfeld (1981, 1982), Svensson and Razin (1981), and Sachs (1983). Actually there are at least two reasons why such models are interesting. First, Dornbusch and Fischer (1980), Mussa (1980), and Rodriguez (1980) have emphasized the role of present and future current account imbalances in driving the exchange rate, following the earlier contribution of Kouri (1976). An important implication of the reemergence of the current account is a renewed interest in the intertemporal allocation of resources and spending among countries which is implied by such surpluses or deficits, and therefore the need to model this process carefully. Another reason is related to the widespread use of the rational expectations assumption. As Muth (1961) pointed out in his original contribution, if one models optimizing agents, one has to assume also that they use all available information in forming their expectations. But then, if they incorporate future anticipated events into their rational expectations, it seems natural to replace static by dynamic optimization.

It has become a standard property of exchange rate models under perfect foresight that the impact effect of an exogenous disturbance is a function of the speed at which some slow-moving variables are able to adjust, as exemplified in Dornbusch (1976). But this effect does not concern the stationary state to which the model converges, which typically remains uniquely defined and easily characterized. The class of models discussed in this paper opens up new interesting possibilities. For example, we show that the degree of flexibility of wages, or the rate at which capital is accumulated, have permanent effects on such variables as the real exchange rate and a country's external indebtedness.

The point made here will seem intuitively clear and is but a special case of the general treatment of linear models under perfect foresight by Blanchard and Kahn (1980) and Buiter (1981). Still, it does not seem to have been directly addressed in the exchange rate literature, although Obstfeld (1982) and Sachs (1983) have signaled its existence. In a completely different setup, Drazen (1980) obtains the same property and argues, as we do, that it presents attractive economic implications.

The problem at hand is illustrated through an example in the next section. The analytical solution is presented in section 10.3, and put to work in section 10.4, where another example shows the role of the labor market in determining the stationary state value of the real exchange rate through its effect on cumulated current account imbalances. Section 10.5 offers some concluding remarks.

10.2 The Nature of the Problem: A First Example

The model presented in table 10.1 assumes perfect foresight and intertemporal optimization. It describes two countries which trade goods and secu-

Table 10.1

(1) $y = y_0 K^\alpha$	$y^* = y_0^* K^{*\alpha}, \; 0 < \alpha < 1$
(2) $C = a\delta A, \quad a > \frac{1}{2},$	$C^* = (1 - a^*)\delta A^*, \; a^* < \frac{1}{2}$
(3) $\lambda C_m = (1 - a)\delta A$	$\lambda^{-1} C_m^* = a^*\delta A^*$
(4) $A = q(K - Z)$	$A^* = q^* K^* + \lambda^{-1} qZ$
(5) $\dot{q} = rq - D/K$	$\dot{q}^* = r^* q^* - D^*/K^*$
(6) $D = y - I + q\dot{K}$	$D^* = y^* - I^* + q^*\dot{K}^*$
(7) $I = \dot{K}\left(1 + \dfrac{\phi}{2}\dfrac{\dot{K}}{K}\right)$	$I^* = \dot{K}^*\left(1 + \dfrac{\phi^*}{2}\dfrac{\dot{K}^*}{K^*}\right)$
(8) $\dot{K} = K(q - 1)/\phi$	$\dot{K}^* = K^*(q^* - 1)/\phi^*$
(9)	$r = r^* + \dot{\lambda}/\lambda$
(10)	$q\dot{Z} = \lambda C_m - C_m^* + DZ/K$
(11) $y = C + C_m^* + I$	$y^* = C^* + C_m + I^*$

Note: The asterisk denotes foreign country's variables.

rities with each other. Each country produces one good, using capital as the sole factor of production. A symmetrical model with labor instead of capital is presented in section 10.4 below. A model with both labor and capital is too large to be solved analytically and has been simulated in Giavazzi, Odekon, and Wyplosz (1982) and in Sachs (1983). The production technology is identical in both countries and exhibits decreasing return to scale (equation [1]). Each good is used for private consumption at home and abroad, and for domestic capital formation. The two goods are imperfect substitutes in consumption, and the demand equations (2) and (3) are derived in Appendix 1 from the intertemporal optimization of an instantaneous Cobb-Douglas utility function.[3] The variable $\lambda = eP^*/P$ is the real exchange rate, with e the nominal exchange rate and P and P^*, respectively, the prices of domestic and foreign goods. With this specification, total real consumption, $C + \lambda C_m$, in each period, is a constant share of real wealth A, the constant being the rate of time preference δ. The assumption that δ is constant and identical across countries is crucial and will be discussed later. Consumption of each good is, by virtue of the Cobb-Douglas assumption, a constant share of total consumption and, in each country, a larger share of consumption falls on the locally produced good ([2] and [3]).

Equity claims on the domestic and foreign capital stocks are the only assets and are taken as perfect substitutes. Consequently, the assumption,

---

3. The essential result does not depend upon the specification of the utility function, because, in the stationary state, total spending $E = C + \lambda C_m$ is always equal to δA. In order to obtain $E = \delta A$ at any point in time, i.e., also outside the stationary state, we need the utility function to be the logarithm of a linear homogeneous function of C and C_m. See Appendix 1 for proofs and a discussion.

implicit in the definition of wealth (4), that only domestic claims are traded is innocuous, and $Z \gtrless 0$ represents the volume of domestic equities held abroad. The variable q in (4) is the market value of installed capital, that is, Tobin's q. It is given in differential form in (5), where the dividends D are defined in (6). The definition of dividends assumes that all capital outlays are financed through issues of equities, so that dividends include the proceeds of the issue of new stocks less spending on investment, I. The investment function (7), in turn, follows the cost of investment literature,[4] in assuming that total investment expenditures exceed the value of actually installed capital $\dot{K}$, this cost being here a simple linear function of K. The optimal rate of investment (8) is derived in Appendix 1,[5] and shows the role of the cost of investment, ϕ. Equation (5) is the arbitrage condition which follows from the assumption of perfect asset substitutability, so that expected real returns, adjusted for expected real exchange rate changes, are equalized. With perfect foresight there is no distinction between expected and actual variables. Finally, in (10), current account deficits at home, the sum of the trade deficit and of dividend payments, are matched by changes in the foreign ownership of domestic stocks, as we assume that these are the only traded assets. The model is closed with the conditions (11) that both goods markets are in equilibrium.

10.2.1 The Stationary State

Assuming away growth, technological changes, and depreciation of capital, stationarity requires that all variables become constant. With $\dot{\lambda} = 0$, real interest rates are equalized. With $\dot{K} = \dot{K}^* = 0$ we need to have $\bar{q} = \bar{q}^* = 1$. Then with $\dot{q} = \dot{q}^* = 0$ and $I = I^* = 0$, (5), (6), and (7) imply that $\bar{y} = \bar{r}\bar{K}$ and $\bar{y}^* = \bar{r}^*\bar{K}^*$, which, together with (1), define uniquely $\bar{K}$ and $\bar{K}^*$ as functions of $\bar{r} = \bar{r}^*$. Next, we consider the two-goods market equilibrium conditions (11). One of them can be replaced by the requirement that world spending equals world income:

$$y + \lambda y^* = (C + \lambda C_m) + (\lambda C^* + C_m^*) = \delta(A + \lambda A^*),$$

which, given the above stationary state conditions, implies

(12) $$\bar{r}(\bar{K} + \lambda\bar{K}^*) = \delta(\bar{K} + \lambda\bar{K}^*).$$

Clearly, then, the two interest rates must equal the rate of time preference.

4. This investment function is described in Abel (1979) and used in Blanchard (1980).

5. In the presence of decreasing returns, one should distinguish the shadow price of investment, Tobin's marginal q, from the present value of installed capital, Tobin's average q. Doing so would increase the order of the dynamic system, making it intractable, so that we approximate marginal q by its average (observable) value. The exact values of the two q's are given in Appendix 1. For a discussion of the issue, see Hayashi (1982). For a simulated version of the model allowing for the two q's, see Giavazzi, Odekon, and Wyplosz (1982). Also, note that the interest rate is not equal to the marginal productivity of capital. This is because, with only one factor of production and decreasing returns to scale, stockholders enjoy a rent which is implicitly redistributed as part of dividend payments so that all earnings are accounted for.

Otherwise, we would have permanent world net saving (when $r > \delta$) or dissaving (when $r < \delta$).

We then consider the current account condition (10). With goods markets in equilibrium, the current account in each country is the excess of income over spending, so that $\dot{Z} = 0$ implies[6]

$$(13) \qquad (\bar{r} - \delta)(\bar{K} - \bar{Z}) = 0.$$

This is where the indeterminacy appears: with $\bar{r} = \delta$, the current account balance condition is always satisfied, so that it is not an active condition. As a consequence, we lose one equation to find the stationary state values of the two variables yet to be determined, λ and Z. The only remaining available condition is any of the two goods market equilibria (11), any one of which gives

$$(14) \qquad \bar{\lambda} = \frac{(1 - a)\bar{K} + (a - a^*)\bar{Z}}{a^*\bar{K}^*},$$

so that any pair of values $(\bar{\lambda}, \bar{Z})$ which satisfy (14) is a priori compatible with the stationary state requirement: the distribution of wealth $\bar{Z}$, and the real exchange rate $\bar{\lambda}$ can take an infinity of values.[7]

The economic reason for this apparent indeterminacy can be made intuitive by considering a transfer of wealth from domestic to foreign residents (an increase in $\bar{Z}$), starting from a stationary state situation. Such a transfer, given perfect asset substitutability, does not affect investment/saving decisions and does not upset world equilibrium as seen in (12). Its only effect is to shift world demand toward foreign goods (when $a > a^*$) and it only requires a real depreciation to restore equilibrium in *both* goods markets.[8]

This indeterminacy of the stationary state is merely apparent; following a disturbance, the economy will converge to a unique stable equilibrium, and the resulting values of $\bar{Z}$ and $\bar{\lambda}$ will be a function of its dynamic characteristics. Unfortunately, these values cannot be found without first spelling out the complete dynamic solution.[9] Although we do not present such a solution

---

6. Thus, at home, income is $y - rZ$, spending is $\delta A = \delta(K - Z)$, and $\dot{Z}$ measures the current account deficit.

7. With $r = r^* = \delta$, (1), (5), and (6) imply $\delta\bar{K} = y_0\bar{K}^\alpha$, so that $\bar{K}$ (and $\bar{K}^*$) are uniquely determined.

8. When $a = a^*$, the transfer has no effect on relative demand for domestic and foreign goods; $\bar{\lambda}$ is determined but $\bar{Z}$ is irrelevant for any other variable: we actually have only one consumer. Also note that Branson (1979) has emphasized that a current account deficit will require a permanent real exchange rate depreciation in order to generate the trade surplus needed to pay for the increased foreign debt. Equation (14) seems to confirm this result when $a > a^*$, but for a totally different reason. The debt effect vanishes in (13) as domestic residents recognize that their wealth is reduced and lower their spending accordingly. Here the effect on the real exchange rate is entirely due to the shift in relative demand for domestic and foreign goods, as discussed in the transfer example, and with $a < a^*$ a current account deficit implies a long-run real *appreciation*.

9. Thus, the general analytical solution provided by Blanchard and Kahn (1980) remains valid in this case and will provide the unique stationary state values. Yet Blanchard and Kahn have not drawn the important consequences of the singularity of the transition matrix, as we shall discuss in the next section.

for this model, it appears that the parameters describing the cost of investment, ϕ and ϕ^* in (7), will influence, not only the adjustment path, but also the ultimate values of Z and λ, and therefore the distribution of spending between the two countries. A higher cost of investment at home will slow down the accumulation (or decumulation) of K toward its optimal value, thus hampering the adjustment of domestic output and, usually, worsening, ceteris paribus, the current account and its total cumulated value as measured by Z. This, in turn, will require a corresponding real exchange depreciation.

10.2.2 How General Is the Problem?

The property shown in the previous example follows from the fact that, with intertemporal optimization, zero savings is an implication of the stationary state, achieved when the interest rate equals the rate of time preference. We now address the question whether this property is truly general or whether it follows from some special assumptions introduced into the model. The answer is that there are several ways of eliminating this property. We now discuss some of them and argue that the assumptions they entail are not obviously superior to those of the above model.

A first possibility is to do away with the perfect assets substitutability hypothesis, which is equivalent to assuming different rates of time preference in each country, since in the stationary state we will still need $\bar{r} = \delta$, $\bar{r}^* = \delta^*$, and we now want $r \neq r^*$. To understand why the indeterminacy is removed, consider again a transfer of wealth ΔZ to the foreign country. Foreign spending increases by $\delta^* \cdot \Delta Z$ while domestic spending falls by $\delta \Delta Z$; the world equilibrium is disturbed, interest rates will have to adjust, and the process will generate current account disturbances leading back to the initial distribution of wealth. Thus the nonuniqueness property is removed. But this solution has some unattractive features. Either it implies a corner solution, where one country has continuously dissaved to the point of selling away all its wealth so that the other country owns the whole world and consumes all output, or else it implies no holding of foreign assets in the stationary state, since such holdings would have spending out of these assets proportional to the holding country rate of time preference, while earnings would be proportional to the issuing country's rate.

Another possibility is to allow for each country to have variable and endogenous rates of time preference. Obstfeld (1981) has introduced such a rate, function of utility. In the stationary state, with perfect asset substitutability, we will still have identical rates of time preference in both countries and consumption is still proportional to wealth, δ being the coefficient of proportionality. But the equalization of the rates of time preference effectively imposes a further condition which eliminates the nonuniqueness property. The reason is that a transfer of wealth—for example, from the domestic to the foreign economy—would reduce wealth and therefore consumption at home, with the opposite effect abroad. This, then, would lower domestic utility, increase foreign utility, and result in different rates of time preference, prompting current account imbalances until the initial situation is restored. In this case, there is a unique distribution of wealth, and a unique real exchange rate, compatible with the stationary state. But the solution of the problem has a cost, because such endogenous rates of time preference are hard to justify: Should the rate of time preference be an increasing or a decreasing function of utility?[10]

A third possibility would be to introduce wealth into the utility function, so that transfer would alter the spending behavior, generating a Metzler-type behavior, and prompting current account adjustments until the unique stationary state distribution of wealth is reached. The question, of course, is whether wealth belongs to the utility function.

The model discussed in the previous section does not include labor as a factor of production. In the following section labor is introduced, and it will be seen that the indeterminacy remains. But could it be removed if leisure were an argument of the utility function?[11] In this case, the stationary state requires that real wages be equal to both the marginal productivity of labor and the marginal utility of leisure. If the utility function is not additive in leisure and consumption but assumes substitutability, a transfer of wealth abroad will reduce domestic consumption and increase the marginal utility of leisure, resulting in a reduction of labor supply. In the corresponding stationary state, the capital stock would be lower at home, higher abroad. Yet, it still is the case that equality between the interest rates in each country and the rate of time preference will guarantee balanced current accounts, so that the nonuniqueness property is preserved. But with labor and capital now depending upon wealth, the nonuniqueness spreads as it also affects these variables, as well as output levels.

Summing up, two-country models with intertemporal optimization are quite likely to exhibit the property that the stationary state is not uniquely determined or, more precisely, that it will be related to some of their dynamic characteristics. The assumptions required to eliminate the property are not necessarily superior, while the indeterminacy may prove to yield interesting and intuitive results. Of course, once we leave the general optimizing framework, the property disappears. It is, of course, the case of ad hoc

10. This issue has been recently revived by Lucas and Stokey (1982). Koopmans, Diamond, and Williamson (1964) had derived a set of postulates conveying the concept of time impatience and characterized the utility functions which satisfy these postulates. They came up with two examples, one with a constant rate of time preference, one with time preference an increasing function of utility. Lucas and Stokey build on Koopmans, Diamond, and Williamson to study the optimum equilibrium allocation in a many-agents growth model. Interestingly, they argue against a constant rate of time preference precisely because any distribution of utility is compatible with the stationary state, that is, they reach the same indeterminacy property but reject it.

11. This case is treated in a simulation context by Lipton and Sachs (1983).

Keynesian consumption functions and models where consumers are facing quantity or liquidity constraints. It should also be the case of models where optimization is carried over a finite period of time, or of models with overlapping generations, unless bequests exist and enter the utility function, although this point is just a conjecture at this time.

10.3 Analysis and Solution for Linear Models

In this section we present briefly the results derived in Giavazzi and Wyplosz (1983). We deal with the general case of a system of linear difference equations, characterize the mathematical aspects of the problem described in the previous section, and sketch its solution. The reader uninterested in these technical aspects can proceed directly to section 10.4 without loss of continuity.

The general form of a system of linear differential equations is:

$$(15) \qquad \dot{x} = Ax - z,$$

where x is an n-vector of endogenous variables, z is an n-vector of (or combination of) exogenous variables, and A is an $n \times n$ matrix. The solution to (15) under perfect foresight is given in Blanchard and Kahn (1980) and in Buiter (1981). They show that the system is stable when A admits as many strictly positive eigenvalues as there exist nonpredetermined variables in x. We assume here this stability condition and consider the special case where A is singular, admitting at least one zero eigenvalue. Denoting steady state levels with a bar, the long run is characterized by:

$$(16) \qquad A\bar{x} = \bar{z}$$

With A singular, (16) normally admits an infinity of solutions[12] so that the stationary state of the model seems not to be unique. Yet, (15) can be solved and shown to converge to a unique stationary state. The procedure is exactly as in Blachard and Kahn (1980) and in Buiter (1981): diagonalize the system,[13] integrate each of the n differential equations, and compute the n arbitrary constants of integration by using either the initial condition for the p predetermined variables or the transversality condition for the n-p nonpredetermined variables. Once we thus obtain $x(t)$ we can take the limiting case when t goes to infinity. The resulting value of $\bar{x}$ is as follows:

$$(17) \qquad \bar{x} = V\Lambda^*V^{-1}\bar{z} + (VEJ)(PVJ)^{-1}(Px(0) - PV\Lambda^*V^{-1}\bar{z}),$$

where Λ^* is a diagonal matrix, with its nonzero elements being the inverse

12. More precisely, (16) admits either no solution or an infinity of solutions. The latter is obtained when the standard rank condition is satisfied, namely that $\bar{z}$ be orthogonal to the eigenvector(s) associated with the zero eigenvalue(s). The case of no solution is uninteresting as it would result from a model ill-specified from the economic point of view.

13. If A cannot be diagonalized, the solution is possible by using the Jordan canonical transformation instead; see Blanchard and Kahn (1980).

of the eigenvalues, the first term(s) corresponding to the zero eigenvalue(s) and being null. (Λ^* is the generalized inverse of Λ.) V is the matrix of eigenvectors ordered conformably. E is an $n \times n$ matrix whose elements are all zero except for the first diagonal term(s) set at unity for each zero eigenvalue(s). P is a $p \times n$ matrix where the first p columns form the identity matrix, the remaining terms being all null, when x is ordered so that its first p elements are the predetermined variables. Then $Px(0)$ represents the initial values of these predetermined variables. Finally J is an $n \times p$ matrix with the first p rows forming the identity matrix, the other terms being zero.

In order to understand (17) consider first the case where A is nonsingular. Then $\Lambda^* = \Lambda^{-1}$ and $E = 0$ so that the second term vanishes and we obtain the standard result $\bar{x} = A^{-1}\bar{z}$. Thus, the effect of the singularity of A is captured by the second term. Inspection of this second term shows that the stationary state will depend upon the initial conditions (as captured by $Px(0)$), the so-called hysteresis property. Furthermore, the effect of $Px(0)$ on $\bar{x}$ will depend on the dynamic characteristics of the system in a nontrivial way which is illustrated in the following section.

10.4 Second Example: Model with Labor Only

10.4.1 Presentation and the Stationary State

In this section, we present a model very similar in spirit to that discussed in section 10.2 but which turns out to reduce to a smaller dimension and allows for an easier analytical solution.[14] This model is presented in table 10.2 below. The difference is that production is now carried out with labor as the only factor of production, instead of capital (1'). The crucial speed of adjustment will be that of the labor market, which functions as follows. Labor supply is infinitely elastic at the going real wage rate w, so that actual pemployment L can differ from the "natural" level $\bar{L}$. Excess demand for labor (respectively excess supply) in turn brings about an increase (respectively a decrease) in the real wage: the speed at which this adjustment proceeds to reestablish full employment is captured in (7') by the parameter γ. Demand for labor follows from the optimizing choice of the firm, so that in (6') the real wage rate is equal to the marginal productivity of labor. Total domestic wealth A is defined in (4') as the present value of domestic output:

$$x(t) = \int_t^\infty e^{-\int_t^s r(V)dV} y(s)ds,$$

---

14. We have been able, so far, to obtain analytical solutions for the model of section 10.2 only in cases where the dynamics is uninteresting and does not lead to current account imbalances, because of the simplifying assumptions which make it tractable.

or

$$\dot{X} = rX - y, \text{ as in } (5'),$$

less domestic indebtedness Z, where Z can be positive or negative. Trade in assets takes the form of indexed bonds, that is, claims to units of output of the issuing country, and (9) ensures that the yields of such bonds are the same, irrespective of which country issues them. Equation $(10')$ describes the current account and $(11')$ represents the two goods markets' equilibrium conditions.

Table 10.2

$(1')$ $y = y_0 L^\alpha$		$y^* = y_0^* L^{*\alpha}$
(2) $C = a\delta A$		$C^* = (1 - a^*)\delta A^*$
(3) $\lambda C_m = (1 - a)\delta A$		$\lambda^{-1}C_m^* = a^*\delta A^*$
$(4')$ $A = X - Z$		$A^* = X^* + \lambda^{-1}Z$
$(5')$ $\dot{X} = rX - y$		$\dot{X}^* = r^*X^* - y^*$
$(6')$ $wL = \alpha y$		$w^*L^* = \alpha y^*$
$(7')$ $\dot{w} = \gamma(L - \bar{L})$		$\dot{w}^* = \gamma^*(L^* - \bar{L}^*)$
(9)	$r = r^* + \dot{\lambda}/\lambda$	
$(10')$	$\dot{Z} = \lambda C_m - C_m^* + rZ$	
$(11')$ $y = C + C_m^*$		$y^* = C^* + C_m$

As in section 10.2, the stationary state implies $\bar{r} = \bar{r}^* = \delta$, and the two-goods markets equilibrium then reduces to

$$(18) \qquad \bar{\lambda} = \frac{(1 - a)\bar{X} + (a - a^*)\bar{Z}}{a^*\bar{X}^*}.$$

As $\bar{X} = \bar{y}/\delta = y_0\bar{L}^\alpha/\delta$ and $\bar{X}^* = y_0^* L^{*\alpha}/\delta$, $\bar{X}$ and $\bar{X}^*$ are clearly defined and we have, again, a relationship linking $\bar{\lambda}$ and $\bar{Z}$, leaving these two variables a priori undetermined.

We will consider a change in domestic productivity $\hat{y}_0 = dy_0/y_0$, which occurs unexpectedly in period $t = 0$. We know that in the new stationary state $\bar{w} = (y_0 + dy_0)\bar{L}^{-(1 - \alpha)}$ and $\bar{w}^*$ is unchanged, so that domestic wealth will change proportionally to the productivity gain with no long-run effect on foreign human wealth.

10.4.2 Solution

We note that the interest rate variables are merely definitional and can be eliminated through $(5')$, $(6')$, and (9) so as to obtain

$$(9') \qquad \dot{\mu}/\mu = y/X - y^*/X^*,$$

where $\mu = \lambda X^*/X$ is the relative value of foreign and domestic gross wealths. The model is then driven by the four equations (7′), (9′), and (10′), together with the goods market equilibrium conditions, which allows us to eliminate X and X^*. The relative value of wealths, μ, is a nonpredetermined variable, while w, w^*, and Z are predetermined.

For the purpose of this example, computations can be greatly reduced by a careful choice of parameters and initial values. Specifically, we assume[15] for $t < 0$, $X = X^* = 1$, $r = r^* = \delta$, $w = w^* = 1$, $y = y^* = \delta$, $\lambda = \mu = 1$, $Z = 0$. The system is linearized and solved around this initial position in appendix 2. The resulting laws of motions of the four driving variables are $w(t) = 1 + \hat{y}_0(1 - e^{-\gamma_1 t})$, $w^*(t) = 1$,

$$(19) \qquad Z(t) = \frac{1 - a - a^*}{a + a^*} \cdot \frac{\alpha}{1 - \alpha} \cdot \frac{\delta}{\gamma_1 + \delta} \hat{y}_0(1 - e^{-\gamma_1 t}),$$

and

$$(20) \qquad \mu(t) - 1 = \frac{1 - a - a^*}{a + a^*} \hat{y}_0 \left(1 + \frac{\alpha}{1 - \alpha} \frac{\delta}{\gamma_1 + \delta} \right)$$
$$+ 2 \frac{1 - a - a^*}{a + a^*} \frac{\alpha}{1 - \alpha} \frac{\delta}{\gamma_1 + \delta} \hat{y}_0(e^{-\gamma_1 t} - 1),$$

where $\gamma_1 = \gamma \bar{L}/(1 - \alpha)$ is a measure of the speed of adjustment in the domestic labor market.

From these formulae, it is easy to obtain the stationary state values for Z and μ:

$$\bar{Z} = \frac{1 - a - a^*}{a + a^*} \frac{\alpha}{1 - \alpha} \cdot \frac{\delta}{\gamma_1 + \delta} \hat{y}_0$$

$$\bar{\mu} - 1 = \frac{1 - a - a^*}{a + a^*} \hat{y}_0 \left(\frac{a + a^*}{a^*} + \frac{a - a^*}{a^*} \frac{\alpha}{1 - \alpha} \frac{\delta}{\gamma_1 + \delta} \right).$$

It appears that the sign of $(1 - a - a^*)$ plays an important role in the evolution of the system: in the following, we discuss the case where the home country captures less additional sales than the foreign country when world wealth increases, that is, $1 - a - a^* > 0$. We also assume $a > a^*$, a "preferred habitat" in consumption.

In order to interpret the solution described by (19) and (20), we turn to figure 10.1. The line LR represents the indeterminacy problem: a priori, in the stationary state, μ and Z can be anywhere along this line which is de-

---

15. Yet we do not assume that the model was resting in a stationary state since, with $Z = 0$ and $X = X^*$, (22) would imply $a + a^* = 1$. In this case we obtain a trivial solution where λ jumps to its new stationary state value, with $Z(t) = 0$, $\forall t$, and no dynamics at all. The reason will appear clearly in the following discussion where we show the role of the assumption $a + a^* \neq 1$.

rived from (18): $a^*\mu \overline{X} = (1 - a)\overline{X} + (a - a^*)\overline{Z}$. We have assumed that, prior to the disturbance, the economy was at point A, with $Z = 0$ and $\mu = 1$. The slope of the line LR increases with $\hat{y}_0$, the disturbance. On impact, Z cannot change instantaneously, but μ is free to jump. As in other models with perfect foresight, the magnitude of the jump is a function of the speed of adjustment of the economy: the more slowly the labor market reacts to a disequilibrium—that is, the smaller γ—the larger the impact increase in μ. What is novel here is that, wherever μ jumps to, there will be a convergence path leading to a stationary state position along LR, as shown on figure 10.1 by the two impact positions B and C, and the corresponding long-run points B' and C'.

In order to understand how this happens, we consider first the long-run effects of the disturbance. We note that foreign output, employment, and the wage rate stay constant. In the stationary state, therefore, world wealth will have increased proportionately to domestic output, making for equal augmentations of world spending and domestic output. With spending directed to both domestic and foreign goods, a real exchange rate depreciation is needed for goods markets to be in equilibrium. Now consider $\mu = \lambda X^*/X$. If we had $a + a^* = 1$, the increase in world wealth per se would not affect the relative demand for domestic and foreign goods so that there would be no need for μ to change; with X^* constant, the increase in λ, proportional to the increase in X, would be enough to maintain both goods markets in equilibrium. If, however, $a + a^* < 1$, as world wealth increases, relative demand tilts toward foreign goods, which requires a further depreciation and an increase in μ; the relative value of foreign wealth, expressed in domestic goods units, must increase in order to eliminate the excess supply of domestic goods. This explains the stationary state value of μ in figure 10.1.

The impact effect of the increase in y_0 is in many respects similar to the

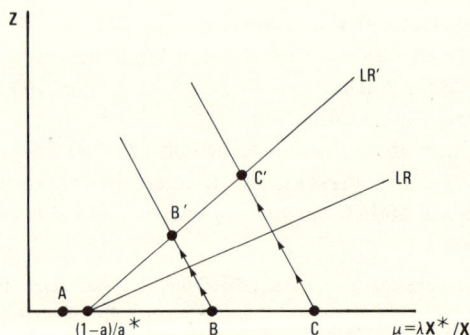

Fig. 10.1

long-run case just described. Domestic output increases but attracts only a fraction $a + a^*$ of the increase in world wealth so that when $a + a^* < 1$, λ and μ increase on impact.

Over time, the domestic labor market adjusts to the increased demand for labor generated by the productivity gain. As the real wage rate increases, demand for labor and domestic output decrease, which requires a real exchange appreciation in order to reduce demand for domestic goods. We thus obtain an overshooting for λ (and μ).[16] This appreciation being correctly anticipated is accompanied, because of (9), by an interest rate differential so that for $t > 0$, $r < \delta$, and $r^* > \delta$. This interest rate effect is important because it leads to a drop in X^*, the present value of the constant flow of foreign output; as a consequence, the foreign current account turns into a surplus as foreign spending is reduced, and this is matched by a domestic deficit.

We can now discuss the role of γ, the speed of adjustment of the domestic labor market. With a high speed of adjustment, the current account imbalances are eliminated faster, thus making for a smaller cumulated debt of the home country and therefore requiring a smaller real exchange rate appreciation.[17] On figure 10.1, the adjustment path BB' describes the response of the economy for a higher γ than along CC'.

10.4.3 Welfare Implications

As the consumption behavior is derived from the optimization of Cobb-Douglas intertemporal utility functions, it is easy to draw implications concerning welfare in the new stationary state. This requires computing the values of total domestic and foreign wealth. As shown in Appendix 2, foreign wealth $A^* = X^* + Z$ has to increase in the long run as X^* goes back to its initial value while Z rises. However, A^* initially drops as X^* is reduced on impact, and Z increases only over time. Domestic wealth $A = X - Z$ increases in the stationary state if the loss in wealth Z through cumulated deficits does not offset the gain in X. The possibility that a productivity gain proves to be "immiserizing" augments when the speed of adjustment is small, as current account deficits are more prolonged. If U and U^* are the domestic and foreign Cobb-Douglas welfare functions, respectively, then we have $U = A\lambda^{-(1-a)}$ and $U^* = A^*\lambda^{a^*}$. While U^* increases unambiguously through both its wealth and its terms of trade arguments, chances that U decreases grow as γ decreases, since it not only reduces

---

16. The overshooting in μ (and in λ) is now a familiar feature in exchange rate models, since Dornbusch (1976) and Black (1977). Here it follows from the stickiness of wages and the corresponding difference in speeds of adjustments on labor and assets markets.

17. While the domestic current account is more quickly eliminated with a high speed of adjustment, its initial size is larger. With a high γ, the exchange rate appreciation, following the depreciation on impact, is faster, pushing r further down and thus leading to larger domestic wealth and spending. Yet the accumulated debt is unambiguously smaller, as shown by (19).

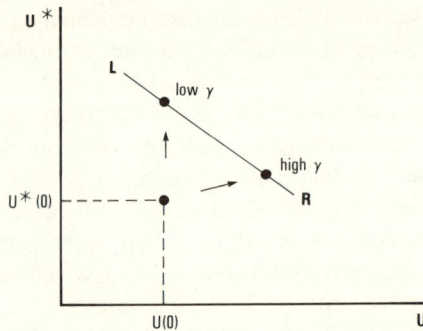

Fig. 10.2

wealth gains but also worsens the domestic terms of trade.[18] The role of the speed of adjustment is illustrated in figure 10.2. The line *LR* shows all the possibilities for the stationary state values of U and U^*. The exact position along *LR* is a priori unknown. With a high speed of adjustment γ, both countries' welfare improves. With a low γ, the gain at home is lower and can even be negative, while the gain abroad is enhanced.

10.5 Conclusion

We believe that the class of models in which the initial conditions and the speed of adjustment parameters have permanent influences on the path of the economy after a disturbance is a large and important one. There are certainly several ways of making different assumptions which eliminate the a priori indeterminacy of the stationary state in these models. We have discussed some of them and argued that they do not necessarily seem more appealing than ours. We think that choosing these assumptions simply because they solve the problem discussed in the paper amounts to discarding what appears to be an intuitively interesting property. It is unnecessary since it turns out that the usual stationarity conditions remain sufficient to pin down a unique and stable long-run equilibrium. The example, which has been solved, shows results which seem to match what one would expect to find.

It is not clear how broad is the potential applicability of this approach. In this paper, the property hinges on the fact that we have two distinct groups of consumers who trade in goods and assets.[19] This is why it has natural

18. At this point, it is worth reemphasizing that the foregoing discussion assumes $1 - a - a^* > 0$. Taking $1 - a - a^* < 0$ would reverse this result and put the burden of potentially decreasing wealth and welfare on the foreign economy.
19. The production part of the models presented here is not required to obtain the result. We have assumed that firms optimize for the sake of coherence only.

applications in macroeconomics for two-country models. It could as well be used in a Kaldorian economy with two classes of consumers who have different spending patterns.

But the same property might also obtain in a one-small-country model, provided its spending is, again, derived from infinite horizon intertemporal optimization, somehow leaving the rest of the world unspecified. The fact that Drazen (1980) reports a similar property arising in the production side is intriguing. His model has heterogeneous capital and labor, both susceptible of "investments," so that the indeterminacy stems from the possibility of adjusting labor to the existing structure of capital, or of adjusting capital to the existing structure of labor. The interesting aspect of this is that investments in capital and in labor (i.e., job training) are sluggish, so that the final stationary state will be uniquely related to the speed of adjustment. There seems to be a scope for a generalization of the mechanisms brought up by Drazen and in the present paper.

Appendix 1: Optimization

1. The Consumer's Problem

The consumer maximizes $\int_0^\infty e^{-\delta t} U(t)dt$ subject to the constraint that total spending $E = C + \lambda C_m$ exhausts, in present value, his wealth A, that is,
$A = \int_0^\infty e^{-\int_0^t r(s)ds} E(t)dt$, or, equivalently, $\dot{A} = rA - E$. We consider the special case where

$$U(C, C_m) = \ln[u(C, C_m)]$$

and where $u(C, C_m)$ is a function homogeneous of degree 1. The first-order conditions are:

(A1) $\partial u/\partial C = \phi u, \quad \partial u/\partial C_m = \phi\lambda u$

(A2) $\dot{\phi} = (\delta - r)\phi,$

where ϕ is the Lagrange multiplier. Using the homogeneity of u through Euler equation, (A1) is reduced to $E\phi = 1$. Differentiating this relationship logarithmically, we then eliminate r to obtain $(\dot{A/E}) = \delta (A/E) - 1$, which, when integrated forward, gives $E = \delta A$. If $u(C, C_m)$ is further specified as a Cobb-Douglas function, (A1) gives (2) and (3) in the text. Note that, in the stationary state, we have $\dot{\phi} = 0$ and $\dot{A} = 0$, so that, given the constraint and (A2), we must have $r = \delta$ and $E = \delta A$ irrespective of the functional form of the utility function $U(C, C_m)$. The reason why the simple formulation $E = \delta A$ also holds outside the stationary state is that the definition of $U(C, C_m)$ as $\ln[u(C, C_m)]$ renders this function Cobb-Douglas over time, thus yielding the usual constant share property.

2. The Firm's Problem

The firm maximizes its present value $\int_0^\infty (y - I)e^{-rt}dt$ given the cost of investment $I = \dot{K}[1 + (\phi/2)(\dot{K}/K)]$. Introducing the notation $\dot{K} = J$, the Hamiltonian is

$$H = \{y_0K^\alpha - J[1 + (\phi/2)(J/K)] + q^m J\}e^{-rt},$$

where q^m is the marginal cost of investment. The first conditions are:

(A3) $\qquad\qquad \partial H/\partial J = 0,$

so $\dot{K} = J = K(q^m - 1)/\phi;$

(A4) $\qquad\qquad -\partial H/\partial K = e^{-rt}(\dot{q}^m - rq^m),$

so $\dot{q} = rq^m - (\alpha y - I + q^m\dot{K})/K$. The average value of installed capital at time t, q^a is the present value of the firm's earnings, the objective function in the previous optimization problem:

$$q^a(t) \cdot K(t) = \int_t^\infty [y(s) - I(s)]e^{-r(s - t)}ds,$$

which after differentiation and dropping the time parameter gives

(A5) $\qquad\qquad \dot{q}^a = rq^a - (y - I + q^a\dot{K})/K.$

Thus (5) and (6) in the text define q to be q^a as specified in (A5), while (8) is (A3) where q^m has been replaced by q^a. Comparison of (A4) and (A5) shows the nature of this approximation, discussed in note 4.

Appendix 2: Solution of the Model

We first linearize the model around its initial position, characterized by $X = X^* = 1$, $\mu = \lambda = 1$, $y = y^* = \delta$, $Z = 0$, and $w = w^* = 1$. The wage adjustment equations (7'), after substitution of (6') into (1') and then plugging L and L^* into (7'), give for a given disturbance $\hat{y}_0 = \Delta y_0/y_0$ in home productivity,

(B1) $\qquad\qquad \dot{w} = -\gamma_1(w - 1) + \gamma_1\hat{y}_0,$

where $\gamma_1 = \gamma\bar{L}/(1 - \alpha)$,

(B2) $\qquad\qquad \dot{w}^* = -\gamma_1^*(w^* - 1),$

where $\gamma_1^* = \gamma^*\bar{L}^*/(1 - \alpha)$.

Clearly, the only solution for (B2) which admits $w^*(0) = 1$ as assumed is $w^* = \overline{w}^* = 1$, a constant. Thus, there will be no departure from full employment abroad. We use, in the following, the fact that w^* remains constant throughout.

From (B1), it is also clear that the stationary state value of w is a priori uniquely determined: $\overline{w} = 1 + \hat{y}_0$. The goods markets' equilibrium conditions (11′) are solved for X and X^* after substitution of $\mu = \lambda X^*/X$. Actually, it is easier first to write that world income is equal to world spending, $y + \lambda y^* = \delta A + \delta \lambda A^*$, which gives

(B3) $$X + X^* = -\alpha/(1 - \alpha)(w - w^*) + \hat{y}_0/(1 - \alpha).$$

Then the domestic goods market condition is solved for X:

(B4) $$\begin{aligned}(a + a^*)(X - 1) = &-[\alpha/(1 - \alpha)](w - 1)\\ &- a^*(\mu - 1) + (a - a^*)Z\\ &+ \hat{y}_0/(1 - \alpha).\end{aligned}$$

The current account equation, when linearized and after substitution of (B3) and (B4), gives

(B5) $$\begin{aligned}(a + a^*)\dot{Z}/\delta = &-(1 - a - a^*)[\alpha/(1 - \alpha)](w - 1)\\ &- a^*(\mu - 1) + (a - a^*)Z\\ &+ (1 - a - a^*)\hat{y}_0/(1 - \alpha).\end{aligned}$$

The asset arbitrage condition (9′), similarly, yields

(B6) $$\begin{aligned}(a + a^*)\dot{\mu} = &\ 2\delta(1 - a - a^*)[\alpha/(1 - \alpha)](w - 1)\\ &+ 2\delta a^*(\mu - 1) - 2\delta(a - a^*)Z\\ &- 2\delta(1 - a - a^*)\hat{y}_0/(1 - \alpha).\end{aligned}$$

The system is reduced to the three equations (B1), (B5), and (B6), and rewritten in matrix form as

$$
\begin{bmatrix} \dot{w} \\ \dot{Z} \\ \dot{\mu} \end{bmatrix} =
\begin{bmatrix}
-\gamma_1 & 0 & 0 \\
-\dfrac{1 - a - a^*}{a + a^*}\dfrac{\delta\alpha}{1 - \alpha} & \delta\dfrac{a - a^*}{a + a^*} & -\delta\dfrac{a^*}{a + a^*} \\
2\dfrac{1 - a - a^*}{a + a^*}\dfrac{\delta\alpha}{1 - \alpha} & -2\delta\dfrac{a - a^*}{a + a^*} & 2\delta\dfrac{a^*}{a + a^*}
\end{bmatrix}
\begin{bmatrix} w \\ Z \\ \mu \end{bmatrix}
$$

$$
+ \begin{bmatrix} \gamma_1\overline{w} \\ u \\ 2u \end{bmatrix},
$$

where $u = -\dfrac{1 - a - a^*}{a + a^*}\dfrac{\delta\alpha}{1 - \alpha} + \dfrac{\delta a^*}{a + a^*} + \dfrac{1 - a - a^*}{a + a^*}\dfrac{\delta\hat{y}_0}{1 - \alpha}.$

It can be checked immediately that the last two columns of the transition matrix are linearly dependent, so that the matrix is singular and we cannot find, a priori, $\overline{Z}$ and $\overline{\mu}$. The eigenvalues are $\lambda_1 = 0$, $\lambda_2 = -\gamma_1$, $\lambda_3 = \delta$, so, with one positive root and one nonpredetermined variable, the model is stable under perfect foresight. The corresponding matrix of eigenvectors is

$$
V = \begin{bmatrix}
0 & \dfrac{a + a^*}{1 - a - a^*} & 0 \\[3mm]
\dfrac{a^*}{a - a^*} & \dfrac{\delta}{\gamma_1 + \delta}\dfrac{\alpha}{1 - \alpha} & -1 \\[3mm]
1 & -2\dfrac{\delta}{\gamma_1 + \delta}\cdot\dfrac{\alpha}{1 - \alpha} & 2
\end{bmatrix},
$$

which contains terms with γ_1, the speed of adjustment.

We can solve for w, Z, and μ:

(B7) $$w(t) = \overline{w} + (1 - \overline{w})e^{-\gamma_1 t}$$

where, again, $\overline{w} = 1 + \hat{y}_0$;

(B8) $$Z(t) = \frac{1 - a - a^*}{a + a^*}\frac{\alpha}{1 - \alpha}\frac{\delta}{\gamma_1 + \delta}\hat{y}_0(1 - e^{-\gamma_1 t});$$

and

(B9) $$\mu(t) - 1 = \frac{1 - a - a^*}{a^*}\left(1 + \frac{\alpha}{1 - \alpha}\frac{\delta}{\gamma_1 + \delta}\right)\hat{y}_0$$
$$+ 2\frac{1 - a - a^*}{a + a^*}\frac{\alpha}{1 - \alpha}\frac{\delta}{\gamma_1 + \delta}\hat{y}_0(e^{-\gamma_1 t} - 1).$$

The stationary state values for Z and μ immediately follow:

$$\overline{Z} = \frac{1 - a - a^*}{a + a^*}\frac{\alpha}{1 - \alpha}\frac{\delta}{\gamma_1 + \delta}\hat{y}_0;$$

$$\overline{\mu} - 1 = \frac{1 - a - a^*}{a + a^*}\left(\frac{a + a^*}{a^*} + \frac{a - a^*}{a^*}\frac{\alpha}{1 - \alpha}\frac{\delta}{\gamma_1 + \delta}\right)\hat{y}_0.$$

Also, note from (B9) that the initial jump of μ at time zero will also be a function of γ_1.

Using (B3), (B4), and the linearized version of $\mu = \lambda X^*/X$, we can now compute

$$X(t) - 1 = \hat{y}_0 + \frac{1}{a + a^*}\frac{\alpha}{1 - \alpha}\hat{y}_0$$

$$\left[1 - (1 - a - a^*)\frac{\delta}{\gamma_1 + \delta}\right]e^{-\gamma_1 t};$$

$$X^*(t) - 1 = -\frac{1 - a - a^*}{a + a^*} \frac{\alpha}{1 - \alpha} \frac{\gamma_1}{\gamma_1 + \delta} \hat{y}_0 e^{-\gamma_1 t};$$

$$\lambda(t) - 1 = \frac{1 - a}{a^*} \hat{y}_0$$

$$+ \left[\frac{(1 - a - a^*)(a - a^*)}{a^*(a + a^*)} \frac{\delta}{\gamma_1 + \delta} \right.$$

$$+ \left. \frac{2 - a - a^*}{a + a^*} e^{-\gamma_1 t} \right] \frac{\alpha}{1 - \alpha} \hat{y}_0.$$

Finally, if the domestic welfare function is $U = kC^a C_m^{1-a}$ with $C = a\delta A$, $\lambda C_m = (1 - a)\delta A$, we obtain $U = A\lambda^{-(1-a)}$ where $k = \delta^{-1} a^{-a} (1 - a)^{-(1-a)}$. Similarly, the foreign welfare function is $U^* = A^* \lambda^{a^*}$. Linearizing and computing the stationary state values gives

$$\frac{\overline{U} - U(0)}{U(0)} = \left[1 - \frac{(1 - a)^2}{a^*} - \frac{a}{a^*} \right.$$

$$\frac{(1 - a - a^*)(1 - a + a^*)}{a + a^*}$$

$$\left. \cdot \frac{\alpha}{1 - \alpha} \cdot \frac{\delta}{\gamma_1 + \delta} \right] \hat{y}_0$$

$$\frac{\overline{U^*} - U^*(0)}{U^*(0)} = (1 - a)\hat{y}_0 + [a + (1 - a^*)]$$

$$\frac{1 - a - a^*}{a + a^*} \frac{\alpha}{1 - \alpha} \frac{\delta}{\gamma_1 + \delta} \hat{y}_0.$$

Comment   Paul Krugman

Giavazzi and Wyplosz have given us an interesting and clear exposition of some consequences of a property which is common to many recent dynamic models: the existence of many possible steady states, and the dependence of the long run on the adjustment path. In my comment, I want to focus on this property, ask how robust it is, and suggest some "realistic" qualifications. I will then argue that what happens in the steady state may not be very important.

The first point to make is that the existence of a continuum of steady states is a characteristic of any model with (i) infinitely lived consumers who (ii) have utility functions which are separable over time, (iii) have the same rate of time preference, and (iv) face perfect capital markets. The reason is simple: in the steady state, the real interest rate will equal the common rate of time preference, so that all individuals will set consumption exactly equal to the interest earnings on their wealth. The result is that *any* distribution of wealth will be self-replicating. It could be, as in Giavazzi and Wyplosz, the distribution of wealth between countries; or it could be the distribution of wealth between groups within a country. The result is the same. And if the different groups have different consumption preferences, relative prices will vary across steady states.

How might we undermine this result? Giavazzi and Wyplosz consider abandoning either assumption ii or assumption iii—that is, replacing a "Ramsey" utility function with an "Uzawa" one, or letting rates of time preference differ, leading to a corner solution. Rightly, in my view, they regard these as unsatisfactory.

In principle, however, we could also drop one of the other assumptions. We could, for example, take a life-cycle approach in which individuals have finite lifetimes. As we know, this leads to a determinate steady-state ratio of wealth to labor income—which is enough to tie down the steady state. Alternatively, we could introduce an imperfection in capital markets; say, a debt ceiling. Add some uncertainty, and we will have a precautionary motive for holding assets which will lead in aggregate to something like a target wealth level, and again tie down the steady state. In either case, the result will to some extent be "as if" wealth were in the utility function—which is the third alternative the paper proposes.

The problem with these alternatives, however, is that they are *hard*. They lead to very intractable models, while the Ramsey world is very clean and straightforward. And is it not clear what one gains for the extra difficulty. Once we understand what the multiplicity of steady states actually means— in particular, once we understand that it does not imply any actual indeterminacy—the existence of zero eigenvalues should not bother us. Infinitely lived consumers and perfect capital markets are not realistic assumptions, but if they clear the ground for more understanding of other issues, the simplification will have been justified.

Turning briefly to substance, the authors are of course right in their point that adjustment speeds affect the steady state. One wonders, however, if they are not making too much of this, because of their focus on *steady-state* utility as a welfare criterion. This is clearly not right: we should use the lifetime utility of the agents in the model. But as soon as we do this, the question of uniqueness of the steady state becomes much less interesting. Even if the steady state were unique, the transition path to that steady state would still affect the lifetime utility levels of the countries—which is a modern dynamic modeler's way of saying that in the long run we are all dead.

An example of how exclusive focus on the steady state can be misleading is Giavazzi and Wyplosz's discussion in section 10.4, and particularly their

figure 10.2. Here it seems that faster adjustment at home necessarily makes the foreign country worse off—as it does, in the steady state, for the steady-state utility possibility frontier is independent of the rate of adjustment. But the true world utility possibility frontier is surely expanded by a higher speed of domestic adjustment, so faster adjustment at home might actually make *both* countries better off.

In sum, this paper is valuable in clearing up a technical issue which has caused some confusion. However, the substantive conclusion that adjustment matters is not something which hinges in any crucial way on whether or not the steady state is unique.

References

Abel, Andrew B. 1979. *Investment and the value of capital.* New York: Garland.

Black, Stanley W. 1977. *Floating exchange rates and national economic policy.* New Haven: Yale University Press.

Blanchard, Olivier J. 1979. Backward and forward solutions for economies with rational expectations. *American Economic Review* 69:114–18.

———. 1980. Demand disturbances and output. Unpublished paper, Harvard University, June.

Blanchard, Olivier J. and Kahn, Charles M. 1980. The solution of linear difference models under rational expectations. *Econometrica* 5:1305–12.

Branson, William H. 1979. Exchange rate dynamics and monetary policy. In *Inflation and employment in open economies,* ed. A. Lindbeck. Amsterdam: North-Holland.

Buiter, Willem H. 1981. Saddlepoint problems in rational expectation models when there may be "too many stable roots." Discussion Paper no. 105/81. University of Bristol, June.

Dornbusch, Rudiger. 1976. Exchange rate dynamics. *Journal of Political Economy* 84:1161–76.

———. 1983. Real interest rates, home goods, and optimal external borrowing. *Journal of Political Economy* 91 (February): 141–53.

Dornbusch, Rudiger, and Fischer, Stanley. 1980. Exchange rates and the current account. *American Economic Review* 70:960–71.

Drazen, Allan. 1980. On the dependence of the natural rate of unemployment on short-run fluctuations in employment and output. Unpublished paper, University of Chicago, November.

Giavazzi, Francesco; Odekon, Mehmet; and Wyplosz, Charles. 1982. Simulating an oil shock with sticky prices. *European Economic Review* 18 (May/June): 11–33.

Giavazzi, Francesco, and Wyplosz, Charles. 1982. The zero root problem: The dynamic determination of stationary equilibrium in linear models. Unpublished paper, INSEAD.

Hadley, G. 1961. *Linear algebra.* New York: Addison-Wesley.

Hayashi, Fumio. 1982. A note on marginal *q* and average *q*. *Econometrica* 50:213–24.

Koopmans, Tjalling C.; Diamond, Peter A.; and Williamson, Richard E. 1964. Stationary utility and time perspective. *Econometrica* 32 (January–April): 82–100.

Kouri, Pentti J. K. 1976. The exchange rate and the balance of payments in the short run and in the long run: A monetary approach. *Scandinavian Journal of Economics* 2:280–308.

———. 1981. Balance of payments and the foreign exchange market: A dynamic partial equilibrium model. NBER Working Paper no. 644, March.

Lipton, David, and Sachs, Jeffrey. 1983. Accumulation and growth in a two country model: A simulation approach. *Journal of International Economics* 15 (August): 135–60.

Lucas, Robert E., Jr., and Stokey, Nancy L. 1982. Optimal growth with many consumers. Discussion Paper no. 518, Northwestern University, March.

Mussa, Michael. 1980. The role of the current account in exchange rate dynamics. Unpublished paper, University of Chicago, October.

Muth, John F. 1961. Rational expectations and the theory of price movements. *Econometrica* 29:315–35.

Obstfleld, Maurice. 1982. Aggregate spending and the terms of trade: Is there a Laursen-Metzler effect?'' Quarterly Journal of Economics 97(May): 251–70.

———. 1981. Macroeconomic policy, exchange rate dynamics, and optimal asset accumulation, *Journal of Political Economy* 89:1142–61.

Rodriguez, Carlos A. 1980. The Role of trade flows in exchange rate determination: A rational expectations approach. *Journal of Political Economy* 88 (December): 1148–58.

Sachs, Jeffrey. 1983. Energy and growth under flexible exchange rates: A simulation study. In *The international transmission of economic disturbances under flexible exchange rates,* ed. J. Bandhari and B. Putnam. Cambridge, Mass.: MIT Press.

Svensson, Lars E. O., and Razin, Assaf. 1983. The terms of trade and the current account: The Harberger-Laursen-Metzler effect. *Journal of Political Economy* 91 (February): 97–124.

Wilson, Charles A. 1979. Anticipated shocks and exchange rate dynamics. *Journal of Political Economy* 87 (June): 639–47.

V   Foreign Exchange Intervention

11   Exchange Market Intervention Operations: Their Role in Financial Policy and Their Effects

Dale W. Henderson

11.1 Introduction and Conclusions

This paper addresses two unanswered questions regarding exchange market intervention operations that leave money supplies unchanged: (1) what role should such intervention operations play in open economy financial policy, and (2) do they have significant effects on macroeconomic variables.[1] First, several versions of a model in which intervention operations have effects are used to delineate the role of these operations in macroeconomic financial policy.[2] Then, attention is focused on some recent theoretical and empirical studies relevant for assessing the likelihood that intervention operations have significant effects.

According to the view adopted here, the home authorities conduct financial policy using two kinds of financial market operations: (1) intervention operations, exchanges of home (currency) securities for foreign (currency)

Discussions with Matthew Canzoneri, Jo Anna Gray, Peter Isard, Maurice Obstfeld, and Kenneth Rogoff led to improvements in this paper. This paper represents the views of the author and should not be interpreted as representing the views of the Board of Governors of the Federal Reserve System or other members of its staff.

1. Stein (1963), Mundell (1968), and Niehans (1968) were pioneers in the analysis of open economy financial policy. Recent contributions include those of Modigliani and Askari (1973), Hamada (1974), Sweeney (1976), Tower and Willett (1976), Turnovsky (1976, 1983), Fischer (1977), Boyer (1978, 1980), Parkin (1978), Flood (1979), Henderson (1979, 1980, 1982), Kaminow (1979), Bryant (1980), Frenkel (1980), Roper and Turnovsky (1980), Artis and Currie (1981), Mussa (1981), Wallich and Gray (1981), Weber (1981), Argy (1982), Canzoneri (1982), Jones (1982), and Canzoneri and Gray (1983).

2. Only in section 11.10 is there brief mention of the use of intervention policy to counter "disorderly markets" or such features of exchange market dynamics as runs or bandwagons. Shafer (1982) and Wonnacott (1982) address these issues among others.

securities with private agents, and (2) monetary operations, exchanges of home money for home securities with private agents.[3] The intervention operation just described is often referred to as "sterilized intervention" because it leaves both the home money supply and the foreign money supply unchanged.[4]

The role of intervention policy is explored in the context of a discrete-time stochastic model in which agents have rational expectations. The description of this model in section 11.2 reveals that it has two features which are especially important. First, intervention operations affect macroeconomic variables. This feature is an implication of the assumptions that private agents regard home and foreign securities as imperfect substitutes and that private agents do not treat the security holdings of the authorities as being implicitly a part of their own portfolios. Second, contemporaneous financial policy feedback rules can dampen the variance of employment caused by disturbances in the markets for goods and assets even though agents have rational expectations. This feature is a consequence of the assumption that labor market participants set a base nominal wage and, in some versions of the model, an indexing parameter before other markets meet.

Whether one open economy financial policy regime is better than another usually depends on the source of disturbances to the economy. In section 11.3 this observation is illustrated by a comparison of the effects of different kinds of transitory disturbances to a single open economy with no indexing under two alternative pure financial policy regimes. Under an "aggregates constant policy" the money supply is kept unchanged and there is no intervention, so the interest rate and the exchange rate vary when disturbances are experienced. Under a "rates constant policy" monetary operations and intervention operations are employed to keep the interest rate and the exchange rate fixed. It is shown that for disturbances to the market for the home good an aggregates constant policy results in less variation in employment and that for disturbances to financial markets a rates constant policy results in less variation in employment. Then it is argued that similar results can be obtained when the economy is subject to one kind of permanent disturbance as well as to transitory disturbances.

Introducing indexing necessitates qualifications to some of the results for pure financial policy regimes. As explained in section 11.4, for disturbances that directly affect only financial markets, a rates constant policy still results

3. Throughout this paper it is the currency of denomination of a security, and not the country of residence of its issuer or holder, that determines whether that security is a home security or a foreign security.

4. Dooley (1979) provides a thorough discussion of intervention operations. Girton and Henderson (1977) compare the effects of intervention operations and monetary operations in a two-country model of financial markets. Black (1980) describes experience with intervention policy in the years 1973–78.

in less employment variation. However, for disturbances that directly affect the market for the home good, the results are less clear-cut with indexing.

To show that the authorities may be able to reduce the variance of employment below that implied by either pure financial policy regime is the main purpose of section 11.5. The authorities may improve the outcome for currently unobserved employment by adopting a contemporaneous financial policy feedback rule that relates a financial variable chosen as an instrument—say, the exogenous supply of home (currency) assets—to a financial variable chosen as an information variable—say, the exchange rate—because the information variable conveys current though incomplete information about the sources of disturbances. Under general conditions macroeconomic outcomes will be better if the financial authorities in a single open economy facing transitory disturbances neither rigidly fix the exchange rate nor allow it to fluctuate freely. In fact, outcomes may be better if they reinforce the movement of the exchange rate that would occur if there were no intervention by "leaning with the wind."

Section 11.6 is a digression from the topic of intervention policy made in order to consider further how exchange rate movements and interest rate movements can be used together to make inferences about the sources of unobserved disturbances. Not surprisingly, it is found that exchange rate movements provide helpful additional information but that they do not completely resolve the problems faced by the authorities in their attempts to discover the sources of disturbances.

Limited support for the contention that intervention policy can be helpful in dampening "vicious circles" is provided in section 11.7. It is shown that when wage contracts are indexed the trade-off between output variance and price variance can be improved when the exchange rate is fixed.

In section 11.8 attention is turned to the interactions in a two-country world economy that must be considered when choosing financial policies. It is emphasized that the overall stance of intervention policy is the result of the intervention policies of both countries. Then it is shown that for two kinds of transitory disturbances the two countries would agree on what the overall stance of intervention policy should be, while for another kind of transitory disturbance a policy conflict would arise.

The message of section 11.9 is that, strictly speaking, imperfect substitutability among securities denominated in different currencies is neither necessary nor sufficient for intervention operations to have significant effects. As noted in section 11.10, recent rejections of the joint hypothesis that securities denominated in different currencies are perfect substitutes and that expectations are rational are consistent with the effects of intervention operations being significant. However, the results of direct tests for these effects suggest that any such effects are quite weak.

11.2 The Model

This section is a description of a discrete-time stochastic model of a two-country world economy in which agents have rational expectations.[5] Special cases of this model are employed in the next six sections.

First, attention is focused on the real sector of the model. The model contains two goods each of which is produced in only one country but is consumed in both. Home output (Y) must be equal to aggregate demand for the home good, and foreign output ($\overset{*}{Y}$) must be equal to the aggregate demand for the foreign good:

$$(1) \quad Y = y_0 + y_1(Y + \overset{*}{Y}) - y_2 r - y_3 \overset{*}{r} + y_4(e + \overset{*}{p} - p) + y_5 e - y_6 p + \alpha,$$

$$(2) \quad \overset{*}{Y} = \overset{*}{y}_0 + \overset{*}{y}_1(Y + \overset{*}{Y}) - \overset{*}{y}_2 r - \overset{*}{y}_3 \overset{*}{r} - y_4(e + \overset{*}{p} - p) - \overset{*}{y}_5 e - \overset{*}{y}_6 \overset{*}{p} - \alpha.$$

Here and in what follows, all coefficients except intercept terms are positive. Increases in home and foreign output raise income at home and abroad and, therefore, spending on both goods.[6] It is assumed that the marginal propensities to consume the home good (y_1), to consume the foreign good ($\overset{*}{y}_1$), and to save ($s = 1 - y_1 - \overset{*}{y}_1$) are the same in both countries and are all positive.[7] Aggregate demand for each good depends negatively on the expected real interest rate on home securities (r) and on foreign securities ($\overset{*}{r}$) because increases in expected real interest rates raise home and foreign saving.

Aggregate demand for the home good depends positively on the (logarithm of the) relative price of the foreign good ($e + \overset{*}{p} - p$). The variables e, $\overset{*}{p}$, and p are, respectively, the (logarithms of the) exchange rate defined as the home currency price of foreign currency, the foreign currency price of the foreign good, and the home currency price of the home good. Aggregate demand for the foreign good depends negatively on the relative price of the foreign good. An increase in the relative price of the foreign good shifts home and foreign spending toward (away from) the home (foreign) good and raises (lowers) foreign (home) income measured in terms of the

---

5. This model is a linear approximation to a nonlinear model sketched out in the Appendix. Explicit expressions for the approximation coefficients are presented in the Appendix.

6. It is possible to add Y and $\overset{*}{Y}$ together because units are chosen so that the relative price of the foreign good is one in the equilibrium about which the approximation is made.

7. Home and foreign residents are assumed to have the same tastes so that shifts of wealth between countries through current account surpluses and deficits will have no effects on the variables of the model. Without this assumption a more complicated, dynamic analysis would be required.

home (foreign) good, thereby stimulating (restraining) spending on the home (foreign) good. It is assumed that trade is initially balanced so that the effect of an increase in the relative price of the foreign good on the demand for the foreign good is equal in absolute value to the effect on the demand for the home good.[8]

A depreciation of the home currency—that is, a rise in e—raises (lowers) home and foreign wealth measured in terms of the home (foreign) good, thereby reducing (increasing) world saving measured in terms of the home (foreign) good and raising (lowering) aggregate demand for the home (foreign) good.[9] An increase in the home (foreign) currency price of the home (foreign) good lowers home and foreign wealth measured in terms of the home (foreign) good thereby raising world saving measured in terms of the home (foreign) good and reducing aggregate demand for the home (foreign) good. The effect of a depreciation of the home currency on demand for the home good is smaller in absolute value than the effect of an increase in the home currency price of the home good ($y_5 < y_6$) because a rise in e raises the home good value of only the foreign currency component of home and foreign wealth, but an increase in p lowers the home good value of all components of home and foreign wealth; $\overset{*}{y}_5 < \overset{*}{y}_6$ by an analogous argument.

Positive values of α represent increases in the demand for the home good at the expense of demand for the foreign good. This stochastic variable and those introduced below to represent other disturbances are assumed to have zero means and to be mutually and serially uncorrelated.

The expected real interest rates on home securities and foreign securities are

$$(3) \qquad r = i - (\bar{q} - q) = i - (\bar{e} - e) - (\bar{\overset{*}{q}} - \overset{*}{q}),$$

$$(4) \qquad \overset{*}{r} = \overset{*}{i} + (\bar{e} - e) - (\bar{q} - q) = \overset{*}{i} - (\bar{\overset{*}{q}} - \overset{*}{q}).$$

The variables i and $\overset{*}{i}$ represent the nominal interest rates on home and foreign securities. The variables q and $\overset{*}{q}$ represent the (logarithms of the) home currency and foreign currency prices of the world consumption bundle:

$$(5) \qquad q = hp + (1 - h)(e + \overset{*}{p}),$$

$$(6) \qquad \overset{*}{q} = h(p - e) + (1 - h)\overset{*}{p}.$$

The constant h represents the proportion of spending that would be allocated

---

8. See the Appendix for proof that the assumption of balanced trade has this implication.

9. The assumptions about asset preferences made below imply that the residents of each country have net claims denominated in the currency of the other country, that is, that there are no "negative net foreign asset positions."

to the home good by residents of both countries if all of the disturbance terms were zero. From (5) and (6) it follows that $\bar{q}$ and $\bar{\overset{*}{q}}$ are given by

$$(7) \qquad \bar{q} = h\bar{p} + (1 - h)(\bar{e} + \bar{\overset{*}{p}}),$$

$$(8) \qquad \bar{\overset{*}{q}} = h(\bar{p} - \bar{e}) + (1 - h)\bar{\overset{*}{p}},$$

where $\bar{q}$, $\bar{\overset{*}{q}}$, $\bar{p}$, $\bar{e}$, and $\bar{\overset{*}{p}}$ are the constant values of q, $\overset{*}{q}$, p, e, and $\overset{*}{p}$ that all agents expect in any period to prevail in the next period.

According to the production functions for home and foreign output,

$$(9) \qquad Y = x_0 + x_1 L + x_2 \beta,$$

$$(10) \qquad \overset{*}{Y} = \overset{*}{x}_0 + \overset{*}{x}_1 \overset{*}{L},$$

home output depends positively on home employment (L), and foreign output depends positively on foreign employment $(\overset{*}{L})$.[10] Positive values of β represent increases in the (marginal) productivity of labor.

Firms and workers in each country enter into a labor contract each period before other markets meet to avoid the costs of ongoing wage negotiations. This contract has two provisions, an employment rule and a nominal wage indexing rule. According to the employment rule, workers must supply whatever amount of labor firms want at the realized real wage. Given this rule, firms in each country employ labor up to the point at which the (logarithms of the) marginal product of labor and the real wage are equal:

$$(11) \qquad w - p = l_0 - l_1 L + \beta,$$

$$(12) \qquad \overset{*}{w} - \overset{*}{p} = \overset{*}{l}_0 - \overset{*}{l}_1 \overset{*}{L}.$$

The variables w and $\overset{*}{w}$ represent (the logarithms of) home and foreign nominal wages measured in home and foreign currency, respectively. The amount of labor employed in the home (foreign) country may be greater or less than the constant "full employment" amount, L_f $(\overset{*}{L}_f)$, that home (foreign) workers would supply in the absence of the labor contract.

The nominal wage indexing rules are

$$(13) \qquad w - \bar{w} = \mu(q - \bar{q}),$$

$$(14) \qquad \overset{*}{w} - \bar{\overset{*}{w}} = \overset{*}{\mu}(\overset{*}{q} - \bar{\overset{*}{q}}).$$

In each country an indexing parameter (μ or $\overset{*}{\mu}$) determines what fraction of deviations of the price index from its base value ($\bar{q}$ or $\bar{\overset{*}{q}}$) will be reflected in deviations of the same sign in the nominal wage from its base value ($\bar{w}$ or

---

10. It is shown in the Appendix that the production function of equation (9) is a linear approximation of a nonlinear production function with a multiplicative disturbance.

$\overset{*}{w}$). The base values $\overline{w}$ and $\overset{*}{\overline{w}}$ are the values of w and $\overset{*}{w}$ which would be consistent with full employment if all disturbances were zero:

(15) $\overline{w} - \overline{p} = l_0 - l_1 L_f,$

(16) $\overset{*}{\overline{w}} - \overset{*}{\overline{p}} = \overset{*}{l}_0 - \overset{*}{l}_1 \overset{*}{L}_f.$

As before, $\overline{q}$ and $\overset{*}{\overline{q}}$ are the constant values of q and $\overset{*}{q}$ expected in any period to prevail in the next. In order to calculate $\overline{p}$, $\overset{*}{\overline{p}}$, and $\overline{e}$ so that they can set $\overline{w}$ and $\overset{*}{\overline{w}}$ and $\overline{q}$ and $\overset{*}{\overline{q}}$, labor market participants must know the parameters of the economic model and the values at which the financial authorities' policy instruments would be set if all disturbances were zero.

Now attention is focused on the financial sector of the model, which consists of markets for three assets: home money, foreign money, and home securities.[11] Residents of each country hold the money of their country but not the money of the other country.[12] The supply of home money (M) must equal the demand for home money by home residents, and the supply of foreign money (N) must equal the demand for foreign money by foreign residents:

(17) $M = m_0 + m_1 p + m_2 Y - m_3 i - m_4(\overset{*}{i} + \overline{e} - e)$
$+ \gamma + \delta,$

(18) $N = \overset{*}{n}_0 + \overset{*}{n}_1 \overset{*}{p} + \overset{*}{n}_2 \overset{*}{Y} - \overset{*}{n}_3(i - \overline{e} + e) - \overset{*}{n}_4 \overset{*}{i}.$

Home (foreign) money demand depends positively on the home (foreign) currency price of the home (foreign) good and on home (foreign) output. Increases in both of these variables raise the transactions demands for money balances.[13] In a given country money demand depends negatively on the nominal interest rate on securities denominated in that country's currency and on the expected nominal return on securities denominated in the other country's currency measured in terms of the given country's currency, which is equal to the nominal interest rate on securities denominated in the other country's currency plus the expected rate of depreciation of the given country's currency. Positive values of γ (δ) represent shifts of home resi-

---

11. The market for the fourth asset, foreign securities, can be omitted by Walras's law; for completeness the equilibrium condition for this market is included in the Appendix.

12. That is, there is no "currency substitution" in this model.

13. The foreign price level does not appear in equation (17), nor does the exchange rate appear as a separate argument. These variables are absent because, as is spelled out in more detail in the Appendix, equation (17) is an approximation of a demand function for nominal balances of the form $PY\lambda(\cdot)$, which has a real income elasticity of unity. If the demand for nominal balances were of the form $[hP + (1 - h)EP]g\{PY/[hP + (1 - h)EP], \cdot\}$ where the real income elasticity was less than one, then $\overset{*}{p}$ and e would appear in equation (17). Assuming that the real income elasticity of the demand for nominal balances is one simplifies the derivation of several results, particularly those for a productivity shock in an economy with no indexing. Under plausible assumptions the qualitative results would be the same if the real income elasticity were less than unity, as is shown in Henderson (1982).

dents' asset preferences toward home money and away from home (foreign) securities.

The supply of home securities (B) must equal the demand for these securities by both home and foreign residents:

$$(19) \qquad B = b_0 - b_1 p - b_2 Y + b_3 i - b_4(\overset{*}{i} + \bar{e} - e)$$
$$+ b_5(i - \bar{e} + e) - b_6 \overset{*}{i} + b_7 e - b_8 \overset{*}{p}$$
$$- b_9 \overset{*}{Y} - \gamma + \epsilon.$$

It is assumed that both home and foreign residents determine the home currency amount that they will hold in securities by subtracting their money demands measured in home currency from the home currency value of their wealth and allocate the same fraction of this amount to home securities.[14] The resulting demand for home securities depends negatively on the prices of the home and foreign goods and on home and foreign output. Increases in prices and outputs raise the transactions demands for money of both home and foreign residents partly at the expense of their demands for home currency securities. It follows that $b_1 < m_1$ and $b_2 < m_2$. It is also assumed that both home and foreign residents regard the three assets they hold as strict gross substitutes. Therefore, the demand for home securities depends positively on the nominal interest rate on home securities and on the expected rate of return on home securities measured in terms of foreign currency, and $b_3 > m_3$. In addition, the demand for home securities depends negatively on the nominal interest rate on foreign securities and on the expected rate of return on foreign securities measured in terms of home currency.[15] The demand for home securities depends positively on the exchange rate because a depreciation of the home currency raises the home currency value of world wealth minus world money demand. The demand for home securities depends negatively (positively) on the disturbance term γ (ϵ). Positive values of γ (ϵ) represent decreases (increases) in the demand for home securities matched by increases (decreases) in the demand for home money (foreign securities).

11.3 Transitory Disturbances and Alternative Pure Financial Policies in a Single Open Economy with No Indexing

In this section a specialized version of the model of section 11.2 is employed to analyze the effects on home employment of some transitory disturbances to macroeconomic equilibrium in the home economy under two

14. The explanation for the assumption that home and foreign residents allocate the same fraction of the home currency value of the difference between their wealth and their money demand to home securities is the same as the explanation in n. 7 for the assumption that these agents have the same tastes for goods.

15. $i - \bar{e} + e$ and $\overset{*}{i}$ are the opportunity costs of holding money rather than the two types of securities in the foreign country.

pure financial policy regimes, an aggregates constant policy and a rates constant policy.[16] The analysis is simplified by the assumption that there is no indexing in the home country ($\mu = 0$).

As a first step the behavior of the home and foreign financial authorities is described. The balance sheet of the financial authorities in the home country has the money supply as a liability and both home and foreign securities as assets. The home authorities' holdings of foreign securities are their only foreign exchange reserves. At a given exchange rate, changes in the three balance sheet items must sum to zero, so values for only two of the three items can be chosen independently. It is assumed that the home authorities do not observe home employment, home output, and the price of the home good in the current period. They can choose as policy instruments and set values for any two of four financial variables: the home money supply (M), private holdings of home securities (B), the interest rate on home securities (i), and the exchange rate (e). The values of the other two variables are determined by the model. The description of the home authorities' balance sheet implies that if the home authorities seek to change B without changing M, they must also change the supply of foreign securities available to private agents through intervention operations. Under an aggregates constant policy M and B are kept unchanged, while under a rates constant policy M and B are allowed to vary to keep i and e constant. Under each policy regime the authorities set and announce the same values for two financial policy instruments before markets meet each period; that is, they either do not observe or, more realistically, elect not to respond to movements in the financial variables for which they do not set values. The announced values of the two policy instruments can be chosen arbitrarily because home country labor market participants set the base nominal wage so that the expected value of L is equal to L_f given these announced values.

Since the objective of this and the next five sections is to focus on financial policymaking in a single open economy, somewhat different assumptions are made about the information available to the foreign authorities and the use they make of this information. It is assumed that the foreign authorities can observe the level of foreign output ($\overset{*}{Y}$) and the price of the foreign good ($\overset{*}{p}$) in the current period and that they act so as to keep these variables as well as the interest rate on foreign securities ($\overset{*}{i}$) fixed.[17]

Given the nature of the disturbances and the behavior of the authorities, it is rational for agents to expect in any period that the values of the price of the home good and the exchange rate in the next period will be equal to

16. The type of analysis used in this section was first employed in the context of a closed economy by Poole (1970) and has been extended by Friedman (1975).

17. The foreign authorities must use monetary operations and two fiscal policy instruments, for example, the level of balanced budget government spending and its allocation between the home good and the foreign good, to achieve these constant values. Flood (1979) makes an interesting alternative set of assumptions about the behavior of the foreign authorities.

the constants $\bar{p}$ and $\bar{e}$, respectively.[18] In addition, it is rational for labor market participants in the home country to set the base nominal wage at the constant value implied by (15) each period before other markets meet.

As a second step the specialized version of the model used in this section is expressed in more compact form. The equilibrium conditions for the markets for the home good, home money, and home securities become[19]

$$(20) \qquad 0 = -y_L\hat{L} - y_i\hat{i} + y_e\hat{e} + \alpha + y_\beta\beta,$$

$$(21) \qquad \hat{M} = m_L\hat{L} - m_i\hat{i} + m_e\hat{e} \qquad -m_\beta\beta + \gamma + \delta,$$

$$(22) \qquad \hat{B} = -b_L\hat{L} + b_i\hat{i} + b_e\hat{e} \qquad + b_\beta\beta - \gamma \qquad + \epsilon,$$

where

$$y_L = y_p l_1 + y_Y x_1, \qquad m_L = m_p l_1 + m_Y x_1, \qquad b_L = b_p l_1 + b_Y x_1,$$

$$y_i = y_2, \qquad m_i = m_3, \qquad b_i = b_3 + b_5,$$

$$y_e = y_p - y_2 - y_6 + y_5, \qquad m_e = m_4, \qquad b_e = b_4 + b_5 + b_7,$$

$$y_\beta = y_p - y_Y x_2, \qquad m_\beta = m_p - m_Y x_2, \qquad b_\beta = b_p - b_Y x_2,$$

and

$$y_p = y_4 + (y_2 + y_3)h + y_6, \qquad m_p = m_1, b_p = b_1,$$

$$y_Y = s + \overset{*}{y}_1, \qquad m_Y = m_2, b_Y = b_2.$$

A circumflex over a variable indicates the deviation of that variable from its constant expected value. It is assumed that relative price and wealth effects outweigh possibly "perverse" expected real interest rate effects so that y_e is positive. With employment held constant, an increase in the productivity of labor tends to create excess demand for the home good because it lowers its price but tends to create excess supply of the home good because it increases the amount supplied. It is assumed that the first effect dominates so that y_β is positive. Assumptions embodied in (9), (17), and (19) imply that an in-

18. This statement is strictly true only if it is assumed that there are "no speculative bubbles." Sargent (1973) explains the implications of this assumption in the context of a closed economy. Parkin (1978), Flood (1979), Roper and Turnovsky (1980), Wallich and Gray (1981), and Weber (1981) analyze open economy financial policies under the assumption of rational expectations.

19. Equations (5) and (7) are substituted into (3), and (6) and (8) are substituted into (4). The resulting versions of (3) and (4) are substituted into (1), and (9) is substituted for Y in (1), (17), and (19). Equations (5), (7), and (15) are substituted into (13). The modified version of (13) is used to eliminate w from (11). The modified version of (11) is employed to obtain an expression for p which depends on e when $0 < \mu \leq 1$ but is independent of e when $\mu = 0$. This expression is substituted for p wherever it appears in the modified versions of (1), (17), and (19). The further modified versions of (1), (17), and (19) with the disturbances set equal to zero are subtracted from the same equations with the disturbances free to take on any value to obtain (20), (21), and (22).

crease in labor productivity leaves nominal income unchanged and that with nominal income unchanged the markets for home money and home securities are unaffected, so that $m_\beta = b_\beta = 0$.[20] Under these assumptions a shift in demand from the foreign good to the home good ($\alpha > 0$) and an increase in the productivity of labor can be analyzed together because they both affect only the market for the home good. Foreign variables do not appear in (20), (21), and (22) because they are fixed by the foreign authorities.

Equilibrium schedules for the markets for the home good, home money, and home securities are shown in figure 11.1. The equilibrium schedule for the home good is $X_0 X_0$. An increase in i, which lowers demand, must be accompanied by a decline in L, which raises excess demand. The equilibrium schedule for home money is $M_0 M_0$. A rise in i, which reduces demand, must be offset by a rise in L, which increases demand. The equilibrium schedule for home securities is $B_0 B_0$. An increase i, which raises demand, must be matched by an increase in L, which lowers demand. The assumptions of the model imply that the MM schedule is steeper than the BB schedule. The effect of an increase in L on the demand for home money

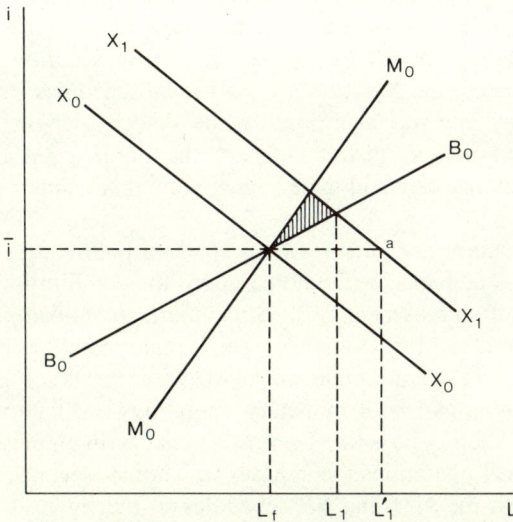

Fig. 11.1   Shift up in excess demand for home goods

20. As stated in n. 13, it is assumed that the demand for home nominal balances has a real income elasticity of unity. Furthermore, it is assumed that p and Y enter the demand for home securities only because home wealth minus home demand for nominal balances is the scale variable for home demand for these securities and that the disturbance term in the production function is multiplicative. These assumptions imply that $m_\beta = b_\beta = 0$ as can be confirmed by reference to the explicit expressions for the relevant approximation coefficients in the Appendix.

is greater than the absolute value of the effect of an increase in L on the demand for home securities: $m_L > b_L$ since $m_1 > b_1$ and $m_2 > b_2$. The absolute value of the effect of an increase in i on the demand for home money is smaller than the effect of an increase in i on the demand for home securities: $m_i = m_3 < b_3 + b_5 = b_i$. Because X_0X_0, M_0M_0, and B_0B_0 are the equilibrium schedules that would result if all disturbances were zero, they intersect at L_f. Changes in the exchange rate or in the balance sheet of the home authorities cause the schedules to shift in a manner described below.

Now consider the employment effects of disturbances to the excess demand for the home good. Such disturbances might result from shifts in the allocation of spending between home and foreign goods either at home or abroad or from a shift up in the productivity of home labor. Suppose an increase in the excess demand for the home good moves the XX schedule from X_0X_0 to X_1X_1 in figure 11.1. If the home authorities pursue an aggregates constant policy, a level of employment between L_f and L_1 results. Employment tends to increase, creating an excess demand for home money and an excess supply of home securities. Those disequilibria can only be removed by a rise in the home interest rate and an appreciation of the home currency. An appreciation of the home currency raises excess supply in the markets for the home good, home money, and home securities. As the home currency appreciates, the X_1X_1, M_0M_0, and B_0B_0 schedules shift toward one another until they intersect at a point in the shaded triangle. Under an aggregates constant policy, disturbances to the home good market induce changes in the interest rate and the exchange rate that dampen the movement in employment.

If instead the authorities pursue a rates constant policy, then following the increase in excess demand for the home good, the equilibrium point is point a, and the level of employment is L_1'. Since there are no dampening changes in the interest rate or the exchange rate, employment raises by the full amount necessary to reequilibrate the market for the home good. The authorities must undertake both monetary operations and intervention operations in order to keep i and e fixed given the change in employment. Expansionary monetary operations, purchases of home securities with home money, shift both the MM and BB schedules to the right. A monetary operation which shifts MM until it passes through point a also shifts BB farther to the right because $m_L > b_L$. Thus, in order to ensure that BB passes through point a, the authorities must undertake an intervention operation, a sale of home securities in exchange for foreign securities. When the only source of disturbances to equilibrium is shifts in the excess demand for the home good, an aggregates constant policy leads to less variation in employment than a rates constant policy.

A different conclusion is reached when disturbances to financial markets are considered. For purposes of illustration, attention is focused on a type of disturbance for which intervention operations are the appropriate remedy, a shift in asset preferences between home and foreign securities. Suppose a shift in asset preferences away from home securities and toward foreign securities moves the *BB* schedule from B_0B_0 to B_1B_1 in figure 11.2. Under an aggregates constant policy a level of employment between L_1 and L_2 results. The decrease in demand for home securities leads to an increase in i, which in turn creates an excess supply of home money. In order for equilibrium in financial markets to be reestablished, the home currency must depreciate. The new equilibrium lies in the shaded triangle. Employment may rise, fall, or remain the same since the changes in financial variables have opposite effects on demand for the home good.

If instead the authorities pursue a rates constant policy, they accommodate the shift in asset preferences with an intervention operation. The *BB* schedule is shifted from B_1B_1 back to B_0B_0, and employment definitely remains unchanged. When the only source of disturbances to equilibrium is shifts in asset preferences between home and foreign securities, a rates constant policy leads to less variation in employment than an aggregates constant policy.

Two other possible sources of stochastic disturbances to equilibrium are (1) shifts in home residents' preferences between home money and foreign securities and (2) shifts in home residents' preferences between home money and home securities. In both these cases, a rates constant policy leads to less variation in employment than an aggregates constant policy. Under a rates constant policy the transmission of financial market disturbances to the market for the home good through interest rate and exchange rate changes is prevented.

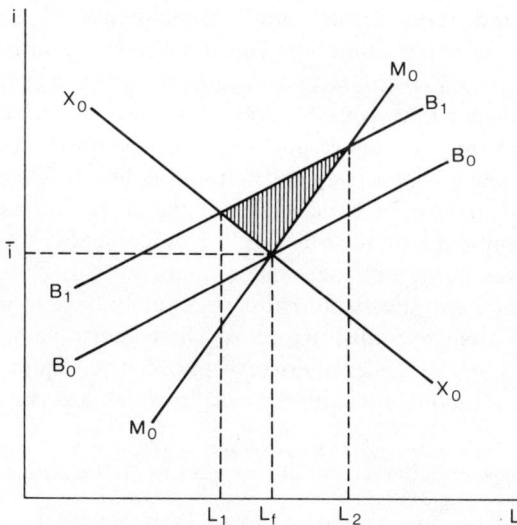

Fig. 11.2   Shift out of home securities into foreign securities

The results just described can be summarized more formally. The variances of home employment (σ_L^2) under rates constant (RC) and aggregates constant (AC) financial policy regimes are given by

(23) $$\sigma_{L|RC}^2 = (1/y_L)^2(\sigma_\alpha^2 + y_\beta^2\sigma_\beta^2),$$

(24) $$\sigma_{L|AC}^2 = (C_1/\Delta_1)^2(\sigma_\alpha^2 + y_\beta^2\sigma_\beta^2)$$
$$+ [(C_2 + C_3)/\Delta_1]^2\sigma_\gamma^2 + (C_2/\Delta_1)^2\sigma_\delta^2 + (C_3/\Delta_1)^2\sigma_\epsilon^2,$$

$$C_1 = m_i b_e + b_i m_e, \quad C_3 = y_i m_e - m_i y_e,$$

$$C_2 = y_i b_e + b_i y_e, \quad \Delta_1 = y_L C_1 + m_L C_2 + b_L C_3.$$

The two sums $C_2 + C_3$ and $m_L C_2 + b_L C_3$ are clearly positive if $y_e > 0$, since $b_i > m_i$, and $m_L > b_L$. It can be shown that they are positive even if $y_e < 0$.[21] Thus, if $\sigma_\gamma^2 = \sigma_\delta^2 = \sigma_\epsilon^2 = 0$ and either σ_α^2 or $\sigma_\beta^2 > 0$, then $\sigma_{L|AC}^2 < \sigma_{L|RC}^2$. If $\sigma_\alpha^2 = \sigma_\beta^2 = 0$ and σ_γ^2, σ_δ^2, or $\sigma_\epsilon^2 > 0$, then $0 = \sigma_{L|RC}^2 < \sigma_{L|AC}^2$.

Of course, financial authorities operating under the assumptions about the availability and use of information specified above and attempting to choose among alternative financial policies would probably be faced with all the types of transitory disturbances considered above. The analysis above provides only limited assistance. For example, given the coefficients of the model and all the other parameters of the joint distribution of disturbances, there exists a variance of the disturbance terms in the market for the home good large enough to ensure that an aggregates constant policy leads to a lower expected loss than a rates constant policy. Additional conclusions must be based on explicit calculations of expected losses. A special assumption yields a few further conclusions. Suppose that the three equilibrium conditions are normalized on employment and that the variances of the normalized disturbances are equal.[22] An aggregates constant policy may or may not be better than a rates constant policy, whereas under similar conditions in a closed economy a money supply constant policy dominates an interest rate constant policy. An aggregates constant policy is superior (inferior) to a rates constant policy for large values of the degree of substitutability between home and foreign securities (the responsiveness of home good demand to changes in the exchange rate).

The financial authorities would almost certainly have to deal with permanent as well as transitory disturbances.[23] The results regarding the effects of transitory disturbances under alternative pure financial policy regimes carry over with minor modifications to the case in which a permanent disturbance

21. For proof of this assertion, see the Appendix.

22. That is, suppose equations (20), (21), and (22) are divided through by y_L, m_L, and b_L, respectively; that $(\alpha + y_\beta\beta)/y_L = \beta'$, $(\gamma + \delta)/m_L = \delta'$, and $(- \gamma + \epsilon)/b_L = \epsilon'$ are disturbances that may be mutually correlated; and that $\sigma_{\beta'}^2 = \sigma_{\delta'}^2 = \sigma_{\epsilon'}^2$.

23. Meltzer (1978) has emphasized the importance of the distinction between permanent and transitory disturbances.

is also present.[24] As an example of a permanent disturbance, consider a once-and-for-all shift in demand from the foreign good to the home good. Of course, if private agents know that this disturbance has occurred and take it into account when setting the nominal wage, it has no effect on the average levels of output and employment. Now suppose that private agents do not realize immediately that this permanent disturbance has occurred. It seems reasonable to assume that the nominal wage would not be changed, at least for a while. During this time the average real wage would be lower and the average level of employment would be higher than their full employment values under either an aggregates constant or a rates constant financial policy regime. However, the deviation of average employment from its full employment level is smaller under an aggregates constant policy than under a rates constant policy because induced changes in the interest rate and the exchange rate dampen the movement in average employment. After a while private agents would recognize that levels of output above the full employment value were being observed more frequently than would be suggested by what was known about the joint probability distribution of the transitory disturbances. They would conclude that the economic structure had changed and would change the nominal wage. Important research on how private agents would go about trying to separate permanent from transitory disturbances under various sets of conditions is well under way, but it is not reported on here.[25]

11.4 Transitory Disturbances and Alternative Pure Financial Policies in a Single Open Economy with Indexing

Here the analysis of the home employment effects of transitory disturbances under alternative pure financial policy regimes is extended to the case in which there is indexing in the home economy ($0 > \mu \leq 1$). The behavior of the home and foreign financial authorities conforms to the description provided in section 11.3.

Allowing for indexing in the home country necessitates some changes in the compact form of the model of equations (20), (21), and (22). The equilibrium conditions for the markets for the home good, home money, and home securities become[26]

(25) $0 = -\bar{y}_L \hat{L} - y_i \hat{i} + \bar{y}_e \hat{e} + \alpha + \bar{y}_\beta \beta,$

(26) $\hat{M} = \bar{m}_L \hat{L} - m_i \hat{i} + \bar{m}_e \hat{e} - \bar{m}_\beta \beta + \gamma + \delta,$

24. Suppose there were a succession of permanent shifts in asset preferences away from home securities and toward foreign securities. A rates constant policy would be appropriate but would require a series of sales of foreign securities by the home authorities. A rates constant policy would still be feasible if the authorities exhausted their holdings of foreign securities since the authorities could sell foreign currency forward.
25. See, for example, Brunner, Cukierman, and Meltzer (1980).
26. See n. 19 above.

(27) $\hat{B} = -\bar{b}_L \hat{L} + b_i \hat{i} + \bar{b}_e \hat{e} \qquad + \bar{b}_\beta \beta - \gamma \qquad + \epsilon,$

where

$$\bar{y}_L = y_p l_1 \rho + y_Y x_1, \qquad \bar{m}_L = m_p l_1 \rho + m_Y x_1, \qquad \bar{b}_L = b_p l_1 \rho + b_Y x_1,$$

$$\bar{y}_e = y_e - y_p \pi \rho, \qquad \bar{m}_e = m_e + m_p \pi \rho, \qquad \bar{b}_e = b_e - b_p \pi \rho,$$

$$\bar{y}_\beta = y_p \rho - y_Y x_2, \qquad \bar{m}_\beta = m_p \rho - m_Y x_2, \qquad \bar{b}_\beta = b_p \rho - b_Y x_2,$$

and

$$\pi = \mu(1 - h), \qquad \rho = 1/(1 - \mu h).$$

A tilde over a coefficient indicates that the coefficient has a different value with indexing. Though $\bar{y}_L$, $\bar{m}_L$, and $\bar{b}_L$ have the same signs as y_L, m_L, and b_L, respectively, they are larger in magnitude. Each of these coefficients is the sum of the reinforcing effects on the market in question of the output and price rises induced by a rise in L. With indexing a given increase in L must be accompanied by a larger increase in p because a given increase in p leads to a smaller decrease in the real wage. The coefficient $\bar{m}_e$ has the same sign as the coefficient m_e and is larger; $\bar{y}_e$ and $\bar{b}_e$ are smaller than y_e and b_e and may even be negative. The coefficients $\bar{y}_e$, $\bar{m}_e$, and $\bar{b}_e$ are each the sum of the direct effect of a rise in e and the indirect effect through the induced rise in p on the market in question. With indexing, increases in e must be accompanied by increases in p if L is to remain constant. The indirect effects of a rise in e may reinforce the direct effect, as in the case of $\bar{m}_e$, or counteract it, as in the cases of $\bar{y}_e$ and $\bar{b}_e$. Algebraically, $\bar{y}_\beta$, $\bar{m}_\beta$, and $\bar{b}_\beta$ are larger than y_β, m_β, and b_β, respectively. The coefficient on β for each market is the result of subtracting the absolute value of the output effect of a positive β from the absolute value of the price effect. With indexing a given positive β induces a larger decrease in p. Positive β's lower nominal income decreasing the demand for home money ($-\bar{m}_\beta < 0$) and increasing the demand for home securities ($\bar{b}_\beta > 0$). Thus, a shift in demand from the foreign good to the home good and an increase in labor productivity can no longer be analyzed together.

The results with indexing can be summarized formally. The variances of home employment ($\bar{\sigma}_L^2$) under rates constant and aggregates constant financial policy regimes are given by

(28) $$\bar{\sigma}_{L|RC}^2 = (1/\bar{y}_L)^2 (\sigma_\alpha^2 + \bar{y}_\beta^2 \sigma_\beta^2),$$

(29) $$\bar{\sigma}_{L|AC}^2 = (\bar{C}_1/\bar{\Delta}_1)^2 \sigma_\alpha^2 + [(\bar{C}_1 \bar{y}_\beta + \bar{C}_2 \bar{m}_\beta + \bar{C}_3 \bar{b}_\beta)/\bar{\Delta}_1]^2 \sigma_\beta^2$$
$$+ [(\bar{C}_2 + \bar{C}_3)/\bar{\Delta}_1]^2 \sigma_\gamma^2 + (\bar{C}_2/\bar{\Delta}_1)^2 \sigma_\delta^2 + (\bar{C}_3/\bar{\Delta}_1) \sigma_\epsilon^2,$$

where

$$\tilde{C}_1 = m_i \bar{b}_e + b_i \tilde{m}_e, \quad \tilde{C}_3 = y_i \tilde{m}_e - m_i \tilde{y}_e,$$
$$\tilde{C}_2 = y_i \bar{b}_e + b_i \tilde{y}_e, \quad \tilde{\Delta}_1 = \tilde{y}_L \tilde{C}_1 + \tilde{m}_L \tilde{C}_2 + \bar{b}_L \tilde{C}_3.$$

For what follows, it is useful to note that since $b_i > m_i$ and $m_p > b_p$,

$$\tilde{C}_1 = m_i b_e + b_i m_e + \pi \rho (b_i m_p - m_i b_p) > 0$$

and that since $\bar{b}_L m_p = \tilde{m}_L b_p$ and $\tilde{m}_L > \bar{b}_L$,

$$\tilde{m}_L \tilde{C}_2 + \bar{b}_L \tilde{C}_3 = y_i (\tilde{m}_L b_e + \bar{b}_L m_e) + \tilde{y}_e (\tilde{m}_L b_i - \bar{b}_L m_i)$$

can be negative if $\tilde{y}_e$ is negative and the second term on the right-hand side of the equals sign is large enough in absolute value to outweigh the first. Only if $\tilde{\Delta}_1 > 0$ do all the disturbances have their usual comparative static effects. It is assumed that $\tilde{\Delta}_1 > 0$ even if $\tilde{m}_L \tilde{C}_2 + \bar{b}_L \tilde{C}_3 < 0$.

It is convenient to discuss the results for financial market disturbances first. Indexing does not change the conclusion that when the only sources of disturbances to equilibrium are shifts in asset preferences, a rates constant policy leads to less variation in employment than an aggregates constant policy because it prevents the transmission of financial disturbances to the market for the home good through interest rate and exchange rate changes. If $\sigma_\alpha^2 = \sigma_\beta^2 = 0$ and $\sigma_\gamma^2, \sigma_\delta^2,$ or $\sigma_\epsilon^2 > 0$, then $0 = \tilde{\sigma}_{L|RC}^2 < \tilde{\sigma}_{L|AC}^2$. The more difficult question of whether indexing increases or reduces the advantage of a rates constant policy is not addressed here.

Indexing necessitates a minor qualification to the result obtained in section 11.3 for a shift in demand from the foreign good to the home good. For this disturbance an aggregates constant policy still leads to less variation in employment than a rates constant policy unless the effect of a change in wealth on the demand for the home good is too large. The greater the degree of indexing (the larger μ and, therefore, $\pi \rho$), the larger the increase in the price of the domestic good induced by a depreciation of the home currency and the smaller the increase in the relative price of the foreign good ($e - p$). The smaller the increase in the relative price of the foreign good, the lower the algebraic value of the increase in the demand for the home good associated with a depreciation of the home currency:

$$\tilde{y}_e = -y_i + (1 - \pi \rho)[(y_2 + y_3)h + y_4 + y_6] + (y_5 - y_6).$$

What is critical for determining whether a positive μ and the associated lower $\tilde{y}_e$ can lead to a reversal of the result that an aggregates constant policy dominates is the size of the effect of a change in wealth on demand for the home good.[27] If this wealth effect is negligible ($y_5, y_6 \rightarrow 0$), then no matter what the degree of indexing ($0 < \mu, \pi \rho \leq 1$) an aggregates constant policy continues to dominate since $\tilde{m}_L \tilde{C}_2 + \bar{b}_L \tilde{C}_3$ remains positive. However, if the

27. For proof of this assertion and the others in the remainder of this section, see the Appendix.

wealth effect is not negligible ($y_6 > y_5 > 0$), then a rates constant policy may dominate since $\bar{m}_L \bar{C}_2 + \bar{b}_L \bar{C}_3$ may be negative. For example, if indexing is complete, then when there is an intermediate degree of substitutability between home and foreign securities an aggregates constant policy dominates for small enough positive values of y_6 and y_5, but when home and foreign securities are highly substitutable, a rates constant policy is as good as an aggregates constant policy for $y_5 = y_6 = 0$, and a rates constant policy dominates for all $y_6 > y_5 > 0$.

The introduction of indexing complicates the comparison of aggregates constant and rates constant policies in the case of labor productivity disturbances. With indexing these disturbances directly affect all three markets. Thus, for labor productivity disturbances a rates constant policy might be preferred even if an aggregates constant policy would be preferred for disturbances that directly affect only the market for the home good.

11.5 Transitory Disturbances and Contemporaneous Financial Policy Feedback Rules in a Single Open Economy with No Indexing

In this section it is assumed that the financial authorities can observe current movements in financial variables not chosen as policy instruments and respond to them in attempting to dampen the effects of transitory disturbances. Furthermore, it is assumed that the authorities change a financial policy instrument in response to current information while the nominal wage remains fixed at a value set before other markets meet. That the authorities rather than private agents should adjust to current information even if it is available to both sets of agents seems reasonable since the costs associated with changing a financial policy instrument are much smaller than the costs associated with renegotiating the nominal wage.[28] Others have shown that in such an environment contemporaneous financial policy feedback rules usually dominate pure financial policies of the type considered in the last two sections.[29] Here it is demonstrated that a contemporaneous intervention

28. It could be assumed that the nominal wage was "indexed" to the financial variables not chosen as policy instruments and that financial policy instruments were not changed. If such an indexing rule were determined optimally, it would result in the same variation in employment as would the authorities' optimal feedback rule as shown in the context of a closed economy model by Canzoneri, Henderson, and Rogoff (1983). It appears that labor contracts involving indexing to financial variables are not negotiated, and conventional indexing is not a perfect substitute for this type of indexing.

29. The superiority of contemporaneous feedback rules was first demonstrated by Poole (1970). Kareken, Muench, and Wallace (1973) and Friedman (1975) significantly generalize and extend Poole's results. Boyer (1978) derives a contemporaneous feedback rule in a model in which home and foreign securities are perfect substitutes and exchange rate expectations are static. Roper and Turnovsky (1980) show how this rule is affected by the incorporation of a more general hypothesis regarding the formation of exchange rate expectations and an additional type of disturbance. Boyer (1980) considers feedback rules for the authorities in a model which is the same as the one used here in all essential respects except that expectations are static. Fischer's (1977) and Frenkel's (1980) optimal rules are derived in models quite different from the one employed here.

policy feedback rule is usually superior to either fixed or flexible exchange rates. This rule may imply reinforcing rather than dampening the movement in the exchange rate that would occur if there were no intervention.

As before, the financial authorities seek to mitigate the fluctuations in unobserved employment caused by different disturbances. The interest rate and the exogenous supply of home (currency) assets are chosen as policy instruments; the interest rate is kept rigidly fixed at an arbitrary value, and the exogenous supply of home assets is varied through intervention operations in response to the current information conveyed by exchange rate movements. Under these assumptions, the model of equations (20), (21), and (22) can be rewritten as

$$(30) \qquad 0 = -y_L \hat{L} + y_e \hat{e} + \alpha + y_\beta \beta,$$

$$(31) \qquad \hat{B}' = b_L' \hat{L} + b_e' \hat{e} \qquad\qquad + \delta + \epsilon.$$

Equation (31) is obtained by summing equations (21) and (22). The change in the exogenous supply of all home assets, $\hat{B}' = \hat{B} + \hat{M}$, represents intervention operations since monetary operations leave the exogenous supply of home assets unchanged. Definitions of y_L and y_e are provided above, and

$$b_L' = m_L - b_L, \text{ and } b_e' = m_e + b_e.$$

Equilibrium schedules for the markets for the home good and home assets are shown in figure 11.3. The equilibrium schedule for the home good is $X_0 X_0$. An increase in e, which raises demand, must be accompanied by an increase in L,

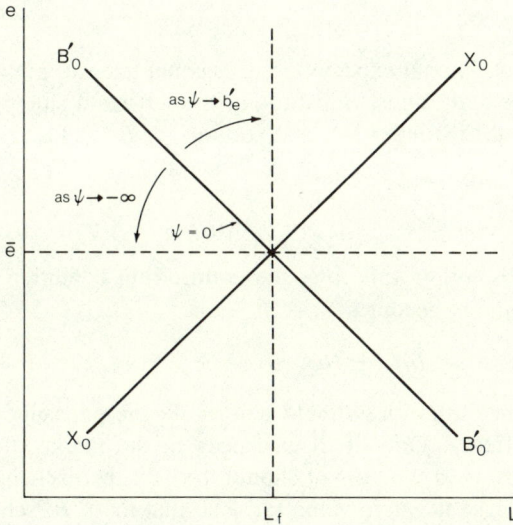

Fig. 11.3   Contemporaneous intervention policy feedback rule: slope of B'B' schedule depends on reaction parameter.

which lowers excess demand. The equilibrium schedule for home assets is
$B_0'B_0'$. A rise in e, which increases demand, must be offset by a fall in L, which
reduces demand. The contemporaneous intervention policy feedback rule alters
the slope of the $B'B'$ schedule in a manner described below.

Since the authorities observe the movement in the exchange rate, they
observe a linear combination of the disturbances. To see this, solve (30) for
$\hat{L}$, subsititute the result into (31), and rearrange to obtain

$$(32) \qquad \hat{L} = (y_e/y_L)\hat{e} + (1/y_L)(\alpha + y_\beta\beta) = (y_e/y_L)\hat{e} + \theta,$$

$$(33) \qquad \hat{B}' - (b_L'y_e/y_L + b_e')\hat{e} = b_L'\theta + \delta + \epsilon = \phi.$$

The authorities can observe the linear combination of disturbances represented by ϕ because they know or can observe everything to the left of the
first equals sign in (33).

The authorities minimize the variance of employment by acting so as to
make the expectation of the employment deviation conditioned on ϕ,
$E(\hat{L}|\phi)$, equal to zero:

$$(34) \qquad E(\hat{L}|\phi) = 0 = (y_e/y_L)\hat{e} + E(\theta|\phi),$$

where $E(\theta|\phi)$ is the expectation of θ conditional on ϕ, and [30]

$$(35) \qquad E(\theta|\phi) = [cov(\theta, \phi)/var(\phi)]\phi,$$

$$cov(\theta, \phi) = b_L'\sigma_\theta^2,$$

$$var(\phi) = b_L'^2\sigma_\theta^2 + \sigma_\delta^2 + \sigma_\epsilon^2,$$

$$\sigma_\theta^2 = (1/y_L)^2(\sigma_\alpha^2 + y_\beta^2\sigma_\beta^2).$$

Setting the conditional expectation of $\hat{L}$ equal to zero implies an intervention rule for the authorities. Substituting the left-hand side of (33) for ϕ in
(35), substituting (35) into (34), and solving for $\hat{B}'$ yields this rule:

$$(36) \qquad B' = \psi e,$$

$$\psi = b_e' - [y_e/(y_Lb_L')][(\sigma_\delta^2 + \sigma_\epsilon^2)/\sigma_\theta^2].$$

If the authorities follow this rule, the equilibrium condition for the market
for home assets (31) becomes

$$(37) \qquad 0 = b_L'\hat{L} + (b_e' - \psi)\hat{e} + \delta + \epsilon.$$

In general, the authorities should neither fix the exchange rate nor allow
it to fluctuate freely. Only if disturbances in the market for home assets
predominate $[(\sigma_\delta^2 + \sigma_\epsilon^2)/\sigma_\theta^2 \to \infty]$ should they fix the exchange rate (choose
an indefinitely large negative value for ψ so that the $B'B'$ schedule becomes
horizontal). By fixing the exchange rate they prevent any transmission of

---

30. In this section it assumed that the disturbances are normally distributed.

purely financial disturbances to the market for the home good. When disturbances to the market for the home good predominate $[(\sigma_\delta^2 + \sigma_\epsilon^2)/\sigma_\theta^2 \to 0]$, the authorities should not simply allow the exchange rate to fluctuate freely (choose a value of zero for ψ so that the $B'B'$ schedule remains unaffected). Rather, they should reinforce any tendency for the home currency to depreciate by selling home assets. By making the market for home assets completely insensitive to exchange rate movements (choosing a value of b'_e for ψ so that the $B'B'$ schedule becomes vertical), thereby amplifying exchange rate movements that would occur in the absence of intervention, the authorities generate exchange rate movements that completely offset disturbances to the market for the home good.

The intervention rule just derived is not the truly optimal contemporaneous financial policy feedback rule except in the extreme cases in which $(\sigma_\delta^2 + \sigma_\epsilon^2)/\sigma_\theta^2$ approaches infinity or zero. The shortcoming of this rule is that it does not reflect the information about θ embodied in the changes in the money supply required to keep the interest rate fixed. The truly optimal intervention policy rule requires intervention to be a linear function of both exchange rate changes and money supply changes. However, few additional qualitative insights can be gained from the considerably more complicated optimal rule.

Even under the optimal financial policy, one policy instrument, the interest rate in the example considered above, can be kept rigidly fixed. It is assumed that the authorities have only a single objective, minimizing the variance of employment, and that the coefficients of the model are known with certainty. Therefore the authorities need vary only one policy instrument, the exogenous supply of home assets, to do as well as they can. If either of these assumptions were relaxed, optimal financial policy would involve variations in both policy instruments as well as in both information variables.[31] Thus, in general, it is optimal for an individual country to opt for managed floating rather than a fixed or freely floating exchange rate whether the exchange rate is chosen as a policy instrument or used as an information variable.

11.6 The Exchange Rate and the Interest Rate as Information Variables

For many years the search for a way to extract information from financial data about the likely realizations of unobserved target variables was a quest

31. Brainard (1967) shows that if the coefficients of the model are stochastic variables which have a joint distribution with the additive disturbances that is known to the authorities, then in general an optimal financial policy requires that all financial variables chosen as policy instruments be set at well-defined values even if the authorities seek to minimize the squared deviations of only a single target variable from its target value. If they operated in this environment, the authorities would have to make inferences about the coefficients of the model as well as about the additive disturbances.

for the best single indicator of the stance of monetary policy. In section 11.5, the current view that more information can be obtained if movements in a number of financial variables are analyzed simultaneously is stated in broad terms. Here there is a more explicit discussion of how the authorities can use exchange rate movements in conjunction with interest rate movements to reduce but not eliminate their uncertainty about the source of disturbances to the economy. It is assumed that the monetary authorities choose the money supply and the supply of home securities as their policy instruments and set them for some interval of time before changing them in response to their inferences about the likely movement in unobserved employment. The tool of analysis is the version of the model used in section 11.3.

Some results have already been obtained. In section 11.3 it was argued that a shift up in excess demand for the home good depicted in figure 11.1 leads to an increase in the interest rate, an appreciation of the home currency, and a rise in unobserved employment. A shift up in excess demand for the home good can be distinguished from a shift in asset preferences away from home securities and toward foreign securities on the basis of movements in financial variables. In the case of a shift in asset preferences represented in figure 11.2, the interest rate rises but the home currency depreciates. As stated above, the effect of this disturbance on unobserved employment is ambiguous in general. However, this effect is likely to be positive. If, as seems probable, the responsiveness of home money demand to the foreign interest rate adjusted for exchange rate expectations (m_4) is small, then with employment held constant a depreciation of the home currency clears the financial markets with little change in the interest rate. The interest rate rises primarily because the employment increase generated by the depreciation raises money demand. Since both of the disturbances probably lead to increases in unobserved employment, the importance of being able to distinguish between them arises because the appropriate responses are different. In the case of a shift up in excess demand for the home good, the authorities would probably want to both reduce the home money supply and intervene to cause an appreciation of the home currency. In the case of a shift in asset preferences away from home securities, the authorities would probably want simply to intervene to prevent the home currency from depreciating.

Now consider a shift up in money demand at the expense of the demand for home securities. As shown in figure 11.4, this disturbance shifts both the MM and BB schedules up, from M_0M_0 to M_1M_1 and B_0B_0 to B_1B_1, respectively; the MM schedule shifts farther up because $m_i < b_i$. If M_1M_1 and B_1B_1 intersect below X_0X_0, as in figure 11.4, then the new equilibrium is in the shaded area. The interest rate rises; the home currency appreciates, and unobserved employment falls. If M_1M_1 and B_1B_1 intersect above X_0X_0, the only difference is that the home currency depreciates. The case in which the home currency appreciates is probably more relevant. The home cur-

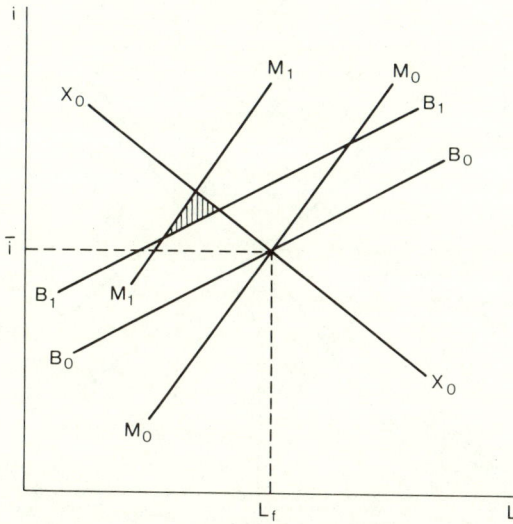

Fig. 11.4   Shift into home money out of home securities

rency is more likely to appreciate the more similar in absolute value are the employment responsivenesses of the demands for home money and home securities, and the better substitutes are home and foreign securities.[32] Thus, exchange rate movements probably make it no easier for the authorities to distinguish between two important sources of disturbances, shifts in excess demand for the home good and shifts in money demand, to which they would want to respond very differently.

There is a presumption that exchange rate movements can help the authorities separate shifts in money demand from changes in expected inflation. Just how to model an increase in expected inflation is not immediately obvious. The experiment conducted here is perhaps the simplest, though clearly not the most realistic. It is assumed that, after nominal wages are set, private agents raise their estimates of next period's price level $(\overline{p})$ and next period's exchange rate $(\overline{e})$ by the same proportion $(\hat{\overline{p}} = \hat{\overline{e}})$ and foresee that the price level and the exchange rate will remain at these new, higher values forever. Such a revision of expectations would be warranted if private agents came to believe that there would be a one-time "helicopter drop" of home money and home securities next period that would increase the stocks of these assets by the same proportion $(\hat{\overline{p}} = \hat{\overline{e}} = \hat{\overline{M}}/\overline{M} = \hat{\overline{B}}/\overline{B})$. As shown in figure 11.5, this kind of increase in expected inflation (with the associated increase in the rate of expected depreciation of the home currency) leads to an increase in the demand for the home good, which shifts the XX schedule from X_0X_0 to X_1X_1, and to decreases in the demands for home money and

32. For proof of this assertion, see the Appendix.

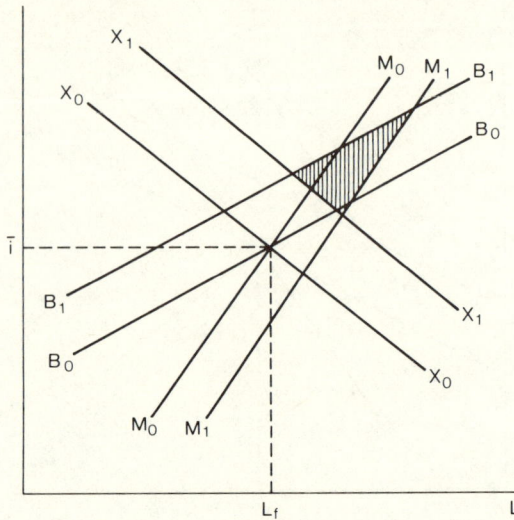

Fig. 11.5   Increase in expected inflation

home securities, which shift the *MM* schedule from M_0M_0 to M_1M_1 and the *BB* schedule from B_0B_0 to B_1B_1, respectively. The *XX* schedule shifts up farther than the *BB* schedule, and X_1X_1 and B_1B_1 intersect above M_1M_1.[33] If M_1M_1 and X_1X_1 intersect above $\bar{i}$, as in figure 11.5, then the new equilibrium is in the shaded area. The interest rate rises, the home currency depreciates, and unobserved employment rises. If M_1M_1 and X_1X_1 intersect below $\bar{i}$, the only difference is that the interest rate may fall instead of rising. The case in which the interest rate rises is probably more relevant. The interest rate is more likely to rise the smaller the responsiveness of home money demand to the foreign interest rate adjusted for exchange rate expectations (m_4)—that is, the smaller the reduction in money demand resulting from the disturbance—and the better substitutes are home and foreign securities. Thus, the presumption is that shifts in money demand need not be mistaken for revisions in inflation expectations. Disturbances of the two types that have the same implications for the interest rate have different implications for the exchange rate. This presumption may turn out to be particularly helpful in the current policymaking environment. Changes in the financial structure have made pinning down money demand more problematic. At the same time, the authorities have undertaken policies explicitly designed to cause private agents to lower their estimate of expected inflation.

33. Given that $(\hat{\bar{e}} = \hat{\bar{p}})$, $(\hat{i}/\hat{\bar{p}})_{XX} = 1$, $(\hat{i}/\hat{\bar{p}})_{BB} = (b_4 + b_5)/(b_3 + b_5) < 1$ since $b_3 > b_4$. X_1X_1 and B_1B_1 intersect above M_1M_1 since the home currency depreciates. For proof of the assertions in this note and those in the accompanying paragraph in the text, see the Appendix.

11.7 Vicious Circles and Intervention Policy

It is often argued that more flexibility in exchange rates has led to the development of so-called vicious (and virtuous) circles.[34] There is no generally accepted benchmark for use in isolating phenomena which are to be designated as vicious circles. All that is really clear is that those concerned about vicious circles have in mind a positive association between depreciations of a country's currency and increases in measures of that country's price level.

The response has been that increased exchange rate flexibility is not really the root cause of vicious circles. Skeptics point out that a country's monetary authorities can cause both a depreciation of their country's currency and an increase in its price indices by initiating an expansion of their country's money supply. Furthermore, these skeptics argue, exogenous disturbances cannot lead to depreciations and price index increases unless monetary policy is accommodating. Thus, the monetary authorities either directly cause vicious circles or allow them to occur.

There is much to agree with in the skeptical view. However, in some policymaking environments with plausible features, allowing the exchange rate to fluctuate rather than keeping it fixed with intervention operations can change the set of outcomes attainable by the financial authorities in a way that they might legitimately regard as unfavorable. The example of such an environment discussed here has two key features: (1) the nominal wage is partially indexed, and (2) intervention operations can affect the exchange rate.

The objective of the financial authorities is assumed to be the stabilization of employment as before. However, in this section it is assumed that the financial authorities obtain complete information about the disturbances that occur in any period and can respond to this information within the period. Given the types of disturbances included in the model of section 11.2, stabilizing employment implies keeping the change in the real wage measured in terms of home output ($\hat{w} - \hat{p}$) equal to the productivity disturbance (β). Given the objective of the home financial authorities and that the foreign authorities stabilize $\overset{*}{p}$, $\overset{*}{Y}$, and $\overset{*}{i}$, the model of section 11.2 can be rewritten in the following compact form:[35]

(38) $$0 = -y_p\hat{p} - y_i\hat{i} + y_e\hat{e} + \alpha + y_\beta\beta,$$

(39) $$\hat{M} = m_p\hat{p} - m_i\hat{i} + m_e\hat{e} \qquad\qquad + \gamma + \delta,$$

---

34. The analysis of this section is based on Henderson (1980) which, in turn, was inspired by Wallich and Gray (1981).

35. The substitutions used to obtain equations (38)–(41) are similar to the ones used to obtain equations (20)–(22) following the procedure of n. 19. However, the expression for p is retained as equation (41) rather than being used to eliminate p from the modified versions of (1), (17), and (19), and L is set equal to zero wherever it appears.

(40) $$\hat{B} = -b_p\hat{p} + b_i\hat{i} + b_e\hat{e} \qquad\qquad - \gamma \qquad\qquad + \epsilon,$$

(41) $$0 = - \hat{p} \qquad + \pi\rho\hat{e} \qquad -\rho\beta.$$

Of course, under both fixed and flexible exchange rates, a shift out of money into home securities ($\gamma < 0$) can be offset with a contractionary open market operation ($\hat{M} = -\hat{B} < 0$) with no change in any other endogenous variable.

Now consider a shift down in the demand for the home good ($\alpha < 0$). Suppose the nominal interest rate is lowered by enough to reequilibrate the market for the home good through an increase in the money supply accomplished by an expansionary open market operation ($\hat{M} = -\hat{B} > 0$). The open market operation which clears the home money market at the new lower nominal interest rate results in an excess supply of home securities since the decline in the nominal interest rate lowers the demand for home securities by more than it raises the demand for home money. The excess supply of home securities gives rise to a tendency for the home currency to depreciate. Under fixed exchange rates, the financial authorities react to the pressure on the exchange rate with an intervention operation, a sale of foreign securities matched by a purchase of home securities ($\hat{B} < 0, \hat{M} = 0$), so that the exchange rate, and therefore the price of the home good and the price index, remain unchanged. However, under flexible exchange rates, the financial authorities allow the home currency to depreciate (e to rise). This depreciation leads to an increase in the price index and the partially indexed nominal wage. In order for the real wage to remain constant (as it must since $\beta = 0$), the price of home output must rise, but the increase in p is less than the rise in e because indexation is only partial. Since both the price of the home good (p) the relative price of the foreign good ($e - p$) rise, the nominal interest rate decline needed to reequilibrate the market for the home good may be larger or smaller under floating exchange rates.[36]

36. If indexing were complete ($\mu = 1$), the relative price of the foreign good would remain unchanged and i would definitely decline by more under flexible exchange rates. In this case, the real wage measured in terms of the consumption basket as well as the real wage measured in terms of home output would remain unchanged. The direct effect of a decline in i on the demand for home output is to raise this demand. However, there are also some induced effects. If i falls, e rises, p increases, and $\hat{M} = -B$ increases. These changes must take place in order to satisfy (39), (40), and (41). The rise in e raises the demand for home output, but the increase in p lowers this demand. Throughout this section, it is assumed that the net result of the direct and induced effects of a decline in i on the demand for home output is an increase in this demand. More formally, it is assumed that

$$y_i > -\bar{y}_e[(b_i - m_i)/(\bar{m}_e + \bar{b}_e)],$$

where $\bar{y}_e$, $\bar{m}_e$, and $\bar{b}_e$ are defined below equation (27). This condition is always met if $\bar{y}_e \geq -y_i$, since it can be shown that the expression in square brackets is positive and less than one. In section 11.4 it is shown that $\bar{y}_e \geq -y_i$ for all $y_5, y_6 > 0$ if the indexing parameter is small ($\mu \to 0$) and that $\bar{y}_e \geq -y_i$ for all $0 < \mu \leq 1$ if the effect of wealth on aggregate demand is negligible ($y_5, y_6 \to 0$).

Next consider a shift down in the productivity of labor ($\beta < 0$). It is useful to begin the analysis of this disturbance by noting that if the exchange rate were fixed, p would have to rise in order to lower the real wage by enough to match the drop in β. Suppose this rise in p occurs. It adds to the excess supply of the home good caused by the direct effect of the decline in β on the market for the home good. Further, suppose that the nominal interest rate is lowered by enough to reequilibrate the market for the home good. To accommodate the rise in p and the decline in i hypothesized above, the authorities must increase the money supply with an expansionary open market operation. The open market operation which clears the home money market at the higher p and lower i may result in either an excess supply or excess demand for home securities. The decline in i lowers the demand for home securities by more than it raises the demand for home money, but the rise in p lowers the demand for home securities by less than it raises the demand for home money. Thus, under fixed exchange rates, the authorities may be required either to purchase or to sell home securities in exchange for foreign securities to stabilize the exchange rate, thereby preventing any further movement in p and the price index. It follows that under flexible exchange rates the home currency may either depreciate or appreciate and the initial increase in p and q may be amplified or dampened according to the logic employed above in the analysis of a shift in demand for the home good.

A similar line of argument can be used to establish that for a shift out of home money into foreign securities ($\delta < 0$) or a shift out of home securities into foreign securities ($\epsilon < 0$), stabilizing employment leads to no change in e, p, q, or i under fixed exchange rates. Under flexible exchange rates, both disturbances lead to a depreciation of the home currency and increases in p and q. Whether i increases or decreases depends on whether the increases in p and $e - p$ which satisfy the condition that the real wage must remain constant, equation (41), lead to an excess demand for, or supply of, the home good.

These results have implications for the trade-off between output variability and price level (home good price and price index) variability under the two alternative exchange rate regimes. In order to achieve the same amount of output variability under both exchange rate regimes, the authorities will have to accept more price variability under floating exchange rates, except perhaps in the case of disturbances in labor productivity. This change in the authorities' trade-off between output and price variability might legitimately be regarded as unfavorable and is suggestive of the concerns of those who emphasize the importance of vicious circles. However, further analysis is necessary before firm conclusions can be drawn about the importance of the results derived above. It is important to establish a basis for the authorities' concern about price level variability and to study the effects of possible responsiveness of the indexing parameter to changes in exchange rate regime.[37]

11.8 Transitory Disturbances and the Scope for Agreement on Intervention Policy in a Two-Country World Economy with No Indexing

In this section it is assumed that neither the home authorities nor the foreign authorities observe the current values of their country's output, employment, or the price of their country's good. As a result, transitory disturbances such as those considered above affect employment in both countries of the two-country world economy. For simplicity, it is also assumed that the authorities in each country use monetary operations to fix the interest rate on securities denominated in the currency of their country. The overall stance of intervention policy is the net result of the intervention operations of the two sets of authorities. Taken together, they can choose as a policy instrument and set a value for either the exogenous supply of home assets (and, by implication, the exogenous supply of foreign assets) or the exchange rate. In this environment it is interesting to consider whether the authorities in the two countries could agree on a fixed or a freely fluctuating exchange rate.[38]

Under the assumptions of this section the relevant version of the model of section 11.2 written in compact form is[39]

$$(42) \qquad 0 = -y_L\hat{L} + y_e\hat{e} + y_L^*\hat{\overset{*}{L}} + \alpha + y_\beta\beta,$$

$$(43) \qquad \hat{B}' = b_L'\hat{L} + b_e'\hat{e} - b_L'^*\hat{\overset{*}{L}} \qquad\qquad + \delta + \epsilon,$$

$$(44) \qquad 0 = \overset{*}{y}_L\hat{L} - \overset{*}{y}_e\hat{e} - \overset{*}{y}_L^*\hat{\overset{*}{L}} - \alpha.$$

Definitions of y_L, y_e, $\hat{B}'$, b_L', and b_e' are provided above, and

37. Flood and Marion (1982) assume that agents choose the indexing parameter in order to maximize expected utility and find that the optimal indexing parameter is different under alternative exchange rate regimes.

38. Sweeney (1976) and Canzoneri (1982) analyze open economy financial policy using two-country models.

39. Equations (5) and (7) are substituted into (3), and (6) and (8) are substituted into (4). The resulting versions of (3) and (4) are substituted into (1) and (2). Equations (9) and (10) are substituted for Y and $\overset{*}{Y}$ in (1), (2), (17), and (19). Equations (5), (7), and (15) are substituted into (13), and equations (6), (8), and (16) are substituted into (14). The modified versions of (13) and (14) are used to eliminate w and $\overset{*}{w}$ from (11) and (12). The modified versions of (11) and (12) are employed to obtain expressions for p and $\overset{*}{p}$ which are independent of e under the assumption that $\mu = \overset{*}{\mu} = 0$. These expressions are substituted for p and $\overset{*}{p}$ wherever they appear in (1), (2), (17), and (19). The modified versions of (1) and (2) and the sum of (17) and (19) with the disturbances set equal to zero are subtracted from the same equations with the distrurbances free to take on any value to obtain (42), (43), and (44).

$$y_{\bar{L}}^* = y_p^* \overset{*}{l_1} + y_Y^* \overset{*}{x_1}, \qquad\qquad \overset{*}{y}_L = \overset{*}{y}_p l_1 + \overset{*}{y}_Y x_1,$$

$$b_{\bar{L}}' = b_{\bar{L}}^* = b_p^* \overset{*}{l_1} + b_Y^* \overset{*}{x_1}, \qquad \overset{*}{y}_e = \overset{*}{y}_p - \overset{*}{y}_3 - \overset{*}{y}_6 + \overset{*}{y}_5,$$

$$\overset{*}{y}_{\bar{L}} = \overset{*}{y}_p^* \overset{*}{l_1} + \overset{*}{y}_Y^* \overset{*}{x_1},$$

and

$$y_p^* = y_4 - (y_2 + y_3)(1 - h), \qquad y_Y^* = y_1, \qquad b_p^* = b_8,$$

$$\overset{*}{y}_p = y_4 - (\overset{*}{y}_2 + \overset{*}{y}_3)h, \qquad\qquad \overset{*}{y}_Y = \overset{*}{y}_1, \qquad b_Y^* = b_9,$$

$$\overset{*}{y}_p^* = y_4 + (\overset{*}{y}_2 + \overset{*}{y}_3)(1 - h) + \overset{*}{y}_6, \quad \overset{*}{y}_Y^* = s + y_1.$$

It is assumed that income, relative price, and wealth effects outweigh possibly perverse expected real interest rate effects so that y_L^*, $\overset{*}{y}_e$, and $\overset{*}{y}_L$ are all positive. In order to simplify the analysis further, it is assumed that the two countries are ''symmetric'' in the sense that $y_L = \overset{*}{y}_L^*$, $\overset{*}{y}_L = y_L^*$, $b_L' = b_{\bar{L}}^*$, and $y_e = \overset{*}{y}_e$.[40]

Equilibrium schedules for the markets for the home good, the foreign good, and home assets are shown in figure 11.6. The equilibrium schedule for the home good is $X_0 X_0$. An increase in L, which reduces excess demand, must be matched by a rise in $\overset{*}{L}$, which increases demand. The equilibrium schedule for the foreign good is $\overset{*}{X}_0 \overset{*}{X}_0$. An increase in L, which raises

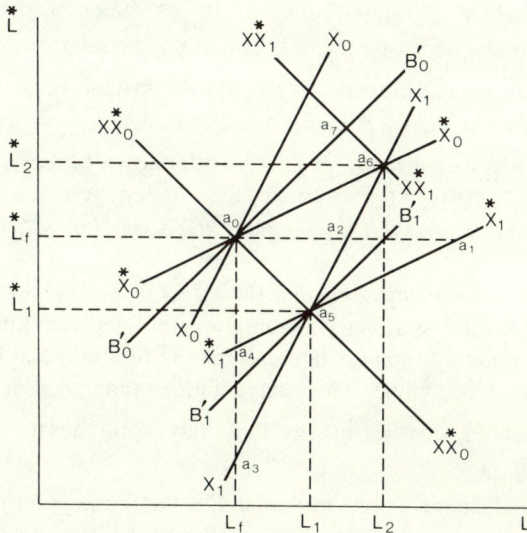

Fig. 11.6   Disturbances in a two-country world economy

40. In Henderson (1982) all these assumptions except the one that $y_e = \overset{*}{y}_e$ are relaxed. Although the analysis is more complicated, the results are basically the same.

demand, must be matched by a rise in $\overset{*}{L}$, which reduces excess demand. Under the symmetry assumption the slope of the XX schedule is greater than positive one, and the slope of the XX schedule is the reciprocal of the slope of the $\overset{**}{XX}$ schedule:

$$(\overset{\hat{*}}{L}/\hat{L})_{XX} = 1/(\overset{\hat{*}}{L}/\hat{L})^{**}_{XX} = y_L/y^*_L > 1.$$

The restrictions on the parameters of equations (42), (43), and (44) imply that $y_L > \overset{*}{y}_L$; the absolute value of the reduction in excess demand for the home good caused by a rise in L which increases home saving as well as home imports exceeds the increase in excess demand for the foreign good caused by a rise in L which increases not only foreign exports (home imports) but also foreign saving. The symmetry assumption implies that $\overset{*}{y}_L = y^*_L$. The equilibrium schedule for the market for home assets is $B'_0B'_0$. An increase in L, which raises the demand for home money plus home securities, must be offset by a rise in $\overset{*}{L}$, which raises the demand for foreign money partly at the expense of the demand for home securities. Under the symmetry assumption, the slope of the $B'B'$ schedule is $+1$. Therefore, the $B'B'$ schedule is steeper than the $\overset{**}{XX}$ schedule.

It is useful to consider first the effects of a shift up in the demand for the home good matched by a shift down in the demand for the foreign good which is equal in absolute value ($\alpha > 0$). Such a shift can be represented by movements in the XX and $\overset{**}{XX}$ schedules from X_0X_0 to X_1X_1 and from $\overset{*}{X}_0\overset{*}{X}_0$ to $\overset{*}{X}_1\overset{*}{X}_1$, respectively. At a constant value of $\overset{*}{L}$, $\overset{*}{XX}$ shifts farther to the right than XX ($a_0a_1 > a_0a_2$) since $y_L > \overset{*}{y}_L$ as argued above. Similarly, at a constant value of L, XX shifts down farther than $\overset{**}{XX}$ ($a_0a_3 > a_0a_4$) since $\overset{**}{y}_L > y^*_L$ from the symmetry assumption. A series of demand shifts of the type under consideration would trace out the $\overset{*}{X}X_0\overset{*}{X}X_0$ schedule in figure 11.6.

As an intermediate step, consider the effect of a depreciation of the home currency. Under the symmetry assumption this depreciation raises demand for the home good and lowers demand for the foreign good by amounts that are equal in absolute value. Thus depreciations (appreciations) move the XX and $\overset{**}{XX}$ schedules down (up) so that they continue to intersect on the $\overset{*}{X}X_0\overset{*}{X}X_0$ schedule.

Now the analysis of a shift in demand to the home good from the foreign good can be completed. The shifted XX and $\overset{**}{XX}$ schedules are X_1X_1 and $\overset{*}{X}_1\overset{*}{X}_1$. Under fixed rates the equilibrium is at point a_5. The shift in preferences for goods causes home employment to rise and foreign employment to fall. Both of these movements tend to raise demand for home currency assets, so the home currency tends to appreciate. However, the authorities undertake intervention operations, sales of home securities for foreign securities which shift the $B'B'$ schedule down. The new $B'B'$ schedule labeled

$B_1'B_1'$ passes through a_5. Under flexible exchange rates the home currency appreciates, dampening the rise in home employment and the fall in foreign employment. The $B'B'$ schedule shifts down and the XX and $\overset{**}{XX}$ schedules shift up along $XX_0\overset{*}{XX}_0$ until an equilibrium is reached somewhere on the line segment a_0a_5 above a_5. Thus, for shifts in demand between home and foreign goods there is less variation in both home and foreign output under floating exchange rates, and there is no policy conflict.

Next, consider a shift in asset preferences toward home assets and away from foreign assets. For convenience, suppose that the initial equilibrium is at a_5. The change in asset preferences shifts the $B'B'$ schedule from $B_1'B_1'$ to $B_0'B_0'$. Under fixed exchange rates the new equilibrium is at a_5, which is also the initial equilibrium. The shift in asset preferences puts pressure on the home currency to appreciate. Under fixed exchange rates this pressure is met by intervention operations, sales of home securities in exchange for foreign securities, which shift the $B'B'$ schedule from $B_0'B_0'$ back to $B_1'B_1'$. Under flexible exchange rates the home currency appreciates, lowering home employment and raising foreign employment. The $B'B'$ schedule shifts down and XX and $\overset{**}{XX}$ shift up along $XX_0\overset{*}{XX}_0$ until a new equilibrium is reached along the line segment a_0a_5 above a_5. Thus, for shifts in asset preferences between home and foreign assets there is less variation in both home and foreign employment under fixed exchange rates, and once again there is no policy conflict.

Finally, consider an increase in the productivity of labor in the home country. Suppose the original equilibrium is at a_0. This disturbance initially affects only the XX schedule, which is shifted from X_0X_0 to X_1X_1. Under fixed exchange rates the new equilibrium is at a_6. Home employment rises and, as a result of induced home demand for foreign goods, foreign employment rises. Since the $B'B'$ schedule is steeper than the $\overset{**}{XX}$ schedule, there is pressure on the home currency to appreciate. Under fixed exchange rates this pressure is countered with intervention operations which cause the $B'B'$ schedule to shift down from $B_0'B_0'$ until it passes through a_6. Under flexible exchange rates the home currency appreciates, dampening the rise in home employment but amplifying the rise in foreign employment. The $B'B'$ schedule shifts down, and the XX and $\overset{**}{XX}$ schedules shift up along the new $\overset{*}{X}X\overset{*}{X}X$ schedule $XX_1\overset{*}{XX}_1$ until a new equilibrium is reached on the line segment a_7a_6 above a_6. Thus, for shifts in home labor productivity there is more variation in home employment under fixed exchange rates and more variation in foreign employment under flexible exchange rates, and there is a definite policy conflict.

The results just described can be summarized more formally. The variances of home employment (σ_L^2) and foreign employment ($\sigma_{\tilde{L}}^2$) under fixed (FI) and flexible (FL) exchange rates given the symmetry assumption are

(45) $$\sigma_{L|FI}^2 = [(y_L - \overset{*}{y}_L)/D_1]^2\sigma_\alpha^2 + (y_L/D_1)^2 y_\beta^2\sigma_\beta^2,$$

(46) $\sigma^2_{L|FI} = [(\overset{*}{y}_L - y_L)/D_1]^2\sigma^2_\alpha + (\overset{*}{y}_L/D_1)^2 y^2_\beta \sigma^2_\beta,$

(47) $\sigma^2_{L|FL} = [b'_e(y_L - \overset{*}{y}_L)/\Delta_2]^2\sigma^2_\alpha + (D_3/\Delta_2)^2 y^2_\beta \sigma^2_\beta + [y_e(\overset{*}{y}_L$

$- y_L)/\Delta_2]^2(\sigma^2_\delta + \sigma^2_\epsilon),$

(48) $\sigma^{2}_{\overset{*}{L}|FL} = [b'_e(\overset{*}{y}_L - y_L)/\Delta_2]^2\sigma^2_\alpha + (D_4/\Delta_2)^2 y^2_\beta \sigma^2_\beta + [y_e(y_L$

$- \overset{*}{y}_L)/\Delta_2]^2(\sigma^2_\delta + \sigma^2_\epsilon).$

$$D_1 = y^2_L - \overset{*}{y}^2_L, \qquad D_3 = y_e b'_L + b'_e y_L,$$

$$D_2 = b'_L(y_L - \overset{*}{y}_L), \qquad D_4 = y_e b'_L + b'_e \overset{*}{y}_L,$$

$$\Delta_2 = b'_e D_1 + y_e D_2.$$

The expressions D_1, D_2, D_3, D_4, and Δ_2 are all positive. Thus if $\sigma^2_\beta = \sigma^2_\delta = \sigma^2_\epsilon = 0$ and $\sigma^2_\alpha > 0$, then $\sigma^2_{L|FL} < \sigma^2_{L|FI}$ and $\sigma^2_{\overset{*}{L}|FL} < \sigma^2_{\overset{*}{L}|FI}$. If $\sigma^2_\alpha = \sigma^2_\beta = 0$ and either σ^2_δ or $\sigma^2_\epsilon > 0$, then $0 = \sigma^2_{L|FI} < \sigma^2_{L|FL}$ and $0 = \sigma^2_{\overset{*}{L}|FI} < \sigma^2_{\overset{*}{L}|FL}$. By manipulating the coefficients in (45), (46), (47), and (48) it can be shown that if $\sigma^2_\alpha = \sigma^2_\delta = \sigma^2_\epsilon = 0$ and $\sigma^2_\beta > 0$, then $\sigma^2_{L|FL} < \sigma^2_{L|FI}$ but $\sigma^2_{\overset{*}{L}|FI} < \sigma^2_{\overset{*}{L}|FL}$.

11.9 The Effects of Intervention Operations: The Theoretical Underpinning

According to the theory of international financial markets developed and elaborated during the 1970s a necessary and sufficient condition for sterilized intervention policy to have effects on the exchange rate and interest rate is that securities denominated in different currencies be imperfect substitutes. Recently this proposition has been challenged: it has been argued that securities being imperfect substitutes is neither a necessary nor a sufficient condition for intervention policy to have effects.[41] That is, proponents of this view argue that resolving the debate about whether securities denominated in different currencies are imperfect substitutes in private portfolios would not settle the issue of whether sterilized intervention has effects.

The argument that intervention policy can alter the exchange rate even if securities are perfect substitutes is considered first. According to this argument, sterilized intervention would not affect the exchange rate if it did not alter expectations about the future values of other variables, perhaps most importantly monetary policy instruments. However, it can have effects if it does alter expectations.[42] Some may regard this argument as a useful extension of previous theory. Others may regard it as simply a precise restatement of an argument often used to justify intervention under the adjustable peg

---

41. Stockman (1979) provides a clear statement of both parts of this argument. Obstfeld (1980, 1982a) develops the second part.

42. Stockman (1979) has explicitly modeled the possible effects of intervention on expectations.

Bretton Woods system. In any case, the argument is not just a trivial special case of the proposition that any policy action might alter expectations. Intervention policy and monetary policy are often, if not always, in the hands of the same authorities. Furthermore, losses on foreign exchange positions can lead to significant political problems for the authorities. Thus, if the authorities undertake an intervention policy which would generate foreign exchange losses if their pronouncements about future monetary policy were not put into effect, there might be more reason for private agents to take these pronouncements seriously. However, private agents do have a number of past episodes on which to base an evaluation of such policy packages, some of which would tend to make them wary.

The argument that intervention policy may not alter the exchange rate when securities are imperfect substitutes represents a more fundamental challenge to previous theory. It has long been recognized that the answers to certain basic questions, such as whether open market operations are neutral and whether replacing tax financing of government expenditure with bond financing is neutral, depend on whether government bonds are net wealth, that is, on whether private agents regard the claims and obligations of the government as their own. For the most part, closed economy models have been used to chart this territory. Recent contributions make clear that whether sterilized intervention can affect the exchange rate when securities are imperfect substitutes also depends on whether private agents "see through" government transactions. The basic insight is that if private agents regard the authorities' holdings of home and foreign securities as their own, then when the authorities decide to alter their holdings through intervention operations, private agents will simply alter their direct holdings in an offsetting way leaving the exchange rate unchanged. This proposition is valid whether or not private agents regard home and foreign securities as imperfect substitutes because of exchange risk. However, it does depend, just as the more familiar closed economy neutrality results do, on the absence of contemporaneous distribution effects and the presence of consumers who either live as long as the (perhaps infinitely lived) government or make bequests that represent the first step along the "time-consistent" path that maximizes the utility of enough (perhaps all) future generations of their offspring.

The discovery that intervention operations do not affect the exchange rate under some fairly strong but nonetheless interesting assumptions is significant in and of itself. More important, it adds urgency to the investigation already under way of the theoretical basis for asset demand functions in open economies and suggests that this investigation may need to focus somewhat more on contemporaneous and intertemporal distribution effects.[43] Some of the results of this investigation are consistent with the type

---

43. Participants in this investigation include Kouri (1977), Frankel (1979), and Dornbusch (1980).

of asset demand functions used earlier in this paper; the one discussed here obviously is not.

11.10 The Effects of Intervention Operations: The Empirical Evidence

A brief discussion of empirical evidence that bears on the question of whether intervention operations affect the exchange rate is in order. Attention is focused on two classes of empirical work: (1) tests of the joint hypothesis that securities denominated in different currencies are perfect substitutes because agents are risk neutral and that expectations are rational and (2) what are called direct tests for effects of intervention.[44]

Under the joint hypothesis the "ex post excess return," defined either as the difference between interest differentials and actual exchange rate changes or equivalently as the difference between forward rates on maturing contracts and realized spot rates, should be white noise. Although some early studies did not reject the joint hypothesis, it has been rejected in most recent studies, some of which incorporate refinements in the testing procedure.[45]

At first, rejections of the joint hypothesis were viewed as evidence against rational expectations. More recently, they have been regarded as refuting the hypothesis of perfect substitutability and providing evidence in favor of the existence of a "time-varying risk premium." Of course, neither of these interpretations is strictly correct. The rejections cast doubt on both components of the joint hypothesis. They are certainly consistent with intervention operations affecting exchange rates. However, even if they are interpreted as evidence in favor of a variable risk premium and, therefore, imperfect substitutability, they do not necessarily imply that the authorities can alter the risk premium and, thus, affect exchange rates with intervention operations.

The ambiguous implications of efficiency tests whet the appetite for more direct tests for effects of intervention. Such tests have been performed by Dooley and Isard (1982), Frankel (1982a, 1982b), and Obstfeld (1983). All these studies focus on the dollar–deutsche mark exchange rate.[46] Although they differ significantly in details, the Dooley and Isard and Frankel studies

44. Genberg (1981) and Obstfeld (1982b) survey empirical work relevant for assessing the likelihood that intervention policy has significant effects. Dooley (1982) points out that since 1973 the intervention policies of several major industrial countries have generated only minor changes in the relative supplies of bonds denominated in those countries' currencies. However, the smaller industrial countries and the developing countries have denominated an increasing share of their total net debt in the currencies of the major countries and have generated relatively large changes in the relative supplies of bonds denominated in the currencies of the major industrial countries.

45. Recent studies include Hansen and Hodrick (1980), Meese and Singleton (1980), and Cumby and Obstfeld (1981).

46. Hooper and Morton (1982) have performed similar tests for the weighted average dollar. Their results are consistent with those reported below.

use the same general approach. Estimating equations are obtained by solving asset demand functions for the risk premium and then imposing rational expectations. The ex post excess return is regressed on an asset stock (and in the first Frankel study on some other variables). In the Dooley and Isard study the coefficient on the asset stock is of the correct sign and in the best regression nearly twice its standard error. However, the authors conclude that their particular representation of the portfolio balance model explains only a small part of the variation in the ex post excess return. Among the many regressions run in the first Frankel study there are no significant coefficients on asset stocks (or any other variable) and coefficients are often of the wrong sign. In his second study Frankel imposes restrictions implied by mean variance optimizing and manages to obtain an asset stock coefficient of the correct sign, but that coefficient is not significant. The results of these studies are consistent with the view that dollar and deutsche mark securities are very good substitutes since changes in asset stocks cause little or no change in expected return. According to this view intervention operations of reasonable size do not have very much effect on the exchange rate.

The results of the Obstfeld study are quite similar. Obstfeld estimates structural equations for German sight deposit demand, German sight deposit supply, German demand for deutsche mark securities, and foreign supply of deutsche mark securities as well as a reduced-form equation for German consumer price index inflation. The differential between Euro–deutsche mark and Eurodollar interest rates is used as a proxy for the expected rate of deprecation of the deutsche mark. Obstfeld finds evidence of lagged adjustment of actual quantities to long-run desired quantities in three of his four structural equations. He simulates two transitory intervention operations under the assumption that market participants have perfect foresight. Each operation is reversed after 9 months. The first operation is a nonsterilized intervention operation that reduces the German monetary base by 10% of its January 1979 level. This operation causes an immediate 3% appreciation of the deutsche mark. Then the deutsche mark begins to depreciate because market participants know that the operation will be reversed. The second operation is a sterilized intervention operation of equal magnitude. This operation causes an immediate appreciation of only 0.04%. These results suggest that sterilized exchange market intervention operations have virtually no effect on the exchange rate.

Appendix

The model of the text is a linear approximation to the one sketched out here at a zero disturbance, balanced trade equilibrium where endogenous variables take on their constant expected values represented by the variables with bars over them. In a linear approximation, output coefficients in aggregate demand equations are familiar marginal propensities to spend, and balance sheet constraints imply straightforward relationships among coefficients of asset demands. Units are defined so that $\overline{E} = \overset{*}{\overline{P}} = \overline{P} = \overset{*}{\overline{Q}} = \overline{Q} = \overset{*}{\overline{W}} = \overline{W} = 1$; thus the differentials of E, $\overset{*}{P}$, P, $\overset{*}{Q}$, Q, $\overset{*}{W}$, and W are equal to the differentials of their logarithms. Symbols are defined at the end of the Appendix. Coefficients displayed below or beside an equation are the coefficients of the approximation to that equation.

The aggregate demand equations for the home and foreign goods are given by

(A1)
$$PY = h(EP/P)\{PY + E\overset{**}{PY} - c[a(r, \overset{*}{r})(PY + E\overset{**}{PY}) - (A + \overset{*}{A})]\} + P\alpha,$$

$$y_1 = h(1 - ca), \quad y_4 = h'(Y + \overset{*}{Y}) + h(1 - ca)\overset{*}{Y},$$

$$y_2 = ca_rY, \qquad y_5 = hc(N + F),$$

$$y_3 = ca_{\overset{*}{r}}Y, \qquad y_6 = hc(A + \overset{*}{A}),$$

(A2)
$$E\overset{**}{PY} = [1 - h(EP/P)]\{PY + E\overset{**}{PY} - c[a(r, \overset{*}{r})(PY + E\overset{**}{PY}) - (A + \overset{*}{A})]\} - EP\alpha,$$

$$\overset{*}{y_1} = (1 - h)(1 - ca), \quad y_4 = h'(Y + \overset{*}{Y}) + h(1 - ca)\overset{*}{Y},$$

$$\overset{*}{y_2} = ca_rY, \qquad\qquad \overset{*}{y_5} = (1 - h)c(M + B),$$

$$\overset{*}{y_3} = ca_{\overset{*}{r}}Y, \qquad\qquad \overset{*}{y_6} = (1 - h)c(A + \overset{*}{A}).$$

In equations (A1) and (A2), $h(\cdot)$ represents a function with $h'(\cdot) > 0$; in the expressions for y_j and $\overset{*}{y_j}$, $j = 1, 4, 5$, and 6, and everywhere else in the paper h represents the value of $h(\cdot)$ at the zero disturbance, balanced trade equilibrium. It is assumed that $0 < h$, $ca < 1$, and that a_r, $a_{\overset{*}{r}}$, and $h' > 0$, so all the approximation coefficients are positive, and $0 < y_1$, $\overset{*}{y_1} < 1$. In deriving y_2, y_3, $\overset{*}{y_2}$, $\overset{*}{y_3}$, and y_4, use is made of the facts that in equilibrium $h(Y + \overset{*}{Y}) = Y$, and $(1 - h)(Y + \overset{*}{Y}) = \overset{*}{Y}$, and that with balanced trade $h\overset{*}{Y} = (1 - h)Y$. The product ca is represented by s in the text.

Expressions for $A + \overset{*}{A}$, r, and $\overset{*}{r}$ are

(A3) $A + \overset{*}{A} = M + B + E(N + F),$

(A4) $r = i - (\overline{Q} - Q)/Q = i - (\overline{E} - E)/E - (\overset{*}{\overline{Q}} - \overset{*}{Q})/\overset{*}{Q},$

(A5) $\overset{*}{r} = \overset{*}{i} + (\overline{E} - E)/E - (\overline{Q} - Q)/Q = \overset{*}{i} - (\overset{*}{\overline{Q}} - \overset{*}{Q})/\overset{*}{Q},$

where

(A6) $\qquad Q = hP + (1 - h)E\overset{*}{P},$

(A7) $\qquad \overset{*}{Q} = hP/E + (1 - h)\overset{*}{P},$

and $\overline{Q}$ and $\overline{\overset{*}{Q}}$ are obtained by replacing P, E, and $\overset{*}{P}$ with $\overline{P}$, $\overline{E}$, and $\overline{\overset{*}{P}}$. The production functions for home and foreign output are given by

(A8) $\qquad Y = e^{\beta}X_0L^{X_1}, \quad x_1 = e^{\beta}X_0X_1L^{X_1-1}, \quad x_2 = Y,$

(A9) $\qquad \overset{*}{Y} = \overset{*}{X_0}\overset{*}{L}\overset{**}{X_1}, \quad \overset{*}{x_1} = \overset{*}{X_0}\overset{*}{X_1}\overset{*}{L}\overset{**}{X_1-1},$

and the marginal productivity conditions for home and foreign firms are given by

(A10) $\qquad W/P = e^{\beta}X_0X_1L^{X_1-1}, \quad l_1 = e^{\beta}X_0X_1(1-X_1)L^{X_1-2},$

(A11) $\qquad \overset{*}{W}/\overset{*}{P} = \overset{*}{X_0}\overset{*}{X_1}\overset{*}{L}\overset{*}{X_1-1}, \quad \overset{*}{l_1} = \overset{*}{X_0}\overset{*}{X_1}(1 - \overset{*}{X_1})\overset{*}{L}\overset{*}{X_1-2}.$

Replacing P and L with $\overline{P}$ and L_f yields $\overline{W}$; replacing $\overset{*}{P}$ and $\overset{*}{L}$ with $\overline{\overset{*}{P}}$ and $\overset{*}{L_f}$ yields $\overline{\overset{*}{W}}$. It is assumed that $0 < X_1, \overset{*}{X_1} < 1$, so $x_1, \overset{*}{x_1}, l_1$, and $\overset{*}{l_1}$ are positive.

The nominal wage indexing rules are given by

(A12) $\qquad (W - \overline{W})/\overline{W} = \mu(Q - \overline{Q})/\overline{Q},$

(A13) $\qquad (\overset{*}{W} - \overline{\overset{*}{W}})/\overline{\overset{*}{W}} = \overset{*}{\mu}(\overset{*}{Q} - \overline{\overset{*}{Q}})/\overline{\overset{*}{Q}}.$

The asset market equilibrium conditions are given by

(A14) $\qquad M = PY\lambda[i, \overset{*}{i} + (\overline{E} - E)/E] + P(\gamma + \delta),$

$\qquad\qquad m_1 = Y\lambda, \; m_2 = \lambda, \; m_3 = -Y\lambda_1, \; m_4 = -Y\lambda_2,$

(A15) $\qquad EN = EP\overset{***}{Y}v[i - (\overline{E} - E)/E, \overset{*}{i}],$

$\qquad\qquad n_1 = \overset{**}{Y}v, \; n_2 = \overset{*}{v}, \; n_3 = -\overset{**}{Y}v_1, \; n_4 = -\overset{**}{Y}v_2,$

(A16) $\qquad B = k[i - \overset{*}{i} - (\overline{E} - E)/E][A + \overset{*}{A} - PY\lambda(\cdot) - EP\overset{***}{Y}v(\cdot)]$

$\qquad\qquad - P(\gamma - \epsilon),$

$$\begin{aligned} b_1 &= km_1, & b_6 &= k'(\overset{*}{A} - N) - kn_4, \\ b_2 &= km_2, & b_7 &= kF, \\ b_3 &= k'(A - M) + km_3, & b_8 &= kn_1, \\ b_4 &= k'(A - M) - km_4, & b_9 &= kn_2, \\ b_5 &= k'(\overset{*}{A} - N) + kn_3, & & \end{aligned}$$

(A17) $EF = \{1 - k[i - \overset{*}{i} - (\bar{E} - E)/E]\}[A + \overset{*}{A}$
              $- PY\lambda(\cdot) - EPY\overset{***}{v}(\cdot)] - \overset{*}{EP}(\delta + \epsilon).$

It is assumed that $0 < k < 1$; that λ, $\overset{*}{v}$, k', $(A - M)$, and $(\overset{*}{A} - N) > 0$; and that λ_1, λ_2, $\overset{*}{v}_1$, and $\overset{*}{v}_2 < 0$. These assumptions imply that all the asset market approximation coefficients except b_4 and b_6 are positive. The assumption that wealth holders in both countries regard the three assets they hold as strict gross substitutes implies that b_4 and b_6 are positive, that is, that the positive effect of the increase in the ratio of wealth minus money demand that home (foreign) wealth holders want to hold in home securities exceeds the negative effect of the increase in home (foreign) money demand. In the equilibrium at which the approximation is made (1) an increase in productivity leaves the demands for home money and home securities unchanged since $m_1 = m_2x_2$ and $b_1 = b_2x_2$ and (2) actual wealth equals desired wealth in both countries, that is, $A = aY$ and $\overset{*}{A} = a\overset{*}{Y}$. Adding (A14), (A15), (A16), and (A17) yields the identity (A3), so only three of the four asset market equilibrium conditions are independent. In this paper the equilibrium condition for foreign currency securities, (A17), is not used.

An assertion made in section 11.3 requires proof. No matter what the size of y_e, $C_2 + C_3$ and $m_LC_2 + b_LC_3$ are positive:

$$C_2 + C_3 = [(y_2 + y_3)h + y_4 + y_5](b_i - m_i) + y_2[b_7$$
$$+ (1 - k)(m_3 + m_4)] > 0,$$

$$m_LC_2 + b_LC_3 = [(y_2 + y_3)h + y_4 + y_5](m_Lb_i - b_Lm_i) + y_2m_Lb_7 > 0.$$

Some assertions made in section 11.4 require proof. It follows from the definitions of y_5 and y_6 under equation (A1) that y_5, $y_6 \to 0$ as $c \to 0$ and that $y_6 > y_5$ for all $c > 0$. If indexing is complete ($\mu = 1$), then

$$\tilde{m}_L\tilde{C}_2 + \tilde{b}_L\tilde{C}_3 = y_i\tilde{m}_Lb_7 + (y_5 - y_6)(\tilde{m}_Lb_i - \tilde{b}_Lm_i).$$

If y_5, $y_6 \to 0$ or if b_i is finite and $y_6 > y_5 > 0$ are small enough, then $\tilde{m}_L\tilde{C}_2 + \tilde{b}_L\tilde{C}_3$ is positive. However, as $b_i \to \infty$, then, for all $y_6 > y_5 > 0$, $\tilde{m}_L\tilde{C}_2 + \tilde{b}_L\tilde{C}_3 < 0$.

Some assertions made in section 11.5 require proof. The effect on the exchange rate of a shift in asset preferences toward home money and away from home securities ($\gamma > 0$) is given by

$$\hat{e}/\gamma = (1/\Delta_1)[y_L(m_3 - b - km) + y_2m_L(1 - k)],$$

$$\Delta_1 = (y_Lm + m_Ly)b + (y_Lm_3 + m_Ly_2)b_7 + km_Lm_4y + y_Lm_4km > 0.$$

The effects on the interest rate, the exchange rate, and employment of an expected helicopter drop in the next period of home money and home securities that would change stocks of both of these assets and the expected price of the home good and the expected exchange rate by the same proportion $(\hat{\overline{M}}/\overline{M} = \hat{\overline{B}}/\overline{B} = \hat{\overline{p}} = \hat{\overline{e}})$ are given by

$$\hat{\imath}/\hat{\overline{p}} = (1/\Delta_1)[m_L yb + km_L m_4 y + (y_2 m_L - m_4 y_L)b_7],$$

$$\hat{e}/\hat{\overline{p}} = (1/\Delta_1)(y_L mb + y_L m_4 km),$$

$$\hat{L}/\hat{\overline{p}} = (1/\Delta_1)(ymb + y_2 mb_7 + m_4 ykm).$$

In deriving the expressions reported above, use has been made of the definitions of the approximation coefficients supplied earlier in the Appendix. The definitions of b, m, and y are the following: $b = b_4 + b_5$, $m = m_3 + m_4$, and $y = y_2 + y_e$. Account has been taken of two implied relationships: $b_L = km_L$ and $b_3 = b_4 + km$. By the gross substitutes assumption, $m_3 - b - km = m_3 - b_i$ is negative, so $\hat{e}/\gamma$ is negative if $0 < k < 1$ is close enough to one (that is, if the employment responsiveness of the demand for money and the demand for home securities are similar enough in absolute value). If b is large enough (that is, if home currency and foreign currency securities are close enough substitutes), $\hat{e}/\gamma$ is definitely negative. If m_4 is small enough (that is, if the demand for home money is insensitive enough to the foreign interest rate adjusted for exchange rate expectations) or if b is large enough, $\hat{\imath}/\hat{\overline{p}}$ is positive. Both $\hat{e}/\hat{\overline{p}}$ and $\hat{L}/\hat{\overline{p}}$ are definitely positive.

The symbols are defined as follows:

P = home currency price of home good.

$\overset{*}{P}$ = foreign currency price of foreign good.

E = home currency price of foreign currency.

Y = aggregate demand for and aggregate supply of home good.

$\overset{*}{Y}$ = aggregate demand for and aggregate supply of foreign good.

A = home residents' wealth measured in home currency.

$\overset{*}{A}$ = foreign residents' wealth measured in home currency.

$h(\cdot)$ = proportion of spending allocated by home and foreign residents to home good.

c = speed of adjustment of actual to desired wealth by home and foreign residents.

$a(\cdot)$ = desired ratio of wealth to income for home and foreign residents.

r = expected real interest rate on home securities.

$\overset{*}{r}$ = expected real interest rate on foreign securities.

i = nominal interest rate on home securities.

$\overset{*}{i}$ = nominal interest rate on foreign securities.

Q = home currency price of world consumption bundle.

$\overset{*}{Q}$ = foreign currency price of world consumption bundle.

W = home currency money wage of home residents.

$\overset{*}{W}$ = foreign currency money wage of foreign residents.

L = employment in home country.

$\overset{*}{L}$ = employment in foreign country.

M = supply of home money measured in home currency.

B = supply of home securities measured in home currency.

N = supply of foreign money measured in foreign currency.

F = supply of foreign securities measured in foreign currency.

$\lambda(\cdot)$ = inverse of velocity in home country.

$\overset{*}{v}(\cdot)$ = inverse of velocity in foreign country.

$k(\cdot)$ = proportion of wealth minus money demand held in home securities by home and foreign residents.

Comment   Rudiger Dornbusch

Henderson's paper is a comprehensive and definitive assessment of what can be said about intervention. It offers little encouragement to anyone who had hoped that intervention, following easily identified rules, might do away with volatility and unnecessary swings in foreign exchange markets. On the contrary, it concludes that there are few instances where intervention is decidedly called for.

The Approach

Henderson analyzes foreign exchange market intervention in terms of a simple general equilibrium model. Its virtue is that asset markets are modeled with great care and are rightly identified as central to the issue of intervention. Henderson distinguishes between sterilized and nonsterilized intervention: In each a purchase of foreign exchange by the authorities is associated with a change in the relative supply of assets in the hands of the world public. However, in the case of nonsterilized intervention there is an increase in money relative to outside debt, and in the sterilized case outside debt rises relative to money. Sterilized intervention thus becomes a change in the currency composition of the world stock of outside debt whereas nonsterilized intervention changes the currency composition of the world money supply.

It is generally accepted that changes in the currency composition of the world money stock should exert effects: money is the medium of transactions and thus there is no foreign demand for home money. Even in models of currency substitution—the theoretical basis of which has never been established—changes in the composition of world money exert effects because of imperfect substitution. In Henderson's paper there is no external money demand and therefore the role of imperfect asset substitution is reserved, rightly, for interest-bearing assets. It serves as the channel through which intervention, by way of sterilization, can affect relative asset supplies and thus equilibrium asset yields, aggregate demand, output, and prices.

Henderson's model is cast in macroeconomic terms in that it establishes a link between money and bond markets and provides for transmission channels between assets and goods markets. But cutting through these details the central point of the finance-theoretic approach remains a link between the depreciation-adjusted interest rate differential and the risk premium on home securities:

$$(1) \qquad i - i^* - \dot{e}/e = \theta(B/e\overline{W}, \ . \ . \ .); \theta' \geq 0.$$

The risk premium, θ, will be an increasing function of the supply of domestic currency assets relative to world wealth, $B/e\overline{W}$. This equation is central to intervention in that it shows the relative supply of assets as one of the determinants in the interest rate–exchange rate relation. Suppose, for example, that domestic interest rates were increased but the exchange rate and depreciation rate were to remain unchanged. Equation (1) suggests that a change in the relative supply of domestic currency assets will do the trick by generating a matching increase in the risk premium. Sterilized intervention then is nothing but management of the risk premium.

The Key Results

Two results come clearly out of Henderson's analysis: first, nonsterilized intervention is effective. If in the face of exchange depreciation the central bank sells foreign exchange and reduces the home money stock, then such intervention cannot fail to dampen the exchange depreciation. Second, sterilized intervention is *the* appropriate policy initiative whenever the disturbance is a portfolio shift between home and foreign currency debt. Sterilized intervention in this case avoids the spreading of purely financial disturbances to interest rates, prices, and exchange rates.

The case for sterilized intervention, when disturbances are primarily portfolio shifts, is parallel to the standard Poole argument that rates should be pegged and supplies endogenized whenever asset demands are random. It is here applied, not to the interest-bearing versus non-interest-bearing government debt, but rather to the currency denomination of debt. Thus, whenever there is a shift out of United States dollar T-bills into French franc bonds, the United States government, or the government of France, would retire dollar debt and issue French franc–denominated debt. Henderson rightly emphasizes that it is rarely the case that we can identify disturbances as being clearly financial as opposed to real. Therefore the accommodation rule retains its interest primarily for those cases where portfolio shifts predominate relative to real disturbances.

In the general case where disturbances can be either real or financial and can originate on the demand or supply side, not much can be said. Henderson considers two policy settings: constant aggregates (money and bonds) and constant rates (exchange rate and interest rate) and asks which setting provides more stability in output and prices. The comparison can be readily made in terms of figure 11.C.1, where AD_r is the aggregate demand schedule along which the interest rate and the exchange rate are held constant, and AD_a is the schedule along which aggregates (money and debt) are constant. The latter is flatter (assuming that certain elasticity conditions are satisfied) since a decline in the price level raises real balances and brings about a fall in interest rates and a depreciation, both of which increase aggregate demand. By contrast, along AD_r the aggregate demand schedule slopes downward only because a decline in prices enhances external competitiveness.

It is immediately apparent from the diagram that an adverse supply shock shifting AS to AS' will bring about a larger increase in prices and smaller decline in output when rates are held constant as opposed to aggregates. When rates are held constant money is accommodating and the supply shock finds its way into prices, not interest rates. Figure 11.C.2 shows the impact of a fiscal expansion or an increase in net exports under the two policy settings. Under a rates constant policy the income expansion is accommo-

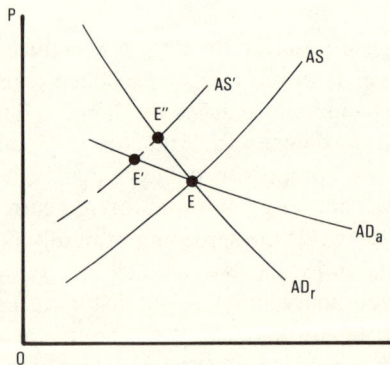

Fig. 11.C.1

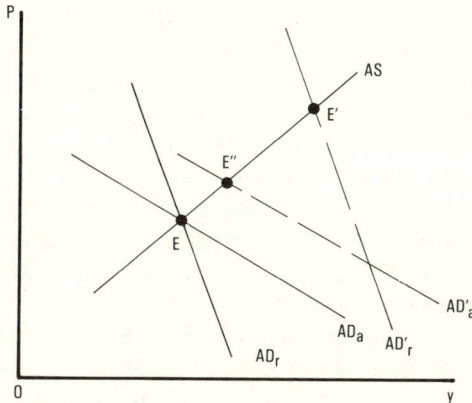

Fig. 11.C.2

dated through an increase in money. With less crowding out, the shift of the aggregate demand schedule is larger than that of AD_a. Thus with a rates constant policy demand disturbances exert larger impacts on output *and* on prices than is the case with constant aggregates. Which policy setting is more conducive to stability then depends on the relative preference for output and price stability and the relative prevalence of demand and supply disturbances. But the answer does not stop here. In a realistic model there would be exchange rate effects on the aggregate supply side—through wage indexing or materials prices—and once that occurs the apparent sharpness of the analysis in figures 11.C.1 and 11.C.2 goes away altogether. Henderson's paper is valuable in showing so strongly that pure portfolio shifts apart there is no case whatsoever for sterilized intervention as a generally good idea.

The Intervention Problem

Henderson's analysis is carefully placed in a macroeconomic, stochastic model. Policymakers face uncertainty about the disturbances that hit the economy and are offered alternative policy menus to select so as to minimize the asymptotic variances of output and prices. The analysis could, and indeed should, also take into account other policy objectives such as real interest rates, which surely matter for the medium-term question of growth. Needless to say, introduction of further trade-offs only weakens the chances that one rigid setting—sterilized intervention—should be optimal. Indeed, we would move further in the direction of Henderson's conclusion that a managed float would be appropriate.

The intervention issue arises in practice in two possible settings. First, should the authorities intervene to reduce "noise" in the foreign exchange market? Here we are concerned with day-to-day fluctuations and for the sake of the argument we might assume that there is no uncertainty about the trend. I can see neither harm nor great advantages to such intervention. One argument is that if the spot exchange rate moves a lot, under these idealized circumstances, it is presumably because it matters very little. Alternatively, noise may be a reflection of the fact that there is insufficient private speculation, which would be the case if there were uncertainty about exchange rate trends. Thus intervention in the case of noise strikes me as sensible only if the central bank can confidently announce financial stability and take bets on it with risk-averse and doubtful speculators.

The more serious intervention problem is the one we face today. Exchange rates have gone far out of line. The real exchange rate of the dollar stands more than 10% above its average of the 1971–81 period and more than 15% above the average of the last 5 years. The exchange rate swings have exerted a major impact on growth and on international inflation differentials. Most important, the overvaluation is the consequence, not of changes in portfolio preferences, but rather of policy decisions to control inflation in the United States. Henderson does not address this critical issue: When one country goes on a disinflation course, is it possible to use intervention and is it advisable to do so? This strikes me as the most important instance where the intervention issue arises, because it is in this case that real exchange rates move so very far from their long-run averages. Henderson's comparative static analysis cannot answer that question, since it is concerned with alternative scenarios of inflation stabilization, credibility, and expectations formation. This is regrettable because the case of intervention response to dyssynchronized inflation stabilization is one of the most serious international financial issues.

References

Argy, Victor. 1982. Exchange-rate management in theory and practice. Princeton Studies in International Finance, no. 50. Princeton: International Finance Section.

Artis, M. J., and Currie, D. A. 1981. Monetary targets and the exchange rate: A case for conditional targets. In *The money supply and the exchange rate,* ed. W. A. Eltis and P. J. N. Sinclair. Oxford: Clarendon.

Black, Stanley W. 1980. Central bank intervention and the stability of exchange rates. In *Exchange risk and exposure,* ed. Richard M. Levich and Clas G. Wihlborg. Lexington, Mass.: Lexington.

Boyer, Russell S. 1978. Optimal foreign exchange market intervention. *Journal of Political Economy* 86:1045–55.

————. 1980. Interest rate and exchange rate stabilization regimes: An analysis of recent Canadian policy. In *The functioning of floating exchange rates: Theory, evidence, and policy implications,* ed. David Bigman and Teizo Taya. Cambridge, Mass.: Ballinger.

Brainard, William C. 1967. Uncertainty and the effectiveness of policy. *American Economic Review* 57:411–25.

Brunner, Karl; Cukierman, Alex; and Meltzer, Allan H. 1980. Stagflation, persistent unemployment and the permanence of economic shocks. *Journal of Monetary Economics* 6:467–92.

Bryant, Ralph C. 1980. *Money and monetary policy in interdependent nations.* Washington: Brookings Institution.

Canzoneri, Matthew B. 1982. Exchange intervention policy in a multiple country world. *Journal of International Economics* 13:267–89.

Canzoneri, Matthew B., and Gray, Jo Anna. 1983. Two essays on monetary policy in an interdependent world. International Finance Discussion Papers, no. 219. Board of Governors of the Federal Reserve System.

Canzoneri, Matthew B.; Henderson, Dale W.; and Rogoff, Kenneth S. 1983. The information content of the interest rate and optimal monetary policy. *Quarterly Journal of Economics* 98:545–66.

Cumby, Robert E., and Obstfeld, Maurice. 1981. A note on exchange-rate expectations and nominal interest differentials: A test of the Fisher hypothesis. *Journal of Finance* 36:697–703.

Dooley, Michael P. 1979. Foreign exchange market intervention. In *The Political economy of policy-making,* ed. Michael P. Dooley, Herbert M. Kaufman, and Raymond E. Lombra. Beverly Hills, Calif.: Sage.

————. 1982. Exchange rate determination in a multicountry model: The importance of industrial country and developing country exchange market intervention policies. *International Monetary Fund Staff Papers* 29:233–69.

Dooley, Michael P., and Isard, Peter. 1982. A portfolio-balance rational-expectations model of the dollar-mark exchange rate. *Journal of International Economics* 12:257–76.

Dornbusch, Rudiger. 1980. Exchange rate economics: Where do we stand? *Brookings Papers on Economic Activity* 1980:143–85.

Fischer, Stanley. 1977. Stability and exchange rate systems in a monetarist model of the balance of payments. In *The political economy of monetary reform,* ed. Robert Z. Aliber. London: Macmillan.

Flood, Robert P. 1979. Capital mobility and the choice of exchange rate system. *International Economic Review* 20:405–16.

Flood, Robert P., and Marion, Nancy P. 1982. The transmission of disturbances under alternative exchange rate regimes. *Quarterly Journal of Economics* 97:43–66.

Frankel, Jeffrey A. 1979. The diversifiability of exchange risk. *Journal of International Economics* 9:379–92.

404   Dale W. Henderson

————. 1982*a*. A test of perfect substitutability in the foreign exchange market. *Southern Economic Journal* 49:406–16.

————. 1982*b*. In search of the exchange risk premium: A six-currency test assuming mean-variance optimization. *Journal of International Money and Finance* 1:255–74.

Frenkel, Jacob. 1980. International reserves under alternative exchange rate regimes and aspects of the economics of managed float. In *The Economics of Flexible Exchange Rates,* ed. Helmut Frisch and Gerhard Schwödiauer. Supplements to *Kredit und Kapital,* vol. 6. Berlin: Duncker & Humblot.

Friedman, Benjamin M. 1975. Targets, instruments, and indicators of monetary policy. *Journal of Monetary Economics* 1:443–73.

Genberg, Hans. 1981. Effects of central bank intervention in the foreign exchange market. *International Monetary Fund Staff Papers* 28:451–76.

Girton, Lance, and Henderson, Dale W. 1977. Central bank operations in foreign and domestic assets under fixed and flexible exchange rates. In *The effects of exchange rate adjustments,* ed. Peter B. Clark, Dennis E. Logue, and Richard J. Sweeney. Washington: Government Printing Office.

Hamada, Koichi. 1974. Alternative exchange rate systems and the interdependence of monetary policies. In *National monetary policies and the international monetary system,* ed. Robert Z. Aliber. Chicago: University of Chicago Press.

Hansen, Lars. P., and Hodrick, Robert J. 1980. Forward exchange rates as optimal predictors of future spot rates: An econometric analysis. *Journal of Political Economy* 88:829–53.

Henderson, Dale W. 1979. Financial policies in open economies. *American Economic Review* 69:232–39.

————. 1980. Analyzing arrangements for reducing exchange rate variability: A comment. In *Monetary institutions and the policy process,* ed. Karl Brunner and Allan H. Meltzer. Carnegie-Rochester Conference Series on Public Policy, vol. 13. Amsterdam: North-Holland.

————. 1982. The role of intervention policy in open economy financial policy: A macroeconomic perspective. In *The political economy of domestic and international monetary relations,* ed. Raymond E. Lombra and Willard E. Witte. Ames: Iowa State University Press.

Hooper, Peter, and Morton, John. 1982. Fluctuations in the dollar: A model of nominal and real exchange rate determination. *Journal of International Money and Finance* 1:39–56.

Jones, Michael. 1982. "Automatic" output stability and the exchange arrangement: A multi-country analysis. *Review of Economic Studies* 49:91–107.

Kaminow, Ira P. 1979. Economic stability under fixed and flexible exchange rates. *Journal of International Economics* 9:277–85.

Kareken, John; Muench, Thomas; and Wallace, Neil. 1973. Optimal open market strategy: The use of information variables. *American Economic Review* 63:156–72.

Kouri, Pentti J. K. 1977. International investment and interest rate linkages under flexible exchange rates. In *The political economy of monetary reform,* ed. Robert Z. Aliber. London: Macmillan.

Meese, Richard A., and Singleton, Kenneth J. 1980. Rational expectations, risk premia, and the market for spot and forward exchange. International Finance Discussion Papers, no. 165. Board of Governors of the Federal Reserve System.

Meltzer, Allan H. 1978. The conduct of monetary policy under current monetary arrangements. *Journal of Monetary Economcs* 4:371–88.

Modigliani, Franco, and Askari, Hossein. 1973. The international transfer of capital and the propagation of domestic disturbances under alternative payment systems. *Banca Nazionale del Lavoro Quarterly Review* 107:296–310.

Mundell, Robert A. 1968. *International economics.* New York: Macmillan.

Mussa, Michael. 1981. The role of official intervention. Group of Thirty Occassional Papers, no. 6. New York: Group of Thirty.

Niehans, Jürg. 1968. Monetary and fiscal policies in open economies under fixed and flexible exchange rates: An optimizing approach. *Journal of Political Economy* 76:893–920.

Obstfeld, Maurice. 1980. Imperfect asset substitutability and monetary policy under fixed exchange rates. *Journal of International Economics* 10:177–200.

———. 1982a. The capitalization of income streams and the effects of open-market policy under fixed exchange rates. *Journal of Monetary Economics* 9:87–98.

———. 1982b. Can we sterilize? Theory and evidence. *American Economic Review* 72:45–50.

———. 1983. Exchange rates, inflation, and the sterilization problem: Germany, 1975–1981. *European Economic Review* 21:161–89.

Parkin, Michael. 1978. A comparison of alternative techniques of monetary control under rational expectations. *Manchester School* 46:252–87.

Poole, William. 1970. Optimal choice of monetary policy instruments in a simple stochastic macro model. *Quarterly Journal of Economics* 84:197–216.

Roper, Don E., and Turnovsky, Stephen J. 1980. Optimal exchange market intervention in a simple stochastic macro model. *Canadian Journal of Economics* 13:296–309.

Sargent, Thomas J. 1973. Rational expectations, the real rate of interest, and the natural rate of unemployment. *Brookings Papers on Economic Activity* 1973:429–72.

Shafer, Jeffrey R. 1982. Discussion of exchange rate volatility and intervention policy. In *The international monetary system: A time of turbulence,* ed. Jacob S. Dreyer, Gottfried Haberler, and Thomas Willett. Washington: American Enterprise Institute.

Stein, Jerome L. 1963. The optimum foreign exchange market. *American Economic Review* 53:384–402.

Stockman, Alan C. 1979. Monetary control and sterilization under pegged exchange rates. University of Rochester.

Sweeney, Richard J. 1976. Automatic stabilization policy and exchange rate regimes: A general equilibrium approach. U.S. Department of the Treasury.

Tower, Edward, and Willett, Thomas D. 1976. The theory of optimum currency areas and exchange rate flexibility. Special Papers in International Economics, no. 11. Princeton: International Finance Section.

Turnovsky, Stephen J. 1976. The relative stability of alternative exchange rate systems in the presence of random disturbances. *Journal of Money, Credit, and Banking* 8:29–50.

———. 1983. Exchange market intervention policies in a small open economy. In *Economic interdependence and flexible exchange rates,* ed. Jagdeep S. Bhandari and Bluford S. Putnam. Cambridge, Mass: M.I.T. Press.

Wallich, Henry C., and Gray, Jo Anna. 1981. Stabilization policy and vicious and virtuous circles. In *Flexible exchange rates and the balance of payments: Essays in honor of Egon Sohmen,* ed. John S. Chipman and Charles P. Kindleberger. Amsterdam: North-Holland.

Weber, Warren E. 1981. Output variability under monetary policy and exchange rate rules. *Journal of Political Economy* 89:733–51.

Wonnacott, Paul. 1982. U. S. intervention in the exchange market for DM. Princeton Studies in International Finance, no. 51. Princeton: International Finance Section.

12

Exchange Rate Unions as an Alternative to Flexible Rates: The Effects of Real and Monetary Disturbances

Richard C. Marston

Although the current period is often characterized as one of flexible exchange rates, many currencies are tied together in joint floats against other currencies, forming exchange rate unions within a system of flexible rates. This paper investigates how a small country fares by joining such an exchange rate union.[1]

The country is assumed to be buffeted by real and monetary disturbances originating at home and abroad. By joining the union, this country is able to fix the exchange rate between its currency and the currencies of the union countries. The central question addressed in the paper is whether or not fixing this exchange rate helps to modify the effects of disturbances on the domestic economy.

The paper shows that the impact of a union depends on several key factors:[2]

This paper was written while I was a visiting professor at the Ecole Supérieure des Sciences Economiques et Commerciales. I would like to thank Joshua Aizenman, Bernard Dumas, Jacques Melitz, and Charles Wyplosz for their helpful comments. Financial support from a German Marshall Fund Fellowship and a National Science Foundation grant (SES-8006414) is gratefully acknowledged.

1. The terminology here is potentially confusing. In this study, the term "exchange rate union" refers to an arrangement in which member countries of each union maintain fixed exchange rates between member currencies, but with each country retaining its own central bank with control over its national monetary policy. This limited type of union, which Corden (1972, p. 3) calls a "pseudo exchange rate union," is to be distinguished from a "complete exchange rate union," or monetary union, with a single central bank and a union-wide currency.

2. Tower and Willett (1976) provide a comprehensive survey of the literature on optimum currency areas which examines the conditions necessary for successful exchange rate or monetary unions; Allen and Kenen (1980, chap. 14) discuss the more recent literature. Among the more important contributions are those of Mundell (1961), McKinnon (1963), Corden (1972), and Ingram (1973). A recent paper by Canzoneri (1981) compares exchange rate unions with more general forms of exchange market intervention.

1. *Wage and price behavior* at home and abroad, a factor emphasized by Corden (1972) in his study of monetary integration. Wage behavior abroad determines the specific form which foreign disturbances take in the domestic economy, while wage behavior at home determines the difference which the choice of regime makes to the behavior of domestic output.

2. *The trade pattern* of the country joining the union. What is important is not just the general openness of the economy, as in McKinnon (1963), but the share of trade between potential member countries relative to trade with the rest of the world.

3. *The sources and types of economic disturbances* giving rise to fluctuations in exchange rates. To some extent the analysis will follow that of the literature on fixed versus flexible exchange rates, of which Mundell's (1963) study is representative. But the decision to join a union is more complicated than that; when there are two foreign countries or regions involved, the specific source of foreign disturbances becomes important, as well as any correlation between disturbances originating in different countries. Of particular interest will be foreign disturbances which are alternatively positively and negatively correlated, since these have very different implications for the choice between regimes.

The paper will investigate two intuitively plausible propositions about these last two factors: that the case for a union is stronger when the home country trades primarily with other countries in the union and when disturbances primarily originate outside the union.

The national models used to investigate the effects of the union consist of three basic equations: an aggregate demand equation dependent on the terms of trade as well as foreign output, an aggregate supply equation derived from a wage indexation model, and a financial equation that determines the exchange rate of the domestic currency relative to one of the two foreign currencies (the other being determined by triangular arbitrage). The paper shows to what extent aggregate supply and demand behavior are important in determining the effects of the union. Supply behavior varies depending upon whether wages respond to prices with a lag or are indexed to current changes in the general price level, while demand behavior is particularly sensitive to price elasticities.

The small country model has the advantage of analytic simplicity, but by itself gives misleading results when foreign disturbances are examined. The model can be used to show, for example, that variations in foreign income due to foreign disturbances anywhere abroad unambiguously lead to greater domestic output variance in the union. But without a model of the two foreign regions, the union countries and the rest of the world, it is difficult to determine the *total* effects of the underlying foreign disturbances, since these disturbances affect the domestic economy through a variety of channels. For example, in addition to changing foreign output, a foreign demand disturbance concentrated in one of the two foreign regions will change the terms of trade between the foreign goods imported by the small country and the exchange rate between the two foreign currencies. The total effects of this foreign disturbance thus may be quite different from the effects of a change in foreign income alone.

To study foreign disturbances, the paper introduces a model of the two foreign trading regions with the same analytical structure as the small country model. This model determines the exchange rate and terms of trade between the two regions as well as the prices, interest rates, and output in each region. Foreign disturbances are studied first within this model, then are traced through the domestic model to determine the effects on the small country.

The first section of the paper introduces the small country model, and the next two sections successively examine the effects of disturbances within the one country and extended models.

12.1 Outline of the Model

Country 1 is a small country which has economic ties with two countries: country 2 is the potential partner of country 1 in an exchange rate union, while country 3 represents the rest of the world. Country 1 has important trade and financial ties with the other two countries; the relative importance of these economic ties will be an issue in the analysis below. Country 1 is assumed to be too small to influence conditions in either foreign country.[3] The two foreign countries affect country 1 through their outputs (Y_t^2, Y_t^3), the prices of their goods (P_t^2, P_t^3), both expressed in logarithms, and interest rates (r_t^2, r_t^3).[4]

In this three-country world, there are three exchange rates to be determined. If the franc is the currency of country 1, the mark the currency of country 2, and the dollar the currency of country 3, then the three exchange rates are as follows (all expressed in logs):

$$X_t^1 = \text{the franc price of the dollar,}$$

$$X_t^2 = \text{the mark price of the dollar, and}$$

$$X_t^{12} = X_t^1 - X_t^2 = \text{the franc price of the mark.}$$

Figure 12.1 illustrates the relationships among the three currencies. X_t^2 is exogenously determined for country 1, while a second exchange rate is determined by triangular arbitrage.

---

3. The two foreign countries could represent blocs of countries with fixed exchange rates within each bloc, in which case country 1 does not need to be small relative to individual countries in each bloc. Country 2, for example, might represent a group of countries in an existing union (e.g., the European Monetary System) and country 3 represent a second group of countries tied to the dollar.

4. A list of variables in provided in Appendix 1.

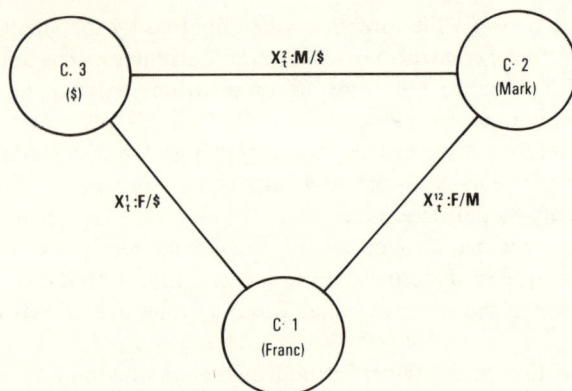

Fig. 12.1   Currencies and exchange rates. Country 1 = domestic country; country 2 = potential partner (or partners) in union; country 3 = rest of world.

12.1.1 Demand Behavior

Unless purchasing power parity is assumed, demand behavior in a country trading with two other countries is inherently complicated. Three national prices are involved as well as at least two exchange rates. I begin by defining the prices of the three countries' goods expressed in francs:

$$P_t^1 = \text{the price of country 1's good,}$$

$$P_t^3 + X_t^1 = \text{the price of country 3's good in francs, and}$$

$$P_t^2 + X_t^{12} = \text{the price of country 2's good in francs.}$$

It is convenient for later analysis to measure country 2's prices relative to country 3. Define the terms of trade between countries 2 and 3 as $T_t = P_t^2 - (P_t^3 + X_t^2)$. Then the price of country 2's good in francs can be written as $P_t^3 + T_t + X_t^1$. The general price level in country 1 can be expressed as a weighted average of the prices of the three goods:

$$I_t^1 = a_{11}P_t^1 + a_{12}(P_t^3 + T_t + X_t^1) + a_{13}(P_t^3 + X_t^1),$$

where a_{1j} is the expenditure weight for country j's good.[5]

There are two relative prices affecting demand in country 1, the price of country 1's good relative to each of the foreign goods. The demand for domestic output can be expressed as a function of these relative prices, output in the two foreign countries, the real rate of interest, and a stochastic factor with a mean of zero and serially uncorrelated:[6]

5. When expressed in levels, this price index has a geometric form with weights $a_{11} + a_{12} + a_{13} = 1$.

6. In Appendix 2 this demand function is derived from a more standard demand function, and the coefficients, g_{pi} and g_{yi}, are expressed in terms of conventional income and price elasticities.

$$(1) \qquad Y_t^1 = g_0 + g_{p2}(P_t^3 + T_t + X_t^1 - P_t^1)$$
$$+ g_{p3}(P_t^3 + X_t^1 - P_t^1)$$
$$g_{y2}Y_t^2 + g_{y3}Y_t^3 - g_r[r_t^1 - ({_tEI}_{t+1}^1 - I_t^1)] + u_t^{d1}.$$

A rise in foreign prices relative to the domestic price is assumed to increase aggregate demand, as is a rise in foreign output. A rise in the real interest rate is assumed to reduce aggregate demand.[7] In the case of perfect substitution between foreign and domestic goods, where either g_{pj} becomes infinite in size, the aggregate demand equation reduces to the familiar purchasing power parity relationship.

12.1.2 Supply Behavior

Supply behavior is based on a labor contract lag of one period with the partial or complete indexation of wages to current prices. Supply behavior is more complicated than in a closed economy because there are two prices important for supply decisions, the price of domestic output (P_t^1) and the general price level (I_t^1). Output is responsive to nominal wages relative to the price of domestic output, but nominal wages may be at least partially indexed to current changes in the general price level.

The supply equation (2) is derived from a Cobb-Douglas production function (2a), a labor market equilibrium condition (2b) determining the contract wage, $W_t^{1'}$, and a wage indexation equation (2c):

$$(2) \qquad Y_t^1 = c(P_t^1 - {_{t-1}EP_t^1}) - cb(I_t^1 - {_{t-1}EI_t^1}) + c_0$$

$$(2a) \qquad Y_t^1 = (1 - c')L_t^1 = -c(W_t^1 - P_t^1) + c\, ln(1 - c')$$

$$(2b) \qquad W_t^{1'} = {_{t-1}EP_t^1} + ln(1 - c') - c'\overline{L}^1$$

$$(2c) \qquad W_t^1 = W_t^{1'} + b(I_t^1 - {_{t-1}EI_t^1}),$$

where $c = (1 - c')/c'$ and $c_0 = (1 - c')\overline{L}^1$. The contract wage, reflecting expectations at time $t - 1$, is based on labor demand (derived from the production function) and an inelastic labor supply ($\overline{L}^1$).[8] The actual wage, W_t^1, will differ from the contract wage if the indexation parameter, b, is different from zero; this parameter is assumed to vary between zero (no

---

7. ${_tEI}_{t+1}^1$ is country 1's general price level for period $t + 1$ expected at period t, so $({_tEI}_{t+1}^1 - I_t^1)$ is the expected change in that price level. ${_tEI}_{t+1}^1$ is assumed to be formed rationally from the rest of the model, as are all other expectations in the model.

8. The desired labor supply is inelastic, but once the contract is signed the amount of labor supplied is determined by the demand for labor as in Gray (1976). The desired labor supply, alternatively, might be sensitive to nominal wages relative to the general price level. None of the results below would be affected by this change in specification, since current output would be a function of the same price prediction errors as in (2). When labor supply is variable, however, an alternative objective function measuring deviations of output from desired output is no longer equivalent to our objective function. (See section 12.2 below.)

indexation) and one (full indexation).[9] With no indexation, only domestic price prediction errors matter, but with partial or full indexation, price prediction errors in the general price index also matter. With full indexation, in fact, equal increases in P_t^1 and I_t^1 leave supply unaffected. When indexation is less than complete, however, equal increases in P_t^1 and I_t^1 *increase* supply since the real wages faced by producers fall.

12.1.3 Financial Behavior

The three countries have two financial assets each: money and bonds (the latter bearing interest rate r_t^i). To keep the financial sector simple, however, the three bonds are assumed to be perfect substitutes so that their expected returns expressed in the same currency are equal:[10]

$$r_t^1 = r_t^3 + ({}_tEX_{t+1}^1 - X_t^1),$$
$$r_t^2 = r_t^3 + ({}_tEX_{t+1}^2 - X_t^2).$$

The demand for money is expressed as a function of real income, with money balances and income being deflated by the general price level, as well as the domestic interest rate:[11]

(3) $$M_t^1 - I_t^1 = (P_t^1 + Y_t^1 - I_t^1) - k_1 r_t^1 + k_0.$$

The behavior of the money supply depends on the exchange rate regime. Under flexible rates, the money supply is assumed to be exogenously determined as follows: $M_t^1 = \overline{M}^1 + u_t^{m1}$. The current money supply is equal to a base level plus a random term, where the latter has a mean of zero and is serially uncorrelated as well as uncorrelated with the demand disturbance. The supply of money in the exchange rate union is described below.

12.1.4 Foreign Behavior

All foreign variables in the model are exogenously determined by the small country assumption. I express each foreign variable as a constant plus

---

9. For studies of wage indexation behavior, see Gray (1976), Fischer (1977), Modigliani and Padoa-Schioppa (1978), Sachs (1980) and Flood and Marion (1982). Flood and Marion provide an interesting analysis of how indexation behavior may respond to the choice of exchange rate regime. Because in many countries indexation behavior is governed by institutional or legal constraints, however, I prefer to assume that the degree of indexation remains the same when the exchange rate regime changes. Thus the analysis will show how the choice of exchange rate regime differs between countries with different types of wage and price behavior.

10. For a more general study of financial behavior in an exchange rate union, see Marston (1984). In that study, where the effects of various financial disturbances are analyzed, foreign and domestic bonds are assumed to be imperfect substitutes.

11. The income elasticity of the demand for money is assumed to be one. If it were not equal to one, a change in the general price level, which could be due to a change in the exchange rate or one of the prices, would have an effect on the net demand for money proportional to one minus this elasticity. Note that the exchange rate can still affect the demand for money in this model by changing the interest rate.

a random variable where the latter is the innovation in that variable for period t:[12]

$$P_t^i = \overline{P}^i + u_t^{pi},$$

$$Y_t^i = \overline{Y}^i + u_t^{yi},$$

$$X_t^2 = \overline{X}^2 + u_t^{x2},$$

$$T_t = \overline{T} + u_t^T,$$

$$r_t^i = \overline{r}^i + u_t^{ri}, i = 2, 3.$$

In the third part of the paper, the random variables will be expressed in terms of the underlying foreign disturbances. Until then these variables are assumed to have zero mean, to be serially uncorrelated, and to be uncorrelated with each other.

12.1.5 Description of the Two Exchange Rate Regimes

The exchange rate union will be compared with a regime of flexible exchange rates where no exchange market intervention occurs. The flexible regime is discussed first.

Flexible Exchange Rates

The basic equations of the model, (1)–(3), determine three domestic variables, Y_t^1, P_t^1, and X_t^1, as functions of all the stochastic and nonstochastic variables (X_t^{12} is then determined by triangular arbitrage). To facilitate comparison between the two regimes, equations (1) and (2) are first solved for Y_t^1 and P_t^1 as functions of X_t^1 and the exogenous variables. The resulting expressions, equations (I) and (II) in table 12.1, describe aggregate demand and supply behavior in *both* exchange rate regimes.[13] The stochastic variables influencing Y_t^1 and P_t^1 include the domestic aggregate demand disturbance, u_t^{d1}, as well as the random components of X_t^1 and the foreign variable.

Under flexible rates, the franc price of the dollar, X_t^1, can be expressed as a function of exogenous variables alone by solving all three equations, (1)–(3), for the reduced form. Equation (IIIa) in table 12.1 presents the expression for X_t^1.

---

12. u_t^{pi} is the innovation in P_t^i, $u_t^{pi} = P_t^i - {}_{t-1}EP_t^i$, and similarly for other variables. The underlying foreign disturbances have a mean of zero and are serially uncorrelated, so the expected value of each variable is equal to its value in a stationary equilibrium; for example, ${}_{t-1}EP_t^i = \overline{P}^i$. (See section 12.3 below.)

13. $\overline{Y}^1$, $\overline{P}^1$ are the solutions for Y_t^1 and P_t^1 when the disturbances in equations (1) and (2) are equal to zero. To obtain the coefficients of u_t^T in table 12.1, I have assumed that the shares of the two foreign goods in the price indexes are proportional to the respective price elasticities in the aggregate demand equation: $a_{12}/a_{13} = g_{p2}/g_{p3}$. This restriction allows trade to be biased toward one foreign country or the other (see below), but the bias must be equally reflected in the a_{1j}'s and g_{pj}'s.

Table 12.1   Country 1's Model

(I)
$$Y_t^1 = \bar{Y}^1 + \frac{c(1 - ba_{11})}{D_1}(u_t^{d1} + g_{y2}u_t^{y2} + g_{y3}u_t^{y3}) + \frac{(g_{p3}c(1-b) - g_rca_{13})}{D_1}(u_t^{p3} + u_t^{x1})$$
$$+ \frac{[g_{p2}c(1-b) - g_rca_{12}]}{D_1}(u_t^{p3} + u_t^{x1} + u_t^T) - \frac{[g_rc(1 - ba_{11})]}{D_1}(u_t^{x3} - u_t^{x1}).$$

(II)
$$P_t^1 = \bar{P}^1 + \frac{(u_t^{d1} + g_{y2}u_t^{y2} + g_{y3}u_t^{y3})}{D_1} + \frac{(g_{p3} - g_ra_{13} + cba_{13})}{D_1}(u_t^{p3} + u_t^{x1})$$
$$+ \frac{(g_{p2} - g_ra_{12} + cba_{12})}{D_1}(u_t^{p3} + u_t^{x1} + u_t^T) - \frac{g_r}{D_1}(u_t^{x3} - u_t^{x1}).$$

(IIIa) *Flexible Rates*

$$X_t^1 = \bar{X}^1 + \frac{D_1}{D}u_t^{ml} - \frac{[1 + c(1 - ba_{11})]}{D}(u_t^{d1} + g_{y2}u_t^{y2} + g_{y3}u_t^{y3}) + \frac{\{k_1D_1 + g_r[1 + c(1 - ba_{11})]\}}{D}u_t^{x3}$$
$$- \frac{\{g_{p3}[1 + c(1 - b)] + a_{13}cb - a_{13}g_r(1 + c)\}}{D}u_t^{p3} - \frac{\{g_{p2}[1 + c(1 - b)] + a_{12}cb - a_{12}g_r(1 + c)\}}{D}(u_t^{p3} + u_t^T).$$

(IIIb) *Exchange Rate Union*
$$X_t^1 = X_t^2 = \bar{X}^2 + u_t^{x2}.$$
where $D_1 = g_{p2} + g_{p3} + g_ra_{11} + c(1 - ba_{11}) > 0$ and $u_t^{x1} = X_t^1 - \bar{X}^1$.
$$D = (1 + k_1)D_1 + c(1 - b)[g_ra_{11} + (g_{p2} + g_{p3}) - 1] > 0.$$

Exchange Rate Union

If country 1 joins an exchange rate union with country 2, the monetary authorities must intervene in the exchange market to ensure that $X_t^{12} = X_t^1 - X_t^2$ remains constant. For convenience I assume that the franc price of the mark is initially equal to one (so that the log of this exchange rate, X_t^{12}, is initially equal to zero). In that case, intervention keeps $X_t^1 = X_t^2$ at all times. Suppose that the foreign intervention is carried out by the monetary authority of country 1 which buys (or sells) country 2's currency and sells (or buys) country 1's currency to keep X_t^{12} fixed. (The results would be the same if country 2 carried out this intervention.)[14] In that case, equation (3) describing money market equilibrium simply determines the money supply consistent with keeping X_t^1 equal to X_t^2. In place of equation (IIIa) determining X_t^1 on the basis of country 1's behavior, I have an exogenously determined exchange rate, $X_t^1 = X_t^2 = \overline{X}^2 + u_t^{x2}$. By joining the union, country 1 has not only fixed its mark exchange rate but has effectively surrendered control over its dollar exchange rate.

Two other characteristics of this regime should be pointed out. First, I assume that the private sector is fully confident that the union is permanent in the sense that the authorities will be able to maintain the fixed exchange rate between the franc and the mark. Thus $_tE\,X_{t+1}^{12} = X_t^{12}$. Since I abstract from inflation and other secular trends, this assumption is not an unrealistic one. But in adopting it, I ignore some interesting problems associated with actual unions such as the European Monetary System where expectations about changes in pegs are important. Second, I ignore any changes in private behavior which the formation of the union might induce. Cooper (1976) and others have pointed out that a change in exchange rate arrangements might lead to changes in trade and financial behavior affecting the parameters of the behavioral functions. While recognizing the importance of this point, I follow previous writers in assuming that these parameters are invariant to the regime since otherwise I would need to model explicitly the microeconomic behavior of trading firms and investors.[15]

12.2 Evaluation of the Union: Domestic Disturbances

The two domestic disturbances in the model, u_t^{d1} and u_t^{m1}, need further discussion. Following Mundell (1963) and other studies of internal-external balance, I might view these factors as deliberate instruments of fiscal and

---

14. The choice of which country to intervene would be important if the intervention took the form of buying or selling foreign bonds (as would be the case if the foreign currency were used as a reserve currency), but here I assume a simple form of intervention with no sterilization of the intervention effects. For an analysis of different types of intervention policy, see Marston (1980).

15. One study which does take into account changes in behavior is that by Flood and Marion (1982), which allows wage indexation to vary with the regime.

monetary policy, respectively, in which case the objective naturally would be to *maximize* their impact on the economy.[16] Given the stochastic assumptions adopted in this paper, these policies would have to be unanticipated and temporary. (See Marston, [1983] for a discussion of stabilization policy in stochastic models.) I prefer to view u_t^{d1} and u_t^{m1} as economic disturbances originating in private sector behavior, however, and to regard the task of policy to *minimize* the effects of these disturbances.

To judge the desirability of an exchange rate union, I also need to specify which macroeconomic variables I am interested in stabilizing, since a union modifies the impact of disturbances on most macroeconomic variables in country 1. Although I discuss the response of other variables such as prices, I follow the traditional literature on the choice between regimes by focusing on one variable only, domestic output. More specifically, the choice between flexible rates and the exchange rate union is based on which regime minimizes the effects of economic disturbances on the variance of domestic output.[17]

Most of the analysis below follows closely that of a country choosing between fixed and flexible rates. That is because country 1's disturbances have no effect on the exchange rate between the mark and the dollar, so that in a union country 1 is affected by the disturbances just as if it had a fixed exchange rate with the dollar as well as the mark. The analysis departs from the traditional literature on fixed and flexible rates, however, in showing how wage indexation modifies the effects of monetary and aggregate demand disturbances. This will be important in the discussion of foreign disturbances to follow.

I begin by examining the effects of the disturbances in the case where there is no wage indexation in the domestic economy, then I consider the effects of indexation. For convenience, I present below the equations for domestic output and the exchange rate (equations [I] and [IIIa] of table 12.1) expressed as a function of domestic disturbances only:

$$(4) \qquad Y_t^1 - \overline{Y}^1 = \frac{c(1 - ba_{11})}{D_1} u_t^{d1}$$
$$+ \frac{(g_{p2} + g_{p3} + g_r a_{11})c(1 - b)}{D_1} u_t^{x1},$$

$$(5) \qquad u_t^{x1} = X_t^1 - \overline{X}^1 = \frac{D_1}{D} u_t^{m1} - \frac{[1 + c(1 - ba_{11})]}{D} u_t^{d1},$$

16. For an analysis of fiscal and monetary policies in a union context, see Allen and Kenen (1980, chaps. 15–18), who study the effects of the policies in an exchange rate union as well as in a full-fledged monetary union where there is a single central bank.

17. Following Gray (1976), we might measure domestic output relative to desired rather than expected output, where the former is defined as that output which would prevail in a frictionless economy without contract lags. As long as labor supply is inelastic, these two objectives are equivalent since desired output, like expected output, is unaffected by the disturbances.

where $D_1 = g_{p2} + g_{p3} + g_r a_{11} + c(1 - ba_{11}) > 0,$

$D = (1 + k_1)D_1 + (g_{p2} + g_{p3} + g_r a_{11} - 1)c(1 - b) > 0.$

In the exchange rate union, u_t^{x1} is equal to zero because X_t^1 is tied to the exogenously determined mark, while under flexible rates u_t^{x1} can be expressed as in equation (5) in terms of both domestic disturbances.

Consider first the effects of a monetary disturbance. A monetary disturbance has no effect on output in an exchange rate union. An expansion of the money supply, for example, leads to pressure on both franc exchange rates, but intervention in the exchange market ensures that $X_t^1 = X_t^2$ where the latter is exogenously determined. The disturbance simply results in an equal and offsetting capital flow.[18] In a flexible regime, in contrast, a monetary expansion leads to a depreciation of the franc and an increase in output, at least when there is no indexation.[19] Thus, as in the case where only one foreign country is involved (see, for example, Mundell [1963]), domestic monetary disturbances cause variations in output only under flexible rates.

An aggregate demand disturbance in country 1, in contrast, leads to greater changes in output in an exchange rate union. An increase in aggregate demand raises domestic output and prices. There is pressure on both franc exchange rates because of the incipient rise in the domestic interest rate, but once again intervention in the exchange market ensures that $X_t^1 = X_t^2$. Under flexible exchange rates, however, the increase in output leads to an appreciation of the domestic currency (X_t^1 and X_t^{12} fall) which dampens the overall increase in aggregate demand.[20] Thus there is less output variation under flexible rates.

When indexation is complete ($b = 1$), however, these familiar results break down. To understand why this is true, notice that the effect of the exchange rate on domestic output is dependent on the degree of indexation in the domestic economy. As equation (4) indicates, the effect is proportional to $c(1 - b)$, with full indexation ($b = 1$) preventing the exchange rate from affecting domestic output at all. For that reason, the difference in

18. If country 1 were not small, its dollar exchange rate could change because the monetary expansion together with the accompanying foreign exchange intervention would also significantly affect the money supply in country 2.

19. The monetary disturbance affects output only through the exchange rate, as equation (4) indicates. The exchange rate depreciates, $u_t^{x1} = X_t^1 - \overline{X}^1 > 0$, so output increases under flexible rates.

20. Under flexible rates, the direct (positive) impact of u_t^{d1} on Y_t^1 in equation (4) is modified by the decline in u_t^{x1} (which reduces Y_t^1). Output nonetheless increases even under flexible rates. In contrast, Mundell's (1961) study of fixed and flexible rates showed that output did not increase at all in response to a demand disturbance (in his study, an increase in government spending); given his assumption that exchange rate expectations were static, only a constant output was consistent with money market equilibrium. In this study, the exchange rate appreciates relative to the expected exchange rate, with the domestic interest rate rising accordingly; so output can increase despite a constant money supply.

output variation *between* the two regimes must be proportional to $c(1 - b)$. And with full indexation, each disturbance must have an identical effect on output in the two regimes. These results can be illustrated in figures 12.2 and 12.3, which show how aggregate demand and supply adjust to the disturbances when indexation is complete.

First consider the monetary disturbance. Under flexible rates, the resulting depreciation leads to an outward shift in the aggregate demand function (to point B in fig. 12.2) because of the sensitivity of aggregate demand to relative prices and the real interest rate. When wages are fully indexed to the general price level, however, there is a corresponding leftward shift in aggregate supply (to point C) because the depreciation leads to a rise in the nominal wage. The price of domestic output accordingly rises further; in fact, the price of domestic output and the exchange rate increase by the same amount, with the constant terms of trade ensuring that output remains fixed at its original level.[21] In the union, in contrast, no depreciation occurs, so the aggregate supply and demand curves remain at point A. With full indexation of wages, therefore, the monetary disturbance leaves output unaffected in both regimes. The two regimes differ with respect to price behavior, however, since prices increase only under flexible rates.

The aggregate demand disturbance does change real output in both regimes. In the union, the demand disturbance shifts equilibrium to point A' in figure 12.3. Under flexible rates, the increase in demand leads to an appreciation of the franc and to a smaller increase in aggregate demand than

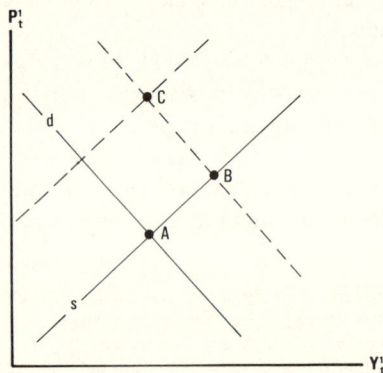

Fig. 12.2   Domestic monetary disturbance.

21. Sachs (1980) and Flood and Marion (1982) also discuss the case of full wage indexation. In the model specified by Sachs, constant terms of trade ensure that the disturbance has no net effect on aggregate demand. In the present model, aggregate demand is also a function of expectations through the real interest rate. But because the expected change in the exchange rate is equal to the expected change in the domestic price as well as in the general price level, the real interest rate also remains constant.

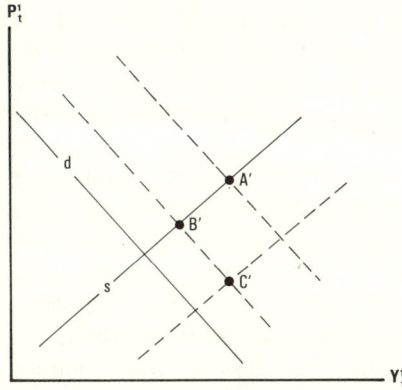

Fig. 12.3   Domestic aggregate demand disturbance

in the union (to point B'). With complete indexation of wages, however, the appreciation of the exchange rate also raises aggregate supply by lowering real wages faced by producers. Point C' is reached where the change in output is the same as in the union. Thus, as in the case of a monetary disturbance, full indexation results in the same variance of output in the two regimes. In both cases, indexation ensures that the shift in aggregate demand due to the exchange rate is matched by an offsetting shift in aggregate supply, so that the exchange rate has no net effect on domestic output.

In the absence of indexation, exchange rate flexibility is preferred in the case of the aggregate demand disturbance, but the union is preferred in the case of the monetary disturbance. The effect of wage indexation is to blur these differences, with full indexation eliminating the advantages or disadvantages of flexibility in stabilizing output.

12.3 Evaluation of the Union: Foreign Disturbances

Foreign disturbances affect the domestic economy through a variety of channels: *(a)* Changes in foreign output directly affect domestic aggregate demand (proportionally to g_{y2} and g_{y3}). *(b)* Changes in foreign prices or in the foreign terms of trade induce substitution with the domestic good (depending on the price elasticities, g_{p2} and g_{p3}). *(c)* In the union, changes in the mark price of the dollar affect aggregate demand (through those same price elasticities). *(d)* Foreign interest rates affect domestic demand indirectly by changing the franc price of the dollar under flexible rates and directly through the real interest rate effect on aggregate demand.

All of these channels are potentially important. For many disturbances, moreover, country 1's output is pushed in contrary directions. The net effect of foreign disturbances on country 1 depends upon which of these channels are most important. That, in turn, depends on the types of economic disturbances encountered as well as on the pattern of trade. One might expect the union to be more desirable if economic disturbances predominantly originate from outside the union and if the pattern of trade is biased so that country 1 trades primarily with country 2. Both of these propositions will be explored in the analysis below.

In order to investigate foreign economic disturbances, I need to specify models of the two foreign countries. To keep the models relatively simple, I adopt the following assumptions:

1. Countries 2 and 3 have identical economic structures. That is, the structural parameters in the aggregate supply and demand equations and in the financial equations are the same for the two countries. Thus I can specify one national model which can apply to both countries.[22] This assumption does not restrict the nature of country 1's relationships with the two foreign countries since any asymmetries in country 1's links with the foreign countries could not affect the latter given the small country assumption. More specifically, country 1 may choose to trade with one country more than the other or may be more sensitive to one country's prices or output.

2. For most of the discussion below, there is complete wage indexation in both foreign countries so that equal increases in domestic prices and exchange rates (or foreign prices) leave aggregate supply unaffected. Foreign output is then solely a function of the terms of trade. This assumption considerably simplifies the analysis of the two foreign countries, making it easier to show the channels through which foreign disturbances affect country 1. Even with the simplifying assumption, some of the effects of foreign disturbances are ambiguous, but I am able to distinguish clearly which factors are important in determining the net impact of the disturbances.

Later in this section I relax the assumption about foreign indexation to consider the opposite case of no wage indexation abroad. The contrast between the two cases is interesting, since it shows once again how wage and price adjustments affect the relative performance of different exchange rate regimes.

12.3.1 The Foreign Country Model

The model closely parallels that specified for country 1. Differences arise primarily because only two countries are involved, given the small country assumption for country 1, and because the aggregate supply equation takes a simple form when wage indexation is complete. Each national model can be expressed in three equations (where $i = 2, 3, j \neq 1$):

---

22. The countries' price indices, for example, are mirror images of one another; the weight of each country's own good in its price index is the same for both countries, $a_{22} = a_{33} = a$. Note that country 1's prices and output are assumed to have a negligible impact on the foreign countries; for example, a_{21} and a_{31}, the weights of country 1's good in the foreign price indices, are assumed to be negligibly small.

$$(1)' \qquad Y_t^i = g_0^f - g_p^f T_t^i + g_y^f Y_t^j - g_r^f[r_t^i$$
$$- ({}_tEI_{t+1}^i - I_t^i)] + u_t^{di},$$

$$(2)' \qquad Y_t^i = c_0^f + c^f(1 - a)(T_t^i - {}_{t-1}ET_t^i),$$

$$(3)' \qquad \overline{M}^i + u_t^{mi} - I_t^i = [P_t^i + Y_t^i - I_t^i] - k_1 r_t^i + k_0,$$

where $T_t^2 = T_t = P_t^2 - (P_t^3 + X_t^2)$, $T_t^3 = -T_t$, $I_t^2 = aP_t^2 +$
$(1 - a)(P_t^3 + X_t^2)$, and $I_t^3 = aP_t^3 + (1 - a)(P_t^2 - X_t^2)$. Aggregate demand
is a function of the terms of trade, T_t, foreign output, and the real interest
rate as well as a disturbance term, u_t^{di}. Aggregate supply is a simple function
of the terms of trade. Money demand and supply in the foreign countries
are assumed to be identical in form to those of country 1.[23]

The two-country model is naturally complex, but one can analyze its behavior relatively easily by focusing on two variables, the terms of trade of
country 2 and the price of country 3's good.[24] The remaining variables can
then be expressed in terms of these two.

The terms of trade of country 2, defined as $T_t = P_t^2 - (P_t^3 + X_t^2)$, can
be expressed as a function of the two aggregate demand disturbances, u_t^{d2}
and u_t^{d3}:

$$T_t = \overline{T} + \frac{(u_t^{d3} - u_t^{d2})}{(N^1 - N^2)}$$

where $N^1 = -g_p^f - c^f(1 - a)(1 + g_y^f + g_r^f/k_1) + g_r^f(1 - a) < 0$,
$N^2 = g_p^f + c^f(1 - a)(1 + g_y^f - g_r^f/k_1) + g_r^f a > 0$.[25]

A rise in aggregate demand in country 3 lowers the terms of trade (since
$N^1 - N^2 < 0$), while a rise in aggregate demand in country 2 raises the
terms of trade. With full indexation, monetary disturbances have no effect
on the terms of trade.

The price of country 3's good is a function of the aggregate demand
disturbances as well as the monetary disturbance in country 3:

$$P_t^3 = \overline{P}^3 + \frac{k_1}{g_r^f(1 + k_1)} \frac{[N^1 u_t^{d2} - N^2 u_t^{d3}]}{(N^1 - N^2)} + \frac{u_t^{m3}}{(1 + k_1)}.$$

A rise in aggregate demand in either country increases the price of country
3's good (as well as of country 2's good), while an increase in country 3's
money supply also raises this price.

23. In particular, I assume that the interest elasticities of the money demand functions are
the same as those in country 1. The disturbance terms, u_t^{di} and u_t^{mi}, are assumed to have mean
zero and to be serially uncorrelated.

24. The price of country 2's good, alternatively, could have been singled out since the model
is symmetric with respect to the two countries. Recall, however, that in country 1's model, the
foreign prices were defined relative to country 3's price.

25. The real interest rate effect on aggregate demand is assumed to be small enough so that
N^1 and N^2 have the signs indicated.

Output in either country is a function of the terms of trade as shown in equation (2'). Note that a rise in the terms of trade increases country 2's output (because it reduces the real wage faced by its producers) but decreases country 3's output. In fact, the increase in country 2's output and decrease in country 3's output are equal in size.

The two remaining foreign variables appearing explicitly in country 1's model, r_t^3 and X_t^2, can be expressed in terms of P_t^3, T_t, and the monetary disturbance by solving the money market equilibrium conditions:

$$r_t^3 = \bar{r}^3 + \frac{1}{k_1} [(P_t^3 - \bar{P}^3) - c^f(1 - a)(T_t - \bar{T}) - u_t^{m3}],$$

$$X_t^2 = \bar{X}^2 - \frac{1}{(1 + k_1)} \{[1 + 2c^f(1 - a)](T_t - \bar{T}) + (u_t^{m3} - u_t^{m2})\}.$$

Monetary disturbances naturally affect both nominal variables, although an equal increase in both money supplies leaves the mark price of the dollar unaffected since there are no asymmetries between the two economies. An aggregate demand disturbance affects both variables by changing the terms of trade and, in the case of the interest rate, by changing country 3's price.

12.3.2 Foreign Monetary Disturbances

This section shows exchange rate unions in their most unfavorable light. That is because flexible exchange rates are so effective in insulating the domestic economy from foreign monetary disturbances, at least when foreign wages are fully indexed. Under flexible rates, monetary disturbances originating abroad have no effect on output or prices in country 1. This is true regardless of the degree of wage indexation in country 1; what matters is that the foreign countries be fully indexed.

Consider first what I term general monetary expansions, disturbances that are perfectly correlated and of the same magnitude in the two foreign countries: $u_t^{m2} = u_t^{m3} = u_t^m > 0$. These disturbances raise the price of country 3's good (and country 2's good) by $u_t^{p3} = P_t^3 - \bar{P}^3 = u_t^m/(1 + k_1)$ but have no effect on foreign output as long as the foreign countries are fully indexed. The interest rate in country 3 (or country 2) falls by $u_t^{r3} = r_t^3 - \bar{r}^3 = -u_t^m/(1 + k_1)$, the same absolute amount by which u_t^{p3} rises.

As far as country 1 is concerned, what matters under flexible rates are the franc prices of the two foreign goods and the franc return on the dollar (or mark) security, since these are the only variables that can affect country 1's aggregate demand or supply. By consolidating price terms, I can write country 1's output as a function of these variables:

$$(6) \qquad Y_t^1 - \bar{Y}^1 = \frac{[(g_{p2} + g_{p3})c(1 - b) - g_r c(a_{12} + a_{13})]}{D_1} [u_t^{p3} + u_t^{x1}]$$

$$- \frac{g_r c(1 - ba_{11})}{D_1} [u_t^{r3} - u_t^{x1}].$$

The foreign prices expressed in francs and the franc return both remain constant under flexible rates since the franc price of the dollar (and of the mark) falls by $u_t^{x1} = X_t^1 - \bar{X}^1 = -u_t^{m3}/(1 + k_1)$, thereby completely insulating country 1 from the disturbance.

Insulation also occurs with respect to any other foreign monetary disturbances under flexible rates, whether the disturbances are negatively correlated, for example, or concentrated in one of the two countries (two types of disturbances considered below). The key to this result lies in the full indexation assumption, but as noted above, it is full indexation abroad rather than in country 1 that insulates the latter.

In an exchange rate union, a monetary disturbance in country 3 still has no effect on country 1. Flexibility in the mark price of the dollar, which falls by $u_t^{x2} = -u_t^{m3}/(1 + k_1)$, simply replaces the franc price of the dollar as the insulating factor (with the franc tied to the mark).

If the monetary disturbance is in country 2, however, then in the union the fixed exchange rate with that country's currency ensures that the disturbance is transmitted to country 1. Consider first the effects of the monetary expansion on the two foreign countries. The price of country 2's good rises while its interest rate falls: $u_t^{p2} = u_t^{m2}/(1 + k_1) = -u_t^{r2}$. The mark price of the dollar rises enough so that country 3 is unaffected by the disturbance: $u_t^{x2} = u_t^{m2}/(1 + k_1)$; that is, country 3's price and interest rate as well as its output remain fixed.

In terms of the franc, country 1's currency, the prices of both foreign goods rise in the union: the franc price of country 2's good rises because its mark price rises, and the franc price of country 3's good rises because of the depreciation of the mark (and hence the franc) relative to the dollar: $u_t^{p2} = u_t^{p3} + u_t^{x1} = u_t^{m2}/(1 + k_1)$. In addition, country 1's interest rate falls. So output in country 1 rises.[26] Thus, if there is a union between countries 1 and 2, monetary disturbances originating in country 2 are transmitted to country 1.

With full indexation abroad, flexible rates have a clear advantage over the union in shielding the domestic economy from foreign monetary disturbances. Later in the paper I consider these same disturbances under the assumption of no indexation. Flexible rates will still generally be superior to the union, but country 1 will not always be insulated from the disturbances.

12.3.3 Aggregate Demand Disturbances

Demand disturbances generally do affect country 1's output under flexible exchange rates as well as in the union. How a country fares in the two

---

26. Country 1's interest rate falls because with a fixed rate between the franc and mark, r_t^1 must decline with r_t^2. Only if there is full wage indexation in country 1 does this purely nominal disturbance leave country 1's output unaffected in the union. (This can be shown by solving equation [6] for u_t^{m2} and simplifying.) The flexibility of wages and prices then makes up for the fixity of the exchange rate.

regimes depends on the specific form which the disturbances take. I will consider three types of demand disturbances because they all provide insight into the effects of the union:

1. Negatively correlated disturbances representing a shift in demand from the products of country 3 to those of country 2. The shift in demand affects country 1 primarily by changing the terms of trade and shifting output (and hence demand for country 1's products) from one foreign country to another. This type of disturbance serves to illustrate the importance of the pattern of trade between country 1 and the other countries.

2. Positively correlated disturbances which have the same magnitude in both countries, representing a general increase in foreign demand. Since the increase in demand is of the same magnitude in both foreign countries, Country 1 responds as if it were trading with one foreign country under flexible and fixed exchange rates, respectively.

3. An increase in demand which is concentrated in one country more than the other, a third case combining the first two to show the importance of where the disturbance occurs.

All of these disturbances have the effect of changing interest rates abroad. If the real interest rate effect on aggregate demand in country 1 is large enough, however, even a general expansion of demand abroad will have ambiguous effects on country 1's output since the resulting rise in foreign interest rates runs counter to other effects on the foreign demand expansion. To avoid this additional ambiguity, I assume in this section that the real interest rate effect in country 1 is zero ($g_r = 0$). Under this assumption, higher foreign interest rates can still have a significant effect on country 1's output, but indirectly by changing exchange rates.

Negatively Correlated Aggregate Demand Disturbances

Suppose that there is a shift in demand to country 2's products from those of country 3 with $u_t^{d2} = v_t^d$, $u_t^{d3} = -v_t^d$, $v_t^d > 0$. Then the terms of trade of country 2 rise by $u_t^T = T_t - \overline{T} = -2 v_t^d/(N^1 - N^2) > 0$. Output rises in country 2 and falls in country 3 proportionately to the change in the terms of trade. Interest rates rise in country 2 but fall in country 3; as a result, the mark appreciates by

$$u_t^{x2} = \frac{-[2k_2 c^f(1 - a) + 1]}{(1 + k_1)} u_t^T < 0.$$

Since the two foreign economies are identical, this shift disturbance moves each economy in equal but opposite directions.

With the two foreign countries responding symmetrically to the disturbance, the effect on country 1 clearly depends on its pattern of trade with the two countries. The expression for Y_t^1 in table 12.1 can be rewritten as a function of the terms of trade and the exchange rates in a form which shows the role of the trade pattern:

(7)
$$Y_t^1 - \overline{Y}^1 = \frac{c(1 - ba_{11})}{D_1} (g_{y2} - g_{y3})c^f(1 - a)u_t^T$$
$$+ \frac{g_{p3}c(1 - b)}{D_1} \left(\frac{-u_t^T}{2} + u_t^{x1} - \frac{u_t^{x2}}{2} \right)$$
$$+ \frac{g_{p2}c(1 - b)}{D_1} \left(\frac{u_t^T}{2} + u_t^{x1} - \frac{u_t^{x2}}{2} \right).$$

As in table 12.1, this expression holds for either exchange rate regime. Under flexible rates, the franc price of the dollar is given by

(8)
$$u_t^{x1} = \frac{u_t^{x2}}{2} - \frac{[1 + c(1 - ba_{11})]}{D} (g_{y2} - g_{y3})c^f(1 - a) u_t^T$$
$$- \frac{\{(g_{p2} - g_{p3})[1 + c(1 - b)] + (a_{12} - a_{13})cb\} u_t^T}{D} \frac{u_t^T}{2}.$$

In these equations, the aggregate demand coefficients, g_{yi} and g_{pi}, and price index weights, a_{1i}, all reflect the pattern of trade between country 1 and the two foreign countries.

Just what is meant by the pattern of trade in this model? I have chosen a definition based on the *share* of country 1's trade with each of the two foreign countries. The price index weight, a_{1i}, reflects the share of country 1's imports from country i expressed as a fraction of domestic expenditure. Similarly, as Appendix 2 shows, the aggregate demand coefficients, g_{yi} and g_{pi}, reflect the share of country 1's exports to country i (as well as the share of imports from country i since trade is assumed to be balanced initially) expressed as a fraction of domestic output. The income coefficients also depend on the income elasticities of demand for country 1's good in the two foreign countries, while the price coefficients also depend on export and import price elasticities. I assume that these elasticities are the same for both foreign countries so that differences in the aggregate demand coefficients solely reflect the share of trade.[27] Alternatively, I could interpret the results obtained below in terms of the elasticities themselves. Country 1 might be particularly sensitive to aggregate demand expansions in country 2, for example, not because its trade is biased toward country 2, but because country 2's demand for its product has a relatively high income or price elasticity. The reader might wish to keep this alternative interpretation in mind, although I will confine this discussion to trade shares alone.

I begin by considering the neutral case where country 1's trade is evenly balanced between country 2 and country 3, so that the output and price elasticities in equation (7) and (8) are equal, $g_{y2} = g_{y3}$ and $g_{p2} = g_{p3}$, as well as the weights in the general price index, $a_{12} = a_{13}$. In this case, the shift in demand has no effect on country 1's output under flexible rates. The

---

27. I assume, for example, that $h_2 = h_3$, so that g_{y2}/g_{y3} is proportional to $(EX^2/Q^1)/(EX^3/Q^1)$, where EX^i denotes the exports of country 1 to country i and Q^1 the output of country 1. (See Appendix 2.)

foreign output term in equation (7) is equal to zero. That is, the change in the terms of trade raises country 2's output and lowers country 3's output by the same amount, so the shift in demand has no direct output effect on country 1's aggregate demand. In addition, the franc appreciates by exactly one-half as much as the mark relative to the dollar: $u_t^{x1} = u_t^{x2}/2$. So the franc prices of goods from the two countries move in equal and opposite directions as follows:

$$\text{country 3's good: } u_t^{p3} + u_t^{x1} = -u_t^T/2,$$

$$\text{country 2's good: } u_t^{p3} + u_t^{x1} + u_t^T = u_t^T/2.$$

This change in relative prices also has opposing effects on aggregate demand. So country 1's output is insulated from the disturbance. The insulation occurs because country 1 can take advantage of its diversified trade pattern, with one foreign country's contraction offset by another country's expansion.[28] The advantage is not confined to demand disturbances, as we shall see below; it is the negative correlation between the foreign disturbances which is important.

Under flexible rates, as noted above, the franc appreciates relative to the dollar; with balanced trade, the franc appreciates one-half as much as the mark. (Recall that the shift in demand toward country 2's products raises country 2's interest rate and lowers country 3's interest rate by the same absolute amount.) In the union, the franc is tied to the mark, so it appreciates more than under flexible rates (i.e., twice as much). The franc prices of both foreign goods fall, so output in country 1 must fall in the union.[29]

For similar reasons, country 1 fares better under flexible rates when trade is biased toward country 3 ($g_{y3} > g_{y2}$, $g_{p3} > g_{p2}$). In that case, the direct effect of the shift in foreign output is to reduce country 1's aggregate demand since the output of its closest trading partner, country 3, drops. Since the appreciation of the franc in the union is greater than under flexible rates, country 1's output falls even further in the union than under flexible rates.[30] The greater appreciation associated with the union adds to the deflationary effects of the shift in demand.

If country 1's trade is biased toward country 2 ($g_{y2} > g_{y3}$, $g_{p2} > g_{p3}$), which may be the more likely case for a country joining a union, then the

---

28. If country 1 produced a variety of goods, the negative correlation between disturbances would not necessarily prevent individual industries in country 1 from expanding or contracting if they were more sensitive to one foreign country's behavior than another's.

29. In the union, the franc price of country 3's good must fall because of the appreciation of the franc. The franc price of country 2's good also falls as long as

$$\frac{u_t^T}{2} + u_t^{x1} - \frac{u_t^{x2}}{2} = -\frac{[2c^f(1-a) - k_1]}{2(1+k_1)} u_t^T$$

is negative, which it will be assuming that $c^f(1-a) > k_1/2$.

30. Note that it can be shown that country 1's output falls under flexible rates even though $u_t^{x1} - u_t^{x2}/2 > 0$ in equation (7).

direct output effect is positive. That is, the shift in output toward country 2 tends to raise country 1's output. Now a greater appreciation of the franc in the union than under flexible rates may help to stabilize country 1's output.[31] So the union may be superior to flexible rates when trade is biased toward country 2. If the price elasticities (g_{pj}'s) are large enough so that the price effects in equation (7) dominate the output effect, however, then once again the greater appreciation of the franc in the union becomes a drawback. Country 1's output then varies more in the union than under flexible rates.[32]

Positively Correlated Disturbances (General Increase in Demand)

There is no longer the same presumption in favor of flexible rates when the demand disturbance is a general one, $u_t^{d2} = u_t^{d3} = u_t^d$. Flexible rates are superior to the union only when price elasticities are high.

If demand increases (or decreases) by the same amount in both countries, there is no change in the terms of trade nor in the mark price of the dollar. Since foreign output is a function of the real wage, which is constant as long as the terms of trade remain fixed, output in both countries is constant.[33] So this demand disturbance has effects only on nominal quantities. Prices in both foreign countries rise:

$$u_t^{p3} = k_1 \frac{u_t^d}{[g_r^f(1 + k_1)]} = u_t^{p2} > 0.$$

Similarly, both rates of interest rise (proportionally to the prices): $u_t^{r3} = u_t^{p3}/k_1 = u_t^{r2}$. The change in output in country 1 can be written

$$(9) \qquad Y_t^1 - \bar{Y}^1 = \frac{(g_{p2} + g_{p3})c(1 - b)}{D_1} (u_t^{p3} + u_t^{x1}),$$

where as before u_t^{x1} depends on the exchange rate regime.

In the exchange rate union, there is no change in the franc price of the dollar since the mark price of the dollar is fixed. But the rise in foreign prices increase output in country 1 with the increase proportional to the price elasticities, $g_{p2} + g_{p3}$.

Under flexible rates as well, country 1's output is increased because $u_t^{p3} + u_t^{x1} > 0$. Whether output is increased more or less under flexible rates, however, depends on whether the franc appreciates or depreciates. The franc price of the dollar can be written

---

31. Since the franc prices of both foreign goods fall in the union, the price effects run counter to the output effect. One may neutralize the other, thus helping to stabilize country 1's output.

32. In equation (7), the price terms increase in (absolute) value relative to the foreign output term as the price elasticities (g_{p2}, g_{p3}) increase.

33. If indexation were less than complete in the foreign countries, this type of demand disturbance would lead to increases in output as well as prices, with the relative importance of changes in output increasing as the degree of indexation fell.

$$(10) \qquad u_t^{x1} = X_t^1 - \overline{X}^1 = -\frac{(g_{p2} + g_{p3} - 1)c(1 - b)}{D} u_t^{p3}.$$

To interpret this equation, note that there are two influences on the exchange rate: higher foreign interest rates lead to a *depreciation* of the franc, while a higher domestic interest rate due to the increase in domestic transactions leads to an *appreciation*. How much the domestic interest rate increases depends on the price elasticities, g_{p2} and g_{p3}, since higher price elasticities imply greater increases in domestic output. The franc appreciates if the sum of these price elasticities exceeds unity and depreciates if the sum is less than unity:[34] $u_t^{x1} \lesseqgtr 0$ as $(g_{p2} + g_{p3}) \gtreqless 1$. If the franc appreciates, then domestic output increases less under flexible rates than in the union. A depreciation, on the other hand, causes domestic output to increase more under flexible rates. Thus in the presence of this general demand disturbance, the union increases or decreases the variation in output depending on whether $(g_{p2} + g_{p3})$ is greater or less than one.[35]

Positively Correlated Disturbances (Increase in Demand Concentrated More in One Country)

The final aggregate demand disturbance to be considered represents a modification of the general demand disturbance to allow for differences in the intensity of the disturbance between the two foreign countries. Many demand expansions or contractions are highly correlated across countries but may be concentrated more in one country than in another. Such demand disturbances can either strengthen or weaken the case for an exchange rate union depending on which country experiences the greater change in demand.

---

34. In the union (when u_t^{x1} is constant), the foreign interest rate rises by $u_t^{r3} = u_t^{p3}/k_1$, whereas the domestic interest rate rises by

$$u_t^{r1} = \frac{u_t^{p1} + u_t^{y1}}{k_1} = [1 + c(1 - b)(g_{p2} + g_{p3} - 1)/D_1]\frac{u_t^{p3}}{k_1}.$$

If $(g_{p2} + g_{p3}) > 1$, then the domestic interest rate rises more than the foreign interest rate; thus under flexible rates, the franc appreciates relative to the dollar and mark. But if $(g_{p2} + g_{p3}) < 1$, the franc depreciates.

35. An analogous condition would apply to a small country choosing between fixed and flexible exchange rates (i.e., where only one foreign country is involved). The above condition resembles the Marshall-Lerner condition, which requires that the sum of the elasticities of export and import demand exceed one. These elasticities, however, are those of the aggregate demand function as a whole; in fact, as Appendix 2 shows, the Marshall-Lerner condition is required in order for these elasticities to be positive. When indexation is less than complete in the two foreign countries, the effect of foreign demand disturbances depends not only on these price elasticities but also on the relative degree of indexation in the domestic and foreign countries. Marston (1982) discusses the effect of different degrees of foreign indexation on the choice between fixed and flexible exchange rates.

The analysis of this more general case, however, can draw on the first two cases, since this disturbance can be regarded as a combination of the first two. Suppose that both countries experience a demand expansion but that the expansion is greater in country 2 (or 3). Then the two disturbances take the form

$$u_t^{d2} = u_t^d \underset{(-)}{+} v_t^d,$$

$$u_t^{d3} = u_t^d \underset{(+)}{-} v_t^d,$$

where each disturbance includes a common element (u_t^d) modified by the shift term (v_t^d).[36]

The general increase in demand (represented by the u_t^d factor) raises output in country 1 under both exchange rate regimes. Under which regime output expands more depends again on the price elasticities. Suppose that $(g_{p2} + g_{p3}) = 1$, so that the general increase in demand has the same effect on output in the union as under flexible rates. Then the choice between regimes depends on which country is more subject to the demand disturbance.

Consider the case where trade is balanced between country 1 and the two foreign countries (the neutral case considered in section 12.1), but where the increase in demand is more concentrated in country 2. Then, strangely enough, country 1 is better off in the exchange rate union—tying itself to the country with greater demand disturbances. That is because changes in relative prices counter the effects of the general expansion.[37] With the disturbance more concentrated in country 2, the terms of trade of that country rise and the mark appreciates. Under flexible rates, the franc also appreciates relative to the dollar, but by less than the mark does. By joining the union, country 1 ties the franc to the mark and finds its output increasing less because of the dampening effect of the mark's appreciation.

When the increase in demand is more concentrated in country 3, in contrast, country 1 is worse off in the union. Now the mark depreciates, and the depreciation of the mark exceeds that of the franc. So joining the union further increases the effect of the disturbance on country 1's output.

Thus the net impact of this disturbance depends not only on price elasticities but also on the location of the disturbance, with output variation being smaller in the union when the disturbance is concentrated in the union country. This disturbance serves well to illustrate the pitfalls in easy generalizations about how the sources of economic disturbances affect the case for a union.

36. I assume that v_t^d is proportional to u_t^d, $v_t^d = \bar{s} \, u_t^d$, where $\bar{s}$ is a fraction less than one so that $(1 - \bar{s}) \, u_t^d > 0$.

37. The demand shift, however, is assumed not to be large enough to lower country 1's output in either regime.

Summary of Results for Demand Disturbances

The form which a foreign demand disturbance takes clearly determines how desirable an exchange rate union would be. Only in the case of a demand shift between countries is there a definite presumption in favor of one regime or the other, but that presumption is in favor of flexible rates. In the second case, that of a general increase in demand, the union is superior only if price elasticities are low. In the third case, where the disturbance is concentrated more in one country than in the other, the result also depends on where the disturbance is primarily located. The final set of disturbances to be considered provides further evidence on the relative advantages of the two regimes, while clarifying the role of foreign wage indexation and trade patterns.

12.3.4 Foreign Monetary Disturbances with No Indexation Abroad

I now briefly investigate the effects of monetary disturbances when there is no wage indexation abroad. I will show that the insulation properties of the flexible regime are very sensitive to the indexation assumption. Flexible rates do not generally provide full insulation from foreign monetary disturbances if the foreign countries are less than fully indexed. But the case for flexible exchange rates still remains quite strong. I will also investigate again the importance of trade patterns. When the foreign countries are less than fully indexed, the trade pattern helps to determine the effects of monetary disturbances, but the influence of trade bias is opposite to that commonly assumed.

I begin by modifying the model of the foreign economies for the case of no wage indexation. With no indexation, the supply equations for countries 2 and 3 are changed to

$$(2'') \qquad Y_t^i = c_0^f + c^f(P_t^i - {}_{t-1}EP_t^i).$$

Since with no indexation wages are fixed throughout the contract period, output in each country is responsive to the price of that output alone. After solving the two-country model, I can express the terms of trade of country 2 and the price of country 3's output in terms of the monetary disturbances.[38]

$$u_t^T = T_t - \overline{T} = -\frac{c^f(1 + g_y^f)(u_t^{m2} - u_t^{m3})}{N^3}$$

$$u_t^{p3} = P_t^3 - \overline{P}^3 = \frac{g_r^f u_t^{m3}}{N^4} + \frac{k_1 c^f N^5}{N^3 N^4}(u_t^{m2} - u_t^{m3}),$$

---

38. For simplicity I have omitted aggregate demand disturbances from these expressions, since I shall consider only monetary disturbances in the analysis below.

where

$$N^3 = (1 + g^f_y)c^f k_1 + \{2g^f_p + g^f_r[a - (1 - a)]\}(1 + k_1 + c^f) > 0,^{39}$$

$$N^4 = k_1 c^f (1 - g^f_y) + g^f_r(1 + k_1 + c^f) > 0$$

$$N^5 = -(g^f_p + g^f_r a)(1 - g^f_y) + g^f_r \gtrless 0.$$

According to these equations, a generalized monetary expansion, where money supplies increase by an equal amount in the two foreign countries, has no effect on the terms of trade but raises country 3's price. A monetary expansion in country 3 alone raises its own price but improves the terms of trade of country 2 by causing an appreciation of the mark relative to the dollar. A monetary expansion in country 2 has an indeterminate effect on country 3's price but lowers country 2's terms of trade.

As in the earlier section, I can express country 3's interest rate and the mark price of the dollar in terms of P^3_t, T_t, and the disturbances:

$$u^{r3}_t = r^3_t - \bar{r}^3 = \frac{(1 + c^f)(P^3_t - \bar{P}^3) - u^{m3}_t}{k_1}$$

$$u^{x2}_t = X^2_t - \bar{X}^2 = \frac{-(1 + c^f)(T_t - \bar{T}) + (u^{m2}_t - u^{m3}_t)}{1 + k_1 + c^f}.$$

Monetary disturbances generally affect both variables, although as before an equal change in both money supplies has no effect on the exchange rate.

Having modified the foreign model to eliminate wage indexation, I will reexamine the relative advantages of the exchange rate union for both positively and negatively correlated monetary disturbances.

Positively Correlated Monetary Disturbances (General Increase in Demand)

If the disturbance is a general one occurring simultaneously in both countries, $u^{m3}_t = u^{m2}_t = u^m_t$, then flexible rates will not generally insulate country 1 from the disturbance when there is no wage indexation abroad. Under flexible rates, in fact, country 1's economy is pushed in two contrary directions by the disturbance. The foreign monetary disturbance raises output in both foreign countries, and so there is an increase in demand for country 1's product via this channel. But at the same time an appreciation of the franc lowers the franc prices of the two foreign goods. The lower foreign prices by themselves cause a reduction in demand for country 1's good. Because

---

39. I assume that N^3 and N^4 are positive. N^3 must be positive if in each country there is no bias in consumption toward the foreign good ($a \geq \frac{1}{2}$). N^4 must be positive if the cross-income elasticity, g^f_y, is less than or equal to one.

the foreign output and price effects oppose one another, country 1's output can increase or decrease under flexible rates.

By using the expression for foreign outputs and interest rates introduced above, output in country 1 can be written as a function of country 3's price and the franc price of the dollar:[40]

$$
(11) \qquad Y_t^1 - \overline{Y}^1 = \frac{c(1 - ba_{11})}{D_1} (g_{y2} + g_{y3})c^f u_t^{p3}
$$
$$
+ \frac{(g_{p2} + g_{p3})c(1 - b)}{D_1} (u_t^{p3} + u_t^{x1}).
$$

Because country 3's price rises (as does country 2's price), foreign output rises proportionally as reflected in the first term above. But under flexible rates, X_t^1 appreciates enough to lower the franc prices of both foreign goods:

$$
(12) \qquad u_t^{x1} = X_t^1 - \overline{X}^1 = -u_t^{p3}
$$
$$
- \frac{[(1 + c(1 - ba_{11}))(g_{y2} + g_{y3})g_r^f + k_1 D_1 (1 - g_y^f)]c^f u_t^{m3}}{(D)N^4}.
$$

So the second term in (11) above, representing the effect of changes in the franc prices of the foreign goods, is negative. Country 1's output rises or falls depending primarily on the sensitivity of aggregate demand to foreign output, on the one hand, and to prices, on the other.

In the exchange rate union, this same monetary disturbance unambiguously raises country 1's output. With the franc exchange rate tied to the mark and the mark-dollar rate constant, the franc prices of both foreign goods rise along with P_t^3 and P_t^2. As a result of higher foreign output and prices, the demand for country 1's good increases, as does its output.

With price effects countering foreign output effects only under flexible rates, the advantage of exchange rate flexibility is evident in the case of this disturbance. Although full insulation only occurs in a razor's edge case where foreign output and price effects exactly offset one another, country 1's output generally changes less under flexible rates than in the union. Only at extreme parameter values does the appreciation of the franc become too much of a good thing, increasing the variance of output beyond that found in the union.[41]

---

40. In this expression and others later in the section, the real interest rate effect on country 1's aggregate demand is assumed to be equal to zero ($g_r = 0$). None of the results would be changed if this assumption were relaxed.

41. What is required is for country 1's aggregate demand to be highly sensitive to relative prices, but even with high price sensitivity flexible rates are superior as long as the change in the foreign interest rate, and hence the change in the franc exchange rate, is not unusually large. For further discussion of this question (in the context of fixed vs. flexible rates), see Marston (1982).

Negatively Correlated Monetary Disturbances

As in the case of an aggregate demand disturbance, flexible exchange rates are advantageous if monetary disturbances are negatively correlated, at least when trade is balanced. Country 1 can then benefit from the opposite movements in output and prices in the two foreign countries. The argument follows the same lines as that in the earlier discussion. If the disturbance takes the form of an increase in country 2's money supply and decrease in country 3's money supply, output rises in the former and falls in the latter. The terms of trade of country 2 fall while the mark price of the dollar rises, with prices in the two foreign countries moving in opposite directions.[42]

The effect on country 1's output can be most easily understood by writing equation (I) in table 12.1 in terms of the prices and exchange rates as follows:

$$
(13) \qquad Y_t^1 - \overline{Y}^1 = \frac{c(1 - ba_{11})}{D_1} (g_{y2} - g_{y3}) c^f(-u_t^{p3})
$$
$$
+ \frac{g_{p2}\, c(1 - b)}{D_1} (u_t^T/2 + u_t^{x1} - u_t^{x2}/2)
$$
$$
+ \frac{g_{p3}\, C(1 - b)}{D_1} (-u_t^T/2 + u_t^{x1} - u_t^{x2}/2).
$$

The first term in (13) represents the effects of changes in foreign output (which are proportional to u_t^{p3}), while the last two terms reflect the effects of changes in the franc prices of the two foreign goods:

country 2's good: $u_t^{p3} + u_t^{x1} + u_t^T = u_t^T/2 + u_t^{x1} - u_t^{x2}/2,$

country 3's good: $u_t^{p3} + u_t^{x1} = -u_t^T/2 + u_t^{x1} - u_t^{x2}/2.$

If country 1's trade is balanced between the two foreign countries, the change in foreign outputs has no net effect on country 1's output (since $g_{y2} = g_{y3}$ in the first term above). As far as price effects are concerned, the franc price of the dollar depreciates by exactly one-half of the depreciation of the mark relative to the dollar: $u_t^{x1} = u_t^{x2}/2$. As a result, the franc prices of the two foreign goods move by the same absolute amount but in opposite directions, so there is no net effect through changes in relative prices. Country 1's output is completely insulated from the disturbance. In the union, in

---

42. Prices and outputs in the two foreign countries will be negatively correlated for many other types of monetary disturbances as well. A monetary expansion in one of the foreign countries, for example, leads to a fall in price and output in the other country (for the case of high price elasticities, at least) because of the appreciation of the latter country's exchange rate. The effects of this disturbance on country 1 are more complicated to analyze than the effects of a negatively correlated disturbance because movements in foreign output are generally not symmetric.

contrast, the franc depreciates as much as the mark, so country 1's output rises.[43]

Biases in trade patterns produce surprising results, however. It is trade biased toward country 3 rather than country 2 that provides a case for the union. The reason lies in the relative movement of the franc in the two regimes. If trade is biased toward country 2, the direct effect of the shift in foreign output is to raise demand for country 1's good. By tying the franc to the mark in a union, the demand for country 1's good is affected by a larger depreciation than in the flexible regime, thus raising country 1's output even further. As in the case of balanced trade, therefore, country 1's output varies more in the union than under flexible rates.

If trade is biased toward country 3, however, the shift in foreign output lowers demand for country 1's good, so a larger depreciation may help to stabilize output. The effect of the disturbance on country 1's output may be smaller in the union than in the flexible regime, depending on the relative magnitudes of the output and price effects. In the union, in fact, domestic output can actually remain constant in the face of this disturbance with the effect of the shift in foreign output being neutralized by the depreciation of the franc relative to the dollar.[44] Thus trade biased toward the rest of the world rather than the union country provides the best case for the union.

12.4 Conclusion

This paper has shown how an exchange rate union would affect a country subject to monetary and aggregate demand disturbances originating at home or abroad. How much difference a union makes depends first of all on domestic wage behavior. Any disturbance has an identical effect on output in the home country under flexible rates or in an exchange rate union if wages are fully indexed to the general price level. Short of full indexation, the case for a union is stronger if monetary disturbances originate at home rather than abroad and weaker if domestic demand disturbances are important. But the advantage of one regime over another diminishes the closer is the country to full indexation.

As far as foreign disturbances are concerned, the form which those disturbances take is crucial. When the disturbances are perfectly correlated general disturbances, the choice between a union and flexible rates is based on

43. In the union, the franc prices of both foreign goods rise. In the case of country 2's good, the franc price rises despite the fall in the terms of trade since $u_t^T/2 + u_t^{x1} - u_t^{x2}/2 = (u_t^T + u_t^{x2})/2 > 0$.

44. In the union the franc prices of both foreign goods always rise, thus tending to raise country 1's output. Only when trade is biased toward country 3 does the foreign output effect run counter to this price effect (since then $(g_{y2} - g_{y3}) < 0$). For some parameter values, $Y_t^1 - \overline{Y}^1 = 0$ in equation (13), so that country 1's output is completely insulated from the disturbance.

the same criteria as the choice between fixed and flexible rates. Other forms of disturbances, however, introduce some of the complexities involved in trading with two or more regions. Among the most important is the correlation pattern itself. The domestic country generally benefits from having foreign disturbances less than perfectly correlated. Indeed, a country may be completely insulated from negatively correlated disturbances under flexible rates, depending on the pattern of trade, even though it might not be insulated from monetary or aggregate demand disturbances when they are perfectly correlated between countries. The key to the insulation lies in the movement of the exchange rate; if the exchange rate is fixed to one of the two foreign currencies, the advantage of the negative correlation is lost. Second, for most disturbances, the pattern of trade is important because it determines how the outputs and prices of different foreign countries affect the domestic economy. But patterns of trade biased toward the rest of the world rather than the union partner strengthen the case for a union, at least in the presence of foreign monetary disturbances. Third, the sources of disturbances are important, although as the last demand disturbance illustrated, sometimes it is best for the disturbances to originate in the union partner rather than the rest of the world.

The effects of an exchange rate union are no doubt complex, and factors which we might think would strengthen the case for a union may sometimes weaken it. As a result, it is difficult to build a case in favor of joining a union. On the other hand, the analysis above provides no overwhelming case for flexible rates either. To choose between the two regimes, empirical evidence is indispensable—evidence on structural behavior, the sources and types of economic disturbances, and other factors emphasized in this paper.

Appendix 1: List of Variables

All variables are in logarithms except interest rates. The innovations in some variables are included in parentheses.

$Y_t^i(u_t^{yi})$ = output in country i,

$P_t^i(u_t^{pi})$ = price of country i's output,

$T_t(u_t^T)$ = terms of trade of country 2, $P_t^2 - (P_t^3 + X_t^2)$,

$X_t^i(u_t^{xi})$ = exchange rate (see figure 12.1),

$r_t^i(u_t^{ri})$ = interest rate of country i,

I_t^i = general price level in country i,

$_tEJ_{t+1}$ = expected value of a variable at $t + 1$, J_{t+1}, based on information available at t,

L_t^i = units of labor of country i,

W_t^i = nominal wage of country i,

$W_t^{i\prime}$ = nominal contract wage of country i,

M_t^i = money supply of country i,

u_t^{mi}, u_t^{di} = monetary, aggregate demand disturbances of country i,

u_t^m, u_t^d = perfectly correlated foreign monetary, aggregate demand disturbances,

v_t^m, v_t^d = negatively correlated foreign monetary, aggregate demand disturbances.

Appendix 2: The Aggregate Demand Function

The foreign output and price coefficients in the aggregate demand equation play a major role in the analysis of foreign disturbances. This Appendix derives the aggregate demand equation from a more traditional equation (in level form) and interprets the output and price coefficients in terms of this more traditional model.

I begin with an expression relating output to expenditure, exports, and imports:

$$(A1) \qquad Q^1 = C^1(Q)^1 + EX^2(Q^2, R) + EX^3(Q^3, R) \\ - R\ IM^2(Q^1, R) - R\ IM^3(Q^1, R).$$

All variables are expressed in level form with the time subscripts omitted. Q^i and C^i are domestic output and expenditure in country i, respectively, while EX^i is the demand for exports of country 1 by country i and IM^i is the demand for imports from country i by country 1. To simplify the analysis, I assume that there are no changes in the terms of trade between the two foreign countries and that the dollar prices of the two foreign goods are initially equal. Thus R can represent the terms of trade between either foreign country and country 1. I also assume that trade is initially balanced with each foreign country so that $EX^i = R IM^i$, and that R is initially equal to one.

Define the following elasticities, where the partial derivative with respect to the first (second) argument of a function has the subscript 1 (2):

h_i = income elasticity of foreign demand for country 1's good,

   = $EX_1^i(Q^i/EX^i)$,

n_{fi} = price elasticity of foreign demand for country 1's good,

   = $EX_2^i(R/EX^i)$,

n^i = price elasticity of domestic demand for country i's good,

   = $-IM_2^i(R/IM^i)$.

Also, define d equal to the sum of the marginal propensities to save and to import by country $1 = (1 - C_1^1) + IM_1^2 + IM_1^3 > 0$. Then equation (A1) can be written in terms of percentage changes as follows:

(A1′)
$$\frac{dQ^1}{Q^1} = \frac{1}{d}\left[h_2 \frac{EX^2}{Q^1}\left(\frac{dQ^2}{Q^2}\right) + h_3 \frac{EX^3}{Q^1}\left(\frac{dQ^3}{Q^3}\right) \right.$$
$$+ (n_{f2} + n_2 - 1)\frac{EX^2}{Q^1}\left(\frac{dR}{R}\right)$$
$$\left. + (n_{f3} + n_3 - 1)\frac{EX^3}{Q^1}\left(\frac{dR}{R}\right) \right].$$

Thus the coefficients of the aggregate demand equation in the text, which is expressed in logarithms, can be written

$$g_{yi} = h_i \left(\frac{EX^i}{Q^1}\right)/d,$$

$$g_{pi} = (n_{fi} + n_i - 1)\left(\frac{EX^i}{Q^1}\right)/d.^{45}$$

The relative sizes of the g_{yi} coefficients depend on the income elasticities in the two foreign countries (h_i) as well as the share of exports to country i as a fraction of total domestic output. The relative sizes of the g_{pi} coefficients depend on the underlying price elasticities as well as the share of exports. The Marshall-Lerner condition for the trade balance between country 1 and country i is $n_{fi} + n_i - 1 > 1$, a condition which is necessary for g_{pi} to be positive.

Comment   Peter B. Kenen

The fundamental problem with which Marston is concerned, the choice of exchange rate regime for a small economy, is one that has been studied frequently. In too many cases, however, the models used to analyze it have been excessively simple. In some models, for example, purchasing power parity deprives the real exchange rate of any role in the adjustment process; in consequence, a flexible exchange rate cannot insulate domestic output from shifts of foreign demand and other real shocks coming from abroad. In many models, the outside world is represented by a single foreign country, and the choice between a fixed and a flexible exchange rate is necessarily posed in all-or-nothing terms; a fixed exchange rate internalizes all external disturbances. Finally, most papers on this subject examine the effects

---

45. In cases where the terms of trade change between countries 2 and 3, there are additional cross effects of changes in the prices of goods in the third country which further complicate the expression for g_{pi}.

of one or two disturbances; one wonders whether the conclusions would stand up to the inclusion of additional disturbances.

Marston's paper is much better than most others in all three of these dimensions. His treatment of goods markets is more general, because it allows the real exchange rate to change. His framework is more realistic, because the country under study trades with two other countries, and an exchange rate union with one of those countries does not internalize all foreign disturbances. His treatment of disturbances is more comprehensive, because there are so many of them. If Marston's results are a bit bewildering, even after he has introduced a number of simplifications, he should be congratulated rather than criticized. The real world is bewildering too.

This is an important paper, and the critical comments made below do not diminish it in any major way. They should be regarded as proposals for more work rather than objections to the work that Marston has reported. My comments fall into three groups. I begin with two comments on the structure of the model. I turn next to the way that Marston has made his comparisons. I conclude with comments on the objective function he uses to assess fixed and flexible exchange rates.

I find it a bit difficult to understand Marston's labor market. If I interpret his equations correctly, his contract wage is set so that the corresponding real wage will clear the labor market. (The contract wage divided by the expected price of the domestic product is equal to the marginal product of labor at full employment output.) Furthermore, the supply of labor is inelastic. It does not depend on either of the two real wages—the one defined by the price of the domestic product or the one defined by the price index. Nevertheless, there is wage indexation, and it takes a strange form. The contract wage is raised or lowered by some fraction of the *error* made in forecasting the price index. If the price index and the forecast of that index do not affect the contract wage, why should the error made in forecasting the index be allowed to influence the actual wage? There may be nothing fundamentally wrong with this specification. But it puzzles me.

Marston's goods markets give the real exchange rate an important role. Home and foreign goods are not perfect substitutes. His assets markets are very much more primitive. Home and foreign bonds *are* perfect substitutes. This assumption makes Marston's model much more manageable but renders his analysis somewhat less interesting. On the one hand, it deprives monetary policy of any influence on aggregate demand, apart from the influence it exercises by way of its effect on the nominal exchange rate and therefore the real rate. On the other hand, it may be responsible for one of Marston's strong results—that a flexible exchange rate can afford full and instantaneous insulation from certain external disturbances.

To illustrate my problem with the way Marston uses his model to study the effects of fixed and flexible exchange rates, I will concentrate on his treatment of domestic disturbances, summarized by his equations (4) and

(5). The effects of these disturbances are clearcut, compared to others, and least dependent on the trade pattern.

When indexation is incomplete, a random increase in domestic demand raises real output, and the increase is larger when the exchange rate is fixed than when it is flexible (because the domestic currency cannot appreciate to dampen the impact of the disturbance). Score 5 points, then, against an exchange rate union. But a random increase in the money supply has no effect on real output when the exchange rate is fixed and increases real output when the rate is flexible. Score 5 points in favor of an exchange rate union.

Is this the right way to keep score? If changes in the money stock are completely random, as in Marston's paper, it may be satisfactory. But there is another way of coming at the problem. Let us give the central bank extraordinary insight. Let it be able to identify immediately the random fluctuations in domestic demand and introduce offsetting fluctuations in the money supply to neutralize their influence on real output. It can do so in principle with a flexible exchange rate. It has merely to set the left-hand side of equation (4) at zero, solve for the exchange rate change that offsets the random change in domestic demand, and insert that change into equation (5) to calculate the change in the money supply that will produce the requisite change in the exchange rate. In other words, it can conduct a managed float to stabilize domestic output. We have therefore to score 10 points against a union. The first 5 are those it lost because fluctuations in domestic demand lead to larger output changes when no one does anything about them. The next 5 are lost because the union emasculates monetary policy.

With full indexation, my objection disappears. The exchange rate term drops out of equation (4), because indexation pegs the real rate, and there is no link between the money stock and real output. In Marston's terms, the central bank is rendered harmless. In my terms, it is rendered helpless. It cannot conduct a managed float to stabilize domestic output.

This illustration raises two broad questions. First, when we compare exchange rate regimes, how should we weigh their impact on economic policies? Do we want to minimize the damage that policies can do when conducted badly or maximize the contribution they can make when conducted well? Second, how should we approach institutional arrangements such as indexation? Should they be regarded as immutable features of the economy, or should we stress the need to change them? (When Marston gave his paper at Bellagio, in January 1982, he and I would probably have said that indexation is pernicious but immutable, and we would therefore have said that exchange rate arrangements must be built around it. This version of my comment was drafted in July 1982, and events in the interim have led me to change my mind. Indexation has been attacked successfully in one of its strongholds, Belgium, and is under attack in another, Italy.)

I have one other problem with the way that Marston treats wage indexation. In most of his paper, he assumes that indexation is complete in the two foreign countries. Having tried to work my way through certain disturbances without making this assumption, I know why he adopts it. Does it make sense, however, to assume that indexation is complete in the foreign countries but incomplete in the small country? This asymmetry is not crucial for some of Marston's main results. It is crucial for others. (I was at first tempted to ridicule this asymmetry by asking a rhetorical question. Would Germany, where wage rates are not indexed, want to join a union with countries whose wage rates *are* completely indexed? But Germany belongs to a union in which indexation is widespread! Marston may have taken the right tack after all.)

My final comment has to do with the objective function implicit in Marston's comparison between fixed and flexible exchange rates. They are compared exclusively in terms of their effects on the volatility of real output. At several important points in his paper, however, Marston notes that they have different effects on prices—on the domestic product price and on the price index. A comprehensive comparison between them, then, should examine their effects on prices as well as their effects on real output. There is, of course, a problem here. When two arguments appear in the objective function, we have to give them weights, and those weights will affect the comparison between exchange rate regimes. But when we look at one argument without looking at the other, we are likewise using weights and failing to confront the choice that we have made.

Marston has constructed an interesting model and used it to produce important results. What more can he do with it?

If I were writing one more paper based on this model, I would adopt two of the suggestions in this comment. First, I would take the "optimistic" view of monetary policy, asking what it can do to stabilize output under alternative exchange rate arrangements rather than asking how those arrangements can minimize its nuisance value. Returning to my earlier illustration, I would use equations (4) and (5) to endogenize monetary policy. Second, I would try to remove the worrisome asymmetry between degrees of indexation, even if this made the analysis more difficult.

If I were amending the model itself, I would introduce imperfect substitutability between home and foreign bonds. Monetary policy would be effective under a fixed exchange rate, if only in the short run, and a flexible exchange rate would not confer full insulation, except in the long run.

I have one more suggestion. It would be interesting to introduce a nontraded good, to assign to monetary policy the task of stabilizing total employment in the face of random shocks, and to look at the effects of fixed and flexible exchange rates on employment in each sector (i.e., on the allocation of the labor force). Critics of current exchange rate arrangements seem to be worrying about this sort of problem. Individual industries and regions, they say, are affected seriously by the short-term changes in real exchange rates brought about by macroeconomic policies and shocks. These sectoral effects may bear some blame for the recrudescence of protectionist pressures and for dissatisfaction with exchange rate flexibility.

References

Allen, Polly Reynolds. 1976. *Organization and administration of a monetary union*. Studies in International Finance, no. 38. Princeton: Princeton University Press.

Allen, Polly Reynolds, and Kenen, Peter B. 1980. *Asset markets, exchange rates and economic integration*. Cambridge: Cambridge University Press.

Canzoneri, Matthew B. 1981. *Exchange intervention policy in a multiple country world*. International Finance Discussion Paper no. 174. Washington: Board of Governors of the Federal Reserve System.

Cooper, Richard N. 1976. Monetary theory and policy in an open economy. *Scandinavian Journal of Economics* 78:146–63.

Corden, W. M. 1972. *Monetary integration*. Essays in International Finance, no. 93. Princeton: International Finance Section.

Fischer, Stanley. 1977. Wage indexation and macroeconomic stability. In *Stabilization of the domestic and international economy,* ed. K. Brunner and A. Meltzer. Carnegie-Rochester Conference Series on Public Policy, vol. 5. Amsterdam: North-Holland.

Flood, Robert P., and Marion, Nancy P. 1982. The transmission of disturbances under alternative exchange-rate regimes with optimal indexing. *Quarterly Journal of Economics* 96:43–66.

Gray, Jo Anna. 1976. Wage indexation: A macroeconomic approach. *Journal of Monetary Economics* 2:221–35.

Ingram, James C. 1973. *The case for European monetary integration*. Essays in International Finance, no. 98. Princeton: International Finance Section.

McKinnon, Ronald I. 1963. Optimum currency areas. *American Economic Review* 53:717–25.

Marston, Richard C. 1980. Cross country effects of sterilization, reserve currencies, and foreign exchange intervention. *Journal of International Economics* 10:63–78.

———. 1982. Wages, relative prices and choice between fixed and flexible exchange rates. *Canadian Journal of Economics,* 15:87–103.

———. 1983. Stabilization policies in open economies. In *Handbook of international economics,* ed. Ronald W. Jones and Peter B. Kenen. Amsterdam: North-Holland.

————. 1984. Financial disturbances and the effects of an exchange-rate union. In *Exchange Rate Management under Uncertainty,* ed. Jagdeep Bhandari. Cambridge: MIT Press.

Modigliani, Franco, and Padoa-Schioppa, Tommaso. 1978. *The management of an open economy with "100% plus" wage indexation.* Essays in International Finance, no. 130. Princeton: International Finance Section.

Mundell, Robert A. 1961. A theory of optimum currency areas. *American Economic Review* 51:657–65.

————. 1963. Capital mobility and stabilization policy under fixed and flexible exchange rates. *Canadian Journal of Economics and Political Science* 29:475–85.

Sachs, Jeffrey. 1980. Wages, flexible exchange rates and macro-economic policy. *Quarterly Journal of Economics* 94:731–47.

Tower, Edward, and Willett, Thomas D. 1976. *The theory of optimum currency areas and exchange rate flexibility.* Special Papers in International Economics, no. 11. Princeton: International Finance Section.

13 Multilateral Exchange Rate Determination: A Model for the Analysis of the European Monetary System

Giorgio Basevi and Michele Calzolari

13.1 Introduction

The purpose of this paper is to build a theoretical framework that will be as simple as possible and yet adequate for econometric estimation and policy analysis of the process of exchange rate determination in a multicountry and multicurrency world. By using a popular model of exchange rates—extended by Frankel (1979) on the basis of an earlier version proposed by Dornbusch (1976)—we also hope to lay the ground for more satisfactory tests of its theoretical foundations. We do this, first, by making the model multilateral—until now it has been cast in a two-country world—and second, by analyzing rationally formed expectations about future exchange rates on the basis of the model's structural version rather than the reduced-form version used by previous commentators.[1]

Our treatment of rational expectations is, however, limited to the extent that we have not assumed rationally expected processes for the exogenous variables. Thus we cannot present in this paper the analysis of the effects of policy changes and of other exogenous shocks. The characterizing feature of this stage of our research is the analysis of the stability properties of the multilateral exchange rate determination mechanism, whose structure we

This work is a part of a larger project developed at the European Community Commission (the Eurolink Project) and aimed at linking the models of at least four European countries: Germany, France, the United Kingdom, and Italy. The Italian model in the project is being developed at Prometeia Associates in Bologna. We thank C. Corradi, F. Giavazzi, and C. Wyplosz for helpful criticism and suggestions.

1. The same criticism of Frankel's model and tests has recently been made by Driskill and Sheffrin (1981), who also present estimates using the rational expectations hypothesis. Their version of the model, however, is still cast in terms of a two-country world.

have estimated under the assumption of given paths for the exogenous variables.[2]

In section 13.2 we outline the basic theoretical specification of the model. Section 13.3 presents a variant of the model together with estimates of behavioral functions for the two alternative specifications of the model, while section 13.4 deals with stability analysis of the system.

In section 13.5 we indicate in which direction our research is currently developing.

13.2 The Theoretical Model

Consider any two currencies (countries) i, k chosen from the set of n countries (currencies) that form the elements of a multilateral trade and payments network. Short-term capital movements ensure a covered interest rate relation that need not be at parity as we consider national markets rather than Euromarkets. We thus allow transaction costs and exchange controls to introduce a wedge δ into

$$(1) \qquad [(1 + i_i^s)/(1 + i_k^s)]_t = [(F_{ik}^s/S_{ik})\ \delta_{ik}^s]_t,$$

where i^s are short-term interest rates, F_{ik}^s is the forward exchange rate (with the same short-term maturity) between currency i and k, s_{ik} is the spot exchange rate, and δ_{ik}^s is the distortion coefficient due to transaction costs and exchange controls.

Because of exchange rate risk, a spread (δ_{ik}^s) may also open between the forward rate and the expected future spot rate,

$$(2) \qquad F_{ik,t}^s = {}_tS_{ik,t+s} \cdot \delta_{ik,t}^s,$$

where ${}_tS_{ik,t+s}$ indicates the value of S_{ik} expected at time t for time $t + s$.

We assume that the nominal quantity of money supplied is demanded according to the following function:

$$(3) \qquad m_{i,t} = \alpha_i p_{i,t} + \beta_i \bar{y}_{i,t} - \gamma_i r^s_{i,t};\ i = 1, \ldots, n,$$

where lowercase letters stand for logs (of money, m; prices, p; real income, y), except that $r^s = \log(1 + i^s)$, and where $\bar{y}$ stands for equilibrium real income.

We now consider (1) and (2) for a maturity $s = 1$, and, taking logs (with $\log S = e$), we write

$$(4) \qquad {}_te_{ik,t+1} - e_{ik,t} = r_{i,t} - r_{k,t} - w_{ik,t};\ i = 1, \ldots, n,$$

where r_i and r_k correspond to 1-period maturity interest rates and $w_{ik} = \log$

2. We are currently extending the model in the direction of policy analysis. Results based on the estimation of monetary authorities' reaction functions were presented at conferences at the University of Illinois and the University of Louvain. We will publish these results in a conference volume edited by P. De Grauwe and T. Peeters. See Basevi and Calzolari (1982).

$(\delta_{ik} \cdot \sigma_{ik})$. In line with the asset market approach to exchange rate determination, we assume that the money market is continuously in equilibrium, so that $m = \bar{m}$; further assuming that equilibrium short-term real rates of interest are internationally equal, substitution of equation (3) into equation (4) yields

$$
\begin{aligned}
(5) \qquad {}_t e_{ik,t+1} - e_{ik,t} = {} & \frac{\alpha_i}{\gamma_i} (p_{i,t} - \bar{p}_{i,t}) - \frac{\alpha_k}{\gamma_k} (p_{k,t} - \bar{p}_{k,t}) \\
& + (\bar{\pi}_{i,t} - \bar{\pi}_{k,t}) - w_{ik,t},
\end{aligned}
$$

where $\bar{\pi}$ are equilibrium rates of expected inflation.

We assume that the deviation of real income from equilibrium level is related to the deviation of the real exchange rate (q) from its equilibrium level $(\bar{q})$ and to the deviation of the dollar price of oil from its trend $(v - \bar{v})$

$$
\begin{aligned}
(6) \qquad y_{i,t} - \bar{y}_{i,t} = {} & D_i(L)(q_{i,t} - \bar{q}_{i,t}) + R_i(L)(v_t - \bar{v}_t); \; i \\
& = 1, \ldots, n,
\end{aligned}
$$

where $D(L) = \sum_j d_j L^j$ and $R(L)$, similarly defined, are polynomials in the lag operator L, such that $L^j x_t = x_{t-j}$.

The real exchange rate q is defined as

$$
(7) \qquad q_i = \left(\sum_{j \neq i} \mu_{ij} \, e_{ij} - p_i + \sum_{j \neq i} \mu_{ij} p_j \right); \; i = 1, \ldots, n.
$$

By assuming that purchasing power parity holds in equilibrium, it follows that $\bar{q}_i = 0$ for all i.

The current rate of price change is assumed to diverge from the equilibrium rate of price inflation $(\bar{\pi}_t)$ because of disequilibrium real income:

$$
(8) \qquad p_{i,t+1} - p_{i,t} = G_i(L)(y_i - \bar{y}_i)_t + \bar{\pi}_{i,t}; \; i = 1, \ldots, n.
$$

Substituting (6) into (8), we obtain

$$
\begin{aligned}
(9) \qquad p_{i,t+1} - p_{i,t} = {} & H_i(L)q_{i,t} + K_i(L)(v - \bar{v})_t + \bar{\pi}_{i,t}; \\
& i = 1, \ldots, n,
\end{aligned}
$$

with $H(L) = G(L) \, D(L)$ and $K(L) = G(L) \, R(L)$.

Taking into account that $e_{ki} = -e_{ik}$, that $e_{kk} = 0$, and that the sum of the weights μ equals unity, it is possible to reduce (g) to a final expression in terms of endogenous (p, e) and of exogenous variables $(\bar{p}, \bar{\pi}, v, \bar{v},$ and $w)$:[3]

---

3. The treatment of $\bar{p}$ and $\bar{\pi}$ as exogenous variables is an intermediate step, to be followed by an explicit analysis of the process generating m (or i); the choice depends upon whether we consider the stock of money or the rate of interest as the authorities' control variable. Moreover, w is only provisionally included among the exogenous variables: a full treatment would include a theory of exchange risk, while δ—the foreign exchange control coefficient—should be included among the control variables. As for the short- and long-run price of oil, it can remain exogenous to the model.

(10)
$$p_{i,t+1} - p_{i,t} = H_i(L)e_{ik,t} - H_i(L)\sum_{\substack{j \neq i \\ j \neq k}} p_{ij}e_{jk,t}$$
$$-H_i(L)\,(p_i - \sum_{j \neq i} p_{ij}p_j)t$$
$$+K_i(L)(v - \bar{v})_t + \bar{\pi}_{i,t}.$$

Mathematical convenience and the theory of international monetary systems suggest choosing a specific country as the one whose currency is used as the numeraire of the system. The obvious candidates for this role are the United States and the dollar. While this choice will be explicitly made in section 13.3, we now simply label the nth country (currency) as the reference country (currency). We thus have a system of linear difference equations in $n - 1$ exchange rates (e_{in}; $i = 1, \ldots, n - 1$) and in n prices (p_i; $i = 1, \ldots, n$), which, considering equations (5) and (10), can be written in matrix form as

(11)
$$x_{t+1} = \Omega x_t + z_t,$$

where the vectors x_{t+1} and x_t of the endogenous variables are defined as

$$x_{t+1} = \begin{bmatrix} \,^t e_{1,n;t+1} \\ . \\ . \\ . \\ \,^t e_{n-1,n;t+1} \\ p_{1;t+1} \\ . \\ . \\ . \\ p_{n;t+1} \end{bmatrix} ;\ x_t = \begin{bmatrix} e_{1,n;t} \\ . \\ . \\ . \\ e_{n-1,n;t} \\ p_{1;t} \\ . \\ . \\ . \\ p_{n;t} \end{bmatrix}$$

and the vector z of the exogenous variables[4] is

$$z_t = \begin{bmatrix} \dfrac{\alpha_1}{\gamma_1}\bar{p}_{1,t} + \dfrac{\alpha n}{\gamma n}\bar{p}_{n,t} + \bar{\pi}_{1,t} - \bar{\pi}_{n,t} - w_{1n,t} \\ \cdots\cdots\cdots\cdots\cdots\cdots\cdots\cdots\cdots\cdots\cdots\cdots \\ \cdots\cdots\cdots\cdots\cdots\cdots\cdots\cdots\cdots\cdots\cdots\cdots \\ \cdots\cdots\cdots\cdots\cdots\cdots\cdots\cdots\cdots\cdots\cdots\cdots \\ \cdots\cdots\cdots\cdots\cdots\cdots\cdots\cdots\cdots\cdots\cdots\cdots \\ \bar{\pi}_{n,t} + K_n(L)(v - \bar{v})_t \end{bmatrix}.$$

4. As already pointed out, endogenization of exchange risk and of the process generating money supply—and hence equilibrium price levels and inflation rates—would change the content of vector z and consequently that of the matrix Ω.

The square matrix Ω is of dimension $2n - 1$ and can be partitioned into

$$= \begin{bmatrix} \Omega_{11} & \Omega_{12} \\ \Omega_{21} & \Omega_{22} \end{bmatrix},$$

where Ω_{11} is an identity matrix of dimension $(n - 1)(n - 1)$, Ω_{12} is a matrix of dimension $(n - 1)n$:

$$\Omega_{12} = \begin{bmatrix} \dfrac{\alpha_1}{\gamma_1} & 0 & \cdots & \cdots & 0 & 0 & -\dfrac{\alpha_n}{\gamma_n} \\ 0 & \dfrac{\alpha_2}{\gamma_2} & \cdots & \cdots & \cdots & \cdots & -\dfrac{\alpha_n}{\gamma_n} \\ \cdot & & & & & & \cdot \\ \cdot & & & & & & \cdot \\ \cdot & & & & & & \cdot \\ 0 & \cdots & \cdots & \cdots & \dfrac{\alpha_{n-2}}{\gamma_{n-2}} & 0 & -\dfrac{\alpha_n}{\gamma_n} \\ 0 & \cdots & \cdots & \cdots & \cdots & \dfrac{\alpha_{n-1}}{\gamma_{n-1}} & -\dfrac{\alpha_n}{\gamma_n} \end{bmatrix},$$

while the remaining parts of Ω are

$$\Omega_{21} = \begin{bmatrix} H_1(L) & & -\mu_{1,n-1}H_1(L) \\ \cdot & & \\ \cdot & & \\ \cdot & & \\ -\mu_{n,1}H_n(L) & \cdots & -\mu_{n,n-1}H_{n-1}(L) \end{bmatrix},$$

$\Omega_{22} = I - \Omega_{21}^*$, and Ω_{21}^* is the Ω_{21} matrix augmented by a last column equal to

$$\begin{bmatrix} -\mu_{1,n}H_1(L) \\ \cdot \\ \cdot \\ \cdot \\ -\mu_{n-1,n}H_{n-1}(L) \\ H_n(L) \end{bmatrix}.$$

13.3 The Estimates

In order to implement the multilateral model of exchange rates just presented we have reduced the "world" to a set of ten countries: the United States, Germany, France, Japan, Canada, the United Kingdom, Italy, the Netherlands, Belgium, and Switzerland. The United States has been chosen as the nth country for its size and for the dominant role of its currency in the international monetary system. In view of our empirical aim—which is to estimate a model to be used for the analysis of the European Monetary System—we also considered Canada, Japan, and Switzerland as an exogenous subset of countries. Moreover, we have provisionally limited the estimates of the structure to five countries: the four large European countries plus the United States.[5] Thus our system (11) is of dimension $2n - 1 = 9$.

The elements of Ω are combinations of the parameters of equations (3), (4), and (6). Thus, for the five specified countries we estimated the parameters determining money demand, disequilibrium income, and price inflation. The sample is made up of monthly observations from 1971.10 to 1980.12; data sources are given in the statistical appendix.[6]

The data were first used to estimate a version of model (11) modified by the use of current income rather than equilibrium income in the money demand functions. From a formal point of view this modification has the consequence of adding a matrix B to the identity matrix Ω_{11}, with

$$
B = \begin{bmatrix}
\left[\dfrac{\beta_1}{\gamma_1}D_1(L) + \dfrac{\beta_n}{\gamma_n}\mu_{n1}\,D_n(L) \quad \cdots \quad \cdots \quad -\dfrac{\beta_1}{\gamma_1}\mu_{1,n-1}\,D_1\,(L)\right. \\
\left. -\dfrac{\beta_n}{\gamma_n}\mu_{n,n-1}D_n\,(L)\right] \\
\cdots \quad \cdots \quad \cdots \quad \cdots \quad \cdots \quad \cdots \quad \cdots \quad \cdots \quad \cdots \quad \cdots \quad \cdots \\
\cdots \quad \cdots \quad \cdots \quad \cdots \quad \cdots \quad \cdots \quad \cdots \quad \cdots \quad \cdots \quad \cdots \quad \cdots \\
\cdots \quad \cdots \quad \cdots \quad \cdots \quad \cdots \quad \cdots \quad \cdots \quad \cdots \quad \cdots \quad \cdots \quad \cdots \\
\cdots \quad \cdots \quad \cdots \quad \cdots \quad \cdots \quad \cdots \quad \cdots \quad \cdots \quad \cdots \quad \cdots \quad \cdots \\
-\left[\dfrac{\beta_{n-1}}{\gamma_{n-1}}\mu_{n-1,1}D_{n-1}\,(L) - \dfrac{\beta_n}{\gamma_n}\mu_{n,1}D_n\,(L) \quad \cdots \quad \dfrac{\beta_{n-1}}{\gamma_{n-1}}D_{n-1}\,(L)\right. \\
\left. +\dfrac{\beta_n}{\gamma_n}\mu_{n,n-1}D_n\,(L)\right]
\end{bmatrix}
$$

and of subtracting its augmented version B^* to the matrix Ω_{12}. The modification does not affect the matrices Ω_{21} and Ω_{22}. In other words, only the exchange rate equations and not the price equations are affected by this alternative specification of the money demand function. The set of estimates based on this modified version of the model are presented in tables 13.1, 13.2, and 13.3. The first rows in the tables correspond to ordinary least squares.

In order to keep the system as small as possible to make the stability analysis in the next section feasible, this first set of estimates—while using

---

5. This choice means that in our empirical use of system (11) the vector z contains, in addition to the variables explicitly written above, the exchange rates and prices of the countries that are left exogenous to the model.

6. In all estimates y is proxied by the index of industrial production and $\bar{y}$ has been constructed by interpolating y on the basis of the following function of time: $\bar{y} = \alpha + \beta t - \gamma t^2$. The same interpolation is used to construct the equilibrium price of oil, $\bar{v}$.

Table 13.1   Demand for Money: Equation (3) (Monthly Observations, 1971.10–1980.12)

		Constant	Q1	Q12	p	y	r	D-W	SE	MDV
United States	OLS	.5148	.0007	.0286	.9409	.3659	-2.4916	.17	.023	6.62
		(.16)	(.008)	(.008)	(.017)	(.043)	(1.08)			
	2SLS	4.7207	.0007	.0288	.9336	.3932	-2.7598	.17	.023	6.62
		(.22)	(.008)	(.008)	(.018)	(.046)	(1.09)			
Germany	OLS	-4.4759	.0096	.0438	1.4426	.8910	-8.9497	.72	.022	6.33
		(.20)	(.008)	(.007)	(.030)	(.063)	(1.03)			
	2SLS	1.5317	.0091	.0447	1.3907	1.0282	-10.2036	.81	.023	6.33
		(.33)	(.008)	(.008)	(.033)	(.071)	(1.09)			
France	OLS	-1.4572	.0018	.0313	1.2642	.4741	-5.9480	.30	.030	6.63
		(.32)	(.010)	(.010)	(.018)	(.082)	(1.71)			
	2SLS	3.7528	.0018	.0330	1.2418	.6076	-7.3811	.36	.030	6.63
		(.46)	(.010)	(.010)	(.020)	(.099)	(1.82)			
United Kingdom	OLS	1.3612	.0042	.0411	.8587	.9468	-4.6581	.32	.043	9.77
		(.48)	(.015)	(.015)	(.013)	(.100)	(1.67)			
	2SLS	4.2493	.0378	.0230	.8461	1.1703	-3.0456	.46	.047	9.77
		(.57)	(.016)	(.016)	(.013)	(.122)	(1.78)			
Italy	OLS	4.4458	.0184	.0421	1.2282	.3196	-5.8491	.24	.039	11.71
		(.28)	(.014)	(.013)	(.018)	(.072)	(1.34)			
	2SLS	9.5919	.0176	.0421	1.2087	.4299	-6.5247	.29	.040	11.71
		(.40)	(.014)	(.013)	(.020)	(.087)	(1.38)			

Notes: Standard errors in parentheses. Q1 and Q12 are dummies for January and December. D-W = Durbin-Watson statistic. SE = standard error of the regression. MDV = mean of the dependent variable.

Table 13.2   Income Disequilibrium: Equation (6) (Monthly Observations, 1971.10–1980.12)

		Constant	y_t	q_t	$(v - \bar{v})_t$	D-W	SE	MDV
United States	OLS	-2.6623	1.5547	.2581	-.1104	.14	.034	4.73
		(.53)	(.11)	(.08)	(.01)			
	2SLS	-2.1006	1.4357	.3900	-.1100	.16	.035	4.73
		(.58)	(.12)	(.09)	(.01)			
Germany	OLS	-1.9620	1.4402	-.0084	-.1214	.21	.033	4.69
		(.48)	(.10)	(.08)	(.02)			
	2SLS	-1.8970	1.4255	-.0545	-.1179	.21	.033	4.69
		(.48)	(.11)	(.09)	(.02)			
France	OLS	-.5248	1.1229	.4584	-.0725	.45	.032	4.67
		(.37)	(.08)	(.09)	(.01)			
	2SLS	-.5312	1.1232	.5262	-.0713	.46	.032	4.67
		(.37)	(.08)	(.10)	(.02)			
United Kingdom	OLS	-12.0961	3.6267	.0398	-.1704	.44	.029	4.66
		(1.48)	(.32)	(.03)	(.02)			
	2SLS	-12.0954	3.6265	.0406	-.1704	.44	.029	4.66
		(1.48)	(.32)	(.03)	(.02)			
Italy	OLS	-1.0072	1.2236	.0295	-.0568	.36	.054	4.71
		(.66)	(.14)	(.097)	(.03)			
	2SLS	-1.0286	1.2281	.0230	-.0567	.36	.054	4.71
		(.67)	(.15)	(.100)	(.03)			

Notes: Standard errors in parentheses. D-W = Durbin-Watson statistic. SE = standard error of the regression. MDV = mean of the dependent variable.

Table 13.3 Price Functions: Equation (8) (Monthly Observations, 1971.10–1980.12)

	Constant	p_{t-1}	y_{t-1}	$-\bar{y}_{t-1}$	$\bar{\pi}_{t-1}$	H	SE	MDV	LR
United States OLS	—	.9957 (.002)	.0271 (.005)	.0290 (.005)	2.3725 (.44)	1.24	.0026	.056	4.43
2SLS	—	.9950 (.002)	.0287 (.005)	.0308 (.005)	2.5411 (.47)	1.23	.0026	.056	—
Germany OLS	—	1	.0107 (.006)		.6212 (.04)	3.17	.0028	.0041	6.28
2SLS	—	1	.0109 (.007)		.6202 (.04)	3.17	.0028	.0041	—
France OLS	—	1	.0190 (.006)		1	2.46	.0027	.0003	11.3
2SLS	—	1	.0204 (.006)		1	2.41	.0027	.003	—
United Kingdom OLS	—	1	.0087 (.02)		1	2.72	.0078	.0005	8.6
2SLS	—	1	.0021 (.02)		1	2.62	.0078	.0005	—
Italy OLS	—	.9965 (.002)	.0405 (.01)		1.2687 (.06)	4.00	.0057	.13	10.3
2SLS	—	.9964 (.001)	.0592 (.01)		1.2805 (.064)	3.69	.0058	.13	—

Notes: Standard error in parentheses. H = Durbin-h statistic. SE = standard error of the regression. MDV = mean of the dependent variable. LR = likelihood ratio to test the linear constraints imposed by the specification.

current rather than equilibrium income in the money demand function—do not allow for lags in endogenous variables; that is, the polynomials $D(L)$ and $G(L)$ are truncated at their first terms d_o and g_o. Possibly as a consequence of this, the estimates in tables 13.1–13.3 denote the presence of first-order serial autocorrelation of residuals, particularly in the income disequilibrium equations (but also in the money demand equations where our theoretical model did not provide for lags).

Even though, as a consequence, their standard errors are underestimated, the coefficients of the money demand functions (table 13.1) all have the theoretically expected sign and are generally of the correct magnitude. Notice, however, that in this first set of estimates we do not constrain the price elasticity of money to equal unity; this homogeneity constraint will, on the other hand, be imposed in the second set of estimates, that is, those using the basic version of the model with $\bar{y}$ in the money demand functions.

In the income equations (table 13.2), the significance of the coefficient of the real exchange rate is particularly low in the case of the United Kingdom and of Italy, while its sign appears contrary to theory, but not significant, in the case of Germany. The price equations reported in table 13.3 are only a subset of our initial estimates. In fact, we have first allowed estimation of a constant in these equations, to account for the fact that the use of the (long-term) nominal interest rate as a proxy for the equilibrium expected inflation rate π introduces into the equations the value of the equilibrium real rate of interest. If this is assumed to be constant (in line with the assumption that $\bar{q} = 0$), its value is estimated by the constant in the price functions. Our initial estimates—not here reported—proved this constant to be insignificantly different from zero for all countries in our sample.

To allow for the possibility that (due to the simultaneity of the model) some of the explanatory variables in each equation are correlated with the error term, we also used two-stage least squares estimation by instrumental variables. We chose as instruments the exogenous variables of the model.[7] The results are also reported in tables 13.1, 13.2, and 13.3, but they do not show a dramatic change of estimated coefficients.

Because the estimates presented in tables 13.1–13.3 are generally plagued by high autocorrelation of the residuals, we performed an autoregressive transformation of the variables using the Cochrane-Orcutt procedure. The results, not reported here, were unfavorable to the theoretical specification of the model in the sense that some coefficients, particularly in the money demand function, acquired the wrong sign and/or became insignificantly different from zero.

We therefore resumed the basic and simpler model, the one with $\bar{y}$ in the

7. For practical reasons, only those pertaining to the five countries of the model were used. The variables pertaining to third countries—Canada, Japan, the Netherlands, and Belgium—did not significantly change the results when they were included among the instruments.

money demand function as formally presented in section 13.2. We estimated it, allowing for 3-period distributed lags in the real exchange rate coefficient of equation (6) and performing a first-order autoregressive transformation in the variables of all three behavioral equations. In addition, we constrained the coefficient of the price variable in the money demand functions to unity, as theoretical considerations would suggest.[8]

Similarly, we chose to follow the theoretical specification of equations (6) and (8) by imposing unitary coefficients to the $\bar{y}$ variable in equation (6) and to the p_{t-1} variable in equation (8), and also by imposing the same estimate (except for sign) to the coefficient of y and $\bar{y}$ in equation (8).

Tables 13.4–13.6 thus report in the first row of each country OLS estimates of equations (3), (6), and (8) according to the specifications just mentioned. In the case of the United States, poor initial estimates of the interest rate coefficient in their demand for money equation and of the real exchange rate coefficient in the income equation induced us to impose values which seem reasonable on the basis of cross-country comparisons or of results of previous studies.

According to an F-test, the imposed constraint is not rejected by the data in case of the latter coefficient (.005), while the value of the former ($-.85$) is at the limit of the critical region of acceptance. On the whole, the values of the D-W or h-statistics in tables 13.4–13.6 indicate that much of the problem of autocorrelation of the residuals has been eliminated in this new set of estimates.

To allow for the possibility that (due to the simultaneity of the model) some of the explanatory variables in each equation are correlated with the error term, and to take into account the interequation covariances in the variance-covariance matrix of residuals, we also used three-stage least squares but, because of limited computer storage capacity, we did it by taking the three structural equations together country by country rather than by using the whole 5×3 system of equations. This is equivalent to assuming that the variance-covariance matrix of the residual is block diagonal, which implies that we disregard cross-country effects. The results of three-stage least squares estimations are reported in the second rows of each country in tables 13.4–13.6.

Relative to their OLS estimates, the coefficients most affected by the three-stage least squares method are those for the income variable in the money demand function and for the real exchange rate variable in the income disequilibrium function. Unfortunately, the coefficients for the latter do not improve their level of significance, which remains very low. While better estimates could be obtained by extending the lags already present and

8. As a matter of fact this homogeneity constraint would be rejected for some countries on the basis of a t-test. We chose, however, to impose it both for theoretical reasons and because in the stability analysis of section 13.4 the results are not significantly affected by the presence or absence of the constraint.

Table 13.4   Demand for Money: Equation (3) (Monthly Observations, 1971.10–1980.12)

		Constant	Time	Q1	Q12	$\bar{y}$	r	$\hat{\rho}$	D-W	SE	MDV
United States	OLS	—	-.003 (.002)	.003 (.002)	.030 (.022)	.462 (.012)	-.85[a] (1.97)	.92	2.10	.009	.031
	3SLS	—	-.36 (.040)	.002 (.002)	.030 (.002)	1.503 (.013)	-.85[a]	.92	2.08	.008	.031
Germany	OLS	—	.25 (.042)	-.002 (.003)	.021 (.003)	.287 (.015)	-3.62 (1.97)	.91	2.01	.011	1.707
	3SLS	—	.05	.001	.022	1.335	-3.61	.93	2.95	.011	1.707
France	OLS	-11.26 (3.86)	-.28 (.16)	.006 (.003)	.038 (.003)	2.92 (.88)	-1.91 (1.66)	.84	1.97	.011	1.954
	3SLS	6.96 (3.96)	.53 (.23)	.006 (.002)	.035 (.003)	3.07 (.92)	-1.60 (1.78)	.85	2.08	.011	1.954
United Kingdom	OLS	—	-.24 (.13)	.008 (.005)	.033 (.005)	1.17 (.05)	-.79 (1.84)	.96	1.68	.017	5.068
	3SLS	—	-.29 (.15)	.006 (.005)	.032 (.005)	2.17 (.06)	-.77 (1.9)	.96	1.70	.016	5.068
Italy	OLS	—	-.36 (.10)	.021 (.003)	.061 (.003)	1.61 (.04)	-.41 (1.09)	.97	1.45	.011	6.973
	3SLS	—	-.54 (.26)	.024 (.003)	.062 (.003)	2.64 (.11)	-.50 (1.1)	.98	1.51	.011	6.973

Notes: Standard error in parentheses. $\hat{\rho}$ estimated with Cochrane-Orcutt method. D-W = Durbin-Watson statistic. SE = standard error of the regression. MDV = mean of the dependent variable.
[a]Value imposed a priori $F(1,109) = 7.6$.

Table 13.5   **Income Disequilibrium: Equation (6) (Monthly Observations, 1971.10–1980.12)**

		Constant	Time	q	q_{-1}	q_{-2}	Σ_q	$(v - \bar{v})_t$	$\hat{\rho}$	D-W	SE	R^2
United States	OLS	.017	−.01	.0015	.002	.0015	.005	−.085	.94	.58	.011	.09
		(.096)	(.06)				(a)	(.026)				
	3SLS	.012	−.01	.0015	.002	.0015	.005	−.115	.92	.61	.011	.11
		(.094)	(.05)				(a)	(.033)				
Germany	OLS	.070	−.04	.0808	.0538	.0269	.161	−.105	.87	2.20	.014	
		(.52)	(.03)				(.125)	(.028)				
	3SLS	.064	−.04	.0243	.0324	.0243	.081	−.118	.86	2.26	.014	
		(.051)	(.03)				(1.30)	(.035)				
France	OLS	.133	−.10	.1125	.1500	.1125	.375	−.076	.76	2.48	.019	.15
		(.039)	(.02)				(.16)	(.025)				
	3SLS	.125	−.09	.1188	.1584	.1188	.396	−.101	.76	2.49	.019	
		(.39)	(.2)				(.17)	(.032)				
United Kingdom	OLS	.019	−.01	.0228	.0304	.0228	.076	−.094	.77	2.12	.018	.13
		(.040)	(.03)				(.07)	(.025)				
	3SLS	.021	−.01	.0186	.0248	.0186	.062	−.120	.77	2.13	.018	
		(.030)	(.02)				(.06)	(.031)				
Italy	OLS	.01	−.01	.0260	.0346	.026	.087	−.073	.81	2.38	.031	.11
		(.09)	(.06)				(.19)	(.048)				
	3SLS	.017	−.02	.0513	.0684	.0513	.171	−.069	.81	2.31	.030	
		(.09)	(.06)				(.21)	(.061)				

Notes: Standard error in parentheses. $\hat{\rho}$ estimated with Cochrane-Orcutt method. D-W = Durbin-Watson statistic. SE = standard error of the regression. R^2 = in terms of changes.

[a]Value imposed a priori; $F(1, 109) = 2.996$.

Table 13.6   Price Functions: Equation (8) (Monthly Observations, 1971.10–1980.12)

		Constant	Time	$(y - \bar{y})_{t-1}$	$\bar{\pi}_{t-1}$	$\hat{\rho}$	H	SE	R^2
United States	OLS	-.004 (.002)	(−)	.026 (.006)	1.546 (.249)	.15	-.171	.003	.42
	3SLS	-.004 (−)	(−)	.026	1.558	.15	-.177	.003	
Germany	OLS	-.002 (−)	(−)	.009 (.008)	.620 (.054)	.30	.002	.003	.34
	3SLS	-.002 (.002)	(−)	.010 (.008)	.618 (.054)	.30	-.038	.003	
France	OLS	-.002 (.002)	.002 (.001)	.017 (.008)	.975 (.320)	.22	-.161	.003	.37
	3SLS	-.002 (.002)	.002 (.001)	.017 (.008)	.983 (.317)	.22	-.121	.003	
United Kingdom	OLS	-.006 (.006)	-.004 (.003)	.023 (.022)	2.269 (.597)	.20	.069	.007	.40
	3SLS	-.006 (.006)	-.004 (.003)	.014 (.023)	2.237 (.588)	.20	.066	.007	
Italy	OLS	.006 (.004)	(−)	.010 (.014)	.555 (.369)	.47	-.132	.005	.25
	3SLS	.006 (.004)	(−)	.014 (.014)	.500 (.358)	.46	-.120	.005	

Notes: Standard errors in parentheses. $\hat{\rho}$ estimated with Cochrane-Orcutt method. H = Durbin's h-statistic. SE = standard error of the regression. R^2 = ... (−) = in terms of changes.

introducing them in the money and price functions, where they are not present, we have chosen not to follow this avenue. In fact, as a result the size of our Ω matrix would be correspondingly enlarged. As it is, with the lags already present in the q variable of the income equations, the dimension of Ω when the system is transformed into its first-order canonical form is $6n - 3$. This, with five countries, makes 27, which is a fairly high order for the characteristic equation to be solved numerically in the next section.

13.4 Stability Analysis

The theoretical model we have used as the basis of our analysis has been estimated and tested for stability by Frankel and many other authors.[9] In our view one of the main weaknesses of the debate about the model and its empirical verification is due to the fact that it has generally been cast in terms of a two-country world.[10] To justify this assertion, we may consider Frankel's original contribution (Frankel 1979). In it, the deutsche mark to dollar (DM/$) exchange rate is shown to converge to a stable path determined by purchasing power parity. The speed of convergence depends only on the parameters of the money demand and price functions of the United States and Germany, regardless of the economic structure and events in third countries. Clearly this is not the case when more than two countries are explicitly introduced into the analysis. The roots of the characteristic equation that determine the stability conditions for the system depend, in the general n-countries case, upon the parameters of the structural equations of all n countries.

Thus, with reference to our system (11), while the vector z drives the endogenous variables along their equilibrium path, the whole structure of the matrix Ω determines whether the system converges again to that path after it is shocked by changes in the exogenous variables.

Although relatively simple as a macroeconomic model, our system is complex enough to require an analytical examination of its stability conditions. We have therefore used the numerical estimates of the structure obtained in the previous section to compute the eigenvalues of matrix Ω. Blanchard and Kahn (1980) have shown that in a linear difference equation system in which a subset of variables is forward looking and the remaining subset is backward looking, uniqueness and stability of solutions are ensured when there are as many roots of the characteristic equation of the system with module larger than one as there are forward-looking variables, and as

9. For criticism and defense of that model, see the exchange comments in the *American Economic Review*, December 1981.

10. The same criticism has also been made by Driskill and Sheffrin (1981). Notice that tests of the model for different pairs of countries (currencies) have been conducted by many authors. All those that we know of, however, remain pairwise tests, and none of them is built within a multilateral exchange rate framework.

many with module smaller than one as there are backward-looking variables. Our system corresponds to this classification, with $n - 1$ forward-looking variables (the $n - 1$ exchange rates) and n backward-looking variables (the n prices).

Table 13.7, in its part A, shows the eigenvalues of matrix Ω based on the numerical parameters obtained in section 13.3 on the basis of the first set of estimates taken from tables 13.1–13.3. We have chosen for this purpose both OLS and 2SLS estimates. The results show that when all five countries are included in the model the eigenvalues do not conform to the Blanchard-Kahn criterion for uniqueness and stability of the solutions. This seems to be due to the wrong coefficient in the income equation for Germany; in fact, when we take Germany out of the system and reduce its endogenous part to a four-country set (and also when we further reduce it to subsets of three or two countries, always excluding Germany), the eigenvalues conform to the Blanchard-Kahn criterion.

Table 13.7A   **Numerical Solution for the Roots of the Characteristic Equation of System (11) Based on Results of Tables 13.1–13.3**

	OLS		2SLS	
	1.0849	.9769	1.1060	.9826
	1.0645	.9838	1.0862	.9786
$N = 5$	1.0434	.9942	1.0623	.9959
	1.0330	.9988	1.0420	.9998
	1.0001		1.0008	
$N = 4$	1.0879	.9769	1.1073	.9854
(excluding	1.0535	.9955	1.0586	.9966
Germany)	1.0425	.9870	1.0766	.9998
		.9993		.9998

Table 13.7B   **Numerical Solution for the Roots of the Characteristic Equation of System (11) Based on Results of Tables 13.4–13.6**

	OLS		3 SLS	
	1.8400	.9999	1.8404	.9999
	1.8397	.9999	1.8395	.9993
$N = 5$	1.8397	.9998	1.8391	.9980
	1.8382	.9998	1.8385	.9968
		−.0260		−.0270

As the estimates of tables 13.1–13.3 are plagued by first-order auto-correlation of the residuals, the set of roots contained in table 13.7A is not very reliable. We have therefore recomputed the eigenvalues on the basis of the estimates contained in tables 13.4–13.6; while the coefficients in these tables generally seem not much more significant than the corresponding coefficients of tables 13.1–13.3, they are less weakened by the phenomenon of autocorrelation. We do not report the 18 additional roots introduced by the two lags of q that appear in each country's income equation; in general, these roots introduce a cyclical movement in the adjustment path which was not present in the unlagged version of the model, but their module is always smaller than unity. As for the remaining nine roots, they are reported in table 13.7B.

Contrary to the results of table 13.7A, this new set of roots conforms to the stability criterion even when all the countries in our sample are included. It is, however, alarming to notice that the roots with modules smaller than unity are dangerously close to the edge of instability. We have therefore engaged in a series of sensitivity experiments, by changing the coefficients of the matrix Ω in the neighborhood of their mean values. The results show that the stability of the system is rather robust except when we change the value of the coefficient of the q variable in the income equations. Thus table 13.8, based only on 3SLS estimates, presents three experiments. In the first of them (part A), the coefficient of the real exchange rate in the United States income equation has been increased from .005 to .009. In the second (part B), the coefficients of q for all countries except the United States have been increased by twice their standard errors. Finally, in the third experiment (part C) we have increased by these amounts the q-coefficients of all countries.

Table 13.8   **Numerical Solutions for the Roots of the Characteristic Equation of System (11) under Alternative Values for the q-Coefficient in Equation (6)**

(a)		(b)		(c)	
1.9404	.9993	1.8436	.9999	1.8436	.9982
1.8396	.9980	1.8404	.9982	1.8404	.9958
1.8391	.9968	1.8389	.9958	1.8389	.9903
1.8386	−.0324	1.8378	.9903	1.8378	−.0328
1.0001			−.0264	1.0001	

It can be seen from the sets of roots thus obtained that the system becomes unstable when the q-coefficient of the United States is increased, whereas it remains stable when only the corresponding coefficients of the other countries are changed.

The robustness of the system's stability with respect to alternative values for the parameters in the money demand functions and in the price functions, together with its sensitivity to different values for the coefficient of the real exchange rate in the income disequilibrium equations of the United States (in the case of the basic version of the model) and for Germany (in the case of the modified version of the model), suggest that the model's underlying theory should allow for structural changes in equilibrium real exchange rates. In other words, the long-run purchasing power parity condition that is still imposed in our model in the form of $\bar{q} = 0$ ought to be relaxed.[11] In view of the fact that the United States and Germany (but also the United Kingdom) are the two countries in our set whose real exchange rate has changed most markedly during the sample period, it is not surprising that the stability of the estimated structure depends so crucially upon those two countries' income sensitivity to their real exchange rate.

13.5 Extensions and Concluding Remarks

In order to perform a detailed analysis of monetary policy in the European Monetary System, our model clearly needs extensions and refinements. Extensions are required in order to include the EMS countries that were left exogenous or absent in our empirical section. More important, theoretical refinement of the model should allow endogenization of the equilibrium price and inflation rates that are here left in the z vector; this must be done by specifying a process for the conduct of monetary policy by the EMS countries and the United States of America. While the minimal assumption is a random walk process,[12] a more relevant approach for our purpose is to specify policy reaction functions for the monetary authorities. These should reflect, in addition to the standard objectives (control of the inflation rate, of unemployment, and of the balance of payments), the effect of the institutional constraints that have ruled exchange rate management of our set of countries during the sample period—for example, the "snake" arrangements—and that still determine monetary and exchange rate policy in the present stage of the EMS.[13]

A set of theoretical and econometric problems that arise in this connection are due to the changing role of policy variables between being policy instruments and being policy objectives, and to the switches in institutional regimes that have been taking place through time and across countries because of the evolution of the European exchange rate arrangements and of the varying participation of European countries to them.

While work in these directions is in progress, we hope that the presentation of our model, its estimation, and the analysis of its stability properties may already be a useful contribution to the theory and practice of exchange rate modeling.

11. See Hooper and Morton (1980) for an exchange rate model oriented in this direction.

12. This is indeed the assumption implicitly made by Frankel (1979). See Driskill and Sheffrin (1981).

13. For an attempt to specify and estimate reaction functions along these lines, see Basevi and Calzolari (1982).

Appendix

Most data, excluding short-term interest rates, are taken from the International Financial Statistics tapes distributed by the International Monetary Fund. Money stocks (defined as M2, rows 34 and 35, except for the United Kingdom where M1, row 34, is used for lack of monthly data on row 35) are end of period and not seasonally adjusted. Price indices, long-term interest rates, and indices of industrial production (seasonally adjusted) are monthly averages. Exchange rates are end of period.

Short-term interest rates are taken from Morgan Guaranty Trust of New York, World Financial Markets, table headed "Representative Money-Market Rates," and they are end of period.

The weights μ_{ij} in the definition of q_i are taken from an unpublished study by the staff of the Bank of Italy, which draws upon data periodically distributed in mimeographed form by the Directorate for Economic Affairs of the European Community Commission.

Comment   Francesco Papadia

J. M. Keynes wrote that "practical men, who believe themselves to be quite exempt from any intellectual influences are usually the slaves of some defunct economist" (1936, p. 383). In a sense I earn my living, either at the EEC Commission or in the Research Department of the Banca d'Italia, attempting to minimize the lag with which practical policymakers are slaves of economists. I should add, incidentally, that slavery is not that bad if you can choose your own master, and the differences existing in the economic profession assure, in this respect, quite a range of choices to a practical policymaker.

I have introduced this autobiographical note just to illustrate the spirit with which I read the Basevi and Calzolari paper on which I have the pleasure of commenting. In my effort to bridge the gap between academic economists and policymakers, I look at models and their empirical estimates as elements to be inserted into the decision-making machinery. I have to see how, for example, Basevi and Calzolari's paper can be made relevant to such mundane activities as building the next phase of the EMS or managing the exchange rate of the lira. From this perspective, there are two questions I would like to put to the authors.

The paper is the newest offshoot of an old but ever-growing tree. The authors explicitly link their model to the one proposed by Frankel (1979). Frankel was extending, using Frenkel-Bilson material, Dornbusch's (1976) model. Dornbusch, in turn, developed the Fleming-Mundell model of the sixties. The new branch provided by Basevi and Calzolari usefully extends the model by (1) making it multilateral instead of limiting it to the two-country case; (2) analyzing rational expectations on the basis of the structural version of the model rather than the reduced-form one; (3) introducing, at least in principle, institutional constraints such as those of the EMS. The two questions I would like to put refer, one to the tree, and one to the new branch.

My first question, which relates to the whole class of models to which Basevi and Calzolari's model belongs, has to do with the issue of price stickiness. Dornbusch (1976) underlines the key role played in this class of models by the stickiness of prices in the real goods markets as compared with the instantaneous clearing of asset markets. Frankel (1979), in turn, builds an alternative hypothesis to his real interest differential model utilizing the Chicago (Frenkel-Bilson) hypothesis of perfectly flexible prices.

Dornbusch states his uneasiness in using, as a building block of his model, price stickiness which has no satisfactory theoretical explanation, but he accepts it as an empirical fact. Let me state my uneasiness in having to choose between the Scylla of perfectly flexible good prices and the Charybdis of price stickiness considered as an act of God, a meta-economic fact of life. Of course it would be nice to have a model in which price stickiness was not a parameter but the outcome of an optimizing process and as such changed according to circumstances. In this model, the optimum degree of stickiness would be reached when the marginal cost of an additional unit of flexibility was equalized to the marginal cost of trading at nonequilibrium prices. That flexibility has a cost is obvious if we look at the resources absorbed by the functioning of auction markets and imagine, in addition, the amount of real resources which would be absorbed if, say, salaries were recontracted every 5 minutes. The cost of trading at nonequilibrium prices, in turn, is obviously in terms of misallocation of resources.

The sort of model closest to the one I have hinted at above, of which I am aware, is the so-called surprise supply function proposed by Lucas (1973). In this model the cost of acquiring information is introduced by assuming that no private operator looks at more than one market to estimate the actual rate of inflation. Since, of course, there is no physical constraint to this effect, this limitation must be derived from an economic choice: it does not pay to incur the expenses of looking at more than one market. The cost of trading at nonequilibrium prices, in turn, is implicit in the fact that operators try to minimize it making optimal use of their limited information.

As is well known, in this model the slope of the Phillips curve (where unemployment is replaced by the deviation between actual income and equilibrium income) depends inversely on the informativeness of the price system expressed by the ratio of the variance of relative to aggregate inflation.

As the latter decreases, so does the informativeness of the price signal as a resource allocator: operators attribute a larger and larger share of observed price movements to aggregate rather than to relative inflation, and the steepness of the Phillips curve increases.

This feature is interesting for a practical policymaker because it gives body to the contention that economic policy has to do with relations among optimizing agents and is not a game against nature. Thus, it shows, for instance, that the agent's reaction to an overactive monetary policy which increases, under normal circumstances, the variance of aggregate inflation, will be a reduced sensitivity to demand policy actions. As I understand it, the Lucas hypothesis on the slope of the Phillips curve is immediately relevant for the class of models to which the Basevi and Calzolari paper belongs. In fact, the price adjustment equation (6) of the Basevi-Calzolari paper, similar to that of Dornbusch (1976, appendix), is just a Phillips curve with the addition of a long-term rate of inflation. In a sense the Phillips curve is a "price stickiness" equation. However, while in a model such as Basevi and Calzolari's, the slope of the Phillips curve is constant, an act of God, and is not derived from economic considerations, in the Lucas model it is explained by an admittedly rough optimizing process.

At the end of this long digression comes my question. The policymaker wanting to use a model similar to Basevi and Calzolari's is confronted with a serious delemma. On one hand, if prices are perfectly flexible there is no overshooting of the exchange rates, the relationship between the nominal interest differential and expected changes in the exchange rate is negative, and monetary policy does not influence real output. On the other hand, if prices show some degree of stickiness it is likely that there will be overshooting, the relationship between interest differential and the exchange rate is positive, and the exchange rate is an important channel of transmission of monetary impulses to real activity. Choosing one or the other assumption makes quite a dramatic difference. Of course, as a complement of these undetermined theoretical results, the policymaker is also given some empirical evidence that, with moderate inflation, the price stickiness hypothesis comes out better. However, he is also warned that during a hyperinflation the flexible price model is more appropriate. This, of course, helps but does not really settle the issue. Is a 20% rate of inflation, like Italy's, moderate? What if inflation reaches 40%? Can one count, for policy purposes, on the constancy of the degree of price stickiness, that is, can one rely on its econometric estimates? Is it by mere chance that the degree of price flexibility, as measured in table 13.6 of the paper, is lower in Germany than in the other four countries and the German Phillips curve is correspondingly flatter than in the other countries?

My questions is whether one could not use a model akin to that of Lucas to answer these points, relieve the policymaker of his dilemma, and get closer to the mythical figure of the "one-handed" economist who cannot present a conclusion with his left hand and its opposite with his right. In other words, what is wrong with the Lucas hypothesis, or some variant thereof, as a theory of price stickiness to be inserted in models of the exchange rate such as the Basevi and Calzolari one?

My second question has to do with the introduction of risk, exchange control, and transaction cost factors in the interest rate parity theory (IRPT) (eq. [1]) and in the expectation theory (ET) of the forward exchange rate (eq. [2]). As I understand it, Basevi and Calzolari assume that transaction costs and exchange controls impinge on the IRPT, while exchange risk impinges on the relationship between forward and expected exchange rates. I have some problems with this distinction. Of course, transaction costs impinge both on the IRPT and on the ET, and they are not trivial even for the latter. I have estimated (Papadia 1981) that the average transaction cost, measured as bid-ask interbank spread, on a forward operation is close to 0.4% for the lira, about 0.2% for the French franc and deutsche mark, and 0.1% for the pound. In addition, one must take into account the fact that the spread changes over time; for instance, on some turbulent days it exceeded 1% on lira-dollar contracts. As far as I know, the most straightforward way (Papadia 1981, pp. 224–25) to take transaction costs into account is to correct the average bid-ask quotes generally used as "forward rates" by adding the spread in the case of expected revaluation and by subtracting it in the case of expected devaluation. This procedure is based on the argument that in the case of expected devaluation one will sell the currency forward until the expected buy spot rate will be equal to today's forward selling rate and vice versa for a revaluation. We can then use the corrected data to make forward/spot rate comparisons.

Exchange controls also impinge on both operations, since foreign exchange transactions are included in both relationships, and one could attempt to measure their effect by the difference between national and international (Euro) rates of interest on similar assets. The issue of exchange risk is notoriously more complicated, and Basevi and Calzolari recognize this. If a satisfactory solution has been found to this problem, I am not aware of it. My question in this respect is whether one could not overlook, in a first approximation, risk factors which are not explicitly considered in the estimation, and try to take into account transaction costs and exchange controls' effects as indicated above. Basevi and Calzolari have substantially improved the estimation method between the version presented at the conference and the present version, and not much can be added here except that I have the suspicion that the residuals of the estimated regressions may not be homoscedastic. In particular, I suspect that the second half of the sample may be noisier than the first. A test to make sure that this is not the case would have been welcome.

References

Basevi, Giorgio, and Calzolari, Michele. 1982. Monetary authorities's reaction functions in a model of exchange rate determination for the European Monetary System. In *Exchange rates in multicountry econometric models* ed. P. De Grauwe and T. Peeters. London: Macmillan.

Blanchard, Olivier J., and Kahn, C. M. 1980. The solution of linear difference models under rational expectations. *Econometrica* 48:1305–11.

Dornbusch, Rudiger. 1976. Expectations and exchange rate dynamics. *Journal of Political Economy* 84:1161–76.

Driskill, R. A., and Sheffrin, S. M. 1981. On testing monetary models of exchange-rate determination. *American Economic Review* 71:1068–74.

Frankel, Jeffrey A. 1979. On the mark: A theory of floating exchange rates based on real interest differentials. *American Economic Review* 69:610–22.

———. 1981. On the mark: A response to various comments. *American Economic Review,* 71:1075–82.

Hooper, P., and Morton, J. 1980. Fluctuations in the dollar: A model of nominal and real exchange rate determination. Mimeographed. Federal Reserve Board, International Finance Discussion Paper, no. 168. October.

Keynes, John Maynard. 1936. *The general theory of employment, interest, and money.* London: Macmillan.

Lucas, Robert E., Jr. 1973. Some international evidence on output-inflation tradeoffs. *American Economic Review.* (June):326–34.

Papadia, Francesco. 1981. Forward exchange rates as predictors of future spot rates and the efficiency of the foreign exchange market. *Journal of Banking and Finance* 5:217–40.

VI Monetary Policy and Exchange Rates

14 Effects of United States Monetary Restraint on the DM/$ Exchange Rate and the German Economy

Jacques R. Artus

14.1 Introduction

This paper assesses the quantitative importance of the effects of a shift to a policy of monetary restraint in the United States on the deutsche mark–dollar (DM/$) exchange rate and the German economy. The paper was motivated by events in 1979–81, when a shift toward monetary restraint in the United States was accompanied by a sharp rise in United States interest rates and in the exchange rate of the United States dollar. This sharp rise is widely viewed as having placed pressures on other industrial countries, in particular Germany, to boost their interest rates in order to limit the depreciation of their currencies. However, it is uncertain exactly how much United States monetary restraint contributed to the appreciation of the United States dollar. It is also uncertain how great were the effects of the depreciation of the other currencies on their corresponding economies, and, therefore, how much constraint the United States policy of monetary restraint imposed on other national authorities. Finally, the costs and advantages of the decision made by other countries to largely match the rise in United States interest rates with a rise in their own interest rates have not been determined. The present paper aims at clarifying these issues, at least with respect to Germany.

Beyond these specific policy issues, the paper also aims at casting some light on a number of theoretical and empirical issues concerning the functioning and interdependence of industrial countries under floating exchange rates. In the area of wage and price formation, the main issues considered in the paper concern the formation of price expectations, the effect of wage

Financial support of the Ford Foundation is gratefully acknowledged.

469

and price long-term contracts, and the effect of variations in import prices. More specifically, the paper addresses itself to the following questions: Do private market participants form their price expectations on the basis of past price developments, or do they take into account information that they have on the monetary policy stance of the authorities? How quickly can changes in price expectations be reflected in actual wages and prices, given the existence of long-term wage and price contracts? Are changes in import prices reflected in wages and prices of domestically produced goods, either because of wage indexation or because of the effect of import prices on price expectations?

In the area of interest rate and output determination, the main issue concerns the effect of monetary policy on interest rates. The crucial question here is whether a reduction in money growth leads to a rapid decrease in interest rates because of reduced inflationary expectations, or whether it may in fact lead to an increase in interest rates for a sustained period of time because of a liquidity squeeze. The squeeze could result from the persistence of inflation either because monetary restraint has no effect on price expectations or because long-term contracts prevent wages and prices from adjusting rapidly. Thus, the interest rate issue is closely related to the issue of price formation. It also has direct implications for output, because an increase in interest rates at a time when inflationary expectations are constant or declining will lead to a reduction in the demand for investment goods and consumer durables, and ultimately to a decline in overall output.

These various theoretical and empirical issues have further implications for the exchange rate determination process. If interest rates rise in real terms, and a fortiori in nominal terms, as a result of a reduction in money growth, the exchange rate may shoot upward at first as a result of the rise in the uncovered interest rate differentials. If output declines, the current account surplus may gradually increase, possibly causing a further appreciation of the exchange rate. The first overshooting effect depends on how persistent the rise in interest rates is expected to be. The second overshooting effect depends both on whether the substitution among assets denominated in different currencies is small and on whether private market participants view new data on the current account balance as containing new information on where the real exchange rate will have to be in the longer run to yield a "reasonable" current balance outturn. The paper examines how large these overshooting effects are and how they may affect domestic inflation.

To deal with these issues, the paper uses a model of a monetary economy developed in Artus (1981). Section 14.2 briefly reviews the main characteristics of this model. Section 14.3 presents the results of the estimation of the parameters of this model for Germany from data through the second quarter of 1981. One of the main findings, consistent with results of a number of previous studies, is that the DM/$ exchange rate is quite sensitive to changes in uncovered interest rate differentials and to inflation rate differentials and current balance developments. A shift to monetary restraint in the United States will influence all these variables and therefore the DM/$ exchange rate. Nevertheless, only a small part of the depreciation of the deutsche mark vis-à-vis the United States dollar in the course of 1980 and the first two quarters of 1981 can be explained by the effects of United States monetary restraint. A large residual remains that for lack of a better name I shall call the "Reagan effect."

Section 14.4 presents the results of five simulations made with the model. The first three simulations concern the effects of United States monetary restraint on Germany. The first simulation assumes that neither the German monetary authorities nor the monetary authorities of other industrial countries change their policies to counter the tendency toward a depreciation of their exchange rates vis-à-vis the United States dollar. The second simulation assumes that the German monetary authorities do not change their policies, while the monetary authorities of other industrial countries change their policies to offset the effect of United States monetary restraint on their exchange rates vis-à-vis the United States dollar. The third simulation assumes that both the German monetary authorities and the monetary authorities of other industrial countries change their monetary policies. In the next two simulations, the consequences of the Reagan effect on Germany are simulated under the assumption that neither Germany nor other industrial countries change their monetary policies, then under the assumption that they all shift to a policy of monetary restraint to offset the consequences of the Reagan effect on their exchange rates.

Finally, section 14.5 summarizes some of the conclusions that can be drawn from this study with respect to international economic interdependence under floating exchange rates.

14.2 The Model

The model developed in Artus (1981) and used in this paper with a few modifications is composed of three blocks of equations: a price block, an output block, and an exchange rate block. The equations are reproduced in table 14.1 and described briefly below.

The price block differentiates between short-run inflationary expectations (for the next quarter) and long-run inflationary expectations (for the next year and a half). Short-run inflationary expectations are assumed to be formed on the basis of recent inflationary developments, while long-run inflationary expectations are assumed to reflect the long-run expected rate of growth of money (for the next year and a half). The assumption underlying this specification is that, in the short run, the relation between money and prices is too tenuous to yield efficient forecasts; private market participants can do better by extrapolating recent inflationary developments. However,

Table 14.1   **Model of a Monetary Economy** ^{a}

Equations

Price block:^{b}

(1) $\dot{m}^{el} = \sum_j \alpha_{1,j}\dot{m}_{-j} - \alpha_2(y - \bar{y})_{-1} - \alpha_3 z_2$

(2) $\dot{p}^{el} = \alpha_5 + \dot{m}^{el} - \dot{\bar{y}}$

(3) $\dot{p}^{es} = \sum_j \alpha_{6,j}\dot{p}_{-j+1}$

(4) $\dot{p}_d^{es} = \sum_j \alpha_{7,j}\dot{p}_{d,-j+1}$

(5) $\dot{p}_d = \alpha_8 + \sum_j \alpha_{9,j}\dot{p}^{el}_{-j} + \sum_j \alpha_{10,j}(y - \bar{y})_{-j}$

(6) $\dot{p} = \alpha_{11}\dot{p}_d + (1 - \alpha_{11})(\dot{p}_m - \dot{e})$

Output block:

(7) $i^l = \alpha_{12} - \alpha_{13}(m - p) + \alpha_{14}y + \alpha_{15}\dot{p}^{el} + \alpha_{16}t + \alpha_{17}(\dot{p}^{es} - \dot{p}^{el})$

(8) $y = \bar{y} + \alpha_{18} + \sum_j \alpha_{19,j}(i^l - \dot{p}^{el})_{-j}$

                $+ \sum_j \alpha_{20,j}[\alpha_{21}\bar{g} + (1 - \alpha_{21})\bar{x}]_{-j}$

(9) $\bar{g} = g - \sum_j \alpha_{22,j}g_{-j}$

(10) $\bar{x} = x - \sum_j \alpha_{23,j}x_{-j}$

Exchange rate block:

(11) $\dot{e} = -(\dot{p}_d^{es} - \dot{p}_{d,\text{U.S.}}^{es}) + \alpha_{24} + \alpha_{25}(\Delta i^s - \Delta i_{\text{U.S.}}^s) + \alpha_{26}[(b - b_{\text{U.S.}})$

                $+ (b - b_{\text{U.S.}})_{-1}]/2$

---

^{a}All variables denoted by small letters are in logs, except for the interest rates (i^s and i^l), the change in foreign assets ($\dot{r}$), and the dummy variables (z_1 and z_2).

The various signs must be interpreted as follows: a dot ($\cdot$) denotes the rate of change of the variable (i.e., $\dot{m} = m - m_{-1}$, with m and m_{-1} in logs); a delta (Δ) signifies that the variable is considered in first-difference terms (i.e., $\Delta\dot{m} = \dot{m} - \dot{m}_{-1}$); a superscript ($el$) denotes the long-run expected value of the variable (i.e., $\dot{m}^{el}$ = the rate of growth of money expected to prevail on average from period t to period $t + 6$ at the time of period t); a superscript (es) denotes the short-run expected values of the variable (i.e., $\dot{p}^{es}$ = rate of increase of domestic demand deflator expected to prevail from period t to period $t + 1$ at the time of period t); a tilde ($\tilde{\ }$) signifies that the variable is expressed in terms of deviation from an average of past values; and, finally, an asterisk ($*$) signifies that the variable refers to the industrial world, minus the Federal Republic of Germany, while a subscript U.S. signifies that the variable refers to the United States. All variables are expressed in deutsche marks, except for the deflator of imports (p_m) and the variables referring to the rest of the industrial world or to the United States that are expressed in United States dollars.

^{b}The coefficients of equation (1) are to be derived by estimating the coefficients of

(1') $\sum_{k=1}^{k=6} \dot{m}_k /6 = \sum_{j=1}^{j=n} \alpha_{1,j}\dot{m}_{-j} - \alpha_2(y - \bar{y})_{-1} - \alpha_3 z_1 - \alpha_4 \sum_{k=1}^{k=6} \dot{r}_k/6$

while the coefficients of equations (3) and (4) are to be derived, respectively, from the estimation of the coefficients of

(3') $\dot{p} = \sum_{j=1}^{i=n} \alpha_{6,j}\dot{p}_{-j}$

and

(4') $\dot{p} = \sum_{j=1}^{j=n} \alpha_{7,j}\dot{p}_{d,-j}.$

Table 14.1   (continued)

(12) $i^s = i^l - \alpha_{27} - \alpha_{28}(m - p) + \alpha_{29}y + \alpha_{30}(\dot{p}^{es} - \dot{p}\dot{e}^{el})$

(13) $x = \alpha_{31} - \alpha_{32}(y - \bar{y}) + \alpha_{33}(y^* - \bar{y}^*) - \sum_j \alpha_{34,j}(p_d - p_d^* + e)_{-j}$

(14) $b = x + p_d - p_m + e.$

List of Variables

Endogenous variables: b, e, $\bar{g}$, i^l, i^s, m^{el}, p_d, p, p^{el}, p^{es}, p_d^{es}, x, $\bar{x}$, y.
Exogenous variables: $b_{U.S.}$, g, $i^s_{U.S.}$, m, p_d^*, $p_{d,U.S.}^{es}$, p_m, t, $\bar{y}$, $\bar{y}^*$, y^*, z_2.

Notation

b = current balance defined as the ratio of exports of goods and services over imports of goods and services

e = nominal exchange rate (value of 1 DM in terms of United States cents)

g = real government expenditures

i^l = long-term interest rate (yield on industrial bonds outstanding)

i^s = short-term interest rate (3-month deposits in local money market)

m = base money adjusted for changes in reserve requirements

p = domestic demand deflator

p_d = GDP deflator

p_m = deflator of import of goods and services (in United States dollars)

$\dot{r}$ = change in net foreign assets component of base money scaled by the proportion of base money accounted for by the net foreign asset component in the previous period

t = time trend

x = ratio of the volume of exports of goods and services to the volume of imports of goods and services

y = GDP (real terms)
$\bar{y}$ = potential GDP (real terms)

z_1, z_2 = dummy variables for announced changes in the stance of monetary policy (see text)

---

in the long run, the amount of money and the overall price level are clearly related, and it makes sense to accept the view that inflationary expectations reflect the monetary policy stance of the authorities as it is perceived by private market participants.[1]

It is the long-run expected rate of inflation that enters the Phillips curve equation. Furthermore, it does so in the form of a distributed lag. The assumption is that participants in labor markets enter into long-run contractual wage arrangements that specify the rate of increase of money wage rates. In each quarter, the arrangements being entered into reflect the expected long-run rate of inflation prevailing at the time.[2] Therefore, in any given quarter

---

1. This view was developed, in particular, by Lucas (1972, 1975), Sargent and Wallace (1975), and Barro (1978).
2. Most of the labor contracts in Germany are for a period of 1 year and require a few months of negotiations, so that the 6-quarter period chosen to evaluate the expected long-run rate of inflation seems adequate.

the increase in the average money wage rate for the whole economy reflects an average of the expected long-run rates of inflation prevailing in a number of past quarters. The behavior of the GDP deflator is assumed to follow the behavior of the average money wage rate. The important consequence of that specification is that, even if an unexpected policy change is immediately reflected in a change in money growth expectations, it will only lead to a gradual change in the actual rate of inflation.

From an empirical standpoint, the difficulty is to find a proxy for the long-run expected rate of growth of money. The standard procedure to derive estimates for the expected rate of growth of money is to assume that the monetary authorities react with a lag to values taken by certain target variables, such as the GDP gap. In each period, the parameters of the policy reaction function can be estimated from the use of past observations on the relevant target variables. The estimates are then used to calculate a proxy for the expected rate of growth of money for the next period on the basis of past and present values of the target variables.[3] I employ this method in the present model with two important modifications. The first is that the policy reaction function (equation [1'] in note b to table 14.1) aims at explaining the average rate of growth of money over overlapping 6-quarter periods. This modification is needed because the proxy that is sought is for the long-run rate of growth of money (over the next year and a half).

The second modification is that two variables that are concurrent with the money growth being explained are introduced in the policy reaction function. The first variable (z_1) is a dummy that identifies the change in the rate of growth of money that tends to follow the announcement of a major discretionary policy change.[4] The effect of the announcement on money growth expectations in equation (1) of table 14.1 is then related to the magnitude of the actual change in the rate of money growth that tended to follow similar announcements in the past. The second concurrent variable introduced in the policy reaction function is the amount of foreign exchange market intervention. In calculating the expected growth rate of money, it is then assumed that private market participants do not anticipate the money growth that results from foreign exchange market intervention because of the erratic nature of this intervention, so that this latter variable can be ignored. In brief, variations in money growth related to exchange market intervention are considered to be unanticipated. The introduction of these two concurrent variables into the policy reaction function allows for a better identification of the unanticipated component of money growth and helps to alleviate some of the identification problems that arise in the estimation of the model.[5]

3. Lagged money growth rates are usually included in the policy reaction function because they may contain information on the normal behavior of the authorities that cannot be readily derived from the way they react to values assumed by specific target variables.

4. See the Appendix for a detailed explanation concerning the use of the z_1 variable in equation (1') and the corresponding z_2 variable in equation (1).

5. For a discussion of these identification problems, see Germany and Srivastava (1979) and Buiter (1980).

The output block assumes that, given a certain level of potential output, the long-term real interest rate and the impulse's coming from real government expenditures and foreign trade determine actual output. The interest rate effect on output is expected to take place with a substantial lag because investment reacts slowly. It takes time to decide on and plan capital projects, and it is costly to stop them before completion. If the impulse comes from real government expenditures and foreign trade, we can expect its effect to be more rapid because no similar lags are involved. At the same time, the model assumes that the effect of this impulse is temporary. Both real government expenditures and the ratio of exports over imports (in volume terms) are introduced in the form of deviations from past tendencies, so that any increase in the growth rate of these variables has first a positive impulse effect on output growth and then a negative effect of equal magnitude spread over time.

The long-run expected rate of inflation having already been determined, the determination of the long-term real interest rate requires only the specification of an equation for the long-term nominal interest rate. This is done by inverting a demand-for-money equation in which the long-term rate of interest represents the opportunity cost of holding money. In the resulting equation (7), it is expected that a lower real money stock leads, by itself, to a higher nominal interest rate, while the sign of the coefficient of the expected long-run inflation term is indeterminate.[6] The last term in equation (7) represents an expected liquidity squeeze or glut, which should have a positive coefficient. As explained in Artus (1981), when a shift to monetary restraint leads to a downward shift in the long-run expected growth rate of money, the slow speed of price adjustment will lead private market participants to expect that the real money stock is going to decline. The excess of the short-run over the long-run expected inflation rate will indicate how severe the liquidity squeeze is likely to become in forthcoming quarters. If this excess is large, private market participants will bid up the interest rate in anticipation of the forthcoming squeeze.

The exchange rate block is based on the asset market theory of exchange rate determination. In the equation that explains the change in the DM/$ exchange rate, the three explanatory variables are the expected inflation rate differential, the change in the uncovered short-term interest rate differential, and the relative current balance position of Germany and the United States.[7] A derivation of this equation was presented in Artus (1981, appendix 1). One of the results of the derivation was that the introduction of the relative current balance position could be justified on two grounds. First, the substitutability of domestic and foreign securities may be limited. For example, if Germany has a large current balance deficit, the spot value of the deutsche

6. See Artus (1981, note 12, p. 508), for a discussion of the sign of the coefficient of the expected long-run inflation term.

7. For the sake of convenience, the current balance variables are expressed as ratios of exports of goods and services over imports of goods and services in logarithmic form.

mark vis-à-vis foreign currencies may have to decline in comparison with its expected future value in order to induce private market participants abroad to increase the share of the deutsche-mark-denominated securities in their portfolios. Second, private market participants may view new data on the current balance as containing new information on where the exchange rate should be in the future and therefore, because of interest rate arbitrage, where it should be in the present.[8]

To complete the exchange rate block, it remains to determine the short-term interest rate and the current balance. The short-term interest rate is determined by specifying an equation for the term structure of interest rate. In this equation, the excess of the short-term interest rate over the long-term interest rate is related to a constant, the real money stock, the real GDP, and the excess of the short-run expected rate of inflation over the long-run expected rate of inflation. The constant measures the liquidity premium and is expected to be negative. The current balance is determined by relating the ratio of exports over imports (in volume terms) to relative real GDP levels and relative GDP deflators in Germany and in the rest of industrial countries. For simplification purposes, the German GDP deflator is taken as a proxy for the deflator of German exports expressed in deutsche marks, while the deflator of German imports expressed in United States dollars is taken as exogenous.

14.3 Econometric Results

Table 14.2 presents the regression results obtained by using quarterly observations and two-stage least squares regression methods to estimate the parameters of the model.[9] The estimation period extends from the third quarter of 1964 to the second quarter of 1981. Two exceptions are equations (1'), (3'), and (4'), which were estimated for each quarter t using observations on the period extending from the first quarter of 1955 to t,[10] and equations (7), (11), and (12), which were estimated from observations on the

---

8. An attempt was made in Artus (1981) to differentiate between these two effects of the current balance by introducing the change in the current balance in the exchange rate equation. This change was viewed as a proxy for unanticipated current balance developments on the grounds that quarterly changes in the current balance are difficult to forecast. The level of the current balance was then assumed to identify the effect of the limited asset substitutability. However, in the empirical analysis, the coefficient of the change in the current balance was found to be small and not significantly different from zero at the 5% significance level, while the coefficient of the level of the current balance was found to be large and significant. This result could be interpreted as suggesting that either the limited-substitutability effect was the important one, or that even the level of the current balance was difficult to anticipate and came often as a "surprise." In the present study, the effect of the change in the current balance was again found to be not significant, and this variable was dropped from the exchange rate equation.

9. The sources of the data are described in Artus (1981, appendix II).

10. The regression results indicated in table 14.2 for equations (1'), (3'), and (4') are those based on the full sample period extending to the second quarter of 1981.

Table 14.2   **Empirical Results**[a]

Price block:

(1') $\sum_{k=1}^{k=6} \dot{m}_k/6 = \sum_j \alpha_{1,j}\dot{m}_{-j} - .0360\ (y - \bar{y})_{-1} - .0072\ z_1 + .1116\ \sum_{k=1}^{k=6} \dot{r}_k/6$

                           (.0163)   (.0011)   (.0164)

$\alpha_{1,1} = .055$	$\alpha_{1,5} = .139$
$\alpha_{1,2} = .154$	$\alpha_{1,6} = .163$
$\alpha_{1,3} = .104$	$\alpha_{1,7} = .143$
$\alpha_{1,4} = .103$	$\alpha_{1,8} = \underline{.072}$
	Total = .933 (.037)
	Mean lag = 4.648 (.782)

$\bar{R}^2 = .959$, SEE = .0047, D-W = .392.

(1) $\dot{m}^{el} = \sum_j \hat{\alpha}_{1,j}\dot{m}_{-j} - .0360\ (y - \bar{y})_{-1} - .0072\ z_2$

(2) $\dot{p}^{el} = .00^b + \dot{m}^{el} - \dot{\bar{y}}$

(3') $\dot{p} = \sum_j \alpha_{6,j}\dot{p}_{-j}$

$\alpha_{6,1} = .123$	$\alpha_{6,4} = .360$
$\alpha_{6,2} = .166$	$\alpha_{6,5} = .163$
$\alpha_{6,3} = .255$	$\alpha_{6,6} = -.048$
	$\alpha_{6,7} = \underline{-.062}$
	Total = .957 (.104)
	Mean lag = 2.877 (.721)

$\bar{R}^2 = .399$, SEE = .0069, D-W = 1.999.

(3) $\dot{p}^{es} = \sum_j \hat{\alpha}_{6,j}\dot{p}_{-j+1}$

(4') $\dot{p}_d = \sum_j \alpha_{7,j}\dot{p}_{d,-j}$

$\alpha_{7,1} = .258$	$\alpha_{7,4} = .298$
$\alpha_{7,2} = .174$	$\alpha_{7,5} = .103$
$\alpha_{7,3} = .051$	$\alpha_{7,6} = -.012$
	$\alpha_{7,7} = \underline{.052}$
	Total = .948 (.106)
	Mean lag = 3.061 (.641)

$\bar{R}^2 = .326$, SEE = .0070, D-W = 1.989.

[a]The period covered by the left-hand-side variables extends from the third quarter of 1964 to the second quarter of 1981, except for equations (1'), (3'), (4'), (7), (11), and (12). As explained in the text, the parameters of equations (1'), (3'), and (4') are estimated for each period t on the basis of observations for the period extending from the first quarter of 1955 to t. To save space, the results are presented here only for the regression equations covering the period extending from the first quarter of 1955 to the second quarter of 1981. The parameters of equations (7), (11), and (12) are estimates from observations on the flexible exchange rate period extending from the fourth quarter of 1973 to the second quarter of 1981. Standard errors of the estimated values of the parameters are shown in parentheses below the coefficients. SEE denotes standard error of the estimate. D-W denotes the Durbin-Watson statistic. Columns may not add to totals shown because of rounding.

[b]$-.05$ from 1976 to 1979.

[c]Almon constraint: polynomial of degree 3, without zero constraint.

[d]Almon constraint: polynomial of degree 3, zero constraint at the end.

[e]Almon constraint: polynomial of degree 3, zero constraints at the beginning and end.

Table 14.2   (continued)

(4) $\dot{p}_d^{es} = \sum_j \hat{\alpha}_{7,j} \dot{p}_{d,-j+1}$

(5) $\dot{p}_d = .0036 + \sum_j \alpha_{9,j} \dot{p}_{-j}^{el} + \sum_j \alpha_{10,j}(y - \bar{y})_{-j} + .0092\, d_1$

  (.0030)   (.0021)

$\quad + .245 \sum_{j=0}^{j=-6} (\dot{p}_m - \dot{e})_j/6$

  (.065)

$\alpha_{9,0} =$	$.422^c$	$\alpha_{10,0} =$	$.017^d$
$\alpha_{9,1} =$	.039	$\alpha_{10,1} =$	.029
$\alpha_{9,2} =$	.025	$\alpha_{10,2} =$	.034
$\alpha_{9,3} =$	.212	$\alpha_{10,3} =$	.033
$\alpha_{9,4} =$	.421	$\alpha_{10,4} =$	.027
$\alpha_{9,5} =$	.349	$\alpha_{10,5} =$	.019
$\alpha_{9,6} =$	$\underline{-.255}$	$\alpha_{10,6} =$	$\underline{.009}$
Total $=$	1.085 (.372)	.168	(.051)
Mean lag $=$	2.253 (1.246)	2.698	(1.186)

$\bar{R}^e = 435$, SEE $= .0054$, D-W $= 1.950$.

(6) $\dot{p} = 0.726\, \dot{p}_d + 0.274\, (\dot{p}_m - \dot{e})$

Output block:

(7) $i^l = -.0025 - .0654\,(m - p) + .0569\, y - .084\, \dot{p}^{el} - .00006\, t$
  (.0696) (.0163)   (.0203)   (.124)   (.00013)

$\quad + .190\,(\dot{p}^{es} - \dot{p}^{el})$
  (.127)

$\bar{R}^2 = .879$,   SEE $= .0014$,   D-W $= .992$.

(8) $y = \bar{y} - .0083 + \sum_j \alpha_{19,j}\,(i^l - \dot{p}^{el})_{-j} + \sum_j \alpha_{20,j}(.41\bar{g} + 0.59\bar{x})_{-j}$

  (.0136)

$\quad + \sum_j \beta_{1,j}(.0092\, d_1 + .245 \sum_{j=0}^{j=-6} (\dot{p}_m - \dot{e})_j/6)_{-j}$

$\alpha_{19,0} =$	$-.093^e$	$\beta_{1,0} =$	$.015^d$	$\alpha_{20,0} =$	.294
$\alpha_{19,1} =$	$-.354$	$\beta_{1,1} =$	.251	$\alpha_{20,1} =$	$\underline{.040}$
$\alpha_{19,2} =$	$-.546$	$\beta_{1,2} =$	.429	Total $=$	.334 (.052)
$\alpha_{19,3} =$	$-.676$	$\beta_{1,3} =$	.555	Mean lag $=$	.120 (.041)
$\alpha_{19,4} =$	$-.753$	$\beta_{1,4} =$	.635		
$\alpha_{19,5} =$	$-.782$	$\beta_{1,5} =$	.674		
$\alpha_{19,6} =$	$-.771$	$\beta_{1,6} =$	.677		
$\alpha_{19,7} =$	$-.726$	$\beta_{1,7} =$	.649		
$\alpha_{19,8} =$	$-.655$	$\beta_{1,8} =$	.597		
$\alpha_{19,9} =$	$-.564$	$\beta_{1,9} =$	.526		
$\alpha_{19,10} =$	$-.461$	$\beta_{1,10} =$	.441		
$\alpha_{19,11} =$	$-.352$	$\beta_{1,11} =$	.348		
$\alpha_{19,12} =$	$-.245$	$\beta_{1,12} =$	.251		
$\alpha_{19,13} =$	$-.146$	$\beta_{1,13} =$	.158		
$\alpha_{19,14} =$	$\underline{-.062}$	$\beta_{1,14} =$	$\underline{.072}$		
Total $=$	-7.197 (1.207)	6.279 (1.029)			
Mean lag $=$	6.208 (1.263)	6.548 (1.643)			

$\bar{R}^2 = .886$, SEE $= .0079$, D-W $= 1.889$, RHO $= .593$.

Table 14.2   (continued)

$$(9)\ \tilde{g} = g - \left(\sum_{j=1}^{j=12} .9^j g_{-j} \Big/ \sum_{j=1}^{j=12} .9^j \right)$$

$$(10)\ \tilde{x} = x - \left(\sum_{j=1}^{j=12} .9^j x_{-j} \Big/ \sum_{j=1}^{j=12} .9^j \right)$$

Exchange rate block:

$(11)\ \dot{e} = -(\dot{p}_d^{es} - \dot{p}_{d,\text{U.S.}}^{es}) - .0396 + 1.371\ (\Delta i^s - \Delta i_{\text{U.S.}}^s)$
$\qquad\qquad\qquad\qquad (.0103)\quad (.822)$
$\qquad\qquad + 2.406\ (\Delta i^s - \Delta i_{\text{U.S.}}^s)_{-1} + .243\ [(b - b_{\text{U.S.}}) + (b - b_{\text{U.S.}})_{-1}]/2$
$\qquad\qquad\quad (.797) \qquad\qquad\qquad\qquad (.054)$
$\qquad\qquad - .027\ d_3 - .062\ d_4 - .065\ d_5$
$\qquad\qquad\quad (.010)\quad\ (.022)\quad\ \ (.019)$
$\bar{R}^2 = .728$, SEE $= .0250$, D-W $= 2.022$.

$(12)\ i^s = i^l - .3641 - .0188\ (m - p) + .0826\ y + .258\ (\dot{p}^{es} - p^{el})$
$\qquad\qquad\quad (.0491)\ \ (.0158) \qquad\qquad (.0204)\quad (.084)$
$\bar{R}^2 = .815$, SEE $= .0012$, D-W $= 1.714$, RHO $= .498$

$(13)\ x = .6166 - 1.585\ (y - \bar{y}) + .952\ (y^* - \bar{y}^*) - \sum_j \alpha_{34,j}(p_d - p_d^* + e)_{-j}$
$\qquad\quad (.1024)\ \ (.308) \qquad\qquad (.163)$

$\qquad + .0598\ d_4$
$\qquad\quad (.0112)$

$\alpha_{34,0} = -.222^c$	$\alpha_{34,9} = -.066$
$\alpha_{34,1} = -.144$	$\alpha_{34,10} = -.081$
$\alpha_{34,2} = -.087$	$\alpha_{34,11} = -.093$
$\alpha_{34,3} = -.050$	$\alpha_{34,12} = -.098$
$\alpha_{34,4} = -.029$	$\alpha_{34,13} = -.093$
$\alpha_{34,5} = -.021$	$\alpha_{34,14} = -.075$
$\alpha_{34,6} = -.024$	$\alpha_{34,15} = -.042$
$\alpha_{34,7} = -.034$	$\alpha_{34,16} = \underline{-\ .010}$
$\alpha_{34,8} = -.049$	Total $= -1.198\ (.258)$
	Mean lag $=\quad 6.509\ (2.095)$

$\bar{R}^2 = .634$, SEE $= .0351$, D-W $= 1.331$.

$(14)\ b = x + p_d - p_m + e.$

floating rate period extending from the fourth quarter of 1973 to the second quarter of 1981. On the whole, the results were similar to those obtained in Artus (1981) for periods with identical starting points but ending in the fourth quarter of 1979. However, there were several important differences.

In the price block, the results obtained for the equations that are used to estimate proxies for inflationary expectations remained similar to those obtained previously. In brief, long-run money growth expectations, and therefore long-run inflationary expectations, are deemed to adjust slowly to actual changes in the rate of growth of money, but they also are deemed to be influenced directly by announcements of major policy changes. Short-run inflationary expectations are deemed to adjust slowly to actual changes in inflation rates.

The results for the Phillips curve equations are also similar to those obtained previously. In particular, the sum of the coefficients on the expectation term is not significantly different from one, but a large part of the effect comes with a significant lag. It takes about 5 quarters for the total effect to take place, which is consistent with the a priori knowledge that most labor contracts in Germany cover a period of 1 year. Similarly, it takes a long time for the output gap to affect the rate of inflation. Furthermore, in this case, even the final effect is not large. Ultimately, an increase of 1 percentage point in the gap between actual and potential GDP reduces the quarterly rate of inflation by 0.17 (0.05) percentage point,[11] or the annual rate by about 0.68 (0.20) percentage point. As in Artus (1981), variables outside the monetary field had to be introduced into the regression equation to account for certain developments. The surge of inflation in 1968–71 is still explained by introducing a dummy variable of the zero-one type. However, contrary to that previous study, the surge of inflation in 1973–75 is no longer explained by the introduction of a dummy variable. Instead, a variable measuring the average change in import prices during the preceding 6 quarters performs that function. The introduction of import prices had not been successful previously, possibly because, except for 1973–75, import prices in deutsche marks were not increasing rapidly during the sample period. It is only when introducing 1980 and the first half of 1981, which were characterized by rapidly increasing import prices in deutsche marks, that the coefficient of the import price variable became relatively large and statistically significant.[12]

These results suggest that German real wage rates are somewhat rigid.[13] For example, a 10% deterioration in the terms of trade due to an increase in import prices will lead to a 2.5% increase in the GDP deflator, presumably because of an increase in nominal wage rates. Given a constant money growth rate, the growth of real GDP will start to decline. But, for many years, the resulting rise in the output gap will fail to bring the decline in real wage rates necessary to restore domestic equilibrium at full employment.

In the output block, the addition of observations for 1980 and the first half of 1981 allows a better identification of the effects of changes in the real money stock on the long-term rate of interest. The coefficient of the real money stock, contrary to previous results, is now statistically significant and is large in magnitude. A 1% reduction in the real money stock is found to lead to an increase of 0.065 percentage point in the long-term interest rate at a quarterly rate, or 0.26 percentage point at an annual rate.[14] The

11. The standard error of the estimate is indicated in parentheses.
12. The expression statistically significant is used in this paper as an abbreviation for "significantly different from zero at the 5% significance level."
13. A similar conclusion is reached in Branson and Rotemberg (1980).
14. The implied elasticity of money with respect to the long-term interest rate is 0.4.

other results in the long-term interest rate equation remained unchanged. In particular, the coefficient of the long-run expected rate of inflation is small and not statistically significant. The coefficient of the expected liquidity-squeeze variable is positive as expected, but also not statistically significant. Together, the two latter coefficients imply that a 1 percentage point decrease in the long-run expected inflation rate initially leads to a 0.27 percentage point *increase* in the long-term nominal interest rate and therefore to a 1.27 percentage point increase in the long-term real interest rate.

The results for the output equation were not affected by the updating. The long-term real interest rate is still found to have a gradual, but ultimately large, effect on output. After 3½ years, an increase in the interest rate of 1 percentage point at a quarterly rate (or 4 percentage points at an annual rate) is found to result in a 7.2% decline in real GDP. By contrast, the impulse effect of an additional 1% increase in real government expenditures and in the ratio of exports over imports in volume terms leads to a 0.33 (0.05)% increase in real GDP after 2 quarters, while government expenditures and exports per se account for about 45% of GDP.

In the exchange rate block, the coefficients of the exchange rate equation were first estimated without making any attempt to isolate the effects of major disturbances such as the oil embargo. The results were as follows:

$$\dot{e} = -(\dot{p}_d^{es} - \dot{p}_{d,U.S.}^{es}) - \underset{(0.0129)}{0.0506} + \underset{(1.016)}{2.799} \,(\Delta i^s - \Delta i_{U.S.}^s)$$
$$+ \underset{(1.026)}{3.209} \,(\Delta i^s - \Delta i_{U.S.}^s)_{-1}$$
$$+ \underset{(.069)}{0.294} \,[(b - b_{U.S.}) + (b - b_{U.S.})_{-1})]/2,$$
$$\overline{R}^2 = .509, \text{ SEE} = .0336, \text{ D-W} = 1.670.$$

While the estimates of the coefficients have the expected signs and are statistically significant, the regression equation explains only 51% of the variations in the exchange rate. The plot of actual and estimated values presented in figure 14.1, part A, clearly shows that the large residuals are to be found in three periods, which follow the oil embargo in late 1973, the collapse of the Herstatt bank in mid-1974, and the election of Ronald Reagan in late 1980.[15] When dummy variables were included for these factors,[16] table 14.2 show that the estimates of the coefficients were not sig-

15. The first half of 1981 was certainly influenced by many factors other than the election of Ronald Reagan, including political problems in Germany and the crisis in Poland, but the anticipation of a new U.S. policy strategy, especially in the fiscal area, was probably the dominant factor.

16. The dummy variable for the oil embargo takes the value 0.5 in the fourth quarter of 1973, 1.5 in the first quarter of 1974, -2 in the second quarter of 1974, and zero otherwise. The dummy variable for the collapse of the Herstaff bank takes the value one in the third quarter of 1974, -0.5 in the fourth quarter of 1974, -0.5 in the first quarter of 1975, and zero otherwise. Finally, the dummy variable for the election of Ronald Reagan takes the value one in the first 2 quarters of 1981 and zero otherwise.

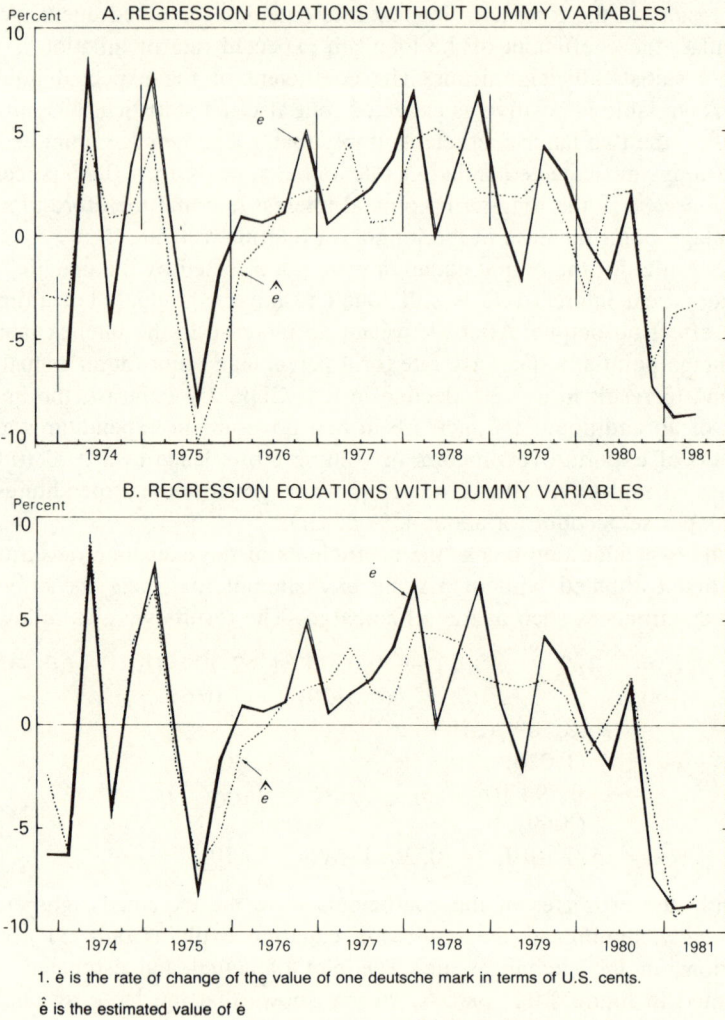

Percent   A. REGRESSION EQUATIONS WITHOUT DUMMY VARIABLES[1]

$\dot{e}$

$\hat{\dot{e}}$

Percent   B. REGRESSION EQUATIONS WITH DUMMY VARIABLES

$\dot{e}$

$\hat{\dot{e}}$

1. $\dot{e}$ is the rate of change of the value of one deutsche mark in terms of U.S. cents.

$\hat{\dot{e}}$ is the estimated value of $\dot{e}$

Fig. 14.1   Actual and estimated values of the change in the DM/$ exchange rate.

nificantly affected, but that their standard errors were greatly reduced. The explanatory power of the equation increased sharply, with 73% of the variations in the exchange rate now accounted for. (See fig. 14.1, part B, for the residuals in the new regression equation.) The results of this latter equation will be used in the rest of this study; they are roughly similar to those obtained in Artus (1981) as far as interest rate and current balance effects are concerned.

The interesting implication of these results is that about half of the 29% depreciation of the deutsche mark against the United States dollar from the fourth quarter of 1979 to the second quarter of 1981 is due to what we have called the "Reagan effect" (see fig. 14.2). The other significant factor during this period is the worsening of the German current balance relative to the United States current balance. Contrary to what is commonly thought, changes in interest rates do not account for much of the net change in the exchange rate from the fourth quarter of 1979 to the second quarter of 1981, mainly because the rise in United States real interest rates was soon offset by an equivalent rise in German interest rates. But the pattern of quarterly changes in the DM/$ exchange rate was strongly influenced by changes in interest rates.

The results for the two remaining regression equations in the exchange

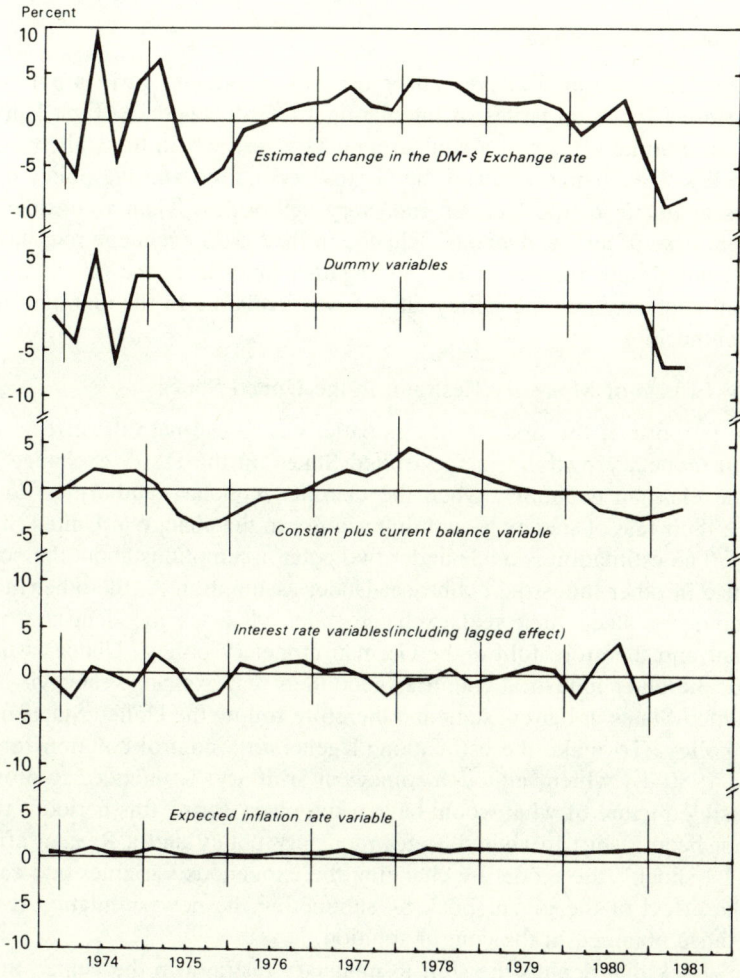

Fig. 14.2   Contributions to the estimated value of the change in the DM/$ exchange rate (these results refer to the regression equation with dummy variables).

rate block call for only brief comments. The results of the equation for the short-term interest rate are reasonable. There is a significant liquidity premium indicated by the negative constant. As expected, an increase in the real money stock decreases the short-term rate by comparison with the long-term rate, while an increase in economic activity increases the short-term rate by comparison with the long-term rate. An excess of the short-run over the long-run expected rate of inflation is reflected by an excess of the short-term over the long-term interest rate. Finally, the trade equation remains characterized, as previously, by a sum of the export and import price elasticities that exceeds one only after a lag of about 3 years.

14.4 Policy Simulations

The model estimated above can be used to investigate various policy issues. Here I focus on issues of international interdependence. First I investigate the normal effects of a shift to monetary restraint in the United States on the DM/$ exchange rate and the German economy, and the policy alternatives available to the German monetary authorities. Then I consider the different case of an "exogenous" change in the DM/$ exchange rate, taking as an example the Reagan effect, and again I investigate the effects on the German economy and the policy alternatives available to the German monetary authorities.

14.4.1 Effects of Monetary Restraint in the United States

The purpose of the first set of simulations is to estimate the effects of a shift to monetary restraint in the United States on the DM/$ exchange rate and the German economy, when the German monetary authorities do not change their rate of money growth in response to the change in United States policy. The estimation is made under two polar assumptions about the policy response in other industrial countries. Under assumption A, the other industrial countries keep their real exchange rates vis-à-vis the deutsche mark constant and therefore follow the German monetary policy. Under assumption B, the other industrial countries keep their real exchange rates vis-à-vis the United States dollar constant and therefore follow the United States monetary policy. To make the estimation, I generate a control solution for the period 1980–84 which, although somewhat arbitrary, is intended to provide a plausible picture of what would have taken place during this period if there had not been a shift in United States monetary policy and a Reagan effect. Then I "shock" the model by changing the exogenous variables and calculate the effect of the given shock by subtracting the new simulation results from those obtained in the control solution.

The shock that depicts the shift to monetary restraint in the United States is represented in figure 14.3. The short-term interest rate (at a quarterly rate) is increased by 1 percentage point in the first quarter, stays at its new level

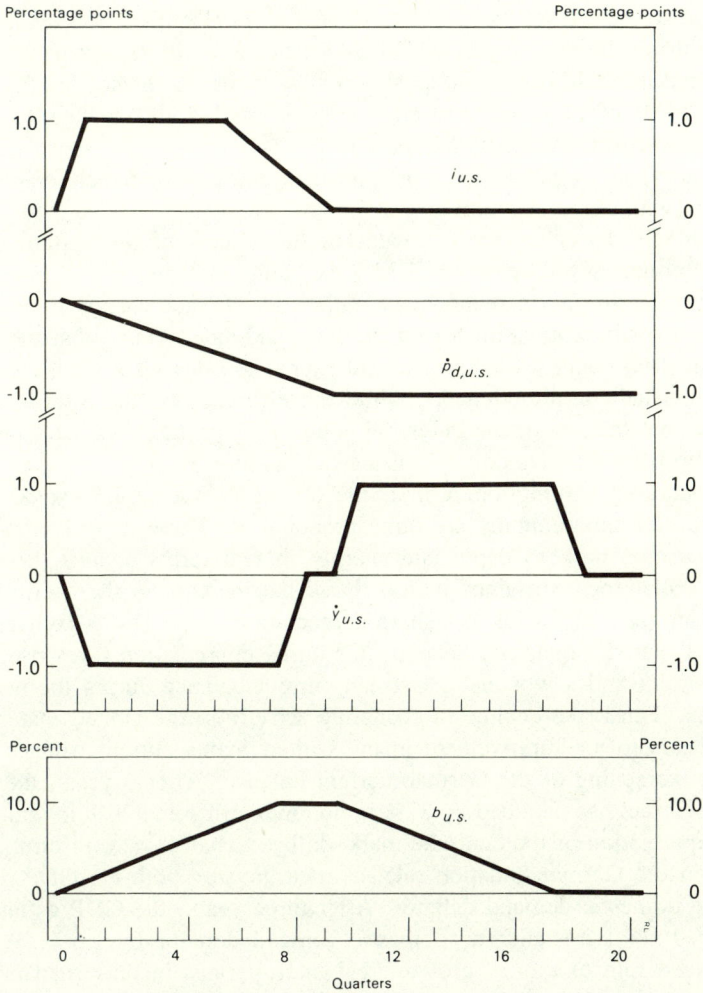

Fig. 14.3   The U.S. shift to monetary restraint (values of variables in terms of deviations from control solution).

for 1½ years, and then declines back to its initial level in 4 quarters. The United States inflation rate (at a quarterly rate) declines gradually, with a total decline of 1 percentage point after 2½ years. The rate of growth of real GNP (at a quarterly rate) is reduced by 1 percentage point in the first quarter, stays at its new level for 2 years, goes back to its initial level for 2 quarters, and then increases by 1 percentage point for 2 years before finally settling back to its initial level. The United States current balance (expressed by the ratio of exports of goods and services over imports of goods and services) increases gradually during the first 2 years for a total gain of 10%

stays at its new level for 2 quarters, then gradually goes back to its initial level during the next 2 years. The choice of these adjustment paths is arbitrary, but it would not be unrealistic to view them as representing the effects of the shift of monetary restraint in the United States in late 1979 in a schematic form. At least this is true if one neglects the sharp quarterly movements in United States money growth and United States interest rates during 1980.

Figure 14.4 depicts the estimates of the effects of the shift in United States monetary policy on the DM/$ exchange rate and the German economy, when the German monetary authorities do not change their rate of money growth. The estimates on the left-hand side assume that the rest of the industrial countries keep their real exchange rates vis-à-vis the deutsche mark constant (assumption A), while the estimates on the right-hand side assume that the rest of the industrial countries keep their real exchange vis-à-vis the United States dollar constant (assumption B).

Considering assumption A first, the effects on the DM/$ exchange rate and the German economy are quite pronounced. Three main factors cause the deutsche mark to depreciate sharply in real terms against the United States dollar for a sustained period. First, the increase in short-term United States interest rates leads to a sharp depreciation of the DM/$ exchange rate during the first 2 quarters. Second, this initial depreciation gives rise to a J-curve effect and a worsening German current balance during the next few quarters. Third, the decline in economic activity in the United States gradually leads to an improvement in the United States current balance and a further worsening of the German current balance. After 3 years, the DM/$ exchange rate has declined by 27% in nominal terms and 20% in real terms. The depreciation of the deutsche mark–dollar exchange rate, in turn, causes a rise in the German inflation rate, as measured by both the GDP deflator and the domestic demand deflator. After three years, the GDP deflator has increased by 1.2% and the domestic demand deflator by 2.9%. With an unchanged rate of money growth, real interest rates increase in Germany, bringing about a small increase in the GDP gap. All these effects become unwound in the long run, but it takes a large number of years at some cost in terms of cumulated lost output in Germany. The cumulated lost output in Germany accounts for 0.5% of a year's GDP already after 3 years and 1.5% after 5 years.

Not surprisingly, the effects under assumption B are similar in their direction, but their magnitude is greater. For example, the rise in the German inflation rate is much larger as a result of a larger rise in import prices. After 3 years, the GDP deflator has risen by nearly 4.0% and the domestic demand deflator by nearly 9.9%. This leads to a larger cumulated lost output in Germany; the lost output amounts to 2.2% of a year's GDP after 3 years and 5.4% after 5 years. These results illustrate how much Germany benefits if other industrial countries keep their real exchange rates vis-à-vis the deutsche mark constant.

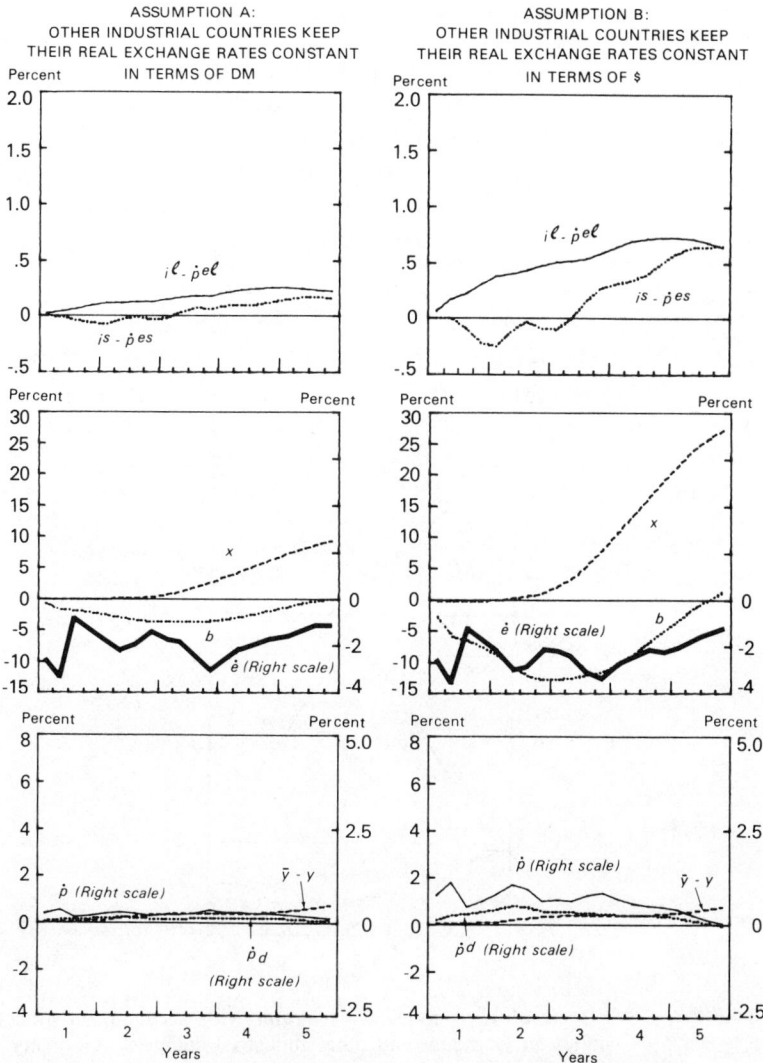

Fig. 14.4   Effects of U.S. monetary restraint without a change in monetary policy in Germany.

A possible policy response of the German monetary authorities is to reduce their rate of money growth in order to offset the effect of United States monetary restraint on the DM/$ exchange rate.[17] The implications of this policy response are depicted in figure 14.5 for the case where other indus-

17. In the simulation, the reduction in money growth in Germany is accompanied by a change in money growth anticipation in the first quarter due to the effect of the dummy variable z_2. (See the Appendix for a description of this variable.) That is, the reduction in money growth is defined as a major policy shift which private market participants view as such.

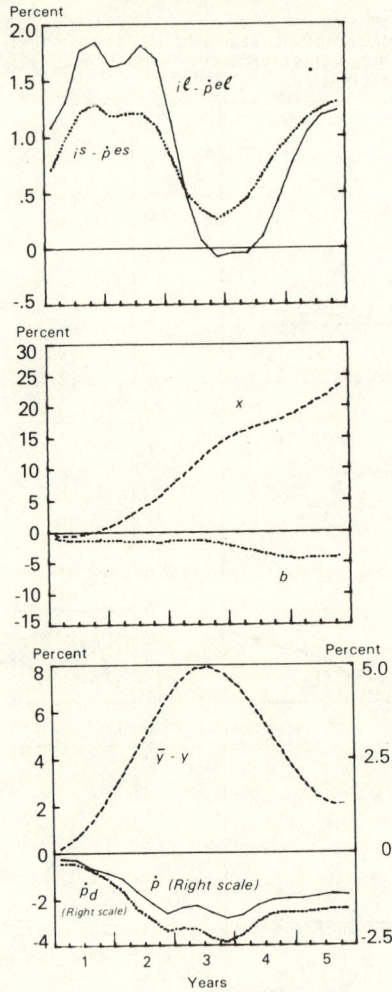

Fig. 14.5   Effects of U.S. monetary restraint with a change in monetary policy in Germany and other industrial countries (Germany and the other industrial countries are assumed to reduce their money growth rates to offset the effect of U.S. monetary restraint on their exchange rates vis-à-vis the $).

trial countries adopt the same response.[18] The favorable effect of such a response is that the rate of inflation declines sharply in Germany. After a year, the rate of inflation has declined by about 1 percentage point (at a

18. In the model, it is not possible to simulate the case where the German monetary authorities stabilize the DM/$ exchange rate while other industrial countries do not adopt any monetary response. In particular, there is no equation in the model that would determine what would happen to the exchange rates of other industrial countries in this case.

quarterly rate), whether the rate of inflation is measured by the GDP deflator or by the domestic demand deflator. Furthermore, this decline in the rate of inflation persists in subsequent years as a result of a permanent decline in the rate of money growth in Germany. However, the cost of such a policy is extremely large in terms of lost output in Germany. The output gap increases gradually to reach about 8 percentage points after 2 years, before declining slowly. By the end of the fifth year, the cumulated lost output accounts for 21.5% of a year's GDP. This can be compared to the cumulated loss of 1.5% in the case where neither Germany nor the other industrial countries respond to the shift in United States monetary policy by an equivalent shift in their own monetary policies.

14.4.2 Changes Generated by the Reagan Effect

To estimate the changes in the German economy generated by a development such as the Reagan effect, I have simulated the model after introduction of an exogenous shift in the value of the deutsche mark against the United States dollar of -6.5% per quarter from the fifth to the sixth quarter of the simulation period. For simplification purposes, it has been assumed that economic activity, inflation, and the current balance in the United States remain as in the control solution. Differences between the new simulation results and those obtained in the control solution are presented in figure 14.6. The results on the left-hand side of the chart assume that the German monetary authorities do not change the rate of money growth, while the results on the right-hand side assume that the authorities reduce the rate of money growth in order to offset the Reagan effect on the DM/$ exchange rate. In both cases, the other industrial countries are assumed to follow monetary policies that keep their exchange rates vis-à-vis the deutsche mark constant in real terms.[19]

The left-hand side results clearly indicate the inflationary impact of a depreciation of the DM/$ exchange rate on the German economy. The rate of inflation measured by the domestic demand deflator increases by more than half a percentage point at a quarterly rate during the first 2 quarters. After about 2½ years, the cumulated effect on the domestic demand deflator reaches 2.5%. The rate of inflation measured by the GDP deflator is less affected; the cumulated effect on the GDP after 2½ years is about 1.5%. In part, the inflationary consequences of the Reagan effect are enhanced because the depreciation of the deutsche mark initially leads to a worsening of the German current balance, which results in a further depreciation. This mechanism maintains the downward pressure on the deutsche mark even after the 2 quarters of the Reagan effect. With an unchanged rate of money

19. In the simulation where the German monetary authorities and the monetary authorities of other industrial countries reduce the rate of money growth, the level of economic activity in other industrial countries is assumed to be reduced in proportion to the reduction in the German level of economic activity.

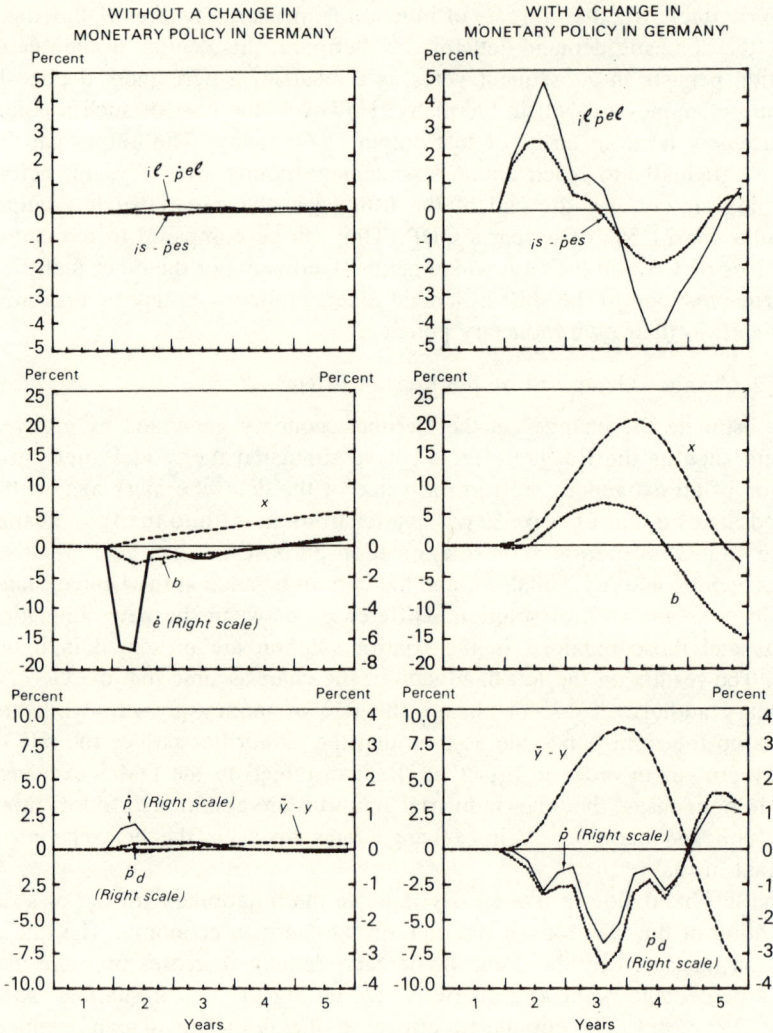

Fig. 14.6   Changes generated by the "Reagan effect"

growth, the increase in the domestic demand deflator gradually brings about a liquidity squeeze and a rise in both short-term and long-term real interest rates. The recessionary effect on output of the rise in long-term interest rates is at first offset by the expansionary effect coming from the increase in the ratio of exports over imports in volume terms, but after 1 year the recessionary effect starts to dominate.

These effects become unwound in the long run, but at a cost. Because of the increase in the output gap, the rate of inflation, measured either by the

GDP deflator or the domestic demand deflator, starts falling in comparison with the control solution. A gradual improvement in the current account, resulting from the lagged relative price effects and the increase in the GDP gap, stops the depreciation of the deutsche mark in time, and then leads to a gradual appreciation. However, it takes a long period of economic slack before the price increases of the first 2½ years are fully offset by subsequent price declines. Five years after the initial shock, the cumulated effect on the domestic demand deflator still amounts to an increase of 2%, which is only 0.5% less than after 2½ years, despite an additional output gap of about 0.5 percentage point maintained continuously from the third year onward.

The alternative strategy for the German monetary authorities and the monetary authorities of other industrial countries is to shift to a policy of monetary restraint in order to offset the effect of the exogenous development that puts downward pressure on their exchange rates. However, the results presented on the right-hand side of figure 14.6 indicate that, at times, the cost in terms of economic slack may be so large that this will not be a realistic alternative. In this case, the model indicates that the German monetary authorities would have had to reduce the rate of monetary growth by about 7 percentage points in each of the 2 quarters directly affected to offset the Reagan effect on the DM/$ exchange rate. Not surprisingly, the model indicates that this would have led not only to a reduction in inflation in Germany, as measured by both the domestic demand deflator and the GDP deflator, but also to a major recession. After 2 years, the output gap would have been increased by about 8.5 percentage points. Then, the German monetary authorities would have had to carry out a major monetary expansion to offset the upward pressures on the DM/$ exchange rate that would have resulted from a sharp increase in the German current balance. This in turn would have led to a sharp economic recovery.

14.5 Conclusions

This paper indicates that a shift to a policy of monetary restraint in the United States has major effects on Germany. If the German monetary authorities keep their rate of money growth unchanged, they will experience a sharp and sustained depreciation of the deutsche mark against the United States dollar in real terms. This will lead to a significant increase in the inflation rate in Germany for a number of years. The GDP gap will also increase gradually. The magnitude of these effects is greatly increased when other industrial countries choose to respond to the United States policy by adopting equivalent policies of monetary restraint. In this latter case, a simulation based on a schematic description of the effects of the 1979 shift to monetary restraint in the United States on United States interest rates, prices, output, and current balances indicates the following effects on the German economy. Prices increase substantially in Germany; after 3 years, the GDP deflator is nearly 4% higher than in the control solution corresponding to no shift to monetary restraint in the United States, and the domestic demand deflator nearly 10% higher. Furthermore, output decreases substantially in Germany by comparison with the control solution. The cumulated lost output amounts to 2.2% of a year's GDP after 3 years and 5.4% after 5 years. It is true that all these effects become unwound in the long run, but the long run seems so far away in this case as to be irrelevant.

If the German monetary authorities respond to the change in United States policy by adopting an equivalent policy of monetary restraint and other industrial countries follow suit, Germany benefits from a marked decline in its inflation rate, but the cost in terms of lost output is extremely large. After a year, the rate of inflation, in terms of the GDP deflator or domestic demand deflator, has declined by about 1 percentage point (at a quarterly rate), and the lower level persists in subsequent years. The output gap increases gradually to reach about 8 percentage points after 2 years before declining slowly. By the end of the fifth year, the cumulated lost output accounts for 21.5% of a year's GDP.

An appreciation of the United States dollar due to an exogenous development gives rise to a similar dilemma for the German monetary authorities. Here again, the dilemma is increased when other industrial countries choose to change their monetary policies in order to stabilize their exchange rates vis-à-vis the United States dollar. If the exogenous development is as large as what I have called the Reagan effect, that is, a depreciation of about 13% within 2 quarters, the analysis indicates that it would be very costly for the German monetary authorities to try to offset the impact of this development on their exchange rate through a policy of monetary restraint. The necessary reduction in money growth would push the German economy into a major recession.

This paper also indicates that the large effects on the German economy of a United States policy of monetary restraint or of an exogenous development affecting the DM/$ exchange rate are mainly due to the following factors: (1) the inflation rate in Germany responds slowly to a change in the money growth rate or the emergence of a GDP gap; (2) there is a direct link in Germany between import prices and domestic factor prices; (3) the DM/$ exchange rate is highly sensitive to variations in uncovered short-term interest rate differentials and to the level of the relative current balance position of the two countries; and (4) the volumes of German foreign trade flows respond slowly to relative price changes.

Appendix: Dummy Variables z_1 and z_2

The dummy variables z_1 and z_2 represent the discretionary component of the monetary policy stance. Consider first the policy reaction function (1'):

(1')
$$\sum_{k=1}^{k=6} \dot{m}_k/6 = \sum_{j=1}^{j=n} \alpha_{1,j} \dot{m}_{-j} - \alpha_2(y - \bar{y})_{-1} - \alpha_3 z_1$$
$$- \alpha_4 \sum_{k=1}^{k=6} \dot{r}_k/6.$$

If the rate of growth of money on the left-hand side of the equation covers a period that includes the beginning of the implementation of a major stabilization program, then its value may deviate substantially from the value that the first two explanatory variables would normally imply. To take this into account, the dummy variable z_1 is given a value that increases from zero to one in proportion to the number of quarters covered by the left-hand-side variable that are affected by the policy shift. If the left-hand-side variable covers a period that immediately follows a policy change, only one or two of the lagged money growth rates included as explanatory variables will be affected by the policy change, so that the historical series cannot be considered to reflect adequately the information available to private market participants. To offset this fact, the value of z_1 is allowed to decay gradually from one to zero in eight quarters. In the empirical study, the rate of decay was chosen to be consistent with the estimates of the values of the lag coefficients of the variables $\dot{m}_{-j}$ in equation (1').

At any point in time, private market participants can look back and estimate the coefficients of the policy reaction function (1') from past data. To predict money growth, they must then forcast the discretionary component of the policy stance. In the present model, it is assumed that private market participants do not anticipate discretionary policy changes but that their long-run expectations are revised once a policy change is announced. The change in their expectations depends on the coefficient of the variable z_1, the magnitude of which depends on the effectiveness of past policy changes.

Thus, in equation (1),

(1)
$$\dot{m}^{el} = \Sigma_j \alpha_{7j} \dot{m}_{-j} - \alpha_2(y - \bar{y})_{-1} - \alpha_3 z_2,$$

which is used to predict money growth, the variable z_1 enters, but in a modified form denoted by z_2. The variable z_2 takes the value of zero up to the period when the policy change is announced; then, like z_1, it takes a value of one when the policy change is announced, after which z_2 decays gradually.

Eight monetary stabilization programs were identified during the period 1955–81 (second quarter) with the following initial impact periods: the second quarter of 1956, the first quarter of 1962, the fourth quarter of 1965, the second quarter of 1972, the fourth quarter of 1972, the second quarter of 1973, the third quarter of 1979, and the first quarter of 1981. The two programs with initial impact in the second quarter of 1972 and the fourth quarter of 1972 were given an intensity that was one half that of the other programs. Following the rules explained above, z_1 and z_2 were given the values presented in table 14.A.1.

Table 14.A.1   Dummy Variables z_1 and z_2

	z_1 Quarter				z_2 Quarter			
Year	1	2	3	4	1	2	3	4
1955	.2	.3	.5	.7	.0	.0	.0	.0
1956	.8	1.0	.9	.8	.0	1.0	.9	.8
1957	.7	.6	.5	.4	.7	.6	.5	.4
1958	.3	.1	.0	.0	.3	.1	.0	.0
1959	.0	.0	.0	.0	.0	.0	.0	.0
1960	.0	.0	.0	.2	.0	.0	.0	.0
1961	.3	.5	.7	.8	.0	.0	.0	.0
1962	1.0	.9	.8	.7	1.0	.9	.8	.7
1963	.6	.5	.4	.3	.6	.5	.4	.3
1964	.1	.0	.2	.3	.1	.0	.0	.0
1965	.5	.7	.8	1.0	.0	.0	.0	1.0
1966	.9	.8	.7	.6	.9	.8	.7	.6
1967	.5	.4	.3	.1	.5	.4	.3	.1
1968	.0	.0	.0	.0	.0	.0	.0	.0
1969	.0	.0	.0	.0	.0	.0	.0	.0
1970	.0	.0	.0	.0	.0	.0	.0	.0
1971	.1	.1	.3	.4	.0	.0	.0	.0
1972	.8	1.1	1.3	1.6	.0	.5	.4	.9
1973	1.6	1.5	1.4	1.1	.7	1.7	1.4	1.3
1974	.9	.7	.5	.4	1.0	.9	.6	.5
1975	.3	.1	.0	.0	.3	.1	.0	.0
1976	.0	.0	.0	.0	.0	.0	.0	0
1977	.0	.0	.0	.0	.0	.0	.0	.0
1978	.0	.2	.3	.5	.0	.0	.0	.0
1979	.7	.8	1.0	.9	.0	.0	1.0	.9
1980	1.1	1.2	1.3	1.3	.8	.7	.6	.5
1981	1.4	1.2			1.4	1.2		

Comment   William H. Branson

This paper analyzes the effects of United States monetary tightness on the German economy using a model in which a combination of expectations effects and nominal price stickiness makes German output extremely sensitive to monetary policy. Artus uses the phrase ''a model of a monetary economy''; I would call it a model of monetary policy. He uses it to analyze recent German experience; I think it may be a better model of 1981–82 recession in the United States.

The model can be interpreted using a conventional diagram of aggregate demand and supply, with the domestic demand deflator on the vertical axis and real GDP on the horizontal. The aggregate demand curve has the usual negative slope. A rise in the price level squeezes real balances, raising the nominal and real long-term interest rate and reducing demand (see equations 7 and 8 in table 14.2). It also reduces real net exports (equation 13). A reduction in the money supply shifts the aggregate demand curve to the left by raising interest rates. The surprising aspect of the model is the flat slope of the aggregate supply curve. The domestic demand deflator (p) is a weighted average of the GDP deflator (p_d) and import prices, with approximately 25% weight to the latter (equation 6). Foreign exchange prices of imports are exogenous, and the exchange rate follows an asset market model (equation 11). The GDP deflator reacts quickly to long-run price expectations and only gradually to the output gap, with a lag that peaks after 2–3 quarters (equation 5). The long-run expected rate of inflation is given by the difference between long-run expected money growth and trend real GDP (equation 2); expected money growth is determined by policy. Thus the model is very similar to the wage contract models of Fischer and Taylor with the addition of long-run price expectations controlled by announcements about monetary policy.

In the Artus model of Germany, an announced and credible tightening of monetary policy shifts the aggregate demand curve by raising real interest rates. In equation (1) the announcement reduces expected money growth through z_2. This immediately reduces the expected long-run rate of inflation in equation (2). The long-term nominal interest rate is estimated from an inverted money demand function in equation (7). Monetary tightening tends to raise the nominal rate directly through the significant coefficient in the real money stock and to reduce it indirectly through the two insignificant coefficients of the expected long-run rate of inflation. The net effect is to raise the long-run real interest rate, which enters the output equation (8) with just a one-quarter lag. Actual prices react with a longer lag, so that the aggregate demand curve shifts leftward along the flat supply curve, reducing output sharply. The effect is shown in figure 14.5. The reduction in demand also comes through an additional channel; the short-term interest rate rises through equation (12). This appreciates the deutsche mark via equation (11), and real net exports are reduced with a lag, as shown in equation (13). Thus the model gives monetary policy announcements a strong influence on actual output.

The main effect of the shift to monetary tightness in the United States comes through an upward shift in the aggregate supply curve in the Artus model. The rise in the United States short-term interest rate causes a depreciation of the deutsche mark, raising the domestic demand deflator. With no effect on long-run expected inflation, the reduction in real balances raises the long-term real interest rate, reducing output. This is partially offset, but with a lag, by the effect of the depreciation on real net exports. The result is an immediate rise in the price level but a very gradual increase in the output gap, shown in part B of figure 14.4.

The relative effects of monetary restraint in the United States and in Germany on the German economy can be seen by comparing figure 14.4B and figure 14.5. In figure 14.4B, the effects of United States monetary restraint are illustrated on the assumption that German monetary policy does not react, but the other industrial countries hold their real exchange rates against the dollar constant. Figure 14.5 shows the effect if Germany also tightens to hold the deutsche mark–dollar rate constant. The result for the output gap is striking. After 3 years it is about 0.5% of GDP with unchanged German monetary policy in figure 14.4B, but with tighter monetary policy in figure 14.5, it is 8%. This illustrates the relative importance of monetary policy as a determinant of German output in the Artus model.

The combination of flexible long-run inflation expectations and sticky nominal prices in the short run is built into the model by assumption. There is a discussion in the text of the paper of foundations of sticky prices in wage contracts, but as far as I can tell this is never tested. The estimates in table 14.2 show sluggish price response to the output gap, but the process of the wage formation is not explicitly modeled. And the adjustment of long-run expectations is built in through equations (1) and (2). Thus I would interpret the Artus model as a model of monetary policy conditional on the assumption of sticky nominal wage and price adjustment, rather than a test of this assumption.

An alternative model would assume that real wages are sticky in Germany. This has been raised as an empirical possibility in several recent papers (e.g., Branson and Rotemberg 1980). The fact that nominal wage contracts are signed annually, noted by Artus, does not eliminate the possibility of wage drift that would make the real wage relatively more sluggish than the nominal wage.

If the real wage were fixed above its equilibrium value, then the economy would be in a state of "classical unemployment." Then the aggregate supply curve would be roughly vertical. The effects on the price level and output in Germany of monetary restraint in the United States would remain much the same as in the Artus model, but they would come from a leftward shift of the vertical supply curve due to a terms-of-trade effect. The demand deflator p would rise relative to the GDP deflator p_d.

In this alternative model, the effects of monetary restraint in Germany would be much different from the Artus model, however. An announced and credible shift to monetary restraint would shift the aggregate demand curve down along the essentially vertical supply curve, reducing the price level (or rate of inflation) with only a small effect on output. In this model German monetary restraint could offset the inflationary effects of United States policy without the major losses of output shown in figure 14.5.

Choice between the alternative assumptions on wage rigidity has little effect on the result in Germany (or in Europe in general) of very tight United States monetary policy: it is stagflationary. The exchange rate effect raises the price level and depresses demand. But the two models have radically different implications for German (or European) policy in the face of this pressure from the United States. In the Artus model, which assumes sluggish nominal wages, monetary tightness generates a large loss in output and an implicit rise in unemployment as the cost of eliminating inflation. With sticky real wages the output and unemployment costs are far less.

The evidence on nominal versus real wage rigidity in Germany is unclear. Econometric work on the 1970s data does not reject the hypothesis of real wage stickiness. These results are supported by the continued rise in the real wage in 1974–75, when productivity growth was sharply reduced by the first oil price jump. On the other hand, the evidence cited in my comment on the May 1982 *EER* paper by de Menil and Westphal suggests that the real wage adjusted immediately to the second oil price jump in 1979–80.

Artus makes beautifully clear the implications of the choice of assumptions on wage rigidity for the analysis of monetary policy in Europe. However, he leaves the alternative assumptions untested in the ex post analysis of monetary policy in the 1970–81 period. But the importance of knowing which is the most nearly correct assumption for current policy analysis comes through as a central message of the paper.

Regardless of the implications for monetary policy, the Artus model provides an excellent articulation of a "stylized European" model of exchange rate effects, which is very different from a "stylized American" view. In the Artus model of Germany, or in the real wage alternative, internal inflation is the main effect of a deutsche mark devaluation. The current account follows a J-curve with very slow adjustment of real trade. In contrast, the American model has changes in the exchange rate mainly influencing trade with small effects on the internal price level. Thus, in the American model exchange rate fluctuations mainly stabilize the current-account balance while in the European model they mainly destabilize the price level. This difference could be the source of recent policy conflicts. It also makes obvious the needs for further careful empirical research and for efforts to understand alternative models underlying policy views on the two sides of the Atlantic.

References

Artus, Jacques R. 1981. Monetary stabilization with and without government credibility. *IMF Staff Papers* 28:495–533.

Barro, Robert J. 1978. Unanticipated money, output, and the price level in the United States. *Journal of Political Economy* 86:549–80.

Branson, William H. 1982. Comment on de Menil and Westphal. *European Economic Review* 18 (May–June): 75–79.

Branson, William H., and Rotemberg, Julio J. 1980. International adjustment with wage rigidity. *European Economic Review* 13:309–41.

Buiter, Willem H. 1980. Some problems of estimation and hypothesis testing in models of unanticipated monetary growth: A simple example. Mimeographed. University of Bristol, Department of Economics, January.

De Menil, Georges, and Westphal, Uwe. 1982. The Transmission of international disturbrances: A French-German cliometric analysis, 1972–80. *European Economic Review* 18 (May–June): 41–73.

Germany, J. David, and Srivastava, Sanjay. 1979. Empirical estimates of unanticipated policy: Issues in stability and identification. Mimeographed. Massachusetts Institute of Technology, March.

Lucas, Robert E. 1972. Expectations and the neutrality of money. *Journal of Economic Theory* 4:103–24.

———. 1975. An equilibrium model of the business cycle. *Journal of Political Economy* 83:1113–44.

Sargent, Thomas J., and Wallace, Neil. 1975. "Rational expectations," the optimal monetary instrument, and the optimal money supply rule. *Journal of Political Economy* 83:241–54.

15   The Relationship between Exchange Rate Policy and Monetary Policy in Ten Industrial Countries

Stanley W. Black

15.1 Introduction

The dichotomy between pegged and floating exchange rate systems goes as far back in economic analysis as Ricardo and has generated an enormous literature on the reasons for choice of different exchange rate regimes (Tower and Willett 1976). More recently, economists have begun to analyze alternative regimes of monetary control, both from analytical (Poole 1970) and institutional (Hodgman 1974) points of view. The analytical and institutional viewpoints on monetary control have been effectively combined by Modigliani and Papademos (1980) in a paper on alternative techniques of monetary control in a closed economy. These latter papers have focused on the domestic aspects of monetary policy, such as the use of interest rates, reserve aggregates, or credit controls as means of influencing the economy. (See also Atkinson, Blundell-Wignall, and Chouraqui 1981.)

A recent notable paper by Dale Henderson (1982) has begun to draw some of the parallels between the analysis of pegged versus floating exchange rate regimes and alternative monetary control techniques. In an elegant generalization of Poole's analysis to the open economy, Henderson shows that when all disturbances affect the financial sector, the authorities should hold interest and exchange rates constant to minimize fluctuations in output, allowing money stocks and international reserves to fluctuate instead. On the other hand, when all disturbances affect the real sector, interest and exchange rates should be allowed to fluctuate, holding constant the stocks of international reserves and money supplies. In general, a managed

499

float is appropriate. Henderson's analytical approach, which is both powerful and revealing, lacks the degree of institutional detail that would enable one to compare actual alternative mechanisms of monetary control and exchange rate policies in different countries. In section 15.2 of this paper I generalize the Modigliani and Papademos model to the open economy in order to provide an effective framework for such an analysis. I show that the choice between alternative methods of monetary control carries with it logical implications for the type of exchange rate regime that is appropriate. There is thus a natural parallelism in exchange rate policy and monetary policy that goes beyond Henderson's analytical results based on the types of disturbances facing the economy.

In section 15.3 of the paper I compare the exchange rate policies and monetary control regimes of ten industrialized countries (Belgium, Canada, France, Germany, Italy, Japan, the Netherlands, Sweden, the United Kingdom, and the United States). The parallelism predicted in section 15.2 is borne out in reality, with some interesting variations. In section 15.4, I then compare some empirical reaction functions for monetary and exchange rate policies in these ten countries. Section 15.5 offers some conclusions.

15.2 An Open Economy Model of Financial Structure

The basic Modigliani-Papademos model for a closed economy contains an IS curve equilibrium condition for the domestic goods market, an LM curve for the M1 money market, an aggregate supply relationship for the price level, and an equilibrium condition in the market for bank credit. This differs from the traditional neo-Keynesian model only by the substitution of intermediated bank credit for the more customary government and/or private bond market. The IS, LM, and BB curves are shown to intersect as usual in (r, Y) space, so that monetary control can focus either on M1 or on bank credit. Under uncertainty, the relative stability of the various curves determines the optimal choice of monetary instruments. Credit rationing appears when the savings deposit rate is not allowed to move to clear the credit market.

An open economy version of this model simply requires the inclusion of a foreign good and its domestic price level ep^*, a foreign component for the domestic monetary base, foreign sources of credit to the domestic economy, and a foreign interest rate r_f in addition to the domestic loan rate r and savings deposit rate r_s. It is assumed that the domestic and foreign goods are imperfect substitutes and that domestic and foreign credit are imperfect substitutes because of differences in currency denomination and the associated exchange risk. Thus r_f is defined to *include* the expected change in the exchange rate e.

Table 15.1 below shows the flow-of-funds accounts for this economy, which is divided into five sectors: deficit units, surplus units, private banks, the central bank, and the rest of the world. Flows are shown in constant price terms, with sources negative and uses positive. Each column of the table represents a sectoral sources-uses statement and hence sums to zero. Each row represents a market equilibrium condition, of which only six are independent, given the columnar balance sheet constraints and the definition of M2 as the sum of M1 and savings deposits. The markets for savings deposits (SD) and foreign loans (NFB) are assumed to face an infinitely elastic supply at, respectively, a constant spread of the loan rate over the deposit rate $r - r_s = d$ and a constant foreign rate of interest r_f. The market for bank reserves (RES) is assumed to face infinitely elastic demand at a zero interest rate. Thus the six independent market equilibrium conditions will be capable of determining the six variables, Y, r, SD, NFB, RES, and e or NFA^{cb}, together with a supply side to determine the price level. We now proceed to specify the behavioral relationships that allow this equilibrium to be analyzed.

The IS equation (1) for equilibrium in the goods market sets domestic investment plus exports equal to private saving plus the value of imports in terms of domestic goods. Expected signs are shown above the arguments.

$$(1) \qquad I(\overset{-}{r},\ \overset{-}{r}_s,\ \overset{-}{r}_f) + EX(p\,/\,ep^*) = S(\overset{+}{Y}) + (ep^*/p)$$

$$IM(\overset{+}{Y},\ \overset{+}{p\,/\,ep^*}).$$

Income is defined as the value of domestic output deflated by the consumer price index

$$(2) \qquad Y = pX(p)/\bar{p}.$$

Consumer prices $\bar{p}$ are given by a weighted average of domestic and foreign prices.

Table 15.1   Flow of Funds

Markets	Deficit Units	Surplus Units	Private Banks	Central Bank	Rest of World
(i) Goods	$\text{Id} - \text{Sd}$	$I_s - S_s$	0	0	$EX - IM$
(ii) Bank reserves	0	0	$\text{RES} - \text{NDA}^{cb}$	$\text{NDA}^{cb} - \text{RES}$	0
(iii) M1	L1_d	L1_s	$-(\text{M1} - \text{C})$	$-\text{C}$	0
(iv) Savings deposits	0	SD_s	$-\text{SD}$	0	0
[(v) M2 = (iii) + (iv)	L2_d	L2_s	$-(\text{M2} - \text{C})$	$-\text{C}$	0]
(vi) Bank loans	$-\text{B}_d$	0	B	0	0
(vii) Foreign loans	$-\text{FB}$	FL	0	0	NFB
(viii) Foreign assets	0	0	NFA^{pb}	NFA^{cb}	$-\text{NFA}$

Note: In constant prices, sources $(-)$ and uses $(+)$.

(3) $$\bar{p} = p^{\mu}(ep*)^{1-\mu}.$$

The supply of real output is taken to be an increasing function of domestic prices $X(p)$ because of the existence of wage contracts set in nominal terms.

The supply of M1 is taken to depend in the product of a money multiplier $k(r)$ and the monetary base, defined as the sum of the net domestic and foreign assets of the central bank. The demand for M1 depends on the usual income, prices, and interest rates.

(4) $$k(r)(\mathrm{NDA}^{cb} + \mathrm{NFA}^{cb}) = p\mathrm{L1}(\overset{-}{r},\ \overset{-}{r}_s,\ \overset{+}{Y})$$

The credit market is analyzed by considering separately deficit units, who are assumed to hold neither savings deposits nor foreign assets, and surplus units, who are assumed not to borrow either at home or abroad but who may lend abroad. The real value of bank borrowing by deficit units is then equal to (table 15.1, column 1) the excess of their investment over their own saving, plus their accumulation of real balances of transactions money, less the real value of their foreign borrowing.

(5) $$B(\overset{-}{r},\ \overset{+}{r}_f,\ \overset{-}{Y}) = I_d(\overset{-}{r},\ \overset{-}{r}_f) - S_d(\overset{+}{Y}) + \Delta\mathrm{L1}_d(\overset{-}{r},\ \overset{+}{Y})$$
$$- \mathrm{FB}(\overset{+}{r},\ \overset{-}{r}_f).$$

The government is not considered separately but may be thought of as an exogenous deficit unit. Acquisition of real balances by surplus units in the form of M1 plus savings deposits is equal to (table 15.1, column 2) the excess of their saving over investment less the real value of their foreign lending. Capital gains and losses are ignored in this accounting.

(6) $$\Delta\mathrm{L2}_s(\overset{+}{r}_s,\ \overset{+}{r}_f,\ \overset{+}{Y}) = S_s(\overset{+}{Y}) - I_s(\overset{-}{r}_s,\ \overset{-}{r}_f) - \mathrm{FL}(\overset{-}{r}_s,\ \overset{+}{r}_f).$$

Subtracting (6) from (5), defining the total change in the liabilities of the banking system as $\Delta\mathrm{L2} = \Delta\mathrm{L2}_s + \Delta\mathrm{L1}_d$ and net foreign borrowing as $\mathrm{NFB} = \mathrm{FB} - \mathrm{FL}$, we have the sources and uses of credit in real terms.

(7) $$S(\overset{+}{Y}) + B(\overset{-}{r},\ \overset{+}{r}_f,\ \overset{-}{Y}) + \mathrm{NFB}\ (\overset{+}{r},\ \overset{+}{r}_s,\ \overset{-}{r}_f)$$
$$= I(\overset{-}{r},\ \overset{-}{r}_s,\ \overset{-}{r}_f) + \Delta\mathrm{L2}(\overset{-}{r},\ \overset{+}{r}_s,\ \overset{\pm}{r}_f,\ \overset{+}{Y}).$$

Thus saving plus bank borrowing plus net foreign borrowing must equal investment plus accumulation of real balances in the form of M2. Equation (7) is equivalent to the sum of the first two columns of table 15.1, and is therefore an identity.

The consolidated balance sheet for the banking system as a whole, including the central bank together with the commercial and savings banks, requires that the additions to M2 be equal to domestic bank lending plus the change in net foreign assets, again as an identity from columns 3 and 4 of table 15.1:

$$(8) \qquad \Delta L2(\overset{-}{r},\ \overset{+}{r_s},\ \overset{\mp}{r_f},\ \overset{+}{Y}) = B(\overset{-}{r},\ \overset{+}{r_f},\ \overset{-}{Y}) + \Delta NFA^{pb}(\overset{-}{r},\ \overset{+}{r_f}) + \Delta NFA^{cb}.$$

Substituting into the foreign asset equilibrium condition from the rest of the world sectoral statement of sources and uses of funds yields the balance of payments:

$$(9) \qquad EX(\overset{-}{p/ep^*}) - (ep^*/p)\ IM(\overset{+}{p/ep^*},\ \overset{+}{Y})$$
$$+ NFB(\overset{+}{r},\ \overset{+}{r_s},\ \overset{-}{r_f})$$
$$= \Delta NFA^{pb}(\overset{-}{r},\ \overset{+}{r_f}) + \Delta NFA^{cb}.$$

15.1.1 Model 1: Control of M1

When monetary control is exercised via manipulation of the monetary base to achieve a target level of M1, the model is similar to the standard IS-LM model. Equations (2) and (3) can be solved for $p(\overset{+}{Y},\ e\overset{+}{p}{}^*)$ which can then be used to eliminate p from the model. Competition in intermediation yields the condition $r_s = r - d$, which can be used to eliminate r_s. In figure 15.1, equation (1) yields the downward-sloping IS curve, equation (4) the upward-sloping LM1 curve, and equation (7) the ambiguously signed CR, or credit-market curve. As usual, the three curves must intersect in a common point A. Under a floating exchange rate regime, the foreign balance curve from equation (9) will also pass through point A with $\Delta NFA^{cb} = 0$. Under a pegged rate this will no longer necessarily be true. The resulting endogenous movements of reserves will directly influence the location of the

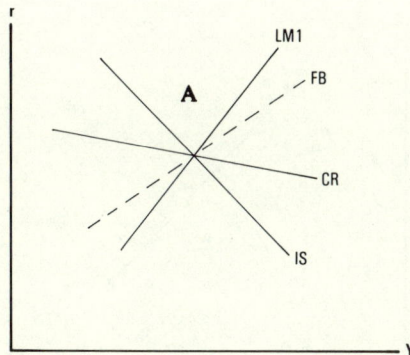

Fig. 15.1

IS-LM-CR intersection, as any nonsterilized portion of reserve flows causes the monetary base to rise or fall.

It is the obvious ability of the floating rate regime to cut off the endogeneity of the monetary base that makes a floating rate attractive to countries that wish to control M1. Note that the ability to sterilize the monetary effects of reserve flows mitigates the institutional attractiveness of a float. On the other hand, if most of the net domestic assets of the central bank are held in the form of direct, nonmarketable claims on the private banks or the government, the central bank may not be willing to offset reserve movements completely.

15.1.2 Model 2: Control of Credit

An alternative method of controlling the monetary system, whose wide use in practice is discussed in section 15.3 of the paper, is direct control of bank lending. Assuming that price movements can be adequately taken into account in setting the limits on bank credit, this can be expressed as a limit to the *real* volume of bank lending.

$$(11) \qquad B(\overline{r},\ \overset{+}{r_f},\ \overline{Y}) = \overline{B}.$$

If we assume that the loan rate adjusts to clear the loan market, stability conditions require the BB curve in figure 15.2 to be flatter than the IS curve.

Credit restriction in this model takes the form of an upward shift in the BB curve, which raises interest rates and reduces investment and income.

As interest rates rise under credit restrictions, nonbanks would be induced to increase their foreign borrowing as an alternative source of finance (see equation [7]), generating a capital inflow. As in model 1, with a pegged exchange rate, the equilibrium point can be above or below the foreign balance, or FB curve. However, the resulting influx or efflux of reserves is not

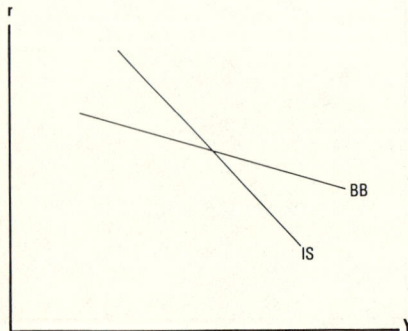

Fig. 15.2

allowed to affect the level of bank credit under this regime. Although the level of M2 will rise or fall with the balance of payments, the primary tool of monetary control is not directly undermined by the international flows. This contrasts sharply with the situation in model 1 under a pegged exchange rate.

On the other hand, credit controls combined with a pegged exchange rate can create problems. Nonbank channels of credit can be opened up to bypass the credit restriction. Controls over bank lending frequently take the form of specifying direct limits on the growth of bank credit by individual banks. This prevents banks from bidding for funds in the credit market and distorts the allocation of investment. An alternative, but seldom used, approach would specify reserve requirements on bank lending and limit the total available reserves.

15.1.3 Model 3: Control of Bank Credit and Net Foreign Assets

As noted above, simply controlling bank credit with a pegged exchange rate leaves the balance of payments free to fluctuate with changes in other internal and external conditions. The level of international reserves may not always be adequate to finance these fluctuations, even if the level of the pegged exchange rate is appropriate in the long-run sense of purchasing power parity. The addition of controls over the net foreign asset position of banks might seem to be a logical way to guarantee external balance along with internal balance in the context of a pegged exchange rate. Unfortunately, it should be obvious from equation (9) that the only way to control the *total* net foreign asset position of private banks together with the central bank is to adopt exchange controls over private sector transactions, with all of the ill effects that such controls can be expected to yield (Bhagwati 1978). Simply controlling the *private* banks' net foreign asset positions will reduce the variability of only one element of the balance of payments, which will often be acting to finance the payments of other sectors.

The adoption of total foreign exchange controls allows M2 as well as bank credit to become independent of balance-of-payments flows. From equation (8), the change in M2 must equal the credit target $\bar{B}$:

$$(12) \qquad \Delta L2(\overset{+}{r}, r\overset{-}{r_f}, \overset{+}{Y}) = \bar{B}.$$

The resulting LM2 curve in figure 15.3 will be downward sloping and, as Modigliani and Papademos argue, steeper than the IS curve for stability.

15.1.4 Model 4: Controls Plus Credit Rationing

The extension of controls over bank credit and possibly exchange market transactions is likely to lead the authorities to prevent interest rates from moving to clear the loan market, as was assumed above. In this case, true credit rationing will arise, in the sense of unsatisfied demand for credit at

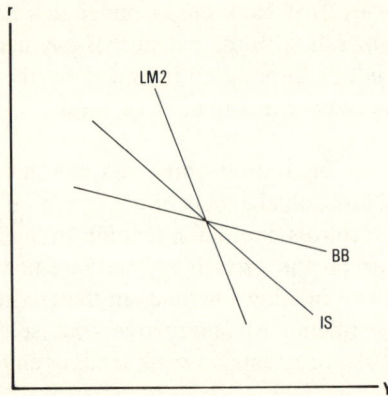

Fig. 15.3

existing interest rates. The inducement to seek nonbank channels of un-regulated finance, including foreign borrowing, will increase dramatically in this situation. Furthermore, the misallocation of credit caused by arbitrary, nonprice rationing will sharply exacerbate the problems raised by credit ceilings on individual banks.

From an analytical point of view, the restriction of credit via an upward shift in the BB curve in combination with interest rate ceilings would be expected to reduce saving and investment at the given interest rate. This could be seen diagrammatically as a clockwise pivoting of the IS curve through the unconstrained equilibrium point, forcing a reduction in output.

Such a monetary policy regime would encourage the use of a pegged exchange rate with exchange controls over all private capital flows, in order to reduce the tendency of unsatisfied borrowers to turn to foreign sources of capital. A floating exchange rate would generate substantial upward pressure on the exchange rate during restrictive periods, followed by downward pressure during expansionary periods.

15.3 A Classification of Exchange Rate and Monetary Policy Regimes in Ten Countries

Actual exchange rate and monetary policy regimes do not fall neatly into pigeonholes labeled "pegged," "floating," "control of M1," or "control of bank credit." Even a pegged exchange rate fluctuates freely between its upper and lower limits and can have the limits changed. And, as recent experience has made clear, most cases of floating rates involve a significant degree of management via central bank intervention in the exchange market. Furthermore, the existence of generalized floating among the major world currencies since 1973 has made it impossible for any country to do more than peg to a subset of the rest of the world's currencies.

The simple classification of a currency as "pegged" or "floating," as seen, for example, in *International Financial Statistics*, thus needs to be supplemented by some additional information on the degree of flexibility allowed in the exchange rate. Table 15.2 shows in column 1 the formal classification of each country's exchange rate regime during the 1970s, but columns 2 and 3 add information on the variability of the effective exchange rate and central bank intervention relative to GDP. As might be expected, countries with floating rates have higher average variability in their effective exchange rates than countries which peg (1.65 vs. 1.29), although Belgium and the Netherlands rank lower than the other "peggers."

The second half of table 15.2 classifies countries according to differences in monetary policy. Column 4 gives the primary monetary target, while column 5 indicates the primary instrument through which monetary policy is carried out. Whenever the primary target is M1 or the monetary base, the main operating instrument is open market operations (or equivalent changes in reserve requirements, as in Germany). By contrast, whenever the main target is domestic credit or M2, credit controls are often used as a primary instrument of monetary policy. (It should, of course, be recognized that this oversimplifies institutional differences and changes in the use of instruments, which are more carefully spelled out in Black [1983]).

Column 6 of table 15.2 gives a measure of the frequency of change of the discount rate in each country, a measure of the authorities' willingness to allow interest rates to fluctuate. This measure is relatively low in France, Italy, Japan, and Sweden. Columns 7 and 8 provide information on the average rate of inflation in each country during the 1970s and its variability. Italy and the United Kingdom of course stand out as high-inflation countries, while Japan has also had a comparably high variability of inflation.

In order to throw more light on the interrelationship between monetary policies and exchange rate policies, table 15.3 cross-classifies the information in table 15.2 according to whether a country was pegged or floating and used credit controls or primarily open market operations in monetary policy. Remarkably, the differences between floaters that use credit controls and floaters that use open market operations are often greater than the difference between the latter and peggers. The parallels between exchange rate policy and monetary policy suggested in the analysis of section 15.2 appear very evident in the data.

The one group of countries that has broken this "law of parallelism" in monetary and exchange rate policy, namely, the countries that float and use credit controls oriented toward M2 or the control of domestic credit, have had higher average inflation, and more variable inflation, as well as more variable exchange rates. Apparently, reliance on market forces to determine exchange rates and credit controls to limit monetary growth is a relatively unstable combination. The German case, by contrast, is stable.

The other two pairings, which might be called "pure" peggers and float-

Table 15.2   Measures of Exchange Rate Policy and Monetary Policy, 1973–79

	Exchange Regime[a]	Variability of Effective Rate[b]	Variability of Inter-vention[c]	Primary Monetary Target[d]	Primary Monetary Instrument[e]	Frequency of use of Discount rate[f]	Inflation Rate[g]	Variability of Inflation[g]
Belgium	Peg	.89	.281	DC	CC	25	7.5	3.17
Canada	Float	1.20	.143	M1	OMO	24	7.8	2.46
France	Peg	1.48	.093	M2	CC	14	9.3	2.50
Germany	Peg	1.65	.165	MO	OMO	19	5.1	1.37
Italy	Float	1.83	.179	DC	CC	15	13.3	5.00
Japan	Float	2.15	.105	M2	CC	15	9.3	6.15
Netherlands	Peg	.98	.171	M2	CC	19	7.4	2.03
Sweden	Peg	1.44	.168	DC	CC	14	8.7	1.81
United Kingdom	Float	1.67	.323	M3	CC	33	13.3	5.14
United States	Float	1.42	.026	M1	OMO	23	7.2	2.63

[a]Countries listed as pegged are members of the EMS/EEC narrow margins arrangement.

[b]Standard deviation of percentage change in monthly effective exchange rate, from International Financial Statistics.

[c]Standard deviation of monthly changes in foreign exchange reserves, adjusted for swaps and foreign borrowing, as percentage of 1980 GDP in United States dollars. See Black (1980) for details.

[d]DC = domestic credit, MO = monetary base. See OECD (1979) and Black (1983, appendix on institutions).

[e]CC = credit controls, OMO = open market operations. See Black (1983, appendix on institutions).

[f]Percentage of months in which discount rate was changed; see Black (1983).

[g]Mean and standard deviation of annual inflation rate of consumer price index.

Table 15.3   **Monetary Policy versus Exchange Rate Policy**

	Peg	Float	F-statistic
A. Variability of effective exchange rate:			
Credit controls	1.20	1.88	
Open market operation	1.65	1.31	$F_{(3,6)} = 4.21$
B. Variability of intervention:			
Credit controls	.178	.202	
Open market operation	.165	.084	$F_{(3,6)} = .72$
C. Frequency of discount rate change:			
Credit controls	.18	.15[a]	
Open market operation	.19	.24	$F_{(3,5)} = 1.53$
D. Average inflation rate			
Credit controls	8.22	12.0	
Open market operation	5.1	7.5	$F_{(3,6)} = 7.20$
E. Variability of inflation:			
Credit controls	2.38	5.43	
Open market operation	1.37	2.54	$F_{(2,7)} = 23.12$

[a]Excluding the United Kingdom, which used a floating discount rate from October 1972.

ers, appear to have performed more acceptably, on this limited but suggestive evidence. The pure peggers, for example, had lower variability of their exchange rates at the cost of higher variability in their reserves, as compared with the pure floaters. The "mixed" floaters, however, intervened about as much as the peggers and had much higher variability of exchange rates, as did Germany.

While the credit control countries, as expected, adjust interest rates less frequently than open market countries, the mixed floaters adjust them least. The pure floaters had Germany appear to have the best inflation performance, with the pure peggers not far behind. The mixed floaters, however, are a poor third in inflation performance.

15.4 Lessons from Studies of Reaction Functions

In two recent papers I estimated central bank policy reaction functions for these same ten industrial countries for domestic monetary policy instruments (Black 1983) and exchange market intervention (Black 1980). It may be useful, in the context of this discussion, to summarize the findings of those studies that appear to be relevant to the relationship between the two types of policies.

A general conclusion, which seems inescapable from the evidence, is that both internal targets such as inflation and unemployment and external targets such as competitiveness, the current account, and reserves are important in determining *both* domestic monetary policy and exchange rate intervention. However, the external targets, as might be expected, play a relatively larger role in determining exchange rate intervention in most countries, judging by the relative number of significant coefficients in reaction functions. And of course for the countries with pegged exchange rates, the proximity of the exchange rate to the peg is a necessarily important factor, which is confirmed in the regressions.

"Leaning against the wind," in the sense of intervention to cushion movements of the exchange rate, appears to be a widespread practice, (the same conclusion is found in Artus [1976] and Quirk [1977]). In addition, movements in competitiveness appear to have set off counteracting intervention policies in some cases (Japan, Canada). Finally, large current account imbalances have led to significant intervention where capital flows have been inadequate to finance them at existing levels of interest rates and exchange rates (Japan, Germany, the United Kingdom).

Interestingly enough, these very same factors appear to be the external variables that affect "domestic" monetary policy, such as interest rates, open market operations, reserve requirements, and credit controls. There is no doubt that the authorities have a choice to respond to external imbalance with either "domestic" or "international" instruments. This distinction of course implies the imperfect substitutability of assets denominated in different currencies, since otherwise the only effective intervention would be indistinguishable from domestic monetary policy.

Less obviously, the authorities can also respond to *internal* imbalances with alternative combinations of domestic and international instruments. For example, in 1973–75 the United Kingdom and Italy both used exchange market intervention to resist the exchange rate implications of domestic expansion in the face of large current account imbalances. Again in 1977 they both used intervention to resist the exchange rate implications of restrictive domestic policies. Conversely, in 1980 and 1981 the United States and the United Kingdom have chosen to accept the exchange rate appreciation that accompanies tight monetary policy, making it an evidently important part of the domestic policy package.

Turning to domestic monetary policy behavior itself, the reaction functions show, not surprisingly, that countries with pegged exchange rates give relatively high policy weights (not necessarily welfare weights) to external target variables. Floaters, on the other hand, typically give more emphasis in policy formulation to internal targets.

As found in section 15.3 above, it is not the case that peggers necessarily do any better or worse in formulating "domestic" monetary policy than floaters. The worst inflation performance during the 1970s was that of Italy and the United Kingdom, both floaters. The best performance was that of Germany and the United States, also both floaters. It is suggestive, however, that the former two are mixed floaters, which use credit controls, while the latter two use open market operations. Clearly, other factors must also be brought into a full explanation of these differences, including fiscal policy and the state of labor relations and indexation.

15.5 Conclusion

In this paper I have argued that there is a natural parallelism between exchange rate and monetary policy regimes, which arises out of the economic logic of models in which monetary control is exercised either through control of bank reserves or control of bank credit. I have shown that the logic of the reserves model leads in the direction of a floating exchange rate, while the logic of the credit control model leads in the direction of a pegged rate.

That logic was supported by showing that six of ten major industrialized countries fell into one of the two "pure" cases, and that these six plus Germany had achieved performances with respect to internal and external measures of economic stability that were superior to those of the three "mixed" countries which used floating exchange rates with credit controls.

Finally, I pointed out that reaction function studies reveal an intimate relationship between the conduct of monetary policy and exchange rate policy, since either policy may support or undermine the other in affecting both domestic and external targets. Differences in exchange rate regime were shown to have a profound impact on the conduct of monetary policy. My argument in this paper is that differences in the monetary policy regime can have an equally profound impact on the choice of exchange rate policy, since credit controls do not mix well with a floating rate.

15.6 Postscript

Following discussion at the Conference, the classification of Germany in tables 15.2 and 15.3 was made consistent with the other Snake countries, with no real changes in the conclusions reached. The comments by Paul de Grauwe suggest an appropriate way to deal with a limitation in the analytical model, and I accept them with enthusiasm. De Grauwe (1982) develops an open economy financial model which addresses some of the issues discussed above.

Comment   Paul de Grauwe

In his paper Stanley Black sets himself the task of adding some institutional detail to a classroom macromodel for an open economy. In particular, he models credit controls and other types of restrictions in order to see how the choice of particular modes of monetary policymaking affects the choice of the exchange rate regime. The attempt is similar to the one made recently by McKinnon and Mathieson (1981) for less developed countries with a heavily "repressed" financial system.

Although I think the problem is important, I feel that the way credit controls are modeled by Stanley Black is unsatisfactory and needs some changes. To show this, I start from the partial equilibrium model of the credit market, as represented by figure 15.C.1. On the vertical axis the loan rate is set out (this is r in Black's paper), on the horizontal axis the quantity of loans is represented. The L_D curve is the demand curve for bank loans, the L_S curve represents the supply of loans by banks. Equilibrium is obtained in E.

Given the banks' balance sheet constraint, L_S is dependent on the willingness of the nonbank public to hold bank deposits (the demand for deposits). In other words, banks receive deposits from the public and lend these out, adding a constant margin over the deposit rate. This is basically the way Stanley Black models the credit market. In figure 15.C.1 this implies that underlying L_S there is a demand for deposit equation D which is a positive function of the deposit rate r_D (represented by r_S in Black's paper). The L_S curve is then nothing but the D curve plus a constant margin d.

The problem arises when credit ceilings are introduced and when one assumes, as Stanley Black does, that the margin between loan and deposit rates is unchanged. Suppose the authorities set a quantitative limit on the amount of bank loans. This is represented in figure 15.C.2. The ceiling is set at $\bar{L}$. It is assumed, first, that loans are the only earning assets of banks. Then it can easily be seen that it will be difficult to maintain a fixed margin d. The credit ceiling reduces the supply of loans to the level $\bar{L}$, so that the loan rate increases. Given their balance sheet constraint, banks will try to reduce the deposit rate in order to ration the amount of outstanding deposits. The result is an increase in the margin from d to d' in figure 15.C.2.

Now add the complication (as in Black's model) that there are other earning assets for the banks, such as foreign assets. In the flexible margin model of figure 15.C.2, this would lead to a combination of an increase in the margin and spillover investment in these other earning assets (the L_S curve shifts upward). In Black's model, however, banks are constrained to keep the margin constant. Thus, as a result of the credit ceiling, both the loan

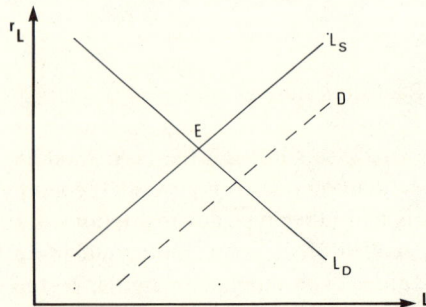

Fig. 15.C.1   Demand and supply of bank loans

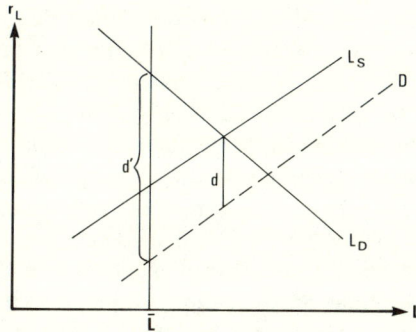

Fig. 15.C.2

and the deposit rate must increase, so that banks acquire more deposits. Since they have to decrease their lending, the excess of deposits over loans must be invested in these alternative assets (net foreign assets).

This fixed margin model yields a surprising result: that credit ceilings necessarily increase the bank's balance sheet—that is, they actually increase the total size of banking intermediation. This result would not necessarily obtain if the margin were allowed to change with the imposition of credit ceilings.

A further problem arises because in Black's model banks will not increase their net foreign assets (NFAp1). As can be seen from equation (8), banks increase their net foreign assets if the loan rate (r) declines or if the foreign rate (r_f) increases. Since after the imposition of a credit ceiling the loan rate increases, banks in Black's model will not increase their net foreign assets. As a result the excess of deposits over loans is invested exclusively in non-interest-bearing reserves (RES). In fact, in Black's model bank reserves perform the role of a slack variable which automatically increases to enforce the balance sheet constraint following the imposition of a credit ceiling.

This implies that banks are willing to let the deposit rate increase, attracting more (and more expensive) deposits which they then invest in non-interest-bearing assets. Profitability necessarily declines and can even become negative in Black's model if credit ceilings are set sufficiently low. This will certainly affect banks' willingness to supply loans and to issue deposits. The preceding criticism has further implications for some of the results obtained in Black's model. One result is that the imposition of credit controls induces a net capital inflow in a pegged exchange rate system and an appreciation of the currency in a flexible exchange rate system. The reason is that unsatisfied borrowers turn to the foreign market and increase their foreign borrowings. In addition, the increased deposit rate leads to increased demand for domestic deposits from the rest of the world. In a fixed rate system this leads to a net capital inflow, in a floating rate system to an appreciation of the currency.

In the alternative formulation of a model with a flexible margin between deposit and loan rate, this effect of credit ceilings is far from obvious. In such a model there are two opposing tendencies. The increase in the loan rate leads domestic borrowers to increase their foreign borrowings (capital inflow); however, the decline in the deposit rate shifts holders of domestic wealth into foreign assets (capital outflow). The net effect is unclear a priori and will depend on the relative strength of the two opposing forces.

A final remark concerns the empirical evidence presented by Black. He finds that peggers rely more often than floaters on credit controls, and interprets this result in the light of his theoretical model. The preceding discussion makes this interpretation less plausible. I would suggest an alternative interpretation: countries which rely on credit controls are countries where the monetary authorities have very little faith in the price mechanism as a device to allocate credit efficiently. For the same reason, these authorities will tend to have little faith in the price mechanism as a device to determine an equilibrium exchange rate in the exchange market. Therefore, it should come as no surprise that countries with an extensive credit control system have resisted more than other countries the move toward flexible exchange rates.

To conclude, Stanley Black has provided us with an important piece of research, which, although not yet finished and in certain respects even unsatisfactory, is one of the first attempts at integrating more institutional detail in our macromodels for open economies.

References

Artus, Jacques R. 1976. Exchange rate stability and managed floating: The experience of Germany. *IMF Staff Papers* 23:312–33.

Atkinson, P. E., Blundell-Wignall, A., and Chouraqui, J. C. 1981. Budget financing and monetary targets, with special reference to the seven major OECD countries. Paper presented at the Conference on Problems and Prospects in National and International Markets, Brasenose College, Oxford, July.

Bhagwati, Jagdish. 1978. *Anatomy and consequences of exchange control regimes.* Cambridge, Mass.: Ballinger.

Black, Stanley W. 1980. Central bank intervention and the stability of exchange rates. Seminar Paper no. 136. Stockholm: Institute for International Economic Studies, February.

————. 1983. The use of monetary policy for internal and external balance in ten industrial countries. In *Exchange rates and international macroeconomics,* ed. Jacob Frenkel. Chicago: University of Chicago Press (for the National Bureau of Economic Research).

De Grauwe, Paul. 1982. The exchange rate in a portfolio balance model with a banking sector. *Journal of International Money and Finance.* 1:225–39.

Henderson, Dale. 1982. The role of intervention policy in open economy financial policy: A macroeconomic perspective. In *The political economy of international and domestic monetary relations,* ed. Raymond E. Lombra and Willard E. Witte. Ames: Iowa State University Press.

Hodgman, Donald R. 1974. *National monetary policies and international monetary cooperation.* Boston: Little, Brown.

McKinnon, R. I., and Mathieson, D. J. 1981. How to manage a repressed economy. Essays in International Finance no. 145, Princeton University, December.

Modigliani, Franco, and Papademos, Lucas. 1980. The structure of financial markets and the monetary mechanism. In *Controlling Monetary Aggregates III.* Conference series no. 23. Boston: Federal Reserve Bank of Boston.

OECD. 1979. *Monetary targets and inflation control.* Paris: Organization for Economic Co-operation and Development.

Poole, William. 1970. Optimal choice of monetary policy instruments in a simple stochastic macro model. *Quarterly Journal of Economics* 84:197–216.

Quirk, Peter J. 1977. Exchange rate policy in Japan: Leaning against the wind. *IMF Staff Papers* 24:642–64.

Tower, Edward, and Willett, Thomas D. 1976. *The theory of optimum currency areas and exchange rate flexibility.* Special Papers in International Economics no. 11. Princeton: International Finance Section.

Contributors

Mr. Jacques Artus
International Monetary Fund
700 19th Street, NW
Washington, D.C. 20431

Professor Giorgio Basevi
Instituto di Scienze Economiche
Universita di Bologna
Via Zamboni 1
40125 Bologna
Italy

Professor John Bilson
Graduate School of Business
University of Chicago
1101 East 58th Street
Chicago, IL 60637

Professor Stanley W. Black
Department of Economics
University of North Carolina
Chapel Hill, NC 27514

Professor William H. Branson
Woodrow Wilson School
Princeton University
Princeton, NJ 08544

Professor Willem H. Buiter
London School of Economics
Houghton Street
London EC2A 2AE
England

Michele Calzolari
Prometeia Associates
Bologna, Italy

Professor Robert Cumby
Graduate School of Business Adminis-
    tration
New York University
100 Trinity Place
New York, NY 10006

Professor Rudiger Dornbusch
Department of Economics
Room E52–564
Massachusetts Institute of Technology
Cambridge, MA 02139

Professor Bernard Dumas
Finance Department
CESA
78350 Jouy En Josas
France

Professor Jeffrey Frankel
Department of Economics
University of California
Berkeley, CA 94720

Professor Jacob Frenkel
Department of Economics
University of Chicago
1126 East 59th Street
Chicago, IL 60637

Professor Hans Genberg
Graduate Institute of International
    Studies
132 rue de Lausanne
Case Postale 53
CH1211 Geneva 21
Switzerland

Professor Francesco Giavazzi
Facolta di Economia
Instituto di Statistica
U. di Venezia-Ca Foscari
Venice, Italy

Professor Jeffrey A. Goldstein
Department of Economics
Yale University
New Haven, CT 06520

Professor Paul de Grauwe
Centrum Voor Economische Studien
Katholieke Universiteit Leuven
E. Van Evenstraat, #2B
B-3000 Leuven
Belgium

Mr. Dale Henderson
Division of International Finance
Board of Governors of the Federal
    Reserve System
Constitution Avenue & 20th Street, NW
Washington, D.C. 20551

Professor Louka Katseli
Scientific Director
Center for Planning and Economic
    Research
Ippokratores 22
Athens, Greece

Professor Peter Kenen
International Finance Section
Department of Economics
Dickinson Hall
Princeton University
Princeton, NJ 08544

Professor Pentti Kouri
Department of Economics
269 Mercer Street
Seventh Floor
New York University
New York, NY 10003

Dr. Paul Krugman
Department of Economics
Massachusetts Institute of Technology
Cambridge, MA 02139

Professor Richard Levich
Graduate School of Business
New York University
100 Trinity Place
New York, NY 10006

Professor Jorge de Macedo
Woodrow Wilson School
Princeton University
Princeton, NJ 08544

Professor Richard C. Marston
Wharton School
3404 Steinberg-Dietrich Hall
University of Pennsylvania
Philadelphia, PA 19104

Professor David M. Meerschwam
Harvard Business School
Harvard University
Cambridge, MA 02138

Professor Michael Mussa
Graduate School of Business
University of Chicago
1101 East 58th Street
Chicago, IL 60637

Dr. Maurice Obstfeld
Department of Economics
International Affairs Building
Columbia University
New York, NY 10027

Mr. Francesco Papadia
Commission of the European Communi-
    ties
Directorate-General for Economic and
    Financial Affairs (DG-II)
Berl. 7/34
200, rue de la Loi
1049 Brussels, Belgium

Professor Charles Wyplosz
INSEAD
Boulevard de Constance
F77305 Fountainebleau Cedex
France

Name Index

Amano, A., 89
Argy, Victor, 69, 287
Artus, Jacques R., 89, 470, 475, 479–80, 482, 510
Ashenfelter, O., 101, 300
Atkinson, P. E., 499

Basevi, G., 311
Baumol, W. J., 68
Bilson, John F., 135, 137, 179, 239, 242
Black, Stanley, 68–69, 248
Blanchard, Olivier J., 65, 336, 342, 457
Blundell-Wignall, A., 499
Branson, William H., 79–80, 89–90, 109, 122, 200, 248–49, 289, 299, 496
Bruno, M., 283, 288
Buiter, Willem H., 108, 323, 329, 336, 342

Card, D., 101, 300
Chouraqui, J. C., 499
Cohen, B. J., 262–63
Cooper, Richard N., 415
Cordon, W. M., 408
Cumby, R. E., 128, 135

De Grauwe, Paul, 311, 511
De Macedo, Jorge, 200, 226, 249
Dhrymes, P. J., 129
Dooley, Michael P., 392
Dornbusch, Rudiger, 72, 79, 121, 139, 168, 175, 241, 249, 284, 324, 336, 443, 462–63
Drazen, Allan, 336, 349
Driskill, Robert A., 178–79

Feige, E. L., 135, 139
Fischer, Stanley, 101, 336
Frankel, Jeffrey A., 136, 178–79, 242, 249, 392, 443, 457, 462
Frenkel, Jacob, 69, 79, 135–37, 139, 141, 169, 239, 293, 299
Frydman, Roman, 72

Geweke, J. F., 135, 139
Giavazzi, Francesco, 337, 342
Girton, L., 122, 248
Goldstein, Jeffrey, 198
Granger, C. W., 327, 329
Grassman, A., 269
Grauer, F., 136

Hakkio, C. S., 135
Haltunnen, Hannu, 89, 249
Hansen, L. P., 128, 135–37, 139
Harvey, A. C., 324
Henderson, D., 122, 200, 248, 499
Hodgman, Donald R., 499
Hodrick, R. J., 129, 135–37, 139, 168
Hsieh, D. A., 135
Huizinga, J., 128

Isard, Peter, 392

Jones, R., 283

Kahn, Charles M., 336, 342, 457
Katseli, L., 283–84, 287
Kemp, C., 68
Kenen, P. B., 90

Keynes, J. M., 135, 283
Kindleberger, C., 262
Koopmans, T. C., 322
Kouri, Pentti J. K., 70–71, 79–80, 136, 200, 248–49, 336
Koutsoyiannis, A., 162
Krasker, W. S., 141
Krugman, P., 141, 249, 251, 265, 283
Kubarych, R., 264–65

Levich, R. M., 135
Litzenberger, R., 136
Longworth, D., 135
Lucas, Robert E., Jr., 71, 233, 462

McCallum, B. T., 142
McCormick, F., 136
Machlup, Fritz, 68
McKinnon, R., 67, 262, 408, 511
Magee, S. P., 141
Marion, N. P., 287
Marston, Richard C., 135, 416
Masson, Paul, 89, 249
Mathieson, D. J., 511
Meerschwam, David, 198, 226
Meese, R. A., 136–37, 176, 179
Melhem, M. F., 193
Merton, Robert, 199
Modigliani, Franco, 499
Montias, J., 322
Mundell, Robert A., 408, 415, 417
Mussa, Michael, 69, 79, 89, 121, 137, 139, 239, 336
Muth, John F., 68, 336

Obstfeld, Maurice, 90, 108, 122, 128, 135, 323, 336, 340, 392
Odekon, Mehmet, 337
Ohlin, B., 283

Papademos, Lucas, 499
Papadia, Francesco, 464

Pearce, I. F., 283
Poole, William, 499
Porter, Michael, 69, 248

Quirk, Peter J., 510

Razin, Assaf, 336
Rodriguez, Carlos A., 336
Rogoff, K., 176, 179
Rogoff, S., 141
Roll, R., 122, 141, 235
Rotemberg, Julio J., 496

Sachs, Jeffrey, 336–37
Salop, J., 287
Sargent, T. J., 101, 300, 329
Schwert, G. W., 328
Shefferin, Steven M., 179
Shiller, R., 66
Sims, C. A., 101, 300, 324–25
Singleton, K. J., 136–37

Solnik, B., 122
Srinivasan, T. N., 283
Stehle, R., 136
Stockman, A. C., 71, 136
Stulz, R. M., 136
Svensson, Lars E. O., 336
Swoboda, A., 262

Taylor, J., 101, 300
Tobin, James, 199
Tower, Edward, 499
Tsiang, S. C., 67, 69, 71
Tyron, R., 135

White, H., 130
Whitman, M. v. N., 90
Willett, Thomas D., 499
Wilson, Charles A., 178
Wyplosz, Charles, 337, 342

Subject Index

Account balance. *See* Current balance

Aggregate demand curve, affected by interest rate changes, 495

Aggregate demand disturbances and interest rate, 424
  output effect in exchange rate union, 417–19, 423–30

Aggregates constant financial policy, 314–15, 370, 372

Arbitrage, 69, 135

Asset demand, 231

Asset market
  bubbles, 65
  equilibrium conditions, 21
  models, 34, 80–89
  theory, 475

Asset prices, 17
  econometric models of, 34, 176
  real exchange rate as, 34–36

Assets. *See also* Interest rates
  Eurocurrency, 136
  financial, short-term, 190, 206–26

Balance of payments
  current accounts, 4, 16 n, 82–83, 99, 341
  equation, 3
  equilibrium, 55
  and exchange rates, 27–37 meaning of, 30–34
  and exchange rates, 27–37, 60–61

Bank lending, control of, 504–5

Bank policy reaction functions, 509–11

Bank regulation, 67

Banks, and foreign exchange market, 90

Belgium
  domestic price response to shocks, 312
  exchange rate movements as determinants of relative price ratio, 302
  exchange rate policy, 508 t
  monetary rate policy, 508 t
  vicious circles, 311, 383–86

Bicherdicke-Robinson-Machlup model, 67–68

Bond prices, correlations with foreign exchange rates, 190

Bonds, in asset models, 4

Bretton Woods system, 1

British pound. *See* Pound

Cagan-Sargent-Wallace model, 69

Canada
  ex ante real interest rate equality comparisons, 131
  exchange rate policy, 508 t
  interest rate differentials, 126 t
  monetary rate policy, 508 t
  spot exchange rates, 157

Canadian dollar, short positions in, 227

Capital asset pricing model, 233. *See also* Asset prices

Capital movements, 68

Carter administration, 23

Consumer Price Index, in ex ante real interest rate equality tests, 132

Consumption patterns, 57, 63

Consumption preferences, 31, 213–14, 216

Credit ceilings, 512

Credit rationing, 505–6

Cross-sectional variations, 191
Currency. *See also* Money; *specific units of currency*
   depreciation, 384
   reserve, 273–74
Current accounts, 82–83, 341
   time series properties of, 4
   balances, 99
      influences on exchange rate, 16 n
Current balance
   Germany, 486
      and U.S. current balance, 483
   and interest rates, 476
   United States, 485–86
      and German current balance, 483

Default risk, and inflation risk,
   distinguishing between, 132 n
Demand behavior, in three-country model,
   410–11
Denmark
   domestic price index, 309
   price index and exchange rate correlations,
      296
Dependent economy model, 3
Deutsche mark, 249
   depreciation, 486; against dollar, 482–83,
      489–91
   and dollar exchange rate, 470
   effects of U.S. shift to monetary restraint
      policy, 484–89
      long positions in, 227
   return on, 223
Discount rate, frequency of change, 507
Discrete-time stochastic model, 362–66
Disequilibrium
   dynamics, 49–59
      and sticky prices, 43–45, 61
   state of, 47
Disturbances, 417–18
   domestic, 312, 415, 438–39
   foreign, 419–23, 430–34
   Herstatt bank collapse, 481
   monetary, 51
   oil embargo, 481
   "Reagan effect," 489
   Reagan election, 481
Dollar. *See also* Canadian dollar
   decline in attractiveness of, 222
   and Deutsche mark exchange rate, 470
   emergence as medium of exchange, 269
   exchange rate, 402, 470

future prospects of, 274
as international medium of exchange,
   265–69
international short positions, 218
as international store of value, 272–74
as international unit of account, 269–72
as intervention currency, 273
long positions in, 227
and "Reagan effect," 482–83, 489–91
real return differential between U.S. and
   Canadian, 224
as reserve currency, 273–74
six roles of, 263–74
substitution effects between United States
   and Canada, 21
Domestic capital formation, 337
Domestic disturbances, and exchange rate
   unions, 415, 438–39
Domestic goods, 56
   conditional equilibrium price of, 51
   relative price of, 48
Domestic monetary policy. *See* Monetary
   policies
Domestic money, nominal demand for, 48
Domestic price ratio, and past exchange rate
   movements, 309
Domestic prices, 56
   response to unexpected shocks, 312
Domestic product, relationship to domestic
   spending, 30
Dornbusch model, 1, 6, 8–9, 72, 179, 181,
   183, 185, 187, 190, 193

Economic models
   asset market, 34, 80–89
   asset price, 54, 176, 233
   Bicherdicke-Robinson-Machlup, 67–68
   Cagan-Sargent-Wallace, 69
   capital asset pricing, 233
   discrete-time stochastic, 362–66
   Dornbusch, 1, 6, 8–9, 72, 179, 181, 183,
      185, 187, 190, 193
   exchange rate, 21–27, 175–80
   flexible price, 7, 239–48
   general equilibrium, 398
   intertemporal optimization, 336
   Keynesian, 55
   labor only, 343–47
   linear, 334, 342–43
   monetary, 21–27
   multilateral, 444–48
   news, 192

open economy, 500–506
payments flows, 17
portfolio, 7
    balance, 72, 248–53, 393
simple monetary, 17 n, 59–60
stationary state, 338–42, 343–47
sticky price, 7, 9
supply-demand, 67–68
three country, 410–12
Employment, disturbances, effects of,
    366–76
England. See United Kingdom
Equilibrium
of exchange rates, 27, 47
path, 47
and price of domestic goods, 51
stocks, 287
Eurocurrency interest rates, 132
Eurocurrency market, 136
European Monetary System, 9, 448, 460
Exchange controls, 464
Exchange market, and banks, 90
Exchange rate determination
    asset market view of, 18–21
    monetary factors in, 37–43
    real factors in, 37–43
Exchange rate dynamics, theoretical model
    of, 177–80
Exchange rate models, empirical
    implementations of, 175–77
Exchange rates. See also Forward exchange
    rates; Nominal exchange rates; Real
    exchange rates; Spot exchange rates
asset market theory, 475
and balance of payments, 27–37, 60–61
behavior characteristics, 15
    theories of, 17–18
and bond prices, 190
conditional equilibrium, 47
correlations
    with bond prices, 190
    with news, 315
    with stock prices, 190
cross-sectional variations, 191
as determinants of relative price ratios,
    302
Deutsche mark, 470
dollar, 402, 470
domestic price ratio and past movements,
    309
economic variables, 57
effects of monetary disturbances, 52–53

effects of U.S. shift to monetary
    restraint policy, 484–89
equilibrium real, 284–89
exogenous shocks, 86–88
expected changes in, 20
flexible, 413–14
floating, 10, 79
and forward premia, 180–84
Germany, 96, 104–5, 470
indices, 289–95
influence of real economic conditions,
    55–56
as information variable, 379–86
and interest rates, 99–108
intertemporal optimization, 336
intervention effects, 89, 114–115, 390,
    509–10
Japan, 96, 106–7
lagged values, 309
monetary models of, 21–27
and monetary policy, 121 n
    classification of, 506–9
money shocks, 188
in multicountry world, 5, 444–48
and national price levels, 141–44
news role in, 169–70, 315
and official intervention, 114–15
overshooting, 47, 56, 169, 185, 188, 463,
    470
pegged, 10
as predictors of inflation rate, 143
problem areas in analysis of, 3
reaction to exogenous shocks, 86–88
and relative prices, 315
stochastic behavior of, 15–17
and stock prices, 190
time series properties of, 4
United Kingdom, 96, 157, 105–6, 292 t,
    508 t
United States, 93–96, 102–4, 288 t,
    508 t
unpredictability, of, 60
variables, 40, 57, 191
Exchange rate unions
    aggregate demand disturbances, 417–19,
        423–30
    defined, 407 n
    domestic disturbances, 415, 438–39
    foreign disturbances, 419–23
    foreign monetary disturbances, 422–23,
        430–34
    and intervention, 415

output effect of monetary disturbances, 417–18
Exchange risk, 464
Expectations, modeling of, 71
External imbalances, response to, 510

Feedback, effects on financial policy, 376–79
  rules, 9
Financial assets, short term, 206–26
Financial authorities, behavior of, 367
Financial behavior, in three-country model, 412
Financial markets disturbances, effects on employment, 370–72
Financial policies, 370–72, 374–75, 400–401
Flexible price model, 7, 239–48
Forecast errors, 4
Foreign behavior, in three-country model, 412
Foreign disturbances. *See also* Monetary disturbances; Shocks
  in exchange rate union, 419–23
Foreign exchange
  a financial asset, 190
  intervention, 8
Foreign exchange market
  equilibrium in, 19
  information shortage, 192
  intervention, 392–93, 398
  risk premium in, 47 n
Foreign goods, 56
Foreign price index, 309
Forward exchange market, analysis of (Tsiang), 4
Forward exchange rates
  Canada, 157
  France, 157
  Germany, 157
  innovations, 190, 193
  Italy, 157
  Japan, 157
  Netherlands, 157
  risk premia effects on, 15
  and spot exchange rates, 15, 20–21, 54, 167–68
  Switzerland, 157
  United Kingdom, 157
Forward markets, theory of, 69
Forward premia, and exchange rates, 180–84
Franc
  emergence as medium of exchange, 267
  positions in, 227

France. *See also* Franc
  domestic price index, 309
  exchange rate indices, 292 t
  exchange rate policy, 508 t
  monetary rate policy, 508 t
  spot exchange rates, 157

General equilibruim model, 398
Germany. *See also* Deutsche mark
  current balance, 483, 486
    vis-à-vis U.S. current balance, 483
  domestic price index, 309
  ex ante real interest rate equality comparisons, 131
  exchange rate indices, 291 t
  exchange rate policy, 508 t
  exchange rates, 96, 104–5, 470
  inflation rate, 486–91
  interest elasticity in, 183
  interest rate differentials, 125 t
  labor contracts, 480
  monetary policies, 5, 89, 489, 508 t
  monetary restraint, effects of, 491, 496
  money stock, reduction in, 480
  "Reagan effect," 489–91
  spot exchange rates, 157
  vector autoregression system, 104–5
  wage rates, 480
Gold
  importance of capital gains, 224
  mean real return on, 223
  optimal portfolios, 206–26
Goods market equilibrium
  and trade balance, 28–30

Herstatt Bank, collapse, 481
Home goods, 370

Imbalances, 510
Indexing, and employment effects, 373–76
Inflationary expectations, 471, 473–75
Inflation hedges, 218
Inflation rate
  exchange rates as predictors of, 143
  in Germany, 486–91
Inflation risk, and default risk, distinguishing between, 132 n

Information
  cost of acquiring, 462
  variables, 379–86
Innovation accounting, 330

Interest arbitrage, 135
Interest elasticity, 183
Interest rate
    causes of increase in, 380
    as information variable, 379–86
    intervention effects, 390
    nominal, as policy instrument, 384–85
Interest rate control, 88–89
Interest rate differentials, 124–27
Interest rate parity, 123, 135
Interest rates, 99. *See also* Real interest
        rates
    and aggregate demand disturbances, 424
    and current balance, 476
    differentials, 135–41
    effects on aggregate demand curve, 495
    equality of, comparisons, 131
    and exchange rates, 99–108
    long-term real, 475
    monetary policy, 470
    and parity relationships, 122–27
    pegging, 399
    United States and United Kingdom,
        equality of, 134
Internal imbalances, 510
International Monetary Fund, 69, 79
International monies, 261
Intervention
    currency, 273
    exchange rates and monetary policy, 509–
        10
    and exchange rate union, 415
    and interest rate, 390
    nonsterilized, 399
    official, in exchange rates, 114–15
    operations
        empirical evidence, 392–93
        theoretical underpinning of, 390–92
    policy, 360
        and transitory disturbances, 386–90
        and vicious circles, 383–86
Invoice currencies, 270
Italy. *See also* Lira
    exchange rate policy, 508 t
    monetary rate policy, 508 t
    spot exchange rates, 157
    vicious circles, 311

Japan. *See also* Yen
    domestic price index, 309
    ex ante real interest rate equality
        comparisons, 131
    exchange rate indices, 291 t
    exchange rate movements as determinants
        of relative price ratio, 302
    exchange rate policy, 508 t
    exchange rates, 96, 106–7
    interest rate differentials, 126 t
    monetary policies, 89, 107, 508 t
    price index and exchange rate correlations,
        296
    spot exchange rates, 157
    vector autoregression system, 106–7

Keynesian model, 55

Labor
    contracts (Germany), 480
    as a factor of production, 341
    productivity of, 385
    wage rates (Germany), 480
Labor only model, 343–47
Lagged price adjustment, 5
Life-cycle consumption patterns, 63
Linear models, 336, 342–43
Lira, short positions in, 227

Magnification effect, definition, 187
Markowitz portfolio theory, 231
Monetary disturbances
    disequilibrium effects of, 51
    foreign, and exchange rate unions, 422–
        23, 430–34
    output effect in exchange rate union,
        417–18
Monetary models, 21–27, 59–60
    criticisms of, 22–23
    failures of, 17 n
Monetary policies. *See also* Financial
        policies
    and exchange rate intervention, 509–10
    and exchange rates, 121 n
    Germany, 5, 89, 491
    Japan, 89, 107, 508 t
    United Kingdom, 5, 89, 508 t
    United States, 5, 107, 508 t
    interest rates, 470
    role of differences in, 165–67
Monetary policy regimes, and exchange
        rates, classification of, 506–8
Monetary restraint, effects of
    in Germany, 496
    in U.S., 496
    U.S. shift to policy of, 484–89
Monetary shocks, 9, 188

Monetary system, control of, 503–5
Money
    foreign, 365
    functions of, 263
    home, 365
    long-run growth expectations, 479–80
    shocks, 188
    as store of value, 272–74
    supply, 385
        control of, 88–89
    as unit of account, 269–72
Money market equilibrium, and exchange
    rates, 23
Multilateral model, 444–48

National price levels, 16, 23
    and exchange rates, 141–44
Netherlands
    domestic price response to shocks, 312
    exchange rate policy, 508 t
    monetary rate policy, 508 t
    spot exchange rates, 157
News
    correlations with exchange rates, 169–70,
        315
    effect on relative prices, 304
    role in exchange rate movements, 169–70
Nominal exchange rates, 23, 37–43, 282–83
    correlations with real exchange rates,
        16–18
    relationship to expected future conditions, 3
    variables affecting, 42
Nominal interest differentials, 135–41
Norway
    domestic price response to shocks, 312
    exchange rate movements as determinants
        of relative price ratio, 302
    price index and exchange rate correlations,
        296

Oil embargo, 481
Open economy
    analysis of, 3
    model, 500–506
Output, interest rate effect on, 475

Parity relationships
    and interest rates, 122–27
    tests of, 6
Payment flows model, 17
Peso problem, 3 61–62, 141

Policies, financial, 370–72, 374–75, 400–
    401
    effect of feedback on, 376–79
Policy actions, 4–5
Policy functions, 509–11
Portfolio, logarithmic, 234
Portfolio balance model, 7, 72, 248–53, 393
    and monetary model, 251
Portfolio choice, microeconomics of, 7
Portfolio rules, 200–206
Portfolios
    inflation hedge, 218
    optimal evolution over time, 217–18,
        221–26
    selection, 199
Pound, 23
    decline as a medium of exchange, 269
    extended period as vehicle currency, 268
    positions in, 227
Price dynamics, 3
Price flexibility, 71
Price indexes, foreign, 309
Price levels, relative, 99
Price ratio
    Belgium, 302
    domestic, 309
    Norway, 302
Prices
    domestic, 312
    effect of news on, 304
    relative, and exchange rates, 315
    sticky, 462
    time series properties of, 4
Pricing formula, 21
Purchasing power parity, 3, 16, 22–23, 53–
    54, 59, 69, 121, 141, 212–14, 227,
    246, 281, 457

Random walk hypothesis, 179
Rates constant financial policy, 370–72,
    374–75, 400–401
Raw materials trade, 270
Reaction function, 509–11
Reagan, Ronald, 481–83, 489–91
Real exchange rates
    as an asset price, 34–36
    correlations with nominal exchange rates,
        16–18
    defined, 16
    dynamics of, 36–37
    problem, 64–65
    and real interest rates, 63–64

relationship to expected future
conditions, 3
Real interest rates, 31
equality of ex ante, 127–44
and real exchange rate, 63–64
Relative price levels, 99
Reserve currency, 273–74
Restraint. *See* Monetary restraint, effects of
Risk aversion, 122
Risk premium, 7, 136, 246, 249, 251
time-varying, 392
Risk sharing, 271

Securities
foreign, 367
home, 365
Shocks. *See also* Disturbances
and domestic prices, 312
Simple asset market model, 21
Simple monetary models, 59–60
Snowballing, 267
Spending behavior, 213–14, 216
of home residents, 31
Spending patterns, 57
Spot exchange rates
Canada, 157
and forward exchange rates, 15, 20–21,
54, 167–68
France, 157
Germany, 157
innovations, 190
Italy, 157
Japan, 157
Netherlands, 157
statistical examination of, 15
Switzerland, 157
United Kingdom, 157
Spot markets, theory of, 69
Stationary state, 338–42
model, 343–47
Sticky price model, 7, 9
Sticky price monetary equation, 241
Sticky prices, 462
and disequilibrium dynamics, 43–45, 61
Stock equilibrium, 287
Stock prices, correlations with foreign
exchange rates, 190
Supply behavior, in three-country model,
411–12
Supply-demand model, 67–68
Sweden
domestic price index, 309

exchange rate conference, 1
exchange rate policy, 508 t
monetary rate policy, 508 t
price index and exchange rate
correlations, 296
Switzerland
ex ante real interest rate equality
comparisons, 131
interest rate differentials, 125 t
spot exchange rates, 157

Three-country model, 410–12
Time impatience, concepts of, 341 n
Time preference, rates of, 340
Trade balance, and goods market
equilibrium, 28–30
Trade contracts, 269
Transaction cost, average, 464

United Kingdom
ex ante real interest rate equality
comparisons, 131
exchange rate indices, 292 t
exchange rate policy, 508 t
exchange rates, 96, 105–6
interest rate
differentials, 124 t
equality, 134
monetary policies, 5, 89, 508 t
spot exchange rates, 157
vector autoregression system, 105–6
United States. *See also* Dollar
current balance, 485–86
vis-à-vis German current balance, 483
domestic price index, 309
ex ante real interest rate equality
comparisons, 131
exchange rate indices, 290 t
exchange rate policy, 508 t
exchange rates, 93–96, 102–4
interest rate
differentials, 124–27
equality, 134
monetary policies, 5, 107, 508 t
monetary restraint, effects of, 496
price increase, and depreciation of foreign
currencies, 211
vector autoregression system, 102–4

Variables
effect on nominal exchange rate, 42
information, 379–86

real role in exchange rate behavior, 40
Vehicle currency, 268
Vicious circles, 311
  and intervention policy, 383–86

Wage rigidity, 497
Wages
  indexation of, 418, 420, 439–40

rates (Germany), 480
Walras's Law, 287
Welfare implications, 347–48
Wholesale price index, in ex ante real
  interest rate equality tests, 132

Yen, long positions in, 227